Cognitive Grammar

Cognitive Grammar

A Basic Introduction

Ronald W. Langacker

OXFORD

UNIVERSITY PRESS

2008

OXFORD
UNIVERSITY PRESS

Oxford University Press, Inc., publishes works that further
Oxford University's objective of excellence
in research, scholarship, and education.

Oxford   New York
Auckland   Cape Town   Dar es Salaam   Hong Kong   Karachi
Kuala Lumpur   Madrid   Melbourne   Mexico City   Nairobi
New Delhi   Shanghai   Taipei   Toronto

With offices in
Argentina   Austria   Brazil   Chile   Czech Republic   France   Greece
Guatemala   Hungary   Italy   Japan   Poland   Portugal   Singapore
South Korea   Switzerland   Thailand   Turkey   Ukraine   Vietnam

Copyright © 2008 by Oxford University Press, Inc.

Published by Oxford University Press, Inc.
198 Madison Avenue, New York, New York 10016

www.oup.com

Oxford is a registered trademark of Oxford University Press

Library of Congress Cataloging-in-Publication Data
Langacker, Ronald W.
Cognitive grammar : a basic introduction / Ronald Langacker.
p. cm.
Includes bibliographical references.
ISBN 978-0-19-533195-0; 978-0-19-533196-7 (pbk.)
1. Cognitive grammar.   I. Title.
P165.L345 2007
415—dc22   2007009457

3 5 7 9 8 6 4

Printed in the United States of America
on acid-free paper

To Sherridan, Julian, and Tre

PREFACE

As you may have guessed from the title, this book presents the linguistic theory known as Cognitive Grammar (CG). Research in CG began in 1976, and the basic framework of the theory has now existed for over a quarter century. Under the rubric "space grammar", it was first extensively described in Langacker 1982, whose numerous and unfortunately rather crudely drawn diagrams must have startled and dismayed the readers of *Language*. The most comprehensive statement of the theory resides in the hulking two-volume mass called *Foundations of Cognitive Grammar* (Langacker 1987, 1991). More accessible—or easier to lift at any rate—is *Concept Image and Symbol* (Langacker 1990), a collection of articles tailored as a single text. A second collection of this sort is *Grammar and Conceptualization* (Langacker 1999a). For ease of reference, these four books are cited here as FCG1, FCG2, CIS, and GC.

First proposed as a radical alternative to the theories then prevailing, CG may no longer seem so drastically different for the simple reason that the discipline has gradually evolved in its direction. There is no longer any clear distinction (if there ever was) between "formalist" and "functionalist" traditions in linguistic theory (Langacker 1999c). Nevertheless, CG is still regarded as extreme by most formalists, and even by many functionalists. And having been trained as a formalist, I myself first placed it at the extreme periphery of the theoretical landscape. But after spending several decades in that outpost, I have come to see it as occupying the very center. I perceive it as striking the proper balance between formalist and functionalist concerns. It straightforwardly reflects the dual grounding of language in cognition and social interaction. I further see it as able to accommodate, integrate, and synthesize the wealth of findings and insights emerging in the varied traditions of cognitive and functional linguistics.

By now there are more opportunities for reading about CG and cognitive linguistics than you probably care to know about. Many references are cited in this book. To appreciate the full scope of the enterprise, you need only peruse the many volumes of *Cognitive Linguistics* (journal of the International Cognitive Linguistics Association) and the monograph series Cognitive Linguistics Research (Mouton de

Gruyter). And these are just the tip of the iceberg. Not yet available, though, are a broad selection of introductory textbooks. Several now exist for cognitive linguistics in general—Ungerer and Schmid 2007, Lee 2001, Croft and Cruse 2004, Evans and Green 2006—as well as two collections of readings (Geeraerts 2006; Evans, Bergen, and Zinken 2006) and a glossary (Evans 2007). For CG in particular, the only current option is Taylor 2002, which covers the basics quite well. Still lacking, however, is an introduction that is less elementary and presented in greater depth and technical detail. Here is my attempt to fill this need.

The book is designed to be usable at different levels and in different ways. Though I have tried to make it accessible to general readers, some basic training in linguistics will be helpful. As a textbook, it is aimed at the advanced undergraduate and beginning graduate levels, having developed out of a course for first-year graduate students. I see it as being ideally suited for a two-semester graduate course, parts I and II being covered in the first semester, parts III and IV in the second. Parts I and II can also stand alone as a basic introduction to the theory. Their chapters are shorter and a bit less challenging, hence more suitable for less advanced students. The four parts do however form an integrated whole, which only collectively affords a real appreciation of CG's vision of language structure and potential for describing it. This being a prime objective, the volume is not conceived exclusively as a textbook. It has enough linguistic depth and substance that it should prove useful for professionals in related disciplines. And for linguists of other theoretical persuasions, it offers a one-stop opportunity to put their assessment and criticisms on a firmer, more accurate basis.

On a personal level, this work brings closure to an initial phase of investigation that has stretched out for several decades. It has been a chance to refine and clarify my thoughts on many issues, to present them more effectively, and to make their rationale more evident. This has led to a fuller, more unified treatment of the interactive and conceptual basis of language structure. There remain, to be sure, important gaps in coverage (e.g. a systematic exposition of phonology). And while the final product is less than perfect (as reviewers will undoubtedly attest), it will have to do. Further attempts at presenting CG will concern a second phase of investigation, which has been under way for a number of years. Some of its major themes are previewed in part IV (Frontiers). The future is harder to predict than the past, but it does seem clear that—even after thirty years—research in CG is only starting.

CONTENTS

PART I

PRELIMINARIES

Orientation

Our topic is the linguistic theory known as **Cognitive Grammar**. This framework offers a comprehensive yet coherent view of language structure, with the further advantages (I would argue) of being intuitively natural, psychologically plausible, and empirically viable. It is nonetheless a decidedly nonstandard view for which orthodox training in linguistics gives little preparation. A presentation of Cognitive Grammar must therefore start by articulating its general nature and basic vision.

1.1 Grammar and Life

Having spent most of my life investigating grammar, I am quite aware that this passion is not shared by the general populace. Let's face it—grammar has a bad reputation. For most people, it represents the danger of being criticized for breaking arcane rules they can never quite keep straight. In foreign-language instruction, grammar is often presented through mechanical exercises, the learning of irregularities, and the memorization of seemingly endless paradigms. Even in linguistics, it is commonly portrayed in a manner hardly designed to inspire general interest: as a system of arbitrary forms based on abstract principles unrelated to other aspects of cognition or human endeavor.

It doesn't have to be that way. Grammar is actually quite engaging when properly understood. Linguists, of course, are concerned with describing language, not prescribing how to talk. They are not responsible for the artificial strictures enforced by would-be grammar police. While grammar does require the learning of many forms, the same is true of lexicon, which inspires much less dread and is often a source of wonder and amusement. Furthermore, portraying grammar as a purely formal system is not just wrong but wrong-headed. I will argue, instead, that **grammar is meaningful**. This is so in two respects. For one thing, the elements of grammar—like vocabulary items—have meanings in their own right. Additionally, grammar allows us to construct and symbolize the more elaborate meanings of complex expressions (like phrases, clauses, and sentences). It is thus an essential aspect of the conceptual apparatus through which we apprehend and engage the world. And instead of being a distinct and self-contained cognitive system, grammar is not only an integral part of cognition but also a key to understanding it.

The meaningfulness of grammar becomes apparent only with an appropriate view of linguistic meaning. In cognitive semantics, meaning is identified as the conceptualization associated with linguistic expressions. This may seem obvious, but in fact it runs counter to standard doctrine. A conceptual view of meaning is usually rejected either as being insular—entailing isolation from the world as well as from other minds—or else as being nonempirical and unscientific. These objections are unfounded. Though it is a mental phenomenon, conceptualization is grounded in physical reality: it consists in activity of the brain, which functions as an integral part of the body, which functions as an integral part of the world. Linguistic meanings are also grounded in social interaction, being negotiated by interlocutors based on mutual assessment of their knowledge, thoughts, and intentions. As a target of analysis, conceptualization is elusive and challenging, but it is not mysterious or beyond the scope of scientific inquiry. Cognitive semantics provides an array of tools allowing precise, explicit descriptions for essential aspects of conceptual structure. These descriptions are based on linguistic evidence and potentially subject to empirical verification.

Analyzing language from this perspective leads to remarkable conclusions about linguistic meaning and human cognition. Remarkable, first, is the extent to which an expression's meaning depends on factors other than the situation described. On the one hand, it presupposes an elaborate **conceptual substrate**, including such matters as background knowledge and apprehension of the physical, social, and linguistic context. On the other hand, an expression imposes a particular **construal**, reflecting just one of the countless ways of conceiving and portraying the situation in question. Also remarkable is the extent to which **imaginative** abilities come into play. Phenomena like metaphor (e.g. *vacant stare*) and reference to "virtual" entities (e.g. *any cat*) are pervasive, even in prosaic discussions of actual circumstances. Finally, these phenomena exemplify the diverse array of **mental constructions** that help us deal with—and in large measure constitute—the world we live in and talk about. It is a world of extraordinary richness, extending far beyond the physical reality it is grounded in.

Conceptual semantic description is thus a major source of insight about our mental world and its construction. Grammatical meanings prove especially revealing in this respect. Since they tend to be abstract, their essential import residing in construal, they offer a direct avenue of approach to this fundamental aspect of semantic organization. Perhaps surprisingly—given its stereotype as being dry, dull, and purely formal—grammar relies extensively on imaginative phenomena and mental constructions. Also, the historical evolution of grammatical elements yields important clues about the meanings of their lexical sources and semantic structure more generally. The picture that emerges belies the prevailing view of grammar as an autonomous formal system. Not only is it meaningful, it also reflects our basic experience of moving, perceiving, and acting on the world. At the core of grammatical meanings are mental operations inherent in these elemental components of moment-to-moment living. When properly analyzed, therefore, grammar has much to tell us about both meaning and cognition.

1.2 The Nature of the Beast

The beast is Cognitive Grammar—CG for short. Some linguists view it with disdain, as it challenges fundamental dogmas and requires alternative modes of thought and analysis. Of course, others like it for just that reason. But whether they are positive, negative, or in-between, most opinions of CG appear to be formed on the basis of a strikingly limited (and often quite erroneous) understanding of it. Even its central claims and basic character are commonly misportrayed. So we need to get a few things straight at the outset.

1.2.1 An Outrageous Proposal

As its name implies, Cognitive Grammar is first and foremost a theory of **grammar**. Rather surprising, therefore, are statements to the effect that "Langacker doesn't believe in grammar—everything is semantics." Rest assured that CG neither threatens nor denies the existence of grammar. Grammar exists. The issue is rather the **nature** of grammar and its relation to other dimensions of linguistic structure.

CG's most fundamental claim is that grammar is **symbolic** in nature. What does this mean, exactly? Let us first define a **symbol** as the pairing between a semantic structure and a phonological structure, such that one is able to evoke the other. A simple lexical item, such as *skunk*, is thus symbolic because it resides in the pairing between a meaning and a phonological shape. Grammar, of course, is concerned with how such elements combine to form complex expressions. The basic tenet of CG is that nothing beyond symbolic structures need be invoked for the proper characterization of complex expressions and the patterns they instantiate. More specifically: **lexicon and grammar form a gradation consisting solely in assemblies of symbolic structures**. An immediate consequence of this position is that all constructs validly posited for grammatical description (e.g. notions like "noun", "subject", or "past participle") must in some way be meaningful.

This is not at all how grammar is viewed in modern linguistic theory. Received wisdom—repeated in every linguistics textbook—holds that notions like noun and subject are purely grammatical constructs not susceptible to any general semantic characterization. Moreover, the reigning theoretical orthodoxy claims that syntax is **autonomous**: that it constitutes a separate linguistic "module" or "component", distinct from both lexicon and semantics, whose description requires a special set of syntactic "primitives". Against this background, the CG position stands out as radical if not heretical. In the words of one distinguished critic: "Many readers will no doubt feel the same sense of outrage at this claim that I did, and I still believe that it is wrong" (Hudson 1992: 507–508).[1]

---

[1] This critic does admit that I make "a surprisingly good case for it" (Hudson 1992: 508).

I have no doubt that this reviewer really did feel a sense of outrage and that other linguists share it. And to the extent that it causes outrage, the position is indeed outrageous. That does not make it wrong, however. It may only indicate that the distorting lenses of contemporary linguistic theory and professional training are able to disguise the very real sense in which the position is both natural and intrinsically desirable. If language serves a symbolic function, establishing systematic connections between conceptualizations and observable phenomena like sounds and gestures, it would seem both natural and desirable to seek an account such that grammar is itself symbolic. If notions like "noun" and "subject" are universal and fundamental to grammar, it would seem both dubious and implausible to deny them a conceptual raison d'être. From a naive perspective (i.e. for those who lack linguistic training), it is hard to fathom why our species would have evolved an autonomous grammatical system independent of conceptual and phonological content. Is it not more reasonable to suppose that grammar, rather than being separate and distinct, is merely the abstract commonality inherent in sets of symbolically complex expressions?

Assessments of CG's central claim have been clouded by confusion on several points. One source of confusion is chronic ambivalence concerning what is meant by "autonomy". A strong version of the autonomy thesis holds that syntactic description requires a special set of purely grammatical primitives, which are not reducible to anything more fundamental. CG denies this by claiming that all valid grammatical constructs are symbolic, hence reducible to form-meaning pairings. A weaker version of autonomy merely asserts that grammar cannot be fully predicted from independent factors (notably meaning and communicative constraints). This weak formulation is fully compatible with CG, and indeed, with virtually every brand of cognitive and functional linguistics. Few would disagree that semantic and functional considerations constrain and motivate grammatical structure but do not completely determine it—speakers still have to learn the specific patterns of their language, and linguists have to describe these explicitly. It should be evident that the weaker version of autonomy does not entail the stronger one: whether grammar is **predictable**, and the **types** of elements needed to describe it, are very different issues. Linguistic theorists sometimes confound them, however, by taking the nonpredictability of grammar as establishing autonomy in the broader sense.[2] This overlooks the possibility of grammar being unpredictable yet fully describable as assemblies of symbolic structures.

Although the reduction of grammar to symbolic assemblies achieves an important conceptual unification, some theorists worry about the fate of syntax. One critic complains that CG "denies it even the status of a definable area within the larger whole of language" (Harder 1996: 260). This erroneous statement betrays a double confusion. First, it confuses the definability of syntax with the existence of a clear and definite boundary. Overlap among lexicon, morphology, and syntax does not prevent us from defining them and drawing useful distinctions, any more than the absence of a precise boundary between green and blue condemns

---

[2] I call this the **type/predictability fallacy**. A prime example is Newmeyer 1983.

us to seeing only grue—a gradation does not imply undifferentiated homogeneity. Second, the statement confuses reduction with elimination. Reducing grammar to symbolic assemblies serves to characterize it, not to deny its status as a definable level of organization. One does not deny the existence of water molecules by analyzing them as consisting in a particular configuration of hydrogen and oxygen atoms.

1.2.2 What Is CG Really Like?

Language is shaped and constrained by the functions it serves. These include the **semiological function** of allowing conceptualizations to be symbolized by means of sounds and gestures, as well as a multifaceted **interactive function** involving communication, manipulation, expressiveness, and social communion. **Functional** approaches to linguistic investigation are most basically distinguished from **formal** ones (notably generative grammar) in terms of whether functional considerations are taken as being **foundational** or merely **subsidiary** to the problem of describing language form. In practice, this matter of emphasis translates into very different substantive claims about the nature of linguistic structure and how to describe it.[3]

Cognitive Grammar belongs to the wider movement known as **cognitive linguistics**, which in turn is part of the functional tradition. Besides CG, important strands of cognitive linguistics include **construction grammar**, **metaphor theory**, the study of **blends and mental spaces**, and various efforts to develop a **conceptualist semantics**. Among other major components of functionalism are **discourse-pragmatic** analyses, the study of **grammaticalization**, and **universal-typological** investigation via cross-linguistic surveys.[4] Naturally, terms like "cognitive linguistics" and "functionalism" are fluid in reference and subsume a diverse array of views. There is at best a broad compatibility of outlook among the scholars concerned, certainly not theoretical uniformity.

A question commonly asked is: "What is **cognitive** about Cognitive Grammar? Or about cognitive linguistics in general?" These do not merit the label merely by proclaiming that language is part of cognition and that linguistic investigation contributes to understanding the human mind—that much is shared by many approaches, both formal and functional. Then what links to cognition do distinguish cognitive linguistics from either formal linguistics or other strains of functionalism? Within functionalism, cognitive linguistics stands out by emphasizing the semiological function

---

[3] See Langacker 1999c. The difference is not a matter of rigor, precision, degree of formalization, or scientific merit. Formal and functional approaches both vary widely along these parameters.

[4] I can do no more than cite a few basic references. For construction grammar, see Fillmore 1988; Goldberg 1995; Croft 2001. For metaphor theory, see Lakoff and Johnson 1980; Lakoff and Turner 1989; Grady, Taub, and Morgan 1996; Kövecses 2000, 2005. For blends and mental spaces, see Fauconnier 1985, 1997; Fauconnier and Sweetser 1996; Fauconnier and Turner 2002. For conceptualist semantics, see Vandeloise 1991; Wierzbicka 1996; Talmy 2000a, 2000b; Tyler and Evans 2003; Hampe 2005. For discourse-pragmatics, see Hopper and Thompson 1980; Givón 1983; DuBois 1987; Chafe 1994; Lambrecht 1994; Verhagen 2005. For grammaticalization, see Traugott 1982, 1988; Heine, Claudi, and Hünnemeyer 1991; Heine 1997; Hopper and Traugott 2003. For universals-typology, see Givón 1984; Bybee 1985; Croft 1990; Talmy 1991; Kemmer 1993; Haspelmath 1997.

of language. It fully acknowledges the grounding of language in social interaction, but insists that even its interactive function is critically dependent on conceptualization. Compared with formal approaches, cognitive linguistics stands out by resisting the imposition of boundaries between language and other psychological phenomena. Insofar as possible, linguistic structure is seen as drawing on other, more basic systems and abilities (e.g. perception, memory, categorization) from which it cannot be segregated. Rather than constituting a distinct, self-contained entity (a separate "module" or "mental faculty"), language is viewed as an integral facet of cognition.

As for CG in particular, care is taken to invoke only well-established or easily demonstrated mental abilities that are not exclusive to language. We are able, for example, to focus and shift attention, to track a moving object, to form and manipulate images, to compare two experiences, to establish correspondences, to combine simple elements into complex structures, to view a scene from different perspectives, to conceptualize a situation at varying levels of abstraction, and so on. Can general abilities like these fully account for the acquisition and the universal properties of language? Or are specific blueprints for language wired in and genetically transmitted? CG does not prejudge this issue. We are evidently born to speak, so it is not precluded that language might emerge owing to substantial innate specification peculiar to it. But if our genetic endowment does make special provisions for language, they are likely to reside in adaptations of more basic cognitive phenomena, rather than being separate and sui generis. They would be analogous in this respect to the physical organs of speech.

Despite its functional nature, CG shares with formal approaches the commitment to seeking explicit characterizations of language structure.[5] For various reasons our capacity to achieve them is subject to strong inherent limitations. Nevertheless, a functional account of language has little chance of proving revealing and empirically adequate unless it is based on reasonably precise and detailed linguistic descriptions. At the same time, I believe that optimal description requires a functional perspective.

The components of a comprehensive functional theory can be conceptualized as a three-level pyramid. The first and lowest level specifies the resources available for describing linguistic structures. Ideally, this inventory of descriptive constructs would enable one to properly characterize any structure encountered in any language. Research in CG has aimed primarily at justifying particular constructs by examining diverse phenomena in numerous languages. If the descriptive inventory is adequate for all structures in all languages, it will necessarily define a very large space of possibilities, many reaches of which are sparsely populated. The second level of the pyramid deals with the "warping" of this space, such that linguistic structures tend to cluster in certain areas while generally avoiding others. A major goal of functional theory is to specify the "attractors" in this space, i.e. the range of structures that are **prototypical** in language, as well as their degree of prototypicality. Cross-linguistic research on typology and language universals is clearly essential for producing a reliable enumeration. Finally, the third and top level of the pyramid

---

[5] CG is thus considered by some functionalists to be a formal model. Formalists tend not to make that mistake.

consists of functional explanations for empirical findings at the second level. Proposing such explanations (e.g. by offering discourse motivation for aspects of clause structure) has been a basic occupation of functional investigation.

While each higher level in the pyramid logically presupposes the lower ones, in practice research at the three levels must proceed simultaneously. By emphasizing the foundational level, CG has been more concerned with structural description than with prototypicality and functional explanation. The theoretical proposals and specific descriptions of CG are, however, envisaged as being embedded in an overall account that encompasses all three levels. Descriptions of particular constructions are not meant to be free-standing, for in themselves they offer no indication of how or to what extent the constructions are functionally motivated. It is only by combining the functional and the descriptive dimensions that we arrive at a full understanding of grammatical phenomena.

Expositions of CG have perhaps not sufficiently emphasized its place within an overall functional account. This has no doubt abetted the common misconception that CG is unconstrained and makes no predictions. If anything, just the opposite is true. This may not be evident given the focus on basic descriptive apparatus: a set of constructs sufficiently flexible to describe the full range of linguistic structures (even the most atypical ones) is unlikely, in and of itself, to be highly constraining. CG's restrictiveness has other sources. A primary source is the information provided at higher levels of the pyramid—that is, enumerations of what is prototypical in language, and why. In my view, positive specifications of this sort offer the proper means of imposing restrictions (since explicit prohibitions are endless and often porous). By stating what **does** tend to occur in language, we implicitly indicate what tends **not** to occur. More precisely, by specifying the location and strength of attractors in the space of structural possibilities, we inherently make predictions about the relative likelihood of particular kinds of structures being encountered in a given language, hence about their cross-linguistic prevalence.

It is not true, then, that CG is unconstrained. I likewise reject the related misconception that I and others misled by me are given to positing wild and fanciful things limited only by the scope of our imagination. The theory and the research are actually notable for their down-to-earth nature, and in §1.3.4 I elucidate the severe restrictions imposed on what can be postulated. For some reason CG appears especially prone to being misapprehended. Competent scholars have confidently but gratuitously asserted, for example, that CG cannot handle metaphor (it can), that it does not account for ungrammaticality (it does), that it is solipsistic (it is not), that it portrays language as a static entity (it does not), and that everything is claimed to be iconic (no such claim is made). These points are all covered later. For now let us turn to the most fecund source of misconceptions about CG, namely the notations it employs.

1.2.3 Those Diagrams

On occasion I resort to diagrams. Of course, those occasions are rather frequent, and critics will no doubt aver that I use them excessively. It is certainly true that works in CG (including this one) are often replete with diagrams, ranging from simple, cartoon-like sketches to elaborate technical displays of great complexity. There is, I suppose, no reason to be apologetic about it. After all, the pages of staid linguistics journals are often splashed with tree-like diagrams drawn by formal syntacticians (not to mention phonologists). The use of diagrams is equally prevalent in the "hard" sciences admired by linguistic theorists. Indeed, we are witnessing the emergence of "scientific visualization" and the growing recognition of its importance to theory and research. Still, since the diagrams used in CG have so commonly been misconstrued, their nature and status need to be clarified.

Among the misconceptions concerning the diagrams of CG are (i) that they are offered as precise and rigorous formal representations and (ii) that they are merely ad hoc, informal "pictures". There is actually a germ of truth in both positions. Some diagrams are just picture-like sketches casually devised to help make a point. Others are meticulously assembled from an inventory of specific notations systematically used with precisely defined values. In all cases, though, I regard the diagrams as being **heuristic** in nature. While even the most carefully drafted fall considerably short of mathematical rigor, the process of producing them forces the analyst to examine myriad details that are commonly ignored in semantic and grammatical descriptions. In my view they provide a level of precision and explicitness sufficient for most purposes, together with a kind of usability that facilitates discovery.

The notations and representational formats developed in later chapters thus do not amount to a mathematically respectable formalization. Many theorists would consider this unfortunate, taking it for granted both that language is amenable to discrete formalization and that scientific progress requires it. Reinforcing this prevalent attitude are such powerful icons as formal logic, computer programming, and Chomsky's archetypal conception of a "generative" grammar (a precise and explicit set of symbol-manipulating rules that enumerate all and only the well-formed sentences of a language). Collectively these engender and sustain certain expectations concerning what linguistic descriptions ought to look like and the level of mathematical rigor to be striven for. I believe, however, that these expectations are inappropriate for natural language, which is not a self-contained or well-defined formal system. I likewise reject the metaphor that likens mind to a digital computer and language to a program that it runs. CG is more at home in the "connectionist" ("neural network") world of dynamic systems, parallel processing, distributed representations, and computation by simultaneous constraint satisfaction.[6]

Since language (for reasons developed later) is neither self-contained nor well-defined, a complete formal description (a "generative grammar" in the classical sense) is held to be impossible in principle. The same is true when any particular dimension or facet of linguistic structure is examined individually. Language does not resemble a collection of computer programs. Rather, it inheres in the dynamic processing of **real** neural networks, and while the patterns that emerge are certainly

---

[6] With the emergence of this psychologically more plausible alternative, algorithmic computation over discrete symbolic representations is becoming progressively less important in linguistics. (In this context, "symbolic" refers to the symbols used in a computation, usually considered contentless. This is quite different from "symbolic" as understood in CG, where a symbolic structure is meaningful by definition.)

amenable to analysis, the discrete notations and static representations devised by linguists can at best only approximate them. But to recognize these limitations is not to
see everything as dissolving into a homogeneous mush. CG acknowledges the existence of highly elaborate linguistic structures, as well as the need to describe them
as precisely and explicitly as possible—both to understand language in its own terms
and to make evident what an adequate model of cognitive processing will have to
deal with. If CG diagrams remain heuristic, notations can nonetheless be developed
to characterize particular phenomena in as much explicit detail as present knowledge
allows. Asking or claiming any more would in my estimation be premature, pointless, and pretentious. Unless and until we have a clear conceptual understanding of
what is going on, there is no point in seeking mathematical precision.

The diagrams used for grammatical constructions come closest to being formal
representations. When worked out in careful detail, they might be considered "quasi-
formal", though I will describe them merely as **systematic**. Certain limitations have
to be noted. The diagrams are necessarily selective; even the more systematic ones
abstract away from many features not presently in focus. If drawn with any specificity, the diagrams representing expressions of even modest size prove quite complex
and unwieldy (e.g. fig. 7.13). Moreover, reading such a diagram takes some time and
effort, especially when the notational conventions have not yet been fully mastered.
I recognize these points but do not accept them as valid criticisms. After all, the same
limitations hold for both formulaic representations and the diagrams used in other
frameworks.

The diagrams used for grammar seem not to raise many eyebrows (tree-like representations being traditional in that domain). When it comes to semantics, however,
misconceptions abound and credulity is ceded more grudgingly. This is not surprising, since meaning is far more complex than grammar, and far more difficult to study
and describe. CG attempts at representing it have consequently been sketchier, more
informal, more preliminary, and less systematic than in the case of grammar.[7] Fair
minds will recognize that, in having an account of semantics which is neither exhaustive nor definitive, CG hardly stands alone. Yet, because it accepts the centrality of
meaning and tries to say something both substantive and psychologically plausible
about it, the deficiencies are especially apparent. Let me then correct a first misconception by stating unambiguously that no semantic representation proposed in CG
is ever considered exhaustive. For reasons outlined in chapter 2, complete semantic descriptions cannot realistically be envisaged. Any actual description must limit
itself to facets of the total meaning that are either central or relevant for a specific
immediate purpose. If they are principled, linguistically revealing, and empirically
supported, even partial characterizations are valid and useful.

What should they look like? With syntax and formal logic as their models, linguists
are accustomed to describing semantic structure by means of formulaic representations
comprising strings of discrete symbols. Hence the use in CG of semipictorial diagrams
(and even crude pictures on occasion) does, I think, raise eyebrows. This is not the place
to debate the very real issue of whether meaning, as an actual cognitive phenomenon,

---

[7] Because grammar is claimed to be symbolic, there is no sharp distinction between semantic and grammatical diagrams. The latter incorporate representations of meaning.

(a) 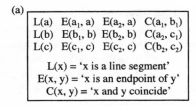   (b)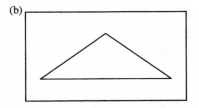

FIGURE 1.1

is better approximated by discrete symbolic representations or by something more analogical in nature. I would only argue that the kinds of diagrams employed in CG are heuristically effective and not inappropriate, given our present level of understanding. One could choose, for example, to represent the concept TRIANGLE in either a propositional or a diagrammatic format, as shown in figure 1.1. Although I certainly appreciate the virtues of the formulaic description, its imagic counterpart is understandably the one I would work with for most quotidian purposes.

From the frequent use of quasi-pictorial diagrams, some critics of CG have leaped to the incorrect conclusion that semantic structure is claimed to be entirely visual or spatial in nature. A related misconception is that CG can only deal with visuospatial notions. On the contrary, the essential constructs proposed for semantic description (e.g. various kinds of **prominence**) are applicable to any cognitive domain and independent of any particular mode of presentation. Another misapprehension is that the diagrams have a consistently analog character; yet another is that the schematic images they employ purport to be direct depictions of conceptual structure. The actual intent of these diagrams is rather more modest: to allow certain facets of conceptual organization to be represented in a format that is both user-friendly and explicit enough to serve as a basis for semantic and grammatical analysis.

I believe the diagrams serve this intended heuristic function reasonably well. While less than fully systematic, they can be made quite precise and force a kind of explicitness that facilitates discovery. The diagrams must, however, be used with caution, for they can be misleading as well as informative: like any other notation, they omit as much as they reveal, and they are biasing if not distorting. Constant awareness of their limitations is well advised.

1.2.4 The Spirit of the Enterprise

From a limited exposure to CG, many people receive the impression that it is "easy", apparently basing their assessment on its intuitive naturalness, its focus on meaning, the liberal use of diagrams, and the seeming absence of constraints. I agree at least in part: it is quite easy to do CG badly, and not so hard to do it indifferently. To do it well is obviously much harder. For various intrinsic reasons, arriving at analyses that will readily be accepted as sound and convincing is arguably more difficult than in other frameworks.

By and large, linguistic theory and training foster a basic expectation of discreteness in language and thus a strong inclination to posit it. This preference is evident in all domains and in every facet of investigation. Although its liabilities are now widely recognized, the following have all been prevalent features of modern linguistic thought and practice: (1) the virtually exclusive reliance on "digital" representations composed of discrete symbols; (2) the presumed adequacy of simple yes/no judgments of well-formedness; (3) the common neglect of linguistic **variation**; (4) the sharp distinction drawn between the **synchronic** study of language structure and the **diachronic** study of how it changes and evolves; (5) the assumption that language is clearly delimited and self-contained (with respect to other mental faculties, as well as associated phenomena like gesture); (6) the division of language into separate **components**, such as phonetics, phonology, lexicon, morphology, syntax, semantics, and pragmatics; (7) the focus on regular patterns permitting crisp generalizations (with the attendant difficulty in handling irregularity and generalizations of limited scope); (8) the default assumption of **classical** categories with strict boundaries, as opposed to **prototype** categories with degrees of membership; (9) the notion that **absolute predictability** ought to be the norm, so that anything which fails to achieve it is held to be of little interest; (10) the usual practice of formulating questions in terms of mutually exclusive alternatives.[8]

This world of discrete units and sharp boundaries is definitely attractive. Dividing makes it easier to conquer. In particular, if meaning can safely be ignored, the description of grammar is greatly simplified (at least superficially). Discrete structures are more readily analyzed and more amenable to perspicuous formalization. Also, the categorical statements and strong predictability afforded by discreteness are highly valued in science. Yet language was not necessarily designed for the convenience or predilections of the analyst. We must therefore ask whether the basic discreteness commonly assumed by linguistic theorists has been **discovered in** language or **imposed on** it. Since my own experience has led me to challenge all of points (1) to (10), I reluctantly conclude that it has largely been imposed.[9] This is not to say, however, that everything in language is continuous—far from it—or to deny the utility of discrete representations, provided that we recognize their possible limitations.

To the extent that language deviates from the expectations embodied in points (1) to (10), accurate descriptions are more difficult to achieve and less likely to satisfy orthodox theorists. Consider just one central issue: the putative autonomy of syntax vis-à-vis semantics. If syntax is separate and self-contained, so that meaning can be ignored, describing it becomes much easier in certain respects. It is easier, for example, to claim that the noun category represents an irreducible syntactic primitive, lacking intrinsic semantic content, than to propose a conceptual characterization that is both linguistically revealing and psychologically plausible (see ch. 4). It is easier just to list grammatical markers and state where they occur than to also determine and represent their meanings. An autonomous form of grammatical description

---

[8] I call this the **exclusionary fallacy** (FCG1: §1.1.6). It is exemplified by the commonly asked question (pointless in CG) of whether something is "in the lexicon" or "in the syntax".

[9] By virtue of training and inclination, I personally favor discreteness, but language has chosen not to cooperate. Points (1) to (10) are all addressed in later discussion.

is more easily extended to a new language or a new structural domain than is a symbolic account requiring semantic analysis.

Adding to the difficulty are the stringent constraints imposed on CG descriptions. A strong limitation on what kinds of elements can be posited is presented in §1.3.4. Further restrictions follow from the requirement of psychological plausibility. CG's nonmodular view of language—approaching it as an integral facet of cognition dependent on more general systems and abilities—implies an ultimate responsibility to the findings of other cognitive sciences. An important additional source of control is the nonautonomy of grammar. If grammar is truly independent of meaning, the analyst is free to describe it paying no heed to semantic considerations. By contrast, the symbolic view of grammar obliges the analyst to accommodate both form and meaning. When properly conducted, their investigation is mutually informing and mutually constraining. Grammatical markings and patterns call attention to subtle aspects of meaning and pose descriptive problems requiring semantic solutions. In doing semantic analysis, a linguist can use these as both a stimulus and a check: besides being psychologically plausible and internally well motivated, semantic descriptions must articulate well with grammar. Basic constructs of CG have in fact been developed through such a dialectic, which can be offered as an optimal working method.

This illustrates the first of several philosophical principles that have guided work in CG: the principle of **integration** favors inclusiveness and unification. It emphasizes the importance of considering and reconciling information from multiple sources (within a language, across languages, and across disciplines). Moreover, it encourages a unified treatment of the various dimensions of language structure (which have much in common at an abstract level) and urges that one avoid imposing dichotomous organization where there is actually a gradation. The principle of **naturalness** maintains that language—when properly analyzed—is by and large reasonable and understandable in view of its semiological and interactive functions, as well as its biological, cognitive, and sociocultural grounding. Cognitive and functional linguists find that virtually everything in language is **motivated** in such terms (even if very little is strictly **predictable**). A third principle, **patience**, amounts to the admonition that one should not put the cart before the horse. An example of patience is the withholding of judgment on questions that are probably premature (e.g. the extent to which language is innately specified). Another is the practice of delaying efforts at formalization until we have a basic conceptual understanding of what is going on. This principle does not imply a reluctance to make strong claims and working hypotheses, however.

1.3 Grammar as Symbolization

Enough preliminaries. It is time to offer an initial sketch of Cognitive Grammar, to be fleshed out in later chapters. The central matters to be addressed are the global organization of a linguistic system and what it means to say that grammar is symbolic in nature.

If it proves empirically adequate, CG represents the kind of theory linguists ought to be seeking. First, it is **natural** in several respects. Moreover, it offers both

conceptual unification and **theoretical austerity**, properties considered desirable in other sciences. CG is natural by virtue of its psychological plausibility, as well as the central place accorded meaning. It is further natural in that its global organization directly reflects the basic semiological function of language—namely, permitting meanings to be symbolized phonologically. To serve this function, a language needs at least three kinds of structures: **semantic, phonological**, and **symbolic**. The pivotal and most distinctive claim of CG is that **only** these are needed. This is one aspect of its theoretical austerity. What makes it possible is the notion that lexicon, morphology, and syntax form a continuum fully reducible to assemblies of symbolic structures. If valid, this notion represents a fundamental conceptual unification.

1.3.1 Symbolic Complexity

Semantic structures are conceptualizations exploited for linguistic purposes, notably as the meanings of expressions. Under the rubric **phonological structure**, I include not only sounds but also gestures and orthographic representations. Their essential feature is that of being overtly manifested, hence able to fulfill a symbolizing role.[10] **Symbolic structures** are not distinct from semantic and phonological structures, but rather incorporate them. As shown in figure 1.2(a), a symbolic structure (Σ) resides in a link between a semantic structure (S) and a phonological structure (P), such that either is able to evoke the other. I describe a symbolic structure as being **bipolar**: S is its **semantic pole**, and P its **phonological pole**. In formulaic representations, a slash is used to indicate a symbolic relationship. The morpheme *cat* can thus be given as [[CAT]/[cat]], where [CAT] stands for the complex conceptualization comprising its semantic pole, and the phonological pole is rendered orthographically in lowercase.

A defining property of human language is the formation of complex structures out of simpler ones. In figure 1.2(b), we see two symbolic structures combining to produce a higher-level symbolic structure, represented by the outer box.[11] These

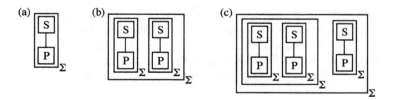

FIGURE 1.2

[10] For most linguistic purposes, we are more concerned with the cognitive representation of phonological structures than with their actual physical implementation. It is thus coherent to posit abstract ("schematic") phonological structures which, per se, cannot be overtly manifested.

[11] To simplify these initial diagrams, the semantic and phonological poles of higher-level structures are not separately depicted. Their semantic and phonological values are based on those of the component elements, though they are not strictly reducible to them.

lower-level and higher-level structures constitute a **symbolic assembly**. Of course, a higher-level symbolic structure is itself capable of entering into a combinatory relationship, producing a more elaborate symbolic assembly, as shown in diagram (c). We can say that a series of structures like (a), (b), and (c) exhibit progressively greater **symbolic complexity**. Through repeated combination, at successively higher levels of organization, assemblies having any degree of symbolic complexity can be formed. A **morpheme** is definable as an expression whose symbolic complexity is zero, i.e. it is not at all **analyzable** into smaller symbolic components. A morpheme can also be thought of as a **degenerate symbolic assembly** comprising just a single symbolic relationship, as in (a).

Corresponding to diagrams (a), (b), and (c) would be a series of expressions such as *moon*, *moonless*, and *moonless night*. Using hyphens for combinatory relationships, we can represent these formulaically as in (1):

(1)   (a) [[MOON]/[moon]]

     (b) [[[MOON]/[moon]] - [[LESS]/[less]]]

     (c) [[[[MOON]/[moon]] - [[LESS]/[less]]] - [[NIGHT]/[night]]]

All of these happen to be fixed, familiar expressions conventionally used in English. Hence they are all **lexical items**, granted CG's definition of **lexicon** as the set of **fixed expressions** in a language. This definition is useful, straightforward, and more or less consonant with an everyday understanding of the term. It is not, however, equivalent to other characterizations proposed by linguists, e.g. lexicon as the set of **words** in a language. Observe that there are fixed expressions larger than words (like *moonless night*), and there are possible words—such as *dollarless*—that are **novel** rather than familiar and conventionally established. Note further that the CG definition suggests the absence of any strict boundary between lexicon and nonlexical expressions, since familiarity and conventionality are matters of degree. The dictionary lists *ireless*, for example, and this word does seem vaguely familiar to me, but for most speakers it is no doubt novel and unfamiliar.

Clearly apparent in lexicon are several very basic phenomena that are quite evident in many other facets of cognition. The central role accorded to them is one aspect of CG's psychological plausibility. They also illustrate the general notion that language recruits, and thus intrinsically manifests in its own organization, a broad array of independently existing cognitive processes. The phenomena in question are association, automatization, schematization, and categorization.

1. Stated most generally, **association** is simply the establishing of psychological connections with the potential to influence subsequent processing. It has numerous manifestations in CG. Here we need only recall the association between a semantic and a phonological structure that defines a symbolic relationship.

2. **Automatization** is the process observed in learning to tie a shoe or recite the alphabet: through repetition or rehearsal, a complex structure is thoroughly mastered, to the point that using it is virtually automatic and requires little conscious monitoring. In CG parlance, a structure undergoes progressive **entrenchment** and eventually becomes established as a **unit**. Lexical items are expressions that have achieved the

status of units for representative members of a speech community. When it is relevant to draw the distinction, units are enclosed in boxes or square brackets; nonunits are in closed curves, boxes with rounded corners, or parentheses. *Dollarless* can thus be given as in (2), since the components *dollar* and *-less* have each achieved **unit status**, whereas the overall expression has not.

(2)   ([[DOLLAR]/[dollar]] - [[LESS]/[less]])

It is important to realize that unit status does not entail the absence or unimportance of components, merely the routinized nature of their execution (which does however tend to diminish their individual salience).[12] Though a unit, *moonless night* is clearly analyzable into *moonless* and *night*, and *moonless* into *moon* and *-less*.

3. By **schematization**, I mean the process of extracting the commonality inherent in multiple experiences to arrive at a conception representing a higher level of abstraction. Schematization plays a role in the acquisition of lexical units, if only because their conventional forms and meanings are less specific than the **usage events** (i.e. the actual pronunciations and contextual understandings) on the basis of which they are learned. For example, the basic sense of *ring*—roughly 'circular piece of jewelry worn on the finger'—is schematic relative to the conception of specific rings in specific contexts, which vary in such details as size, material, identity of the wearer, and so on. Schematization can be carried to different degrees, depending on the diversity of the elements it is based on. Since *ring* is also used for adornments worn in other places than on the finger, we can posit for it the more schematic value 'circular adornment worn on the body', with respect to which 'circular piece of jewelry worn on the finger' constitutes an **elaboration** or specific **instantiation**. Still more abstractly, *ring* can mean 'circular object' (consider the *rings* in gymnastics) or even just 'circular entity' (e.g. the *ring* of dirt left around a bathtub).

4. **Categorization** is most broadly describable as the interpretation of experience with respect to previously existing structures. A **category** is a set of elements judged equivalent for some purpose; for example, the alternate senses of a lexical item constitute a category, equivalent in having the same phonological realization. If structure A belongs to a category, it can be used to **categorize** another structure, B, which may then become a category member. Categorization is most straightforward when A is **schematic** for B, so that B **elaborates** or **instantiates** A. For this I use a solid arrow: A → B. The arrow indicates that B is fully compatible with A's specifications but is characterized with greater precision and detail. For instance, (3)(a) might represent the categorization responsible for *ring* being applied to circular arenas, as used in circuses and bullfighting.

(3)   (a) CIRCULAR ENTITY → CIRCULAR ARENA

        (b) CIRCULAR ARENA ---> RECTANGULAR ARENA

---

[12] Likewise, when reciting the alphabet in automatized fashion we still have to say all the letters.

However, it can also happen that B conflicts with A's specifications but is nonetheless assimilated to the category on the basis of an association or perceived similarity. A is then a **prototype** (at least locally), and B an **extension** from it. For this I use a dashed arrow: A ---> B. A possible example is (3)(b), the extension applying *ring* to rectangular arenas, as used in boxing.

1.3.2 Lexicon and Grammar

If lexicon resides in assemblies of symbolic structures, can we say the same for grammar? Not according to the current orthodoxy, where grammar is sharply distinguished from lexicon and described using a special set of primitives with no intrinsic meaning. Here I argue that a clear demarcation between lexicon and grammar is far from evident. I also indicate how grammar can be described with symbolic assemblies that vary along the same parameters as those describing lexicon, and within the same ranges of values.

In the standard conception, lexical items are essentially syntactic atoms. They are "inserted" into particular slots at the bottom of syntactic tree structures, as sketched in figure 1.3(a). The individual lexical items are continuous, self-contained, and nonoverlapping. While they may be complex, their internal structure is morphological rather than syntactic. *Healthy*, for example, is analyzable into the component morphemes *health* and *-y* (or, more tenuously, into *heal*, *-th*, and *-y*). Yet it functions syntactically as a simple adjective analogous to *big*.

This neat partitioning between lexicon and syntax can only be maintained by imposing artificial boundaries, however—in particular, by ignoring lexical items larger than words. Consider **idioms**. As fixed expressions whose meanings are not predictable from their parts, idioms satisfy both the CG definition of lexicon and a

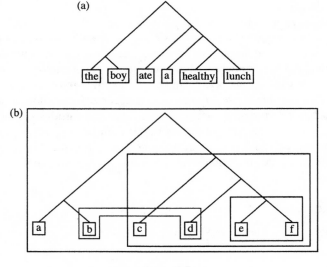

FIGURE 1.3

more restrictive one requiring semantic idiosyncrasy. They can nonetheless be of any size and exhibit internal structure that is clearly syntactic. For instance, *tall tale* represents an adjective + noun combination, *bury the hatchet* consists of a verb and its noun phrase object, while *A bird in the hand is worth two in the bush* is a full sentence. Rather than being syntactic atoms confined to particular slots in syntactic tree structures, idiomatic expressions subsume various portions of such trees, as is shown abstractly in figure 1.3(b) by the different-size boxes. The diagram also indicates that idioms can be manifested discontinuously (note the box enclosing [b] and [d]). A stock example is *keep tabs on*:

(4) (a) *The police **kept tabs on** all the leading activists.*

     (b) ***Tabs** were **kept** by the police **on** all the leading activists.*

The point is still more evident if we discard the requirement of semantic irregularity (which, in any case, is a matter of degree) and simply define lexicon as the set of fixed expressions in a language. Becoming a fluent speaker involves learning an enormous inventory of expressions larger than words, representing usual ways of conveying certain notions. These conventional expressions can be of any size and undeniably subsume varying portions of syntactic tree structures, in the manner of figure 1.3(b). Numerous examples can be found in any text. Conventional among linguists, for instance, are the following expressions, all culled from the previous paragraph: *neat partitioning, lexicon and syntax, artificial boundaries, impose artificial boundaries, in particular, larger than, satisfy... definition, more restrictive, any size, of any size, internal structure, tree structures, syntactic tree structures, idiomatic expressions, various portions of, stock example, a stock example.* According to standard linguistic doctrine, many of these are excluded from the linguistic system on grounds of being semantically and grammatically regular (hence derivable by rules). Their exclusion is arbitrary, however, if a language is characterized as the set of internalized structures (conventional units) that enable its users to speak and understand. Without a substantial inventory of prefabricated expressions, fluent real-time speech would hardly be possible. Theorists have grossly exaggerated the novelty of "novel sentences".

We have seen that lexical units can be ordered in terms of their degree of symbolic complexity (e.g. *moon < moonless < moonless night < a moonless night < on a moonless night*). A second parameter along which they vary is **schematicity,** or its converse **specificity**, pertaining to the precision and detail of their characterization. From taxonomic hierarchies like those in (5), it is evident that lexical items run the full gamut semantically from highly schematic, coarse-grained descriptions to those of a specific, fine-grained nature:

(5) (a) *thing → creature → animal → dog → poodle*

     (b) *do → act → propel → throw → fling*

It is less commonly appreciated that their phonological characterizations also vary along this parameter. For example, the English past-tense morpheme has the regular allomorphs [d], [t], and [əd] (as in *failed*, *rocked*, and *heeded*). Since the choice is phonologically predictable, linguists often posit a schematic representation that specifies only the presence of an alveolar stop (leaving voicing and the possible occurrence of [ə] to be filled in by rules). Many languages have morphemes manifested phonologically by reduplication. Thus a plural morpheme might have the schematic form CV-, i.e. a prefix consisting of a consonant plus a vowel, whose specific instantiations match the initial CV of the stem. In the Semitic languages, roots are traditionally described as comprising just a sequence of consonants (typically three), although in any actual form these occur with vowels contributing other lexical and grammatical information. In CG terms, the roots are phonologically schematic in regard to the placement and identity of the supporting vowels.

Many multiword lexical units contain schematic elements. A well-known example is *X crane X+POSS neck*, where *X* refers schematically to the agent and neck possessor. It represents the commonality inherent in an open-ended set of expressions in which *X* is instantiated by a specific nominal element: *I craned my neck, She was craning her neck, Phil always cranes his neck*, and so on. Another partially schematic unit is V_s *X in the* N_b, where V_s is a verb of striking like *hit, kick, strike*, or *poke* and N_b is a body-part noun like *shin, back, face, eye*, or *knee*. Certain partial instantiations of this schema are themselves established units ("collocations"), e.g. *hit X in the back, kick X in the shin, poke X in the eye*. Even more schematic is the template *a* N_1 + *less* N_2, instantiated by specific unit expressions such as *a moonless night, a childless couple, a hopeless situation, a treeless plain, a fruitless search, a cordless phone*, and so on.

It should be apparent that this list of partially schematic unit expressions could be extended indefinitely. They constitute an essential—perhaps even the preponderant—component of a fluent speaker's conventional linguistic knowledge. Yet standard linguistic theory hardly recognizes their existence, let alone accommodate them in any straightforward manner. The problem is that they conform to the stereotype of neither lexicon nor grammar, and by combining features of each, they subvert the claim that these are sharply distinct. Units like *X crane X+POSS neck*, V_s *X in the* N_b, and *a* N_1+*less* N_2 are nonstereotypical for grammar by virtue of containing specific lexical elements. They are nonstereotypical for lexicon because of their partial schematicity. They are not themselves full-fledged expressions but patterns abstracted from them and potentially used in forming new ones. To this extent they are grammar-like, since grammar by definition comprises the patterns used in forming complex expressions. In an effort to preserve the standard dichotomy, *X crane X+POSS neck* could be assigned to the lexicon, as it contains the indisputably "lexical" elements *crane* and *neck*, whereas *a* N_1 + *less* N_2 might be considered grammatical because its only specific components (*a* and *-less*) are "grammatical markers". This will not solve the problem, however. Apart from being aprioristic, it leaves us with an arbitrary choice in cases like V_s *X in the* N_b, where V_s and N_b are intermediate in specificity (V_s designating a certain type of action, and N_b a body part). What the linguistic data seems to be trying to tell us is that lexicon and grammar form a gradation instead of being sharply dichotomous. That, of course, is a central claim of CG, which further contends that the full gradation reduces to assemblies of symbolic structures.

1.3.3 Grammar as Symbolic Assemblies

We have seen that symbolic assemblies range widely along three main parameters. First, they vary in symbolic complexity, as sketched in figure 1.2 and exemplified by a series of lexical units like *sharp < sharpen < sharpener < pencil sharpener < electric pencil sharpener*. Second, they vary in their degree of specificity (or conversely, schematicity), as seen in (5), and also in a series like (6), where the initial structure is wholly schematic, the next partially instantiated, and the last fully specific:

(6) V_s *X in the* $N_b \rightarrow$ *kick X in the shin* $\rightarrow$ *kick my pet giraffe in the shin*

Third, symbolic assemblies vary in the extent to which they achieve the status of units and become conventional within a speech community.[13] The first two structures in (6) are plausibly ascribed the status of conventional units in English, whereas the last one—taken as a whole—is surely novel. The different facets of lexicon and grammar can all be characterized as symbolic assemblies occupying various regions in the abstract space defined by these three parameters. Bear in mind, though, that we are dealing with graded phenomena. The regions corresponding to particular traditional notions are expected to overlap, and specific lines of demarcation are held to be arbitrary.

Full-fledged **expressions**—those we could actually use—are specific at the phonological pole, for they have to be capable of being spoken, signed, or written down.[14] At the semantic pole there is more flexibility, though actual expressions tend to be rather specific. Since expressions can obviously be of any size, they range freely along the dimension of symbolic complexity. They can also have any degree of conventionality. To the extent that expressions become entrenched and attain the

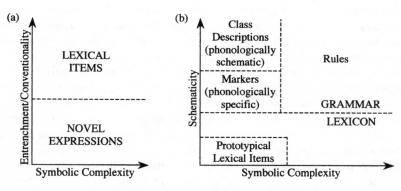

FIGURE 1.4

---

[13] For ease of discussion, I am conflating two parameters that eventually have to be distinguished: **entrenchment** or **unit status** (pertaining to a particular speaker) and **conventionality** (pertaining to a speech community).

[14] This is basically what the term **expression** is meant to convey. The notion involves many subtleties, but they will not concern us (FCG1: §11.2.1).

status of conventional units, they constitute **lexical items**. To the extent that they do not, they are **novel**. This is sketched in figure 1.4(a), where the dashed line indicates the absence of any sharp boundary.

The lexicon and grammar of a language consist of symbolic assemblies that in substantial measure have achieved the status of conventional units. Figure 1.4(b) shows their arrangement with respect to the parameters of schematicity and symbolic complexity. The elements traditionally recognized as (prototypical) lexical items are phonologically and semantically specific expressions with only limited symbolic complexity: *dog, moonless, carefully, toothbrush*. I suggest, however, that drawing any particular line of demarcation along either parameter would be arbitrary. A broader array of structures are therefore accepted in CG as lexical items, including symbolic units that are schematic either phonologically (like Semitic roots) or semantically (e.g. *do, a, -less*), as well as assemblies of indefinite symbolic complexity (such as idioms and proverbs). Also subsumed under lexicon are symbolically complex assemblies that are both semantically and phonologically schematic in certain positions, like *X crane X+POSS neck* or *X take Y over X+POSS knee and spank Y*.

Where does lexicon stop and grammar begin? The point, of course, is that there is no particular place. But this is not to say that no distinction can be drawn. The key parameter is specificity. To the extent that symbolic assemblies are specific, they would tend to be regarded as lexical, both traditionally and in CG. To the extent that they are schematic, they would generally be considered grammatical. Thus **lexicon** can be characterized as residing in fairly specific symbolic assemblies, and **grammar** in more schematic ones. Toward the two extremes are clear cases unequivocally identifiable as lexical or grammatical (e.g. *dog* vs. a pattern for forming relative clauses). In between lie many structures (such as $V_s X$ *in the* N_b) validly thought of either way, depending on one's purpose.

The claim, then, is that grammar reduces to schematic symbolic assemblies. But what exactly does this mean? How does symbolic grammar work? Later sections and chapters answer these questions in some detail. For now, let us focus on three basic matters: grammatical markers, grammatical classes, and grammatical rules. These are all describable by means of symbolic assemblies. What distinguishes them are the regions they occupy in the abstract space defined by the parameters of schematicity and symbolic complexity.

1. As parts of expressions, **grammatical markers** are specific at the phonological pole, since they have to be capable of overt realization.[15] Even those reasonably ascribed a schematic phonological value, like a reduplicative morpheme or the regular English past tense, acquire specific segmental content in a given expression. On the other hand, grammatical markers tend to be quite schematic at the semantic pole—otherwise they would simply be lexical items. There is little agreement among linguists concerning which elements to identify as "grammatical" rather than "lexical". Examples commonly treated both ways include prepositions (e.g. *for, to, at, like*), modals (*may, can, will, shall, must*), and indefinite pronouns (*someone, anywhere, everybody, whatever, who*). These all resemble canonical lexical items

---

[15] Alternate terms for grammatical markers include "grammatical morpheme", "function word", "empty word", "formative", and "closed-class element".

in having clearly discernible meanings. At the same time, their meanings resemble those of classic grammatical markers in being tenuous, abstract, and hard to elucidate. From the standpoint of CG, which posits a gradation, such uncertainty is unproblematic; because schematicity is a matter of degree, it is actually expected that certain elements should be ambivalent as to their lexical or grammatical status. The essential point, though, is that even the most "grammatical" of grammatical markers—forms like *be*, *do*, *of*, the infinitival *to*, agreement markers, case inflections, and derivational affixes—are viewed in CG as being meaningful.

2. Grammatical markers are closely related to **grammatical classes**, which they often serve to derive or signal. A class per se, however, is not overtly manifested but resides in a set of symbolic structures that function alike in certain respects. CG maintains that grammatical classes are definable in symbolic terms and, more controversially, that basic classes like noun, verb, adjective, and adverb can be given uniform semantic characterizations (see ch. 4). Hence the members of a class all instantiate a schematic description representing their abstract commonality. For instance, the bipolar schema defining the noun class can be written as [[THING]/[...]], where [THING] specifies that a noun refers to a **thing** (in the most general sense of that term), and [...] indicates that no particular phonological properties are specified. What it means for an expression to be a noun is that it instantiates this schema:

(7)   (a) [[THING]/[...]] → [[MOON]/[moon]]

    (b) [[THING]/[...]] → [[[TOOTH]/[tooth]] - [[BRUSH]/[brush]]]

    (c) [[THING]/[...]] → [[[[MOON]/[moon]] - [[LESS]/[less]]] - [[NIGHT]/[night]]]]

Moon, *toothbrush*, and *moonless night* are all nouns because each is a symbolic structure that designates a thing.[16] Most nouns elaborate the schema both semantically and phonologically. Arguably, though, the grammatical element *thing*—the one appearing in forms like *something*, *nothing*, and *anything*—is more specific only at the phonological pole: [[THING]/[thing]]. Thus, in accordance with figure 1.4(b), the noun class description is schematic at both poles, the grammatical formative *thing* is schematic semantically but phonologically specific, and a typical lexical item like *moon* is also semantically specific.

3. **Grammatical rules** occupy the remaining portion of the abstract space depicted in figure 1.4(b). By **rule** I simply mean the characterization of some pattern.[17] In CG, rules take the form of schemas: they are abstract templates obtained by reinforcing the commonality inherent in a set of instances. Since grammatical rules are patterns in the formation of symbolically complex expressions, they are themselves symbolically complex as well as schematic. Complex expressions consist of specific

[16] This semantically based characterization is not limited to traditionally recognized lexical items, or even to fixed expressions. In this broad sense, even a full noun phrase (fixed or novel) is classed as a special kind of noun.

[17] The term "rule" is often used more narrowly, e.g. for "constructive" statements (like the rewriting rules of generative grammar) as opposed to templates.

symbolic assemblies, and the rules describing them are schematic assemblies that embody their common features.

Schematization can be carried to any degree. If particular expressions give rise to low-level schemas like *hit X in the back*, *kick X in the shin*, and *poke X in the eye*, these in turn support the extraction of the higher-level schema V_s *X in the* N_b. This may then instantiate a still more abstract schema based on a wider array of data. For instance, V_c *X P the* N_b (where V_c is a verb of contact) would also subsume such patterns as *kiss X on the cheek*, *grasp X by the wrist*, *chuck X under the chin*, and *grab X around the waist*. These examples further show that the different components of a complex symbolic assembly can be schematic to varying degrees.

The schematic assemblies describing grammatical patterns can also exhibit any degree of symbolic complexity. Simpler schemas are often incorporated as components of more complex ones. For instance, adjectives like *moonless*, *childless*, *hopeless*, *treeless*, *fruitless*, and *cordless* instantiate a derivational pattern that we can write as *N+less*.[18] This schematic symbolic assembly is one component of N_1*+less* N_2 (as in *moonless night*, *childless couple*, *hopeless situation*, *treeless plain*, *fruitless search*, *cordless phone*), which in turn is part of *a* N_1*+less* N_2.

A speaker's knowledge of grammatical patterns resides in a vast inventory of symbolic assemblies ranging widely along the parameters of schematicity and symbolic complexity. It is a highly structured inventory, in that the assemblies bear a variety of relations to one another, such as instantiation, overlap, and inclusion. These schemas are abstracted from occurring expressions, and once established as units they can serve as templates guiding the formation of new expressions on the same pattern. For example, once abstracted to represent the commonality of fixed expressions like *moonless night*, *childless couple*, *hopeless situation*, etc., the schematic assembly N_1*+less* N_2 is subsequently available to **sanction** the occurrence of novel expressions like *moonless world*, *dollarless surgeon*, and *ireless dwarf*.[19] All of this holds for both morphological and syntactic patterns. If we wish to make a distinction, we can do no better than follow the tradition of drawing the line at the level of the word. **Morphology** is then described by schematic assemblies (like *N+less*) whose instantiations are no larger than words, and **syntax** by assemblies (like N_1*+less* N_2) with multiword instantiations. Even so the boundary is fuzzy, if only due to expressions (such as compounds) that are intermediate between single words and multiword sequences.

1.3.4 The Content Requirement

Compared with the descriptive machinery routinely invoked in other frameworks, CG is quite conservative and highly restrictive in what it allows the analyst to posit. Any flights of fancy cognitive grammarians might be prone to are seriously

---

[18] Formulaic representations like *N+less*, N_1*+less* N_2, and V_s *X in the* N_b are merely abbreviatory. Actual CG descriptions of such assemblies have to specify in some detail both the internal structure of the symbolic elements and the relations they bear to one another.

[19] The extraction of a schema need not require fixed expressions. Schematization is just the reinforcing of recurring commonalities, which can perfectly well inhere in novel expressions, none of which ever coalesces as a unit.

constrained by the **content requirement**. Adopted as a strong working hypothesis, this requirement states that **the only elements ascribable to a linguistic system are (i) semantic, phonological, and symbolic structures that actually occur as parts of expressions; (ii) schematizations of permitted structures; and (iii) categorizing relationships between permitted structures.** The thrust of the content requirement is that the linguistic knowledge we ascribe to speakers should be limited to elements of form and meaning found in actually occurring expressions, or which derive from such elements via the basic psychological phenomena listed in §1.3.1: association, automatization, schematization, and categorization. By keeping our feet on the ground, this restriction assures both naturalness and theoretical austerity.

Provision (i) of the content requirement imposes the symbolic view of grammar and grounds linguistic descriptions in the sounds and meanings that occur in actual usage. These are **directly apprehended**, in the sense that we hear or produce the sounds of a usage event and understand it in a certain way. They also have intrinsic **content** related to broader realms of experience—the sounds of speech represent a particular class of auditory phenomena, and linguistic meanings are special cases of conceptualization. By contrast, grammar is not per se something that untrained speakers are aware of. It is not directly apprehended in the same way that sounds and meanings are, nor does it manifest any broader experiential realm. Having no independently discernible content, grammar is reasonably seen as residing in the abstracted commonality of sound-meaning pairings—that is, as being symbolic in nature.

Let us see how the content requirement applies, starting with phonological structures. Provision (i) allows us to posit specific elements such as segments, syllables, and any larger sequences sufficiently frequent to become entrenched as units. As speakers of English, for example, we master particular sound segments ([a], [t], [m], [s], etc.) and a substantial number of recurring syllables (e.g. [hap], [liv], [mɛk]).[20] Provision (ii) permits schematized segments and syllables. At different levels of abstraction, for instance, schemas can be posited representing what is common to the high front vowels of a language, the front vowels, or the vowels in general. Each schema characterizes a **natural class** of segments. Similarly, the schematic template [CVC] embodies the abstract commonality of [hap], [liv], [mɛk], and many other syllables. Provision (iii) lets us posit categorizing relationships, such as those between schemas and their instantiations. Thus [[CVC] → [hap]] indicates that [hap] is categorized as an instance of the [CVC] syllable type.

Analogously, the content requirement allows the postulation of specific and schematic semantic structures, as well as relationships of semantic categorization. Conceptual units are most clearly linguistically relevant—and thus qualify as semantic units—by virtue of being individually symbolized.[21] Permitted under provision (i) of the content requirement are conceptions functioning as the conventional meanings of

---

[20] Considering them as purely phonological units, it is irrelevant whether these segments and syllables can function as morphemes. Prosodic elements naturally have to be posited as well.

[21] Semantic units need not be individually symbolized (any more than phonological units need be individually meaningful). For instance, there is no everyday term for the maximal extension of a category, i.e. the union of all instances. Yet this notion is one conceptual component of *all*, *most*, and *some*, which refer to various proportions of the full extension.

lexical items. Given an array of similar semantic units, such as [ROSE], [DAISY], and [TULIP], provision (ii) sanctions a more schematic structure representing their abstract commonality, in this case [FLOWER]. While [FLOWER] is itself a lexical meaning, hence directly available under (i), we can readily imagine schemas that are not. It is plausible, for example, that from notions like [HORSE], [DONKEY], and [ZEBRA] many speakers extract a schematic conception, [HORSE-LIKE CREATURE], that they have no lexical means of expressing (*equine* being a learnèd form). In either circumstance, relationships of semantic categorization are ascribable to the linguistic system in accordance with provision (iii): [[FLOWER] → [TULIP]], [[HORSE-LIKE CREATURE] → [DONKEY]]. Also permitted are relationships of semantic extension, such as [[HORSE] ---> [DONKEY]], where a donkey is categorized as an atypical kind of horse.

Examples of symbolic units allowed by clause (i) of the content requirement are specific nouns like [[MOON]/[moon]], [[TULIP]/[tulip]], and [[HOPE]/[hope]]. Clause (ii) permits the class schema [[THING]/[...]], describing what nouns have in common, and (iii) lets us classify particular elements as nouns, e.g. [[[THING]/[...]] → [[MOON]/[moon]]]. We must also consider symbolically complex expressions, for instance *moonless*, *cordless*, and *toothless*. These are permitted by clause (i), the N+*less* pattern by (ii), and their categorization as instances of the pattern by (iii). For *moonless*, we see this formulaically in (8)(a)–(c), respectively:

(8) (a) [[[MOON]/[moon]] - [[LESS]/[less]]]

    (b) [[[THING]/[...]] - [[LESS]/[less]]]

    (c) [[[[THING]/[...]] - [[LESS]/[less]]] → [[[MOON]/[moon]] - [[LESS]/[less]]]]

It is claimed that grammar resides in vast networks of symbolic assemblies such as these, with varying degrees of abstraction and symbolic complexity.

The content requirement keeps the analyst from resorting to several kinds of devices commonly used in formalist theories. Since patterns can only arise by the schematization of occurring expressions, this requirement rules out derivations from underlying structures with divergent properties.[22] Also ruled out are formless, meaningless elements (e.g. "traces") posited solely to drive the machinery of autonomous syntax. Last but not least, the content requirement proscribes the use of "filters", rules specifically stating what **cannot** occur in well-formed expressions. CG assumes that languages are learned and that they are learned primarily by reinforcement of the commonality inherent in what actually **does** occur. I cannot yet claim to have demonstrated that negative statements are avoidable altogether, that descriptions using only positive specifications prove optimal for all linguistic structures and strictures. This is nonetheless quite natural and desirable as a working hypothesis, if only because it offers the most straightforward account of language learning.

---

[22] Provision (iii) is intended to permit extensions (and chains of extensions) from a prototype, however. (For discussion of the difference, see FCG1: §11.3.3.)

2

Conceptual Semantics

In a rare instance of consensus, linguists agree that grammar is extremely complex and hard to properly describe. Why should it be so difficult? The reason, I suggest, is precisely the fact that grammar is meaningful. Rather than being autonomous, it resides in schematized patterns of conceptual structuring and symbolization. For this reason we need a conceptual semantics. We cannot describe grammar revealingly without a principled and reasonably explicit characterization of the conceptual structures it incorporates.

2.1 Meaning and Semantic Representations

How we think about grammar depends on our view of linguistic meaning. Unfortunately, there is no general agreement on this score. Even the most basic issues—for example, the role of cognition in semantics—are points of chronic and continued contention. Let me then outline the rationale for certain positions adopted in CG.

2.1.1 Are Meanings in the Head?

Our concern is with the meanings of linguistic expressions. Where are these meanings to be found? From a cognitive linguistic perspective, the answer is evident: meanings are in the minds of the speakers who produce and understand the expressions. It is hard to imagine where else they might be. Yet there are many scholars who resist or reject that answer.[1] A conceptualist view of meaning is not as self-evident as it might first seem and has to be properly interpreted.

What are the alternatives? The first two options, in their extreme form, leave the human mind and body out of the picture altogether. The **platonic** view treats

---

[1] In fact, semantics textbooks often specifically argue against the identification of meanings with concepts (e.g. Palmer 1981: 24–29).

language as an abstract, disembodied entity that cannot be localized. Like the objects and laws of mathematics (e.g. the geometric ideal of a circle), linguistic meanings are seen as transcendent, existing independently of minds and human endeavor. More traditional is the **objectivist** position—still prevalent in philosophy, logic, and formal semantics—identifying the meaning of a sentence with the set of conditions under which it is true. These "truth conditions" pertain to what the world is like objectively, irrespective of how it might be conceptualized. Both options stand in sharp contrast to the cognitive semantic view that meaning derives from embodied human experience. This book should amply demonstrate the critical role of mental processes in semantics and grammar.

More reasonable is the **interactive** alternative, which does take people into account but claims that an individual mind is not the right place to look for meanings. Instead, meanings are seen as emerging dynamically in discourse and social interaction. Rather than being fixed and predetermined, they are actively negotiated by interlocutors on the basis of the physical, linguistic, social, and cultural context. Meaning is not localized but distributed, aspects of it inhering in the speech community, in the pragmatic circumstances of the speech event, and in the surrounding world. In particular, it is not inside a single speaker's head. The static, insular view ascribed to cognitive semantics is deemed incapable of handling the dynamic, intersubjective, context-dependent nature of meaning construction in actual discourse.

In and of itself, the interactive alternative is certainly correct. It is not however an alternative—its essential ideas are in fact accepted as basic tenets of cognitive semantics. Though common, the portrayal of cognitive semantics as being static and insular is simply wrong. Conversely, a revealing account of communicative interaction needs to acknowledge and characterize the conceptualizations employed in discourse. The cognitive and interactive approaches are therefore quite compatible, provided that the former is correctly portrayed and the latter adequately formulated. It is only with an extremist formulation of interactionism—one which denies cognition a central role—that any conflict arises.

The CG position on these issues accommodates both the cognitive and the interactive perspectives. We can best appreciate it by contrasting it with certain extreme positions standing in polar opposition to one another. Consider the opposing positions that **everything** of consequence is inside the head, and that **nothing** of consequence is inside the head. According to the former (a kind of solipsism), cognition takes place within a hermetically sealed skull affording no input from or access to the exterior; it is thus asocial and acontextual, contemplation being limited to what goes on inside. According to the latter, meaning is created through communicative interaction between people whose heads—for all intents and purposes—are totally empty. To state these positions explicitly is to see how silly they are. Even so, cognitive linguists are not infrequently charged with solipsism, and interactionist rhetoric sometimes gives the impression that anything inside the head is irrelevant.

The cognition envisaged by cognitive linguists is noninsular, being grounded in perception and bodily experience. Since mental development is stimulated and guided by social interaction, the skills and knowledge acquired are very much attuned to the sociocultural surroundings. The conceptualizations we entertain are undeniably internal, in the sense of taking place in the brain, yet reach beyond it in the sense of being conceptualizations **of** some facet of the world.[2] In speaking, we conceptualize not only what we are talking about but also the context in all its dimensions, including our assessment of the knowledge and intentions of our interlocutor. Rather than being insular, therefore, conceptualization should be seen as a primary means of engaging the world. And empty heads cannot talk, interact, or negotiate meanings.

Closely related is the issue of localization. Can meanings be **localized**, contained in the minds of individual speakers, or are they **distributed** over a speech community, the immediate context of speech, as well as the physical and sociocultural world? I take it as evident that the extreme version of distributionism, where nothing at all is ascribed to individual minds, is simply untenable. Its polar opposite—the extreme version of localism, putting everything of relevance inside a single mind—is likewise untenable. But provided that some subtle but crucial distinctions are made, I find it reasonable to say that a single speaker grasps an expression's meaning.

We must first distinguish between, on the one hand, the various circumstances that create the potential for meaningful interaction and, on the other hand, the actual mental experience of an individual engaging in such an interaction. Countless aspects of our surroundings do carry meaning potential: the fact of facing a particular interlocutor in a particular social situation, an artifact clearly designed for a certain function, an action conforming to a familiar cultural practice, and so on. Thus, if a doctor extends a tongue depressor toward my mouth and says *Open wide*, my understanding of what the doctor intends and what I am supposed to do is far more comprehensive than anything derivable from the linguistic expression alone. (I know, for example, that I will not satisfy the request by approaching a cabinet and pulling a drawer out all the way.) It would not be unreasonable to describe the relevant circumstances as being "imbued with meaning" or as "part of the meaning" an expression has in context. Yet I think we gain in clarity and analytical precision by reserving the term "meaning" for how a speaker understands an expression (in either a speaking or a listening capacity). It thus incorporates a speaker's apprehension of the circumstances, and exploits the meaning potential they carry, but cannot be identified with those circumstances. So defined, an expression's meaning resides in the conceptualizing activity of individual speakers.

But does a single individual really ever know an expression's meaning? One objection is that linguistic meanings are conventional and thus reside at the social rather than the individual level. Another is that many expressions have meanings that are only partially known by any particular speaker. The term *electron*, for instance, is understood very differently by a theoretical physicist, by an electrical engineer, and by someone like myself with only a vague, partial, and metaphorical idea of its import. It is thus concluded that meanings are distributed over the entire speech community and cannot be found in any single person's head.

While these observations are true enough, the conclusion depends on the simplistic assumption that just one kind of entity counts as "the meaning" of an expression.

---

[2] Of course, the "world" includes both the real world and the mental worlds we construct, as well as the body and even our mental experience itself (to the extent that we can reflect on it, as opposed to merely undergoing it).

We can validly distinguish, however, between what a single speaker knows and the collective knowledge of a whole society. The former is arguably more basic, since collective knowledge consists in (or at least derives from) the knowledge of individuals.[3] For purposes of studying language as part of cognition, an expression's meaning is first and foremost its meaning **for** a single (representative) speaker. This is not to deny or diminish the social aspect of linguistic meaning. An individual's notion of what an expression means develops through communicative interaction and includes an assessment of its degree of conventionality in the speech community. By their nature, moreover, certain questions have to be studied at the population level (e.g. how norms are established and maintained, the extent to which consensus is achieved, and the range of variation actually encountered). Still, these questions cannot be fully answered unless the knowledge of individual speakers is taken into account.

Lastly, consider the accusation that cognitive semantics—owing to the fixed, static nature of concepts—cannot accommodate the dynamicity of actual language use: rather than being fixed, the values of linguistic elements are actively negotiated; and rather than being static, the meanings of complex expressions emerge and develop in discourse. Though frequently made, this accusation is groundless. In the first place, meaning is not identified with concepts but with **conceptualization**, the term being chosen precisely to highlight its dynamic nature. Conceptualization is broadly defined to encompass any facet of mental experience. It is understood as subsuming (1) both novel and established conceptions; (1) not just "intellectual" notions, but sensory, motor, and emotive experience as well; (3) apprehension of the physical, linguistic, social, and cultural context; and (4) conceptions that develop and unfold through processing time (rather than being simultaneously manifested). So even if "concepts" are taken as being static, conceptualization is not.

The remaining issue is whether linguistic meanings are fixed and predetermined or whether they are actively negotiated by interlocutors. It ought to be evident that the latter is quite compatible with a conceptualist semantics—Why would anyone assume that conceptualization has to be rigid and inflexible? Once more we can usefully consider two extreme positions, neither of which is tenable. At one extreme is the notion that there is no flexibility whatever: a lexical item has a fixed, invariant meaning, and the meaning of a sentence is completely predicted by rules of semantic composition. Cognitive semantics explicitly rejects this option. At the opposite extreme is the view that nothing at all is conventionally established: an element's meaning is negotiated from scratch every time it is used, with no prior expectation whatever about its possible value. I doubt that anyone actually believes this (though interactionist rhetoric sometimes suggests it). Clearly, there must be something inside the head. Speakers must have some preconception of what the words they use are normally expected to mean. Otherwise the meanings negotiated would be completely random, and *cat* would have no greater likelihood of meaning 'feline' than 'walnut', 'book', or 'through'. While everything may be negotiable, something has to be learned and conventionalized as a basis for negotiation.

---

[3] Societal knowledge is also stored in books, databases, the design of artifacts, and so on, but ultimately these reduce to the activity of individual minds in creating or using them.

2.1.2 What Are Meanings Made Of?

Admitting that meaning resides in conceptualization does not itself solve anything but merely lets us formulate the problem. What do we actually mean by "conceptualization"? What are its general nature and specific properties? How do we go about investigating it? How can we describe it? At present there are no definitive answers to such questions. Considerable progress is, however, being made in cognitive linguistics, in the broader context of cognitive science. I would argue that CG embodies a coherent and plausible view of conceptualization, allowing a principled basis for characterizing many facets of semantic and grammatical structure.

Ultimately, conceptualization resides in cognitive processing. Having a certain mental experience resides in the occurrence of a certain kind of neurological activity. Conceptualization can thus be approached from either a **phenomenological** or a **processing** standpoint: we can attempt to characterize either our mental experience per se or the processing activity that constitutes it. Cognitive semantics has focused on the former, which is obviously more accessible and amenable to investigation via linguistic evidence. As for processing, it can be studied at different levels (both functional and neurological) and by such varied means as psycholinguistic experiment, clinical research (notably on aphasia), neurological imaging, and now even computer modeling (Holmqvist 1993; Regier 1996; Lakoff and Johnson 1999: appendix). Still, these approaches rely on phenomenological characterizations for guidance and as the basis for interpreting results. And despite the rapid progress being made, a secure and detailed understanding of how specific linguistic structures are neurologically implemented remains a long-term goal.

Yet even at this early stage, speculative but plausible connections can be posited between the phenomenological and processing levels. What we experience as the prominence of conceived entities is reasonably ascribed to a high level of neural activation.[4] The spreading of activation is the evident basis for association and can thus be implicated in many linguistic phenomena (Deane 1992). I further suggest that any conceptual ordering or sequenced mental access implies a corresponding seriality in the processing that constitutes it. In mentally reciting the alphabet, for instance, we run through the letters in sequence, each prompting the next. It seems evident that this ordered conception resides in the ordered occurrence of the neural operations representing each letter, and that our knowledge of the proper sequencing resides in processing routines where the operations representing one letter precede and activate those representing its successor.

As neurological activity, conceptualization has a temporal dimension. Even the simplest conception requires some span of time for its occurrence, and with a more elaborate conception its temporal progression is subject to awareness. The meaning of a complex sentence (like this one) can hardly be apprehended instantaneously; more likely it unfolds on a clause-by-clause basis, there being no instant when all facets of it are simultaneously active and accessible. Conceptualization is **dynamic**

---

[4] Chafe characterizes discourse status in terms of activation levels: for "given", "accessible", and "new" information, he posits the respective levels "active", "semiactive", and "inactive" (1994: ch. 6).

in the sense that it unfolds through processing time, and also because the specific course of development is a significant aspect of our mental experience. Thus a pair of sentences like (1)(a)–(b) are not semantically equivalent, despite using the same words to characterize the same objective situation:

(1)   (a) *A line of trees extends from the highway to the river.*

(b) *A line of trees extends from the river to the highway.*

Although the situation described is static, the sentences evoke dynamic conceptualizations in which we mentally scan along the line of trees in one direction or the other. These opposing ways of building up to the full conception, through processing time, result in subtly different mental experiences and different linguistic meanings.

Dynamicity bears on the fundamental issue of whether conceptual structure is basically **propositional** in nature or whether it has an **imagistic** character. What kind of format should we ascribe to thoughts and concepts, especially at lower levels of organization? Should they be formulaic in nature, comprising strings of discrete symbols? Or should they be more analogical, more directly depictive of the structure represented?[5] The propositional view, still prevalent if not predominant, treats concepts as expressions formulated in a "language of thought" (Fodor 1979), consisting of conceptual "primitives" (the "vocabulary") and principles for their combination (the "syntax"). The meaning of *enter*, for example, might be mentally represented by something comparable to the following formula (Jackendoff 1983):

(2) $[_{\text{Event}} \text{ GO } ([_{\text{Thing}} \text{ X}], [_{\text{Path}} \text{ TO } ([_{\text{Place}} \text{ IN } ([_{\text{Thing}} \text{ Y}])])])]$

Cognitive linguists incline more to imagistic accounts. The best-known proposal posits a set of **image schemas**, described as schematized patterns of activity abstracted from everyday bodily experience, especially pertaining to vision, space, motion, and force. Image schemas are seen as basic, "preconceptual" structures that give rise to more elaborate and more abstract conceptions (or at least provide their skeletal organization) through combination and metaphorical projection.[6] As shown in figure 2.1, for instance, the concept ENTER can be analyzed as a combination of the image schemas object, source-path-goal, and container-content.

An imagistic approach is no less capable than a propositional one of precisely describing complex structures in terms of simpler conceptual components. It is arguably

---

[5] The issue is whether conceptualization per se is discrete and propositional in nature, independently of the discrete, propositional format imposed by linguistic encoding. Is thought itself "language-like" at all levels? Does the concept of a triangle, for example, decompose into propositions in the manner of fig. 1.1(a)?

[6] Johnson 1987; Lakoff 1987, 1990; Hampe 2005. Examples cited by Johnson are container, blockage, enablement, path, cycle, part-whole, full-empty, iteration, surface, balance, counterforce, attraction, link, near-far, merging, matching, contact, object, compulsion, restraint removal, mass-count, center-periphery, scale, splitting, superimposition, process, and collection. Note that diagrams like those in fig. 2.1 are not to be identified per se as image schemas (which are patterns of mental activity) but are merely intended to evoke them and suggest their nature.

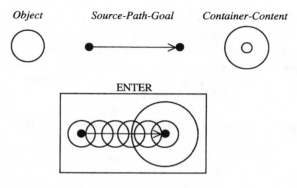

FIGURE 2.1

advantageous because—as seen by comparing (2) with figure 2.1—the nature of a mental experience is reflected more directly in a complex image than in a complex formula. Also, images seem particularly well suited (and formulas unsuited) for certain aspects of conception. Central to the concept of a trumpet, for instance, is a visual image of its shape, as well as an auditory image of its sound. Furthermore, the characterization of image schemas as patterns of activity dovetails quite nicely with the intrinsic dynamicity of conceptualization. I thus look with favor on an image-schematic approach to conceptual structure. Certainly I assume that the notions cited as image schemas function as components of more elaborate conceptual configurations.

Still, there has been some vagueness about the notion of image schemas, their inventory, and the criteria for identifying them. I am not at all sure that the examples commonly cited (n. 6) form a coherent or naturally delimited class. While adopting an imagistic orientation, for my own purposes I prefer to distinguish several kinds of fundamental notions, each "basic" in its own way and useful for the characterization of more complex structures:

1. Basic in one sense are **minimal concepts** in particular domains of experience. I have in mind such notions as line, angle, and curvature, in the spatial domain; brightness and focal colors, in vision; precedence, in time; and the kinesthetic sensation of exerting muscular force.
2. Also minimal, but independent of any particular experiential domain, are highly schematic **configurational concepts**, e.g. contrast, boundary, change, continuity, contact, inclusion, separation, proximity, multiplicity, group, and point vs. extension. Being abstract and applicable to most any domain, these come closest to the apparent spirit of image schemas.
3. Some notions commonly cited as image schemas fall instead in my third class, **conceptual archetypes**. These are experientially grounded concepts so frequent and fundamental in our everyday life that the label archetype does not seem inappropriate. Here are some examples: a physical object, an object in a location, an object moving through space, the human body, the human face, a whole and its parts, a

physical container and its contents, seeing something, holding something, handing something to someone, exerting force to effect a desired change, a face-to-face social encounter. These notions are fairly schematic, but considerably less so than the configurational concepts. Some are incorporated as components of others. While they can be quite complex and hard to describe explicitly (try explaining what a physical object is!), they are basic in the sense that they are readily apprehended as coherent conceptual gestalts at an early developmental stage.

I do not regard this three-way distinction as either clear-cut or the only useful classification. Certainly connections can be established among elements of the different groups. The minimal concept of a line, for example, bears an obvious affinity to the configurational notion of extension, as well as to the conceptual archetype of an object moving along a spatial path. Moreover, since all conceptions are dynamic (residing in processing activity), there is no sharp boundary between simple concepts and certain basic **cognitive abilities**. We can describe focal red as either a minimal concept or else the ability to perceive this color. Instead of describing contrast, group, and extension as configurational concepts, we can equally well speak of the ability to detect a contrast, to group a set of constitutive entities, and to mentally scan through a domain.

The essential point is that conceptions can be "basic" in very different ways. This makes possible a general CG proposal about certain grammatical notions that are fundamental and possibly universal. Minimally, these notions include noun, verb, subject, object, and possessive. The proposal has several parts:

1. Each such notion can be characterized semantically in terms of both a **prototype**, valid for central instances, and a **schema** instantiated by all instances.
2. The prototypical meaning consists of an experientially grounded conceptual archetype.
3. The schematic meaning resides in a domain-independent cognitive ability.
4. The basic abilities are initially manifested in the corresponding archetypes. Presumably innate, the abilities make it possible for structured experience, based on these archetypes, to occur in the first place.
5. At a later developmental stage, these same abilities are extended to other domains of experience, where their application is less automatic (hence more apparent).

Let us see how this works in the case of nouns.[7]

1. The noun category has both a semantic prototype and a semantic schema.
2. The prototype is the conception of a physical object.

---

[7] All the notions cited are described semantically in later chapters (nouns in ch. 4).

3. Providing the schematic characterization is our capacity for conceptual grouping.
4. Developmentally, conceptual grouping is first manifested in the apprehension of physical objects, the noun category prototype.
5. It figures subsequently in the apprehension of the many other kinds of entities also coded by nouns.

I view the ability to perceive a discrete physical object, like a ball, as a low-level, essentially automatic manifestation of the same capacity more transparently involved in mentally forming a single entity by grouping the constitutive elements of an orchard, team, stack, alphabet, or archipelago. For most linguistic purposes, a noun like *ball* and a noun like *orchard* function alike (as singular, common, count nouns). Although the constitutive elements and their conceptual grouping are more evident with *orchard*, in each case the conception of a unitary entity emerges through cognitive processing at some level. The world does not present itself to us as a finished, predetermined structure, nor is apprehending the world like xeroxing a document. Even in the realm of concrete reality, its apprehension resides in dynamic, interactive processing activity. This is not to deny that the world is highly structured, so that certain ways of apprehending it are most likely to prove successful for both individuals and species. Because our own species has evolved to cope with the world successfully, we all comprehend it in largely commensurate ways that are grounded in common bodily experience. We all perceive physical objects and employ the same grouping capacity to recognize collective entities like an orchard or an archipelago.

Our apprehension of the world is thus active, dynamic, and constructive in nature. A fundamentally important consequence is that the conceptions evoked as linguistic meanings are **nontransparent**: they do not simply reflect or correspond to the world in a wholly straightforward manner, nor are they derivable in any direct or automatic way from objective circumstances. Instead, a conceptualist semantics must start by recognizing the prevalence—indeed, the utter pervasiveness—of imaginative devices and mental constructions. It is not merely that we frequently talk about imaginary worlds (like those of movies, fairy tales, soap operas, mythology, and linguistic theories). We further demonstrate our imaginative capacity in constructing and manipulating an extraordinary variety of **mental spaces** (Fauconnier 1985, 1997). Some types of mental spaces, respectively exemplified in (3), are those representing a hypothetical situation, a particular person's beliefs, the situation obtaining at a certain time or place, and the content of reported speech.

(3)   (a) *If we were rich, we could fly first class.*

(b) *My lawyer thinks that the judge is incompetent.*

(c) *Meanwhile, back at the ranch, a heated discussion was going on.*

(d) *She indicated that they were having trouble with termites.*

Various other imaginative phenomena prove essential to conceptualization and linguistic meaning. A primary means of enhancing and even constructing our mental world is **metaphor**, where basic organizational features of one conceptual domain—usually more directly grounded in bodily experience—are projected onto another (Lakoff and Johnson 1980, 1999; Turner 1987). In (4), aspects of the **source domain**, pertaining to the manipulation of physical objects, are projected metaphorically onto the **target domain** of understanding and communicating ideas.

(4) (a) *I couldn't grasp what she was saying.*

　　(b) *We were tossing some ideas around.*

　　(c) *The message went right over his head.*

　　(d) *He didn't catch my drift.*

Metaphor is one source of **blending**, in which selected features of two conceptions are combined to form a third (Fauconnier and Turner 1998, 2002). As hybrid mental constructions, blends are often quite fanciful but nonetheless are genuine objects of conception and linguistic expression. The entities portrayed in (4) as being grasped, thrown, and caught—combining as they do the abstract nature of ideas with certain physical properties of balls or other projectiles—cannot exist in reality. Neither do such blended creatures as mermaids and werewolves (let alone beagles who think in English sentences and imagine themselves as World War I pilots), but that does not stop us from thinking and talking about them. Even for the kinds of entities that do exist, what we refer to linguistically is often a **virtual** (or **fictive**) instance, i.e. an imaginary instance "conjured up" for some purpose. Cars exist, for example, but the car referred to in (5)(a) does not (it makes no sense to ask *Which car doesn't your brother have?*). It is rather an imagined instance invoked for the purpose of specifying the circumstance that is being negated.

(5) (a) *My brother doesn't have a car.*

　　(b) *A kitten likes to chase a piece of string.*

Likewise, the kitten and the piece of string mentioned in (5)(b) are virtual entities conjured up to make a global generalization. The statement does not pertain to any particular kitten or piece of string, nor to any actual chasing event.

2.1.3 Where Does Meaning Stop?

At any given moment, we engage in conceptualizing activity at different levels of awareness and in varied domains of mental experience. It draws on many types of abilities (perceptual, motor, intellectual) and vast stores of knowledge (particular and general; physical, social, and cultural; individual, conventional, and contextual). The problems we now address pertain to the boundary between "linguistic" and "extralinguistic" concerns. What in all this counts as **language**? Which particular skills and bits of knowledge can we specifically characterize as being **linguistic**? Accompanying the production or understanding of any linguistic expression is a complex and multifaceted stream of conceptualization. How much of this should we identify as its **linguistic meaning**?

Standard doctrine holds that discrete boundaries ought to be expected. Language is commonly viewed as an autonomous mental "faculty" (Fodor 1983), so that knowledge of a language is fully describable by a large but limited set of statements. Linguists who reject this modular outlook still tend to posit a definite boundary between linguistic and extralinguistic knowledge, dividing the global understanding of expressions into linguistic meaning per se versus what can be pragmatically inferred. Nevertheless, received wisdom often proves erroneous. We need to ask whether these discrete boundaries are **discovered** by linguists or **imposed** on the basis of theoretical preconception. The answer, I believe, is clearly the latter: the linguistic and the extralinguistic form a gradation rather than being sharply distinct. While there are limits to linguistic meaning, and valid distinctions can be drawn, imposing specific boundaries is both arbitrary and misleading.

These issues arise for any aspect of language (FCG1: §2.1.2), but here the focus is meaning. We can start with lexical items, where two basic questions need to be considered. First, how many distinguishable meanings—often called **senses**—should be attributed to a given lexeme? Second, how much information do these senses include?

A lexical item used with any frequency is almost invariably **polysemous**: it has multiple, related meanings that have all been conventionalized to some degree. Among these related senses, some are more central, or **prototypical**, than others, and some are **schemas** that are elaborated (or instantiated) by others. To some extent the senses are linked by **categorizing relationships** to form a network.[8] Figure 2.2 is a partial network plausibly suggested for the noun *ring* (briefly discussed in §1.3.1). The boxes drawn with heavy lines indicate the most prototypical senses. The arrows represent categorizing relationships: solid arrows for the elaboration of a schema, and dashed arrows for extension from a more central meaning.

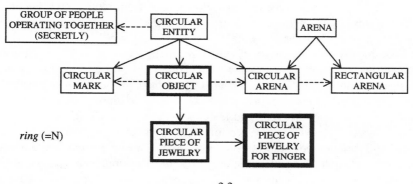

FIGURE 2.2

[8] For examples and discussion, see the following: Geeraerts 1993; Tuggy 1993, 2003a, 2003b; Tyler and Evans 2003; Riemer 2005. This network model is useful up to a point, but it may imply greater discreteness and specificity than is psychologically realistic. An alternative metaphor for complex categories is proposed at the end of §8.1.3.

An alternative is to claim that lexical items are **monosemous**, each having a single abstract meaning from which all its uses can be predicted (Ruhl 1989; Huffman 1997). Positing more specific senses, it is argued, leads to an uncontrolled proliferation of putative "meanings" that are better regarded as contextual interpretations of an item's abstract semantic value. I would counter by denying that a single abstract meaning enables one to predict, in full and precise detail, the actual range of specific senses in which a lexical item is conventionally employed. I can imagine a highly schematic meaning for *ring*—perhaps some abstract notion of enclosure—that would subsume all the more specific values depicted in figure 2.2. From this alone, however, one could hardly predict that *ring* would have exactly the set of particular uses that it manifests, to the exclusion of countless others (equally motivated by cognitive and communicative factors) that it lacks. Why should the term be used for arenas and groups of smugglers but not, say, for rubber bands?

Thus a single abstract meaning does not fully describe a lexical item's established semantic value. Such a meaning should always be sought, and—if found—incorporated in the polysemy network. By itself, though, it fails to represent a speaker's knowledge of how the expression is conventionally used and understood. This knowledge (surely part of knowing a language) resides in the entire network. To allay any fears, positing such networks does not result in an uncontrolled proliferation of senses. Meanings (like other linguistic structures) are recognized as part of a language only to the extent that they are (i) entrenched in the minds of individual speakers and (ii) conventional for members of a speech community. Only a limited array of senses satisfy these criteria and qualify as established **linguistic units**. But since entrenchment and conventionalization are inherently matters of degree, there is no discrete boundary between senses which have and which lack the status of established units. We find instead a gradation leading from novel interpretations, through incipient senses, to established linguistic meanings.

What does a particular lexical meaning include? If a lexical item (in one of its senses) refers to a certain type of entity, how much of our total knowledge of such entities constitutes its linguistic semantic value? Is there some portion of this knowledge that one possesses just by virtue of speaking a language?

Traditionally, this last question is answered in the affirmative. A lexical meaning is thought to consist of relatively few semantic features or descriptive statements, specifically linguistic in character, that are clearly distinguished from general knowledge concerning the type of entity referred to. The basic sense of *bull*, for example, is often represented by the semantic features [MALE], [ADULT], and [BOVINE], to the exclusion of anything else we might know about these creatures (e.g. their role in bullfights and rodeos). In this respect a lexical meaning would be more like a dictionary entry than an article in an encyclopedia. This approach is thus described metaphorically as the **dictionary view** of linguistic semantics, diagrammed in figure 2.3(a). The circle represents the total body of knowledge speakers have about the type of entity in question. Indicated by the heavy-line box is the small, discrete set of specifications constituting the lexical item's meaning.

These "purely linguistic" meanings have proved elusive. It has not been shown that precise boundaries can be drawn in a principled manner (Bolinger 1965; Haiman 1980), nor can descriptions like [MALE ADULT BOVINE] be considered

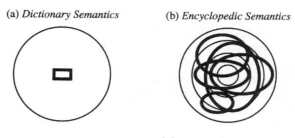

(a) *Dictionary Semantics*   (b) *Encyclopedic Semantics*

FIGURE 2.3

linguistically adequate. An alternative view, metaphorically referred to as **ency-clopedic semantics**, is generally adopted in cognitive linguistics (FCG1: §4.2; cf. Wierzbicka 1995). In this approach, a lexical meaning resides in a particular way of **accessing** an open-ended body of knowledge pertaining to a certain type of entity. This knowledge is represented in figure 2.3(b) by a series of concentric circles, indicating that the knowledge components have varying degrees of **centrality**. This ranking for centrality is one facet of a lexical item's conventionally established value. For a given lexical meaning, certain specifications are so central that they are virtually always activated whenever the expression is used, while others are activated less consistently, and others are so peripheral that they are accessed only in special contexts. In figure 2.3(b), each heavy-line ellipse stands for the set of specifications activated on a single occasion. There need be no specification activated on every occasion, and every use may well involve a unique pattern of activation.

On the encyclopedic view, a lexical meaning is neither totally free nor totally fixed. It is not totally free because the expression evokes a certain range of knowledge and specifies a particular way of accessing it. It is not totally fixed because centrality (preferential access) is a matter of degree and subject to being overridden by contextual factors. This conception (developed further in §2.2) is both linguistically and psychologically realistic. While it does have the consequence that no discrete boundary can be drawn between linguistic and extralinguistic knowledge, any such boundary ought to be drawn on empirical grounds, not imposed a priori.

A comparable issue arises with respect to the meanings of complex expressions, such as sentences. When uttered in context, a sentence may invoke or convey considerably more than what it actually says. Owing to the previous discourse, to interpretive abilities, as well as to general and contextual knowledge, its full understanding may be far more elaborate than anything derivable from the meanings of overt elements. How much of this global understanding is properly identified as the expression's linguistic meaning? Or as the question is usually posed, which facets of it belong to **semantics** (reflecting the language per se) and which are better left for **pragmatics**?

The traditional position, that there is a definite boundary, reflects a **modular** view of language. This supposed modularity starts at the lexical level. Lexical items are thought of as building blocks, discrete units that are stacked in various arrangements to form complex expressions fully determined by the units and the patterns followed in arranging them. In semantics, this is known as the principle of **full compositionality** (an expression's meaning is predictably derivable from the meanings of its parts). The assumption of full compositionality implies a clear and definite distinction between semantics (compositionally determined meaning) and pragmatics (contextual interpretation). This is crucial for the claim of modularity made at a higher level, with respect to a language overall: that it is a well-delimited, self-contained system sharply distinct from other facets of cognition.[9]

Though standard, this modular conception is gratuitous and (I would argue) erroneous. I do not believe that a fixed boundary between semantics and pragmatics can be drawn on a principled basis in a way that makes linguistic sense.

A distinction can indeed be made between semantics and pragmatics. An expression's full contextual understanding goes beyond what can be determined from established linguistic units. Suppose we are looking at a cat, and I say *The bird is safe*. With this statement I may **implicate** that the cat is lazy or incompetent (relying on the context, encyclopedic knowledge of cats, and a general presumption of relevance), but I would not consider this to be part of its linguistic meaning. I therefore object when Levinson (1997: 19) characterizes me as a "stubborn ostrich" who "refuse[s] to countenance the existence of pragmatics."[10] He misinterprets my statement that "the distinction between semantics and pragmatics...is largely artifactual" by ignoring the further clarification that a viable linguistic semantics needs to avoid "such false dichotomies" (FCG1: 154). What is being denied is the strictly dichotomous view depicted in figure 2.4(a), with a fixed and definite boundary between two separate components. This denial does not entail either the nonexistence of pragmatics, as sketched in diagram (b), or the absence of any differentiation, as in (c). The claim, instead, is that semantics and pragmatics form a gradation, as shown in (d), with no precise boundary between the two. But toward either extreme of the scale lie phenomena that are indisputably either semantic or pragmatic.

At issue, then, is whether a discrete boundary can be found (not just arbitrarily imposed). Can we justifiably ascribe to complex expressions a level of "purely

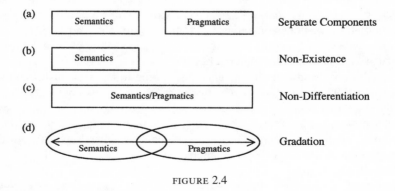

FIGURE 2.4

---

[9] It is further assumed that a linguistic system is divisible into discrete "components" (such as lexicon, morphology, and syntax). I argue against this in §1.3.

[10] If I am a stubborn ostrich, it is for other reasons.

linguistic" meaning that is strictly predictable from the meanings of their parts? A variety of considerations suggest that the answer is negative. For one thing, the very question presupposes that the parts have clearly delimited linguistic meanings. That is, it presupposes the dictionary view of lexical semantics, which we have seen to be problematic. The alternative, encyclopedic approach entails that even the putative "building blocks" are flexibly construed. Rather than being fully pre-formed modules, with fixed and limited content, lexical items reside in conventional paths of access to domains of knowledge—not exclusively linguistic—that are evoked both variably and probabilistically. Even at this level we find a gradation between linguistic and extralinguistic knowledge.

When we consider semantic composition, the inappropriateness of the classic building block metaphor is even more evident. This is not to deny the existence of compositional patterns (in CG they constitute the semantic poles of schematic symbolic assemblies). The question is whether, starting from lexical meanings, these patterns alone give rise to semantic representations that are sufficiently coherent and self-contained to have any kind of independent cognitive status, or approximate anything recognizable as the meanings of complex expressions. Instead (ironically), I agree with Levinson (1997: 18–19) that indisputably "semantic" representations of this sort—compositionally derived from lexical building blocks—are "deeply inadequate mental orphans, which serve so effectively in human communication only through the rich interpretive principles we bring to bear on their development."

Among these interpretive principles are those discussed in the previous section: metaphor, blending, mental space construction, and the invocation of fictive entities. Calling me a *stubborn ostrich* was presumably not an attempt at biological classification but rather an instance of metaphor. By projecting selected features of the source domain (ostriches) onto the target domain (people), this metaphor creates the blended conception of a person who exhibits the fancied ostrich behavior of burying its head in the sand. This hybrid creature is only fictive; nobody believes that it actually exists. Yet, without describing it explicitly, the expression was specifically intended to evoke it metaphorically. Furthermore, the statement that this fictive ostrich/person *refuses to countenance the existence of pragmatics* induces the construction of mental spaces representing a belief and an attitude. It ascribes to the blended creature the belief that pragmatics does not exist, with the aim of imputing this belief (incorrectly) to its correspondent in the target domain (me). The attitude consists of being unwilling to even entertain the possibility that pragmatics exists. Since unwillingness implies that an option must at least be considered, the expression sets up a mental space that contains it, but only as an imagined potential occurrence. The creature's contemplating the possible existence of pragmatics is thus invoked as a virtual entity, conjured up just for purposes of indicating what might have been the case but actually is not.

The example is not at all unusual. When producing or understanding linguistic expressions, we engage in elaborate, highly sophisticated processes of **conceptual construction**, drawing on many and varied resources. Among these are lexical meanings and compositional patterns, as traditionally recognized. Another resource is our impressively rich imaginative capacity, featuring such devices as metaphor, blending, fictivity, and mental spaces. Moreover, the mental constructions evident in normal language use are critically reliant on general and contextual knowledge. For instance, my characterization as a *stubborn ostrich* exploited the folk conception, prevalent in our culture, that an ostrich buries its head in the sand to avoid facing up to problems. It is this notion (hardly part of a dictionary definition) that makes the full expression coherent, by providing a link between *ostrich* and *refuses to countenance the existence of pragmatics*.

Or consider once more *The bird is safe*, uttered while looking at a cat. The word *safe* implies potential danger, which in this context the speaker and hearer understand as residing in the feline. *Safe* might then be analyzed as an abbreviated way of saying *safe from the cat*, the context permitting elliptic expression. Though tacit, reference to the cat is not unreasonably viewed as part of the expression's linguistic meaning; after all, it corresponds to something (a source of danger) inherent in the meaning of *safe*.[11] Furthermore, in the same context it would also be felicitous to say the following: *The bird is safe, because it's smarter*. Here the cat is invoked not only as a source of danger but also, more saliently, as a standard of comparison. I doubt that a conceptualization excluding it would actually occur or be recognizable as what the utterance means.

An expression's meaning presupposes an extensive, multifaceted **conceptual substrate** that supports it, shapes it, and renders it coherent. Among the facets of this substrate are (i) the conceptions evoked or created through the previous discourse; (ii) engagement in the speech event itself, as part of the interlocutors' social interaction; (iii) apprehension of the physical, social, and cultural context; and (iv) any domains of knowledge that might prove relevant. Contributing in no small measure to both the substrate and its subsequent elaboration are imaginative and interpretive phenomena (such as metaphor, blending, fictivity, and mental space construction). All of this provides the setting for lexical interpretation and semantic composition. Contrary to the traditional modular view, these do not proceed autonomously or in a vacuum. A lexical item does not have a fully determinate meaning. Instead, its semantic value resides in conventional paths of access (some well-trodden, others less so) to open-ended domains of knowledge. Precisely what it means on a given occasion—which portions of this encyclopedic knowledge are activated, and to what degree—depends on all the factors cited. Likewise, patterns of semantic composition are only one of the resources exploited in the process of conceptual construction producing the meanings of complex expressions. This overall process results in highly elaborate conceptualizations whose construction is merely **prompted** by lexical meanings and compositional patterns, which are usually not themselves sufficient to **derive** them. I thus describe language as exhibiting only **partial compositionality.**

What should then be recognized as an expression's **linguistic meaning**? I suggest the following, nontechnical definition: besides elements that are indisputably semantic, an expression's meaning includes as much additional structure as is needed to render the conceptualization coherent and reflect what speakers would naively regard as being meant and said, while excluding factors that are indisputably pragmatic and not necessary to make sense of what is linguistically encoded. Admittedly, this is vague and

---

[11] This is not so for the possible implication that the cat is lazy or incompetent, cited previously as a case of pragmatic inference beyond the scope of linguistic meaning.

does not allow one to draw a line in any particular place, even for specific examples. But I also consider it appropriate. I prefer a realistic notion of linguistic meaning that is only fuzzily delimited and partially compositional, as opposed to one that (by definition) is precisely delimited and fully compositional, but whose cognitive status is quite dubious. My feeling is that focusing on the latter represents an artificial exercise, directed at something that may not exist at all, has no autonomous status if it does, and in any case represents only a small portion of the overall problem.

2.2 Conceptual Content

Linguistic meaning resides in conceptualization, which I have so far characterized as being dynamic, interactive, imagistic (as opposed to propositional), and imaginative (involving metaphor, blending, fictivity, and mental space construction). Important though they are, these general properties are not themselves adequate for describing conceptual structure in explicit detail. As the basis for semantic and grammatical description, we must now consider more specific proposals.

Most broadly, a meaning consists of both conceptual **content** and a particular way of **construing** that content. The term **construal** refers to our manifest ability to conceive and portray the same situation in alternate ways.[12] An initial example is sketched in figure 2.5. The content in question is the conception of a glass containing water occupying just half of its volume. At the conceptual level, we are presumably able to evoke this content in a fairly neutral manner. But as soon as we encode it linguistically, we necessarily impose a certain construal. Four such options are shown in the diagram, each corresponding to a distinct expression. The semantic contrast depicted (by means of heavy lines) lies in what the expressions designate (or refer to) within the conceived situation:[13] (1) *the glass with water in it* designates the container; (2) *the water in the glass* designates the liquid it contains; (3) *the glass is half-full* designates the relationship wherein the volume occupied by the liquid is just half of its potential volume; and (4) *the glass is half-empty* designates the relationship wherein the volume occupied by the void is just half of its potential volume.

The distinction between content and construal is not at all a sharp one. For instance, **level of specificity**—an aspect of construal—has a direct bearing on the content evoked: precisely because they differ in specificity, *the glass with water in it* has more content than *the container with liquid in it* (another way of coding the situation in figure 2.5). The distinction is nonetheless useful for expository purposes, as it highlights the essential point that conceptual meaning involves more than just truth conditions or the objective circumstances being described. Indeed, the meaning of many linguistic elements—especially those considered "grammatical"—consists primarily in the construal they impose, rather than any specific content. Yet every element evokes some content (however schematic it might be), and conversely, any content evoked is construed in some fashion. Content is the topic of this section. Construal is addressed in chapter 3.

---

[12] The term **construal** is preferable to **imagery**, used in certain earlier works, since the latter lends itself to confusion with more familiar applications (FCG1: 110).

[13] Called **profiling**, this aspect of construal is discussed in §3.3.1.

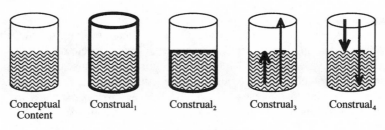

FIGURE 2.5

2.2.1 Domains

Linguistic meaning involves both conceptual content and the construal imposed on that content. To have a uniform way of referring to content, the term **domain** is adopted in CG. An expression is said to invoke a set of cognitive domains as the basis for its meaning (i.e. as the content to be construed).[14] Collectively, this set of domains is called a **matrix**. For most expressions the matrix is **complex** in the sense of comprising multiple domains.

What is a domain, exactly? To serve its purpose, the term is broadly interpreted as indicating any kind of conception or realm of experience. Among the domains figuring in the content of figure 2.5, for example, are space, the sensation of wetness, the specific concept WATER (partly defined in terms of wetness), the more schematic concept LIQUID (immanent in WATER), the conception of a container and its contents, the more elaborate conception of filling a container with liquid, notions of volume and equality (hence equality of volume), as well as our knowledge of the cultural practice of filling a glass with water for the purpose of drinking it. We should not expect to arrive at any exhaustive list of the domains in a matrix or any unique way to divide an expression's content among them—how many domains we recognize, and which ones, depends on our purpose and to some extent is arbitrary. The important thing is to recognize the diverse and multifaceted nature of the conceptual content an expression evokes.

Obviously, many conceptions incorporate others or are in some sense reducible to more fundamental notions. Domains for which this is not the case are said to be **basic**. A basic domain is therefore cognitively irreducible, neither derivable from nor analyzable into other conceptions. Though I cannot give a definite inventory, some prime examples are space, time, and the ranges of unanalyzed experience associated with the various senses: color space (the range of colors we are capable of experiencing), pitch (the range of pitches we can perceive), temperature, taste and smell, and so on. In and of themselves, basic domains are not concepts or conceptualizations. They are better thought of as realms of experiential

---

[14] The selection of domains is itself an aspect of construal, reinforcing the point that the distinction between content and construal is not absolute.

potential, within which conceptualization can occur and specific concepts can emerge. For instance, color space—as the range of possible color sensations—is not the same as any particular color experience on a particular occasion (a kind of conceptualization), nor is it a color concept (e.g. RED). Likewise, space supports the conception of spatial configurations and time the conception of change. As basic domains, however, these are not themselves concepts but simply the spatial and temporal extensionality in which configurations are manifested and change unfolds.[15]

Most domains are **nonbasic**.[16] Of the ones listed above for figure 2.5, all are nonbasic except for space. Any kind of conceptualization counts as a nonbasic domain capable of being exploited for semantic purposes. Conceptions fall under this rubric whether they are sensory or intellectual, static or dynamic, fixed or novel, simple or complex. Included as nonbasic domains are instances of immediate sensory, emotive, and motor/kinesthetic experience (e.g. the sensation of wetness, of being afraid, or of blowing up a balloon), as well as the abstracted products of intellectual operations (e.g. concepts like JUSTICE, VERTEBRATE, and BATTING AVERAGE). Also included are conceptions manifested instantaneously at the level of conscious awareness (e.g. the image of a circle), as well as elaborate scenarios that we can only conceptualize stage by stage through processing time (like the successive steps in a complicated recipe). There is no requirement that a nonbasic domain be fixed, established, or conventionally recognized. Apprehension of the situational context thus qualifies as a cognitive domain, as does the previous discourse.

Nonbasic domains vary greatly in their degree of conceptual complexity. They range from minimal concepts (e.g. RED), to more elaborate conceptions (like the configuration of the human body), to entire systems of knowledge (such as everything we know about baseball). To some extent they arrange themselves in hierarchies, such that a conception at a given level presupposes and incorporates one or more lower-level conceptions. For instance, the concept APPLE incorporates RED; NECK invokes the overall shape of a body; and BATTING AVERAGE presupposes some knowledge of both arithmetic and baseball. In cases of this sort, where one conception—asymmetrically—presupposes another as part of its own characterization, they are said to occupy higher and lower **levels of conceptual organization**. Numerous levels of conceptual organization can often be discerned even in simple examples. In the case of ENTER (fig. 2.1), the concept of a physical object is one component of the higher-level conception of an object moving from source to goal along a spatial path. Along with the container-content schema, this is then incorporated as part of

---

[15] These basic domains are not per se the meanings of the words *space* and *time*. Their meanings are higher-order conceptions in which the dimensions function in their own right as objects of contemplation, rather than merely supporting spatial and temporal conceptualization. Similarly, the metaphorical construal of basic domains (e.g. *in a moment, bright sound, sharp taste*) results in conceptions that are not irreducible and are hence nonbasic.

[16] The term **abstract domain**, used in previous works, is infelicitous because many nonbasic conceptions pertain to physical circumstances.

ENTER, at the next higher level. In turn, ENTER is invoked for the characterization of ENTRANCE, and so on indefinitely.

Such hierarchies are a fundamental aspect of conceptual structure and thus essential to semantics. Few linguistic meanings lend themselves to being directly and solely described in terms of basic domains or a putative set of primitive concepts.[17] Most expressions are best characterized with respect to higher-level notions whose relation to basic ones can be mediated by any number of intervening levels. As the basis for their meaning and hence the starting point for semantic description, expressions invoke conceptualizations at any level of organization and with any degree of complexity.

Consider the word *sophomore*. Among the elements that figure in its meaning are the basic domains of time and space, as well as such lower-level concepts as PERSON, KNOW, YEAR, and TWO, and higher-level notions such as LEARN, STUDY, STUDENT, and SCHOOL. Clearly, though, the meaning of *sophomore* further—and crucially—invokes a still higher-level conception of the sort that Fillmore (1982) calls a **frame** and Lakoff (1987) refers to as an **idealized cognitive model** (or ICM). This is the idealized conception, quite familiar in our culture, of a nonelementary educational institution offering a course of study lasting precisely four years. While it incorporates the lower-level concepts, this ICM taken as a whole is the natural starting point for semantic description: with respect to it, we need only specify that *sophomore* designates a person in the second year of study. We can say that the ICM provides the expression's conceptual content, the basis for its meaning, which results from construing this content in a certain manner. In particular, *sophomore* is construed as designating (profiling) a student in the second year (as opposed to *freshman*, *junior*, and *senior*, which have the same basic content but designate students in other years).

At this point some terminological clarification may be helpful. We seem to have a lot of terms that might all be applied to the same conceptual phenomenon: *concept*, *conception*, *conceptualization*, *(nonbasic) domain*, *frame*, and *idealized cognitive model*. Although usage varies and the contrasts are subtle, I should at least indicate how I myself tend to understand the terms.

The distinction between the first three terms and the second three is basically a matter of perspective: the former pertain to a notion considered in its own right, whereas the latter highlight its role in describing linguistic meanings. Within the first group of words, *conception* neutralizes the distinction between *concept*, which suggests a fixed or static notion, and *conceptualization*, which suggests dynamicity. However, since every conception is dynamic if viewed on a small enough time scale, *conceptualization* is also employed as a fully general term. The terms in the second group are often interchangeable. We can say, for instance, that *sophomore* derives its meaning by imposing a particular construal on the content supplied by a *domain*, a *frame*, or an *ICM*.[18] Yet these terms are not quite equivalent. *Domain* has the greatest

---

[17] This is clearly recognized by Wierzbicka (1996), who does base her descriptions on a set of irreducible semantic primitives (identified as lexical universals), but also posits hierarchies where a concept at any level incorporates simpler concepts previously assembled.

[18] Naturally, the resulting *concept((ualizat)ion)* may function in turn as a *domain/frame/ICM* for another expression (e.g. *sophomore yearbook*).

generality, since neither *frame* nor *ICM* applies very well to basic domains (e.g. time or color space). A *frame* may be roughly comparable to a *nonbasic domain*. If the words *idealized* and *model* are taken seriously, *idealized cognitive model* has the narrowest range of application. It would not, for example, apply to the ongoing discourse or the physical circumstances of the speech event.[19]

2.2.2 Accessing Domains

The set of domains an expression invokes is called its conceptual **matrix**. Usually there are multiple domains, in which case the matrix is said to be **complex**. In describing an expression's matrix, it is not sufficient merely to list the constitutive domains. How they relate to one another, and how they are mentally accessed, are an important dimension of linguistic meaning.

An instructive way to start is by considering one example in fair detail. The expression chosen is *glass*, in the ordinary sense whereby it designates a container used for drinking. Here are some of the domains that evidently figure in its conceptual characterization:

1. Space [a basic domain].
2. Shape [roughly that of a cylinder, closed at one end]. This nonbasic domain presupposes space, as the domain in which a shape conception is manifested.
3. Typical orientation in space [long dimension aligned along the vertical axis, with the closed end at the bottom]. Among the other domains this incorporates are space, verticality, and the shape conception.
4. Function$_1$ [container for liquid]. This presupposes the typical orientation, the concept of a liquid, and that of a container (which in turn incorporates such notions as spatial inclusion, potential motion, force, and constancy through time).
5. Function$_2$ [role in the process of drinking]. This incorporates function$_1$, as well as the conception of the human body, of grasping, motion with the arm, ingestion, etc.
6. Material [usually the substance glass].
7. Size [easily held in one hand].
8. Others [domains pertaining to cost, washing, storage, dropping and breaking, position on a table at mealtime, matching sets, method of manufacture, and so on].

According to the encyclopedic view of linguistic semantics (§2.1.3), the potentially relevant domains are an open-ended set. The example clearly indicates that, rather than being disjoint, the domains of a complex matrix overlap with one another, often to the extent of full inclusion. An attempt to convey this diagrammatically is made in figure 2.6, where domains are shown as ellipses. The heavy-line circle

---

[19] Of course, there are still more terms. For instance, *script* refers to an idealized sequence of actions. *Domain* and *mental space* are compared in §2.2.3.

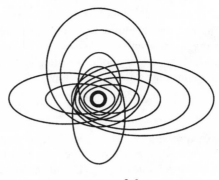

FIGURE 2.6

represents the entity designated by the expression (its profile), which has some role in all the domains of the matrix.

Not captured in figure 2.6 are the varying degrees of centrality ascribable to the domains of a complex matrix.[20] Centrality (FCG1: §4.2.2) is the likelihood of a particular domain being activated when an expression is used on a given occasion. Certain domains are so central that we can hardly use the expression without evoking them, some are activated less consistently, and others are so peripheral that we invoke them only in special circumstances, when they happen to be relevant. In our example (*glass*), domains 1 to 7 are clearly quite central, those listed under 8 more peripheral. A ranking for degree of centrality is depicted in figure 2.7. In this "exploded" diagram, the domains of a matrix are separately shown (ignoring their extensive overlap). The dotted lines, used for **correspondence**, indicate that the heavy-line circles all represent the same entity (namely the expression's designatum, represented just once in figure 2.6).

The relative centrality of constitutive domains is one facet of linguistic meaning, important for the characterization of lexical items. As part of its conventional semantic value, a lexeme not only gives access to a set of domains, but does so preferentially, making some especially likely to be activated. Occasionally a semantic contrast

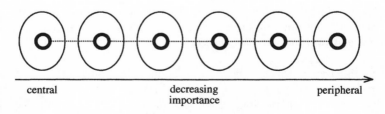

central   decreasing   peripheral
                           importance

FIGURE 2.7

---

[20] In fig. 2.3, degrees of centrality are indicated by concentric circles. The ellipses in fig. 2.6 represent domains (not individually shown in the former diagram).

resides less in the inventory of accessible domains than in their degree of accessibility. Although the same object might be referred to as either a *knife* or a *dagger*, and either can be used for stabbing someone, this possible function is far more central to the meaning of *dagger*. Or consider the contrast between *snail* and *escargot* (accepting that the latter is now an English word). Encyclopedic semantics implies that the two expressions afford potential access to the same domain inventory: it is part of our encyclopedic knowledge of snails that they are sometimes cooked and eaten (especially in French restaurants), and we know that escargots are the same creatures that infest our gardens. Yet *snail* and *escargot* clearly have different meanings, the contrast residing in how the domains are ranked (i.e. degree of centrality). With *escargot*, the domain of fancy cuisine is ranked very high; it is primarily this domain that is accessed, others—like the domain of garden pests—being activated only if there is special motivation. With *snail*, on the other hand, the domain of fancy cuisine is peripheral but fairly accessible. It is therefore natural (at least linguistically) to say *The snails were delicious*, but hardly **My garden is crawling with escargots*.[21]

Ranking for centrality implies that a lexical meaning, even if open-ended, is not totally free or unconstrained. A lexical item is partly defined by the likelihood (sometimes approaching categorical status) of particular domains being activated. It thus incorporates conventional ways of accessing a certain range of encyclopedic knowledge. At the same time, a lexical meaning is never totally fixed or invariable, for several reasons. First, the inclination for a given domain to be activated is probabilistic rather than absolute. A second reason is that the probabilities are subject to contextual modulation. Finally, they vary through time depending on the vicissitudes of usage.

These points seem fairly evident. That domains are activated with a certain probability is precisely what is meant by degree of centrality. Nor is there any doubt that the probabilities are altered by context and use. Contextual factors can obviously focus attention on a domain that might otherwise not be accessed at all or only at a lower level of activation. This in turn might lessen the activation of an otherwise salient specification. If (6)(a) induces a canonical construal of *glass*, with domains 1 to 7 all being accessed, examples (6)(b)–(d) skew the pattern by highlighting various domains of lesser centrality: breaking, matching, placement, and washing.

(6) (a) *He took another sip from his glass.*

    (b) *This antique glass is quite fragile.*

    (c) *The glasses on that table don't match.*

    (d) *Plastic wine glasses are hard to wash.*

Directing attention to such notions tends to push more central specifications (like the role of a glass in drinking) into the background. They can even be suppressed

---

[21] Following standard linguistic practice, asterisks (and sometimes question marks) indicate that an expression is in some respect deviant or "ungrammatical". The basis for these assessments is discussed in ch. 8.

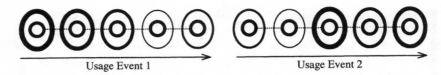

| Usage Event 1 | Usage Event 2 |

FIGURE 2.8

or overridden. In (6)(d), *wine* and *plastic* override the default specifications of *glass* with respect to shape and material. Moreover, their collocation with *glass* occurs so commonly these days that the default status of these specifications may well be diminished. Usage has a constant impact by either reinforcing the probabilities or adjusting them.

A ranking of domains for centrality measures their likelihood of being accessed and strongly activated, other things being equal. Yet other things are never really equal, since language use is never truly acontextual; an expression's manifestation is always subject to influence from the physical, linguistic, social, and psychological circumstances. Given a particular ranking, as depicted in figure 2.7, such influence results in specific patterns of activation representing a lexical item's contextual implementation in actual usage events. This is shown in figure 2.8, where the thickness of a line indicates the degree to which a domain is activated. From one usage event to the next, the domains accessed are likely to vary, as well as their level of activation. This variable activation is one reason why an expression appears to have different values on different occasions. It may be that, strictly speaking, a lexeme is never used twice with exactly the same meaning.

Followed to their logical conclusion, these observations have certain theoretical consequences that I consider quite natural (though some would regard them as unfortunate). They imply the absence of any specific line of demarcation that strictly separates linguistic meaning from either general knowledge or contextual interpretation. Since the conceptualizations that function as linguistic meanings are neither distinct from these nor well delimited, semantic structure cannot be exhaustively described. Nor is semantics fully compositional, if only because the putative building blocks—lexical meanings—do not have constant values. Moreover, since language necessarily incorporates semantics, it does not constitute an autonomous, self-contained "module" or "mental faculty".[22]

2.2.3 Domains and Mental Spaces

A cognitive **domain** was defined as any kind of conception or mental experience. The definition is very broad, intended to provide a uniform way of referring to anything exploited as the conceptual basis of linguistic meaning. Equally broad, and for a similar reason, is Fauconnier's definition of a **mental space** (1997: 11): "Mental spaces... are partial structures that proliferate when we think and talk, allowing a

---

[22] Cf. Fodor 1983. CG posits only semantic, phonological, and symbolic structures, the latter consisting in the pairings of semantic and phonological structures. Without semantics, therefore, only phonology is left.

fine-grained partitioning of our discourse and knowledge structures." It is not obvious that any conceptual structure is strictly excluded by either definition, and in practice the terms have overlapping ranges of application. What, then, is the relation between these notions? Are both terms really necessary?

As I see it, anything called a *domain* could also be referred to as a *mental space*, and conversely. From a purely referential standpoint, therefore, a single term would be sufficient. Yet referential coverage is not the only measure of a term's utility; even in the technical sphere, the same entity is often describable by means of alternate expressions that highlight different facets of it.[23] The terms *domain* and *mental space* represent nonequivalent ways of viewing conceptual structure, each reflecting a certain range of analytical concerns. *Domain* focuses on a conception's unity and internal coherence. As a way of referring to conceptual content, it tends to be used for established conceptions in relation to lexical meanings. By contrast, *mental space* emphasizes conceptual discontinuities, the partitioning of conceptual structure into semiautonomous regions. It tends to be employed for the products of imaginative operations and the structures created dynamically in discourse. These are only tendencies, however, and both terms are vague enough for general application.

The phenomena generally dealt with in mental space theory, and the analyses proposed, are readily accommodated in CG. This is actually quite evident, since any kind of conception counts as a domain, and no restrictions are imposed on how the domains of a matrix are related to one another. Thus any mental space configuration—including both the spaces and the connections linking them—can simply be incorporated as part of a matrix.

By way of illustration, consider the following metaphorical expression:

(7)   *The thought just flew right out of my head.*

Metaphor resides in a set of **connections** among a **source space**, a **target space**, and a **blended space**.[24] The target space is the one being structured metaphorically. In (7), it is the common experience of entertaining a thought but subsequently—when wanting to express it—being unable to access it. The source space is the (usually less abstract) notion serving as the basis for metaphorical projection. On one interpretation of (7), the source is identified as the conception of a bird flying out of a cage, with the consequence that the bird is no longer available for viewing. The blended space is the result of projecting the source onto the target. It is a hybrid conception, fictive in nature, combining selected features of each input space.

The spaces and connections evoked in (7) are roughly depicted in figure 2.9. The elements of the source space are a bird (B), a cage (C), and a viewer (V). The bird is in the cage, where the viewer can see it (as indicated by a dashed arrow), but then

[23] Referring to the same entity, for instance, a developer speaks of a *unit*, a contractor talks about a *structure*, and a realtor calls it a *home* (while the buyer just wants a *house*).

[24] This is the terminology used in blending theory, based on mental spaces (Fauconnier 1997; Fauconnier and Turner 1998, 2002). Previously (starting with Lakoff and Johnson 1980), cognitive linguists working on metaphor spoke (equivalently) of **mappings** between a **source domain** and a **target domain**, without positing a blend.

flies away (solid arrow) and becomes inaccessible. The elements of the target space are a thought (T), a person's head (H), and that person's "subject" (S)—that is, the subjective center of consciousness (Lakoff 1996). The dashed arrow represents the experience of having a thought, which subjectively occurs inside the head. Though not shown, the target scenario also includes a subsequent phase in which that thought is absent. Connections between spaces are given as dotted lines. Observe that connections are established between the bird and the thought, between the cage and the head, and between the viewer and the subject of consciousness. Further connections (not indicated, to simplify the diagram) hold between relationships in the two spaces: viewing a bird is likened to having a thought; and the bird flying away is likened to the thought becoming inaccessible. These connections are the basis for the metaphorical construal.

The blended space is formed from the other two by merging connected elements into new, hybrid entities retaining some, but not all, of their properties. The fictive, even fanciful nature of these imaginative creations does not make them mysterious or insignificant—on the contrary, they are crucial both conceptually and linguistically. The entity labeled T′ blends the abstract nature of a thought with physical attributes of a bird, which enable it to fly through space. H′ is a head, but more specifically it is a head conceived as a container that can hold an object (the way a cage holds a bird). And while S′ is still a "subject" (or center of consciousness), it combines with this the properties of a viewer able to look inside a container (H′) and examine its contents. This blended space provides the essential content of (7): despite its fictive character, the event that takes place there is precisely what the sentence directly describes.

In CG terms, each space in figure 2.9 qualifies as a domain, as does the entire space configuration. These spaces are part of the complex matrix comprising the expression's conceptual content. The connections between spaces conform to the general observation that the domains of a matrix are related to one another in various ways, rather than being separate or disjoint. Connections are a special case of

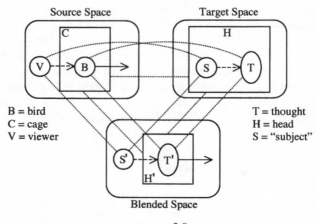

FIGURE 2.9

correspondences (represented as dotted lines), which have multiple applications in CG (FCG1: §2.3.2).

The example raises the broader issue of how domains are related to particular linguistic expressions. The kind of relationship discussed in the previous section—where a fixed expression provides a conventional way of accessing a certain set of domains—is by no means the only possibility. Besides simple lexical items (like *glass*), the overall picture must accommodate both novel and complex expressions, as well as their contextual and discourse interpretations.

For the most part, domains exist independently of any particular expression. They are not specifically linguistic, but conceptual resources that can be exploited for linguistic purposes. A given domain can thus be recruited for any number of different expressions. This is obviously true for basic domains such as time and space, which figure in the meanings of innumerable expressions without depending on any for their cognitive status. It is also true for many basic concepts (e.g. person, motion, physical object) and, on a lesser scale, for higher-order conceptions. For example, the practice of keeping a bird in a cage is easily accessible as part of the encyclopedic characterization of both *bird* and *cage* and is central to the meaning of *birdcage*. Moreover, this practice is commonly exploited in metaphorical expressions, even when there is no explicit reference to it, as seen in (7) and figure 2.9.

What happens when simpler expressions combine to form a more complex one? In principle, the matrix for the overall expression incorporates all the domains of the components. But it is not just the union of the component matrices. For one thing, as shown by *birdcage*, the composite expression provides its own way of accessing the constitutive domains. While the notion of keeping birds in cages is not peripheral with either *bird* or *cage*, taken individually, it is absolutely central to the meaning of the compound as a whole.[25] By the same token, *birdcage* affords only indirect access to certain domains that are fairly central to its components (e.g. hatching from eggs for *bird*, zoo for *cage*). Moreover, it is possible for a composite expression to invoke a domain that does not figure saliently in the meaning of any component. For instance, the compound *lipstick* pertains to the cultural practice of females coating their lips with a colored substance, typically packaged in small cylinders encased in metal or plastic and carried in purses. This cultural model cannot be ascribed to the matrix of *stick*, and for *lip* it is quite peripheral (*lip* would seldom evoke it in a neutral context). More clearly, the conception of a British soldier is central to the meaning of *redcoat* but absent from the matrices of *red* and *coat*. Nor does any word in (7) evoke by itself the idea of someone looking in an empty birdcage—this only emerges through a process of conceptual construction triggered by the entire expression.

Among the domains evoked as the basis for meaning, but not conventionally associated with component elements, are those consisting in a speaker's apprehension of the current discourse context. Suppose you are helping me put away the groceries. I see you there in the pantry holding several cans of tomatoes, with a quizzical

---

[25] By itself, neither *bird* nor *cage* necessarily evokes the practice, but *birdcage* is virtually certain to do so. Each component reinforces this aspect of the other's encyclopedic semantics.

look on your face. In this context, I might use any of the expressions in (8) to convey what is effectively the same message:

(8)   (a) *I want you to put the canned tomatoes on the top shelf of the pantry.*

    (b) *Put the tomatoes on the top shelf of the pantry.*

    (c) *Put them on the top shelf.*

    (d) *Tomatoes, top shelf.*

    (e) *On the top shelf.*

    (f) *On top.*

Our shared apprehension of the situational context provides a conceptual substrate, various facets of which are overtly expressed. By virtue of this substrate, even the most fragmentary expressions are coherent and meaningful (indeed, the first two seem needlessly verbose). I have defined an expression's meaning as including not only the content directly coded by overt elements but whatever additional structure is needed to render a conceptualization coherent and reflect what speakers would naively regard as being meant and said (§2.1.3). By this criterion, the meanings of all the expressions in (8) include at least the content expressed in (8)(a).[26]

This runs counter to conventional wisdom, which insists on a clear distinction between linguistic meaning and contextual interpretation. An expression's meaning would be limited to what is strictly derivable from the (nonencyclopedic) meanings of its parts, and as such would be well-delimited, self-contained, acontextual, and fully compositional. It is thus no accident that sentence "fragments" like (8)(d)–(f) are traditionally ignored, for it is only the context that renders them coherent or supplies enough content to make them conceptually or communicatively useful. Such fragments are both normal and highly frequent in everyday language use, however. As seen in (8)(a)–(f), moreover, expressions cover the full spectrum in terms of what proportion of their essential content is contextually induced and what proportion is explicitly encoded. Insofar as possible, the entire spectrum of cases should be treated analogously. An expression is always understood with respect to some actual or imagined context. Only by avoiding an artificial dichotomy between linguistic meaning and contextual interpretation can we handle the full range of data in a unified manner.

---

[26] If all the expressions in (8) should have the same content, they are nevertheless semantically non-equivalent owing to construal. In particular, they contrast in regard to which facets of the overall content are explicitly mentioned and thereby rendered prominent in relation to tacit elements.

3

Construl

An expression's meaning is not just the conceptual content it evokes—equally important is how that content is construed. As part of its conventional semantic value, every symbolic structure construes its content in a certain fashion. It is hard to resist the visual metaphor, where content is likened to a scene and construal to a particular way of viewing it. Importantly, CG does **not** claim that all meanings are based on space or visual perception,[1] but the visual metaphor does suggest a way to classify the many facets of construal, if only for expository purposes. In viewing a scene, what we actually see depends on how closely we examine it, what we choose to look at, which elements we pay most attention to, and where we view it from. The corresponding labels I will use, for broad classes of construal phenomena, are **specificity**, **focusing**, **prominence**, and **perspective**. They apply to conceptions in any domain.

3.1 Specificity

One dimension of construal is the level of precision and detail at which a situation is characterized. I can describe the temperature by saying that it is *hot*, but also—with progressively greater specificity—by saying that it is *in the 90s*, *about 95 degrees*, or *exactly 95.2 degrees*. Similarly, *aunt* is more specific than *relative*, and *large brown rat* is more specific than *rodent*. Alternate terms are **granularity** and **resolution**. A highly specific expression describes a situation in fine-grained detail, with high resolution. With expressions of lesser specificity, we are limited to coarse-grained descriptions whose low resolution reveals only gross features and global organization.

The converse of specificity is **schematicity**. Thus *relative* is schematic with respect to *aunt*, and *rodent* with respect to *large brown rat*. A schematic characterization is **instantiated** by any number of more specific ones, each serving to **elaborate**

---

[1] This fact has not prevented uninformed commentators from claiming that it does. To the extent that **conception** and visual **perception** are analogous, I use the term **viewing** for both (GC: ch. 7). Talmy (1996) refers to them both as "ception".

its coarse-grained specifications. Elaborating *rodent*, in different ways and to different degrees, are *rat, large brown rat, vole, curious mouse, ground squirrel, ferocious porcupine with sharp quills*, and so on indefinitely. An elaborative relationship is represented by a solid arrow: A → B. Expressions can often be arranged in elaborative hierarchies, as in (1), where each expression is schematic with respect to those that follow.

(1)   (a) *rodent → rat → large brown rat → large brown rat with halitosis*

      (b) *hot → in the 90s → about 95 degrees → exactly 95.2 degrees*

Participating in elaborative relations are both lexical items and novel expressions of any size. In lexicon, such relations constitute **taxonomies**, i.e. hierarchies of conventionally recognized **types**, like the one in (2)(a). An elaborative hierarchy containing novel expressions, in this case full sentences, is given in (2)(b).

(2)   (a) *thing → object → tool → hammer → claw hammer*

      (b) *Something happened. → A person perceived a rodent. → A girl saw a porcupine.*
           → An alert little girl wearing glasses caught a brief glimpse of a ferocious
           porcupine with sharp quills.

We can make an expression as specific as we like, for it can be of any length. By making it longer, we can always describe a situation more precisely and in greater detail. There are practical limits, however. Being of finite length, a particular expression can only be specific to a certain extent, and only with respect to certain facets of the overall situation. The sentences in (2)(b) are actually rather unnatural because in each case the major elements are all presented at a comparable level of specificity. More typical are expressions like (3), exhibiting a mixture of schematic and specific description:[2]

(3)   *Somebody saw a ferocious porcupine with sharp quills.*

Lexical meanings are likewise specific in only some respects, schematic in others. For instance, *carnivorous* and *nocturnal* are each specific concerning one aspect of an animal's behavior but otherwise are quite schematic. The verb *crush* designates a fairly specific type of interaction, yet the participants it invokes are only vaguely characterized: as an agent (or energy source) and a deformable object.

Schematization is fundamental to cognition, constantly occurring in every realm of experience. The extraction of a schema is simply the reinforcing of something inherent in multiple experiences, at whatever level of granularity their commonality emerges. A schema should therefore be seen as **immanent** in its varied instantiations, not as separate and distinct (even if shown individually for analytical purposes). By its very nature, a schema serves a **categorizing** function: capturing what is common

---

[2] In spontaneous speech, there is a strong tendency for a single clause or a single "intonation unit" to contain just one element introducing a substantial amount of new and important information (Du Bois 1987; Chafe 1994: ch. 5).

to certain previous experiences, it can be applied to any new experience exhibiting the same configuration.

Schemas and elaborative relationships are essential in every aspect of language structure. CG claims that all linguistic generalizations arise via schematization from more specific structures. In semantics, schemas and categorizing relationships (based on either elaboration or extension) constitute the network representing the senses of a polysemous lexical item (fig. 2.2). In phonology, schemas characterize "natural classes" (like [VOICELESS STOP]) as well as phonotactic patterns (e.g. [CCVC], specifying a permissible type of syllable). The schemas expressing grammatical regularities are symbolic, each consisting of a semantic and a phonological pole. Here too schemas characterize both natural classes (such as verbs) and combinatory patterns (e.g. a passive construction). Finally, as representations of conventional patterns, schemas provide the basis for assessing linguistic well-formedness. An expression is judged well-formed to the extent that it bears relationships of elaboration (rather than extension) to the schemas invoked to categorize it.

3.2 Focusing

Through linguistic expressions, we access particular portions of our conceptual universe. The dimension of construal referred to here as focusing includes the **selection** of conceptual content for linguistic presentation, as well as its arrangement into what can broadly be described (metaphorically) as **foreground** vs. **background**.[3]

The encyclopedic view of lexical meaning illustrates both aspects of focusing. As part of its conventional value, a lexical item provides direct access to a set of cognitive domains (its matrix) ranked for centrality (likelihood of activation). The domain inventory represents a selection of conceptual content. Also, central domains are foregrounded (in the sense of being more accessible) vis-à-vis peripheral ones. Focusing is further evident in how a lexical item is actually understood in the context of a usage event. Of all the domains in the matrix, only a limited number can be activated on a given occasion (fig. 2.3(b)). This is a kind of selection. Moreover, the domains selected are activated to varying degrees (fig. 2.8). A high level of activation is a kind of foregrounding.

Focusing is thus a matter of degree. It is also relative to particular purposes, dimensions of structure, and levels of organization. In a complex matrix, a domain in the foreground—by virtue of being central (highly susceptible to activation)—may nonetheless remain in the background (being only weakly activated) on a certain occasion. We saw previously, for the compound *lipstick*, that the cultural practice of painting lips has a different status at the two levels of structural organization. At the lower level, this domain is not selected at all by *stick* and is rather peripheral to *lip*. Yet it is very much in the foreground at the higher level, being strongly evoked by *lipstick* as a whole.

---

[3] To unify these aspects of focusing, observe that selected content is foregrounded relative to unselected content. Also, certain kinds of prominence (e.g. profiling) can be thought of as extreme cases of focusing/foregrounding.

3.2.1 Foreground vs. Background

Many kinds of asymmetries lend themselves to metaphoric description as foreground vs. background. Though distinguishable, they can all be seen as manifesting a very general feature of cognition. Most broadly, they all involve departure from a baseline, the exploitation of previous experience (what has already been established) for the interpretation of subsequent experience.[4] A manifestation in perception is the phenomenon known as **figure** vs. **ground**. For instance, a sudden noise stands out as figure against the ground of silence, or a small, moving cursor against the more stable background on a computer screen. Another manifestation is categorization, which succeeds to the extent that the categorizing structure is recognized within the experience being categorized. The categorizing structure lies in the background, taken for granted as a preestablished basis for assessment, while the target is in the foreground of awareness as the structure being observed and assessed.

We can reasonably speak of background and foreground for any case where one conception precedes and in some way facilitates the emergence of another. In this broad sense, we can say that expressions invoke background knowledge as the basis for their understanding. Such knowledge is presupposed even by a detailed sentence like *I want you to put the canned tomatoes on the top shelf of the pantry*. Though seemingly explicit, its default interpretation relies, inter alia, on cultural knowledge pertaining to food storage and pantry organization. Without this background knowledge, we might interpret the sentence as indicating that the tomatoes should be removed from the cans before being placed on the shelf, or that the cans should be glued to the face of the shelf instead of being placed on its upper surface. Further in the background, but equally essential, is basic knowledge of our physical world as we experience it (e.g. the experience of reaching upward, or the knowledge that objects will fall to the ground unless supported).

In similar fashion, the source domain of a metaphor has a kind of precedence vis-à-vis the target domain. Usually more concrete or more directly anchored in bodily experience, the source domain provides a conceptual background in terms of which the target domain is viewed and understood. Viewing the target against this background results in a hybrid domain, or blended space (fig. 2.9). We can also say, with equal validity, that the source and target domains jointly constitute the background from which the blended conception emerges. Not only does the blend inherit selected features of both the source and the target, but it is also foregrounded in the sense of being most directly coded linguistically. In *The thought just flew right out of my head*, it is only a hybrid, bird-like thought that is capable of flight.

Foreground and background have numerous manifestations in discourse (ch. 13). In a narration, for example, static descriptions of the characters and situation serve as the background against which the "story line"—a series of bounded events—stands out as a kind of figure (Hopper and Thompson 1980). Along another axis, we can distinguish the important content a speaker foregrounds as the actual target of

---

[4] Although terms like "foreground", "background", and "baseline" are visual and spatial in origin, the asymmetries in question most likely have some temporal basis in cognitive processing. Even in vision, to perceive something as standing out against a background is to register a contrast presupposing the background as a basis for comparison (FCG1: §3.1).

discussion from subsidiary comments pertaining to its status or assessment. I have in mind examples like (4)(a)–(b), where smaller print represents this communicative backgrounding. Phonologically, it corresponds to the phrases in question being unaccented and lower in pitch.

(4) (a) *Victoria would, I think, make a good candidate.*

  (b) *Victoria would make a good candidate, I believe.*

  (c) *I think Victoria would make a good candidate.*

  (d) *I definitely anticipate that Victoria would make a good candidate.*

  (e) *Jason stated that Victoria would make a good candidate.*

In sentence (c) we observe that even a "main clause" (i.e. one foregrounded in a structural sense) can be backgrounded in this manner. The main-clause situation stays in the foreground when described in fuller detail, as in (d), or when the opinion is attributed to someone other than the speaker, as in (e).

As discourse unfolds, at each step the current expression is constructed and interpreted against the background of those that have gone before. The prior discourse is a major determinant (along with context, background knowledge, etc.) of what I call the **current discourse space** (CDS). The CDS is a mental space comprising everything presumed to be shared by the speaker and hearer as the basis for discourse at a given moment. Starting from that basis, each successive utterance updates the CDS in some fashion. In (5), for example, speaker A's question updates the CDS by introducing a proposition to be considered ('Victoria will agree to be a candidate'), as well as the expectation that an interlocutor will answer concerning its possible validity. This forms the basis for speaker B's response, which in turn creates the updated CDS presupposed by C's continuation.

(5) **A:** *Will Victoria agree to be a candidate?* **B:** *She may not.* **C:** *But Stephanie will.*

As this discourse fragment shows, reference to the CDS is inherent in the meanings of many linguistic elements. A personal pronoun, like *she*, carries the supposition that its intended referent is established, salient, and uniquely identifiable in the CDS (van Hoek 1997). Negation evokes as background the positive conception of what is being denied.[5] Speaker B's use of *not* is thus interpreted as applying to the previously introduced notion of Victoria agreeing to be a candidate. *But* indicates a contrast with what has gone before. In using it, speaker C is contrasting Stephanie's agreement to be a candidate with Victoria's possible nonagreement, just invoked by B.

The CDS also figures in various phenomena collectively referred to as **information structure**. Information is said to be **given** or **new**, depending on whether it has already been presented; if given, it can sometimes be left implicit. While *agree to be a candidate* is new for speaker A, its occurrence in A's question makes it given

---

[5] I would have no reason to say *My car isn't purple* unless the possibility of it being purple had already been mentioned or somehow brought up for consideration.

for B and C, whose responses can therefore be elliptic. When a new proposition is expressed, the portion departing from what was previously established is called the **focus**. In C's utterance, *Stephanie* is the focus, since that is the point of difference between the proposition 'someone will agree to be a candidate' (already in the CDS) and 'Stephanie will agree to be a candidate' (the contextual interpretation of C's elliptic statement). Finally, the entire sequence in (5) is construed as pertaining to a particular discourse **topic**, which—once established as such—need not be explicitly mentioned. From earlier statements, for instance, it might be clear that the entire discourse fragment relates to the next president of the local chapter of the ACLU.

3.2.2 Composition

Let us now turn to focusing that is inherent in the meanings of individual expressions. Most expressions are **symbolically complex**, being assembled out of smaller symbolic elements (§1.3.1). For example, *lipstick* has *lip* and *stick* as symbolic components. These are **component** symbolic structures, *lipstick* as an integrated whole being the **composite** symbolic structure. Likewise, *make* and *-er* are symbolic components of the composite expression *maker*. A composite structure can itself function as a component structure in an expression of greater symbolic complexity. *Lipstick* and *maker* are thus components of the higher-level composite structure *lipstick maker*. Linguists refer to this hierarchical arrangement as **constituency** and represent it in tree-like diagrams (e.g. fig. 1.3). One version of such a diagram is given for *lipstick maker* in figure 3.1.

As the diagram indicates, the relation between component and composite structures is an instance of background vs. foreground. The relative degree of foregrounding is represented here by the thickness of lines.[6] When we use the composite expression *lipstick maker*, we certainly access the individual meanings of *lipstick* and *maker*. We do not evoke them for their own sake, however, but only as a way of "reaching" the novel composite conception, LIPSTICK MAKER. Because the

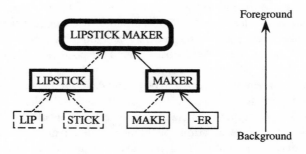

FIGURE 3.1

[6] Also, since LIPSTICK MAKER is a novel conception, the box enclosing it has rounded corners. The dashed and solid arrows connecting the boxes indicate relationships of categorization (extension and elaboration, respectively). Their rationale is discussed in ch. 6.

notions LIPSTICK and MAKER are individually symbolized, and thus facilitate the emergence of the composite conception, they exhibit the conceptual precedence characteristic of background status. Analogously, the conceptual components LIP and STICK are backgrounded in relation to LIPSTICK, as are MAKE and -ER in relation to MAKER. Of course, when there are multiple levels of composition, the highest-level composite structure (in this case LIPSTICK MAKER) is foregrounded with respect to the structures at all lower levels.

Composite expressions exhibit varying degrees of **analyzability**; that is, they vary in how salient the component structures are in relation to the composite conception, and how strongly they contribute to its emergence. A novel expression, such as *lipstick maker*, is fully analyzable precisely because it is novel. Since LIPSTICK MAKER is not a prepackaged conceptual unit, it has to be actively constructed on the basis of the individually symbolized notions LIPSTICK and MAKER, which are therefore highly activated and salient within the whole. With a fixed expression, on the other hand, the composite conception does constitute a prepackaged unit, so instead of being newly constructed it need only be activated. No longer is it essential that the symbolic components be recognized and their individual meanings accessed. For fixed expressions, consequently, we can posit degrees of analyzability, depending on how consistently and saliently the component conceptions are accessed along with the composite conception. *Maker*, for instance, seems more analyzable than *lipstick* (as shown by the dashed-line boxes in fig. 3.1). The discrepancy is quite evident in cases like *complainer*, *computer*, and *propeller*. We immediately understand *complainer* as 'someone who complains', but *computer* is not necessarily apprehended as 'something that computes', and *propel* may not be recognized at all in *propeller*.

How an expression's composite meaning relates to those of its components (at successive levels of organization) is called its **compositional path**. Figure 3.1 sketches the compositional path of *lipstick maker*. An important claim of CG is that an expression's meaning does not consist of its composite semantic structure alone, but further includes its compositional path, the two standing in a foreground/background relationship. While the composite conception is primary, it is viewed against the background of the component semantic structures at all lower levels. How strongly a particular component contributes to this secondary dimension of meaning depends on its proximity to the composite structure along the compositional path, as well as the expression's degree of analyzability at the various levels. LIPSTICK and MAKER are thus quite salient by virtue of proximity—*lipstick* and *maker* being **immediate** constituents of *lipstick maker*—and also because the composite expression is fully analyzable at that level. MAKE and -ER are less salient within the overall expression since they are backgrounded relative to MAKER, while LIP and STICK are less salient still since *lipstick* has a lower degree of analyzability.

Why should we define an expression's meaning as including its compositional path? For one thing, it just seems right—this is a very real dimension of conceptual organization, and to ignore it is simply pointless. More significantly, it helps explain the commonplace observation that no two expressions are exactly the same in meaning. A classic example is *pork* vs. *pig meat*. Suppose, for sake of argument, that their composite semantic structures are taken as being identical. They are nevertheless semantically nonequivalent, since they arrive at this composite conception via different compositional paths: a **degenerate** path in the case of *pork* (consisting of just the composite structure, since there are no individually symbolized components); and for *pig meat*, a path incorporating both PIG and MEAT. The semantic difference, then, is that *pig meat* evokes the component notions PIG and MEAT more saliently than does *pork*. Similar examples abound. The word *cousin*, being unanalyzable, directly invokes a particular kinship configuration, viewed holistically, whereas *parent's sibling's child* arrives at the same configuration step by step, in effect taking us on a tour of the family tree. By the same token, *triangle* does not have the same meaning as *three-angled polygon*, irrespective of whether their composite semantic structures are identical. The notions THREE and ANGLE figure in both expressions but are less salient in *triangle*, which has a low degree of analyzability. Being individually symbolized, the schematic concept POLYGON is necessarily accessed in *three-angled polygon* but remains implicit with *triangle*. It should further be evident that *three-angled polygon* and *three-sided polygon* are semantically distinct, despite their referential identity.

By acknowledging the semantic contribution of compositional paths, we can also explain why expressions that are **semantically anomalous**—having no coherent composite structure—nonetheless seem meaningful. Consider *four-sided triangle*. It is semantically anomalous because the component conceptions FOUR-SIDED and TRIANGLE are inconsistent with one another; when we attempt to combine them in the manner specified by the grammatical construction, the composite semantic structure is either defective or vacuous (depending on how we choose to look at it). The expression is not semantically empty, however: its semantic pole consists of a compositional path with meaningful components arranged in a particular configuration. By virtue of their distinct compositional paths, different anomalous expressions are nonsynonymous. While both *four-sided triangle* and *four-angled triangle* are incoherent at the composite structure level, they contrast in meaning because their compositional paths incorporate different elements (SIDE, SIDED, and FOUR-SIDED vs. ANGLE, ANGLED, and FOUR-ANGLED).

3.2.3 Scope

In addition to foregrounding, focusing includes the initial selection of conceptual content for linguistic presentation. One facet of selection is the access an expression affords to a particular set of cognitive domains, in general or on a given occasion. A second facet is the extent of an expression's "coverage" in the domains accessed: which portions of these domains it actually evokes and utilizes as the basis for its meaning. For each domain in its matrix, an expression has a **scope** consisting of its coverage in that domain.[7]

Scope has an evident cognitive basis: there is only so much that we can mentally encompass at any one moment. For example, our visual apparatus limits what we can see at any one time. Experientially, we have a restricted "viewing frame"—the visual field—delimiting what we can visually encompass when "looking out" at the world. At any one instant, only a limited portion of our spatial surroundings falls within the

---

[7] Full coverage (where scope and domain are coextensive) is allowed as a special case.

scope of vision. We can recognize an analogous delimitation for other domains of experience. For each domain it evokes, an expression's scope is the conceptual content appearing in the subjective viewing frame inherent in its apprehension.

A scope is always **bounded**, in the abstract sense of having only limited expanse. Consider a word like *glass*, which evokes the domain of space for the specification of its characteristic shape. Entertaining this shape conception requires a certain spatial expanse, extensive enough to support its manifestation, but this spatial scope does not subsume the entire universe. Similarly, conceptualizing an event—e.g. *stumble*—requires that we mentally access a span of time long enough to encompass its occurrence, but this temporal scope does not include all of eternity. A term like *cousin* evokes a nonbasic domain comprising a network of kinship relations. While a kinship network can be extended indefinitely far in any direction, a mere fragment is sufficient to conceptualize the *cousin* relationship.

Bounding (in this abstract sense) does not imply that a scope's boundary is objectively discernible. It may only be implicit, imposed by the subjective viewing frame, and not necessarily with any great precision. Indeed, a viewing frame subjectively constant in size may subtend a region of virtually any (objective) size in the domain being viewed. Subjectively, our visual field is fixed in size (try expanding it!), yet by adjusting for distance we can greatly modify how much of the surrounding world it delimits; when viewing a distant mountain range, our visual scope is vastly greater than when looking at a painting from close up. This subjective constancy despite variation in scope is quite significant linguistically. Because of it, the same expression is often applicable to situations observable at any **scale**. The description *X is close to Y* is equally felicitous when applied to the distance between two neurons, two cities, or two galaxies. We can use the word *horse* not only for a real equine of normal stature but also for a small toy or an enormous sculpture carved from a mountain. It is not just a matter of perceiving their common shape and ignoring the gross disparity in their sizes; in relation to the subjective viewing frame (either the visual field or its conceptual analog), they may in fact be of comparable size.

One reason for grouping selection and foregrounding under a common rubric (focusing) is that scope—a matter of selection—can itself be arranged in terms of foreground vs. background. We sometimes need to distinguish between an expression's **maximal scope** in some domain, i.e. the full extent of its coverage, and a limited **immediate scope**, the portion directly relevant for a particular purpose. The immediate scope is thus foregrounded vis-à-vis the maximal scope. Metaphorically, we can describe it as the "onstage region", the general region of viewing attention.

Consider a word like *elbow*. Clearly, one domain it selects—quite central in its matrix—is the conception of the human body.[8] But it is equally clear that *elbow* is not characterized directly with respect to the human body as an undifferentiated whole. A body has major parts, including arms, and an elbow is first and foremost part of an arm. In conceptualizing an elbow, the conception of an arm in particular is most directly relevant ("onstage"). There is a conceptual hierarchy, such that BODY

---

[8] Linguists thus refer to such expressions as "body-part terms".

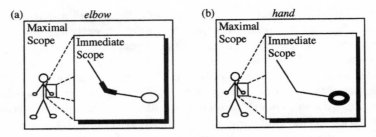

FIGURE 3.2

figures directly in ARM, which in turn figures directly in ELBOW, but BODY figures only indirectly in ELBOW (via ARM). For *elbow*, then, we can say that BODY functions as maximal scope and ARM as immediate scope. This is shown diagrammatically in figure 3.2(a).

Distinctions between maximal and immediate scope are quite significant in hierarchies consisting of successive whole-part relations. While body-part terms afford the clearest examples, there are similar hierarchies in other domains of experience:

(6)   (a) *body > arm > hand > finger > knuckle*

       (b) *body > head > face > eye > pupil*

       (c) *house > door > hinge > screw*

       (d) *car > motor > piston > ring*

A striking feature of such hierarchies is that each part functions as immediate scope for the next term in the sequence. The conception of an arm is thus the immediate scope for *hand* (fig. 3.2(b)), a hand for *finger*, and a finger for *knuckle*. This type of arrangement is depicted abstractly in figure 3.3(a), where MS and IS indicate maximal and immediate scope, and a heavy-line box represents the entity designated by each successive expression (its profile). The dotted correspondence lines equate the entity designated by each expression with the immediate scope for the next. As a consequence, each term incorporates in its matrix the essential content of all the terms that precede it in the hierarchy. The result, as shown for Part$_3$ in figure 3.3(b),

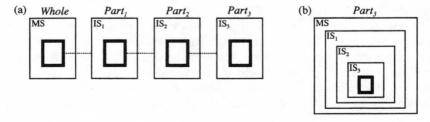

FIGURE 3.3

is a layered arrangement of successively embedded scopes. For a given expression, degree of embedding correlates with degree of foregrounding and directness of mental access. *Knuckle*, for instance, provides direct mental access to FINGER (its immediate scope), which in turn evokes HAND, and so on. The conception of a finger, a hand, an arm, and the body as a whole all figure in the meaning of *knuckle* but lie progressively farther in the background.

This layering has various linguistic manifestations. To take just one, a part can often be labeled by a compound: *fingertip, ear lobe, eyeball, toenail, bellybutton, kneecap, thigh bone, door knob, window pane, toilet seat, piston ring*, and so on. A noteworthy feature of these compounds is that the component nouns represent adjacent levels in a whole-part hierarchy. More specifically, the entity designated by the first element of the compound functions as immediate scope for the second element, as well as for the composite expression; the referent of *toilet*, for instance, constitutes the immediate scope for interpreting both *seat* and *toilet seat*. Skipping levels usually results in an infelicitous expression. We can therefore speak of a *door hinge* or a *hinge screw*, but the same entities could hardly be referred to as a **house hinge* or **door screw*. And as alternatives to *fingernail, eyelash*, and *shoulder blade*, compounds like **armnail, *facelash*, and **body blade* would simply not work.

The distinction between maximal and immediate scope is not confined to whole-part hierarchies. A rather different example is found in the contrast between a verb designating a bounded event (e.g. *examine*) and the corresponding progressive (*be examining*), formed by adding *be...-ing*. The domain of interest is time, indicated in figure 3.4 by the arrow labeled t.

For the verb itself (*V*), there is no reason to distinguish maximal and immediate scope, so the box delimiting the temporal scope in diagram (a) is labeled MS/IS. The heavy line represents the event designated by the verb, viewed in its evolution through time. The entire bounded event, including its endpoints, appears "onstage" within the temporal scope. Diagram (b) shows the effect of adding the progressive *be...-ing*. Its meaning resides in the construal it imposes on the content supplied by the verb. Specifically, it "zooms in" and imposes a limited immediate scope that excludes the endpoints of the bounded event. The composite expression *be Ving* therefore has both a maximal and an immediate scope in the temporal domain: its maximal scope encompasses the entire bounded event, of which only some internal portion falls within the immediate scope. Because the immediate scope is foregrounded, only this onstage portion of the overall event stands out as the composite expression's referent. So in contrast to *She examined it*, which designates a complete act of examination and specifies its past occurrence, *She was examining it* merely indicates that such an act was under way.

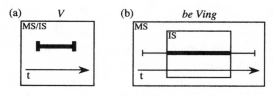

FIGURE 3.4

3.3 Prominence

Language structure displays numerous kinds of asymmetries that are reasonably considered matters of prominence. The terms **prominence** and **salience** (used here interchangeably) are not self-explanatory. Because something can be salient in many different ways, describing it as such is not an adequate characterization but only a starting point for analysis.

What are some dimensions of prominence? Focusing fits comfortably under this rubric, since anything selected is rendered prominent relative to what is unselected, and a foreground is salient relative to its background. Within a category, the proto-type has greater prominence than its various extensions.[9] Space and vision have a privileged cognitive status vis-à-vis other realms of experience. More generally, an intrinsic disparity in salience seems clearly evident between the members of various oppositions: concrete vs. abstract, real vs. imaginary, explicit vs. implicit, and so on. Whether such asymmetries can all be grouped under a single label is less important than properly distinguishing them and determining which ones figure in particular phenomena.

Here I concentrate on two particular sorts of prominence: **profiling** and **trajector/landmark alignment**. Though not equivalent, they are similar in that each involves the focusing of attention (a strong kind of foregrounding). Both constructs are strongly justified on semantic grounds. They also prove essential in grammatical description.

3.3.1 Profiling

As the basis for its meaning, an expression selects a certain body of conceptual content. Let us call this its conceptual **base**. Construed broadly, an expression's conceptual base is identified as its maximal scope in all domains of its matrix (or all domains accessed on a given occasion). Construed more narrowly, its base is identified as the immediate scope in active domains—that is, the portion put "onstage" and foregrounded as the general locus of viewing attention. Within this onstage region, attention is directed to a particular substructure, called the **profile**. Thus an expression's profile stands out as the specific **focus** of attention within its immediate scope.[10] The profile can also be characterized as what the expression is conceived as designating or referring to within its base (its conceptual referent).

Consider *elbow*, diagrammed in figure 3.2(a). With respect to spatial configuration, its maximal scope is the overall shape of the human body.[11] Within this, the conception of an arm is put onstage as the immediate scope, or general locus of attention. Within the immediate scope, the expression singles out a certain substructure as

---

[9] Also, in taxonomies a **basic level category** (e.g. *hammer*) has greater cognitive salience than either a **subordinate** category (*claw hammer*) or a **superordinate** one (*tool*) (Taylor 2004: §3.3).

[10] The immediate and maximal scopes are not necessarily distinct (see fig. 3.4).

[11] Space and spatial configuration are not the only domains in the matrix of *elbow*, but they are obviously highly central. I emphasize that the semantic descriptions offered here do not purport to be exhaustive but are merely illustrative of the phenomena being discussed.

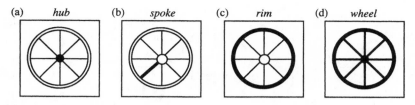

FIGURE 3.5

its profile, or referent. The profile—drawn with heavy lines—is the specific focus of attention within the onstage region.

If we now compare *elbow* with *hand*, sketched in figure 3.2(b), we see that *hand* has the same maximal and immediate scopes as *elbow* but a different profile. In fact, it is quite common that two or more expressions evoke the same conceptual content yet differ in meaning by virtue of profiling different substructures within this common base. For instance, *Monday*, *Tuesday*, *Wednesday*, etc. all evoke as their base the conception of a seven-day cycle constituting a week, within which they profile different segments. Similarly, as shown in figure 3.5, the conception of a wheel functions as the base for *hub*, *spoke*, and *rim*, which contrast semantically because they designate different parts. *Wheel*, of course, profiles the whole.

An expression can profile either a **thing** or a **relationship**.[12] The ones considered so far profile things despite incorporating relationships in their base (notably whole-part relations). Indeed, it is common for an expression to invoke a relationship for its essential conceptual content even though it profiles a thing. A good example is a kin term, such as *aunt*, diagrammed in figure 3.6. The essential content of this lexeme is the kinship relation between a female and a reference individual, R (the one with respect to whom the person is an aunt). It is this relationship that is critical for characterizing the female in question. *Aunt*, however, does not profile the relationship but rather the female it serves to identify—its referent is a person, albeit one characterized as a female relative. Note that the profile is not defined as the most important or distinctive content, but rather as the entity an expression designates, i.e. its referent within the content evoked.

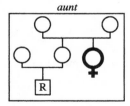

FIGURE 3.6

---

[12] This fundamentally important conceptual distinction is discussed in ch. 4. For now I simply note that these terms are defined abstractly (hence things are not limited to physical objects, nor does a relationship necessarily involve multiple participants).

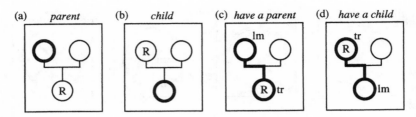

FIGURE 3.7

This distinction—between crucially invoking a relationship and actually profiling it—is exemplified in figure 3.7. All four expressions invoke the conception of a nuclear kin relation (involving one instance of reproduction). Their semantic non-equivalence derives from the different profiles they impose on this common base. *Parent* and *child* (in the 'offspring' sense) are like *aunt*, in that each profiles a thing characterized by its role in the relation; the latter remains unprofiled, since the referent of *parent* or *child* is a person, not a relationship. This relationship is, however, profiled by the composite expressions *have a parent* and *have a child*. These designate the relationship itself, viewed as a stable situation continuing through time. The semantic contrast between *have a parent* and *have a child* resides in their opposite directionality: each portrays the relationship as proceeding from the reference individual (R) of the kin term it incorporates.[13]

Although *have a parent* and *have a child* contrast in directionality, they do not have different profiles. An expression's profile is its referent, and the relationship designated is the same referentially with either direction of mental access. It is, however, common for expressions that profile relationships (like those which profile things) to have the same conceptual base and yet be semantically distinct because they profile different facets of it. For a grammatical example, consider any verb and its corresponding progressive (e.g. *examine* vs. *be examining*), diagrammed in figure 3.4. The verb designates an entire bounded event, while the progressive, without altering the overall content, singles out just an arbitrary internal portion of that event for profiling. A lexical example is *come* vs. *arrive*, diagrammed in figure 3.8. As their base, both verbs evoke the conception of a thing (represented as a circle) moving along a spatial path (arrow) to an end location (LOC). Each verb invokes a relationship in which the mover, through time, successively occupies all the positions defining the path. The difference in their meanings is that *come* profiles the full motion event, in which the mover traverses the entire path, whereas *arrive* designates only the segment in which the mover finally reaches the goal.

---

[13] The labels tr and lm indicate **trajector** and **landmark,** to be discussed shortly. The choice of trajector is responsible for the difference in directionality.

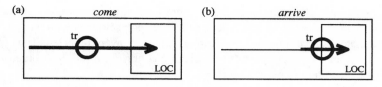

FIGURE 3.8

Profiling figures crucially in the pervasive phenomenon known as **metonymy**. In a narrow sense, we can characterize metonymy as a shift in profile. For example, a customer who says (7)(a) to a waiter is not claiming to be an Italian dessert. While this would be the usual referent of *tiramisu*, in the restaurant context its profile shifts from the dessert to the person who ordered it. Similarly, in (7)(b) the entity absent from the phone book is not the famous golfer per se but rather his name, address, and telephone number. The profile of *Tiger Woods* shifts from the person to the associated information (or its printed representation).

(7) (a) *I'm the tiramisu.*

(b) *She couldn't find Tiger Woods in the phone book.*

Mediating the shift in profile is a cognitive domain establishing some connection between the two entities: the restaurant scenario of customers placing orders, or else the knowledge of what a phone book is for. More precisely, then, we speak of metonymy when an expression that ordinarily profiles one entity is used instead to profile another entity associated with it in some domain. A single expression is susceptible to any number of metonymic extensions, reflecting different associations.[14] For instance, *Miró* would ordinarily be understood as referring to a person, as in (8)(a). Since Miró was a famous artist, reference to this person tends to evoke the conception of his works, as well as the more elaborate conceptions of exhibits or books featuring a single artist's works. Mediated by these domains, *Miró* is interpreted metonymically in (8)(b)–(d) as designating a work of art, a collection of works, and a book, respectively.

(8) (a) *Miró died in 1983.*

(b) *She bought an original Miró.*

(c) *Miró is in Gallery B, at the end of this corridor.*

(d) *Miró is at the bottom of the stack, right under Tamayo.*

There are many conventional patterns of metonymy, like the extension from artist to artistic creation. These can be applied productively. If Tiger Woods should give

---

[14] Being based on association in a single domain, metonymy is distinct from metaphor; instead, metaphor involves an abstract similarity between two domains (source and target).

up golf for sculpture, we can immediately refer to one of his creations by saying *This is a Tiger Woods.* Metonymy is a regular source of polysemy, which results when a particular metonymic usage becomes entrenched and conventionalized. Thus *church* can profile either a building used for religious meetings or a religious organization that meets in such buildings:

(9)   (a) *They built a new church just out of town.*

      (b) *The church he belongs to has very odd beliefs.*

And while the usual examples of metonymy pertain to things, we can also observe it in expressions that profile relationships. Consider these two uses of *come*:

(10)   (a) *They came all the way from Los Angeles.*

       (b) *He came at precisely 7:45 PM.*

In (10)(a), *come* profiles the full event of moving along an extended spatial path, as shown in figure 3.8(a). In (10)(b), however, it designates only the final stage of arriving at the goal (making it comparable to *arrive* in figure 3.8(b)). Because they profile different substructures within a common base, the two senses are related metonymically, and since they are both conventionally established, *come* is polysemous.

We have now seen numerous cases where a difference in meaning stems from alternate choices of profile within the same conceptual base. Since the content is effectively equivalent, these semantic contrasts are matters of construal—in particular, the directing of attention to a thing or relationship thereby singled out as an expression's conceptual referent. Profiling is not the only descriptive construct needed pertaining to focus of attention, however. One can easily find expressions that are semantically distinct despite having the same conceptual base and profiling the same relationship within it. An additional construct is therefore required to properly distinguish the meanings of relational expressions. This is **trajector/landmark alignment**, another kind of prominence.

3.3.2 Trajector/Landmark Alignment

When a relationship is profiled, varying degrees of prominence are conferred on its participants. The most prominent participant, called the **trajector** (tr), is the entity construed as being located, evaluated, or described. Impressionistically, it can be characterized as the **primary focus** within the profiled relationship. Often some other participant is made prominent as a **secondary focus**. If so, this is called a **landmark** (lm). Expressions can have the same content, and profile the same relationship, but differ in meaning because they make different choices of trajector and landmark.[15]

---

[15] In earlier works, every relational expression was said to have a trajector and a landmark, defined as the entities between which the profiled relationship holds (FCG1: §6.3). Under that definition, the trajector and landmark are not necessarily distinct or individually salient. I now reserve the terms for entities with focal prominence.

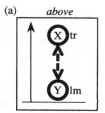 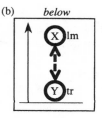

FIGURE 3.9

The prepositions *above* and *below* differ in this manner. They are clearly not synonymous. Where, however, does their contrast in meaning lie? They have the same content: each indicates the relative spatial location of two things, primarily with respect to the vertical axis. Moreover, as shown in figure 3.9, they also profile the same relationship: referentially, *X above Y* is the same relationship as *Y below X*. The semantic contrast can only reside in the degree of prominence conferred on the relational participants. We use *X above Y* to specify the location of X (the higher participant), and *Y below X* to locate Y (the lower participant). This makes X and Y their respective trajectors. In each case the other participant functions as a spatial landmark for that purpose. This difference in trajector/landmark alignment, a matter of construal, is solely responsible for *above* and *below* being semantically distinct.

If *above* and *below* contrast in their choice of trajector, characterized as the participant being located or assessed, the discourse context should sometimes determine which preposition will be used. This prediction is borne out by data like the following:

(11)   (a) *Where is the lamp?*

(i) *The lamp (tr) is above the table (lm).*

(ii) **The table (tr) is below the lamp (lm).*

(b) *Where is the table?*

(i) *The table (tr) is below the lamp (lm).*

(ii) **The lamp (tr) is above the table (lm).*

The question in (11)(a) makes it clear that the lamp is interpreted as the thing being located. In this context, the answer is felicitous only when *the lamp* specifies the trajector, as in response (i), not the landmark, as in (ii). In (11)(b), where the table is the entity being located, these judgments are naturally reversed.

Many relational expressions have only a single focal participant. By default, the sole focal participant must be the primary focal participant, which makes it the trajector. With verbs like *come* and *arrive*, the mover has this status (fig. 3.8). The relationship they profile is the mover's translation through space, which clearly involves a series of locations that the mover successively occupies. But while these successive locations support the conception of spatial movement, they remain in the background rather than standing out as focused elements.[16] These verbs thus have a trajector but no landmark.

It is important to realize that a trajector does not have to be a mover (nor is a mover necessarily a trajector). Instead, trajector and landmark are defined in terms of primary and secondary **focal prominence**, not in terms of any specific semantic role or conceptual content. The notions are therefore applicable to any kind of cognitive domain. We can see this with the non-motion expressions *have a parent* and *have a child*, diagrammed in figure 3.7. Although they profile the same relationship, which is static and abstract, they are semantically distinct due to their opposite trajector/landmark alignments: *have a parent* is the description of a child, while *have a child* describes a parent. Note further that focal prominence is not restricted to things—a relationship can also be put in focus as trajector or landmark. In (12), for instance, *before* and *after* profile a relationship of temporal precedence between two events, which are thus the relational participants; but since these events are expressed as finite clauses, they are themselves relational expressions:

(12)   (a) *The other guests all left before we arrived.*

      (b) *We arrived after the other guests all left.*

Once again, as shown in figure 3.10, *before* and *after* designate what is referentially the same relationship. The semantic contrast between them resides in their choice of trajector and landmark, not in content or profiling.

As a final word on prominence, let us ponder the issue of where to look for it. If a certain element is salient, as either a profile or a focal participant, where exactly does its salience lie? It does not lie in the outside world. If we look at our surroundings, we do not see objects bordered with heavy lines to mark them as profiles, nor is something intrinsically a trajector or a landmark. Like other aspects of construal, prominence is a conceptual phenomenon, inhering in our apprehension of the world,

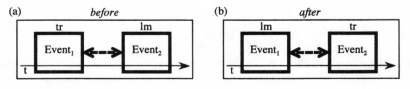

FIGURE 3.10

---

[16] That is, the locations are viewed merely as part of the spatial medium in which the motion occurs. Even the end location, which (as goal) has a certain amount of salience, lacks the focal prominence of a landmark and is often not expressed (*They finally came*; *We just arrived*).

not in the world per se.[17] However, merely acknowledging its conceptual nature is insufficient. Even at the conceptual level, the objects of our mental universe have no inherent status as profile, trajector, or landmark. These pertain specifically to the conceptualizations evoked as the meanings of linguistic expressions. How prominent a particular entity is—whether it functions as profile, trajector, landmark, or none of the above—depends on the construal imposed by the linguistic elements employed, in accordance with their conventional semantic values.

Consider *The lamp is above the table*. The lamp has trajector status only by virtue of how the situation is linguistically expressed. It reflects the speaker's decision to say where the lamp is, and thus to use *above*, which puts primary focus on the vertically higher participant. Yet nothing forces the speaker to construe and describe the scene this way. In another discourse context (e.g. when discussing a certain table), the speaker might say instead *The table is below the lamp*. Here the same lamp is only a landmark.

Crucially, these kinds of prominence hold for particular levels of structural organization. As we combine elements to form progressively larger expressions, the composite structure at each level has its own profile; and if that expression profiles a relationship, it has its own trajector/landmark alignment. By itself, for instance, *table* profiles a thing, as does *the table*. But at a higher structural level, *above the table* profiles a spatial relationship. It is only when we reach this level that *the table* functions as landmark. At a still higher level, where the prepositional phrase modifies a noun, the latter imposes its own profile on the composite expression: *the lamp above the table* profiles the lamp, not the table or the *above* relationship. This entire nominal can then be used as a subject or object, as in the sentence *She detests the lamp above the table*. At the sentence level, the profiled relationship is *detest* (not *above*), the trajector is *she*, and the landmark is the lamp (not the table). In sum, each structure in a symbolic assembly makes its own assignments of focus, so an entity focused in one structure need not have comparable salience in another.

3.4 Perspective

If conceptualization (metaphorically) is the viewing of a scene, perspective is the **viewing arrangement**, the most obvious aspect of which is the vantage point assumed. Under the rubric of perspective I also consider **dynamicity**, pertaining to how a conceptualization unfolds through processing time.

3.4.1 Viewing Arrangement

A **viewing arrangement** is the overall relationship between the "viewers" and the situation being "viewed". For our purposes, the viewers are conceptualizers who apprehend the meanings of linguistic expressions: the speaker and the hearer.

---

[17] This is not to deny that the world imposes itself in particular ways, thereby constraining and biasing our apprehension of it. Likewise, normal patterns of conceptualization constrain and bias the conceptualizations invoked for linguistic purposes. We nevertheless have enormous conceptual flexibility, and the biases at each level are easily overridden.

One particular viewing arrangement, common in everyday conversational inter-actions, arguably has default-case status, being presupposed unless there is reason to assume the contrary. In the default arrangement, the interlocutors are together in a fixed location, from which they observe and describe actual occurrences in the world around them. This default arrangement is tacitly invoked for the kinds of example sentences invented by linguists for basic illustrative purposes, e.g. *The lamp is above the table* or *John kissed Mary*.

Precisely because of its default-case status, this arrangement tends to be invisible to us. But though we take it for granted, the default arrangement is an essential part of the conceptual substrate that supports an expression's meaning and shapes its form. The default arrangement becomes more visible when we consider various departures from it, noting the changes in form and meaning that ensue. Most apparent are expressions that perform an action other than mere description, such as questions and commands:

(13)   (a) *Is the lamp above the table?*

(b) *Kiss her!*

Semantically, these do not report on what is happening but actually comprise a particu-lar kind of speaker-hearer interaction, traditionally called a **speech act**. This special meaning is signaled by distinct forms (involving word order, intonation, and/or absence of an overt subject). However it is not just the meanings of "special" sentence types like interrogatives and imperatives that incorporate speech acts signaled by their forms. Simple description also represents a kind of speaker-hearer interaction, and basic declarative form (i.e. the absence of special marking) can be seen as a way of indicat-ing it.[18] We tend to ignore this specification only because it reflects the default viewing arrangement, for which zero marking is both natural and iconic (Haiman 1985).

A glance at some other noncanonical viewing circumstances reveals how much of a special case the default arrangement really is. First, a large proportion of what we describe fails to qualify as actual occurrences observed or known to be real. We often say what did not happen, as well as what may or may not occur in the future. We readily invoke hypothetical situations, even some known to be false, and trace their nonfactual development (e.g. *If you had asked for directions we wouldn't have gotten lost*). Moreover, we refer to all manner of entities that are virtual, imaginary, blended, abstract, and/or internally contradictory (*every flea, Santa Claus, pet rock, compassionate conservative, four-sided triangle, the square root of minus one, the last digit in the decimal expansion of pi*).

Rather different are departures from the default arrangement involving the rela-tive position of the viewers. For example, instead of occupying a fixed location, the viewer is often conceived as being in motion. In (14)(a), *through this valley* describes the path of the viewer's motion, which otherwise remains implicit. In (14)(b), it is

---

[18] Simple description is usually (but misleadingly) called **assertion**. Note that questioning, ordering, and assertion are only the prototypical values of the interrogative, imperative, and declarative sentence types (viewed as forms). The same forms can be used for other speech acts, and the same speech acts can be expressed in other ways. (See §13.2.3.)

only the presupposed journey that makes it coherent to characterize the length of a nap by means of a spatial distance.

(14) (a) *It's pretty through this valley.*

(b) *She's been asleep for 30 miles.*

(c) *The trees are rushing past at 90 miles per hour.*

(d) *The forest is getting thicker.*

Movement by the viewer can also engender a perception of change which, though virtual in nature, is described as if it were actual. While it is possible in (14)(c) that the trees actually are in motion, the more likely interpretation is that a moving viewer (perhaps riding in a train) is describing the visual impression obtained by imagining the default arrangement where the viewer is static. Similarly, the more likely interpretation of (14)(d) does not involve any actual change in the forest. Rather, movement through the forest brings the viewer into contact with different portions of it, which—when fictively construed as the same entity—are seen as increasing in density. Although these expressions make no explicit reference to the viewer's motion, it is nonetheless part of their conceptual substrate, in no small measure being responsible for their conceptual coherence as well as their form.

Another possibility is for the interlocutors to be separated in space or time. Consider the banal statement *It's warm here*. In a face-to-face conversation, *here* refers to the area where both the speaker and the hearer are located. But in the context of a long-distance phone call, the proximate region it designates is defined in relation to the speaker alone: *It's warm here, but it must be cold where you are*. Illustrating displacement in time is the recorded message one hears when making a phone call and reaching an answering machine. This message might begin with the statement *I'm not here right now*, which is contradictory presuming the default viewing arrangement (by definition, where I am right now is *here*). In recording the message, however, the speaker interprets *right now* as referring to the later time when a caller will hear it, and at that time the speaker will not be at home (*here*). What makes the message coherent and easy to understand is our apprehension of the overall communicative situation, part of the tacit conceptual substrate. An extreme example of spatiotemporal displacement is a sign or warning label, e.g. *Shake well before using* (Sadock 1974). Here the expressive medium is writing rather than speech. Moreover, the writer is not a particular person but a generalized voice of authority (perhaps the manufacturer), the reader is whoever should happen to use the product, and a usage event occurs whenever and wherever the label is read. The specific time and place of writing are unknown and irrelevant.

One component of the viewing arrangement is a presupposed **vantage point**. In the default arrangement, the vantage point is the actual location of the speaker and hearer. The same objective situation can be observed and described from any number of different vantage points, resulting in different construals which may have overt consequences. Many expressions undeniably invoke a vantage point as part of their meaning (arguably, all expressions do). In one of their basic uses, for example, *in front of* and *behind* rely on vantage point to specify the trajector's location

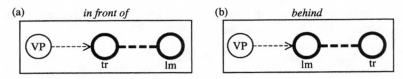

FIGURE 3.11

vis-à-vis the landmark. This is sketched in figure 3.11, where VP labels the vantage point and a dashed arrow indicates the viewer's line of sight. In both cases, one focal participant intervenes in the line of sight leading from the vantage point to the other participant. As in previous examples, the semantic contrast resides in choice of trajector and landmark, there being no significant difference in content or profiling.

If we imagine a scene with a large rock and a tree, how we code it linguistically depends on the vantage point we assume. Let us suppose that the rock, tree, and vantage point are roughly in alignment, as indicated in (15)(a). Then, if the vantage point is such that the rock intervenes in the line of sight (VP$_1$), we can happily use either sentence in (15)(b). If the vantage point is such that the tree intervenes (VP$_2$), the sentences in (15)(c) are appropriate instead.

(15)   (a) VP$_1$ ---> (**rock**)————(**tree**) <--- VP$_2$

     (b) **VP$_1$:** *The rock **(tr)** is in front of the tree **(lm)**. The tree **(tr)** is behind the rock **(lm)**.*

     (c) **VP$_2$:** *The tree **(tr)** is in front of the rock **(lm)**. The rock **(tr)** is behind the tree **(lm)**.*

Of course, the vantage point assumed for linguistic purposes need not be the speaker's actual location. We can easily adopt a fictive vantage point and imagine what the scene would look like from there. The following would thus be appropriate and readily understood when uttered at VP$_1$:

(16)   **VP$_1$:** *If you were standing over there* [at VP$_2$], *the tree would be in front of the rock.*

This capacity to fictively adopt or at least accommodate a nonactual vantage point enables us to describe a situation from the perspective of the hearer or some other individual.

While the term suggests space and vision, vantage point is a useful descriptive construct for other domains as well, notably time. As shown in figure 3.12, the phrase *next year* evokes as its base the conception of a series of years, within which it profiles the year immediately following the one containing the temporal vantage point. In the default situation, this vantage point is equated with the time of speaking, as in (17)(a).

(17)   (a) *Next year will be full of surprises.*

     (b) *Joe believed that next year would be full of surprises.*

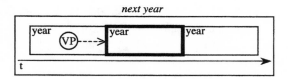

FIGURE 3.12

But here too we can easily adopt a vantage point other than the one defined by the speech event. In (17)(b), *next year* invokes a temporal vantage point identified as the time of the main-clause occurrence: the year in question is the one immediately following the year when Joe entertained his belief (not the year when the sentence is produced).

Closely related to vantage point is a subtle but important aspect of construal known in CG as **subjectivity** vs. **objectivity**. Though quite general in application, it is best introduced with reference to visual perception. Imagine yourself in the audience of a theater, watching a gripping play. All your attention is directed at the stage, and is focused more specifically on the actor presently speaking. Being totally absorbed in the play, you have hardly any awareness of yourself or your own immediate circumstances. This viewing arrangement therefore maximizes the asymmetry between the **viewer** and what is **viewed**, also called the **subject** and **object** of perception. In this polarized arrangement, where the asymmetry in viewing role is maximized, the viewing subject is said to be construed with maximal **subjectivity** and the object with maximal **objectivity**. Subjective construal is characteristic of the viewer's role as such—as an offstage locus of perceptual experience that is not itself perceived. Conversely, objective construal characterizes the onstage focus of attention, which (at least in that capacity) does not engage in viewing. By virtue of being attended to, an entity construed objectively is clearly more prominent than it is when construed subjectively.[19]

For linguistic purposes, we are interested in the general conceptual analog of this perceptual asymmetry. The subjects of conception are the speaker and hearer, who apprehend the meanings of expressions. When they function exclusively in this capacity, as a tacit conceptualizing presence that is not itself conceived, they are construed with maximal subjectivity. At the opposite extreme, construed with maximal objectivity, is the focused object of attention: the entity an expression puts onstage and profiles. Objective construal thus correlates with profiling and explicit mention, and subjective construal with an implicit locus of consciousness. Being implicit is not the same as being absent, however. The conceptualization constituting an expression's meaning extends beyond its onstage content (which does not exist in isolation), further encompassing its mode of apprehension by the offstage conceptualizers in the context of the overall viewing arrangement.

---

[19] When I am wearing my glasses, for instance, they are essentially part of my visual system, hence subjectively construed and nonsalient. They help shape my visual experience, but barely, if at all, do I see the glasses themselves. They become salient, however, when I construe them objectively by taking them off and looking at them.

In their tacit role as subjects of conception, the speaker and hearer are always part of the conceptual substrate supporting an expression's meaning.[20] If that is their only role, they are always implicit and construed with maximal subjectivity. To varying degrees, however, they can themselves function as objects of conception, in which case they are more salient by virtue of being construed more objectively. The extreme is to put them onstage as the focus of attention: with the first- and second-person pronouns (*I, you, we,* and their variants), the speaker and hearer are profiled, explicitly mentioned, and objectively construed. There are also intermediate possibilities. In (15), the speaker and hearer are not merely the subjects of conception, they are also the viewers whose vantage point and line of sight are invoked by *in front of* and *behind* (fig. 3.11). To this extent they figure in the scene described, so their role is not wholly subjective. But neither is it fully objective, for even in this additional viewing capacity they are offstage, unprofiled, and implicit.

The term **ground** is used for the speaker and hearer, the speech event in which they participate, and their immediate circumstances (e.g. the time and place of speaking). As the "platform" for apprehending the content evoked, the ground enters into the meaning of every expression, even when construed with maximal subjectivity. Usually, though, facets of the ground are themselves evoked as part of that content, so that to some degree they function as objects of conception. Quite often they are profiled; since we are naturally concerned with ourselves and our own circumstances, words like *I, you, here,* and *now* are highly frequent. It may however be more typical for facets of the ground to be offstage and construed with only minimal objectivity. They tend to function as implicit points of reference for specifying the location of more objectively conceived entities vis-à-vis the ground. We have already seen this in (15) and (17)(a): just as the place of speaking is tacitly invoked as the spatial vantage point for *in front of* and *behind*, so the time of speaking functions implicitly as a temporal point of reference for *next year.*

The ground's role as tacit point of reference is in fact ubiquitous. Even when implicit and construed with a substantial degree of subjectivity, the ground functions in this capacity for every full nominal and every finite clause (ch. 9). For example, tense is usually reckoned from the ground: *was, is,* and *will be* are past, present, and future with respect to the time of speaking. In the nominal sphere, a comparable parameter is definiteness, as in the contrast between *a rock* (indefinite) and *the rock* (definite). Definiteness relates to the speaker and hearer, for it depends on whether the nominal referent is uniquely apparent to both interlocutors in the current discourse context. Observe that the grammaticized markers for tense and definiteness invoke some facet of the ground but do not mention it explicitly: *now* is not incorporated in the tense markers (e.g. *-ed, -s, will*), nor do markers of definiteness (like *a* and *the*) incorporate the pronouns *I* and *you.*

---

[20] If we view an expression abstractly, independent of specific usage events, the speaker's and hearer's subjective role is just that—a **role** to be instantiated by particular individuals whenever the expression is actually used.

3.4.2 The Temporal Dimension

Conceptualization is inherently dynamic—not something that statically exists, but rather something that happens. It resides in mental processing (or neurological activity) and therefore occurs through time. When time is viewed in this capacity, as the **medium** of conception, it is referred to as **processing time**. Every conceptualization requires some span of processing time for its occurrence. Even one that we experience as instantaneous (e.g. feeling the prick of a pin) has a duration and a course of development when examined on a small enough scale. As an aspect of construal, dynamicity pertains to how a conceptualization develops and unfolds through processing time, especially on larger time scales where its consequences are introspectively accessible.[21]

Processing time has to be distinguished from **conceived time**—that is, time as an **object** of conception. Time is construed most objectively when a span of time is profiled, for instance by expressions like *moment, period, week*, and *next year* (fig. 3.12). Time is also construed objectively, though not as the focus of attention, when it functions as the cognitive domain in which a profiled relationship is manifested, as with *before* and *after* (fig. 3.10). It figures as well in the conception of any event, since events occur through time. The verb *enter*, for example, designates a relationship in space (fig. 2.1), but the change in spatial configuration constituting the profiled event can only be implemented along the temporal axis. Conceived and processing time can be hard to disentangle, if only because the conceptualization **of** time necessarily occurs **through** time. Still, for semantic purposes they have to be clearly separated. In understanding a sentence like (18), we require only a brief interval of processing time (perhaps a second) to scan through a distinct and much longer interval of conceived time (perhaps an hour).

(18)   *The long procession slowly entered the city.*

There is a natural tendency for conceived time and processing time to be coaligned, such that the order in which events are conceived as occurring dovetails with the order in which they are conceptualized and described. This **temporal iconicity** is well known from examples like (19)(a), which would normally be interpreted as indicating that the resignation preceded the marriage and that the marriage preceded the birth, although the sentence does not actually say this.

(19)   (a) *I quit my job, got married, and had a baby.*

         (b) *I had a baby, got married, and quit my job—in reverse order, of course.*

Such iconicity is only a tendency, however. We can mentally access events and describe them linguistically in a sequence that diverges from their order of occurrence or even runs directly counter to it. Thus a sentence like (19)(b) could perfectly

---

[21] This dynamic view of conceptualization fits well with a psychological theory of meaning based on **mental simulation** (Barsalou 1999).

well be used in the proper context (e.g. in response to the question *What are the most important things that happened to you last year?*).

Temporal iconicity of the sort observed in (19)(a) is represented in figure 3.13(a). The upper and lower arrows respectively indicate conceived time (t) and processing time (T). E_1, E_2, and E_3 are three events (e.g. quitting a job, getting married, and having a baby). A, B, and C stand for the conceptualization of each event as it occurs in constructing or understanding a linguistic expression describing it, while the corresponding lower-case letters stand for those expressions themselves (e.g. *I quit my job*, *[I] got married*, and *[I] had a baby*). When a sentence like (19)(a) is uttered, the component expressions are spoken in a certain order (a > b > c), which either reflects or induces an ordering of the conceptualizations they symbolize (A > B > C). Both expression and conception occur (and are coaligned) through processing time (T). Iconicity obtains when the events thus conceptualized are further conceived as occurring in that same order (E_1 > E_2 > E_3) through conceived time (t). There is full harmonization in the sequencing of events, event conceptions, and event descriptions.

Diagrammed in figure 3.13(b) is the noniconic alignment of a sentence like (19)(b). As always, the sequence in which the component expressions occur (a > b > c) correlates with an ordering of the conceptualizations they symbolize (A > B > C). Here, though, this coalignment at the two poles in processing time does not extend to corresponding events in conceived time. Via the linguistic expression, these events are mentally accessed in the order E_3 > E_2 > E_1, while they are conceived as actually occurring in the opposite order, E_1 > E_2 > E_3. We can certainly accomplish this, conceptually and linguistically, but it does carry a processing cost. The need for extra processing effort is signaled by the appendage in (19)(b): *in reverse order, of course.* This directs the listener to **reconceptualize** the events described, by mentally running through them again, but in a sequence directly counter to the order of their initial presentation. Only through such **backtracking** can the listener arrive at a proper apprehension of their actual temporal sequencing.

The order of presentation is conceptually and semantically consequential even when event order is not a factor. A case in point is the semantic effect of preposing a locative expression, as illustrated by the following contrast:

(20)   (a) *A dead rat lay in the middle of the kitchen floor.*

          (b) *In the middle of the kitchen floor lay a dead rat.*

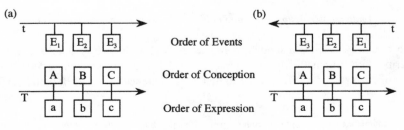

FIGURE 3.13

Despite having the same elements, the sentences have different meanings. Their semantic contrast does not reside in the objective situation described but in how it is mentally accessed. The atypical word order in (20)(b) accommodates the general discourse tendency for given information to precede new information, while also allowing the introduction of a new participant as grammatical subject (cf. Birner 1994). The sentence first directs attention to an already accessible location, and then brings a new participant (*a dead rat*) into the discourse by establishing it in that location. Evidence that the construction in (20)(b) has this special semantic value comes from the infelicity of expressions whose information structure conflicts with it.[22] For instance, (21)(b) is awkward because the subject refers to the speaker, who is always taken as given, as already established in the discourse. Conversely, (21)(c) is infelicitous because the preposed locative represents new information. Compare this with (21)(d), where the garage is mentioned in the first conjunct and is therefore given for purposes of the second.

(21) (a) *I lay in the middle of the kitchen floor.*

  (b) *?*In the middle of the kitchen floor lay I.*

  (c) *?*In a garage sat an old truck.*

  (d) *There was a garage behind the house, and in this garage sat an old truck.*

Order of presentation also has an evident semantic impact in examples like these:

(22) (a) *Your camera is upstairs, in the bedroom, in the closet, on the shelf.*

  (b) *Your camera is on the shelf, in the closet, in the bedroom, upstairs.*

Once again, the two sentences are semantically distinct, even though they contain the same elements and describe the same objective situation. They represent two variants of the "nested locative" construction (GC: 60–61), which specify the subject's location through a series of locative expressions pinning it down to successively nested spatial areas. The difference is that the first variant "zooms in" from the largest area to successively smaller ones, whereas the second variant starts from the smallest area and "zooms out". While the two sentences succeed in evoking the same overall spatial configuration, they build up to it in different ways, thereby providing very different conceptual experiences. They contrast semantically precisely because each conceptualization has its own time course, unfolding in a particular way through processing time.

The words of an expression occur in a certain temporal sequence, which linguists (unwittingly using spatial metaphor) refer to as "linear order". This temporal sequencing defines one salient path of access to the conceptions symbolized. Since

---

[22] Many scholars would say that the contrast in (20) is not one of semantics but rather of pragmatics. I would argue, however, that information structure is conceptual in nature, being special only in that the relevant cognitive domain is the apprehension of the discourse itself.

we necessarily encounter these words sequentially, in either speaking or understanding, linear order always has some effect on meaning—a difference in word order always implies a semantic contrast (though in practical terms it may be slight or even negligible). But linear order is not the only factor influencing the sequence of mental access, nor is the cognitive processing of a sentence limited to a single "left-to-right" pass through it. Processing occurs simultaneously in multiple structural dimensions, at different levels of organization, and on vastly different time scales. Even as we are attending to individual words, we must also be making more global projections at various syntactic and even discourse levels. Much of the relevant conceptual structure is not expressed at all by overt elements, which are merely prompts for the requisite meaning construction. And those notions which are expressed can be reaccessed and reconceptualized as needed, through backtracking (as in (19)(b)).

Sequencing at the conceptual level is thus not always driven by the order of overt elements in speech. We can see this from pairs of examples like (23), which describe the same spatial configuration but have contrasting meanings nonetheless:

(23) (a) *The hill gently rises from the bank of the river.*

    (b) *The hill gently falls to the bank of the river.*

The difference lies in the direction of **mental scanning**. The conceptualizer, in building up to a full conception of the profiled relationship, constructs an image of the hill by tracing a mental path along it in either an upward or a downward direction. However, the direction of scanning is not determined by the order in which the words occur, but rather by their meanings: *rises from* induces upward mental scanning, and *falls to*, downward scanning. Note further that *rise* and *fall*, whose basic senses pertain to spatial motion, are used here to describe a situation that objectively is totally static. While motion is indeed involved, it is subjectively construed. In the case of objectively construed motion (e.g. *It fell*), an onstage entity moves along a spatial path through conceived time. By contrast, the mover in (23) is the offstage conceptualizer, who traces a mental path in space through processing time.

Mental scanning is not restricted to space. Directed scanning through a nonspatial domain is pivotal to the meaning of many expressions and is often reflected in their form. Commonly it consists of running through a set of conceived alternatives arranged in a certain order. Here are a few examples:

(24) (a) *Gestation period varies greatly from one species to the next.*

    (b) *I'll never get into a size 8, and a size 9 is probably still too small.*

    (c) *Don't mention calculus—elementary algebra is already too advanced for him.*

In (24)(a), the alternatives are an imagined set of species, the variation in gestation period being observed as we move subjectively *from one … to the next*. In (24)(b), we scan in a positive direction along a scale of possible sizes. This mental scanning is signaled by *still*, which normally indicates persistence in time (e.g. *Is she still asleep?*). It has the same value here, apart from being construed subjectively. It does not describe the insufficient size as persisting through conceived time, but through processing time, as the conceptualizer scans through a range of alternative sizes. The temporal persistence is subjectively construed by virtue of inhering in the conceptualizing activity itself. Similarly, in (24)(c) the conceptualizer moves subjectively along a scale in which mathematical subjects are ranked for difficulty. The word *already* indicates that the property of being too advanced is encountered sooner than expected (cf. *Are you done already?*). However, this imagined encounter only occurs in processing time: in scanning through the list of subjects, the conceptualizer comes upon it at the level of elementary algebra, well before reaching calculus.

Mental scanning can follow a path that is either continuous or discrete. In (23), the conceptualizer traces a continuous path along the hill's expanse in building up a conception of its overall configuration. By contrast, the scanning in (24) follows a path consisting of discrete steps (species, sizes, or mathematical subjects), but here too the sequenced mental access is a means of building up to an overall conception of some complexity. These are two forms of a general process I refer to as **summary scanning**. As we scan through a complex scene, successively attending to various facets of it, the elements apprehended at each stage are summed, or superimposed. In this way a detailed conception is progressively built up, becoming active and available as a simultaneously accessible whole for a certain span of processing time.[23]

Of considerable grammatical importance is a particular type of scanning called a **reference point relationship**. The term is best reserved for cases where the mental path is discrete, each element accessed is individually salient, and the reason for scanning along this path is primarily to find or identify the element ultimately arrived at. We can best appreciate this from a perceptual example. We often direct attention to a perceptually salient entity as a point of reference to help find some other entity, which would otherwise be hard to locate. In (25)(a), for instance, the speaker wants to direct the hearer's attention to the duck, but from a distance the boat is easier to pick out. Once the hearer has located the boat, the duck can be found by searching in its vicinity.

(25) (a) *Do you see that boat out there in the lake? There's a duck swimming right next to it.*

      (b) *Do you remember that surgeon we met at the party? His wife just filed for divorce.*

This perceptual phenomenon has a general conceptual analog, exemplified in (25)(b). The speaker first directs attention to one conceived entity (the surgeon) for the specific purpose of locating another that is mentally accessible in relation to it (the surgeon's wife).

Clearly, then, we have the ability to invoke the conception of one entity in order to establish "mental contact" with another. The entity first invoked is called a **reference point**, and one accessed via a reference point is referred to as a **target**. A particular reference point affords potential access to many different targets. Collectively, this set

---

[23] To some extent, this kind of summation is always going on as we process words in their sequence of occurrence. The examples show it to be a general conceptual phenomenon independent of word order. In ch. 4 I discuss the grammatical relevance of summary scanning.

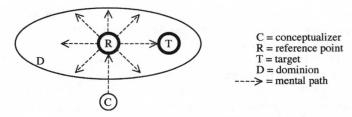

FIGURE 3.14

of potential targets constitute the reference point's **dominion**. Thus a reference point relationship comprises the elements depicted in figure 3.14. In the case of (25)(a), the reference point is the boat, the target is the duck, and the dominion is every-thing—including the duck—in the boat's vicinity. In (25)(b), the reference point is the surgeon, his wife is the target, and the dominion is anything readily associated with (hence mentally accessible via) the surgeon.

It is no accident that the target in (25)(b), *his wife*, contains a possessor pronoun refer-ring back to the reference point. There is good evidence that a reference point relation-ship represents the essential meaning of a basic possessive construction (GC: ch. 6). Here I offer just two brief observations. First, the characterization is independent of any specific conceptual content. Thus it has the abstractness and flexibility needed to accommodate the full range of possessive expressions, e.g. all those in (26)(a).[24]

(26)   (a) *the boy's shoe; Jeff's uncle; the cat's paw; their lice; the baby's diaper; my train;*
            Sally's job; our problem; her enthusiasm; its location; your candidate; the city's
            destruction

       (b) **the shoe's boy; *the paw's cat; *the diaper's baby; * the destruction's city*

Second, the characterization explains why it is usually infelicitous to reverse the choice of possessor and possessed, as seen in (26)(b). This irreversibility reflects the intrinsic asymmetry of a reference point relationship, where conceiving of one entity makes it possible to mentally access another. As a schematic and fully general description, it is thus proposed that a possessor functions as a reference point, and the possessed as its target.

A reference point relationship is often conflated with specific conceptual content, such as spatial proximity in (25)(a). Still, its essential semantic import resides in the very act of mental scanning: evoking first the reference point and then a target it renders accessible. It is thus inherently and quintessentially dynamic, for how it unfolds through processing time actually constitutes its value. As shown by the arrows in figure 3.14, a reference point relation involves two phases of focused awareness, their temporal sequence defining its directionality and intrinsic asymmetry. The first phase consists of

---

[24] As a general description, the notion 'ownership' is too narrow, applying only to the first example cited. While 'ownership' (along with 'kinship' and 'whole-part') does appear to be prototypical for possessive constructions, a schematic characterization valid for all instances has to be devoid of specific content.

mentally accessing the reference point, which is thereby placed in focus. Its activation creates the conditions for accessing elements of the reference point's dominion, one of which is focused as the target. As focus shifts to the target, the reference point—having served its purpose—fades into the background. Hence the reference point and target are both salient, each at a certain stage of processing.

Once focused, of course, the target provides access to its own dominion and may then be invoked as reference point to reach another target. In this way we often scan along a **chain** of successive reference points. One such case is a chain of possessives, e.g. *Harry's cousin's lawyer's therapist*. Another is the chain of successive locations specified in the nested locative construction, as in (22)(a): *upstairs, in the bedroom, in the closet, on the shelf*. Once a particular location is singled out, it affords ready access to any smaller location within it, one of which is put in focus as the target and the next locative reference point.

3.5 Evidence for Semantic Claims

A conceptual semantics lets us make sense of how language makes sense. In and of itself, however, a conceptualist stance does not make semantic description any easier (quite the contrary). Nor does it offer any assurance that we are describing meanings in a principled and appropriate manner. How can we tell whether a proposed description has any validity?

We cannot just rely on intuition or introspection. A conceptual view of meaning does not imply that semantic structure is directly accessible to introspective awareness: engaging in conceptualization is not the same as knowing how it works, any more than seeing is knowing how vision works. We apprehend meanings (i.e. we understand the expressions we use), but this is quite different from subjecting them to explicit analysis. Indeed, at the level of conscious analysis we are generally quite oblivious to construal—both the fact that we construe the content evoked and also the specific ways in which we do so. In normal, unreflective language use our primary interest lies in what is being said, not the underlying mechanisms. These mechanisms are in any case inaccessible to conscious awareness, just as the mechanisms of vision are themselves invisible to us.

It is only through careful linguistic analysis that we can arrive at a principled and revealing characterization of semantic structure. The semantic descriptions proposed in CG utilize a particular set of theoretical constructs—notions like domain, profile, trajector, vantage point, scanning, mental space, immediate scope, and reference point relation. These constructs have all been adopted on the basis of substantial and varied empirical evidence. The general strategy employed is to seek converging evidence from each of three general sources: (i) what we know about cognition (independently of language), (ii) what is needed for viable semantic descriptions, and (iii) whether the constructs support an optimal account of grammar.

With respect to (i), the descriptive constructs proposed in CG are all based on well-known or easily demonstrated cognitive phenomena. Many have direct analogs in vision, although they clearly extend to other aspects of cognition. For example, the focusing of attention is quite apparent in both visual and auditory perception, as well as nonlinguistic thought. There is no question that we apprehend our surroundings from a particular vantage point and have the ability to mentally adopt a vantage point other than our actual one. In the same way that we can visually scan through a scene, we can mentally run through a range of options. The use of reference points is evident in perception and fundamental to conception in general. Hence the descriptive constructs adopted in CG are not in any way exotic or even problematic from the psychological standpoint. In fact, it would be peculiar to suppose that such phenomena lack an important role in linguistic meaning.

As for (ii), the primary means of justifying constructs empirically is by showing that they are needed for adequate semantic descriptions. For instance, profiling is supported by the need to distinguish expressions that differ in meaning despite evoking the same content (e.g. *parent* vs. *child*, *come* vs. *arrive*, *examine* vs. *be examining*). Likewise, trajector/landmark alignment is supported by the need to distinguish semantically nonequivalent expressions that are the same in both content and profiling (e.g. *before* vs. *after*, *precede* vs. *follow*, *have a parent* vs. *have a child*). I would argue that the constructs adopted in CG are quite successful in allowing principled representations of the similarities and differences among expressions with comparable content. Moreover, the same, limited set of constructs prove systematically applicable to an extremely broad array of diverse data.

A final source of evidence is (iii), whether the constructs adopted support an optimal account of grammar. In later chapters, I show that the constructs of CG score very highly on this count. For example, profiling turns out to be crucial for the characterization of basic grammatical classes. Subject and object are defined in terms of trajector/landmark alignment. The constructs also work well in the description of particular grammatical constructions. We have already noted the role of immediate scope in both the progressive construction (fig. 3.4) and whole-part compounding (e.g. *eyelash* vs. *°facelash*, *shoulder blade* vs. **body blade*).

Let us now turn from general constructs to the characterization of particular expressions. How can a proposed semantic description be supported empirically? At least at this level, I suggest that native speaker intuition is not entirely irrelevant. We obviously cannot expect naive speakers to produce semantic descriptions or even to articulate the subtle differences between expressions. Still, speakers do have semantic intuitions that bear on descriptive issues and are probably no less reliable (or no more unreliable) than the grammaticality judgments traditionally employed in formal syntax. With large samples and appropriate statistical techniques, for example, speaker judgments could help determine whether *ring* 'circular piece of jewelry' and *ring* 'arena' represent alternate senses of a polysemous lexical item (as opposed to being unrelated homonyms), or whether *computer* is in fact more analyzable than *propeller*. Speaker reactions to more elaborate semantic descriptions may also be pertinent. If a proposed characterization strikes speakers as being intuitively natural and revealing, we can at least feel encouraged and prefer this to the opposite judgment.[25]

---

[25] Positive reactions of this sort are quite common in cognitive linguistics and, ironically, are one reason it tends to be underappreciated. Semantic descriptions achieved through considerable effort and ingenuity are often so natural and revelatory that they give the impression of having been obvious all along, so nothing seems to have been accomplished.

Evidence can sometimes be sought by looking at other languages (Haiman 1978). Consider the issue of whether the *if* occurring in conditional clauses (*If it rains we'll stay home*) and the *if* occurring in interrogative clauses (*I wonder if it will rain*) are semantically related. Supporting a claim of polysemy is the fact that a single form is used in both ways in numerous other languages (e.g. French). Were this merely a case of accidental homonymy, it should not be prevalent cross-linguistically. Another source of evidence is language change. It is known, for example, that particular kinds of grammatical markers evolve historically from particular kinds of lexical items. Such paths of **grammaticalization** can tell us something about the meanings of the elements involved. One common path is for a lexical verb like *have*, used for possession (*She has a cat*), to develop into an auxiliary verb marking perfect aspect (*She has finished*). This provides a measure of corroboration for the proposal that possessive constructions are based on reference point relations. It is generally accepted that perfect constructions involve a reference point in time. For instance, *He had left by 3 PM* takes 3 PM as a temporal reference point and portrays the leaving as being accomplished prior to it. This path of grammaticalization is most easily analyzed if a possessive verb is itself characterized in terms of a reference point relationship.

More consistently available as empirical evidence are the predictions a semantic description lets us make. Implicit in any such description are expectations that certain kinds of expressions ought to be semantically well-formed and others judged anomalous. Suppose it is claimed that in (27)(a) the inanimate subject is construed metaphorically in terms of the human body. The choice among *sit*, *stand*, and *lie* should thus depend on whether—by analogy to a person assuming these postures—the subject's referent is relatively compact (as in sitting) or whether it is saliently extended along the vertical or horizontal axis.[26]

(27)   (a)   *The clock is {sitting/standing/lying} on the table.*

(b)   *The {vase/?pen/?football/?*watermelon/*mat/*peach} is standing on the table.*

This prediction is in fact borne out, as seen from data like (27)(b). *Stand* is unproblematic with *vase*, as such objects are commonly tall and thin. *Pen* and *football* are questionable, since the vertical orientation suggested by *stand* is hard to achieve in practice. They are acceptable, however, if we imagine that the pen is standing on end (possible with certain pens) or that the football is on a kicking tee. Because it has rounded ends, a watermelon can only *lie* on a table unless we concoct a bizarre context (e.g. it might be impaled on a spike). Neither a mat nor a peach has the right shape for a verb demanding salient vertical extension. Of course, encyclopedic knowledge tells us that mats are sometimes rolled up, and a rolled-up mat could well be stood on end; under this interpretation we can perfectly well describe it as *standing*. On the other hand, a peach is roughly spherical, with no conspicuously long dimension, so regardless of orientation it can only *sit*.

Other predictions pertain to the discourse contexts in which an expression can occur. Recall, for instance, that the characterization of trajector/landmark alignment,

---

[26] Matters are slightly more complex in that *sit* also functions as the general term, i.e. it has a schematic sense that abstracts away from the differences in posture, making it broadly applicable.

and the description of *above* and *below* as contrasting in that regard, predicted the distribution in (11): a sentence like *The lamp is above the table* is felicitous in response to the question *Where is the lamp?*, and *The table is below the lamp* in response to *Where is the table?*, but not conversely. Recall as well the discourse-based characterization of sentences like (20)(b), *In the middle of the kitchen floor lay a dead rat*. The description correctly predicts that such expressions will be infelicitous if the postposed subject represents given information (*In the middle of the kitchen floor lay I*), or if the preposed locative represents new information (?*In a garage sat an old truck).

We can sometimes make predictions to be tested experimentally. I would claim, for example, that the semantic contrast between (28)(a) and (28)(b) resides in the direction of summary scanning. The conceptualizer builds up to a full conception of the scar's configuration by scanning mentally along its extension in one direction or the other, as specified by the *from-* and *to-*phrases. Moreover, the order of words in speech induces us to access the conceptions they symbolize in the corresponding order. In (28)(a)–(b), these two conceptual orderings are in alignment: we first encounter the *from-*phrase, specifying where the mental scanning begins, and then the *to-*phrase, specifying where it ends. This coalignment of paths is optimal from the processing standpoint.

(28)   (a) *An ugly scar extends from his wrist to his elbow.*

(b) *An ugly scar extends from his elbow to his wrist.*

(c) *An ugly scar extends to his wrist from his elbow.*

In (28)(c), however, the two paths run counter to one another. Scanning along the scar starts at the elbow, but word order first directs attention to the wrist, at the endpoint of the scanning path. Hence a conceptual account based on dynamicity implies the need for backtracking: after initially processing the whole expression, the conceptualizer needs to back up and reconceptualize the full scanning path in the proper sequence in order to properly apprehend the overall configuration. This makes an experimental prediction: namely, that (28)(c) should take longer to process and require greater effort than the other expressions.

A frequent criticism of cognitive linguistics, that it makes no predictions, is therefore erroneous. It is, however, true that its predictions tend to be relativistic instead of absolute. For instance, one cannot predict in absolute terms precisely which nouns can occur in the construction in (27)(b). In particular, one cannot make a yes/no prediction about a noun's cooccurrence with *stand* just by examining objectively discernible properties of the nominal referent. What counts is how a situation is construed, which involves general and contextual knowledge as well as our full range of imaginative and interpretive abilities. It is not a matter of deciding categorically whether a certain combination is or is not grammatical, but rather of ascertaining the kind and degree of motivation it has in view of all relevant factors—hence the dictum in cognitive linguistics that, while virtually everything is **motivated**, very little is subject to **absolute** predictability.

A standard view, long predominant in semantic theory, is that a conceptual account of meaning is either impossible or necessarily unscientific. A scientifically respectable semantics is presumed to be objectivist in nature, subject to discrete for-malization, and capable of strict predictability. However, I have tried to indicate that this approach to meaning is not the only game in town. Conceptual semantics is pos-sible, and it is developing into a rigorous scientific enterprise. Ideally, and increas-ingly in practice, cognitive semantic descriptions are based on careful analysis, supported by empirical evidence, and formulated in terms of well-justified descrip-tive constructs. And in no small measure, conceptual semantics derives support from its efficacy as the basis for characterizing grammatical structure. This will be our focus in the chapters that follow.

PART II

FUNDAMENTALS

4

Grammatical Classes

We speak of a **class** (or **category**) when different elements are treated alike for certain purposes. Without categorization, we could not discern patterns or regularities, as these involve the recurrence of configurations judged to be "the same". Categories can be established for any facet of language structure. In the case of phonology, for instance, we posit such classes as consonant and high front vowel. Here we focus on classes relevant to grammar, such as noun, verb, and adjective.

A fundamental question is whether basic grammatical categories are definable in terms of meaning. After arguing that they should be (§4.1), I propose specific meanings for the noun and verb categories (§4.2) and subsequently for others (§4.3). Then, in chapter 5, I examine an important conceptual opposition dividing both nouns and verbs into two major subclasses.

4.1 Are Conceptual Characterizations Conceivable?

In elementary school, I was taught that a noun is the name of a person, place, or thing. In college, I was taught the basic linguistic doctrine that a noun can only be defined in terms of grammatical behavior, conceptual definitions of grammatical classes being impossible. Here, several decades later, I demonstrate the inexorable progress of grammatical theory by claiming that a noun is the name of a thing.[1]

4.1.1 Traditional Views and Fallacies

That grammatical classes **cannot** be defined semantically constitutes a fundamental dogma of modern linguistic theory. Statements like the following, proclaiming the impossibility of conceptual characterizations, are prominently displayed in every introductory text and every book intended for a popular audience:

---

[1] My definition of "thing" is highly abstract. It subsumes people and places as special cases and is not limited to physical entities.

No constant semantic effect is associated with the functioning of a morpheme as a noun, as a verb, or as any other part of speech. (Langacker 1968: 83)

Let's ask whether each part of speech really denotes a consistent kind of meaning. . . . Now it is true that any word that names an object will be a noun. But on the other hand, not every noun names an object. *Earthquake* names, if anything, an action, as does *concert*; *redness* and *size* name properties; *place* and *location* pretty obviously name locations. In fact, for just about any kind of entity we can think of, there exist nouns that name that kind of entity. So the grammatical notion of noun can't be given a definition in terms of what kind of entity it names. . . . A particular kind of entity need not correspond to a single part of speech either. . . . We conclude that parts of speech . . . are not definable in terms of meaning. (Jackendoff 1994: 68–69)

As they stand, the traditional definitions criticized in such passages are definitely unworkable. Not so clearly justified, however, is the attitude of smugness and scientific certainty often detectable in the dismissive comments of linguistic theorists. I suggest, in fact, that no persuasive case has actually been made against the semantic characterization of grammatical classes. The inadequacy of particular definitions (e.g. that a noun names an object) does not imply that notional characterizations are impossible in principle—conceivably there are others that might work. Moreover, the standard type of argument against a conceptual approach is quite simplistic and rests on very questionable assumptions.

The passage just cited from Jackendoff typifies this standard line of argument. It is simplistic because, as possible notional definitions, it considers only a limited class of concepts representing a particular level of generality: notions like 'object', 'action', 'property', and 'location'. While these are quite general, they are certainly not the most schematic conceptions we are capable of handling. Each incorporates substantial conceptual content distinguishing it from the others (e.g. a physical object comprises a continuous expanse of material substance, whereas an action per se is nonmaterial, consisting instead of a change that unfolds through time, typically involving force). These notions represent experientially grounded **conceptual archetypes** (§2.1.2) and as such are appropriate as the **prototypes** for linguistic categories. Objects and actions, for instance, are respectively prototypical for the noun and verb categories. At issue, however, is whether such classes are susceptible to **schematic** definitions satisfied by **all** members (not just central members). Characterizations appropriate for all class members will obviously have to be considerably more abstract than the archetypal notions considered. The standard argument against notional definitions fails to even contemplate the possibility of more abstract formulations.

The standard argument is further simplistic because it presupposes a common yet untenable view of linguistic meaning: an objectivist view that ignores cognition and our capacity for construing the same situation in alternate ways (ch. 3). In the passage cited, an expression's meaning is taken as being established by the objective nature of the entity designated—not by how it is conceptualized. It is assumed, for example, that the objective nature of an earthquake, as a kind of action (or event), implies that the noun *earthquake* necessarily names an action. Cognition is not seen as having any significant role in determining the expression's meaning. Ignored, for instance, is our conceptual capacity for construing events as abstract objects. If this capacity for **conceptual reification** is recognized, one can argue that *earthquake* does name a kind of object—namely, a conceptually reified event. An expression's meaning always incorporates a particular way of construing whatever content is evoked.

A verb like *explode* and a noun like *explosion* can both refer to the same event. According to standard doctrine, this proves that the verb and noun classes are not semantically definable: if they were, *explode* and *explosion* would belong to the same category, since they have the same meaning. This reasoning hinges on the fallacious assumption that referring to the same event makes the two expressions semantically equivalent. They are not. While invoking the same conceptual content, they differ in meaning because of how they construe it: unlike *explode*, which directly reflects the event's processual nature, *explosion* construes it as an abstract thing derived by conceptual reification. It is precisely by virtue of this conceptual contrast that the expressions belong to different grammatical categories.

On grounds of plausibility and interest, we should start with the expectation that such fundamental grammatical notions as noun and verb are definable in terms of meaning.[2] Reasons have been given for rejecting the standard argument—really the only argument—for claiming they are not. Of course, rejecting the argument does not prove that conceptual characterizations are indeed feasible. In the pages that follow, reasonably explicit semantic definitions are proposed for nouns, verbs, and other categories. They should at least demonstrate that such definitions are possible in principle.

4.1.2 The Nature of the Claim

What precisely is intended by the CG claim that basic grammatical classes are semantically definable? Several points need clarification.

First, the claim pertains to the schematic level of description rather than the prototype level.[3] By now it is widely accepted that conceptual characterizations are possible for the central or prototypical members of basic categories. Thus a prototypical noun is one that names a physical object (e.g. *spoon, car, dog, umbrella*). It is likewise prototypical for verbs to designate actions or events (*run, explode, hit*) and for adjectives to specify properties (*blue, tall, intelligent*). Far less obvious is the possibility of schematic definitions applicable to all members of a class. In the case of nouns, for instance, a schematic characterization must subsume not only physical objects but also the vast and heterogeneous array of entities designated by nouns like *air, beauty, team, integer, concert, earthquake, orbit, explosion,* and *philosophy*. Counter to standard doctrine, CG claims that characterizations of this sort can in fact be achieved.

What is the scope of this claim? For which grammatical categories are schematic conceptual definitions held to be possible? A preliminary answer is that the claim is

---

[2] For some psychological evidence bearing on this issue, see Gentner 1981, 1982 and Kellogg 1994, 1996.

[3] An integrated model of categorization, accommodating both schemas and prototypes, is presented in ch. 8 (also in FCG1: ch. 10). For prototype categorization, see Taylor 2004, Lakoff 1987, and Rosch 1978.

limited to classes reasonably considered **universal** and **fundamental** (respectively measured by how many languages and how many constructions they figure in). The most obvious cases are noun and verb. At the opposite extreme, there is no expectation that a class based on a particular grammatical idiosyncrasy in a single language should be semantically definable. It is not expected, for instance, that the verbs in English which form their past tense in -*ought*/-*aught* (*bring, seek, fight, buy, catch, teach*) can be specified on the basis of their meaning. Of course, limiting the claim to classes that are universal and fundamental raises a number of theoretical issues, if only because these criteria are matters of degree.

Even noun and verb are sometimes denied the status of universal categories. Such denials are based on the observation that in some languages virtually every lexical item can be used either way; it is only in the context of a higher-level grammatical construction (nominal or clausal) that a lexeme takes on noun-like or verb-like properties. This observation, however, bears only on the status of noun and verb as universal **lexical** categories—that is, whether particular lexemes are learned and stored specifically as nouns or as verbs. For CG, which views lexicon and grammar as a continuum, this is not a crucial issue. The essential claim is merely that noun and verb have a role in the grammatical description of every language. It is not precluded that a lexeme's meaning might consist of conceptual content alone, with the construal characteristic of particular categories being imposed by the grammatical configurations it appears in. (I would argue, however, that regular occurrence in a certain type of configuration leads to the entrenchment and conventionalization of the construal it induces, and that this itself amounts to the lexeme having a variant belonging to the class in question. Languages may simply differ in the proportion of lexical items for which a particular categorization is strongly established.)

CG is not at all wedded to the traditional "parts of speech" or the classes implied by standard grammatical terminology. Traditional terms lack precise definition, are inconsistent in their application, and are generally inadequate (let alone optimal) for describing grammar. Still, certain standard notions (e.g. preposition, adverb, participle) are useful enough and so frequently invoked that they can hardly be avoided. Their CG characterizations are meant to capture the conceptual basis for whatever descriptive utility they have (at least as first approximations). Nevertheless, CG draws category boundaries in different ways, based on its own fundamental notions. The classes thus defined are not precisely coextensive with traditional ones, even when standard terms are retained.

A pivotal issue concerning grammatical categories is how they relate to grammatical constructions. Based on the supposed impossibility of conceptual definitions, standard doctrine holds that all classes—even noun and verb—must be defined for each language in terms of their grammatical behavior (e.g. nouns occurring with determiners and modifying adjectives, verbs being inflected for tense). Because languages vary greatly in their specific inventories of grammatical constructions, basing definitions solely on the constructions elements occur in has the consequence that no class will be truly universal. It has in fact been proposed that constructions (rather than categories) are the basic units of linguistic structure (Croft 2001). Every construction in a language defines a category, specific to that language, consisting of just those elements that occur in it. From this perspective, there might be no need to posit any general classes analogous to the traditional parts of speech.[4]

A descriptive framework must indeed allow one to specify the range of elements that appear in a given construction. In providing a means of doing so (ch. 8), CG accommodates the classes implicitly defined by occurrence in particular constructions. For such classes it is neither required nor expected that semantic characterizations be possible (the past-tense verbs in -*ought*/-*aught* are a case in point). At the same time, their membership tends not to be wholly arbitrary. Unusual at best is a construction where the occurring elements have nothing more in common than the mere fact of appearing in it. On the contrary, construction-based classes show varying degrees of semantic or phonological cohesiveness. The similarity among class members may be quite tenuous (e.g. most of the -*ought*/-*aught* verbs involve some notion of acquisition). Or there may be a valid generalization that is nonetheless insufficient to distinguish members from nonmembers (e.g. the -*ought*/-*aught* verbs are monosyllabic). At the extreme, class membership—ability to occur in the construction—might be wholly predictable on the basis of meaning and/or form.

The semantic properties that figure in these regularities are not a random collection. Across languages, a certain array of notions are especially prevalent in characterizing grammatical behavior and contributing to the semantic cohesiveness of construction-based classes. Particular conceptions evidently have sufficient cognitive salience that they are often invoked for grammatical purposes, inducing classes to coalesce around them. Their degree of cognitive salience determines to what extent the corresponding classes are universal and fundamental. The most universal and fundamental categories coalesce around a highly salient conceptual archetype, as well as a basic cognitive ability (presumably inborn) that is initially manifested in the archetype and responsible for its emergence. The former functions as category prototype, while the latter provides its schematic characterization. In the case of nouns, for example, the archetype is the conception of a physical object, which emerges due to the basic ability referred to here as conceptual reification (§4.2).

Because cognitive salience is a matter of degree, CG does not posit any fixed, definite inventory of universal categories. In terms of their salience, the notions anchoring the noun and verb categories are analogous to the highest peaks in a mountain range: while they may stand out, they do not stand alone. We can further recognize categories with somewhat lesser but still substantial degrees of universality and grammatical importance, for instance adjectives (Dixon 1977). How many classes we acknowledge depends on how far down these scales we go. Any specific cut-off point would no doubt be arbitrary.

A basic category of this sort does not necessarily coincide exactly with any construction-based class. Suppose, for instance, that a particular construction applies primarily to nouns, so that reference to this category figures in any cogent description. The construction might nonetheless incorporate a semantic specification that is incompatible with the meanings of certain nouns and thus precludes their occurrence.

---

[4] If posited, such categories would constitute abstractions over a range of constructions. This is not incompatible with the CG view, which also sees lexical items as deriving their category membership from participation in grammatical constructions (ch. 8; GC: ch. 4; Langacker 2005b).

Conversely, the construction might be extended beyond the prototype (nouns) to encompass members of another class.[5] Grammatical constructions are generally quite complex, with many factors determining the precise array of elements that appear in them. A basic category can thus be strongly motivated for its utility in describing varied constructions, regardless of whether its own conceptual characterization—taken alone—is sufficient to specify the membership of any construction-based class.

4.1.3 Initial Characterizations

If basic categories are indeed semantically definable, why has this not been evident all along? Why were viable category meanings not proposed long ago and generally accepted? We can largely blame objectivist semantics, the identification of meaning with objective features of the situation described. This long-predominant outlook eliminates just what is needed to solve the problem. It is only by recognizing the crucial role of cognition—how situations are apprehended and conceptualized—that semantic characterizations become feasible. Especially relevant are two aspects of construal: profiling and level of specificity.

I have noted the relevance of specificity, arguing that the concepts usually considered (e.g. 'object', 'event', and 'location') are too specific to serve as schematic characterizations valid for all members of basic classes. If general definitions can indeed be found, it will be at a higher level of schematicity.

Profiling is critically important for the following reason: **what determines an expression's grammatical category is not its overall conceptual content, but the nature of its profile in particular**. It stands to reason that the profile should have a determining role in categorization, for it is what an expression designates; the profile is the focus of attention within the content evoked. The content of *bat*, for example, includes the conception of someone swinging a long, thin piece of wood in order to hit a ball. This domain is central to its meaning, whether it functions as a noun (*He uses a heavy bat*) or as a verb (*It's your turn to bat*). Its categorization as a noun or as a verb depends on whether it profiles the wooden implement or the action of using it.

For defining basic categories, it is useful to have a term that is maximally general in its application. The word **entity** is adopted for this purpose. It thus applies to anything that might be conceived of or referred to in describing conceptual structure: things, relations, quantities, sensations, changes, locations, dimensions, and so on. It is specifically **not** required that an entity be discrete, separately recognized, or cognitively salient. In schematic diagrams, like figure 4.1, entities are shown as rectangles.

Preliminary definitions of some basic classes can now be presented. Each category is characterized in terms of what an expression profiles. Thus a noun is defined schematically as an expression that profiles a **thing**. It must be understood that *thing* is used here as a technical term, whose precise import will be spelled out in §4.2.2. For now we can simply note that its characterization is quite abstract (any product of conceptual reification), so things are not limited to physical objects. In diagrams, a thing is represented by a circle or an ellipse.

---

[5] As a case of the former, the unique reference of proper nouns may preclude their occurrence with determiners. A case of the latter would be the marking of plurality not just on nouns but also on adjectives.

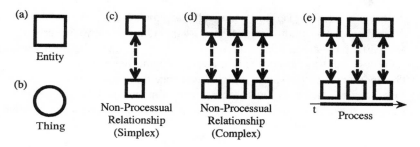

FIGURE 4.1

The members of other basic classes profile **relationships**. The term *relationship* is also used in an abstract, technical sense to be further explicated. In diagrams, relationships are often depicted by lines or arrows connecting the entities participating in them. Consistent with the characterization of entities, it is **not** required that relational participants be salient, discrete, or individually recognized.

Various kinds of relationships can be distinguished and used to characterize basic categories. Most fundamental is the distinction between a **process** and a **non-processual** relation. As the term is defined in CG, a process develops through time, represented in figure 4.1(e) by the arrow labeled t. The bar along the time arrow indicates that its evolution through time is focused rather than backgrounded. A process is further **complex**, in the sense that its manifestation at any one instant—any "time-slice" of the overall relationship—is itself a relationship.[6] A relation that lacks these properties is thereby nonprocessual. It can be nonprocessual by virtue of being **simplex**, residing in a configuration fully manifested at a single instant. While a simplex relationship may persist through time, its temporal evolution is not essential to its characterization or recognition. For example, the spatial relationship profiled by *on* in (1)(a) might endure indefinitely, but it is fully instantiated at any single moment (hence recognizable in a photo).

(1)   (a) *She is sitting **on** the roof.*

      (b) *She climbed up **onto** the roof.*

A relationship which does develop through time can be nonprocessual by virtue of being viewed holistically, so that its temporal evolution is backgrounded. In (1)(b), for instance, *onto* profiles a spatial relation that develops through time, defining the path of motion, yet the preposition itself construes it holistically, as a single gestalt (in the manner of a multiple-exposure photograph). Whether it is simplex or viewed holistically, a nonprocessual relation is **atemporal** in the sense that evolution through time is not in focus.

---

[6] Just three component relationships are depicted in fig. 4.1(e). But since a process unfolds through a continuous span of time, how many time-slices are explicitly shown is arbitrary (a matter of diagrammatic convenience).

We can now define a verb, schematically, as an expression that profiles a process. A number of other traditional categories—including adjective, adverb, preposition, and participle—are all characterized as profiling nonprocessual relationships. Although these can be distinguished on the basis of further properties (§4.3), from the CG standpoint they constitute a global category that subsumes them as special cases. Because it is not traditionally recognized, this category has no ready label. Thus I simply speak of relational expressions that are nonprocessual (or atemporal).

4.1.4 Initial Illustrations

As a preface to detailed discussion, a few examples should help clarify these characterizations and make them tangible. Let us first examine *choose* together with the derived nouns *chooser* and *choice*. Being a verb, *choose* profiles a process, sketched in figure 4.2(a). It designates the relationship between a trajector (tr), the one who chooses, and a landmark (lm), the entity chosen. For our purposes, it suffices to indicate that the trajector engages in mental activity (represented by a dashed arrow) serving to single out the landmark from a range of alternatives (given as a vertical, double-headed arrow). Clearly, the relationship profiled by *choose* unfolds through time, and is thus processual, even though time is omitted from the diagram.[7]

The nouns *chooser* and *choice* derive from *choose* and evoke the process it designates as their conceptual base. They are nouns precisely because their derivation consists in shifting the profile from the process per se to a thing characterized in relation to it. In the case of *chooser*, the profiled thing is the one who does the choosing

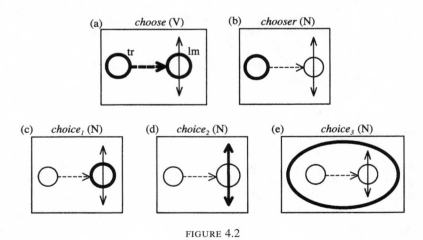

FIGURE 4.2

---

[7] For ease of representation, the time arrow is often omitted when it is not crucial for the point at issue, especially when (as here) the component relationships (time-slices) are all summarized in a single diagram. The profiled process should nevertheless be imagined as unfolding through time, as depicted in fig. 4.1(e).

(i.e. the verb's trajector).[8] *Choice* has three basic meanings. On one interpretation, exemplified in (2)(a), it designates the thing chosen (the processual landmark). Alternatively, as in (2)(b), it profiles the range of options. Finally, in (2)(c), it profiles an abstract thing obtained by conceptual reification of the base process. Shown as an ellipse in figure 4.2(e), this reified event consists of one instance of choosing.

(2)   (a) *Unfortunately their top choice proved incapable of doing the job.*

       (b) *They offer a wide choice of investment options.*

       (c) *She made her choice in just seconds.*

Consider next the boldfaced expressions in (3). As their essential content, they largely share the conceptual base sketched in figure 4.3. The circle stands for a mover, the solid arrow for the path of motion, and the partial box for a container with an opening. Starting from outside the container, the mover ends up inside it. Representing this final locative relationship is a dashed, double-headed arrow. Diagrams (a)–(e) respectively indicate the profiles imposed on this content by the highlighted forms in (3)(a)–(e).

(3)   (a) *The anthropologist is now **in** the tomb.*

       (b) *The **inside** of the tomb was elaborately decorated.*

       (c) *The **entrance** to the tomb is narrow.*

       (d) *He reluctantly **enter**ed the tomb.*

       (e) *His **entry** into the tomb took only a few seconds.*

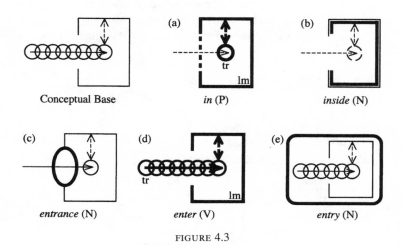

Conceptual Base   *in* (P)   *inside* (N)

entrance (N)   *enter* (V)   *entry* (N)

FIGURE 4.3

[8] Some readers may recall the use of *chooser* in reference to a Macintosh desk accessory, where it designated a place in which choosing occurred.

In (3)(a), *in* profiles a simplex spatial relationship between a trajector and a landmark, both characterized as things. This makes it a preposition, which per se is atemporal. While the trajector presumably moved to reach the specified location, the preposition does not itself designate (or necessarily even evoke) this motion. The word *inside* can also be a preposition, roughly equivalent to *in*, but in (3)(b) it functions as a noun. In this particular use it profiles the container's interior surface. Although a container suggests the idea of something being in it, here this notion is very much in the background. *Entrance*, of course, is a noun. It has an abstract sense (like *entry* in (3)(e)), but in (3)(c) it merely designates the opening in a container through which admission is gained. In (3)(d), the verb *enter* profiles the process of the trajector moving along a spatial path to the landmark's interior. Finally, *entry* in (3)(e) is a noun designating an abstract thing, derived from the verb by conceptual reification. The profile consists of one instance of the verbal process.

As a last example, consider the various senses of *yellow* exemplified in (4), respectively diagrammed in figure 4.4.

(4) (a) **Yellow** *is a nice color.*

    (b) *This* **yellow** *would look good in our kitchen.*

    (c) *The ball is* **yellow.**

    (d) *Gradually the paper* **yellow**ed.

    (e) *There's a lot of* **yellow** *in this painting.*

In (4)(a), *yellow* functions as a kind of proper noun, for its referent is unique. Its profile is an abstract thing, consisting of a certain region (labeled Y) in the basic domain of color space. In (4)(b), *yellow* designates a bounded area within region Y, corresponding to some particular shade of yellow. Since there are many possible shades, in this use *yellow* is a common (rather than a proper) noun. Moreover, since the profiled area is bounded, it is also categorized as a count noun (rather than a mass noun).

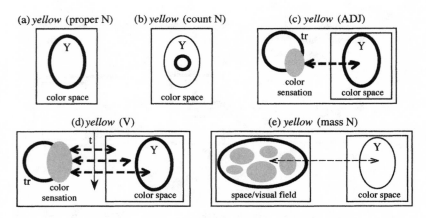

FIGURE 4.4

As an adjective, in (4)(c), *yellow* profiles an atemporal relationship whose single focal participant (its trajector) is a thing. The nature of this relationship (shown as a dashed arrow) is that a color sensation associated with the trajector falls within the yellow region of color space.[9] Suppose, now, that the color sensation changes through time, progressing from a color outside region Y to one inside it, as described in (4)(d). When classed as a verb, *yellow* profiles this entire complex relationship and foregrounds the change through time. In (4)(e), finally, *yellow* functions as a mass noun, taking the mass-noun quantifier *a lot of*. Here it refers collectively to various patches of yellow color manifested within the spatial extension of the painting. The thing profiled by a mass noun is not inherently bounded, has no intrinsic shape, and need not be spatially continuous (cf. *There's a lot of mud on this carpet*).

4.2 Nouns and Verbs

CG advances the controversial (if not outrageous) proposal that essential grammatical notions can be characterized semantically, not just at the prototype level but also at the schema level. Their prototypes consist of experientially grounded conceptual archetypes. Their schematic characterizations (valid for all instances) make reference to basic cognitive abilities initially manifested in those archetypes and later extended to other cases. Though its ultimate scope remains to be determined, the proposal is made at least for certain notions reasonably considered both fundamental and universal: noun, verb, subject, object, and possessive. Here we consider noun and verb.

4.2.1 Prototype Level

For nouns, the archetype functioning as category prototype is the conception of a physical object. For verbs, it is the conception of participants interacting energetically in a "force-dynamic" event (Talmy 1988a). Both figure prominently in a more elaborate conceptual archetype which I refer to as the billiard-ball model:

> We think of our world as being populated by discrete physical objects. These objects are capable of moving about through space and making contact with one another. Motion is driven by energy, which some objects draw from internal resources and others receive from the exterior. When motion results in forceful physical contact, energy is transmitted from the mover to the impacted object, which may thereby be set in motion to participate in further interactions. (FCG2: 13)

This cognitive model represents a fundamental way in which we view the world. The featured role within it of the noun and verb archetypes is thus concomitant with their status as the most fundamental grammatical categories.

---

[9] It is not required that the color sensation coincide with the trajector, only that they be associated. For instance, the yellow portion of a *yellow croquet ball* may be limited to a stripe around its circumference. In this case, the stripe is said to be the croquet ball's **active zone** with respect to the *yellow* relationship.

It is usual in categorization for the greatest differentiation between the members of two classes to be observable in their prototypes. Accordingly, the noun and verb prototypes are polar opposites with regard to the billiard-ball model, contrasting in all their basic properties. The archetype for nouns is as follows:

1. A physical object is composed of material substance.
2. We think of an object as residing primarily in space, where it is bounded and has its own location.
3. In time, on the other hand, an object may persist indefinitely, and it is not thought of as having any particular location in this domain.
4. An object is **conceptually autonomous**, in the sense that we can conceptualize it independently of its participation in any event.

In each respect the archetype for verbs stands diametrically opposed:

1. An energetic interaction is not itself material, consisting instead of change and the transfer of energy.
2. Thus an event resides primarily in time; it is temporally bounded and has its own temporal location.
3. By contrast, an event's location in space is more diffuse and also derivative, as it depends on the locations of its participants.
4. This is so because an event is **conceptually dependent**; it cannot be conceptualized without conceptualizing the participants who interact to constitute it.

These archetypes are so elemental and pervasive in our experience that we generally take them for granted. Still, their conceptual emergence is seen here as presupposing certain basic cognitive abilities. Four in particular seem essential: our capacity for **grouping**, for **reification**, for **apprehending relationships**, and for **tracking relationships** through time. That we have these abilities can hardly be disputed. Once recognized, they allow plausible schematic characterizations of the noun and verb categories.

4.2.2 The Noun Schema

Our capacity for grouping is readily demonstrated at the level of basic perception. Let us first examine figure 4.5(a). In viewing it, we automatically perceive a group of two black dots, on the left, and another group of three, on the right. So strong is this grouping tendency that we cannot just see the five as a bunch of dots with no particular clustering. Nor, without special mental effort, can we see them as being grouped in any other way (e.g. a group of three dots on the left, and one of two on the right). Several factors encourage grouping, the primary ones being **contiguity** and **similarity**.[10] The dots in figure 4.5(a) clearly form groups of two and three on the basis of spatial contiguity. On the other hand, the dots in figure 4.5(b) sort themselves into

[10] Similarity might be regarded as an abstract sort of contiguity (adjacency in **quality space**, discussed in ch. 5).

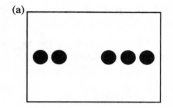 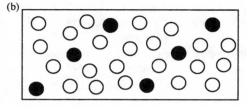

FIGURE 4.5

groups on grounds of similarity: despite their spatial admixture, we can readily perceive a group of six black dots whose color sets them apart from the larger group of white ones. We are likely as well to perceive the black dots as forming two groups of three on the basis of spatial proximity. This further clustering illustrates an essential point: namely, that grouping (like many other cognitive phenomena) occurs at multiple **levels of conceptual organization**. In this case, higher-level groups based on contiguity emerge within the lower-level group based on similarity.

A further basis for grouping is the recognition of familiar configurations. The conception of any such structure resides in mental operations that tie together—or **interconnect**—the entities interpreted as constituting it. These interconnections single out the constitutive entities and establish them as a group. In figure 4.5(b), for instance, the three black dots on the left are perceived as forming a straight line, as are the three on the right. The perception of a line functions as an interconnecting operation that in each case reinforces the grouping based on spatial contiguity. A more elaborate example of a group established in this manner is a constellation. When we look at the nighttime sky and see the Big Dipper, the stars comprising it do not stand out from the rest due to any special similarity (all stars look pretty much alike), nor even by spatial proximity (since other stars are interspersed). What causes their emergence as a group is their interpretation as points defining a familiar schematic image, whose recognition consists in mental operations through which the component stars are interconnected.

Once a group is established, it can function as a single entity at higher levels of conceptualization. For instance, the two lines that emerge by grouping in figure 4.5(b) (each consisting of three black dots) are further perceived as being parallel. They function as **unitary** entities with respect to this higher-level assessment: the judgment of parallelism does not pertain to the dots individually, but to the lines they constitute. This capacity to manipulate a group as a unitary entity for higher-order cognitive purposes is what I refer to as **reification**. Thus each emergent line in figure 4.5(b) is reified by virtue of being treated as a single element in the perception of parallelism, and in any other conception invoking them as such (e.g. in counting them, comparing their length, or observing their slope).

We can now define a **thing** as any product of grouping and reification.[11] Since these are general cognitive phenomena, not limited to space or perception, things can

---

[11] Equivalently, I have also defined a thing as a **region**, characterized abstractly as a set of interconnected entities (FCG1: §5.2). By avoiding this intermediate term (and the spatial metaphor it incorporates), the definition presented here is a bit less cumbersome.

emerge from constitutive entities in any domain or at any level of conceptual organization. Consider a *recipe*, for example. Though it may be written down, a recipe per se does not exist in space. By our abstract definition, however, a recipe is a thing whose constitutive entities are the successive steps involved in preparing some dish. These steps are interconnected and established as a group just by virtue of being conceived as occurring in a certain sequence. They are reified by being conceptualized as a single, unified procedure with the overall goal of creating the dish. Similarly, a *committee* qualifies as a thing even if its constitutive entities—the members—never assemble in one place. Their grouping and reification are effected by the very conception of their consulting and working together with a common purpose. Rather different in nature, but still a thing, is a *moment*. As a continuous span of time, its constitutive entities (points in time) are grouped on the basis of temporal contiguity. The group is reified through its conception as being a single unit of temporal experience, quite brief in overall duration.

A thing produced by grouping and reification can itself function as a constitutive entity with respect to a higher-order thing. Through successive application of these mental operations, things representing any level of conceptual organization can be arrived at. For instance, a *plate* is a thing. So is a *stack* of plates, obtained by placing such objects one on top of the other. If four such stacks are arranged in a certain configuration, they can be perceived as a *square*. A number of these squares can be put together to form a *row* of squares. Imagining several such rows being laid out in parallel gives rise to the conception of *three parallel rows*, which can further be thought of as a single *array*. And so on indefinitely. Despite its complexity, an expression like (5) poses no particular conceptual problems. (It could plausibly occur as a catalog entry describing a work of modern art.)

(5)   *an array of three parallel rows of squares each consisting of four stacks of plates*

More abstractly, a sports *league* might consist of two *conferences*, each with three *divisions*, each having several *teams*, each comprising a number of *players*.

We are ready now to consider the basic CG proposal that **a noun profiles a thing** (in the technical sense just outlined). This schematic characterization would seem to have a real chance of proving viable. Note first that it straightforwardly accommodates the many nouns whose referents clearly consist of multiple, individually recognizable elements. Here is just a small sample: *group, set, pair, collection, stack, team, orchestra, row, archipelago, trio, constellation, list, association, library, silverware, repertoire, herd, flock, colonnade, tribe, family, bunch, alphabet, chord, squadron, forest, six-pack, deck [of cards], choir, staff, [offensive] line, crew, colony, place setting, litter [of kittens], fleet, triptych, convoy, lexicon, audience*. For nouns like these, a description of the sort proposed—where constitutive entities are grouped and reified to form a unitary entity at a higher level of organization—seems not just workable but absolutely necessary.

If the definition works well for cases like these, what about the nouns considered prototypical, which designate physical objects? Here it would seem problematic, since we do not think of a *rock, board, mattress, cat,* or *potato* as a group. Nor is it obvious what their constitutive entities might be.[12] Moreover, it is problematic that the definition is problematic, for if valid it should certainly apply unproblematically to the prototype. The difficulty, though, is only apparent. There is in fact a good rationale for the grouping of constitutive entities being least evident in the prototype.

A thing is a set of interconnected entities which function as a single entity at a higher level of conceptual organization. A key point is that an entity (as defined in §4.1.3) need not be discrete, cognitively salient, or individually recognized. Thus even something continuous and homogeneous, like a *board*, can be described without inconsistency as having constitutive entities. These might be identified as the patches of wood—indefinite in number and arbitrarily delimited—which collectively occupy the full volume of its spatial extension. That a board comprises a continuous expanse of this substance is obviously central to its conception.[13] The very act of apprehending this continuity, of registering the existence of substance at every point, serves to interconnect the constitutive entities and establish them as a group. It is **not** implied that there is discretization at any level of processing, such that a board is perceived as a constellation of separate elements. Indeed, the absence of individuation is precisely what makes physical objects prototypical. They represent the special circumstance where grouping and reification are so automatic that constitutive entities are never consciously accessible. It is only when these operations are extended to other cases, where they are nonautomatic if not atypical, that we can be cognizant of their effect.

With physical objects it is thus the product of grouping and reification, the conception of a unitary entity, that predominates at the conscious level. A typical object is both continuous and has a definite spatial boundary. Yet, since neither property is specified by the abstract definition of a thing, substances lacking these properties also qualify as things. The category schema therefore accommodates mass nouns, which prototypically designate substances. Though a substance may be spatially manifested, its essential characterization is qualitative. Of course, any particular instantiation of a substance, e.g a puddle of *water*, may be continuous and bounded, exhibiting a certain shape. These spatial properties are not crucial for identifying the substance, however, nor are they specifically implied by the mass noun's meaning. We can identify water as such even if it totally surrounds us, with no evident boundary. Likewise, separate puddles of water are construable as a single instance of the substance, as in the expression *all that water on the floor*. Despite their spatial discontinuity, the discrete patches form a group on the basis of their qualitative similarity.[14]

The schematic characterization must of course accommodate the many kinds of nouns that designate abstract entities. Some of these are treated in chapter 5 (see also

---

[12] The constitutive entities cannot be identified as parts. Many objects lack discernible parts, which in any case are best characterized in relation to the whole rather than conversely (§3.2.3).

[13] We can speculate that this aspect of its conception resides in a kind of mental scanning (below the level of conscious awareness) serving to register the continuous existence of the substance throughout the board's extension (FCG1: §3.1).

[14] Directly analogous is the mass-noun sense of *yellow*, as in *There's a lot of yellow in this painting*, diagrammed in fig. 4.4(e). The constitutive entities are an indeterminate number of patches of color, which emerge as a group on the basis of similarity (they all project to the same region in color space).

FCG2: §1.2). Here I simply note that the proposed schema makes no direct reference to physical entities, but only to cognitive abilities, so its applicability to abstract things poses no intrinsic difficulty. To be sure, this discussion in no way constitutes a proof that the noun schema is correct or adequate as it stands. Still, in view of the prevailing doctrine that grammatical categories are not semantically definable, the mere existence of a seemingly plausible candidate is rather significant. At the very least, it may demonstrate that a semantic characterization of nouns is not impossible in principle.

4.2.3 The Verb Schema

The schema for verbs presupposes two fundamental cognitive abilities: the capacity for apprehending relationships and for tracking relationships through time. These are so basic and obvious that discussion might seem superfluous. Nonetheless, they involve certain subtleties that need to be exposed.

In the most elemental terms, apprehending a relationship is a matter of conceptualizing multiple entities as part of the same mental experience. They must somehow be brought together within a single processing "window" (whether through memory, imagination, or direct observation). There must further be some mental operation that involves them both and thereby establishes a connection between them. Consider the perception of two tones. If we hear them an hour apart, they will almost certainly constitute separate and unrelated experiences.[15] But if we hear them just a second apart, we cannot avoid connecting them through some mental assessment—observing, for example, that the second tone is higher in pitch than the first, that they have the same duration, or simply that there are two of them close together. Hence they are not conceived in isolation but in relation to one another.

Entities conceived in relation to one another are **interconnected** by the mental operations that link them. Thus they implicitly form a group, i.e. a set of interconnected entities. These are, of course, the same notions used for the characterization of a thing. The question therefore arises whether the present account can properly distinguish between things and relationships. In fact it can, because additional factors come into play: focusing and reification. When entities are interconnected, we can focus either on the interconnecting operations or on the group they establish. By focusing on the interconnections, we conceptualize a relationship. We conceptualize a thing by focusing instead on the group that emerges and construing it as a single entity for higher-level purposes.

Like things, relationships can be apprehended at multiple levels of organization, with the group emerging at each level having the potential to be focused and reified. Recall figure 4.5(a), which we cannot see as merely a collection of dots. Through assessments of proximity, we automatically connect the two dots on the left, as well as the three on the right, and establish them as groups. At a higher level of organization, we might observe that these groups are unequal in size, or that they have the

---

[15] Naturally, the tones can be experienced together if the first is reactivated via memory. This would usually only happen in the context of a psychological experiment.

same location along the vertical axis. In figure 4.5(b), relationships are evident at several levels: certain dots stand out from the rest by being the same in color; within the group thus established, subgroups emerge through assessments of spatial proximity; in scanning through each subgroup, the path connecting the dots is seen as being straight; finally, the lines perceived in this manner are judged to be parallel.

Relationships like these are **simplex**, in the sense that each consists of a single configuration fully manifested at a single point in time. We can also apprehend relationships that are **complex**, consisting of multiple component relationships, typically manifested successively through a continuous span of time (fig. 4.1). Event conceptions have this character. Imagine a simple (as opposed to simplex) event, such as a ball rolling down an incline, sketched in figure 4.6. The event unfolds through time. At each instant the ball occupies some position in space, but in each case a different one; collectively these positions define its spatial path. The situation obtaining at any one moment constitutes a simplex relationship: a single configuration in which the ball occupies one particular location. The overall event comprises an indefinite number of such relationships and is therefore complex.

Experientially, apprehending an event is similar to watching a motion picture, as opposed to examining a series of still photographs. An event's conception is continuous rather than discrete, even though each time-slice consists of a simplex relationship. These component relationships—referred to as **states**—are neither individuated nor separately examined at the level of conscious awareness. Instead, we conceptualize an event as seamlessly unfolding, with each state developing organically out of its predecessor. The notation of a wedge (>) is used in figure 4.6 to represent this continuity (and counteract the discreteness suggested by static diagrams).

In their seamless continuity, an event's component states (simplex relationships) are quite analogous to the patches of substance constituting a physical object. The nonindividuation of their constitutive entities results in both objects and events being perceived as continuous.[16] This perception of continuity implies some kind of mental operation serving to register the uninterrupted occurrence of constitutive entities throughout their expanse. We can plausibly describe this as **scanning**. It is by means of scanning—through space in the case of objects, and through time for events—that

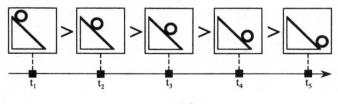

FIGURE 4.6

---

[16] These comments pertain to low-level processing, where the constitutive entities are elemental. It is not denied that many objects have discernible parts or that many events have recognizable phases. Presumably these emerge at higher levels of conceptual organization.

their constitutive patches or states are integrated to create the seamless conception of their spatial or temporal extensionality. The scanning that occurs with events constitutes our capacity for tracking a relationship through time.

Essential here is the distinction made earlier (§3.4.2) between **conceived time** and **processing time**. The arrow in figure 4.6 represents conceived time (t), time as an **object** of conception. We conceive **of** time whenever we conceptualize an event (which by definition is manifested temporally). Of course, since conceptualization is a mental activity, it happens **through** time and has its own temporal duration. Time functioning as the **medium** of conception is referred to as processing time (T). Every conception—even of a static situation—requires some span of processing time for its occurrence. Naturally, both sorts of time play a role in the conception of events. When we track a relationship through time, the tracking occurs in processing time and the event itself in conceived time.

Let us now elaborate the previous diagram so that both conceived time (t) and processing time (T) are represented. Depicted once more in figure 4.7 is the conceptualization of a ball rolling down an incline. The conceptualizing activity itself occurs during span T_1–T_5 of processing time. Each of the larger rectangles corresponds to the conception active at a given moment, wherein the ball occupies a particular location at a certain point in time. Collectively these points define the temporal interval t_1–t_5 during which the event is conceived as occurring.[17]

One way in which we conceptualize events is by directly observing their actual occurrence. In this circumstance, the distinction between conceived time and processing time might seem superfluous, since the temporal intervals coincide. If figure 4.7 represents the actual, real-time observation of a ball rolling down an incline, the time span during which the conceptualization occurs (T_1–T_5) is precisely the same as the time during which the event occurs (t_1–t_5). However, the direct observation of actual events is only one of the many viewing arrangements that provide the conceptual substrate for linguistic expressions (§3.4.1). Suppose, instead, that the conceptualization in figure 4.7 is one of either recalling a past event or imagining a future one.

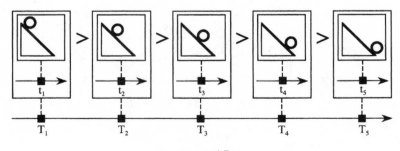

FIGURE 4.7

---

[17] Once more, it is arbitrary how many component states and temporal locations are indicated diagrammatically, since the conceptualization is actually continuous.

In this case the time of conceptualization and the time of the event's occurrence are clearly distinct. Moreover, they are usually not even the same in duration: how long it takes to conceptualize an event (by mentally running through its component states) and how long it takes for it to actually occur are very different matters.

In principle, then, we need to distinguish the time of an event's conception from the time of its occurrence, even in cases where they happen to coincide. The notation in figure 4.7 is meant to be neutral as to whether the intervals T_1-T_5 and t_1-t_5 represent the same span of time or different ones, and also as to their relative duration. Its essential import is rather that the component states are mentally accessed through processing time in the order of their occurrence through conceived time, and further, that just one component state is strongly activated at a given processing moment. Stated more technically, the component states are sequentially accessed through processing time such that, at a given instant T_i, the only state in focus is the one obtaining at the corresponding instant t_i. This amounts to mentally tracking an event as it unfolds through time, that is, scanning sequentially through it along the temporal axis. Accordingly, it is referred to as **sequential scanning**.

While it may seem mysterious, sequential scanning is actually quite pedestrian. In fact, we engage in this mode of scanning whenever we directly observe an event. Suppose we actually watch a ball roll down an incline. In our real-time viewing of this occurrence, we see the ball in just one position at any moment, and we necessarily access these component states in the precise sequence of their temporal manifestation. Sequential scanning is thus inherent in this viewing arrangement (without being restricted to it). If a relationship develops through time, the most natural way of apprehending it is to track it through time in this manner. Hence sequential scanning is equally applicable whether an event is observed, remembered, or imagined.

We are nonetheless capable of viewing events in another manner, sketched in figure 4.8. In this mode of scanning, it is no longer the case that only one component state is focused at a given moment of processing time. While the states are still accessed in their natural sequence, they undergo **summation**: that is, they are mentally superimposed, resulting in their simultaneous activation. Therefore, at each moment T_i of processing time, the focused conception comprises all the configurations thus far encountered in scanning through the conceived time interval t_1-t_i. The end result is that all the component states are simultaneously active and available. They form a single gestalt comparable to a multiple-exposure photograph. Our capacity for **summary scanning** is not in doubt. It occurs, for example, whenever we watch an object move—say a golf ball rolling on a putting green—and then represent its trajectory by means of a line with a corresponding shape. Indeed, television replays sometimes make the summation explicit by successively superimposing the images of the ball in each position, just in the manner of figure 4.8, until the final picture shows the ball in all positions simultaneously.

Sequential and summary scanning should not be thought of as mutually exclusive but as two facets of the normal observation of events. Sequential scanning represents the actual nature of the real-time viewing experience, where just one component state is accessible at any given instant. As we view an event sequentially, the successive states are retained in short-term memory, producing a transient record that can

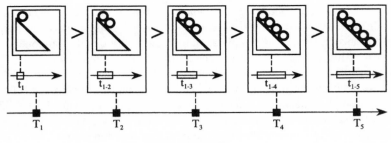

FIGURE 4.8

then be accessed in summary fashion. We thus have the option of conceptualizing an event by focusing selectively on either mode of scanning. Depending on which mode predominates, we can either highlight its inherent sequentiality or impose a holistic construal.

The term **process** is adopted for a complex relationship that develops through conceived time and is scanned sequentially along this axis. This characterization makes reference not only to schematic conceptual content (a complex relation extending through time) but also to a particular way of mentally accessing it (sequential scanning). The same content can therefore be construed as either a process or a nonprocessual relationship, depending on whether it is accessed via sequential scanning (in the manner of fig. 4.7) or summary scanning (as in fig. 4.8). A basic proposal of CG is that **a verb profiles a process**. Sequential scanning is thus implied by categorization as a verb.[18] When the same content is viewed in summary fashion, the resulting expression belongs to another grammatical category (e.g. an infinitive or a participle).

4.3 Classes of Relational Expressions

The noun and verb prototypes—physical object and energetic interaction—are maximally distinct with respect to the billiard-ball archetype (§4.2.1). A glance at figure 4.1 reveals that the noun and verb schemas are also polar opposites. These schemas are based on different cognitive abilities (grouping and reification vs. apprehending and tracking relationships). They contrast in the nature of their profile (thing vs. relationship), degree of elaboration (simplex vs. complex), and mode of scanning (summary vs. sequential). Between the two extremes lie expressions that differ from nouns because they profile relationships, and from verbs because these relations are nonprocessual. We must now consider the characterization and classification of these intermediate cases, which correspond to such traditional categories as preposition, adjective, adverb, infinitive, and participle.

---

[18] In diagrams like fig. 4.1(e), the bar along the time arrow represents sequential scanning. The span of time through which the relationship is tracked sequentially is called its **temporal profile**. (I acknowledge that this term is potentially misleading, for a verb does not profile the span of time per se, but the **relationship** scanned sequentially through it.)

4.3.1 Focal Participants

No single classificatory scheme makes all the necessary distinctions and captures all the significant similarities among linguistic elements. There are different grounds for categorization, yielding cross-cutting classes that are equally and simultaneously valid. The factors used for the characterization of nouns and verbs suggest a number of natural groupings (analogous to "natural classes" in phonology), none of which coincide with traditional categories. One such class consists of expressions that profile relationships. These relational expressions include both verbs, which profile processes, and expressions designating nonprocessual relationships. The latter are themselves a natural category. Also natural would be a category based on summary scanning (subsuming everything but verbs). We will find some evidence for each of these classifications.

For relational expressions, an additional basis for classification resides in the number and the nature of their focal participants (§3.3.2). A profiled relationship construes its participants at different levels of prominence. It is usual for one participant to be made the primary focus, as the entity being located, evaluated, or otherwise described. This is called the **trajector** (tr). Additionally, there is often a secondary focal participant, called the **landmark** (lm).[19] These constructs were initially adopted on purely semantic grounds. They are necessary to distinguish many pairs of expressions that are otherwise semantically identical, like *above* and *below* (fig. 3.9). Trajector/landmark organization is thus inherent in the meanings of relational expressions, even when the focused elements fail to be overtly manifested. The verb *swallow*, for instance, has both a trajector (the swallower) and a landmark (the swallowee) as part of its internal semantic structure. In a sentence like *He swallowed it*, these are specified by the subject and object pronouns. Yet the verb itself evokes these participants schematically and accords them focal prominence, even in the absence of a subject or object nominal (e.g. *Swallow it!*; *the pill he swallowed*).

Thus one basis for categorizing relational expressions is whether they have just a single focal participant (by definition, the trajector) or two. There is nothing contradictory about a relationship having only one participant. The abstract characterization in §4.2.3 merely specifies that a relationship consists of interconnections. Since it is not required that the interconnected entities be salient, explicit, or even individuated, the notion of a one-participant relationship is perfectly coherent. The verb *rise*, for example, designates the process of its trajector moving through space in an upward direction. The profiled relationship consists of the trajector occupying a spatial location at any given moment and how this location changes through time. In contrast to the mover, however, these locations are neither individuated nor singled out for separate focus. Similarly, an adjective like *pretty*, *tall*, or *stupid* situates its

---

[19] Since the characterization of relationships (§4.2.3) does not specify focal prominence of the interconnected entities, there may well be relational expressions best analyzed as having more than two focal elements or none at all. A possible case of the former are verbs like *give*, which occur with two object-like nominals: *She gave us a kitten* (§11.3.3). The latter may be illustrated by certain verbs of Cora (a Mexican language of the Uto-Aztecan family) that occur in subjectless clauses: *nʸeeri'i* 'be all lit up', *suuna* '[water] pour', *tʸee* 'be long', *kun* 'be hollow' (CIS: ch. 2).

trajector vis-à-vis a scale representing the degree to which it exhibits a certain property. There is just one focal participant because the adjective itself specifies both the property and the scalar position. Neither is construed as an independently existing entity requiring separate identification.

A relational expression also has only one focused participant when the profiled interconnections hold between different facets of the trajector itself (not between the trajector and a distinct landmark). Consider the adjective *square*, which describes its trajector as having a certain shape. The conceptualization of this shape resides in a number of mental operations assessing particular subparts with respect to one another: that there are four sides, that each side is straight, that opposite sides are parallel, that adjacent sides are perpendicular, and that all sides are equal in length. Collectively these assessments constitute the profiled relationship, manifested within a single participant. This participant—the adjectival trajector—is the same element that is profiled when *square* is used as a noun. As shown in figure 4.9, the noun and the adjective have the same conceptual content, involving both a thing and a specification of its shape. They differ in what they profile within this base: the noun profiles the thing, while the adjective profiles the configurational assessments (represented diagrammatically for both by dashed arrows).

A relationship is conceptually dependent on its participants; it evokes its participants (if only schematically) as an intrinsic aspect of its own conception. Consequently, the focal participants in a profiled relationship are themselves part of the relational profile, as shown for *square* in figure 4.9(b). Bear in mind that focal prominence is one dimension of construal, a matter of how a situation is conceived and portrayed, not something objectively discernible in it. Hence the same situation can often be described by expressions that confer focal prominence on different elements, even elements at different levels of conceptual organization. The sentences in (6), for example, might all be used to describe the same event:

(6) (a) *The bride hugged the groom.*

   (b) *The groom hugged the bride.*

   (c) *The couple embraced.*

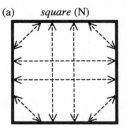
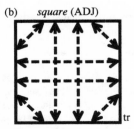

FIGURE 4.9

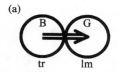 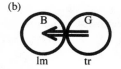 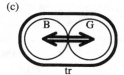

FIGURE 4.10

Even if the bride and groom participate equally, the speaker has the option of focusing either on what the bride does, resulting in (6)(a), or on what the groom does, yielding (6)(b). The contrast is sketched in figure 4.10(a)–(b), where the circles labeled B and G stand for the bride and groom, and a double arrow represents the exertion of force. Choosing either person as trajector (primary focal participant) has the effect of selecting that person's action as the profiled process (in which the other person functions as landmark). Yet the speaker need not risk charges of gender discrimination by making this arbitrary choice. A safer option is (6)(c), diagrammed in figure 4.10(c). Here the profiled process subsumes the actions of both people and portrays them as symmetrical. Accordingly, trajector status is not conferred on either one individually, but rather on the group comprising them. This group—a thing that emerges at a higher level of conceptual organization—is the only focal participant in the profiled relationship.[20]

A relationship's focused participants are thus not restricted to any particular level of conceptual organization. Nor are they limited to things: the trajector or the landmark of a relational expression can itself be a relationship. The boldfaced elements in (7) exemplify the various possibilities. In (7)(a), the trajector of *in* is a process, instantiated by the clausal expression *their baby was born*. In (7)(b), the landmark of *intend* is specified by *to complain*—an infinitival expression designating a complex nonprocessual relationship. It is even possible for both focal participants to be relationships. In (7)(c), the trajector and landmark of *before* are both processes, respectively expressed by the clauses *the guests all left* and *she got there*.

(7)   (a) *Their baby was born **in** July.*

(b) *I **intend** to complain.*

(c) *The guests all left **before** she got there.*

Focal participants prove crucial for characterizing several traditional parts of speech—namely adjective, adverb, and preposition. Each profiles a nonprocessual relationship. What distinguishes them is their trajector/landmark organization, shown abstractly in figure 4.11. Adjectives and adverbs differ from prepositions in having only a single focal participant (a trajector but no focused landmark). They differ from

[20] This is another kind of circumstance where a profiled relationship holds between subparts of the single focused participant.

one another in the nature of their trajector: a thing in the case of adjectives, a relationship for adverbs. On the other hand, a preposition has two focal participants, its landmark being a thing. Since a preposition's trajector can either be a thing or a relationship, it is characterized schematically as an entity (represented by a rectangle).[21]

Traditionally, an adjective is said to modify a noun. Its trajector is thus a schematic thing, which the modified noun specifies in finer detail. In *square tablecloth*, for example, *tablecloth* elaborates the schematic trajector of *square*. The relationship profiled by an adjective holds between its trajector and an entity which fails for some reason to stand out as a separate, focused participant. This might be because the relation holds between subparts of the trajector, as in the case of *square* (fig. 4.9). Alternatively, the nontrajector entity may be abstract and fully specified by the adjective itself. A degree adjective like *tall* locates the trajector on a scale indicating the extent to which it exhibits a particular property. A color adjective, such as *yellow* in figure 4.4(c), connects a thing to a particular region in color space. In such cases, where the adjective itself uniquely identifies the nontrajector entity (a scalar region or a certain quality), the latter is neither independently salient nor individually focused.

An adverb is traditionally defined as modifying a verb (e.g. *work fast*), a preposition (***directly** into the fire*), an adjective (***exceedingly** handsome*), or another adverb (***almost** excessively brilliant*). These are precisely the basic categories characterized as profiling relationships (processual and nonprocessual), so they constitute a natural grouping in CG. The notation in figure 4.11(b) is meant to indicate that a relationship functions as trajector, while being neutral as to what kind of relationship it is. The minimal contrast with adjectives is apparent from pairs like *work fast* and *fast worker*. In both cases, *fast* locates some activity at the positive end of a scale assessing its rate of execution. The only difference is that the adverb confers focal prominence (trajector status) on the activity itself, whereas the adjective confers it on the actor.[22]

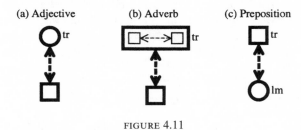

FIGURE 4.11

---

[21] Once more, these traditional categories are neither fundamental nor essential to CG, which can however reveal the conceptual coherence responsible for their evident utility in describing grammar. The characterizations are devised for basic lexical examples, so they will not apply without adjustment to all phenomena for which the traditional labels have been employed.

[22] To be sure, the actor can only be assessed for rapidity relative to some activity it engages in. This activity, which mediates the actor's placement on the scale, is its **active zone** with respect to the profiled relationship.

In contrast to adjectives and adverbs, prepositions are indifferent as to the nature of their trajector. The distinctive property of this class is the conferring of secondary focal prominence on a thing. This landmark is expressed by the prepositional object (e.g. *in August*; *under the bed*; *with a screwdriver*). Normally the same preposition has both "adjectival" uses, where its trajector is a thing (*the last weekend in August*; *the dust under the bed*; *a boy with a screwdriver*), and also "adverbial" uses, where its trajector is a relationship (*They got married in August*; *It's hot under the bed*; *She opened it with a screwdriver*). This overlap is one reason for thinking that the traditional categorization—where adjectives, adverbs, and prepositions are viewed as mutually exclusive classes—is less than optimal.

4.3.2 Complex Relationships

The relationship profiled by a preposition can either be simplex or complex. In the case of spatial expressions, a simplex preposition specifies a single location: *in the garage*; *under a tree*; *near the exit*. In contrast, a complex preposition describes a series of locations amounting to a spatial path: *into the garage*; *along the river*; *through a tunnel*. A specific example is the difference between *in* and *into*, diagrammed in figure 4.12(a)–(b). Because *in* profiles a single spatial configuration, it has just one component state. By contrast, the profile of *into* consists of multiple configurations and thus comprises a continuous series of states (only three of which are shown). The dotted correspondence lines indicate that the trajector is the same throughout, as is the landmark. Observe that the single configuration profiled by *in* is the same as the final state of *into*.

Since the relationship profiled by a verb is also complex, we must pose the question of how a verb differs from a path preposition. It cannot just be a matter of conceptual content, for this can sometimes be the same. In some uses, for example, the verb *enter* would seem to have the same content as the preposition *into*. This is shown in figure 4.12(c), where the component states are identical to those in 4.12(b). In the CG analysis, the crucial difference resides not in content but in construal. There are two respects in which the verb construes the content **temporally** and the preposition **atemporally**. First, the verb specifically invokes conceived time (t) and portrays the complex relationship as developing along this axis. While the temporal dimension is not excluded from the preposition's meaning, neither is it focused—it

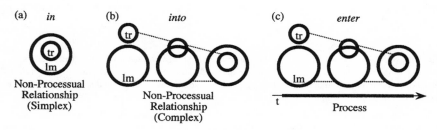

FIGURE 4.12

remains in the background and may even be absent altogether.[23] Second, the verb highlights temporality by scanning through the component states sequentially (indicated by the bar along the time arrow), whereas the preposition achieves a holistic view by scanning them in summary fashion (compare figs. 4-7 and 4-8).

The expressions that profile complex relationships are not restricted to verbs and path prepositions. Also having this character are some of the elements traditionally referred to as participles and infinitives.[24] In English, these include the kinds of expressions exemplified in (8): infinitives with *to* (e.g. *to enter*), present participles (*finding*), past participles that occur in the perfect (*[have] painted*), and those occurring in the passive (*[be] demolished*).

(8)   (a) *The firemen tried* **to enter** *the burning building.*

    (b) *They kept* **finding** *errors in the manuscript.*

    (c) *I have already* **painted** *the fence.*

    (d) *The building was completely* **demolished** *by the explosion.*

For the moment, we can limit our attention to infinitives. What is the meaning of an infinitival phrase like *to enter*? In particular, how does it contrast semantically with the verb *enter*, on the one hand, and the preposition *into*, on the other? Since there is no apparent difference in conceptual content, the component states are the same as in figure 4.12(b)–(c). The contrast must therefore reside in construal, with temporality suggesting itself as the relevant factor. Yet merely describing *to enter* as either temporal or atemporal would be insufficient, for it has to be distinguished from both *enter* (which is temporal) and *into* (atemporal). There is a ready solution, however. Since the verb differs from the preposition in two respects—by specifically and saliently invoking conceived time, and by scanning sequentially along this axis—the infinitive can be seen as intermediate, resembling the verb in one respect and the preposition in the other. Because it derives from the verb, the infinitive certainly views the component states in relation to time. Its atemporality must therefore be due to scanning—evidently, the infinitival *to* imposes summary scanning on the verbal process. Thus the infinitive *to enter* preserves the component states of *enter*, still conceived as extending through time, but scans them in summary fashion. Its diagrammatic representation would be the same as figure 4.12(c), minus the bar for sequential scanning on the time arrow.

Since the varied elements referred to as infinitives and participles all derive from verbs, the process designated by the verb stem figures prominently in their meaning.

---

[23] In expressions like *the road into the forest*, the spatially extended trajector (the road) simultaneously occupies all the specified locations vis-à-vis the landmark. Here there is no development through time, since the entire spatial configuration obtains at any one instant. (The expression does tend to evoke the idea of something moving along the road, but this is tenuous and unprofiled.)

[24] Participles and infinitives are actually quite diverse, and often the same form has uses representing different categories. Hence the present discussion does not apply to everything bearing these traditional labels.

They share the further property of imposing a summary view on the verbal process. Consequently, the derived structure—representing a higher level of conceptual organization—is nonprocessual. Despite their verbal base, infinitives and participles are not themselves verbs. Typically they profile nonprocessual relationships.

It is also quite common for the same forms to function grammatically as nouns. For instance, *to*-infinitives occur in certain environments which (at least arguably) are reserved for nominal expressions:

(9)   (a) **To complain** *would be futile.*

       (b) *What I really want is* **to live forever***.*

As nouns, they profile a thing identifiable as a conceptual reification of the verbal process.[25]

This extension to nominal use is quite straightforward, given the CG description of basic categories. Things and nonprocessual relationships represent a natural grouping since both construe a situation in summary fashion. Consequently, the holistic view imposed by infinitival or participial marking is one of two essential factors involved in deriving a noun from a verb. The other requisite factor is a shift in profile from the relationship to a thing. Suppose, then, that an infinitive or participle should undergo such a shift. If there is no additional marking to signal it, the same form will profile a thing and thus be classed as a noun. This is neither implausible nor unlikely. An implicit shift in profile is nothing other than the ubiquitous linguistic phenomenon known as **metonymy** (§3.3.1).

These steps are shown abstractly in figure 4.13.[26] Diagram (a) represents a process. Its profile is a complex relationship, scanned sequentially. Diagram (b) shows the minimal adjustment brought about by infinitivalization or participialization: the imposition of summary scanning (indicated by the absence of a bar along the time

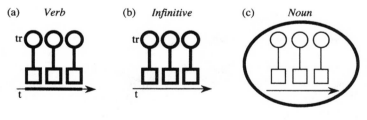

FIGURE 4.13

---

[25] More clearly nominal are participles marked by *-ing* that take possessives: **Your being so stubborn** *really complicates matters*; *The judge's leniency was attributed to* **his having a clean prior record***.* These too profile an abstract thing obtained by reification. Rather than a reification of the process, nouns based on participles often profile a processual participant. English exploits this option quite sparingly (e.g. *the damned*; *his betrothed*).

[26] As is often done in this volume, correspondence lines are omitted to simplify the diagrams. The relational participants are presumed to be the same in all the component states.

arrow). This does not itself imply a change in profile. As exemplified in (8), an infinitive or participle may still profile a complex relationship comprising all the component states of the verbal process. A summary view does however constitute one essential step toward nominalization. The other step is a shift in profile to a thing, which can be either a participant in the original process or else a conceptual reification of that process itself. The latter option is depicted in diagram (c).

In CG, the grammatical markers deriving infinitives and participles are necessarily considered meaningful. One facet of their meaning consists in their suspension of the verb's sequential scanning. The resulting holistic construal of the verbal process is the only property shared by all infinitival and participial expressions. They differ from one another in regard to what additional effect they have on the processual base. Elements considered infinitival usually have the least effect. Indeed, the suspension of sequential scanning may be the only change they bring about. As shown in figure 4.13(b), an infinitive profiles all the component states of the process and has the same trajector/landmark alignment. If it undergoes the further step of nominalization, depicted in 4-13(c), all the component states are included in the abstract thing it profiles. At least as a first approximation, these diagrams might serve as a characterization of the English infinitival *to*.[27]

By contrast, the elements referred to as participles have a more substantial impact on the processual base. Affected are not only the mode of scanning but additional factors like profiling and focal prominence. In one way or another, participles invoke a certain vantage point for viewing the processual content. English shows this fairly clearly. The so-called present participle, formed with *-ing*, takes an "internal perspective" on the verbal process. The so-called past participle, derived by *-ed* (and a variety of irregular inflections), adopts a "posterior" vantage point.

Among their central uses, present participles occur in the progressive, as noun modifiers, and as clausal adverbs:

(10)   (a) *A monkey **is climbing** the tree.*

　　　　(b) *The monkey **climbing the tree** is very cute.*

　　　　(c) ***Climbing the tree**, the monkey lost its grip.*

In these constructions the participle profiles a complex relationship, whose characteristic feature is that it represents an internal portion of some longer process. Stated in CG terms, *-ing* imposes a limited **immediate scope** (IS) in the temporal domain (§3.2.3). Since the immediate scope is the "onstage" region, the locus of viewing attention, those portions of the processual base that fall outside its confines are excluded from the profile. This is seen in figure 4.14, where the beginning and end of the verbal process lie outside the immediate temporal scope, which delimits the relationship profiled by the participle. The ellipses (…) indicate a further effect of *-ing*: to abstract away from any differences among the focused states, thus viewing

---

[27] Certainly more is involved. Most obviously, *to*-infinitives usually have a future orientation relative to the main-clause event (cf. Wierzbicka 1988: ch. 1).

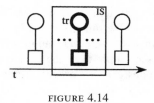

FIGURE 4.14

them as effectively equivalent. Hence the profiled relationship is construed as mass-like and homogeneous.

Past participles occur in the perfect construction (with *have*), the passive (with *be*), and as adjectives formed on both intransitive and transitive verbs:

(11) (a) *The students **had collected** a lot of money for the trip.*

(b) *This building **was designed** by a famous architect.*

(c) *The pond is **frozen**.*

(d) *The **demolished** cathedral took a century to rebuild.*

The perfect indicates that the profiled relationship is prior to a time of reference, given as R in figure 4.15(a). Its apprehension from this posterior vantage point provides a connection to the meanings exhibited by *-ed* (and its morphological variants) in other constructions. They all highlight the **end** of the verbal process, focusing either the final participant or the final state. The passive *-ed* confers primary focal prominence on the final participant. The bold arrows in diagram (b) represent the direction of influence: the participant shown at the top acts on the one at the bottom or somehow initiates their interaction. The more active participant would normally be chosen as trajector. However, the participial morpheme overrides the trajector/

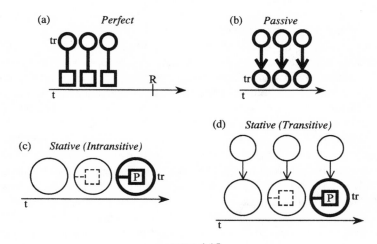

FIGURE 4.15

landmark organization of the verb stem, conferring trajector status on the more passive participant that would otherwise function as landmark.

The participial forms in (11)(c)–(d) are appropriately described as "stative-adjectival", for they restrict the profile to a single state and function grammatically as adjectives. The verb stem designates a process in which a participant undergoes a change of state (e.g. from liquid to solid, in the case of *freeze/frozen*). As a result, this participant—represented by the larger circle in diagrams (c) and (d)—exhibits a property, P, that it did not have previously. The stative-adjectival *-ed* imposes on the processual base a profile restricted to the participant's manifestation of this property. Since there is only one profiled participant, it functions as trajector. This is so even for transitive verbs (like *demolish*), where the verb's trajector acts to induce a change in its landmark (the trajector of the participle). In either case, the participle's profile is limited to the resultant situation of a single participant exhibiting a property, so the profiled relationship conforms to the CG characterization of adjectives (fig. 4.11(a)).

In all the cases examined, the formation of a participle or infinitive has the effect of **atemporalizing** the process designated by the verb it derives from. The processual base loses its temporality in various ways: by nominalization, by the restriction of its profile to a single component state, or just by imposition of summary scanning. However it happens, the resulting expression is not a verb, for it is no longer **temporal** in the sense of profiling a complex relationship scanned sequentially through conceived time.

4.3.3 Structural Motivation

If they are not pushed too far, traditional grammatical classes have considerable descriptive utility over a wide spectrum of diverse languages. It is not without reason that terms like noun, verb, adjective, adverb, preposition, infinitive, and participle are constantly and unavoidably used by linguists of all persuasions. The conceptual characterizations proposed for these categories both explain their descriptive efficacy and make them available for a symbolic account of grammar. To the extent that they are valid and useful, CG is able to exploit them.

They are not adopted uncritically, however. Their CG characterizations reveal the limitations of traditional classifications that view the parts of speech as disjoint lexical categories. For example, if one accepts that a noun profiles a thing, it can be shown that the same description applies to pronouns, demonstratives, and articles. Hence these are most reasonably seen not as disjoint from but as belonging to the class of nouns, being distinguished from "lexical" nouns by their additional, special properties (chs. 9–10). Also problematic is the traditional division among adjectives, adverbs, and prepositions (fig. 4.11). Treating them as separate and on a par fails to capture the fact that prepositions (and prepositional phrases) function either adjectivally or adverbially, depending on whether their trajector is a thing or a relationship. Rather than positing disjoint classes, it seems preferable to recognize a broader category of expressions designating nonprocessual relationships. Overlapping subclasses can then be defined (as needed) based on cross-cutting properties such as complexity, nature of the trajector, and the presence of a landmark.

The CG account of categorization meets the requirements of being flexible, allowing cross-cutting classifications, and accommodating both construction-based and meaning-based classes (ch. 8). Still, classification per se is less important than elucidating the conceptual factors that underlie it. In describing basic classes, we have focused on conceptual phenomena reasonably considered fundamental. These same phenomena allow the characterization of other categories that might well prove grammatically significant, even though they are not traditionally recognized. Three in particular seem worth considering: expressions that profile relationships (rather than things); expressions that profile nonprocessual relationships; and expressions based on summary (as opposed to sequential) scanning. At least some motivation can be found for each of these higher-level groupings.[28]

If nothing else, the first potential category—expressions that profile relationships—permits a succinct characterization of adverbs: an adverb profiles a relationship whose trajector is also relational (fig. 4.11(b)). This is admittedly rather tenuous, and there is no assurance that this grouping will prove to be strongly motivated. It may just be that, taken as a whole, the class of relational expressions is too variegated to exhibit any common behavior distinguishing them from nouns.

The other two groupings are supported by general features of nominal and clausal organization. Let us first consider nominal expressions, often referred to (infelicitously) as "noun phrases". A noun phrase profiles a thing, typically expressed by a noun called the **head**. Elements like articles (*a*, *the*) and demonstratives (*this*, *that*, *these*, *those*) serve to **ground** the profiled thing by relating it to the context of speech (ch. 9). Various sorts of **modifiers** may also be included. In (12), modifiers are given in bold.

(12)　(a)　*an **expensive** dress*

　　　(b)　*the box **on the top shelf***

　　　(c)　*the only student **to hand in her assignment***

　　　(d)　*that man **complaining to the waiter***

　　　(e)　*the brand **preferred by most customers***

　　　(f)　*this **broken** cup*

　　　(g)　**the **break** cup*

　　　(h)　*that man **complain to the waiter***

A pattern is evident: the kinds of elements able to modify nouns are just those described as profiling nonprocessual relationships. Included are expressions headed by adjectives (*expensive*), prepositions (*on*), infinitives (*to hand in*), present participles (*complaining*), and past participles (the passive *preferred* and the stative-adjectival *broken*). However, a noun cannot be modified directly by a verb (*break*) or a complex processual expression headed by a verb (*complain to the waiter*); (12)(g)–(h) are

---

[28] I have no evidence worth mentioning for a grouping based on complexity (simplex vs. complex). This factor may be inherently nonsalient.

clearly "ungrammatical". We can therefore make a generalization concerning the structure of English nominals: namely, that **noun modifiers designate nonprocessual relationships**. Its role in capturing the regularity indicates that this class of expressions constitutes a natural grouping.[29]

The same data suggests the naturalness of a grouping based on summary scanning. This higher-level category consists of nouns together with their possible modifiers—that is, relational expressions other than verbs. If nouns can be modified by numerous kinds of relational expressions, why should verbs be excluded? Apparently nouns and their modifiers have some affinity, something in common that sets them apart from verbs. That something is their summary mode of scanning. A noun phrase profiles a thing, which—as primary focus—tends to impose its holistic perspective on the construal of other nominal elements. The overall nominal conception is thus most coherent (and easiest to process) when the other elements share that perspective to begin with. Because the sequentiality of verbs is inconsistent with a summary view, languages generally do not permit them to directly modify nouns.[30] To serve in this capacity, they must first be rendered atemporal by infinitivalization or participialization.

The relation between a noun and a full noun phrase is parallel in many respects to the relation between a verb and a full, "finite" clause. For the moment, we can characterize a finite clause (in English) as one specified for tense (present vs. past). A basic descriptive generalization of CG is that **a finite clause profiles a process**. In simple examples like (13), the lexical verb is the head, since the process it designates is also profiled by the clause as a whole. The tense marking grounds this process by relating it to the time of speaking.

(13)   (a) *His new hairstyle **resembles** a porcupine.*

(b) *My cup **broke**.*

Being processual, a verb cannot itself modify a noun, as we saw in (12)(g)–(h). Conversely, the kinds of elements that modify nouns cannot stand alone as clausal heads, since they profile nonprocessual relationships. The following sentences are therefore ungrammatical:

(14)   (a) **Her dress **expensive(s)**.*

(b) **The box **on(s) the top shelf**.*

(c) **The students **to hand in their assignments**.*

(d) **That man **complaining to the waiter**.*

---

[29] This is not just a regularity of English but represents a strong universal tendency. Bear in mind, though, that since noun modification is a complex matter involving numerous factors, no single generalization can serve as a full description of noun modifiers in any language.

[30] Why, then, can verbs and clauses be modified by relational expressions based on summary scanning? I imagine this reflects an intrinsic processing asymmetry. It is quite possible for a holistic conception to be evoked at any instant in the course of sequential scanning. In contrast, the sequentiality of a verb or clause cannot be implemented in the simultaneous view effected by summary scanning.

(e) *This brand **preferred by most customers**.

(f) *The cup already **broken** when I found it.

Observe that a well-formed clause can in each case be produced by adding the verb *be*:

(15) (a) Her dress **is expensive**.

(b) The box **is on the top shelf**.

(c) The students **are to hand in their assignments**.

(d) That man **is complaining to the waiter**.

(e) This brand **is preferred by most customers**.

(f) The cup **was** already **broken** when I found it.

Be is a verb, so it profiles a process, albeit a highly schematic one. In (15) it is *be* that functions as clausal head—the schematic process it designates is profiled by the clause as a whole. When *be* is added to an atemporal expression, it lends its processual profile to the latter's more substantial content, which can thus be presented in clausal form. The shared property of occurring in this construction further supports the higher-level category of expressions that profile nonprocessual relationships.

An additional point in favor of these CG characterizations is that they let us make sense of the English "verbal auxiliary" system. In a finite clause, the lexical verb can be accompanied by markings for the passive, the progressive, the perfect, or any combination thereof. Each marking consists of two elements: a schematic verb (either *have* or *be*) and a participial inflection (*-ing* or *-ed*) on the following verb.

(16) (a) The child **was** frightened by a loud noise.   [passive: *be* + *-ed*]

(b) My father **is** contemplating retirement.   [progressive: *be* + *-ing*]

(c) They **have** silenced all their critics.   [perfect: *have* + *-ed*]

Though long noted (e.g. in Chomsky 1957), this dual marking has generally been taken as arbitrary and unprincipled, a case of pure grammatical idiosyncrasy. Indeed, the constitutive elements (*have, be, -ing, -ed*) are often considered individually meaningless. These views are quite erroneous. The CG analysis not only posits specific, motivated meanings for each element but also provides a principled explanation for why they occur in pairs.

The meanings of *-ing* and *-ed* have already been described (Figs. 4.14 and 4.15(a)–(b)). Each views a process from a certain perspective and scans the component states in summary fashion. Their effect is thus to atemporalize a verbal process, deriving a participial expression that designates a complex nonprocessual relationship. Being nonprocessual, this expression can modify a noun, as in *a child frightened by thunder* or *a person contemplating retirement*.[31] For the same reason,

---

[31] Perfect participles are exceptional in this regard (see FCG2: 232).

however, a participle cannot stand alone as the head of a finite clause. A clause pro-files a process. If it is to head a finite clause, consequently, a participial expression must first be rendered processual. The verbs *have* and *be* serve this purpose. Though quite schematic in their content, they incorporate the temporality (sequential scan-ning through conceived time) characteristic of verbs and clauses. When *have* or *be* combines with a participle, the former imposes its temporality on the latter's more specific content. The resulting composite expression profiles a specific process and can therefore function as a clausal head.

Why bother? Since a participle derives from a verb in the first place, why not simply use that verb alone to head a finite clause? We bother because participializa-tion imposes a particular perspective on the verbal process. *X frightened Y* is not the same as *X was frightening Y*, which takes an internal perspective on the event, nor the same as *Y was frightened by X*, which focuses the experiencer instead of the stimu-lus. To adopt these special perspectives, we therefore resort to complex expressions involving multiple levels of conceptual and grammatical organization. The verb first evokes a type of process (e.g. *frighten*). At a higher level of organization, participial inflection imposes a certain perspective on that process and views it atemporally (*frightened*). Through combination with *have* or *be*, the participial expression can then be "retemporalized", yielding another process at the highest level of organiza-tion (*be frightened*). This higher-order process is not the same as the original one, however. While their content is the same, the derived process differs in either profil-ing or trajector/landmark alignment.

Because the perspectives they embody are compatible with one another, the pas-sive, progressive, and perfect constructions can occur in any combination. When they all occur together, they apply in that order at successively higher levels of orga-nization, each operating on the basic or higher-level process already assembled. Moreover, each consists of atemporalization (by the participial morpheme) and then retemporalization (by *have* or *be*). The maximal sequence is shown in (17), where boldface indicates the element added at each level.

(17)   *criticize* (processual) > *criticized* (atemporal) > **be** *criticized* (processual) > **being** *criticized* (atemporal) > **be** *being criticized* (processual) > **been** *being criticized* (atemporal) > **have** *been being criticized* (processual)

The highest-level process can then be grounded (by tense), and its participants speci-fied, to form a full finite clause:

(18)   *The disgruntled employee had been being criticized by his coworkers.*

In sum, the conceptual characterizations proposed for basic grammatical catego-ries prove instrumental in revealing, describing, and explaining important regulari-ties of nominal and clausal structure. In particular, they allow the formulation of two broad generalizations (possibly universal): that noun modifiers designate nonproces-sual relationships, and that a finite clause profiles a process. They further show the principled nature of the dual marking for the passive, progressive, and perfect in

English, and explain why infinitives and participles only combine with *be* or *have* in their clausal use (not when they modify nouns).

A final point concerns a major exception to the generalization that noun modifiers are nonprocessual. Standing in clear violation (as the generalization is currently formulated) are finite relative clauses. A relative clause is one that modifies a noun. In many languages, relative clauses can be finite, from which it follows (granted the second generalization) that they are processual. For example, the relative clauses in (19) are grounded via their inflection for past and present tense:

(19)   (a) *the documents **that I shredded***

      (b) *a woman **who loves adventure***

To accommodate this exception, the generalization can be revised as follows: **ungrounded noun modifiers designate nonprocessual relationships**. Because they are grounded, finite clauses are now excluded from the statement's scope.

Rather than being problematic, the exclusion of finite clauses turns out to have a principled basis. A noun modifier is nonprocessual because the thing profiled by the noun—the primary focus of the nominal expression—imposes its holistic view on the relationships designated by modifying elements. Finite relative clauses are exceptional in this regard precisely because they (in contrast to other modifiers) are internally grounded. Through tense marking, they incorporate their own specification of how the profiled relationship relates to the context of speech, and thus to the speaker and hearer. Since grounding provides an independent point of access to the clausal content, the profiled process is viewed primarily in its own terms, as a grounded clause, and only secondarily in relation to the modified noun. Internal grounding insulates it from the holistic view imposed by the noun, making it sufficiently autonomous to be scanned sequentially.

5

Major Subclasses

The most fundamental grammatical categories, noun and verb, are polar opposites with respect to their conceptual characterizations. At the prototype level, the spatially compact material of a physical object contrasts with the temporally extended interaction constituting a force-dynamic event. At the schema level, where thing and process are defined in terms of mental operations, the unitizing effect of grouping and reification contrasts with the expansive nature of apprehending a relationship and tracking its evolution through time.

Despite this maximal opposition, nouns and verbs have a lot in common. The higher-level grammatical structures they respectively head, nominals and finite clauses, show extensive parallels (discussed in later chapters). Moreover, each category divides into two major subclasses, and these too exhibit extensive parallelism. The basic types of nouns, traditionally known as **count** and **mass**, correspond to the conceptual archetypes **object** and **substance**. The basic types of verbs, referred to here as **perfective** and **imperfective**, correspond to the archetypal notions **event** and **state**. We will see that the count/mass and perfective/imperfective distinctions are essentially the same.[1]

5.1 Count and Mass Nouns

Why are nouns divided into two basic subclasses? Grammarians make the distinction initially on the basis of their contrasting grammatical behaviors. Nonetheless, the traditional labels "count" and "mass" suggest the possibility of distinguishing them on conceptual grounds. In this section, I explore the components of a semantic characterization and the many subtleties of their application. The differing grammatical properties of count and mass nouns prove to be merely symptomatic of a fundamental conceptual opposition.

---

[1] Although the following discussion is primarily based on English, comparable distinctions are likely to be found in most (if not all) languages.

5.1.1 Grammatical Basis

Along one axis, English nouns are divisible into two broad categories, exemplified in (1).[2] Typical for count nouns are the names of physical objects (e.g. *diamond, book, cup*), and for mass nouns, the names of physical substances (*gold, meat, water*). Yet each class includes the terms for other sorts of entities. For instance, count nouns also label creatures (*cat*), parts of larger wholes (*tail*), and geographical regions (*county*), as well as entities that are either nebulous (*cloud*) or abstract (*idea*). Likewise, mass nouns designate entities whose substantial nature is rather tenuous (*air, electricity*) or which are wholly nonphysical (*nonsense, righteousness*).

(1)   (a) **Count nouns:** *diamond, book, cup, pencil, house, tree, apple, cat, tail, pancreas, edge, county, lake, cloud, question, idea, integer, complaint...*

   (b) **Mass nouns:** *gold, meat, water, wood, coal, glue, beer, skin, steel, air, moisture, electricity, nonsense, anger, righteousness, complaining...*

It is not at all obvious, therefore, that either category is susceptible to a semantic description valid for all members (i.e. a schematic characterization). The descriptive labels that readily come to mind, object and substance, are straightforwardly applicable only to **prototypical** members, not to **all** members. The conclusion generally drawn is that the count/mass distinction can only be established and characterized in terms of grammatical behavior. As a practical matter, the classes are indeed posited—and members assigned to them—on the basis of their distinctive grammatical properties.

Some of these properties are shown in (2), taking *diamond* and *gold* as representative instances of the count and mass noun categories. We see first, in (2)(a), that only a mass noun can stand alone as a complete nominal expression, without a determiner. Other contrasting properties pertain to the kinds of determiner each allows. Only a count noun permits the indefinite article. Conversely, a number of determiners—including the quantifiers *most, all*, and *a lot of*—only occur with mass nouns. The same judgments hold for all the examples in (1).

(2)   (a) *They're looking for {*diamond/gold}.*

   (b) *a {diamond/*gold}*

   (c) *most {*diamond/gold}*

   (d) *all {*diamond/gold}*

   (e) *a lot of {*diamond/gold}*

Count nouns are so called because they designate entities that can be counted: *one diamond, two diamonds, three diamonds*, etc. Countability correlates with the

---

[2] Cross-cutting this classification is the distinction between **common** and **proper** nouns (ch. 9). The examples in (1) are all common nouns. Proper nouns can also be categorized as either count (e.g. *Wal-Mart, Connecticut, Tiger Woods*) or mass (*Coca-Cola, Clorox, Tylenol*).

possibility of forming a plural (e.g. *diamonds*), designating multiple instances of the type specified by the singular noun (*diamond*). By contrast, mass nouns do not form plurals (**golds*), nor are their referents countable: **one gold*, **two gold(s)*, **three gold(s)*. As suggested by the term, the referent of a typical mass noun lacks the discreteness required for the recognition and counting of multiple instances.

What, then, is the status of plurals in regard to the count/mass distinction? Only a count noun can be pluralized. Strikingly, however, a plural functions grammatically as a mass noun. Going through the properties in (2), we find in every case that *gold* and *diamonds* behave alike, in opposition to *diamond*:

(3)   (a) *They're looking for {*diamond/gold/diamonds}.*

    (b) *a {diamond/*gold/*diamonds}*

    (c) *most {*diamond/gold/diamonds}*

    (d) *all {*diamond/gold/diamonds}*

    (e) *a lot of {*diamond/gold/diamonds}*

Diamonds is further like *gold*, and unlike *diamond*, in that it cannot itself undergo pluralization: **diamondses*. Grammatical behavior thus argues for the classification in figure 5.1. The mass noun category—in a broad sense of the term—includes both plurals and mass nouns "proper" (such as *gold*).

Plurals do not behave identically to other mass nouns, however. By its very nature, a plural (e.g. *diamonds*) refers to multiple instances of the same type (*diamond*). It thus portrays the mass it designates as consisting of individual "particles" salient enough to be countable. As a consequence, plurals occur with numerals, whereas other mass nouns do not (*eight diamonds* vs. **eight gold*). Also sensitive to the contrast between a "particulate" mass and a "continuous" one are demonstratives and certain quantifiers:

(4)   (a) *those diamonds* vs. *that gold*

    (b) *these diamonds* vs. *this gold*

    (c) *many diamonds* vs. *much gold*

    (d) *few diamonds* vs. *little gold*

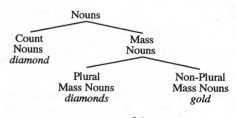

FIGURE 5.1

(e) *several diamonds* vs. **several gold*

(f) *numerous diamonds* vs. **numerous gold*

Hence there is a clear grammatical basis for distinguishing plurals from other mass nouns, as well as for their grouping in a higher-level category.

Ultimately, though, I am arguing that these grammatical properties are symptomatic of underlying conceptual differences. The discussion has already suggested the semantic characterizations roughly sketched in figure 5.2. A count noun profiles a thing construed as being discretely bounded in some fashion, whereas a mass noun referent is amorphous and not inherently limited. As a convenient notational device, I use a circle to represent the former, an ellipse for the latter. Within the mass-noun category, plurals contrast with nonplurals by highlighting the particulate nature of the profiled mass. It is not precluded that a nonplural mass might have discernible particles—we know, for instance, that *sand* consists of particles, and we even have a name for them (*grains*). The point is rather that nouns of this sort foreground the perceived continuity of the mass at the expense of constitutive entities. It does so by naming the mass directly, as an undifferentiated whole, whereas a plural is based on the term for an individual particle.

It cannot be emphasized too strongly that categorization depends on how things are conceptualized, which to some extent is independent of their objective nature. We are perfectly capable of construing the same conceived entity in alternate ways, each of which highlights certain aspects of it and downplays others. Collectively, for example, some oblong pieces of wood can be referred to as either *boards* or *lumber*. Although they are referentially identical, the plural *boards* renders salient the individual constitutive entities, whereas *lumber* suppresses their individuation in favor of their apprehension as an effectively homogeneous mass: *three boards* vs. **three lumber*, *these boards* vs. *this lumber*, etc. These different construals are incorporated as part of the established meanings of these forms, a matter of shared linguistic convention. We have the conceptual flexibility to construe the situation in either fashion and select the form whose meaning best suits our communicative intent.

A further consequence of our conceptual dexterity is the great fluidity of the count/mass distinction. It is anything but a rigid lexical opposition such that a given noun definitively belongs to one or the other category. A slight adjustment in how we construe the content evoked by a form is sufficient to change its categorization and thus its grammatical behavior. We see in (5)(a), for example, that *diamond* functions as a mass noun when we do not care whether the constitutive substance is discretely

Count Noun   Plural Mass Noun 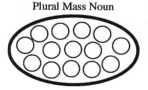   Non-Plural Mass Noun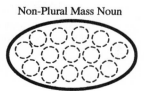

FIGURE 5.2

instantiated, but focus exclusively on its qualitative properties. In (5)(b), on the other hand, *gold* functions as a count noun because it refers to a **kind** of gold (a discrete though abstract entity) rather than the substance per se.

(5)   (a) *Diamond is a very hard substance.*

    (b) *I'm looking for a gold that is just the right color for a ring.*

To varying degrees, particular forms are entrenched and conventionally established as either a count noun or a mass noun—or often both. Learning such conventions is part of mastering a language. Yet there is always the option of a novel construal, hence an altered grammatical potential. Indeed, general patterns for extending count nouns to mass noun use, and also the reverse, ensure that most every noun can in principle be employed in either manner.

It should not be thought that every noun fits comfortably in the classificatory scheme depicted in figure 5.1.[3] For instance, *cattle* is not a plural in form (there is no corresponding singular), yet it behaves like one grammatically: *those cattle, few cattle, several cattle,* etc. Conversely, many nouns are plural in form but diverge from typical plurals in meaning and grammatical behavior (cf. Wierzbicka 1985). A well-known example is *oats*, which appears to be the plural of *oat*, a stem that does occur (e.g. *oatmeal*). But this stem cannot be used as a singular count noun to designate one of the salient constitutive particles (**an oat, *this oat*), nor are the particles countable (**five oats, *numerous oats*). Slightly different are words like *scissors, pliers, tweezers, binoculars,* and *shorts,* which designate a single object with two prominent parts. Grammatically, they exhibit varying mixtures of singular- and plural-noun behaviors (e.g. *a scissors,* but *These scissors are broken*). Thus, while plural morphology may always indicate that the nominal referent is internally complex, the nature of this complexity is not limited to the prototypical case of multiple individuals each describable by the nonplural stem.

5.1.2 Conceptual Basis

The grammatical distinction between count and mass nouns manifests a basic conceptual distinction. I have so far described this opposition, rather vaguely, as a matter of whether the nominal referent is "discretely bounded in some fashion" or else "amorphous and not inherently limited". Obviously, this characterization needs to be refined and clarified.

A more precise definition runs as follows. A noun profiles a thing, defined as any product of grouping and reification (§4.2.2). In the case of a count noun, this thing is construed as being **bounded within the immediate scope in the domain of instantiation**. The profile of a mass noun is **not** construed as being bounded in this fashion. The key notions, then, are bounding, immediate scope, and domain of instantiation. Each term requires explanation.

---

[3] Though we must largely ignore the many idiosyncrasies of these less typical nouns, their description is not inherently problematic in CG, which accommodates both general and idiosyncratic phenomena (ch. 8).

The notion **immediate scope** was introduced in §3.2.3. For a given domain, an expression's immediate scope (IS) is the portion of its maximal scope (MS) that is directly relevant for some purpose. Metaphorically, it is the onstage region, the general **locus** of attention. An expression's profile—being the specific **focus** of attention—is confined to its immediate scope.

The count/mass distinction hinges on whether bounding occurs within the immediate scope, as shown in figure 5.3. Limiting our attention momentarily to physical entities (where the domain of instantiation is space), the shaded region in each diagram represents an expanse of material substance. For a count noun, this region is bounded, and the boundary falls within the immediate scope. The noun *board*, for example, profiles an expanse of wood which is bounded in each spatial dimension to give it a characteristic oblong shape defined by flat surfaces, straight edges, and right angles. Crucially, the existence of the boundary (and the shape it defines) is part of what needs to be apprehended in order to identify the substance as an instance of *board*. The presence of a boundary is put onstage by *board* as something that must be attended to. It is thus included in the noun's immediate scope.

But discerning a boundary is not necessary to identify something as an instance of *wood*. Suppose you remove a section of plaster from a wall and reveal a smooth surface underneath. No boundary is apparent; the material visible through the hole extends beyond it in all directions. By seeing it and feeling it, you can nonetheless determine—from the accessible portion alone—that the material is wood. A mass noun like *wood* names a kind of substance, distinguished from other substances by **qualitative** factors. The distinguishing qualities are apparent in any portion we might sample, irrespective of shape or size. The portion observable within a restricted immediate scope (like the hole in the plaster) can thus be identified as an instance of the type of substance in question.

Consequently, a mass noun has the organization shown in figure 5.3(b). While a mass can certainly be bounded, this is not required for its identification; a mass noun does not itself invoke a boundary as an onstage element to be attended to. Hence there is no bounding within its immediate scope. Moreover, it is only within the immediate scope (the general locus of attention) that focused viewing is possible. An expression's profile—its specific focus of attention—is thus confined to this region. While the substance it names may have indefinite expanse, a mass noun profiles only what is put onstage as the viewing focus. Should you look through the hole in the plaster and say *I see wood!*, you would only be referring to the visible portion.

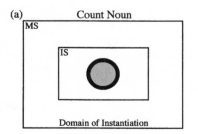 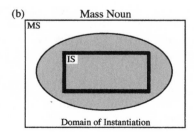

FIGURE 5.3

A noun names a **type** of thing and specifies the properties an entity must have to qualify as an **instance** of this type. Usually this **type specification** invokes a number of cognitive domains, collectively referred to as its matrix (§2.2.2). Within the matrix, a particular domain stands out as the one where instances of the type are primarily thought of as residing. It can thus be called the **domain of instantiation**. Conceptually, what distinguishes an instance from a type is that an instance is specifically thought of as occupying a particular location in this domain. Instances of the same type are distinguished from one another by virtue of occupying different locations.[4] The domain of instantiation is further characterized as the domain in which the presence or absence of bounding determines a noun's categorization as count or mass.

Let us once more consider the count noun *board*. As is usual for physical objects and substances, the domain of instantiation is space. A board has both spatial and temporal existence: it takes up space, and it endures through time. Obviously, though, we primarily think of a board as existing in space, taking for granted its persistence through time. The question *Where is the board?* is thus quite sensible, but **When is the board?* is something we would never think to ask.[5] A type like *board* has many instances, and at a given moment every instance occupies a distinct location (whereas the type itself, representing the abstracted commonality of all these instances, is a "floating" entity that cannot be localized). Even if they should be identical, two boards at different locations constitute different instances of the type—if they occupied precisely the same location, they would be the same board. By contrast, a board that occupies the same location at different times can nonetheless be recognized as the same instance (even if altered). Space being the domain of instantiation, *board* functions as a count noun because its type specification includes the notion of spatial bounding. It fails to specify temporal bounding, but since time is not the domain of instantiation, this does not make *board* a mass noun.

Domain of instantiation does however vary in the case of nouns, and time is one of the options. Among the many nouns invoking time in this capacity are *time* itself, as well as terms for spans of time of different lengths, such as *moment, minute, hour, month, year*, and *century*. In one of its senses, *time* functions as a mass noun (e.g. *We have a lot of time*; *Time passes slowly*). Its abstract referent is conceived as stretching endlessly in either direction—hence as being intrinsically unbounded. *Time* can also be used as a count noun, in which case it designates just a point in time (*What time is it?*) or a span of limited duration (*a short time*). The many terms for particular lengths of time are, of course, count nouns. The time span profiled by *moment* is construed as being quite short but not precisely measured. By contrast, words like *minute, hour, month, year*, and *century* presuppose elaborate conceptual frameworks in terms of which we measure the passage of time and specify temporal locations (fig. 3.12). Each of these terms designates one bounded unit in such a grid. Also invoking time as their domain of instantiation are nouns referring to events, such as *beep, flash,*

---

[4] This does not imply that we can **identify** their locations. In imagining two rocks, we imagine them as being spatially disjoint (hence in two distinct locations), regardless of where they might be.

[5] The question is perhaps conceivable if *the board* is interpreted metonymically as referring to the object's anticipated delivery.

shout, birth, sneeze, bath, explosion, and *earthquake.* These are nouns because, via conceptual reification, the events they profile are construed as abstract things. They are count nouns because the occurrences they designate are bounded in time. For instance, the continuous sound emitted by a malfunctioning car horn is quite annoying but is not *a beep.* A sound can only be identified as *a beep* if it is fairly short in duration, and if its onset and offset are observed.[6]

Despite the preponderance of nouns invoking space or time as their domain of instantiation, any number of other options are available. An example is color space, another basic domain. Recall that a color term, such as *yellow,* has two count-noun uses. As a proper noun (e.g. *Yellow is a soothing color*), it profiles a unique region in color space bounded by being distinguished from other colors (fig. 4.4(a)). As a common noun (e.g. *We need a brighter yellow for the kitchen*), it designates any limited portion of the yellow region, corresponding to a particular shade of yellow (fig. 4.4(b)).[7] Providing illustration of a different sort are terms like *chapter, paragraph, introduction, conclusion, preface,* and *preamble,* which profile restricted parts of a written work. Though writing usually has a spatial manifestation (on paper or a computer screen), this is not the essential aspect of these terms, for if a book is committed to memory and recited orally it can still have chapters and paragraphs. These words pertain primarily to functional units within a linguistic composition, and they are count nouns because they profile limited portions of the overall text. The domain of instantiation is thus the conception of the composition as an abstract textual entity, however it might be manifested.

Determining a noun's domain of instantiation raises a number of subtle issues. They stem from the fact that a noun's meaning draws on multiple cognitive domains, some incorporated as part of others, which are activated to varying degrees on different occasions (§2.2.2). Often, for example, we ignore the role of a *paragraph* as a textual unit, instead conceptualizing it as a spatially manifested entity, visually delimited by the left and right indentations of its initial and final lines. A *book* can likewise be characterized as either a physical or a textual entity (*Her book took five years to write and weighs two pounds*). We can use the term *walk* for a bounded spatial path (*It's a five-mile uphill walk*), an event (*I took a walk*), or a manner of walking distinguished from other walking styles (*His walk is peculiar*). In cases like these, each interpretation presupposes a different domain of instantiation, where instances are thought of as occupying locations that distinguish them from other instances.

Identifying a unique domain of instantiation is problematic when one domain is incorporated as part of another. Consider a body-part term, such as *arm.* One domain crucial to its meaning is a conception of the overall shape of the human body. *Arm* qualifies as a count noun because it profiles a bounded region within this whole. However, since a body exists in space, it is no less true that an arm occupies space and

---

[6] Because time is *beep*'s domain of instantiation, identical sounds heard at different times constitute different instances of this type.

[7] The region profiled by the proper noun functions in turn as immediate scope for the common noun (cf. fig. 3.3). The latter's profile is therefore bounded (limited) within the immediate scope (yellow region) in the domain of instantiation (color space)—which is precisely the definition of a count noun.

has a spatial boundary. Should space then be regarded as the domain of instantiation? If so, an arm is nonetheless characterized and delimited by its position within the overall configuration of the body. A time expression, such as *hour*, poses an analogous problem. Should its domain of instantiation be identified as the basic domain of time or, alternatively, as the conceptual framework imposed on time to effect its segmentation and measurement? The choice would seem to be arbitrary, for a measured temporal segment is bounded in both the basic domain and the conceptual framework incorporating it. Similarly, an *octave* constitutes a bounded segment with respect to both a musical scale and the basic domain of pitch. In such cases, there is no obvious basis for singling out one or the other as an exclusive domain of instantiation.

5.1.3 Bounding

Compared with immediate scope and domain of instantiation, the notion "bounding" may seem self-evident, but it too requires elucidation. For many count nouns, the profiled thing is bounded in the straightforward sense of having a discernible boundary. A *lake*, for example, is a body of water bounded in all directions by land. Moreover, its boundary—the line delimiting water and land—gives it a particular shape. It is not the case, however, that every count noun referent has a boundary or a shape in any usual sense of those terms. A general definition of bounding has to be more abstract.

We generally speak of a shape only in regard to spatially manifested entities. What is the shape of an *hour*, an *introduction*, a *beep*, an *octave*, or *yellow*? The term "boundary" is used more flexibly but is still awkward with nonspatial things. An *hour* has a beginning and an end, but does it have a boundary? Though dawn might be described (metaphorically) as the boundary between night and day, it is less natural to say that a *night* has boundaries. It is not evident that a *team*, whose members may be scattered all over a playing field, has either a boundary or a shape. What about an *alphabet*? While it may have an initial and a final letter, these hardly seem like boundaries. And what is an *alphabet* bounded **from**? The notion of a boundary is problematic even for a physical object like a *board*. By analogy to *lake*, it might plausibly be suggested that a *board* is a continuous mass of wood bounded on all sides by... by what? Not by air, since we can easily imagine a board submerged in water or floating in the vacuum of outer space. We can only say, in general, that it is bounded by the absence of wood. A bit of a reach, perhaps. We think of a *board* as having a surface and a shape, but not a boundary.

Defined more abstractly, a thing is bounded when there is **some limit to the set of constitutive entities**. What this means, in conceptual terms, is something like the following. Recall that a thing is characterized schematically as a set of interconnected entities, grouped and reified to form a unitary entity for higher-level cognitive purposes (§4.2.2). Let us then imagine the process of mentally scanning through the set of constitutive entities—accessing them in some natural sequence—in building up to the full conception of an instance of the type in question. A thing is bounded if, in carrying out this scanning operation, the requisite set of entities is eventually exhausted. The instance conception is then complete, in the sense that further scanning through constitutive entities amounts to conceptualizing another instance of the same type. In short, there is some notion of reaching the limits of a single instance, making it possible to begin the conception of another, distinct instance.

There are various ways of recognizing that the limits have been reached. The most obvious basis for bounding is **contrast with surroundings**. One aspect of conceptualizing a *board*, for example, resides in mental scanning serving to register the continuous extension of the material substance constituting it. The constitutive entities are patches of wood (indefinite in number and arbitrarily delimited). In scanning through them in any direction, we eventually reach a point at which this substance fails to be manifested. The limit (in any given direction) is defined by this point of contrast, where we detect a transition from wood to nonwood. Analogously, a *beep* is the occurrence of a certain kind of noise bounded by silence on either end. In hearing or imagining a beep, we first encounter a transition from the absence of that noise to its presence, and then from its presence to its absence. If further scanning through time reveals more of the sound, it represents the onset of another beep (not the continuation of the previous instance).

Bounding can also be effected on the basis of **internal configuration**. For example, a *bicycle* consists of a certain set of parts connected in a particular manner to form a structured whole. To recognize an instance of this type, it is sufficient to observe the requisite parts in the appropriate configuration—contrast with surroundings (transition from bicycle to nonbicycle) seems inessential. Moreover, if all the parts are present and properly configured, the instance conception is complete. Introducing further parts (a second seat, a third pedal, etc.) would hardly serve to augment or enhance its conception; more likely they would be taken as initiating the conception of another, distinct instance. The noun *alphabet* provides a more abstract example of bounding by configuration. An alphabet is constituted by a set of letters whose names we learn to recite in a well-rehearsed sequence (A > B > C > ... > X > Y > Z). The letters are limited in number and bounded by the first and last elements in the sequence. In mentally scanning through our alphabet, we fully expect to finish: we start with A secure in the knowledge that once we reach Z we are done.

A third basis for bounding is the **function** served by a count noun referent. Consider a wooden baseball bat. Physical examination reveals no obvious boundary between the portions referred to as the *handle* and the *barrel*. The bat gets thicker as we scan from handle to barrel, but continuously, with no evident point of transition. The demarcation depends primarily on the function served: the *handle* is where we grip the bat, and the *barrel* is the part that hits the ball. Similarly, the *introduction* to an article may be visually continuous with the remainder and typographically indistinguishable. It can nonetheless be identified and delimited by the textual function it serves. What about a *team*? Its constitutive entities (the team members) are grouped on the basis of their cooperative action toward achieving a common goal. There need be nothing at all that sets them apart from nonmembers other than their participation in this endeavor.

The various means of bounding—by contrast with surroundings, internal configuration, and function—are in no way mutually exclusive. An *alphabet* is delimited not only by configuration (a fixed sequence with initial and final letters) but also by function: it comprises the full set of letters used together to represent the sounds of a certain language. Form and function are of course interdependent. The configuration of a *bicycle* is just what is needed for its function as something to ride on; if bikes were used instead for drying clothes, they would have a different form. To some extent, we can also see a bicycle as being bounded by contrast with surroundings. Its spatial expanse is limited in all directions by points of transition between the presence and absence of the substances constituting its various parts.

Conceiving of something as being bounded does not depend on being able to impose a precise line of demarcation in any specific place. Boundaries are often "fuzzy", but entities bounded fuzzily are bounded nonetheless. There is no precise boundary between the *handle* of a bat and its *barrel*, yet each is a bounded region distinguished from the other. We conceptualize an article's *introduction* as being of limited extent even when it merges imperceptibly with the main part of the text. And where, exactly, would you draw a line delimiting a *shoulder* from the rest of your body? While there is no specific place where shoulder gives way to nonshoulder, the region is clearly bounded—along the arm, for example, it does not extend as far as the elbow.

The fuzziness of many boundaries is one indication that they need not be objectively discernible. In the last analysis, bounding that "counts" for linguistic purposes is always conceptually imposed. This is not to say that we go around imposing arbitrary boundaries just for the sake of doing so. The bounding imputed to a count noun referent always has substantial motivation, for otherwise—if there were no natural basis for delimitation—we would have no reason to talk about it. The strongest grounds for delimitation are afforded by physical discontinuities that we can readily perceive, especially when the bounded entity, taken as a whole, has some culturally recognized function or significance (e.g. a *knife*, a *lake*, or a *goat*). These are matters of degree, however, with no single factor being invariant or indispensable.

Even for physical entities, bounding is commonly imposed on functional or sociocultural grounds in the absence of any perceptible discontinuity. Often, for example, territorial boundaries established by political convention (e.g. between two *nations*, *states*, *counties*, *districts*, or *precincts*) have no inherent physical basis and are thus invisible (there being no replication in nature of the lines of demarcation drawn on a map, or the contrasting colors used for different regions). This does not prevent them from being precisely defined and very real in terms of their legal and social consequences. Even more clearly imposed, yet equally real in our mental and social life, is the bounding effected by units of temporal measurement. An *hour*, for instance, can start or end at any point whatever, since time and its passing are intrinsically homogeneous. Despite this arbitrariness, an hour can be precisely measured, is rendered observable through "material anchors" (such as timers and clocks), and serves numerous functions in the organization of our daily lives.

Further indication that bounding is conceptually imposed, even when strongly motivated objectively, are the many cases where some portion of a boundary is **virtual** in nature. One such case is a container like a *tub*, *bin*, *pitcher*, *cup*, or *fish tank*, which is thought of as effecting a spatial enclosure despite being open on top. We do conceptualize the container as having an upper boundary, albeit one that is nonmaterial, hence represented by the dashed line in figure 5.4(a).[8] Not dissimilar is the

---

[8] This virtual boundary is invoked for computing the container's volume, as well as for delimiting the region where something is said to be *in* it.

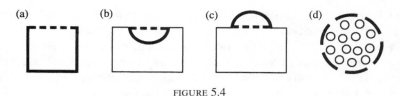

FIGURE 5.4

virtual bounding of a *hole*, *dent*, *depression*, *pit*, or *cavity*, sketched in figure 5.4(b). We impose a boundary on one side by mentally extrapolating the surface expected to be there were it not for the "concavity". An analogous extrapolation delimits a "convexity", such as a *bump*, *welt*, *hump*, *mound*, or *swelling*, as shown in diagram (c). At the extreme, a boundary can be entirely virtual. One illustration, in diagram (d), is the spatial boundary circumscribing a contiguous collection of distinct entities, e.g. a *swarm*, *herd*, *forest*, *mob*, or *archipelago*.

A collection virtually bounded in this manner is the product of another mental operation: conceptual grouping based on spatial contiguity (§4.2.2). This spatial contiguity may itself be virtual in nature: mentally created rather than actually observed. We can speak of a *herd of cattle*, for instance, even when its constitutive elements (individual bovines) are scattered all over the range. Indeed, we can do so even if they have never been assembled in one place and never will be, provided that there is some basis for their grouping (e.g. their collective function as the livestock of a single ranch). We nevertheless have a strong tendency to visualize them as forming a spatially contiguous, virtually bounded thing, as depicted in figure 5.4(d).[9] Our propensity for virtual grouping and bounding is quite apparent when we deal with abstract entities, such as numbers. Prime numbers, for example, are commonly described as constituting a *set*, written in a form that presents them as being spatially contiguous and bounded by brackets: $\{1, 2, 3, 5, 7, 11, \ldots\}$. Despite its evident utility, this visual representation is fictitious in every respect. The prime numbers have no spatial location and cannot be seen. They are not contiguous in the number sequence. And since there are infinitely many of them, in actuality they are unbounded. The bounding represented by brackets is virtual, imposed by the very fact of viewing them as a *set*. In terms of its linguistic semantics, the count noun *set* profiles a bounded entity metaphorically construed as a container for its members (Lakoff 1987). A *set* is thus bounded at this level of conceptual organization even when it is further stipulated (at another level) that its membership is infinite.[10]

5.1.4 Other Sides of the Coin

In the task of distinguishing count and mass nouns, bounding does not stand alone. It shares this burden with three additional conceptual factors: homogeneity, contractibility,

---

[9] This imagined spatial clustering might even be necessary for their conception as a unitary entity.

[10] This metaphorical bounding of infinite sets is foundational to modern mathematics (Lakoff and Núñez 2000). My description of nouns in terms of mental operations is not incompatible with one based on spatial metaphor.

and replicability. So closely related are these factors that I like to think of them as four sides of the same coin.

A mass is construed as being internally homogeneous. A typical mass noun, such as *water*, designates a substance identified by various **qualities**: a liquid of low viscosity, largely transparent, tasteless, odorless, nonalcoholic, and so on. Ideally, sampling any portion of a mass is sufficient to reveal those properties. Homogeneity thus consists of being qualitatively the same throughout. Contrast this with a typical count noun, such as *pencil*. Here there is no presumption of qualitative uniformity. Instead, it is usual for different parts (lead, shaft, eraser) to consist of different substances (graphite, wood, rubber). With respect to qualitative properties, a typical count noun referent is internally heterogeneous.

What matters linguistically, of course, is conceived rather than actual homogeneity. Objectively, no mass is truly homogeneous. Examined in fine enough detail, any two samples of water will exhibit some qualitative difference (e.g. concentrations of pesticides measured in parts per billion). We nonetheless use the word *water* every day, feeling no obligation to first engage in chemical analysis. By ignoring minor variations in quality, we construe a substance as being effectively homogeneous for purposes of identification and linguistic labeling.

How does this work for nouns such as *sand*, *corn*, *grass*, *gravel*, and *lumber*? The masses they designate consist of discrete, easily discernible particles, which we label with terms like *grain*, *kernel*, *blade*, *piece*, and *board*. Saying that a mass is homogeneous might seem problematic when it is clearly recognized as being noncontinuous, with spaces between the constitutive entities. Recall, however, that conceptualization is multifaceted and highly flexible. Inherent in the meaning of any linguistic element is a particular way of construing conceptual content, so that certain facets are focused while others remain in the background. A particulate mass can therefore be seen as either homogeneous or heterogeneous, depending on which aspects of this complex notion are put in focus. The mass-noun status of forms like *sand*, *corn*, *grass*, *gravel*, and *lumber* indicates that their conventional meanings emphasize aspects of homogeneity.[11]

A particulate mass exhibits several kinds of homogeneity. First, the constitutive particles are often not individually perceived or functionally important. When walking on a beach, we see what appears to be a continuous expanse of substance; we notice individual grains of sand only on closer inspection. With grass we likewise have the visual impression of continuity. If individual blades are apparent at a glance, your lawn is too sparse. A particulate mass is further homogeneous in that any portion is essentially equivalent to any other portion. Examine any patch of sand on a beach, or any patch of grass in a lawn, and what you will find is basically the same: a densely packed array of particles so numerous that you would not want to have to count them. Moreover, for all intents and purposes these particles are identical. We are quite oblivious to their individual differences, knowing them only in relation to the mass they constitute. And only collectively do they exhibit the functional and

---

[11] Homogeneity also prevails in the case of plurals (e.g. *boards*, *pebbles*, *blades of grass*), but to a lesser extent, since there is greater awareness of their particulate nature (fig. 5.2).

qualitative properties characteristic of the mass. It is hard to walk on a single grain of sand or blade of grass, and hard to build a house with a single board. Individually a pebble lacks the grainy feel of gravel, nor can a single kernel of corn give us a very good idea of its taste and texture.

The effective identity of constitutive particles is much less obvious with nouns like *silverware*, *furniture*, and *equipment*. Not only do we use their component elements individually, but also we group them into different categories: for example, *silverware* consists of knives, forks, and spoons. Yet they function grammatically as mass nouns, indeed as nonplural mass nouns, where particles are not accorded any salience. We are, though, quite capable of apprehending an abstract commonality that renders them equivalent from a functional standpoint. Knives, forks, and spoons are alike in being basic implements (comparable in size and material) used in eating. Shared by chairs, tables, beds, sofas, desks, and lamps are the properties of being fairly large, hence movable only with some difficulty, and serving collectively to *furnish* a house and make it livable. And while the term *equipment* applies to a more diverse array of entities, they are generally physical devices collectively used in some endeavor. So even though the component elements belong to different categories, a noun of this sort imposes a construal of homogeneity by focusing on very general similarities, including a common function. The degree of abstraction required is no greater than for a high-level category such as *animal*. While a monkey, an elephant, and a crocodile are very different, they are nonetheless equivalent when viewed at a certain level of abstraction. The term *animal* portrays them at this level, and the plural form *animals* relies on this common schematic characterization to construe them as a homogeneous mass.

If mass nouns regularly construe their referents as homogeneous, is it also true that a count noun referent is always heterogeneous? This might at first seem doubtful. A *lake*, for example, consists of water throughout, with no imputation of any qualitative variation. But a lake is not merely an expanse of water. Another essential feature is that the water be surrounded by land—*lake* is a count noun precisely due to this bounding. The conception of a lake, one sufficient to identify it as such, must therefore include the boundary within its immediate scope. A boundary, however, is a very different kind of entity from the substance it delimits. It is, rather, a discontinuity: the point of transition between the substance and its absence. The boundary of a lake is not water but resides in the water/land interface. Thus, even though the substance may be homogeneous, the presence of a boundary introduces a measure of heterogeneity in the overall conception. A noun like *lake* represents the extreme case where the only aspect of heterogeneity is the boundary itself. There are many nouns of this sort: *lawn*, *puddle*, *meatball*, *brick*, *stain*, *beep*, *hour*, *hole*, *intermission*, etc. Each profiles a bounded entity that is otherwise homogeneous, whether the "substance" it comprises is physical or more abstract (like a sound, time, or the absence of something).

The homogeneity of a mass is thus dependent on the lack of intrinsic bounding. These two factors are in turn responsible for a third property, namely **contractibility**. What I mean by this is simply that any portion of a mass of a given type is itself a valid instance of that type. If we start with the *water* in a lake, any portion selected for individual examination can itself be described as *water*. The sample can be of any size: whether an acre-foot, a gallon, or a single drop, it is still *water*.[12] This does not hold for count nouns. Part of a lake is not itself a *lake*, for it lacks the property of being wholly circumscribed by land. By themselves, a pedal and seat are not a *bicycle*, the sequence MNOP is not an *alphabet*, and the tail of a cat is not a *cat*.

The homogeneity and lack of bounding characteristic of a mass also lead to the converse property, **expansibility**: the mass obtained by combining any two instances of a given type is also a valid instance of that type. By adding some flour to the flour already in a bowl, we obtain a larger mass that also counts as a single instance of *flour*—we can describe it as *that flour* or *the flour in the bowl*, but not as **those two flours*. On the other hand, combining two instances of a count noun type, such as *bowl*, does not result in a single larger instance, but in multiple instances: *those two bowls*. Because a count noun specifies bounding, hence some limit to the constitutive entities, it provides a way of determining when one instance ends and another begins. I refer to this property—the opposite of expansibility—as **replicability**. These opposing properties of mass and count noun referents are indicated, respectively, by *more* vs. *another*: when two instances are combined, the result is *more flour* but *another bowl*.

Since a mass is characterized qualitatively, identification of an instance does not require bounding, any particular shape, or even spatial contiguity. Consider the land of 10,000 lakes (also known as Minnesota). What counts as an instance of *water*, with respect to those lakes, is whatever we wish to single out and construe as such. As shown in (6), the instance profiled by a nominal expression may be from a single lake, from more than one, or from all of them; it may comprise all the water in a lake or just part; or any combination of these factors. The possibilities are clearly endless.

(6) (a) *the water in that lake*

(b) *the water near the surface of that lake*

(c) *the water in those two lakes*

(d) *the water in the lakes in the northern part of Minnesota*

(e) *the water in all the lakes of Minnesota*

(f) *the water near the surface in most of the lakes in the southern part of Minnesota*

5.1.5 Variable Construal

Being conceptual in nature, the count/mass distinction reflects our capacity for conceiving and portraying a situation in alternate ways. The dexterity we exhibit in this regard has the consequence that categorization is rather fluid. In one way or another, probably every noun can be used in either manner.

---

[12] Obviously, the sample must be large enough to preserve the defining qualitative properties. Perhaps a molecule of water still counts as an instance of this type, but an oxygen atom does not. In the case of plurals, a minimum of two elements are needed to instantiate the type.

This is not to say that everything is random or solely a matter of whim. Particular categorizations are thoroughly familiar to speakers and firmly established in linguistic convention. In using *lake* as a count noun, or *water* as a mass noun, I am not doing anything inventive or unanticipated. And while many uses depart from these basic categorizations, they usually follow conventionally established patterns. Though novel, the mass-noun use of *lake* in (7)(a) manifests a general pattern for construing a bounded entity as an unbounded mass. Conversely, the count-noun use of *water* in (7)(b) follows a general pattern for construing a mass as a bounded entity. In this case, the extended meaning and the categorization it engenders are also entrenched and conventional.

(7)   (a) *You need **a lot of lake** for a speedboat race.*

      (b) *I want two lemonades and **a water**.*

For a large number of nouns, both a count-noun variant and a mass-noun variant are well established as conventional linguistic units. Either variant can be more thoroughly entrenched and thus perceived as basic, the other then constituting a semantic extension. For *water*, the mass-noun sense is clearly primary. In contrast, *diamond* is primarily a count noun, with a secondary mass-noun use (e.g. *Diamond is one of the hardest substances known*). There are also many nouns where the two variants are roughly comparable in status: *rock, stone, brick, tile, glass, hair, fur, cloth, rope, string, cake, squash, steak, meatloaf, thought, insight, pain, rest, law, principle*, etc. As a mass noun, each names a physical or abstract "substance", whereas the count-noun variant designates a bounded entity composed of that substance.

The mass-noun use of *lake* in (7)(a) instantiates a general pattern applicable when a referent's shape and boundary are irrelevant:

(8)   (a) *In my dream I attempt the winning shot and hit nothing but **net**.*

      (b) *You'll have to stand—there's not enough **bench** for another big person.*

      (c) *After he dug through the wall with his knife, there was very little **blade** left.*

      (d) *With pre-owned vehicles, you get a lot of **car** for your money.*

The effect of this pattern is to shift attention away from the overall contour of a bounded entity and focus instead on a quantifiable expanse that enables it to serve some function. Conceptually, it is a matter of "zooming in", so that the boundary recedes from focused awareness. A more technical representation is given in figure 5.5. Starting from the count-noun sense, the mass-noun sense is obtained by imposing a limited immediate scope that excludes the contours of the count-noun profile. By definition, an expression's profile is confined to its immediate scope (the onstage region). The mass-noun profile is therefore limited to some internal portion (construed as homogeneous) of the count-noun referent.

Another count-to-mass pattern reflects the everyday activity of grinding, mashing, crushing, or pulverizing one or more discrete objects, thereby converting them into a homogeneous substance. As seen in (9), a count noun that names such an

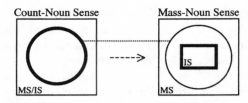

FIGURE 5.5

object comes to be used instead to designate the mass obtained by destroying its shape and structural integrity.

(9)   (a) *By mashing a dozen potatoes, you get enough **potato** for this recipe.*

(b) *After a cat got in the way of our SUV, there was **cat** all over the driveway.*

(c) *Putting powdered **rhinoceros horn** on his cereal failed to enhance his virility.*

The simplest pattern for extending a mass noun to count-noun use likewise reflects an everyday activity, that of eating and drinking. Illustrated by the count-noun use of *water* in (7)(b), it is just a matter of restricting the profiled mass to a bounded quantity, typically the amount that constitutes a single serving. This extended meaning is well established for certain foods (notably desserts) and numerous beverages: *an ice cream, a crème brûlée, a tiramisu, a cherries jubilee, a clam chowder, a beer, a coke, a soda, a lemonade, an iced tea, a whiskey, a Grand Marnier, a gin and tonic,* and so on.

Another common pattern of mass-to-count conversion pertains not to quantity but to quality. If I speak of *a dry wine, a tasty beer, a hard steel,* or *a good glue,* I am not referring to any particular quantity of the substance. My concern is with the qualitative properties that differentiate one kind or brand from another. In technical terms, the shift in meaning involves a change in what is taken to be the domain of instantiation—the domain where instances primarily reside and are distinguished by their locations. For expressions like *a dry wine,* the profiled instance is not distinguished from others by its location in space (the usual domain of instantiation for physical substances) but by qualitative differences. The domain of instantiation is therefore one that we can describe metaphorically as **quality space**. Constituting this multidimensional "space" are all the qualitative properties relevant for the characterization of various substances. A particular substance is characterized by a typical range of values with respect to each of these dimensions.

These values delimit a bounded region in quality space, as shown in figure 5.6. The diagram on the left represents the basic meaning of a mass noun designating a physical substance. Although it is characterized by a bounded region in quality space (serving to distinguish it from other substances), it is in physical space—the domain of instantiation—that instances occur, and in this domain no bounding is imposed. We can thus identify an instance without it having an evident boundary, a particular shape, or even spatial continuity (recall the examples in (6)). Instead it is identified qualitatively, as shown by dashed lines, which indicate that any portion sampled projects to the defining region in quality space.

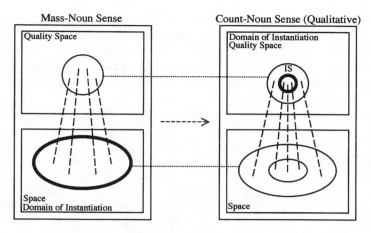

Mass-Noun Sense   Count-Noun Sense (Qualitative)

FIGURE 5.6

Depicted on the right in figure 5.6 is the extended meaning observed in expressions like *a dry wine* and *a tasty beer*. The essential change is that the domain of instantiation is shifted from physical space to quality space. It is therefore in quality space that instances occur and have distinguishing locations. Each instance represents a particular kind selected from the range of possible kinds for the substance in question, so it profiles a subpart of the region defining that substance qualitatively. Because it contains the profile, that region constitutes the immediate scope. Hence the qualitative sense of a mass noun fully satisfies the technical definition of a count noun: the thing it profiles is bounded within the immediate scope in the domain of instantiation.

The same sort of relationship between mass- and count-noun senses obtains in more abstract examples. We observed it previously for nouns naming colors:

(10)   (a) ***Yellow*** *is a cheerful color.*   [proper noun; fig. 4.4(a)]

       (b) *We need a bright **yellow** for the baby's room.*   [common (count) noun; fig. 4.4(b)]

       (c) *There's a lot of **yellow** in this picture.*   [mass noun; fig. 4.4(e)]

For color terms, quality space is simply color space (the range of colors we can perceive). When used as a proper noun, *yellow* profiles a bounded region in this domain, which functions as domain of instantiation. The common noun use, corresponding to the diagram on the right in figure 5.6, takes that region as immediate scope and profiles some portion of it. *A bright yellow* thus designates a shade of yellow, just as *a dry wine* designates a kind of wine. The mass-noun sense corresponds to the lefthand diagram in figure 5.6. Here the domain of instantiation is space (or perhaps the visual field). The profile is a spatially extended mass—possibly discontinuous—consisting of an abstract substance characterized solely by the quality of the visual impression engendered.

Emotion terms like *anxiety*, *hate*, *anger*, *happiness*, and *depression* exhibit a precisely analogous trio of senses, exemplified in (11). In this case, quality space consists of whatever dimensions are taken as characterizing and distinguishing the various kinds of emotive experience. Space and time function jointly as domain of instantiation: a patch of emotive "substance" occurs wherever and whenever somebody experiences the emotion in question. Numerous discontinuous patches of this sort may constitute a single instance of this abstract type of substance.

(11)   (a) *Anxiety is one of the hardest conditions to treat.*   [proper noun]

    (b) *I feel a very intense anxiety.*   [common (count) noun]

    (c) *There's a lot of anxiety around here.*   [mass noun]

Also analogous are the respective nouns in (12), each derived from the verb *walk* by a different pattern of **nominalization**. Here quality space comprises the various parameters serving to distinguish and characterize different types of actions and, more specifically, different types of locomotion. The proper noun, which names a general means of locomotion, profiles a bounded region in this domain, a restricted portion of which is designated by the common noun indicating a particular walking style. For the mass noun, space and time function jointly once again as domain of instantiation. A patch of this *walking* "substance" occurs wherever and whenever somebody engages in this action. Any number of such patches, possibly discontinuous, may constitute a single instance of this type.

(12)   (a) *Walking is very good exercise.*   [proper noun]

    (b) *He has a peculiar walk.*   [common (count) noun]

    (c) *There's a lot of walking going on in this neighborhood.*   [mass noun]

These are but three of the numerous patterns of nominalization that a verb like *walk* can undergo. As a verb, it profiles a process unfolding through time (the domain of instantiation) in which the trajector moves along a spatial path in a normal mode of bipedal locomotion. A noun is derived by shifting the profile to a thing somehow involved in this process. The things profiled in (12) are abstract and rather tenuous (regions of different size in "quality space"; a "substance" comprising patches of activity projecting to the larger region). Generally, though, the profile shifts to something more tangible and salient. As shown in (13), it may be the actor, an instrument of walking, or the path traversed. It can also profile an event consisting of one instance of the process (see figs. 4.2(d) and 4.13(c)), as well as an organized social event involving multiple instances.

(13)   (a) *Tell that walker to keep off the grass.*

    (b) *My walker is broken again.*

    (c) *It's a very difficult walk—7 miles and uphill all the way.*

    (d) *Did you enjoy your walk?*

    (e) *We're organizing a 5 K run and walk to support cancer research.*

5.2 Perfective and Imperfective Verbs

Like nouns, verbs in English divide into two basic subclasses initially distinguished by their grammatical behavior. You will not be shocked to learn that these two subcategories are semantically definable. More surprising, perhaps, is the further claim that the semantic contrast between them is exactly the same as for nouns. The conceptual factors responsible for the count/mass distinction are applicable to processes as well as things.

5.2.1 Flexible Categorization

A verb profiles a process, schematically defined as a relationship scanned sequentially in its evolution through time. The two major subclasses are referred to in CG as **perfective** and **imperfective** verbs.[13] The terms reflect the conceptual characterization of perfectives as being bounded in time, whereas imperfectives are not specifically bounded. Moreover, perfectives construe the profiled relationship as internally heterogeneous, involving some kind of change through time, while imperfectives construe it as homogeneous, the continuation through time of a stable situation. Some typical examples are listed in (14).

(14)　(a) **Perfective verbs:** *fall, jump, kick, bite, throw, break, ask, tell, persuade, learn, decide, cook, melt, evaporate, die, kill, create, calculate...*

　　　(b) **Imperfective verbs:** *be, have, know, doubt, believe, suspect, like, love, detest, appreciate, hope, fear, resemble, contain, reside, exist...*

The conceptual distinction is quite apparent. The verbs in (14)(a) designate occurrences with a beginning and an end. Something happens—some change is observed in the situation described. For instance, to *fall* is to rapidly change location along the vertical axis, and to *learn* something is to change from not knowing it to knowing it. By contrast, the verbs in (14)(b) profile stable situations of indefinite duration. Nothing changes, and nothing happens. This is not to say that the profiled relationship has no beginning or end, only that the verb itself excludes them from what it puts onstage for focused viewing. To say that something *exists* does not imply that it has always existed or that it always will but does portray the situation as constant during whatever is taken to be the relevant span of time (the temporal immediate scope). And while learning something constitutes a change, to *know* it represents a steady situation with no intrinsic endpoint.

Despite its conceptual basis, the perfective/imperfective distinction first calls attention to itself through contrasting grammatical behavior. The usual diagnostics are occurrence in the simple present tense (*-s* for third-person singular) and in the progressive (marked by *be...-ing*). As shown in (15), a perfective (e.g. *learn*) does

---

[13] Other terms are often used, e.g. "active" vs. "stative". With respect to another common classification—into "accomplishment", "achievement", "activity", and "stative" verbs (Vendler 1967)—perfectives subsume the first three, while imperfectives correspond to the fourth.

not occur in the present but does take the progressive. An imperfective (such as *know*) displays the opposite behavior.[14] We will see that these grammatical properties are a consequence of how perfectives and imperfectives are characterized conceptually.

(15) (a) *He learns the poem.*   (a') *He is learning the poem.*

   (b) *He knows the poem.*   (b') *He is knowing the poem.*

Numerous verbs that appear to designate stable situations nonetheless function grammatically as perfectives. Thus, in reference to something going on right now, the verbs in (16) resist the present tense and take the progressive instead:

(16) (a) *She {sleeps/swims/dreams/perspires/meditates/wears a very expensive gown}.*

   (b) *She is {sleeping/swimming/dreaming/perspiring/meditating/wearing a very expensive gown}.*

The processes in question are readily construed as internally homogeneous. This is so even for a verb like *swim*, involving activity, force, and motion: the process is homogeneous in the sense that any stretch of swimming is comparable to any other, with repetitive movement of arms and legs resulting in steady progress through the water. It is also true, however, that we normally conceive of these processes as occurring in bounded episodes. They are therefore comparable to the things profiled by count nouns such as *lake*, *lawn*, *brick*, *beep*, and *hole*, which are likewise homogeneous yet bounded. In both cases the boundary itself provides a measure of heterogeneity. And in both cases, inclusion of the boundary within the expression's immediate scope is sufficient to effect its categorization as either a count noun or a perfective verb.

Like the count/mass distinction, the perfective/imperfective contrast is anything but a rigid lexical specification. While it is usual for a verb to have a primary classification as either perfective or imperfective, many verbs are comfortably used both ways. Categorization is flexible and subject to subtle conceptual influence from a variety of sources.

The verbs in (17) are among those well established in both perfective and imperfective use. In each case the first example profiles a bounded event, and the second a stable situation. Being imperfective, the verbs in the second column are able to occur in the simple present tense. The perfectives in the first column cannot, so the past is used for illustration. To describe the same events occurring at the present time, one would have to use the progressive (e.g. *The SWAT team is surrounding the house*).

(17) (a) *The SWAT team surrounded the house.*   (a') *A hedge surrounds the house.*

   (b) *She covered the hole with a picture.*   (b') *A picture covers the hole.*

---

[14] For this diagnostic purpose, one must only consider the "true" present tense, which indicates an occurrence of the profiled process at the time of speaking. Excluded are various "special" uses involving other conceptual factors, like its use for generics (*A cat chases birds*), habituals (*She works out every day*), and scheduled future events (*We leave next week*).

(c) *He demanded my resignation.*   (c') *That problem demands attention.*

(d) *We connected the wires.*   (d') *A tunnel connects the two buildings.*

(e) *I realized the enormity of the problem.*   (e') *I realize the enormity of the problem.*

Flexible categorization is nicely illustrated by the basic posture verbs *sit, stand,* and *lie.* Each can be used perfectively to profile the act of assuming the posture in question, as in (18)(a), in which case they normally occur with *down* or *up.* Each also occurs alone in another perfective sense, shown in (18)(b), where it designates a bounded episode of being in that posture. Like the verbs in (16), this use requires the progressive to describe a present situation, even though the profiled process is internally homogeneous. The posture verbs can also be used imperfectively, as in (18)(c), which suggests that the park is the statue's permanent home. Suppose, however, that the statue is placed there only temporarily, while its permanent location is being prepared. The standing would then be construed as constituting a bounded episode—hence perfective—so in (18)(d) the progressive is employed. With a human subject, like *Sam* in (18)(e), a posture verb is normally construed perfectively, for the simple reason that people are mobile, so that any particular postural configuration is bounded in duration. By contrast, a country that lies between two others does so indefinitely, so in (18)(f) *lie* behaves imperfectively.[15]

(18)   (a) *Rebecca sat (down), then she stood (up) again.*

(b) *He is {sitting/standing/lying} on the couch.*

(c) *A statue of the president stands in the middle of the park.*

(d) *A statue of the president is standing in the middle of the park.*

(e) *Sam {*lies/is lying} on the beach right now.*

(f) *Belgium {lies/*is lying} between Holland and France.*

These examples illustrate the general point that a verb's **participants** (i.e. the entities participating in the profiled relationship) influence its categorization as perfective or imperfective. In (18)(e)–(f) the choice reflects the nature of the subject. A case of the object exerting influence is provided by basic verbs of perception. Note first that these can be used imperfectively: *I see light*; *I hear music*; *I feel pain.* This itself is interesting, for sensations are usually fairly brief, not your typical "stable situation of indefinite duration". Linguistically, however, stability and duration are not absolute but relative to some concern. What matters is whether a situation is construed as stable for the purpose at hand (with no requirement of absolute invariance) and whether this stability endures through the stretch of time considered relevant.

---

[15] Using the progressive would signal a perfective construal and thus suggest that Belgium could be picked up and moved somewhere else. (Of course, this is perfectly acceptable when working on a jigsaw puzzle where each piece represents a nation of Europe.)

This scope of concern constitutes a verb's immediate temporal scope—the span of time put onstage for focused viewing. Its absolute length is thus quite variable and depends on what kind of event is being talked about (e.g. the formation of the solar system, the rise and fall of an empire, or a trip to the store). Because perception is a moment-to-moment affair, for verbs like *see*, *hear*, and *feel* the time frame for assessing change or stability is very short.

Object nouns such as *light*, *music*, and *pain* imply a perceptual experience capable of enduring for a certain span of time, if only a matter of seconds. It can thus be presented as constant throughout the brief temporal interval relevant for describing immediate sensations. This allows the perception verbs to be used as imperfectives. Sometimes, however, an imperfective construal is precluded: **I see a flash*; **I hear a shot*; **I feel a twinge of pain*. Here the object nominals impose a **punctual** interpretation. Since they themselves are point-like in nature, so is the perceptual experience they engender; it essentially consists of just an onset and an offset, with nothing in between. The sensation is thus too brief to be viewed as stable, even for a limited period. It does however constitute a bounded event, resulting in a perfective interpretation: *I saw a flash*; *I heard a shot*; *I felt a twinge of pain*.[16]

Various other factors can influence a verb's construal as perfective or imperfective. Normally, for instance, the verb *like* describes a stable attitude and is therefore imperfective, as in (19)(a). But as seen in (19)(b), the adverbial *more and more* facilitates a perfective construal by introducing the notion of change.

(19)   (a) *She likes her new teacher.*

        (b) *She's liking her new teacher more and more.*

Another factor is scope. Responsible for the contrast between the imperfective use of *wind* in (20)(a) and the perfective use in (20)(b) is whether the spatial configuration is apprehended in global fashion, as in looking at a map, or locally, from the perspective of someone traveling along the road. On the one hand, with a global view, the entire road-mountain configuration is simultaneously visible within the immediate spatial scope. That configuration is stable through time, so the verb describing it is imperfective and occurs in the simple present tense. On the other hand, with the local view afforded by driving along the road, only a small portion of the overall configuration is visible at any one moment. In (20)(b) that portion is construed as the immediate spatial scope for the subject nominal—what constitutes *this road* is that segment of the entire road which is visually accessible at any one time. While driving through the mountains, therefore, what counts as *this road* is perceived as moving, and indeed, as *winding* through them (much like a snake is perceived as winding through the grass). *Wind* is thus perfective, and takes the progressive, because it profiles a change unfolding through time rather than a stable configuration.

---

[16] Although these expressions are conceptually perfective (by virtue of profiling bounded events), they do not allow the progressive: **I'm seeing a flash*. Their punctual nature makes them semantically incompatible with the progressive, which profiles an ongoing situation internal to a bounded event (and excludes its endpoints).

(20)   (a) *According to the map, this road winds through the mountains.*

   (b) *The way this road is winding through the mountains, we'll never get there on time.*

The choice between a perfective and an imperfective construal is not necessarily determined by anything inherent in the scene described. It often depends on general or contextual knowledge, or it may simply be a matter of how the speaker decides to portray the situation. If you came upon a statue in the park, how would you describe it? The choice between (18)(c) and (18)(d) depends on knowing the intention of whoever put it there. Or suppose your professor, obviously deep in thought, happens to strike the exact same posture as Rodin's famous statue *The Thinker*. To describe this you might very well say (21)(a). The perfective construal reflects our general knowledge that the sitting and meditating done by people occurs in bounded episodes. For the statue itself, however, (21)(b) is more appropriate.

(21)   (a) *Our prof is sitting and meditating.*

   (b) *Rodin's* Thinker *sits and meditates perpetually.*

The contrast in (22) represents a case where a perfective vs. an imperfective construal is purely a matter of speaker choice. Recall that *see* allows both options, depending on the nature of its object: *I see light* vs. **I see a flash.* An imperfective construal is possible with *light* but hardly with *a flash,* since only the former has sufficient duration to allow a stable perceptual experience for even the brief period constituting the immediate temporal scope. Hence *see a flash* is normally perfective, even though its punctual nature precludes the progressive: **I'm seeing a flash.* Part of what we know about flashes, however, is that sometimes they induce an afterimage which, in contrast to the flash itself, may endure for some moments. We can thus say either (22)(a) or (22)(b), where *flash* is understood metonymically. Both options are permitted, since the afterimage has no fixed length in relation to the immediate temporal scope. The perfective construal in (22)(a) specifically portrays this visual experience as a bounded episode. In (22)(b), the speaker decides instead to focus on its constancy during the relevant span of time. Though presumably not ignorant of its temporary nature, the speaker chooses to ignore this.

(22)   (a) *I'm still seeing that blinding flash which occurred a moment ago.*

   (b) *I still see that blinding flash which occurred a moment ago.*

5.2.2 The Count/Mass Analogy

A noun profiles a thing, defined abstractly as any product of grouping and reification. A verb profiles a process, defined abstractly as a relationship scanned sequentially in its evolution through time. Despite their maximal conceptual opposition, nouns and verbs show certain parallels, one being their division into two major subclasses. Remarkably, for each category this major division has the same conceptual basis: the count/mass distinction for nouns is precisely analogous to the perfective/imperfective distinction for verbs. In both cases, the distinction involves the interrelated factors of bounding, homogeneity, contractibility, and replicability.

The count/mass distinction hinges on whether the thing profiled by a noun is construed as being bounded within the immediate scope in the domain of instantiation. For physical objects (the category prototype), the domain of instantiation is space, and bounding is effected by the spatial boundary defining an object's shape. For nouns in general, however, the domain of instantiation varies, and bounding needs to be characterized more abstractly: a thing is bounded when there is some limit to the set of constitutive entities.

For verbs, the domain of instantiation is always time. The perfective/imperfective contrast therefore hinges on whether the profiled process is bounded within the immediate temporal scope, and it is bounded if there is some limit to the set of constitutive entities. But what are these entities? What aspects of a process should we identify as being analogous to the patches of substance constituting a physical object, or the discrete particles of a group (e.g. *stack*) or plural mass? The answer lurks in the characterization of a process as a **complex** relationship, one consisting of **component** relationships distributed through a continuous span of time (fig. 4.6). These time-slices—the **component states** of the process—are naturally taken as being its constitutive elements. For the most part, of course, we do not apprehend them separately but only as facets of a continuous whole, where each morphs seamlessly into the next. In this respect, they resemble the arbitrarily delimited patches of substance constituting a physical object, which are likewise perceived as continuous. Recall that, as defined, an **entity** need not be discrete, salient, or individually recognized.

The essential difference between perfectives and imperfectives is depicted in figure 5.7. In the simplified format adopted, a line represents a relationship evolving through time. Hence each point on the line corresponds to a component state—that is, the relationship obtaining at a single moment.[17] In diagram (a), for perfective verbs, vertical bars indicate that the profiled relationship is bounded in its temporal extension. These are transition points marking the beginning and end of the relationship's manifestation. Crucially, its entire manifestation falls within the immediate temporal scope. The profiled process is therefore bounded within the immediate scope in the domain of instantiation (time). Such bounding is not intrinsic to the characterization of imperfective verbs. In diagram (b), ellipses (...) indicate that the relationship extends indefinitely. The immediate temporal scope segments out some portion of this ongoing situation and puts it onstage for focused viewing. The verb's profile is restricted to just that portion. Though limited by the immediate scope, the profiled relationship is not bounded in the sense of there being a beginning and end to its manifestation—the relationship itself extends beyond the immediate scope in either direction. The limitation is not inherent in the situation described but extrinsic, pertaining to how it is viewed. Thus the profiled relationship is not specifically bounded within the immediate scope in the domain of instantiation.

---

[17] Compare this with the slightly less simplified format of fig. 4.13(a), where representative component states are shown explicitly as relationships. For present purposes there is no need to portray each state's internal structure. Also omitted is the bar along the time arrow, indicating sequential scanning.

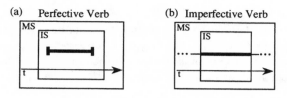

FIGURE 5.7

Comparing figure 5.3, for count vs. mass, and figure 5.7, for perfective vs. imperfective, reveals that the two distinctions are essentially the same. The only differences in the diagrams reflect its application to things in the first instance and to processes in the second. This parallelism observed with respect to bounding continues when we turn the coin over to examine its other sides: homogeneity, contractibility, and replicability.

Like a count-noun referent, a perfective process is construed as being internally heterogeneous. And like a mass-noun referent, an imperfective process is construed as being internally homogeneous. The "geneity" of a verb (hetero- vs. homo-) is a matter of whether the component states of the process are conceived as being effectively identical. Perfectives are therefore heterogeneous because the profiled relationship changes through time. Imperfectives are homogeneous because they profile the continuation through time of a stable situation. You can see the parallelism by comparing the leftmost and rightmost diagrams in figure 5.8, where a wavy line indicates heterogeneity and a straight line homogeneity. The diagrams in the

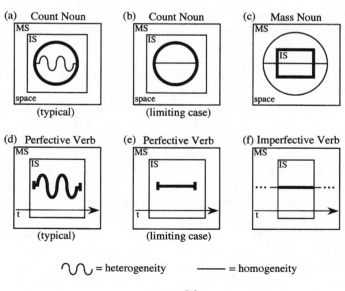

FIGURE 5.8

middle show that the noun/verb parallelism extends even further. For each category, we have noted examples construed as bounded despite being uniform throughout: count nouns such as *lake*, *lawn*, and *beep*; perfective verbs like *sleep*, *swim*, and *meditate*. These represent the limiting case of heterogeneity, where the thing or process is homogeneous apart from the measure of heterogeneity introduced by the boundary itself.

A mass is contractible in the sense that any portion of an instance is itself a valid instance of the mass-noun type. The analogous property holds for imperfective verbs. Suppose I learn a poem and manage to remember it for over a month. During this time span, the statement *I know the poem* is valid for any interval of any length (*I knew the poem last week, I know it right now, and I will still know it tomorrow*). There is no need to consider the entire month-long situation—whatever interval is selected for focused viewing (as the temporal immediate scope) is sufficient to manifest an instance of the profiled process. Contractibility is not characteristic of count nouns or perfective verbs. Part of a *lake* is not itself a lake. Analogously, if it takes me an entire month to learn a poem, the statement *I learned the poem* is inappropriate for describing the progress made during a single day or week.

In addition to being contractible, a mass is also expansible in the sense that combining two instances yields a single, larger instance. Count nouns lack this property due to bounding, which limits the extent of an instance. They instead exhibit the property called replicability, which simply means that putting instances together yields multiple instances. Hence *the water in those two lakes* invokes one instance of *water* but two instances of *lake*, despite their referential identity. It is therefore as expected that imperfectives are expansible and perfectives replicable. If I knew a poem in March and also knew it in April, it is equally valid to say that I knew the poem during the entire two-month period. But if a full instance of learning it occurred in March, and another in April, they would constitute two separate instances of learning: *I knew the poem* once, but *I learned the poem* twice.

A specific indication of replication is the adverbial phrase *again and again*. As expected, it only occurs with perfectives. While a sufficiently forgetful person might well say *I learned the poem again and again*, it is a bit strange to say *??I knew the poem again and again* for the same series of alternating periods of knowing the poem and not knowing it. *Learn* replicates because an event of learning is inherently bounded and (alas) gives no guarantee that the resulting knowledge will endure—it may have to be learned on multiple occasions. But since *know* is imperfective, it induces the expectation of indefinite continuation. For *know* to be replicable, we need to make a semantic adjustment and construe the profiled relationship as occurring in bounded episodes. We have the conceptual flexibility to do this if we can imagine a plausible scenario, and here we can, owing to the frailty of human memory. In similar fashion, *??She resembled her mother again and again* strikes us as semantically anomalous until we start to think of plausible interpretations. We need only imagine a scenario in which resembling someone constitutes a bounded episode able to recur. And indeed, since people change we can imagine a person resembling her mother for numerous periods during her life, interspersed with periods of nonresemblance. Alternatively, she might resemble her mother just in a certain respect manifested on multiple occasions, as in her tone of voice while angry.

Such examples illustrate a number of general points. First, the grammatical well-formedness of sentences ("grammaticality") cannot be judged independently of what they are interpreted as meaning. Moreover, semantic interpretation is not exclusively linguistic but depends on what we know or can imagine about the world. And finally, because it is influenced by these factors, linguistic categorization is flexible.

5.2.3 Interaction with Tense and Aspect

The usual basis for distinguishing perfective and imperfective verbs is contrasting grammatical behavior, primarily their interaction with tense and aspect: English perfectives take the progressive but resist the simple present tense; imperfectives do the opposite. From the CG perspective, the behavior of perfectives and imperfectives is merely symptomatic of their conceptual characterizations. These allow us to explain not only the basic distributional pattern but also some apparent exceptions.

For semantic explanations, we must first describe the meanings of the relevant grammatical elements: progressive aspect (marked by *be...-ing*) and tense (both present and past). As suggested by its form, the progressive combines the meanings of *-ing* and *be*. The former was briefly discussed in §4.3.2. It is one of several elements (others being participial *-ed* and infinitival *to*) that construe a process holistically, thus making the profiled relationship nonprocessual. Moreover, *-ing* takes an "internal perspective" on this relationship. What this means, in technical terms, is that *-ing* imposes an immediate temporal scope delimiting some internal portion of the overall relationship and selecting it for focused viewing. Hence only this portion is profiled, as was shown in figure 4.14, which also indicates a third property of *-ing*: namely, that the profiled relationship is construed as homogeneous. This is so even when the verb that *-ing* attaches to describes a change. While the component states may then be different, they are nonetheless equivalent when viewed at a certain level of abstraction. In particular, they all qualify as representative internal states of the same base process.[18]

Starting with a verb like *climb*, then, *-ing* derives a participial expression, *climbing*, which profiles—and construes as homogeneous—a relationship comprising some internal portion of the verbal process. The profiled relationship is nonprocessual by virtue of being scanned in summary fashion (rather than sequentially). This holistic construal enables it to modify a noun, as in *the monkey climbing that tree*. Alternatively, it combines with *be* to form a progressive, *be climbing*. Since *be* is a schematic verb, it lends its processual nature to the relationship profiled by the participle. A progressive can therefore serve as the head of a finite clause (§4.3.3): *A monkey is climbing that tree*.

The overall effect of a progressive is thus to convert a perfective process into an imperfective one, as sketched in figure 5.9. The bounded occurrence profiled by the former functions as conceptual base for the latter, which profiles an internal portion that excludes the endpoints. Two subtle matters bear emphasizing. First, while a verb

---

[18] The level of abstraction required to construe them as homogeneous is no greater than the one implied by mass nouns like *furniture*, *equipment*, and *silverware*, or the plural *animals* used in reference to a monkey, an elephant, and a crocodile (§5.1.4).

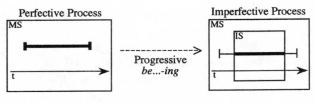

FIGURE 5.9

and its progressive are both processual, they profile **different processes**, one characterized in relation to the other. Second, while a progressive indicates that the verb it is formed on is perfective, the expression as a whole is imperfective.[19]

This semantic characterization explains why the progressive only occurs with perfectives. Quite simply, because its function is to imperfectivize a verb, there is no point in using it with a verb that is already imperfective. It thus makes perfect sense that the conventions of English preclude this option. While it cannot be claimed that languages are maximally efficient and always avoid redundancy, the added complexity of a progressive imperfective would serve no apparent purpose.[20]

Also explained is why the progressive does not occur with perfectives that are punctual, e.g. *I'm seeing a flash. A punctual event is just too brief to allow an internal perspective. It essentially consists of just an onset and an offset, with nothing in between, so excluding the endpoints leaves nothing to view and profile within the immediate temporal scope. There are of course exceptions to this exception, and these too can be explained. I noted in (22)(a) that see a flash permits the progressive when used in reference to an afterimage. Another example is blink. One cannot say *He is blinking with respect to a single blink viewed in the normal fashion. There is simply not time to say it or to observe the event's interior phase. Yet He is blinking is a perfectly normal, grammatical expression. It would usually be understood as referring not to one blink but to a series of blinks, construed as constituting a single overall event of bounded duration. On this **repetitive** interpretation, blink profiles a higher-order perfective process with sufficient length to be rendered progressive. The sentence then profiles some internal portion of this bounded series. Or imagine that a single blink has been recorded using high-speed photography and is now being projected on a screen at a normal viewing rate. We thus observe a single blink occurring over a time span of several seconds. Since blink is no longer punctual, He is blinking is quite acceptable.

The remaining question is why perfectives do not occur in the simple present tense. Indeed, out of all four combinations of tense and perfectivity, only the present perfective is problematic:

---

[19] Progressives behave like other imperfectives grammatically: they occur in the present tense (A monkey is climbing that tree) and do not themselves take the progressive (*A monkey is being climbing that tree).

[20] Although the progressive as a whole is limited to perfectives, -ing by itself occurs with either sort of verb: the monkey **climbing** that tree; a monkey **resembling** my uncle. This does serve a purpose, since either a perfective or an imperfective process must be viewed holistically when it is used to modify a noun (§4.3.3).

(23)   (a) *He learned the poem.*   [PAST PERFECTIVE]

    (b) **He learns the poem.*   [PRESENT PERFECTIVE]

    (c) *He knew the poem.*   [PAST IMPERFECTIVE]

    (d) *He knows the poem.*   [PRESENT IMPERFECTIVE]

Why do we find this particular distribution rather than some other? Also needing explanation are various exceptions, where a perfective does occur in the present.

We must first examine the meanings of the English tense inflections.[21] In the traditional view (sufficient for immediate purposes), tense relates an occurrence to the moment of speaking. Translating this into CG terminology, we can say that tense imposes an immediate temporal scope, positioned with respect to the speech event, within which the profiled process must be manifested. Obviously, for past tense the immediate scope is prior to the speech event. Perhaps less obviously, for the present tense in English it precisely coincides with the time of speaking (Langacker 2001a). This is shown in figure 5.10, using a box with squiggly lines to indicate the speech event. The profiled process is represented with a simple line (without bars or ellipses) because these structures themselves are neutral in regard to the perfective/imperfective contrast. The past tense indicates that an instance of the process occurs prior to the time of speaking, and the present tense indicates that an instance exactly coincides with the time of speaking.

Consider, then, the result of applying these tense morphemes to a perfective or an imperfective verb. With the past tense, the immediate temporal scope can be of any duration—it need only occur prior to the time of speaking. Therefore, it can always be large enough to encompass a perfective process instance, including its endpoints, as shown in figure 5.11(a). Past imperfectives are also unproblematic because imperfectives are mass-like in nature, hence contractible. Suppose a stable situation endures indefinitely and thus extends beyond the immediate scope in either direction, as shown in diagram (c). Owing to contractibility, that portion which falls within the immediate scope qualifies as a valid instance of the imperfective process type. This portion, segmented out for focused viewing, satisfies the requirement of an instance occurring prior to the speech event. The same holds for

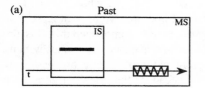 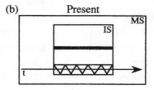

FIGURE 5.10

---

[21] Since future *will* is noninflectional (belonging instead to the modal system), English is usually analyzed as having just two grammatical tenses. The brief description offered at this juncture is justified more fully in ch. 9. Until then, we are only concerned with the "true" present, pertaining to things happening at the moment of speaking (see n. 14).

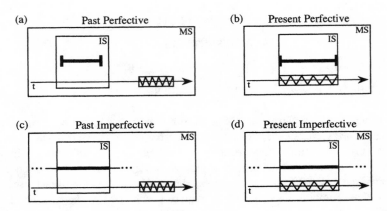

FIGURE 5.11

present imperfectives, as seen in diagram (d). The time of speaking is quite brief (the second or so it takes to utter a finite clause), so a stable present situation will normally extend beyond it in both directions. Nevertheless, the contractibility of an imperfective process ensures that the small sample coinciding with the speech event is a valid instance of the process type.

That leaves present tense perfectives, diagrammed in figure 5.11(b). There would seem to be nothing wrong with this configuration; conceptually, it is perfectly coherent for a bounded event to precisely coincide with the speech event. So why do present perfectives give the impression of being semantically anomalous? It is not because they are internally inconsistent, but rather because the configuration in diagram (b) is hard to achieve in normal language use. By "normal use", I refer to the default-case viewing arrangement where the speaker observes and describes actual events and situations (§3.4.1). Relative to this arrangement, diagram (b) represents the description of an actually observed, bounded event. This is problematic in two respects. First, it is seldom the case that an observed event is the same in duration as the utterance of its verbal description. It takes just a second to say *He learns the poem* or *She changes the tire*, but few actual occurrences of these events are so brief. The second problem can be posed as a question: What does the speaker know, and when does he know it? To describe an observed event, the speaker must first observe it, or at least enough of it to know what it is. But by the time the speaker has accomplished this, it is already too late to initiate an utterance describing the event that exactly coincides with it.

Present tense perfectives are therefore not problematic owing to any intrinsic conceptual incoherence. The reason, instead, is that the configuration in figure 5.11(b) is incompatible with the default-case viewing arrangement. Yet there are many other viewing arrangements where the same problems do not arise. It turns out, in fact, that present perfectives are very common. If they are usually considered anomalous, it is simply because the default arrangement is taken for granted as the basis for their interpretation.

In one departure from the default arrangement, the speaker not only describes an action but actually performs it by virtue of the speech event itself. The expressions in

(24) are called **performatives** (Austin 1962; Searle 1969). A verb like *order*, *promise*, or *sentence* names a type of **speech act** and is therefore perfective. For an utterance to count as a performance of that act, the verb must be in the present tense, with the speaker coded as subject. Moreover, the speaker must intend to perform the action profiled by the verb, and the conditions required for its successful performance must all be satisfied (e.g. the speaker in (24)(c) must have the requisite authority).

(24) (a) *I order you to leave at once.*

(b) *I promise to stop smoking.*

(c) *I hereby sentence you to 30 days in the county jail.*

In performative use, perfective verbs are more than happy to occur in the present tense. The problems that arise in the default viewing arrangement are absent when the speaker actually performs the action named. There is no problem of temporal duration. Indeed, the profiled event and the speech event have to be the same in length, since—as shown in figure 5.12—a performative represents the special case where the event profiled by the sentence is the speech event itself. Nor is there any problem of speaker knowledge. Since the speaker performs the action described, and necessarily intends to do so, he does not have to observe its occurrence in order to identify it. He simply performs the action he intends to perform. And because he performs it by speaking, the action coincides exactly with the time of speaking.

Present tense perfectives are extremely prevalent in the "play-by-play" mode of speech practiced by sportscasters:

(25) *He hits a high fly to left. Jones comes in a few steps…he shades his eyes…he grabs it for the final out.*

This definitely approaches the default viewing arrangement, in that the announcer observes events and describes them. Yet it is special in certain ways that eliminate (or at least mitigate) the problems of duration and speaker knowledge. For one thing, the events described have a typical duration that roughly approximates the length of their description.[22] For another, these events are highly stereotypical, so the announcer

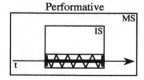

FIGURE 5.12

---

[22] A home run cannot be observed in just a second or so, since the ball has to travel quite a distance, and one has to observe its entire flight to be sure it clears the fence. Hence the announcer does not say *He homers to left!* but rather something like the following: *He hits a long fly to left…it's going, going, gone!* (not *It goes!*).

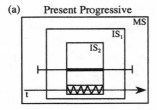 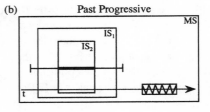

FIGURE 5.13

can either anticipate them or identify them virtually at their onset. Usually, then, a play-by-play account can shadow the events described with a very small time lag. In apprehending this mode of speech, we adopt the convention of ignoring whatever time lag there may be. Equivalently, it might be said that our conception of this genre incorporates the fiction of coincident description.

Other nondefault arrangements sanctioning present tense perfectives are examined later (§9.4.2 and §14.2.2). But what about the default viewing arrangement? How do we describe an actual perfective process observed as occurring at the present moment? For this we use the progressive, e.g. *He is learning the poem*, as shown in figure 5.13(a). We start with a bounded process (*learn*) whose overall occurrence includes the time of speaking. From this perfective process, the progressive derives an imperfective (fig. 5.9). It does so by imposing an immediate temporal scope, IS_1, that excludes the endpoints of the bounded event, and by construing the onstage portion as homogeneous. Of the original perfective process, the resulting imperfective (*be learning*) profiles the segment delimited by IS_1, which likewise includes the time of speaking. It is to this imperfective process that the present tense applies. The present imposes its own immediate scope, IS_2, coincident with the speech event (cf. fig. 3.3(b)). Hence the composite expression (*is learning*) profiles just that segment, which—owing to contractibility—is a valid instance of the imperfective process type (*be learning*).

For bounded events in the past, the progressive is not required (*He learned the poem*). We need only impose an immediate scope large enough to encompass the entire occurrence (fig. 5.11(a)). A past progressive is nonetheless possible: *He was learning the poem*. Diagrammed in figure 5.13(b), the past progressive lets us focus the portion of an overall event that was observable at some previous moment.

6

Constructions

General Characterization

Most of the expressions we employ are symbolically complex, to some degree analyzable into smaller symbolic elements. Grammar consists of the patterns for constructing such expressions. Accordingly, the expressions and the patterns are referred to as **constructions**. In this chapter and the next, I consider the general nature of constructions and then examine some basic aspects of their description.

6.1 Symbolic Assemblies

CG makes the fundamental and highly controversial claim that grammar is **symbolic** in nature. More specifically, it holds that grammar and lexicon form a continuum residing exclusively in **assemblies** of symbolic structures. Constructions are symbolic assemblies. The objective of grammatical analysis is to describe such assemblies in clear and precise detail.

6.1.1 Composition, Integration, and Symbolization

A symbolic structure (Σ) consists in the pairing of a semantic structure (S) and a phonological structure (P): $[[S]/[P]]_{\Sigma}$. It is thus bipolar, S being its semantic pole and P its phonological pole. As shown in figure 1.2, symbolic structures combine with one another to form more elaborate symbolic structures: $[\Sigma_1] + [\Sigma_2] = [\Sigma_3]$. These three structures constitute a symbolic assembly. At a higher level of organization, $[\Sigma_3]$ may itself combine with another symbolic structure to form one that is still more elaborate: $[\Sigma_3] + [\Sigma_4] = [\Sigma_5]$. And so on indefinitely. In this way, expressions exhibiting any degree of symbolic complexity can be progressively assembled: words, phrases, clauses, sentences, even discourses.

With respect to a particular level of organization, we can say that the **component structures** [Σ_1] and [Σ_2] are **integrated** to form the **composite structure** [Σ_3]. For instance, the component expressions *jar* and *lid* can be integrated to form the composite expression *jar lid*. All three structures are symbolic. The construction can thus be represented as follows, where uppercase and lowercase letters respectively indicate the semantic and phonological poles: [[JAR]/[jar]] + [[LID]/[lid]] = [[JAR LID]/[jar lid]].[1] These structures and the relationships among them constitute a symbolic assembly.

Shown abstractly in figure 6.1(a) are the structures and relationships inherent in a simple construction. The component symbolic structures, [Σ_1] and [Σ_2], as well as the composite structure [Σ_3], each consist of a semantic structure and a phonological structure connected by a relationship of **symbolization** (s). At each pole, the two component structures participate in relationships of **integration** (i) with one another and relationships of **composition** (c) with respect to the composite structure. Moreover, the integration of P_1 and P_2 symbolizes the integration of S_1 and S_2. The same structures and relationships are shown in diagram (b) for the specific case of *jar lid*. Of course, this representation is still quite abstract. A serious analysis of this or any other construction requires that each structure and each relationship be described in explicit detail.

Consider first the component semantic structures [JAR] and [LID]. A full description of either component involves semantic specifications in numerous cognitive domains ranked for centrality (recall the discussion of *glass* in §2.2.2). For sake of practicality, we must therefore confine our attention to those facets of these complex meanings that play some role in the construction of concern, and even here we can hardly avoid oversimplification. In the case of [JAR], relevant specifications include the fact that it profiles a thing, further identified as a physical container open at the top. The pictorial representation at the left in figure 6.2(a) is merely an informal, mnemonic abbreviation for these and other properties—it is **not** claimed that

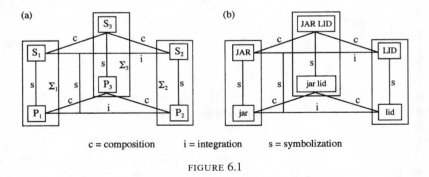

c = composition   i = integration   s = symbolization

FIGURE 6.1

---

[1] In formulaic representations, it is convenient to abbreviate by omitting the composite structure. *Jar lid* would then be given as follows: [[[JAR]/[jar]] - [[LID]/[lid]]]. Despite this simplified notation, the composite structure is a distinct entity whose presence must always be understood.

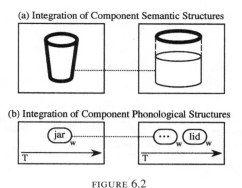

<figure (a) Integration of Component Semantic Structures; (b) Integration of Component Phonological Structures>

FIGURE 6.2

the meaning of *jar* is a picture. Likewise, the sketch on the right in 6.2(a) abbreviates the relevant specifications of [LID]. It too profiles a thing, further characterized as the cover for an opening in the upper side of a container. [LID] itself does not specify any one kind of container (consider *pot lid*, *box lid*, *coffin lid*) and thus evokes it schematically. The dotted line in 6.2(a) shows how [JAR] and [LID] are integrated. It indicates that the container profiled by [JAR] **corresponds** to the schematic container evoked by [LID]: that these are two representations of the same conceived entity. Corresponding elements are superimposed, and their specifications merged, in forming the composite conception.

Analogously, figure 6.2(b) shows the integration of the component phonological structures [jar] and [lid]. Here, too, the representations are highly abbreviatory. In lieu of comprehensive phonological descriptions (cf. FCG1: §9.1), it is merely indicated that [jar] and [lid] are words (w), each occurring at a certain point in the flow of speech. The arrow labeled T is processing time—in particular, speech time. One aspect of the characterization of a word is the potential for other words to precede or follow it along this axis. This provides a basis for phonological integration. In 6.2(b), a correspondence line identifies [jar] with the word directly preceding [lid] in the temporal sequence.[2] Hence the merger of corresponding elements produces the word sequence *jar lid* at the composite-structure level.

Composition is largely a matter of combining component structures in accordance with the correspondences holding between their elements at the semantic and phonological poles. Component-structure elements that correspond to one another correspond to the same element at the composite-structure level. In this way, the structures and correspondences shown in figure 6.2 give rise to the configuration in figure 6.3, representing the construction as a whole. The composite semantic structure profiles the cover for a container identified not just schematically but as a jar in particular. The composite phonological structure is the two-word sequence *jar lid*, with the first word bearing

---

[2] [lid] itself evokes this word only potentially and in schematized form (indicated by ellipses). Its role in the construction brings it to the fore. The notation is arbitrary in the sense that one could equally well show [lid] as corresponding to the word following [jar].

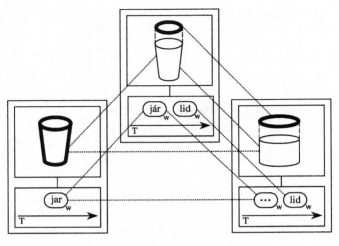

FIGURE 6.3

stress: [jár lid]. These composite structures stand in a relationship of symbolization to one another, and one of composition to their respective component structures.

6.1.2 Composition as Categorization

A crucial point is that the composite structure is not merely the sum of the component structures it is based on, at either pole. The composite structure is an entity in its own right, usually with emergent properties not inherited or strictly predictable from the components and the correspondences between them. From figure 6.2(a) alone, one could not predict that the composite expression *jar lid* profiles the lid rather than the jar. Likewise, from figure 6.2(b) one could not predict that stress falls on the first word of the compound rather than the second. These are properties of the expression as a whole, emerging only at the composite-structure level. As a general matter, component structures should be thought of as resources drawn on—along with others—in arriving at the composite expression. While they motivate the composite structure to varying degrees, and may supply most of its content, they should not be thought of as building blocks that need only be stacked together to form the composite whole. As discussed in §2.1.3, the relation between them is one of partial (rather than full) compositionality.

Since the composite structure is a distinct entity, not reducible to its components, together they form an **assembly** of symbolic structures. They form an assembly (as opposed to being separate and unrelated) precisely by virtue of being linked by correspondences. "Horizontal" correspondences constitute the relationship of integration, which links the component structures. "Vertical" correspondences constitute the relationship of composition, which links the component structures to the composite structure. And as shown in figure 6.1, the phonological integration symbolizes the semantic integration. In the case of *jar lid*, the fact that *jar* directly precedes *lid* in the temporal sequence symbolizes the fact that the container evoked by *lid* is specifically the one profiled by *jar*. Though easily taken for granted, this symbolizing relationship between semantic and phonological integration is a critical aspect of constructional meaning. It ensures that integration at the two poles is coordinated, and is thus responsible for the symbolic link between [S_3] and [P_3] at the composite-structure level. Without it, nothing would ensure that in a sentence like *They found a jar lid under the coffin* the lid is interpreted as belonging to the jar rather than the coffin.

The structures in a symbolic assembly are linked not only by correspondences but also by relationships of **categorization** (§1.3.1). At the semantic pole of *jar lid*, for example, the component and composite structures exhibit the categorizing relationships shown in figure 6.4. First, as indicated by a solid arrow, [LID] is schematic with respect to [JAR LID]: while the two are consistent in their specifications, the latter is more specific. This "vertical" elaborative relationship is due to a "horizontal" one, whereby [JAR] provides a finer-grained description of the schematic container evoked by [LID]. Finally, a dashed arrow indicates that [JAR LID], taken as a whole, constitutes a semantic extension vis-à-vis [JAR]: that is, they are inconsistent in their specifications. The discrepancy resides in their profiling. Although [JAR] profiles the container, the composite structure inherits its profile from [LID], so [JAR LID] designates the cover.

In a categorizing relationship, the categorizing structure lies in the background. Occupying the foreground—as the structure of concern—is the **target** of categorization (the structure being categorized). This asymmetry can be observed in symbolic assemblies, where a composite structure is foregrounded relative to its components (fig. 3.1). It is the composite structure that we primarily attend to and employ for further composition at higher levels of organization. The component structures are not invoked for their own sake, but as "stepping-stones" for purposes of "reaching" the composite conception. Moreover, a categorizing structure is usually not exhaustive of its target but merely provides a way of apprehending it.[3] In this we find a

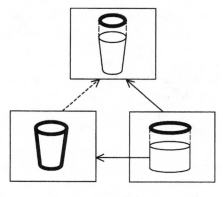

FIGURE 6.4

---

[3] While [DOG] categorizes [POODLE], for example, the latter is semantically more elaborate: [[DOG] → [POODLE]].

general basis for the point that a composite structure is more than just the sum of its components. Though standard and unavoidable, the metaphor inherent in terms like "construction" and "composition" should not be pushed too far. While component structures serve to evoke a composite structure, and provide a way of apprehending it, the latter should not be thought of—in any strict or literal sense—as being constructed out of them. Stepping-stones are not the same as building blocks.

The potential for being misled by the "construction" metaphor is one motivation for speaking of component and composite structures as forming a symbolic "assembly". Within an assembly, the composite structure stands in the foreground by virtue of being the target of categorization.[4] Thus far, of course, we have only considered simple symbolic assemblies representing a single level of composition. But assemblies can be of any size, representing multiple levels of grammatical organization. In a complex assembly, it is typical for the composite structure at a given level of organization to function as a component structure with respect to another, "higher" level of organization. If the component structures are stepping-stones for reaching the composite structure, that in turn may be a stepping-stone for reaching another composite structure, and so on indefinitely. Hence the structures in a complex symbolic assembly define a **compositional path** that can be of any length (§3.2.2).

Illustrating an assembly with just two levels of grammatical composition is the compound *jar lid factory*. At the first ("lower") level of organization, the component structures *jar* and *lid* are integrated to form the composite structure *jar lid*. At the higher level, *jar lid* functions as a component structure, combining with *factory* to form the full expression. It would be possible to continue—for example, by adding *supervisor* to derive the more complex expression *jar lid factory supervisor*. That in turn might combine with the compound *training school*, yielding the still more complex *jar lid factory supervisor training school*. And so on.

To keep things manageable, let us confine our attention to *jar lid factory*. Its semantic pole is sketched in figure 6.5, showing only correspondences (not categorizing relationships).[5] The assembly of *jar lid* is just as described in figure 6.3. Its composite structure is one of the two component structures at the higher level of organization. The other component, *factory*, profiles a building or facility used for manufacturing some product, represented as a circle. Effecting the integration of *jar lid* and *factory* is a correspondence between the profile of the former and the schematic product evoked by the latter: a *jar lid factory* is one that manufactures jar lids. The result is the structure shown at the top, the composite structure for the overall

---

[4] Given the limitations of a two-dimensional printed page, this foregrounding is normally shown by placing the composite structure above the component structures.

[5] For sake of practicality, every diagram is selective in what it portrays, being limited to what is essential for the point at hand. The labels in fig. 6.5 (*jar, lid, jar lid*, etc.) are meant to be suggestive of the phonological pole, but not to actually describe it in even the minimal fashion of fig. 6.3. Though seldom represented in explicit detail, the phonological pole must always be understood as a crucial part of symbolic assemblies.

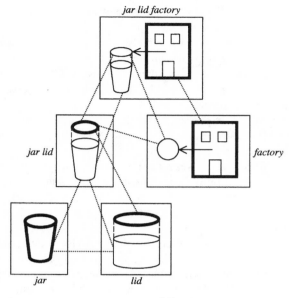

FIGURE 6.5

expression. What it profiles is the facility, since a *jar lid factory* is a kind of factory (not a kind of lid or jar).

The five structures indicated in figure 6.5 constitute a symbolic assembly of modest complexity. Within this assembly, component structures serve as stepping-stones for arriving at composite structures, at two successive levels of organization. The ultimate target, shown at the top, comprises the composite form and meaning of the full expression. These stand in the foreground. At either pole, the other structures define a compositional path leading to the final target. Though it lies in the background, this path is not unimportant. The path followed in reaching the final composite structure is a secondary but significant aspect of an expression's form and meaning.

6.2 Constructional Schemas

Symbolic assemblies can either be specific or schematic. Specific assemblies constitute linguistic expressions (like words, phrases, clauses, and sentences). More schematic assemblies are referred to in CG as **constructional schemas**. These provide the basis for semantic and grammatical composition.

6.2.1 Role in Compositionality

An expression is said to be compositional to the extent that its composite structure derives in a regular, predictable way from its component structures. Compositionality is an essential feature of language, enabling us to create and understand an endless supply of new expressions. Thus we need to be clear about its nature, as well as its limitations.

The simplest hypothesis would merely identify an expression's composite meaning with the set of its component meanings. Composition would then be just a matter of viewing the component meanings collectively. On this account, the composite meaning of *jar lid factory* would be the unordered set {[FACTORY], [LID], [JAR]}. It is readily seen, however, that there is more to composition than mere summation. Otherwise, distinct expressions with the same components would always be semantically equivalent. But they are not. We cannot, for instance, ignore the semantic differences of *jar lid factory* (factory for making jar lids), *lid factory jar* (jar used in a lid factory), and *jar factory lid* (cover for a roofless jar factory). An expression's composite meaning is not just a pile of component meanings, but an integrated structure where elements relate to one another in very specific ways. These structural relationships are spelled out by correspondences, categorizations, and profiling at the semantic pole of symbolic assemblies, as shown for *jar lid factory* in figure 6.5. When arranged in other configurations, the same component elements give rise to other meanings.[6]

What guides us in putting assemblies together? How do we know which elements correspond, or what is profiled within the composite conception? What tells us, not only that the semantic assembly in figure 6.5 is possible, but also that it represents the phonological sequence *jar lid factory* (as opposed to *lid factory jar* or *jar factory lid*)? We know such things by virtue of knowing the grammar of our language. Grammar consists of conventionally established **patterns** for putting together symbolic assemblies. As viewed in CG, these patterns are themselves symbolic assemblies, precisely analogous to the complex expressions they characterize except for being schematic rather than specific. Since they are both constructions and schematic, they are naturally called **constructional schemas**. They are acquired through a process of **schematization**, being abstracted from occurring expressions as skeletal representations of shared organizational features. Once learned, a schema serves as a template for dealing with novel expressions on the same pattern.

The examples considered so far all instantiate a basic compounding pattern of English. The constructional schema describing that pattern is sketched in figure 6.6. Apart from the greater schematicity of semantic and phonological elements, this diagram is just the same as figure 6.3. At the phonological pole, it simply refers to words (not to *jar* and *lid* in particular). Semantically, the component and composite structures are equally schematic: they merely profile things (which makes them nouns). The only further specification—general enough to be almost vacuous—is that the thing profiled by the second component is somehow associated with some other thing. A correspondence identifies this associated entity with the one profiled by the first component.

Learned by exposure to innumerable compounds of this sort (*toothbrush, alarm clock, pear tree, peanut butter, tablespoon, baby sitter, belly button, can opener, cowboy, fingernail, pie crust, ski-plane, birthday party, football*, etc.), this constructional

---

[6] Describing the semantic poles of *lid factory jar* and *jar factory lid* (by means of diagrams analogous to fig. 6.5) is left as an exercise for the reader.

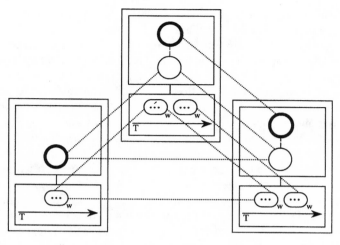

FIGURE 6.6

schema guides the formation and interpretation of new ones.[7] We noted previously that certain features of these composite expressions are not apparent from just the component structures and the correspondences connecting them: from *jar* and *lid* alone, one could not know that the compound as a whole profiles the lid rather than the jar, or that the first word bears primary stress: *jár lid*. These features are quite regular, however. Rather than being idiosyncrasies of this one expression, they are characteristic of the general compounding pattern. The pattern itself specifies that the first component bears stress (*tóothbrush, alárm clock, péar tree,* etc.) and that the second component determines profiling (thus a *toothbrush* is a kind of brush, an *alarm clock* a kind of clock, and so on). Accordingly, these specifications are incorporated in the constructional schema the expressions all instantiate.

Can we say, then, that *jar lid* is compositional? Are its composite form and meaning predictable from the components *jar* and *lid*? That depends on what is presumed available as the basis for prediction. Since composition is more than just summation, the component structures alone are insufficient; the basis for prediction also has to include a conventionally established compositional pattern. The issue of compositionality must therefore be formulated in terms of whether the composite structure derives from component structures in the manner specified by a constructional schema. By this definition, *jar lid* approximates full compositionality.[8] In CG, of course, compositionality is claimed to be a matter of degree. If *jar lid* and *tabletop* come close to being fully compositional, the same cannot be said for *laptop*, whose

---

[7] It is not important that certain compounds are written as single words, others as two words, and still others as words separated by hyphens. This is simply a matter of orthographic practice that does not reliably correlate with actual phonological differences.

[8] *Jar lid* is arguably not quite fully compositional because the constructional schema does not guarantee that the association between jar and lid will be the obvious one of the lid serving as cover for the jar. Conceivably, for example, *jar lid* could be interpreted as a lid decorated with the picture of a jar.

expected meaning (roughly 'top of lap') is related only metonymically to its actual meaning ('portable computer'). At the extreme, there may be no connection at all between component and composite meanings. The meanings of *under* and *stand*, for example, play no apparent role in the composite meaning of *understand*. Though morphologically complex, this verb is semantically unanalyzable (§3.2.2).

Discrepancies between an expression's expected meaning and its actual meaning arise because the component structures and constructional schema are not the only resources available in creating or understanding it. Also available for exploitation are general knowledge, apprehension of the context, and imaginative capacities like metaphor, metonymy, fictivity, and blending. Their effect can range from the minor one of merely supplementing the contributions of component structures, to more substantial adjustments like metonymic shift (§3.3.1), all the way to cases where the composite conception is drastically different from either component. As a consequence, most expressions are only partially compositional, their actual meaning diverging in some respect from anything derivable by strictly compositional means. Normally, though, the compositional meaning does have a major part in determining the actual semantic value, and for many purposes discrepancies can often be ignored. Despite their limitations, therefore, composition and compositional patterns have to be a central focus of linguistic investigation. It is thus the compositional aspects of meaning that primarily concern us in this chapter and the next.

In accordance with the standard view that syntax is autonomous (§1.2.1), linguists generally make a clear-cut distinction between patterns of grammatical composition ("rules of grammar") and patterns of semantic composition ("rules of semantic interpretation"). CG, on the other hand, views grammar as symbolic in nature and therefore meaningful. It thus proposes a fundamentally different organization, where grammar (along with lexicon) consists solely of symbolic assemblies. On this account, patterns of grammatical composition are characterized by schematic assemblies, i.e. constructional schemas (like fig. 6.6). Patterns of semantic composition are simply the semantic poles of those assemblies. Hence they are not distinct from grammar, but an inherent and indispensable facet of it.

6.2.2 Categorization of Expressions

A constructional schema invoked for producing or understanding an expression participates in a categorizing relationship with that expression. If the latter fully conforms to the schema's specifications, so that it fully **instantiates** the schema, the relationship is one of **elaboration**: [SCHEMA] → [EXPRESSION]. If there is some conflict in their specifications, the relationship is one of **extension**: [SCHEMA] ---> [EXPRESSION]. In either case, the categorization constitutes the expression's interpretation with respect to established linguistic convention, as embodied in the schema. An elaborative relationship represents a judgment of conventionality (often referred to as "grammaticality"). While an expression that conflicts with a schema is to that extent nonconventional ("ungrammatical"), this need not be grounds for stigma. The pleasures of innovation and the pressures of actual language use are such that we are always pushing the envelope of established convention. Thus a certain measure of nonconventionality is usual and readily accepted.

By way of illustration, *jar lid* conforms to the compounding pattern and therefore elaborates the constructional schema describing it. This categorizing relationship, involving the entire assemblies in figures 6.3 and 6.6, is shown in figure 6.7. Of course, this overall configuration is itself a kind of symbolic assembly, pertaining to a different dimension of linguistic organization. Internally, both schematic assemblies (constructional schemas) and specific ones (expressions) describe the combination of simpler symbolic structures to form one of greater complexity. Such relationships—those internal to constructions—are traditionally labeled **syntagmatic**. The term is used in contrast to **paradigmatic**, which pertains to relationships of categorization. Paradigmatic relationships hold between schemas and their various instantiations and are thus external to constructions.[9]

While all the details in figure 6.7 are descriptively important, we can often get by with less cumbersome representations. In one abbreviatory format, the same

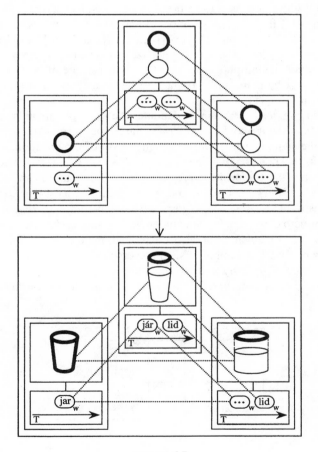

FIGURE 6.7

---

[9] Hence all constructions are symbolic assemblies, but not conversely, since the latter include both syntagmatic and paradigmatic relationships.

assembly is sketched in figure 6.8. The constructional schema's component and composite structures are given as N_1, N_2, and N_3 (since each profiles a thing and is thus a noun). There is no indication of correspondences, as corresponding elements are not represented individually. Relationships of categorization are, however, shown, both within constructions and between them. Within both the constructional schema and the instantiating expression, the first and second component structures categorize the composite structure in relationships of extension and elaboration, respectively (cf. fig. 6.4). These relationships are syntagmatic. In the paradigmatic plane, the entire assembly constituting the constructional schema categorizes the entire assembly constituting the expression. This global categorizing relationship resolves itself into local ones, whereby the component and composite structures of the schema categorize those of *jar lid*.

If we adopt instead a formulaic representation, where the composite structure is left implicit, the global categorization can be given as follows: $[[N_1] - [N_2]] \rightarrow$ [[[JAR]/[jar]] - [[LID]/[lid]]]. This global relationship comprises the local categorizations $[N_1] \rightarrow$ [[JAR]/[jar]], $[N_2] \rightarrow$ [[LID]/[lid]], and $[N_3] \rightarrow$ [[JAR LID]/[jar lid]]. Of course, any of these can further be resolved into categorizing relationships at the semantic and phonological poles. For instance, if N_1 is represented as [[THING]/[...]] (the noun schema), the first local categorization decomposes into [THING] $\rightarrow$ [JAR] plus [...] $\rightarrow$ [jar].

When the composite structure instantiates the same grammatical category as a component structure, it may be possible for the former to function as a component structure in the same construction, at a higher level of organization. English commonly exploits this potential with respect to the first element of the basic compounding pattern: since the composite expression *jar lid* is a noun, it can function as the first component of the higher-order compound *jar lid factory*. Figure 6.9 shows that the same constructional schema categorizes the compounds at both levels of organization.[10] In principle, we can continue indefinitely, using each successive composite structure as the first element of another compound: the owner of a *jar lid factory* is a *jar lid factory owner*; a number of such owners may form a *jar lid factory owner association*; if there are many such associations, it may be necessary to assemble a *jar lid factory owner association list*; someone who does so is a *jar lid factory owner*

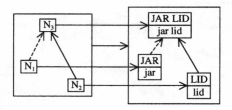

FIGURE 6.8

[10] To handle this and other cases, the constructional schema must actually be slightly more general than the version sketched in fig. 6.6. In particular, it must allow the possibility for either component structure to consist of multiple words instead of just a single word.

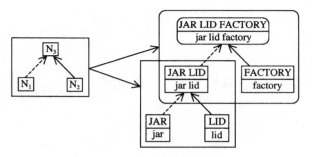

FIGURE 6.9

association list compiler; and so on for as long as imagination permits. While this is hardly the best example, it illustrates the general point that a limited set of constructional schemas (in this case just one) can sanction an open-ended set of potential instantiating expressions.

In practice, of course, there quickly comes a point where such compounds are too specialized and unwieldy to be very useful. (When is the last time you needed to refer to someone who compiles lists of associations of owners of factories making lids for jars?) English compounds of this sort seldom go beyond two levels of organization, and most of those established as lexical units exhibit just one. Thus, while *jar lid* is to some extent familiar and conventional, *jar lid factory* is certainly not. This difference in degree of entrenchment and conventionalization is represented in figure 6.9 by the boxes enclosing the two constructions. When it seems relevant to make the distinction, boxes with rounded corners are used for novel structures, regular boxes for those with the status of conventional units.

Two-level compounds are quite common in English, however, and a fair number are established as fixed expressions (e.g. *baseball bat, toothpaste tube, birthday party, pancake batter, football helmet, laptop user*). Among the conventional units of the language, we must therefore recognize a two-level compounding pattern, shown on the left in figure 6.10. The constructional schema representing this pattern incorporates two instances of the basic schema, where the composite structure of one instance functions as the first component of the other. The conventional basis for a form like *jar lid factory* is thus not limited to the individual elements and the single-level constructions bracketed in figure 6.9—in using this complex expression, a speaker follows the established precedent of embedding one compound as the first component of a higher-level compound. To the extent that complex expressions conform to patterns of composition encompassing multiple levels of organization, we can posit constructional schemas to capture these regularities. In principle, constructional schemas, like expressions, can exhibit any degree of symbolic complexity.

Let me end this section on a cautionary note. Every notation has its limitations and is bound to be misleading in some respect. One potentially misleading aspect of the present diagrams is the representation of schemas and their instantiations (and more generally, categorizing structures and the targets of categorization) as separate,

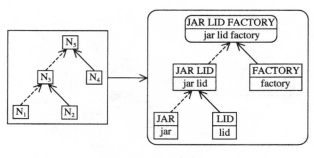

FIGURE 6.10

nonoverlapping boxes. While this is necessary for analytical purposes, such elements should not be thought of as discrete, as independent, or as bounded containers stored in different parts of the brain. Indeed, they are not "stored" as such, but reside in patterns of neural processing. It is thus implausible to suppose that schemas are either self-contained or wholly distinct from their instantiations. They are better seen as being **immanent** in their instantiations (i.e. as "lying within" them). What I mean by this is that schemas reside in certain aspects of the processing activity in which their instantiations reside.

6.3 Unipolar vs. Bipolar Organization

The conventional units posited in CG are restricted by the content requirement (§1.3.4) to semantic, phonological, and symbolic structures. A symbolic structure reduces to the pairing of a semantic and a phonological structure (its two poles). Linked together in assemblies, symbolic structures provide a seamless account of lexicon, morphology, and syntax. In this way, CG achieves a natural, restrictive, and unified conception of linguistic organization that directly reflects the semiological function of language: permitting meanings to be symbolized by sounds.

If every symbolic structure comprises a semantic structure and a phonological structure, the converse fails to hold. It is not the case that every semantic or phonological structure directly participates in a symbolic relationship. For both semantics and phonology, we have to distinguish two kinds of structures and dimensions of organization: those based on symbolic considerations (hence **bipolar**) and those whose basis is purely semantic or phonological (**unipolar**).

6.3.1 Delimitation of Structures

The phonological units of a language are not limited to those which serve as the phonological poles of symbolic structures. A large number of units must be recognized whose role is purely phonological—they contribute to the formation of phonological structures but do not themselves participate in symbolizing relationships. Examples of such units are individual sounds ([p], [ɪ], [k], [e], [n], etc.), as well as permitted sound combinations like consonant clusters ([bl], [mp], [str]) and syllables ([pɪk], [bley], [nɪks]). Also included are phonological schemas representing such abstract entities as classes of sounds ([VOICELESS STOP], [HIGH FRONT VOWEL]), permitted syllable types ([CV], [CCVC]), and accent patterns (e.g. [(. . . ớσ)$_w$], whereby stress falls on the penultimate syllable of a word).

Consider *picnics*, for example. On purely phonological grounds, we can describe it as a word of two syllables, with accent on the first: ((pík)$_σ$ (nɪks)$_σ$)$_w$. Each syllable instantiates a syllable schema ([CVC] and [CVCC]), consists of a series of sounds, which belong to various classes, and so on. Note that a linguist could arrive at this description without knowing anything about the word's meaning or grammatical analysis. The structural elements in question are posited on a strictly phonological basis, with no reference to symbolic relationships or the semantic pole. Such elements are said to be **unipolar**, since just a single pole figures in their delimitation and characterization.

The word *picnics* is thus divisible on unipolar grounds into the major parts *pic* and *nics*. But obviously, it can also be analyzed into the basic elements *picnic* and *s*. Here, though, the rationale is nonphonological. While *picnic* and *s* do comprise phonological structures, the only reason for dividing the form into these two parts pertains to meaning: these are the parts that symbolize the semantic components [PICNIC] and [PLURAL]. It is by virtue of functioning as the phonological poles of symbolic units that these portions of the word are recognized as being structurally significant. Since two poles figure in their delimitation and characterization, these elements are said to be **bipolar**.

At the phonological pole, we can thus distinguish between unipolar and bipolar organization, depending on whether structural elements are delimited on the basis of strictly phonological considerations (like *pic* and *nics*) or in terms of their symbolizing function (*picnic* and *s*). There is a definite tendency for phonological structures with bipolar motivation to coincide with those having unipolar motivation.[11] Yet, since unipolar and bipolar phonological structures have different functions and different rationales, this tendency is easily overridden. Also, a phonological structure that does participate in a symbolizing relationship does not necessarily do so in all its occurrences. The syllable [pɪk], for example, has bipolar motivation in *pick*, but not as part of *picnics* or *picture*. Likewise, [nɪks] has symbolizing function in *nix*, *nicks*, and *Nick's*, but not as part of *Phoenix*. In and of themselves, syllables are unipolar structures, so their exploitation for symbolic purposes is purely contingent. Thus, while [bley] occurs as a syllable in *blatant*, *blazon*, and *blazing*, it does not itself contribute to their meanings (i.e. it is not a morpheme).

The distinction between unipolar and bipolar organization has to be made at the semantic pole as well. Semantic structures with bipolar motivation are those which directly participate in symbolic relationships (functioning as the semantic poles of symbolic structures). On the other hand, semantic structures have unipolar motivation

---

[11] They coincide in the case of *toothless*, *unhelpful*, *jar lid*, and indeed, in most multiword expressions. Their coincidence no doubt facilitates language processing.

when they are conventionally exploited in constructing linguistic meanings but lack individual symbolization.[12] An example is the notion of an immediate part, i.e. the relationship between two successive levels in a whole-part hierarchy (fig. 3.3). For instance, the head is an immediate part of the body, the ears are immediate parts of the head, and so on. This relationship plays a small but significant role in the structure of English. Notably, it provides the associative link between N_1 and N_2 in many noun compounds: *fingernail, tabletop, tree branch, bicycle seat, window pane, weekend*, etc. When the whole-part relationship is nonimmediate, such a compound is generally infelicitous; we say *ear lobe, doorknob*, and *book chapter* but not **head lobe, *house knob*, or **book paragraph*. Yet the notion of whole-part immediacy is not specifically symbolized in these expressions. It remains covert, despite its role in this and other patterns.

6.3.2 Dimensions of Composition

Being symbolic in nature, lexicon and grammar are primarily concerned with bipolar organization. Aspects of this organization include both minimal symbolic structures and their arrangement in symbolic assemblies of any degree of complexity. At either pole, it subsumes not only the ultimate component structures but also the composite structures at every level of organization. The disparity between unipolar and bipolar organization becomes most apparent when we consider the compositional path these structures define, the stepping-stones for arriving at the composite form and meaning of a symbolically complex expression.

This disparity starts with morphemes, which are symbolically minimal in the sense that they cannot be decomposed into smaller symbolic elements. Though minimal from a bipolar standpoint, by virtue of participating in an irreducible symbolic relationship, a morpheme's semantic and phonological poles are usually complex in unipolar terms. Phonologically, for example, *picnic* consists of two syllables, each comprising three sound segments, but only as a whole does this complex structure enter into a symbolic relationship. The semantic pole of *picnic* is also quite elaborate, involving numerous conceptions (of a social event, of certain kinds of food, of eating outdoors in a natural setting, etc.) none of which is symbolized individually. A major source of the great expressive power of language lies precisely in the fact that symbolizing structures are not limited to individual sounds (for this would imply a restricted inventory) and that one such structure can evoke a conceptualization of indefinite complexity.

In symbolically complex expressions, the disparity pertains to paths of semantic or phonological composition. What can we identify as a path of composition in the case of unipolar structure? The most obvious candidate is the combination of smaller elements into larger and larger ones. At the phonological pole, segments are grouped

---

[12] The distinction between unipolar and bipolar organization is not equivalent to the one drawn between phonetics and phonology or between conceptualization and semantics. Phonology and semantics represent the conventional exploitation of general phonetic and conceptual potential in accordance with the structure of a language. Unipolar and bipolar organization are two aspects of this **linguistic** structure, at each pole.

into syllables, syllables into words, and words into phrases.[13] An evident semantic analog is the conception of constitutive entities forming groups at successively higher levels of organization. In American professional football, for example, players form teams, which are grouped as divisions, which make up conferences, which constitute a league. There are other natural ways of building up progressively "larger" conceptions. We often build up the conception of a complex path by invoking its segments one at a time in proper sequence (imagine arranging flights from San Diego to Kansas City to Chicago to Milwaukee). Another natural progression leads through a whole-part hierarchy (e.g., from body to leg to knee), where each conceived entity provides the configuration required to conceptualize the next, which thus incorporates it.

At the semantic pole, the composition of bipolar elements often goes against the grain of natural, unipolar paths such as these. The description of a journey, for instance, need not reflect its inherent, chain-like sequencing. In contrast to (1)(a), which presents it iconically, (1)(b) imposes conceptual groupings on the cities that conflict with their sequence of access in the composite conception.

(1)   (a) *I traveled from San Diego to Kansas City to Chicago to Milwaukee.*

(b) *I traveled between San Diego and Milwaukee via Chicago and Kansas City.*

A second example pertains to the combination of smaller elements into larger ones. In its bipolar structure, a plural noun reflects the organization intrinsic to the conception of constitutive entities forming a group. The compositional path from *pea* to *peas* follows the natural conceptual progression from a single particle to a mass of such particles. However, this coalignment of paths is not observed in the case of *corn*. While the masses designated by *peas* and *corn* are quite analogous in unipolar terms, each comprising particles of roughly comparable size, their bipolar paths proceed in opposite directions. For *peas*, the path of composition goes from particle (*pea*) to mass (*peas*), but *corn* takes the mass as its starting point. To speak of a single particle, we resort to a composite expression with *corn* as one component—for example, *corn kernel*. The difference between unipolar and bipolar organization is also apparent from cases where different compositional paths lead to composite conceptions that—in unipolar terms—are essentially the same. The sentences in (1) are one illustration. Or consider *corn kernel* vs. *kernel of corn*. Unlike the former, the latter specifically evokes the notion 'intrinsic relationship' as one step in its compositional path. Individual symbolization by *of* serves to reinforce this facet of the composite conception (GC: ch. 3).[14]

With respect to phonological composition, the disparity between unipolar and bipolar organization was already shown with *picnics*. The unipolar compositional

---

[13] A fuller description would recognize other kinds of structures and dimensions of unipolar phonological organization (e.g. prosody). Also, the hierarchy does not imply any claims about the order in which structures emerge in language development or are accessed in linguistic processing.

[14] Providing a more elaborate example is the trio of expressions *triangle, three-sided polygon*, and *three-angled polygon*. Ultimately they all lead to the same composite conception (fig. 1.1(b)), but they reach it through very different paths.

path starts with segments, continues with the syllables *pic* and *nics* as intermediate stepping-stones, and terminates with the composite form, the full word *picnics*.[15] By contrast, the bipolar path arrives at the same composite form in just a single step, starting from the irreducible symbolizing structures *picnic* and *s*. The disparity is further evident from cases where two different paths of symbolic composition yield identical composite forms (indistinguishable in regard to intrinsically phonological properties like sound segments and their grouping into syllables). For example, *tolled* and *told* are pronounced exactly alike. In unipolar terms, each is a word consisting of a single syllable: $((towld)_\sigma)_w$. Yet their phonological composition is quite different in bipolar terms. Whereas *tolled* decomposes straightforwardly into *toll* plus *-ed*, the symbolic organization of *told* is more abstract. One component is *tell*, which is not directly observable as part of *told*. The other component—the symbolization of past tense—does not consist of just the ending *-d*, but of that together with the contrast between the vocalic nucleus [ow] and the vowel [ɛ] that would otherwise appear. What marks the past tense in this form is the overall discrepancy between the component structure $((tɛl)_\sigma)_w$ and the composite structure $((towld)_\sigma)_w$.

This illustrates an important general point—namely, that bipolar structures are more varied in nature and often more abstract than unipolar ones. In performing their symbolizing function, bipolar structures are not limited to providing explicit phonological "substance" of their own but may also reside in "operations" on the substance provided by another component. The modification effected on this component—the discrepancy between the composite form and what its form would otherwise be—may itself constitute a symbolizing structure.[16] The verb *sat*, for instance, does not divide naturally into a part meaning [SIT] and a part meaning [PAST] (the way *tolled* divides into *toll* plus *-ed*). We do not isolate [s...t] as the symbolization of [SIT], nor is [PAST] symbolized by the vowel [æ] per se. What we want to say, instead, is that [sæt] consists morphologically of [sɪt] plus a pattern of vowel modification: [[...ɪ...] ---> [...æ...]]. The phonological pole of *sat* is thus as sketched in figure 6.11(a). This variant of the past-tense marker (which also occurs in *sang*, *began*, *swam*, *rang*, and *spat*) makes schematic reference to both the stem and the composite form: [...ɪ...] and [...æ...]. These schematic elements respectively categorize [sɪt] and [sæt], which elaborate them. The categorizations shown (also correspondences, which are not shown) serve to link these symbolizing structures in a phonological assembly, the phonological pole of a symbolic assembly.

An analogous assembly, for *rose* (the past tense of *rise*), is given in figure 6.11(b). Compare this to diagram (c), representing the phonological pole of the homophonous noun. As unipolar structures, their composite forms are precisely the same, but viewed

---

[15] Like any other, the path metaphor has its limitations. It should not be taken as implying that the stepping-stones are arranged in strictly linear fashion, since at any level two or more stepping-stones must be accessed simultaneously in order to reach the next. This metaphor captures the directionality of composition (from categorizing structures to successive targets of categorization) but not the notion of convergence from multiple sources.

[16] The modification may consist of altering sound segments, changing their order, deleting them, adding or changing prosodic features (like stress and tone), or any combination of these (FCG1: §9.1.3). Such modifications generally symbolize highly schematic meanings (those characteristic of "grammatical" elements).

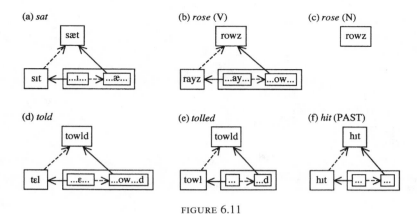

FIGURE 6.11

in bipolar terms the path to [rowz] leads through [rayz] in the case of the verb, but reaches it directly in the case of the noun.[17] Diagrams (d) and (e) show the contrasting bipolar paths of *told* and *tolled*, whose composite forms are likewise indistinguishable. The notation for *tolled* is meant to indicate that affixation can be regarded as a special case of a modifying operation, that where the only modification consists in the addition of segments at the beginning or end of a stem. Another special case is zero modification, illustrated by the past-tense form of *hit*. At the extreme, when there is no discrepancy between a component structure and the composite structure, the modification effected by the other component amounts to an identity mapping.

We can usefully think of unipolar and bipolar composition as proceeding along two different axes. This is shown for *picnics* in figure 6.12, where horizontal and vertical arrows respectively indicate these two dimensions of phonological organization. Along the vertical axis, the symbolically delimited components *picnic* and *s* categorize the composite form *picnics*. In the manner of figure 6.11(e), the plural suffix -*s* effects the modification of a schematically specified stem by adding [s] as its final segment. Each of these structures—internally—can also be analyzed in unipolar terms; this involves their segmental composition, the grouping of segments into syllables and of syllables into a word. Each structure is thus complex from the unipolar standpoint. For the component structure *picnic* and the composite structure *picnics*, this unipolar composition is partially represented along the horizontal axis: the word *picnic* decomposes into $(pik)_\sigma$ and $(nik)_\sigma$, and *picnics* into $(pik)_\sigma$ and $(niks)_\sigma$. Of course, each of these syllables further decomposes into segments.

Thus, as bipolar composition proceeds from component to composite structures at successively "higher" levels of organization, each structure along the compositional

---

[17] We can still speak of a compositional path—it is simply degenerate. In the case of a nondegenerate path, the ultimate composite structure is the one that is actually pronounced. Though tacit, other structures along the path represent a secondary aspect of the expression's phonological value. In this way, the noun *rose* and the verb *rose* are phonologically distinct, just as *pork* and *pig meat* are semantically distinct by virtue of reaching the same composite conception by alternate routes.

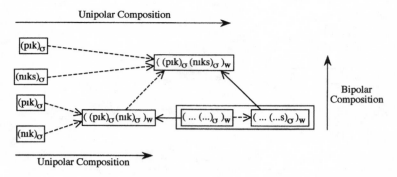

FIGURE 6.12

path is individually configured in unipolar terms in accordance with the "tactic" patterns of the language. That is, each is structured internally as specified by schemas describing conventionally permitted elements and combinations of elements (like segments, syllables, and words). This structuring need not be consistent from one level to the next, since the addition of another symbolizing element can trigger a reconfiguring of the unipolar structure. A reconfiguration of this sort is apparent in figure 6.12 from the discrepant syllabic organization of *picnic* and *picnics*. Specifically, the segment sequence [nɪk] constitutes an entire syllable in the former but not in the latter, where it is only a portion of (nɪks)$_\sigma$. The addition of final [s] to symbolize pluralization induces an alternate syllabification at the composite-structure level.

6.3.3 The Nonproblem of Mismatch

By clearly recognizing the distinction between unipolar and bipolar organization, CG reveals the straightforward nature of phenomena often considered problematic. Consider a possessive phrase like *the king of Denmark's castle*. The apparent problem it poses concerns the placement of the possessive ending *'s*, which shows up on *Denmark* even though the actual possessor of the castle is the king. Hence there seems to be a "mismatch" between the form of the expression and what it actually means. Another sort of example involves the definite article in expressions like *the big dog*. In normal speech, *the* loses its phonological independence and cliticizes (i.e. loosely attaches) to the following word: *th'big dog*. Once more, we find an evident mismatch between form and meaning: whereas *the* is phonologically associated with *big*, semantically it pertains to the dog.

There is no real problem, however. The apparent mismatches are simply a manifestation of unipolar and bipolar composition representing two different axes of phonological structure. In fact, the examples cited differ only in degree from a case like *picnics* (not usually considered problematic). We see in figure 6.12 that, in strictly phonological terms, the plural ending *-s* specifically combines with *nic* to produce the augmented syllable *nics*. This aspect of unipolar organization is quite consistent with the fact that, for purposes of semantics and grammar, plural *-s* combines with *picnic* as a whole. Delimited by symbolic considerations, these elements are integrated along the "vertical" axis of bipolar composition. In particular, *picnic* elaborates the schematic

stem invoked by the plural morpheme, which modifies it by adding [s] as the final segment. The incorporation of [s] in the stem's final syllable is then a consequence of the
structure at each level being configured in accordance with general unipolar patterns.

Analogously, the symbolic components of *the king of Denmark's* are unproblematically identified as *the king of Denmark* and *'s*, despite their disparity in size (a
matter of unipolar structure). Their bipolar integration instantiates a pattern whereby
's is added to the final word of the possessor nominal. The phonological pole of this
construction is sketched in figure 6.13(a).[18] For *th'big dog* we can likewise take the
symbolic components to be the ones expected on semantic and syntactic grounds:
the and *big dog*. The apparent mismatch results from the article's unipolar characterization as a clitic attaching to the immediately following word, even when the other
component is a multiword expression. If only for sake of discussion, I describe a clitic
as an element that combines with a word to form a larger structure also analyzed as a
word. The phonological pole of *th'big dog* is then as shown in diagram (b).

The composition observed in a unipolar hierarchy (segment > syllable > word >
etc.) is basically additive in nature. At each level, phonological elements of roughly
comparable size combine to form a larger structure where they are still evident with
only minimal distortion. Bipolar composition can also have this character. It is often
effected simply by juxtaposing structures roughly equal in size and complexity, as in
jar lid (fig. 6.2(b)). In general, though, bipolar composition is more flexible and more
abstract. Simple juxtaposition is not the only kind of operation deriving composite
phonological structures from component structures. The components are often quite

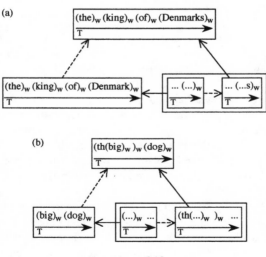

FIGURE 6.13

<hr>

[18] For convenience, orthography is used and syllabification is omitted. To make it clear that the order
of words is relevant, I have reintroduced the arrow representing speech time (T). This dimension of
phonological space is always present even when not explicitly shown.

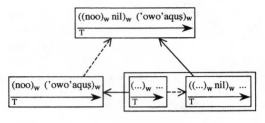

FIGURE 6.14

disparate in size, complexity, or type, and they may not be discernible in undistorted form at the composite structure level. *Sit*, for example, is only partially evident in *sat*.

Such disparities and distortions are not confined to morphology. Consider a syntactic example from Luiseño.[19] It is typical in a Luiseño clause for a clitic to occur following the initial word or phrase. In (2), the clitic *=nil* appears following the first word of a clause that would otherwise have the form *Noo 'owo'aquṣ* (which is also possible). The clitic offers a basic indication of how the clausal process and its trajector relate to the speech situation. Here it specifies that the trajector is first-person singular (1s) and that the profiled process lies in the past. In this case (though not always) the information turns out to be redundant, since the same information is supplied by the subject pronoun *noo* 'I' and the past durative suffix *-quṣ*.

(2)   *Noo=nil   'owo'a-quṣ.*   'I was working.'

  I=1s:PAST work-PAST:DUR

How should we describe this construction? Semantically and grammatically, we want to say that the two component structures are the basic clause *noo 'owo'aquṣ* and the clitic *=nil*, which invokes a clause schematically. Phonologically, though, the clitic appears on the subject pronoun. Stated more generally, the clitic occurs **inside** the clause, following whatever happens to be the first word or phrase. There seems to be a mismatch, where the clitic combines phonologically with an element other than the one it pertains to semantically and combines with grammatically. It should now be clear, however, that this is a false impression which only arises by failing to properly distinguish unipolar and bipolar organization. The component structures are indeed *noo 'owo'aquṣ* and *=nil*, integrated as shown in figure 6.14. But while *=nil* combines with an entire clause in bipolar terms, the combinatory operation consists in placing it after the initial word, so it winds up inside the clause in terms of unipolar organization. With respect to their overt segmental content, the two component structures are drastically different in size, and instead of their being juxtaposed, one is incorporated in the other. As a consequence, the clausal component *noo 'owo'aquṣ* is not preserved without distortion at the composite structure level, since the clitic interrupts it. The construction is nonetheless straightforwardly described in CG.

---

[19] Luiseño is a Native American language, formerly spoken in southern California, belonging to the Uto-Aztecan family.

7

Constructions

Descriptive Factors

Describing the grammar of a language consists primarily of describing its constructions. To understand grammar in any depth, we must therefore look at constructions in more detail. The following sections examine four basic factors in their description: **correspondences**, **profiling**, **elaboration**, and **constituency**. While the phonological pole will mostly be ignored (doubtless to your relief), bear in mind that the semantic structures under discussion represent just one pole of **symbolic** assemblies.

7.1 Correspondences

Of the four descriptive factors to be considered, correspondences are perhaps the most fundamental. They indicate how component and composite structures fit together in a coherent assembly (as opposed to being an arbitrary collection of unrelated elements). At the semantic pole, they specify the **conceptual overlap** between component structures, thus providing the basis for their integration. They also specify how each component structure overlaps with the composite structure, thereby indicating what it contributes to the unified conception that emerges. Viewed from the opposite perspective, these "vertical" correspondences represent the selection of certain facets of the composite conception for individual symbolization by component structures.

A word about notation. The dotted lines employed here for correspondences are at best a rather blunt descriptive instrument. Though sufficient for present purposes, they (and the diagrams containing them) lack formal precision. To properly understand their import, an intelligent user has to rely on certain tacit but natural principles of interpretation. For example, the correspondence line in figure 6.2(a) is meant to indicate that the jar as a whole is identified with the schematic container as a whole. You probably had no trouble interpreting it in this fashion, even though the line, in fact, connects just the side of the jar and the side of the container (and indeed, just particular locations on each). There is also a certain arbitrariness in how many correspondences are explicitly shown. For instance, the global correspondence in 6.2(a) could perfectly well be resolved into any number of local correspondences equating various parts of the two containers (e.g. the bottoms, the sides, the openings on top). Usually the number shown is the minimum needed for proper interpretation. When it is clear how structures are supposed to overlap, correspondences may even be omitted altogether (as they were in figs. 6.11 to 6.14).

7.1.1 Multiple Correspondences

Often it suffices to indicate a single global correspondence between component-structure elements (e.g. fig. 6.5). In other constructions multiple correspondences must be posited. A correspondence line is fairly unobtrusive from a notational standpoint, yet adding one to a construction has semantic and grammatical consequences that can be quite substantial. Let us briefly consider two examples.

The first case concerns a well-known construction in French (and other Romance languages), illustrated by the sentences in (1). They describe the causation of motion, where the thing moved is part of the body. The part moved is expressed by means of a nominal consisting of a definite article plus a body-part noun. Literally, then, the sentences translate as *I raise the hand, She closes the eyes*, etc. In English such sentences would usually be interpreted as indicating that the body part moved belongs to some person other than the actor.[1] But in French they are normally understood to mean that the body part in question is indeed an intrinsic part of the actor's own body. The sentences do not convey this explicitly, however. Whereas English specifies the possessor by means of a pronoun like *my* or *her*, in French one merely says the equivalent of *the hand* or *the eyes*. How do speakers know that the body part belongs to the person designated by the subject?

(1)   (a) *Je lève la main.*   (I raise the hand)   'I raise my hand.'

    (b) *Elle ferme les yeux.* (she closes the eyes) 'She closes her eyes.'

    (c) *Il ouvre la bouche.*   (he opens the mouth)   'He opens his mouth.'

It must first be acknowledged that this is not the only conceivable interpretation. In the proper context, these sentences might indeed indicate that the subject acts on a part belonging to some other body. In this event they simply instantiate the general direct object construction of French, and the object happens to be some contextually identifiable body part. As a strongly favored default, however, the sentences do imply that the actor is the possessor. We can account for this by also positing for French, as a special case of the general object construction, a more specific construction that incorporates the default interpretation. The constructional schema describing the

---

[1] For instance, a therapist might say *I raise the hand* in regard to patients too weak to raise it themselves. Alternatively, the sentence might refer to the hand of a mannequin or even a disembodied hand that for some reason needs elevation.

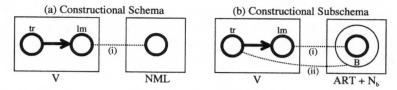

FIGURE 7.1

latter constitutes a particular, conventionally established elaboration of the schema describing the general pattern. The general schema and the more specific subschema are sketched in diagrams (a) and (b) of figure 7.1 (showing just the component structures and their integration).

The elements of the general schema are a verb (V) and an object nominal (NML). The verb profiles an interaction (represented as an arrow) between its trajector and landmark. The nominal profiles a thing. The pivotal feature of the object construction is the correspondence labeled (i), which identifies the verb's landmark with the nominal profile. All of these elements are also present in the constructional subschema, which is, however, more specific. In particular, the nominal is specifically characterized as consisting of the definite article (ART) plus a body-part noun (N_b).[2] The large circle labeled B represents the body as a whole, with respect to which the profile is a part. Another feature of this subschema—the crucial one—is correspondence (ii). This second correspondence equates the verb's trajector with the body evoked by the object nominal. It is this additional correspondence that imposes the default interpretation.

The semantic consequences of this second correspondence are seen more concretely in figure 7.2, which compares the composite structures that result from invoking the general schema and the subschema. They represent the specific expression *lever la main* 'raise the hand', which can instantiate either the general pattern or (by

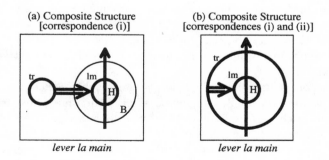

FIGURE 7.2

[2] This characterization takes the form of a lower level of composition (not indicated). The resulting composite structure functions as a component structure in this subschema.

default) the subpattern. The verb *lever* 'raise' profiles an event consisting of the trajector exerting force (double arrow) so that the landmark moves (single arrow) in an upward direction. The letter H abbreviates the multifaceted semantic specifications of *main* 'hand'. Though not irrelevant, the meaning of the definite article is omitted (see ch. 9).

Constructed in accordance with the general schema, based on correspondence (i) alone, *lever la main* merely indicates that the trajector induces the upward motion of a contextually identifiable hand. There need be no connection between the actor and the hand other than their coparticipation in this relationship. This is shown in diagram (a). Comparison with diagram (b) shows the effect of adding correspondence (ii), in accordance with the subschema. This tighter integration of verb and object yields a more compact composite conception, where the same individual serves as both actor and as host for the body part. This construction implies that the trajector induces the upward motion of his own hand.

Actually, the integration is tighter still. The default interpretation further specifies that the causal force is internally transmitted, and that the landmark moves in the manner characteristic of the body part in question. Thus (1)(a) would not be used, for instance, if the speaker were to grasp the left hand with the right and pull it upward.[3] Observe that these further specifications are not an automatic consequence of adding correspondence (ii). Strictly speaking, they represent still another correspondence, whereby the force profiled by the verb is identified with that inherent in our cognitive model of the body part in question and how we normally move it. In schematized form, all of these specifications are incorporated in the constructional subschema describing the default interpretation. They are aspects of the **constructional meaning** this schema imposes on instantiating expressions.

Also illustrating the effect of adding a correspondence are phrases like *tall giraffe*, *intelligent ape*, and *honest politician*. They consist of a noun modified by a "scalar" adjective, one attributing to its trajector a property whose presence is a matter of degree. The point at issue is that a phrase like *tall giraffe* has two very different meanings. On the one hand, it might indicate that the giraffe is tall in relation to the scale of normal human experience. At the zoo, for instance, a father might say to his child *Look at that tall giraffe!* meaning only that the giraffe is tall relative to the things usually encountered by the child. The giraffe might actually be quite small as giraffes typically go, but to the child it looms quite large. On the other hand, a *tall giraffe* may be one that is tall *for a giraffe* (the kind of giraffe who would wind up playing basketball).

The component structures of *tall giraffe* are roughly sketched in figure 7.3. Being an adjective, *tall* profiles a nonprocessual relationship whose trajector is a thing and which lacks a focused landmark. Its trajector is characterized schematically as a physical entity with a salient vertical dimension when in its canonical orientation; thus we use it with respect to vertically aligned entities like people, buildings, mountains, trees, and flagpoles (but not, say, for snakes). The arrow represents a scale measuring degree of extension along the vertical axis from a horizontal surface

---

[3] In that case one would say *Je me lève la main* (literally, 'I raise me the hand').

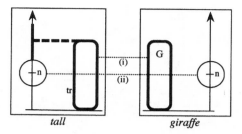

FIGURE 7.3

(usually the ground). Along this scale, the region labeled n comprises the range of values considered normal. The relationship profiled by *tall* is that of the trajector (when upright) projecting to some location beyond the scalar norm. As for the noun *giraffe*, I have basically just shown it as a thing with vertical alignment. Also shown is an arrow representing our knowledge that giraffes typically fall within a certain range (n) in regard to their height. The letter G stands for all the other specifications constituting the noun's encyclopedic meaning.

The two interpretations of *tall giraffe* do not stem from any difference in the meanings of the component structures but are, instead, a matter of how they are integrated, as seen in the diagram. Correspondence (i) represents the basic conceptual overlap defining the ADJ + N construction. If this is the only correspondence, no connection is made between the scales evoked by the adjective and by the noun. The height specified by *tall* can then be interpreted with respect to any norm that might suggest itself, the default being typical human experience. More likely, though, the adjectival norm will be identified with the characteristic height of giraffes in particular. Their identification is effected by correspondence (ii). This additional correspondence reflects a well-entrenched, conventionally established pattern for combining scalar adjectives with nouns. It is part of a constructional subschema that instantiates the schema describing the ADJ + N construction in general.

7.1.2 Redundancy and Inconsistency

Correspondence lines are a graphic indication of conceptual overlap. Component and composite structures can overlap to any extent, even completely. A case in point is the Luiseño example from the previous chapter, *Noonil 'owo'aquṣ* 'I was working'. Here the clitic =*nil* evokes no element not specified in as much or greater detail by the clausal component *noo 'owo'aquṣ*. The construction's semantic pole is roughly sketched in figure 7.4 (its phonological pole is given in figure 6.14). The clausal component profiles the specific process of working, represented as a solid arrow. Its trajector is identified by the subject pronoun *noo* as being the speaker (S), and the past durative suffix -*quṣ* places it prior to the time of speaking. The clitic =*nil* also evokes a process, but only schematically (hence the arrow representing it contains ellipses). It serves to identify the trajector as the speaker and to locate the process in the past. Thus all the basic elements of one component have counterparts in the other.

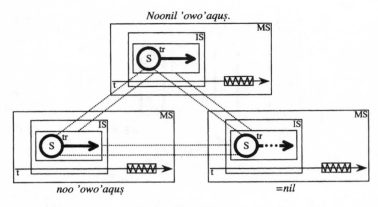

FIGURE 7.4

In particular, the specific process profiled by the clause corresponds to the schematic one profiled by the clitic.[4] This entails that the processual trajectors also correspond. The clitic, however, provides no information that is not also supplied by the clause, so when corresponding elements are superimposed to form the composite conception, the latter proves identical to the clausal component.

The clitic is thus redundant. Redundancy is not to be disparaged, for in one way or another every language makes extensive use of it. By providing the listener with extra clues, it helps ensure that a partially degraded message can still be understood. It allows the speaker to either emphasize a certain notion through repetition or to portray it from multiple perspectives. The second-position clitics of Luiseño exemplify the natural cognitive strategy of "zooming in" from general to particular. Anchored by the initial element, they "frame" the clause by introducing a schematic depiction of the profiled process, its central participant, and their relationship to the speech situation. By introducing a skeletal representation of the global situation, the clitics facilitate apprehension of the remaining clausal elements, which then flesh it out.

The redundancy afforded by grammatical elements is traditionally referred to as "agreement". The Luiseño clitics would thus be described as agreeing with the subject in person and number and with the inflected verb in tense. The traditional notion of agreement is highly problematic, however; often the "agreeing" elements have nothing to agree with or provide differing information about the entity characterized (Barlow 1992). CG takes another approach. The kinds of redundancy in question are not handled by "copying" information from one part of an expression to another, but simply as matters of multiple symbolization. That is, information about some entity is symbolized by more than one component structure within the same symbolic assembly and thus has multiple manifestations in a single complex expression. The representations of that entity (like the trajector in fig. 7.4) correspond to one another and map onto the same element in the composite conception.

---

[4] The inner boxes enclosing these processes are included just as a way of indicating that the processes participate as wholes in this correspondence.

So-called agreeing elements are therefore analyzed as making independent semantic contributions that happen to overlap with information provided elsewhere. Yet this overlap varies in extent, and sometimes the "agreeing" element is the only source of the information in question. In Luiseño, for example, a subject can be omitted, so in a sentence like (2) the clitic is the only element serving to identify the trajector. In this case each component structure evokes a highly schematic entity that the other specifies in greater detail. The clausal component *waxaam 'owo'aquṣ* evokes a schematic trajector which the clitic *=nil* identifies as the speaker. Conversely, the clitic evokes a schematic process which the clause identifies as that of working. When pieced together, the two component structures afford a full characterization of the profiled event.

(2) *Waxaam=nil* *'owo'a-quṣ.* 'Yesterday I was working.'

yesterday=1s:PAST work-PAST:DUR

When elements of two component structures correspond, they each correspond to the same composite-structure element, and each component structure provides some information about it. Often one characterization is schematic, the other specific. Usually the two are consistent and in some way complementary. But nothing guarantees this. Rather than complementing one another, two characterizations may be exactly equivalent, as for the trajector in the case of *noo* and *=nil* in *Noonil 'owo'aquṣ*. Nor does any divine or linguistic force prevent two characterizations from being inconsistent. For instance, a speaker of Luiseño might produce a sentence like (3), whether from inattention, some special motive, or sheer perversity. Here the subject pronoun and the clitic make contradictory specifications concerning the trajector: whereas *noo* describes it as first-person singular ('I'), the clitic *=chamil* specifies first-person plural ('we'). This is not a good sentence of Luiseño. But what exactly is the import of "good"?

(3) **Waxaam=chamil* *noo* *'owo'a-quṣ.* 'Yesterday {I/we} {was/were} working.'

yesterday=1p:PAST I work-PAST:DUR

Linguists mark such expressions with an asterisk and describe them as "ungrammatical" or "ill-formed". In most expressions so labeled, the problem turns out to be semantic inconsistency. Now inconsistency (like redundancy) has its uses. One can imagine special circumstances where a sentence like (3) might actually be employed to good effect.[5] But as they evolve through usage, the conventions of a language are shaped for communicative efficiency in typical situations, so in general they avoid the salient presentation of blatantly contradictory specifications. The conventions of Luiseño naturally reflect the usual situation of wanting to characterize the clausal trajector in a single, consistent manner. There are constructional schemas describing clauses in which a subject and a clitic are compatible in regard to the person and

---

[5] For instance, it might allow a speaker to subtly acknowledge having the psychiatric disorder of multiple personalities.

number of the trajector. There are none for cases where they are incompatible. A sentence like (3) is thus perceived as nonconventional ("ungrammatical") because it conflicts with the only schemas available to sanction it.

7.1.3 A Nonargument for Autonomy

Conformity to relevant constructional schemas does not itself guarantee that an expression is internally consistent semantically. A famous example is (4):

(4)   *Colorless green ideas sleep furiously.*

Chomsky (1957: 15) cited this sentence in arguing for the **autonomy** of syntax (§1.2.1)—that is, its independence from meaning. He claimed that (4) is perfectly well-formed grammatically despite its semantic incoherence. In terms of its grammar, (4) is precisely analogous to (5)(a). Conversely, we see from (5)(b) that a semantically impeccable expression can nonetheless be completely ungrammatical:

(5)   (a)   *Friendly young dogs bark harmlessly.*

     (b)   **Dogs harmlessly young bark friendly.* [with the meaning of (5)(a)]

It was thus concluded that grammar is properly described without essential reference to meaning.

    Critics of the autonomy thesis have tried to deny that (4) is semantically anomalous. They correctly point out that speakers try to make sense of seemingly incoherent expressions, and that this is not impossible, even in such extreme examples. For instance, *green* could be interpreted as meaning 'new, unproven, immature' (cf. *greenhorn, green banana*), and *colorless* as 'plain, uninteresting' (cf. *colorless personality*). Likewise, *sleep furiously* might conceivably describe a person clinging so tenaciously to sleep that all attempts to wake him are futile. One could then construe the sentence metaphorically as indicating that uninteresting new ideas remain dormant and resist all efforts to make them catch on.

    I believe, however, that such criticisms are beside the point. Chomsky is certainly correct that a sentence like (4) is semantically anomalous if each word is given its normal, default interpretation. And while the words do not then fit together to yield a coherent meaning, we can nonetheless recognize the sentence as being put together in accordance with regular syntactic patterns. Where Chomsky goes wrong is in claiming that this proves the autonomy of grammar. We can see this by observing that the facts are readily accommodated in CG, which—as a symbolic account of grammar—represents the antithesis of the autonomy thesis.

    The semantic sins committed in (4) are violations of **selectional restrictions**. *Green*, for instance, selects for the noun it modifies some physical entity capable of exhibiting color, but *ideas* fails to satisfy this restriction. It is thus sufficient to examine a single case of this sort (rather than tackling (4) in all its complexity). Consider the phrase *tall idea*. Now certainly we can give it a coherent interpretation. It might well be taken as referring to a "big", audacious idea (cf. *tall tale*). Relevant here,

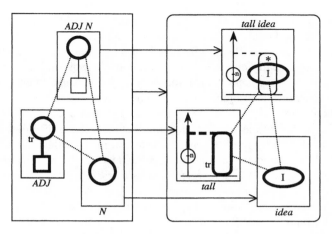

FIGURE 7.5

though, is the literal meaning, where each word is strictly understood in its most basic sense. So interpreted, *tall idea* is semantically anomalous.

In its strict, literal sense, the adjective *tall* characterizes its trajector as a physical entity that exists in space and has salient vertical extension in its canonical orientation. When *tall* modifies *idea*, a correspondence equates the adjectival trajector with the thing profiled by the noun, as shown on the right in figure 7.5. But an idea (I) is abstract, hence it does not exist in space and has no shape or spatial orientation (notationally, the ellipse is meant to indicate its amorphous, nonphysical nature). *Tall idea* is thus anomalous because the noun fails to satisfy the restrictions imposed by the adjective on its trajector. When corresponding elements are superimposed to form the composite semantic structure, their specifications clash instead of merging into a coherent conception—attempting their unification is like trying to fit an elliptical peg into a rectangular hole. An asterisk is added to the diagram to highlight this conceptual inconsistency.

Despite this semantic anomaly, *tall idea* is "grammatical". It follows the regular pattern by which adjectives modify nouns in English (e.g. *tall giraffe, good idea, green apple*). What this amounts to, in CG terms, is that *tall idea* instantiates the constructional schema describing that pattern. An adjective profiles a nonprocessual relationship with a thing as trajector but with no focused landmark. As shown on the left in figure 7.5, a correspondence identifies the adjectival trajector with the thing profiled by the noun, which is also profiled at the composite-structure level. Phonological integration consists of the adjective occurring directly before the noun. The diagram indicates that *tall idea* fully conforms to this schema. Examined individually, all the schema's specifications are satisfied: *tall* is an adjective, *idea* is a noun, the thing profiled by *idea* corresponds to *tall*'s trajector, it is also profiled by the composite structure, and *tall* directly precedes *idea*. Yet integrating an adjective and a noun in the manner specified by the schema does not itself guarantee that the lexemes chosen will be semantically compatible. As conventions for putting together complex expressions, constructional schemas are a critical resource for speaking and understanding. But they are not the only resource employed, and speakers cannot necessarily be trusted to use them in a conceptually coherent way.

Let us now return to the original examples. Sentence (5)(a) is fully grammatical and semantically coherent. It conforms to the appropriate constructional schemas, at both the semantic and phonological poles, and semantic integration in accordance with those schemas yields a consistent composite conception. The other two sentences are "ill-formed", albeit in different ways. On the one hand, sentence (4) is comparable to *tall idea*: grammatical in the sense that it conforms both semantically and phonologically to sanctioning schemas, yet conceptually incoherent when component elements are integrated in the manner they specify. On the other hand, (5)(b) is semantically well formed, on the assumption that it employs the same constructional schemas as (5)(a) and has the same composite meaning. Its blatant ungrammaticality stems from how the component structures are integrated phonologically. Words do not occur in the order specified by constructional schemas to symbolize their semantic integration (e.g. adjectives do not precede the nouns they modify).[6]

I conclude that the possibility of distinguishing between semantic anomaly and "ungrammaticality" fails to establish the autonomy of syntax. The contrast is straightforwardly handled in a symbolic account of grammar.

7.2 Profile Determinance

It is typical in constructions for the composite semantic structure to profile the same entity as one of the component structures. As a composite whole, for instance, *jar lid* profiles the same entity as *lid*: a *jar lid* is a kind of lid, not a kind of jar (fig. 6.3). Similarly, *jar lid factory* has the same profile as *factory* (fig. 6.5), and—despite its semantic anomaly—*tall idea* designates the idea, not the relationship profiled by the adjective (fig. 7.5). Metaphorically, we can say that the composite structure generally "inherits" its profile from a component structure. The component structure that "bequeathes" its profile to the composite structure is referred to in CG as the **profile determinant**.

The profile determinant is often indicated by using heavy lines for the box enclosing it. This notation is first employed in figure 7.6, showing the integration of the preposition *in* and the nominal *the closet* to form the prepositional phrase *in the closet*. The nominal component profiles a thing depicted as a rectangle, both to indicate its status as a location and to mnemonically represent its usual shape. The letter C abbreviates all its other semantic specifications (relation to a room, approximate size, storage function, and so on). No attempt is made at this stage to include the meaning of the definite article (see ch. 9). The preposition *in* profiles a simplex,

---

[6] For sake of completeness, we can note another kind of ill-formedness, in which an expression violates the specifications a constructional schema makes at its semantic pole. An example is **happily girl* (instead of *happy girl*). Here an adverb is used in lieu of the adjective specified by the constructional schema in fig. 7.5.

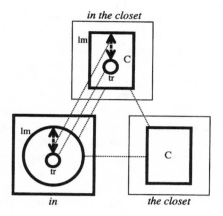

FIGURE 7.6

nonprocessual relationship between two things, typically one in which the trajector is spatially included in the landmark.[7] The nominal and the preposition are integrated through a correspondence between the profile of the former and the landmark of the latter. The heavy-line box indicates that the preposition functions as profile determinant in this construction. As a composite whole, *in the closet* designates a relationship of spatial inclusion, not the closet.

By calling attention to profile determinants, heavy-line boxes prove useful in dealing with complicated diagrams. A separate notation for this purpose is actually redundant, however. Profile determinance is based on other features of symbolic assemblies that are separately specified, namely profiling and correspondences. We can thus identify a profile determinant by examining component and composite structures, as well as the correspondences connecting them. By definition, the profile determinant is the component structure whose profile corresponds to the composite-structure profile. *Lid* is thus the profile determinant in *jar lid* because, as seen in figure 6.3, the profiles of *lid* and *jar lid* correspond (whereas neither corresponds to the profile of *jar*). From figure 7.6, we can tell that *in* functions as profile determinant because the relationship it profiles corresponds to the relationship profiled by *in the closet*.[8] Thus heavy-line boxes merely highlight an aspect of constructions which can be ascertained independently.

A construction's profile determinant is roughly equivalent to what is traditionally called a **head**. As most commonly defined, the head (at a given level of organization)

---

[7] This is at best an oversimplification, for even "spatial" prepositions have other dimensions to their semantic characterization, notably function. In the case of *in*, the landmark's function as a container for the trajector is arguably more fundamental than the purely spatial relationship (Vandeloise 1991, especially ch. 13).

[8] This is shown by correspondence lines connecting their trajectors, their landmarks, and the arrows representing the relationships. To keep diagrams simple, the latter correspondence is often omitted (e.g. in figs. 7.5 and 7.8). Corresponding participants are a consequence of a correspondence between two relationships and can thus be exploited as a shorthand way of indicating the correspondence.

is the component element that represents the same grammatical category as the composite expression.[9] The equivalence of head and profile determinant is then entailed by a basic claim of CG: that an expression's grammatical category is determined by the nature of its profile. From this it follows that a component element which bequeathes its profile to a composite expression thereby determines its grammatical category. Thus, in accordance with general CG principles, the notion head is defined conceptually with respect to the semantic pole of symbolic assemblies (rather than being an irreducible grammatical construct, as per the autonomy thesis).

Although it is usual for a single component structure to function as profile determinant, not every construction conforms to this prototype. Departures from the canonical arrangement fall into three broad categories: cases of **corresponding profiles**, **conflated profiles**, and **exocentricity**.

Illustrating the case of corresponding profiles are Luiseño clauses containing clitics, e.g. *Noonil 'owo'aquş* 'I was working'. In figure 7.4, we see that both the clause and the clitic profile a process—respectively, the specific process of the speaker working in the past and the schematic process evoked by the clitic. A pivotal feature of this construction is the identification of these two processes: the clause and the clitic offer specific and schematic characterizations of what, in referential terms, is precisely the same occurrence. Because the component-structure profiles correspond to one another, they each correspond to the composite-structure profile. Hence there is no basis for singling out either one as profile determinant to the exclusion of the other.

Another such example is nominal **apposition**, involving the juxtaposition of two expressions each of which profiles a thing. There are various patterns of nominal apposition. The two component structures can be simple nouns, as in *pussycat*, or full nominals, as in *Billy the Kid*, *my son the doctor*, and *our good friend Hillary Clinton*. In one such pattern, exemplified by *his strange belief that chickens are immortal*, the second nominal represents the conceptual reification of a clause. Here the reified proposition expressed by the second component (*that chickens are immortal*) constitutes the very belief profiled by the first (*his strange belief*). The details distinguishing these various constructions do not presently concern us. What matters is that they all instantiate the abstract configuration in figure 7.7: both component structures profile things, and their profiles correspond, so both correspond to the composite-structure profile. Hence the composite expression designates a single entity characterized by two sets of semantic specifications (X and Y). But since both component-structure profiles correspond to this entity, which component is the head?

The issue posed by corresponding profiles is largely terminological. Faced with the configuration of figure 7.4 or figure 7.7, we might want to say that both component structures are heads, since each of their profiles corresponds to the composite-structure profile. Alternatively, because neither component-structure profile does so exclusively, we might want to say that neither component is a head. The choice is

---

[9] Alternatively, a head is defined as a lexical element that provides an overall expression's essential semantic content. The two definitions sometimes conflict. In the progressive *be playing*, for example, *be* determines the category of the overall expression (imperfective verb), but the "lexical head" is *play* (a perfective verb).

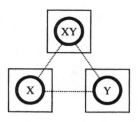

FIGURE 7.7

immaterial. Somewhat arbitrarily, I follow the second course and reserve the term "profile determinant" for instances where just a single component structure has the same profile as the composite structure.

An analogous terminological question arises in cases of conflated profiles. These are cases where the composite-structure profile is not identified with that of any single component structure, taken individually, but rather with the more complex entity obtained by conflating them. Thus, while each component-structure profile corresponds to some facet of the composite-structure profile, only collectively do they match it as a whole. Should we then say that all the components function as profile determinants, or that none of them does? Once more I take the second option.

An example of this sort is the nested locative construction (previously discussed in §3.4.2). Sentence (6) locates its trajector by successively "zooming in" to smaller and smaller areas. Each locative element places the trajector within a restricted location, which the next locative takes as the immediate scope for its interpretation. In this path of search, *upstairs* confines the trajector to the upper story of a house. The following locative, *in the bedroom*, is interpreted relative to this location—only upstairs bedrooms are relevant—and the definite article implies that there is only one. Only this bedroom is invoked for interpreting *in the closet*, and only the bedroom closet for *on the shelf*.

(6)   *Your camera is upstairs, in the bedroom, in the closet, on the shelf.*

To keep things simple, we will limit our attention to the last two locatives. We must therefore consider how *in the closet* and *on the shelf* are integrated to form a complex locative expression. This is sketched in figure 7.8, where the two component structures are the composite structures of the respective prepositional phrases. *In the closet* profiles a relationship of spatial inclusion (fig. 7.6). *On the shelf* profiles a relationship in which the trajector makes contact with the upper surface of a shelf, which supports it. In the context of an overall expression like (6), it is pertinent to represent both the immediate spatial scope (IS) and the maximal scope (MS). For each prepositional phrase, the profiled relationship is manifested within a restricted scope of attention (the "onstage" region) selected from a larger spatial setting.

Two correspondences are responsible for the integration of component structures. First, their trajectors correspond. The same entity—in (6), the camera—is located both in the (upstairs bedroom) closet and on the shelf. A second correspondence accounts for the "zooming in" effect of nested locatives. It needs to specify that the

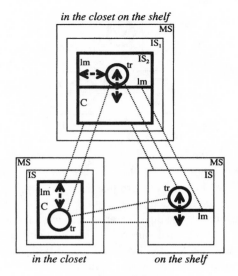

FIGURE 7.8

area to which the first component confines its trajector functions as the immediate scope for interpreting the second locative. The first locative, *in the closet*, confines the trajector to the closet's interior, which is essentially coextensive with the closet itself. This region is thus connected by a correspondence line to the box representing the immediate spatial scope of *on the shelf*. As a consequence, the composite structure shows two nested immediate scopes, reflecting the successive loci of attention for the two component structures. IS_1 is the immediate scope imposed by *in the closet*, and within it, IS_2 is the immediate scope for *on the shelf*.

In a complex locative of this sort, what does the composite structure profile? It would be both arbitrary and counterintuitive to claim that it designates either component structure relationship to the exclusion of the other. Instead, the profiled relationship is itself complex, representing the conflation of the component relations. The trajector is located simultaneously with respect to two landmarks, the closet and the shelf.[10] By itself, then, neither component has the same profile as the composite expression. Each component structure profile corresponds to a single facet of the conflated profile observed at the composite-structure level. Thus neither component structure is singled out as profile determinant.

There is one more type of situation where a profile determinant cannot be identified. This is the case of constructions in which neither component-structure profile corresponds to the composite-structure profile. In traditional terminology, expressions of this sort are said to be **exocentric**. The term is appropriate, for it indicates that the "center" (i.e. the composite expression's profile) is "external" (not being profiled by either component).

---

[10] In sentence (6) as a whole, the camera's position is specified by a complex locative with four component relationships and four landmarks.

A simple illustration is the compound *pickpocket*. It is one instance of a compounding pattern (some others being *scarecrow, breakwater, killjoy, cureall, turnkey,* and *spoilsport*) in which the two components are a verb and a noun corresponding to its landmark (cf. Tuggy 2003b). *Pick* has various meanings, but in this compound it profiles an action of removing something from a location (cf. *pick up*). Figure 7.9 thus shows the trajector exerting force (double arrow) to induce this motion (single arrow). Relevant here is a more specific sense, in which the original location (given as a box) is focused as the landmark.[11] A *pocket* is a kind of location. In the diagram, small and large circles respectively indicate the contents of the pocket and the article of clothing it is a part of. Correspondences identify the pocket with the landmark of *pick*, and its contents with the object removed.

It is normal in English for the second element of a compound to function as profile determinant. This is the case for the $[[N_1] - [N_2]]$ compounds considered earlier (e.g. *jar lid*), representing the basic pattern, and also for $[[ADJ] - [N]]$ compounds (e.g. *blueberry, happy face, Big Bird*). $[[V] - [N]]$ compounds are exceptional in this regard: a *pickpocket* is not a pocket, and a *scarecrow* is not a crow. Nor do they designate the process profiled by the verb. So neither component structure imposes its profile at the composite-structure level. Instead, the composite expression designates the actor: a *pickpocket* is a person who picks pockets, while a *scarecrow* supposedly scares crows. Even though the composite-structure profile is not inherited from either component, its choice follows a regular pattern, consistently corresponding to the verb's trajector. Their correspondence is therefore specified in the constructional schema for $[[V] - [N]]$ compounds. This is not to say that these expressions are fully compositional. Indeed, the composite forms derive their specific import from cognitive domains (e.g. the practice of picking pockets) not evoked by either component structure individually.

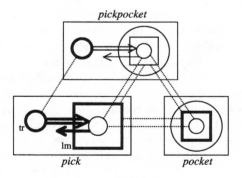

FIGURE 7.9

---

[11] This sense of *pick* is also found in expressions like the following: *Buzzards had picked the bones clean; He was picking his teeth with a knife; Don't pick your nose!; There wasn't much left on the bargain shelf—shoppers had pretty much picked it over.* The action is normally one of probing with the tip of an elongated instrument (like a beak, fingers, or tooth**pick**).

7.3 Elaboration

The structures constituting a symbolic assembly are linked by both correspondences and categorizing relationships. We have so far emphasized correspondences, and secondarily the categorizing relationships between component and composite structures. The latter define an expression's compositional path at either pole. What we have not yet considered in any detail are the categorizing relationships that link component structures to one another.

7.3.1 Elaboration Sites

It is typical in a construction for one component structure to contain a schematic substructure which the other component serves to **elaborate**, i.e. characterize in finer-grained detail. In *jar lid*, for example, *lid* evokes a schematic container specified in finer detail by *jar* (figs. 6.3 and 6.4). Similarly, *giraffe* elaborates the schematic trajector of *tall* in *tall giraffe* (fig. 7.3), and *pocket* the landmark of *pick* in *pickpocket* (fig. 7.9). A schematic element elaborated by another component is called an **elaboration site**, or **e-site** for short.

 As in the case of profile determinants, it is useful to mark e-sites explicitly, even though such marking is actually redundant in fully described assemblies. The notation adopted here is hatching, as shown in figure 7.10. Diagram (a) represents the component structures in a prepositional phrase construction, such as *in the closet* (fig. 7.6). The preposition profiles a nonprocessual relationship between two things, and a correspondence equates its landmark with the profile of the following nominal. The box with hatching identifies the landmark as an e-site. Only schematic within the preposition itself, this element is specified in finer detail by the nominal component. The solid arrow indicates that this schematic substructure categorizes the other component in a relationship of elaboration.

 Observe that the correspondence line in diagram (a) connects two circles, while the arrow for elaboration runs between two boxes. The reason for the difference is that correspondence pertains to conceptual **reference**, whereas elaboration is a matter of **characterization**. On the one hand, the correspondence line indicates that the prepositional landmark and the nominal profile refer to the same entity: they are two manifestations of a single entity in the composite conception. On the other hand, the boxes represent the total information provided about the corresponding entities—the conceptual **base** evoked for their characterization, within which they stand out as profiles. Referentially, it is specifically the nominal profile that is identified with the preposition's landmark, but the entire conceptual base of the nominal contributes to

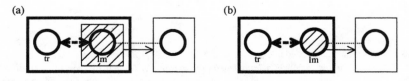

FIGURE 7.10

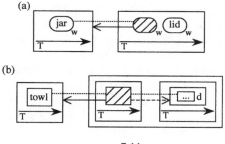

FIGURE 7.11

the landmark's description. From the standpoint of diagrammatic clarity, however, it is sometimes awkward to include a separate box representing the elaboration site. The notation in diagram (b) is thus employed for abbreviatory purposes.

Elaboration and elaboration sites can also be recognized at the phonological pole. Two examples are given in figure 7.11. Diagram (a) shows the phonological integration of *jar* and *lid* in *jar lid* (cf. fig. 6.2(b)). Part of the overall characterization of every word is its potential for preceding and following other words, which can thus be invoked as e-sites. In this construction, the word preceding *lid* functions as an e-site, which *jar* elaborates. Diagram (b) depicts the integration of *toll* and *-ed* in the past-tense form *tolled* (cf. fig. 6.11(e)). The representation of *-ed* reflects an essential feature in the characterization of an affix: it inherently makes schematic reference to a stem and specifies how that stem is modified by adding segmental material. Here the schematic stem evoked by *-ed* is an e-site elaborated by *toll*.

7.3.2 Autonomy and Dependence

Elaboration sites point to a fundamental aspect of linguistic organization. They indicate that certain structures, by their very nature, do not stand alone but require the support of others—they are **dependent** on other, more **autonomous** structures for their own manifestation. Thus dependent structures cannot be described independently, in their own terms, but only in relation to the autonomous structures that support them. As a consequence, a dependent structure refers schematically to an autonomous, supporting structure as an intrinsic aspect of its own characterization. This schematic substructure functions as an e-site when the dependent structure combines with an autonomous one.

The asymmetry between autonomous and dependent components, referred to as **A/D-alignment**, is a general feature of language design. It is found in both unipolar and bipolar organization, at both the semantic and the phonological poles. In the case of unipolar phonological organization, an obvious example is a prosodic element like tone or stress, which requires the support of segmental content for its manifestation (one cannot put high tone or primary stress on silence). At the segmental level, vowels are autonomous and consonants in the same syllable are dependent on them. The autonomous, self-contained nature of vowels allows them to occur independently as full syllables. Consonants, on the other hand, consist primarily in modulating or interrupting the sonority provided by vowels and thus require the support of vowels to be fully manifested and clearly perceived. The stem/affix distinction exemplifies A/D-alignment in the case of bipolar phonological organization. Stems and affixes both consist of sound segments, and the same segment or segment sequence can function in either capacity. What distinguishes them is that a stem is autonomous, and thus potentially stands alone, whereas an affix intrinsically makes reference to a stem, as seen in figure 7.11(b).[12] More obviously dependent are morphemes that actually change the segmental composition of a stem, e.g. the symbolization of past tense by changing *sit* to *sat* (fig. 6.11(a)). It is only in relation to the vowel that would otherwise be expected that the vowel of *sat* has symbolizing function.

At the semantic pole, a prime example of unipolar A/D-alignment is the distinction between things and relationships. For typical cases (and with certain oversimplifications), we can say that things are conceptually autonomous and relationships are dependent. It is possible for a physical entity (e.g. a rock, a table, or a cat) to be conceptualized in and of itself, without its relationship to other objects being invoked in any crucial or salient way. By contrast, a relationship is conceptually dependent on its participants. For example, we cannot conceptualize a spatial relation (like *on*, *under*, or *near*) without to some extent (if only schematically) invoking the entities that participate in it. As the term suggests, apprehending a relationship resides in conceiving entities in relation to one another. Thus it does not exist independently of those entities.

Our main interest lies with A/D-alignment in bipolar semantic organization, at the semantic pole of grammatical constructions. Here a component structure is said to elaborate whatever schematic portion of the other component its profile corresponds to. Thus in figure 7.10, representing the prepositional object construction, the nominal component elaborates the preposition's landmark. Since a landmark is salient as a matter of definition, and the object nominal specifies it in finer-grained detail, the preposition is dependent with respect to its object. This nominal is generally autonomous with respect to the preposition. It does not feel conceptually "incomplete" if used in some way other than as a prepositional object.

Thus, in a prepositional phrase like *near the door*, the component structure *near* is dependent with respect to the more autonomous component *the door*, which elaborates its schematic landmark. But can we not also say that *near* elaborates *the door*, since *near the door* represents a more detailed and elaborate conception than just *the door*? Certainly we can. Part of our encyclopedic knowledge of doors is that, as physical entities, they participate in spatial relationships with other such entities. *Near* can therefore be taken as instantiating this schematic specification. These two elaborative relationships are depicted in figure 7.12. *Near* locates its trajector somewhere in the landmark's neighborhood, given as an ellipse. Diagram (a) shows its landmark being elaborated by *the door*. Conversely, diagram (b) shows *near* elaborating a schematic locative relationship implicit in the meaning of the nominal.

---

[12] The crucial factor is whether one element makes intrinsic reference to the other, not whether it actually occurs independently. On this basis, a stem can be distinguished from an affix even when it never occurs in unaffixed form. Likewise, vowels are autonomous vis-à-vis consonants even in languages where the minimal syllabic form is CV, so that a vowel never stands alone as a syllable.

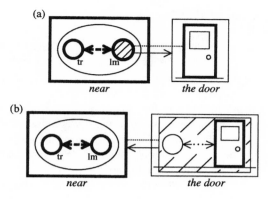

FIGURE 7.12

These two elaborative relationships are not equal in status, however. They differ in both the salience of the e-site and the extent to which the other component elaborates it. The e-site of *near* is highly salient (the landmark being a focused participant) and quite schematic relative to *the door*. By contrast, the e-site ascribed to *the door* is rather peripheral to its semantic characterization. The spatial relationships that a door bears to other objects are not part of the nominal profile and may not even come to mind in using the expression. Moreover, the degree of elaboration effected by *near* is somewhat limited. Although the *near* relationship per se is more specific than the one implicit in the nominal, the latter is more specific in regard to the landmark. The example is not untypical. Each component structure can usually be thought of as elaborating something evoked at least potentially by the other. To some extent, therefore, each component structure is dependent on the other. Yet there tends to be a marked asymmetry, such that the dependence in one direction is stronger and more clearly evident. In the case at hand, *near* is more strongly dependent on *the door* than conversely.

A/D-alignment is thus a relative matter. One structure is dependent on another to the extent that the latter elaborates a salient substructure within it. The key notions here are **salience** and **elaboration**, both of which are matters of degree. When, based on these factors, the degree of dependence is substantially greater in one direction than the other, we can reasonably simplify by focusing just on that direction. If a construction were a trial, a jury given these instructions would render the judgment "dependent" for *near* and "autonomous" for *the door*, based on the preponderance of evidence. But some trials result in hung juries. In many cases the component structures exhibit little or no A/D-asymmetry, either because each is dependent on the other to a significant extent or because both are largely autonomous.

Illustrating bidirectional dependence are Luiseño sentences like (2), *Waxaamnil 'owo'aquş* 'Yesterday I was working'. In one direction, the clausal component *waxaam 'owo'aquş* 'yesterday...was working' depends on the clitic to specify its schematic trajector. It is identified as being the speaker by the initial segment of *=nil*. However, as shown in figure 7.4, the clitic itself invokes a schematic process elaborated by the clausal component (except in regard to its trajector). While on balance the clitic is more highly dependent, its elaboration of the clausal trajector is hardly trivial.[13]

A case where the judgment hangs in balance, there being no preponderance of evidence, is the phonological pole of a compound like *jar lid*. In figure 7.11(a), *jar* was shown as elaborating the word schematically evoked by *lid* as the one preceding it. The choice, though, is arbitrary. *Lid* could just as well have been shown as elaborating the schematic word following *jar*. Although the degree of elaboration in the two directions is equal and quite substantial, neither component is strongly dependent on the other, owing to the salience factor. A word is phonologically autonomous, capable of being pronounced in isolation as a self-contained whole. Moreover, since words like *jar* and *lid* are not limited to any particular grammatical environment, they are phonologically independent in bipolar terms as well. Thus it cannot be said that a preceding or a following word is a salient feature of their phonological description. The elaboration site shown in the diagram reflects an aspect of the "encyclopedic" characterization of words: the background information that words are strung together in sequences and can therefore precede and follow other words. The e-site's nonsalience has the consequence that the extent to which either *jar* or *lid* is dependent on the other is fairly minor. Both are largely autonomous.

7.3.3 Complement and Modifier

To appreciate the grammatical significance of A/D-alignment, we can best start by considering a typical example. Figure 7.13 depicts the semantic pole of the nominal expression *a table near the door* (still ignoring articles, for the time being).[14]

At the lower level of organization, *the door* elaborates the landmark of *near* to form the prepositional phrase *near the door. The door* is thus autonomous, and *near* is dependent. Since the composite structure inherits its profile, *near* is the profile determinant. At the higher level of organization, *(a) table* elaborates the trajector of *near the door* to derive the full expression. The former is thus autonomous and the latter dependent. At this level *table* functions as profile determinant, since the overall expression designates the table (rather than the spatial relationship).

In traditional terminology, *near* and *table* function as **heads** at their respective levels of organization. At the lower level, *the door* is said to be a **complement** of *near*; at the higher level, *near the door* is a **modifier** with respect to *table*. The descriptive utility of these notions implies, from the CG perspective, that they must have conceptual characterizations. We have seen that a head is a profile determinant, characterized in terms of a typical feature of symbolic assemblies: that of a component structure profile corresponding to the composite structure profile. The notions complement and modifier are likewise definable with reference to symbolic

---

[13] The clitic is more highly dependent because the clause elaborates the schematic process to a greater extent than the clitic elaborates the schematic trajector (i.e. the clause provides far more detailed information). Also, the clausal trajector is specified only by the first element of the clitic (*n* marks first-person singular), whereas the clause combines grammatically with the clitic as a whole.

[14] I take no position on whether the indefinite article combines directly with *table* (as shown here) or with the complex expression *table near the door.*

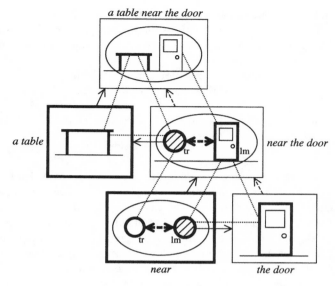

FIGURE 7.13

assemblies. Each represents a commonly observed configuration in which the head participates in an elaborative relation with the other component structure. The difference between them resides in the direction of elaboration, as shown in figure 7.14. A complement is a component structure that **elaborates** a salient substructure of the head. The head is thus dependent, and the complement is autonomous. Conversely, a modifier is a component structure that contains a salient substructure **elaborated by** the head. In this case the head is autonomous, and the modifier is dependent.

By these definitions, *the door* is a complement in figure 7.13, since *near* is the head and *the door* elaborates its landmark. At the higher level, *near the door* is a modifier because its trajector is elaborated by the head noun *table*. The definitions extend straightforwardly to other standard instances of complement and modifier constructions. In a phrase like *tall giraffe* (fig. 7.3), *tall* is said to modify *giraffe*. This is so because the noun is the head and elaborates the adjective's trajector. Like the object of a preposition, the object of a verb is a complement, since the verb functions as head and the nominal elaborates its landmark (fig. 7.1). It is unproblematic

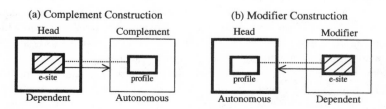

FIGURE 7.14

that the definitions extend to cases the terms are usually not applied to.[15] The CG strategy is not to adopt traditional notions uncritically, but rather to offer explicit conceptual characterizations that preserve their valid insights while avoiding their limitations.

The status of an element as a complement or a modifier plays a role in many grammatical phenomena. As a simple case, consider the following contrast:

(7)   (a) *He tried to annoy his mother.*   [complement construction]

    (b) *He cried to annoy his mother.*   [modifier construction]

While the two sentences seem quite parallel, there is one crucial difference: the infinitival clause *to annoy his mother* functions as complement with respect to *try* but as a modifier with respect to *cry*. It is a complement of *try* because it specifies a schematic activity essential to the meaning of this verb, the target toward which the subject's effort is directed. By contrast, *cry* designates a typically spontaneous emotional reaction; conscious effort to achieve a purpose is not inherent in its meaning. Sentence (7)(b) does indicate that the crying is intended to annoy the mother, but this does not reflect the meaning of the verb; rather, it manifests a grammatical construction in which an infinitival clause expresses the purpose for an action. *To annoy his mother* is thus an adverbial modifier of the clausal nucleus *he cried*, which specifies that action. One consequence of the complement/modifier distinction in such examples pertains to word order. As seen in (8), the infinitival clause can readily occur in sentence-initial position when it functions as a modifier, but hardly as a complement.

(8)   (a) **To annoy his mother he tried.*   [preposed complement]

    (b) *To annoy his mother he cried.*   [preposed modifier]

Not every construction involves a complement or a modifier. Though typical, the configurations in figure 7.14 are just two of the varied forms symbolic assemblies can assume. As defined, for example, a complement or modifier only has that status in relation to a head. The terms are thus not applicable in constructions that lack a profile determinant, such as nominal apposition (fig. 7.7) and nested locatives (fig. 7.8). They are also not applicable when neither component structure contains a salient substructure corresponding to the other's profile. One such case is *go away angry*, in which a complex verb combines with an adjective. Their integration is sketched in figure 7.15.

Go away designates an event in which the trajector moves out of an original location that serves as a point of reference (R). The bar along the time arrow indicates sequential scanning of the profiled process. *Angry* profiles an atemporal relationship in which the trajector exhibits a certain emotional state (a). Being nonprocessual, this relationship is not profiled in its evolution through time. The conceptual base for *angry* does, however, include the specification that this emotion typically occurs in episodes of limited duration. An unfilled bar represents the time span of one such episode. *Go away* and *angry* are integrated by means of two correspondences. First, their trajectors correspond: the

---

[15] In *jar lid*, for instance, *jar* is a complement to *lid* (fig. 6.3). Why? By now it should be evident.

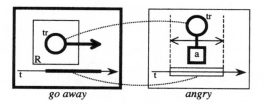

FIGURE 7.15

person who goes away is also the person who is angry. Second, the time spans correspond: the episode of anger is coextensive with (or at least includes) the time of leaving. *Go away* is the head, since the composite expression is processual.

In this expression, *angry* is neither a complement nor a modifier with respect to *go away*, for neither elaborates a salient substructure within the other. While we know that a person who goes away may well do so while in a certain emotional state, this is quite peripheral to the meaning of the verb, which would generally not evoke it independently. Nor is spatial motion central to the meaning of *angry*, although we certainly know that a person in this state is usually capable of it. A component structure which, like *angry*, fails to either elaborate the head or be elaborated by it is sometimes called an **adjunct**.

Although CG is able to characterize traditional grammatical notions like head, adjunct, complement, and modifier, these terms are not themselves the basic units of CG description. They are more accurately thought of as convenient labels for certain kinds of configurations commonly observable at the semantic pole of symbolic assemblies. Thus it is not expected that every construction will have a head, or that every component structure combining with a head will be clearly and uniquely identifiable as a complement or a modifier. Like the factors defining them, these latter notions are matters of degree and are not mutually exclusive.

7.4 Constituency

Constituency is a fundamental construct in both traditional grammar and modern syntactic theory. It is also recognized in CG and readily accommodated. However, CG has a very different take on the nature of constituency, as well as its role in language structure.

7.4.1 Two Conceptions of Constituency

Syntacticians generally describe constituency by positing fixed hierarchical structures that are metaphorically conceived as inverted "trees". Styles change and details vary, but in one classic format the nominal *a table near the door* might have the tree representation in figure 7.16.[16]

---

[16] This is the counterpart of fig. 7.13, which however does not show the decomposition of *a table* and *the door* into article plus noun. NP stands for **noun phrase**, a standard but infelicitous term that CG replaces with **nominal**.

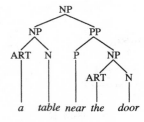

FIGURE 7.16

In theories assuming the autonomy of grammar, these tree structures are conceived as purely syntactic objects, with no intrinsic semantic or phonological content. While the trees play a role in semantic and phonological "interpretation", based on the content supplied by the lexical items "inserted" into them, syntactic structure per se is seen as a separate level of representation distinct from both semantics and phonology. CG is more highly constrained; owing to the content requirement (§1.3.4), it cannot posit autonomous syntactic objects of this sort. Nor are they necessary. An account of grammar based solely on symbolic assemblies proves not only adequate but more revealing.

Syntactic tree structures represent three kinds of information: grammatical category (through labels like N, P, NP, etc.), "linear order" (left to right on the page), and constituency (hierarchical grouping). All of these are also provided by the symbolic assemblies of CG.

Information concerning category membership is intrinsic to the semantic pole of each symbolic structure in an assembly. It inheres in the nature of the profile. Depending on the profile, a symbolic structure instantiates one or another class schema defined primarily on this basis, e.g. [[[THING]/[...]] → [[JAR]/[jar]]]. Recall that schemas are **immanent** in their instantiations even when, for analytical purposes, they are shown separately.

Information concerning linear order is intrinsic to the phonological pole of each symbolic structure. "Linear order" is actually temporal order, the sequencing of elements in the flow of speech. Time is a basic dimension of phonological structure and is thus inherent in its characterization, even when left implicit in diagrams. When it is shown explicitly, as in figure 6.3, time is represented by an arrow labeled T.[17]

---

[17] Observe that such arrows are placed at the phonological pole of each symbolic structure in an assembly, both component and composite structures. Time and temporal sequencing are aspects of a symbolic structure's own internal characterization at any level. It is thus at the composite-structure level that temporal ordering is specified for the elements in a complex expression. To ascertain their ordering from a diagram, one must therefore look at the composite structure's phonological pole—it is not indicated by the placement of component structures relative to one another on the page. Of course, it does facilitate the reading of diagrams if component structures are arranged left to right in a way that mirrors their phonological sequencing. But that is not essential, and sometimes diagrammatic convenience dictates otherwise. In fig. 6.13(b), for instance, a simpler diagram results from placing *big dog* on the left and *the* on the right, despite their being pronounced in the opposite order: *th'big dog*.

Constituency is observed in symbolic assemblies when a composite structure at one level of organization functions in turn as component structure with respect to a higher level. Though it plays a role in grammar, it is quite wrong to suppose that constituency is solely or even primarily a grammatical phenomenon. It is simply one manifestation of hierarchical organization, evident in virtually every realm of human functioning. It is evident, for example, in perceptual grouping (fig. 4.5), in the apprehension of whole-part hierarchies (body > arm > hand > finger > knuckle), in hierarchical categorization (thing → object → vehicle → truck → pickup truck), in planning a complex endeavor (with goals, subgoals, sub-subgoals, etc.), in dealing with collections of different sizes (army > division > brigade > batallion > company > platoon > soldier), and even in complex motor routines (decomposable into subroutines, sub-subroutines, and so on). What these share is the capacity to operate at multiple levels of organization, where a single entity at one level in some way arises from multiple entities at another level.

All the information provided by tree structures is thus inherent in symbolic assemblies. From the standpoint of CG, extracting this information and presenting it separately as an autonomous formal object is not just superfluous but a kind of gerrymandering. Of course, in their hierarchical arrangement, symbolic assemblies like figure 7.13 do resemble syntactic tree structures. Nevertheless, the two are quite different in their fundamental nature: whereas each structure in an assembly has both a semantic and a phonological pole, the "nodes" in a tree structure (NP, P, PP, etc.) are seen as purely grammatical elements with no intrinsic semantic or phonological value. A further difference is that syntactic constituency is considered a basic and invariant aspect of grammatical description, so that a particular kind of expression should always be assigned the same, definite tree structure. In CG, on the other hand, constituency is viewed as flexible, variable, and nonessential. Rather than being basic to grammatical description, "classic" constituency hierarchies like figure 7.16 emerge from other phenomena and represent just one of the configurations that symbolic assemblies can assume (GC: ch. 5).

Specifically, "classic constituents" represent the special situation where a particular kind of conceptual grouping is symbolized by a particular kind of phonological grouping. The conceptual grouping is that of two component structures being integrated through correspondences involving salient substructures (notably profile, trajector, and landmark). The phonological grouping is based on temporal contiguity, the component structures being adjacent in the flow of speech. The groups arising in this fashion—the composite semantic and phonological structures—may themselves participate in further grouping at a higher level of organization. When this occurs at multiple levels, the phonological grouping in each case symbolizing the semantic grouping, it results in configurations of the sort represented in standard syntactic tree structures like figure 7.16.

7.4.2 Limitations of the Classic View

It may be that classic constituents have a privileged status owing to their prevalence and the obvious nature of the factors invoked as the basis for grouping. If so, it must still be recognized that there are numerous dimensions of semantic and phonological organization, as well as various grounds for grouping elements and delimiting structures of different sizes. The same semantic and phonological content can thus be grouped and organized in alternate ways that are incommensurate yet simultaneously valid. Hence there are more facets to the structure of a complex expression than can be represented in any one constituency hierarchy.

We have seen, for example, that unipolar and bipolar organization present two dimensions of composition that cannot be conflated in a single hierarchical structure (fig. 6.12). Beyond this, unipolar and bipolar organization are themselves multifaceted. For unipolar structure, I will merely note in passing the need to distinguish, at the phonological pole, between prosody and segmental composition. With respect to bipolar organization, let us briefly consider two aspects of linguistic structure usually excluded from "grammar" in the narrow sense: lexical units and focus. They represent symbolically motivated groupings that often cross-cut the constituency hierarchies posited in syntactic analysis.

Lexical items are fixed expressions, familiar to speakers and conventional in the speech community. Most are symbolically complex. I point out in §1.3.2 that lexical units need not coincide with syntactic constituents, and, indeed, the elements constituting them need not even be adjacent. One example is the sequence *take it for granted that*, which is certainly an established unit with its own global meaning.[18] While this lexical unit is arguably a syntactic constituent in (9)(a), if we take it as including schematic reference to the clause introduced by *that*, it cannot be one in (9)(b), where its elements are noncontiguous:

(9)   (a) *Most commentators **take it for granted** [**that** money is the primary source of political influence].*

    (b) ***It** has been **taken** more or less **for granted** by most commentators [**that** money is the primary source of political influence].*

This lexeme represents a coherent conceptual grouping whose components are linked by correspondences at the semantic pole and are individually symbolized by phonological elements. It is thus a symbolic assembly, entirely defined by semantic structures, phonological structures, and symbolic links between the two, even though—in its most general description—the phonological components do not form a group based on temporal adjacency. Though symbolic in nature, this lexical unit is delimited on the basis of entrenchment and conventionality in a way that cross-cuts classic constituency hierarchies.

Similar in this respect is focus, one aspect of information structure (§3.2.1). Very roughly speaking (and most descriptions are pretty rough), an expression's focus is that portion of it which the speaker wishes to foreground as a significant departure from what has already been established in the immediately preceding discourse.

---

[18] It is of course decomposable into smaller meaningful structures—notably *take...for granted* (cf. *You've been taking me for granted!*) and an independent construction involving *it* and a *that*-clause (e.g. *I resent it that he treats us so badly*). This is perfectly consistent with the entire sequence being established as a unit in its own right.

In English, nonfocused elements tend to be reduced in stress, so that the focus stands out phonologically by virtue of having full, unreduced stress (indicated here by small caps). For instance, the first sentence in (10) provides a discourse context with (a) and (b) as possible continuations. The focus in (a) is *likes*, since the other elements are merely restatements of what has just been said. In (b), the focus consists of *sister* and *coffee*, for both elements stand out as being new and significant.

(10)   *My mother puts orange juice on her cereal.*

   (a)   *She LIKES it that way.*

   (b)   *My SISTER puts it in her COFFEE.*

The focus in cases like (b) is not a syntactic constituent in the classic sense. It is none-theless a symbolic structure recognized in CG as one facet of an expression's gram-matical organization. At the semantic pole, its component elements form a group apprehended as such because they collectively constitute what is new and significant in the discourse. At the phonological pole, they are grouped on the basis of unreduced stress. This distinguishing phonological property (pertaining to prosody) symbolizes the distinguishing conceptual property (pertaining to information structure).[19] While structures delimited in this fashion tend to coincide with syntactic constituents of the classic sort, there is no reason to expect that they would always do so.

Hence the structures and relationships captured in a constituency hierarchy of the sort depicted in figures 7.13 and 7.16 tell only part of the story. Though central and essential, they are by no means exhaustive of the semantic, phonological, and symbolic structures that need to be described in a complete account of linguistic structure. These can all be accommodated in CG, within the limits imposed by the content requirement. Permitted by this requirement are semantic and phonological groupings of any size, effected on any basis, and delimited in any way. Semantic and phonological structures representing any level or dimension of organization can be linked to form symbolic structures. Further permitted are categorizing relationships (both syntagmatic and paradigmatic), giving rise to assemblies of structures. Out of the broad spectrum of structures and relationships thus afforded, classic constituency hierarchies emerge as a special case.

When they do emerge, such hierarchies do not themselves incorporate every semantic, phonological, and symbolic structure that figures in an expression's full characterization. They do not represent focus, for example. They also fail to accommodate semantic structures that happen not to be individually symbolized. For instance, while both sentences in (9) invoke the global meaning of the lexical unit *take it for granted that*, in (9)(b) there is no phonological structure serving to symbolize this lexical meaning as a unitary whole. Classic constituency hierarchies

---

[19] Their relationship is both iconic and symbolic, for at each pole the focused elements stand out from the background with respect to a natural dimension of prominence (loudness or informativeness). While they are often excluded or marginalized, CG considers prosody and information structure to be integral parts of phonology and semantics. Likewise, symbolic structures based on them are integral parts of grammar.

are further problematic in cases where phonological integration is not effected by juxtaposition in the temporal sequence. An example from Luiseño is the integration of a clitic with a clause, where the clitic neither precedes nor follows the clause but occurs inside it (fig. 6.14).

7.4.3 Grammatical Relationships

In theories of autonomous syntax, constituency is commonly invoked for the representation of basic grammatical relationships. Prime examples are the **subject** and **object** relations. In an early and well-known account (Chomsky 1965), these notions were defined in terms of particular tree configurations. The definitions presupposed the constituency shown in figure 7.17(a), where S = "sentence" and VP = "verb phrase". A subject was defined as a noun phrase (NP) attached as a "daughter" to S and a "sister" to VP, whereas an object NP is a daughter to VP and a sister to V. In the sentence *Alice admires Bill*, *Alice* is thus the subject and *Bill* the object. The definitions are purely grammatical, making no inherent reference to meaning.

Compare this with the CG account, where subject and object receive a conceptual characterization. They are defined in terms of several factors observable at the semantic pole of symbolic assemblies: correspondences, profiling, and trajector/landmark alignment. This is shown for *Alice admires Bill* in figure 7.17(b).[20] A subject is characterized as a nominal whose profile corresponds to the trajector of a profiled relationship, and an object as one whose profile corresponds to a landmark (ch. 11). Only conceptual factors are invoked in these definitions.

The diagrams in figure 7.17 show the same constituency, with *admires* and *Bill* forming a group that combines as a whole with *Alice*. Presumably this represents the default-case grouping, reflected in the most natural placement of a slight hesitation: *Alice / admires Bill*. But there is a crucial difference between the syntactic definitions of subject and object and the CG definitions: the former **rely** on this constituency,

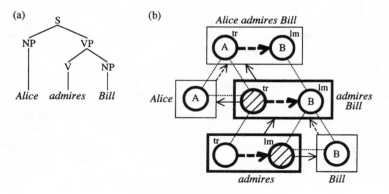

FIGURE 7.17

---

[20] Tense is ignored, and the process profiled by *admire* is represented by a dashed arrow, often used for mental relationships.

whereas the latter are **independent** of it. Reliance on syntactic tree structures for defining grammatical relationships makes it necessary to posit a definite, invariant tree structure for a given type of expression. There is no such necessity in CG, for rather than being "purely syntactic", the relationships in question are taken as being conceptual in nature. Their manifestation in a symbolic assembly does not require any particular constituency. As a consequence, CG allows variable constituency for expressions that exhibit the same grammatical relationships. While these relationships often correlate with particular constituency configurations, their characterization does not depend on them. Hence there is no need to force expressions into rigid constituency hierarchies which they appear not to manifest.

Consider an alternate pronunciation of *Alice admires Bill*, possible in slow, deliberate speech: *Alice/admires/Bill*. Intonation suggests a "flat" constituency—that is, the three components combine with one another at a single level of organization, with no internal grouping. This is shown in figure 7.18, where *Alice* and *Bill* respectively elaborate the trajector and landmark of *admires* at the same level. By virtue of correspondences, *Alice* is still identified as the subject and *Bill* as the object, despite the absence of constituency grouping. The syntactic definitions of subject and object preclude this option. Since *Alice* is the subject and *Bill* the object with either intonation, the constituency in figure 7.17(a) must be posited for both.

Provided that *Alice* elaborates the trajector and *Bill* the landmark, the former qualifies as subject and the latter as object even with the third possible constituency, where *Alice* first combines with *admires* to form *Alice admires*, which then combines with *Bill* at a higher level of organization. The grouping of subject and verb to form a constituent that excludes the object is in fact observed in English, at least in the context of certain larger constructions. We find it, for example, in clause-internal topic constructions like (11)(a), as well as certain cases of coordination, as in (11)(b). Subject and verb also form a constituent in relative clauses like the one in (11)(c).

(11) (a) *Bill Alice admires (Harvey she doesn't).*

  (b) *Alice admires, but Sharon detests, their new teacher.*

  (c) *The teacher [Alice admires] speaks fluent Arabic.*

Relative clauses further illustrate the advantages of the flexible constituency afforded by a conceptual characterization of grammatical relationships. Usually a

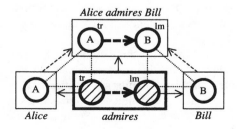

FIGURE 7.18

relative clause in English directly follows the noun it modifies, as in (12)(a). In this case they clearly form a syntactic constituent of the classic sort. What, then, do we say about sentences like (12)(b), where the clause is separated from its head?

(12)   (a) *The package [that I was expecting] arrived.*

    (b) *The package arrived [that I was expecting].*

In autonomous approaches to syntax, it is commonly claimed that a sentence like (12)(b) is "derived" from an "underlying structure" like (12)(a) by a rule that "moves" the relative clause to the end. This analysis follows from the assumption that grammatical relationships are properly represented by particular configurations in syntactic tree structures. Since the relative clause bears the same grammatical relationship to its head in (12)(a) and (12)(b), the two must form a syntactic constituent in both expressions. This is overtly the case in the former, but not in the latter, where they are separated. To preserve the assumption, it must therefore be maintained that (12)(b) has the same syntactic tree structure as (12)(a) in a hypothetical underlying structure. A rule that moves the relative clause is then hypothesized to account for the fact that it does not form a constituent with its head at the "surface structure" level.

By acknowledging the conceptual basis of grammatical relationships, CG accommodates the data without resorting to the dubious theoretical constructs of underlying structures and transforming operations. Neither expression in (12) "derives" from the other. Instead, they represent two alternate ways of successively grouping the same component elements in arriving at the same composite conception. These alternate compositional paths are respectively shown in diagrams (a) and (b) of figure 7.19. As usual, irrelevant details are suppressed (namely tense, the definite article, progressive aspect, and the subordinator *that*). For the relative clause, only the composite structure is represented. It profiles a mental relationship (dashed arrow) whose trajector is identified as the speaker (S) through elaboration at a lower level of organization, but whose landmark remains schematic.

In diagram (a), this landmark is elaborated by *the package*, which serves as profile determinant. The resulting composite expression, *the package that I was expecting*, is a standard example of a head noun being modified by a relative clause. Note that *the package* functions semantically as the clausal object, because its profile corresponds to the landmark of *I was expecting*. At the higher level of organization, the complex nominal *the package that I was expecting* elaborates the trajector of *arrived* and is therefore its subject. *Arrived* is the profile determinant at this level, since (12)(a) as a whole designates an instance of arriving (not the package or the process of expecting).

In diagram (b), we find the same three components: *the package*, *arrived*, and *that I was expecting*. Observe also that the same elements correspond as in diagram (a), and their composite semantic structures are identical. The only difference resides in the order of composition, i.e. constituency. Here, in accordance with the general subject construction, *the package* combines with *arrived* to form the composite expression *the package arrived*. At the higher level of organization, *the package*

(a)

the package that I was expecting arrived

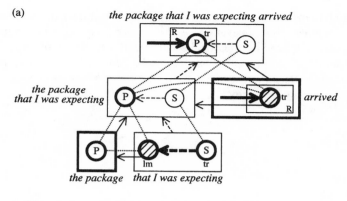

(b)

the package arrived that I was expecting

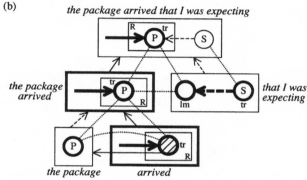

FIGURE 7.19

arrived is integrated with the relative clause by virtue of a correspondence between the former's trajector (the package) and the latter's schematic landmark. This correspondence ensures that the package is understood semantically as the object of the relative clause, even though (12)(b) is not a classic relative clause construction (since *the package* and *that I was expecting* do not combine directly to form a higher-order nominal).

Despite the difference in constituency, both assemblies in figure 7.19 provide all the essential semantic and grammatical information. Since the composite semantic structures are identical, the sentences in (12) are basically the same in meaning. The only semantic contrast resides in a secondary dimension of meaning, namely the compositional path leading to the ultimate composite structure: in (12)(a), one step along this path consists of the nominal expression *the package that I was expecting*; in (12)(b), we find instead the clausal expression *the package arrived*. Both represent natural conceptual groupings. *The package* forms a conceptual group with *that I was expecting* because they jointly offer a full characterization of the central clausal participant. By the same token, *the package* forms a conceptual group with *arrived* because they jointly specify the profiled event. Each sentence chooses one of these natural groupings for explicit symbolization by juxtaposition, thereby yielding a classic constituent. But only one can be symbolized in this manner, so whichever one is chosen, the other remains implicit. While remaining unsymbolized may lessen the salience of a grouping, this does not entail its total absence at the conceptual level. Recall a general point made earlier: there are more facets to the structure of a complex expression than can be represented in a single constituency hierarchy.

8

Rules and Restrictions

$\mathbf{A}$ language allows its speakers to construct and understand an endless supply of new expressions. We might say that it **licenses** or **sanctions** their formation. However, it does not give speakers license to do whatever they want. To be considered normal or correct, expressions have to be put together in certain ways and not others. Linguists therefore talk about the "rules" of a language and the "restrictions" on possible expressions. But what does this actually mean? Applied to language, terms like "rule" and "restriction" are metaphorical, hence potentially misleading. Thus we need to consider how they might realistically be interpreted. What is the nature of linguistic rules and restrictions? Where do they come from? How can we describe them? How do they relate to actual language use?

8.1 Networks and Schemas

In a preliminary way, the questions just posed have already been answered. The rules and restrictions of a language reside in large numbers of **schemas** arranged in **networks**. Schemas are abstracted from occurring expressions and can then be used in constructing and understanding new expressions. We must now examine these matters in greater depth and detail. A good way to start is by posing another fundamental question.

8.1.1 What Is a Language?

Actually, there is no such thing as "a language", at least as this term is commonly understood, both by linguists and by ordinary people. To a large extent this understanding is metaphorically constituted. A very general metaphor, applied to language in many ways, construes linguistic entities as physical entities. We can *pick up a language* (like our clothes pick up cat hairs) or *acquire* it (the way we might acquire an art collection). Linguists talk about *linguistic structure* and *constructing sentences*. When we speak of *empty statements*, *putting ideas into words*, and *getting something out of what someone says*, we are thinking of expressions as containers and meanings as their content (Reddy 1979). A language too is conceived as a container, an elaborate one with a number of compartments, each holding an array of separate objects. Thus a linguist might ask (quite pointlessly from the standpoint of CG) whether a certain rule is *in the lexicon* or *in the syntax*. Another metaphor likens knowing a language to knowing a set of facts. This engenders the common supposition that a language is fully describable with a grammar book and dictionary, hence available for inspection once these materials are prepared. Linguistic theorists subscribe to this metaphor when they talk about *linguistic knowledge* (as if knowing Finnish were comparable to knowing U.S. history) or the *internal grammar* of a language (the mental counterpart of the grammar a linguist might write to describe it).

Such metaphors reflect and support the conception of a language as a distinct, discretely bounded, clearly delimited entity that is basically stable and uniform within a community of speakers. Accordingly, linguists refer to "the linguistic system" or "the grammar of a language", view this as a separate mental "component", and often represent it diagrammatically with a box labeled L. The idealization and reification underlying these notions is unavoidable and perhaps even helpful if not taken too seriously. Indeed, I continue here to talk about "a language" or "linguistic system", sometimes using a box labeled L to represent it. But this conception is just a convenient fiction that must be recognized as such. A language does not reside in grammar books and dictionaries, and looking in a speaker's brain does not reveal a box labeled L.[1]

The basic reality is simply that people talk, in ways that are similar to varying degrees. Talking is a complex **activity**, so ultimately a language must be viewed dynamically, as something people do rather than something they have. The various facets of this activity—motor, perceptual, and mental—are either controlled or constituted by neural processing, so in a broad sense talking is **cognitive** activity. Moreover, since a language is acquired and used by way of interacting with others in a social and cultural context, the activity is **sociocultural** in nature.

Talking can thus be characterized as socioculturally grounded cognitive activity. Like any complex activity (e.g. building a house, running a business, or playing baseball), it draws on a wide array of resources and requires an elaborate set of general and specific abilities. Constituting the more specific abilities are recurring patterns of activity, which emerge with increasing robustness as we develop them and continue to refine them. Among these patterns are those we reify and identify as the units of a language. Such units thus consist in recurring aspects of processing activity. To different degrees, these patterns of neural processing have coalesced as entrenched cognitive routines that can be activated whenever needed. They might be thought of as mental or mentally directed skills employed in various combinations in the complex task of talking. Knowing a language is a matter of controlling a vast repertoire of skills collectively used for talking in certain sociocultural contexts.

Granted that linguistic units are dynamic in nature, residing in aspects of cognitive processing, we must next consider their status vis-à-vis other facets of cognition. It is important not to be misled by the metaphorical conception of a language as

---

[1] If there actually is a grammar in our head, who is in there to consult it?

a bounded container holding discrete and separate objects. Several expectations induced by this metaphor are almost surely incorrect. One property of physical containers which we cannot ascribe to the units of a language—individually or collectively—is that of occupying a definite, limited location. While certain regions in the brain are strongly implicated in language, the processing activity constituting linguistic units cannot be strictly localized to any one area. Nor are linguistic structures distinct or independent from nonlinguistic phenomena. Instead, they recruit and incorporate knowledge and abilities that are not specifically linguistic, without which they could not be manifested.[2] They can only emerge in the context of a broader processing matrix, as strands of activity intertwined with others to form a cohesive fabric. Finally, linguistic units are not separate and independent with respect to one another; some units overlap with others or include them as components. And rather than being distinct from their instantiations, schemas are best envisaged as inherent aspects of the processing activity in which they reside. They are immanent in their instantiations in much the same way that the schematic shape of a letter inheres in all the specific shapes the letter assumes in different fonts.

Everybody talks a bit differently. You will not find any two speakers, for example, who control exactly the same vocabulary and ascribe exactly the same meaning to every lexical item. If we reify the skills deployed in talking, referring to them individually as linguistic units and collectively as a linguistic system, we have to recognize that every speaker's linguistic system is different from everyone else's. When two systems are sufficiently similar, the differences do not impair communication and are usually not even noticed. Speakers simply talk and manage to understand each other fairly well. Having no conscious access to the system per se, they focus their attention on expressions and the contexts supporting their occurrence. But if everybody has a different linguistic system, what do we then identify as "a language", such as English (to choose one at random)?

Objectively, there is no single entity that can be so identified. There are simply lots of people—hundreds of millions of them—who talk in roughly similar ways (sometimes very roughly indeed). Strictly speaking, each person has a distinct linguistic system (or "idiolect"). These individual systems do exhibit a strong family resemblance, however, and like the members of an extended family, some systems resemble one other quite closely, others more distantly. On this basis we can group them into "dialects" of various sizes and degrees of cohesiveness. Yet we can only do this by abstracting away from individual differences and imposing artificial boundaries. If thought of as a clearly delimited entity with definite boundaries, neither a dialect nor a language exists in the wild, but only as a mental construction—the product of idealization, reification, and metaphor. The mental construction of a language is itself grounded in social interaction and cultural attitudes. Idealizations and metaphors commonly used in thinking and talking about language are part of socially transmitted cultural knowledge. The very notion that an element belongs

---

[2] Recall the discussions of encyclopedic semantics (§2.1.3) and conceptual archetypes functioning as linguistic category prototypes (ch. 4). Also exploited for linguistic purposes are basic mental phenomena like perception, association, abstraction, categorization, reification, rhythm, temporal sequencing, and motor control.

to "a language", in the sense of being regularly and intrinsically used in speaking it, constitutes one dimension of its conventional linguistic import.

It is pointless to ask whether language is cognitive or sociocultural in nature, for it is obviously both. A linguistic system comprises a vast array of skills employed in talking. Ultimately, those skills reside in recurrent patterns of neural and neurally guided processing activity. They do not develop in isolation, but as the product of social interaction in a cultural context (Tomasello 2003). In learning to talk, an individual's linguistic system converges on those of other individuals the learner interacts with. Acquisition is never really completed, for the system a person acquires continues to be refined, adjusted, and extended throughout linguistic life. These adaptations as well are effected through sociocultural interaction, and are thus coordinated to some extent among individuals who interact with one another.

In the sea of talking individuals, there is thus a constant inclination for structure to emerge and maintain itself. Individuals tend to be organized in self-perpetuating groups whose speech is very much alike and who think of themselves as speaking the same language or dialect. These "speech communities" vary greatly in size, social cohesiveness, and the degree to which they approximate linguistic uniformity. The key word, of course, is "approximate", since even the closest-knit community exhibits linguistic variation. The differences among individual linguistic systems may nevertheless be overshadowed by the extensive commonality enabling members of a speech community to freely communicate. To the extent that this is so, both speakers and linguists are prone to abstract away from the differences and focus on the massive similarities. It is through this process of idealization and reification that languages and dialects emerge as mental and sociocultural constructions.

8.1.2 Schemas

To ignore these factors, pretending that languages and linguistic units are wholly discrete, would have to be regarded as misguided. It would be equally misguided to embrace the opposite extreme and regard them as wholly continuous—a sea of infinite variation with no discernible structure. The fact is that structures do emerge with varying degrees of robustness, definition, and stability. Language is patterned, organized activity exhibiting extensive regularities that need to be discovered and described. Their characterization should, however, accommodate the inherent dynamicity and variability of linguistic structure.

The regularities that we reify and collectively refer to as "a language" consist of conventional linguistic units. They are "units" in the sense of being entrenched cognitive routines, and "conventional" by virtue of representing established linguistic practice in a certain speech community. These conventional units embody the rules of a language and the restrictions imposed on its expressions. As there are various forms such units might in principle assume, we must consider the basic nature of linguistic rules and the source of their restrictiveness.[3]

---

[3] I am using the term "rule" in a neutral sense, to indicate whatever is responsible for the patterns and regularities of a language. Theorists often use it more narrowly, for what are here called "constructive rules".

Linguists conceive of rules in one of three general ways: as **constructive rules**, as **filters**, or as **schemas**. Constructive rules are like instructions to be followed step by step in putting together expressions (giving them as "output"). Prime examples are the "phrase structure rules" and "transformations" of classic generative grammar (Chomsky 1957, 1965). Phrase structure rules are instructions for building syntactic tree structures like figures 7.16 and 7.17(a). Transformations specify how the "under-lying" structures thereby constructed are successively modified—by operations like insertion, deletion, and movement—to yield an expression's "surface" form. Rules and expressions are thus conceived as being fundamentally different in nature. To make an analogy, if rules are the steps in a computer program, expressions are the images it generates on the screen. Hence there is no reason to expect individual rules to resemble the expressions they help produce. The sole requirement is that the rules function collectively to give only well-formed expressions as output.

Linguistic rules can also be cast in negative form, as statements of what is **not** permitted in well-formed expressions. Such a rule, for instance, might brand as ill-formed any clause in which a verb and its subject disagree in number (*it are*; *they is*). Theorists have occasionally entertained the notion that grammar might consist entirely in filters of this sort. Such an account would take as its starting point the set of all possible "strings" of words drawn from the lexicon of the language. Most of these are simply incoherent—only a very small proportion (but still infinitely many!) would be accepted as grammatical expressions. This determination is made by check-ing the candidate strings against the long list of prohibitions in which the grammar of the language resides. Most strings are filtered out by virtue of being flagged for violations. Expressions that draw no flags are judged grammatical.[4]

In contrast to constructive rules (which **need not** resemble expressions) and filters (which by definition **cannot**), schemas **must** resemble the expressions they characterize. Schemas emerge from expressions through reinforcement of the com-monalities they exhibit at some level of abstraction. Or to phrase it more accurately, they arise within expressions, as recurring aspects of the processing activity that constitutes them. They differ from the expressions they characterize only in level of specificity, representing the coarse-grained similarities revealed by abstracting away from fine-grained details.

In CG, rules take the form of schemas. Patterns and regularities of any sort, at any level of specificity, reside in schematic units abstracted from occurring expres-sions. Even lexical items have this character. Though often regarded as idiosyncratic,[5] lexical items are better thought of as regularities of limited scope. The lexeme *cat*, for instance, embodies the generalization that creatures of a certain sort are con-ventionally designated by this form. There is no inconsistency in describing lexical items as specific fixed expressions, on the one hand, and as schemas, on the other. A lexical unit like *cat* is certainly specific compared with the schema describing

---

[4] This filtering approach is reminiscent of the old, lame joke about how to sculpt an elephant: you start with a huge block of marble, and then knock off anything that doesn't look like an elephant.

[5] Lexical items are so regarded by theorists who claim a sharp distinction between lexicon and syntax, the latter supposedly consisting of general rules. Because CG recognizes grammatical patterns at all levels of generality, lexicon and grammar are seen as a continuum.

count nouns or nouns as a general class. It is nonetheless schematic compared with any particular manifestation of *cat* in actual language use. A particular occurrence may be highly specific (if not unique) in terms of both its contextually determined meaning and the fine details of its pronunciation. But as an established unit—psychologically entrenched and conventional in the speech community—a lexical item neutralizes the fine-grained features that vary from one occasion to the next.

An actual instance of language use, in all its complexity and specificity, is referred to as a **usage event**. The essential aspect of a usage event is how the expression employed is apprehended by the speaker and hearer—their full contextual understanding of its import and the full detail of its phonetic manifestation. Importantly, the relevant context subsumes far more than just the immediate physical circumstances. Speech interactions unfold at all levels of the interlocutors' awareness: physical, mental, social, cultural, emotive, and evaluative. Part of an expression's contextual import is thus an assessment by each interlocutor of what the other knows and is currently attending to, as well as their attitudes, intentions, and desires. Further included is their awareness of the ongoing discourse itself and how the current expression fits into it.

CG is a **usage-based** model of language structure (Barlow and Kemmer 2000; Bybee and Hopper 2001; GC: ch. 4). One motivation for this label is the claim that usage events are the source of all linguistic units. The relationship between units and the usage events that spawn them is tightly constrained by the **content requirement** (§1.3.4). According to the content requirement, units are limited to structures that arise from usage events through two basic cognitive processes: schematization and categorization. Semantic units are abstracted from the contextual understanding of occurring expressions, phonological units from apprehension of their phonetic properties, and symbolic units from the pairing of the two. In each case, units emerge via the progressive entrenchment of configurations that recur in a sufficient number of events to be established as cognitive routines.[6] Since only recurring features are reinforced, the units that emerge are far less comprehensive and detailed than the usage events giving rise to them. A unit corresponds to just selected aspects of the source events, and the commonality it reflects is only apparent at a certain level of abstraction.

Units are thus schematic relative to both the source events and the further events in which they figure. Once established, they function as templates in constructing and interpreting new expressions. The relationship they bear to the corresponding aspects of subsequent usage events amounts to categorization. The categorizing relationship is one of elaboration if the schema is fully manifested, without distortion, in the target; otherwise it is one of extension. Moreover, either sort of categorization is itself capable of recurring and being established as a conventional linguistic unit. We will also see that categorizing relationships are themselves subject to schematization and categorization.

---

[6] Under some conditions a unit (e.g. a new lexical item) can be learned from a single exposure. Thus the sheer number of usage events may be less important than some measure of cumulative psychological impact (involving additional factors like cognitive salience).

Linguistic units are limited by the content requirement to schematized representations of configurations inherent in usage events. Since schemas are the reinforced commonalities of occurring expressions, they amount to positive characterizations of what actually occurs in language use. This direct relation between structure and use offers an account of language acquisition that in principle is quite straightforward.[7] By contrast, certain devices employed in other theories—such as filters, constructive rules, and underlying structures—are problematic from that standpoint because their connection with actual expressions is far more indirect. The content requirement precludes their adoption in CG.

Schemas have now been given two descriptions that might seem contradictory. On the one hand, they are positive characterizations of what actually occurs. On the other hand, they are said to embody the rules and restrictions of a language. The apparent difficulty is that "rule" and "restriction" are basically negative terms, referring to what **must not** be done or what **must** be done if one is **not** to face a penalty. The question, then, is whether schemas, being positive specifications, can achieve the restrictiveness imputed to linguistic systems. If only schemas are posited, how can speakers know that certain expressions are not permitted, even some that conform to general patterns (e.g. *mans* as the plural of *man*)? On what basis can an infinite set of potential expressions be ruled out as "ungrammatical"?

Detailed answers to such questions are provided in later sections. For now, we can simply observe that limitations need not come about through explicit prohibitions. In language as in life, a single positive model may be more effective in controlling and directing behavior than any number of injunctions. This is especially so given that conventionally sanctioned structures represent just small enclaves in the vast space of structural possibilities. As ready-made resources available for exploitation, schemas function as attractors within this space, thus inhibiting the exploration of other areas. In this way, the positive characterization of conventional patterns can indicate implicitly (and quite effectively) that options outside their range are nonconventional and will be judged ill-formed.

8.1.3 Networks of Schemas

A language comprises an enormous inventory of conventional linguistic units, all abstracted from usage events. This is sketched in figure 8.1, where the small squares stand for individual units, and the large box labeled L for the language as a whole. By now you should certainly be aware of the gross distortions inherent in this representation, which is nonetheless useful for limited purposes. The discreteness suggested by the diagram and the container metaphor it is based on must not be taken seriously.

In particular, the units of a language are not like ping-pong balls in a box. Even if ping-pong balls were square, linguistic units would still be quite different owing to their intrinsically dynamic nature. More directly relevant here is the further difference that ping-pong balls are separate and unconnected, whereas units are neither. We have seen,

---

[7] Tomasello 2003 provides a comprehensive (though necessarily preliminary) description of language acquisition in a usage-based perspective.

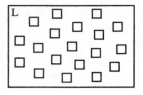

FIGURE 8.1

for example, that units combine with one another in assemblies that are themselves conventional units (fig. 6.6). Some units are schematic vis-à-vis others, and schemas, rather than being distinct, are immanent in their instantiations. More generally, units are connected by relationships of categorization, both elaboration and extension. They can thus form **networks** of any size (as shown in fig. 2.2 for the alternate senses of *ring*).

On this basis, we can describe a language as a **structured** inventory of conventional linguistic units. This structure—the organization of units into networks and assemblies—is intimately related to language use, both shaping it and being shaped by it. To see just how, we need to examine the interaction between occurring expressions and the linguistic system invoked for constructing or understanding them. Expressions do not exist independently, but only as manifestations of a language. A conceptualization and a sequence of sounds do not constitute an expression in and of themselves, but only via their interpretation with respect to some linguistic system. Expressions are linguistic objects whose structure and status depend on the conventional units used by the speaker and hearer in apprehending them. The relationship they bear to these units amounts to categorization.

Consider, then, the relation between a language (L) and a usage event (U) interpreted as an utterance in that language. Its interpretation as such is a matter of categorization: it resides in particular units of L being invoked to categorize particular facets of U. Quite a number of units may be invoked, representing elements of different sizes in the various dimensions of linguistic structure. It is precisely by virtue of these categorizations that the utterance counts as an expression of the language. Collectively, the categorizations provide the expression's **structural description**, its characterization with respect to L.

One such categorization is depicted in figure 8.2. [A] is a conventional unit of L, and (B) is the facet of U it categorizes. These can be structures of any size or any kind (e.g. sounds, lexical items, grammatical constructions). Their relationship can either be one of elaboration ($\rightarrow$) or extension (--->). [A] is enclosed in a box to indicate its status as a unit. (B) is enclosed in a circle, on the presumption that it is novel when apprehended in full detail as part of a usage event. If (B) is novel, so must be its categorization by [A]. This is shown by enclosing it in a box with rounded corners. Formulaically, using brackets and parentheses for units and nonunits, the categorizing relationship can thus be given as either ([A] $\rightarrow$ (B)) or ([A] ---> (B)).[8]

---

[8] The speaker and hearer must both effect this categorization, since both interpret U as an instance of L. The relationship between L and U is referred to in CG as **coding** because it figures in both the speaker's task of "encoding" situations and the hearer's task of "decoding" expressions.

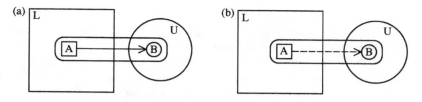

FIGURE 8.2

(B) is thus interpreted as manifesting [A] in a usage event. When (B) manifests [A] fully and without distortion, as in diagram (a), the expression is perceived as conventional ("well-formed") with respect to this particular facet of its structure. When (B)'s manifestation of [A] is only partial or distorted, as in diagram (b), the expression is perceived as nonconventional ("ill-formed") in this particular respect. The extent to which the expression as a whole is judged well-formed is thus a function of all the individual categorizations that figure in its structural description. Since we are always pushing the envelope in language use, stretching available resources to meet new linguistic challenges, a measure of nonconventionality is readily accepted if it is even noticed. Only the more blatant distortions are likely to attract attention and cause an expression to be judged "ill-formed" or "ungrammatical".

Whether it involves elaboration or extension, [A]'s categorization of (B) need not be a one-shot affair. If it is useful for [A] to be invoked and realized as (B) in the context of one usage event, the same might well prove useful in other such events. Both (B) and [A]'s categorization of (B) will then occur on multiple occasions. Should they occur sufficiently often, they will undergo entrenchment and achieve the status of units: ([A] ---> (B)) > [[A] ---> [B]].[9] Now suppose they eventually achieve unit status not just for one speaker but for most or even all members of a speech community. In this case, both [B] and the categorization [[A] ---> [B]] are nothing other than conventional linguistic units. By definition, then, they have been incorporated in the language. This overall development is summarized in figure 8.3.

Let us take some concrete examples. Imagine first that [A] is the syllable [ma], a phonological unit that occurs as part of many words. It would not be unexpected

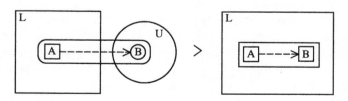

FIGURE 8.3

---

[9] Strictly speaking, the unit [B] is schematic relative to the version of (B) that occurs in any particular usage event (since every such event is unique when examined in fine enough detail).

that a speaker might occasionally pronounce it with a nasalized vowel (a natural phonetic development, essentially just a matter of relaxing the timing of oral and velic closures). In a particular usage event, [ma] would then be manifested in slightly distorted form, as (mã). Despite this discrepancy (which will probably go unnoticed), the latter is easily interpreted as a realization of the former: ([ma] ---> (mã)). An alternate pronunciation of this sort might very well occur on many occasions, on the part of many speakers. In this way, it can eventually establish itself as a conventional unit of the language: ([ma] ---> (mã)) > [[ma] ---> [mã]]. The result of this minor linguistic change is that [mã] is now a regularly expected pronunciation of [ma].[10]

Consider next a case of semantic extension. The noun *mail*, originally referring to physically embodied messages delivered through a postal system, is now well established for what is also known as *email*—messages delivered electronically by computer. At one stage this use of *mail* was innovative. The lexical unit *mail*—at that time limited to what is now called *snail mail* or *hard mail*—was invoked to designate its electronic counterpart. This extension implies the categorization in figure 8.4(a). The occurrence of *mail* in the utterance is interpreted as manifesting the symbolic unit [MAIL/mail] even though, in the context of the usage event, it is understood as referring to electronic messages: (EMAIL/mail). This usage is now well established, so both the symbolic structure [EMAIL/mail] and its categorization by [MAIL/mail] have the status of conventional units. This is shown in diagram (b), which can be given more compactly as (c) by collapsing the two representations of [mail]. Since the original unit has not been lost, *mail* is now polysemous, having both 'hard mail' and 'email' as well-entrenched meanings. To some extent, the latter sense is still understood as an extension from the former, just as indicated in diagram (c). But this motivation is well on its way to being lost; more and more [EMAIL/mail] stands alone as an independently accessed symbolic unit.[11]

The categorization in figure 8.4 is a case of extension, rather than elaboration, because certain features of the categorizing structure are absent or distorted in the target. In lieu of messages being written down on paper is the notion of their appearing on a computer screen. Electronic transmission replaces physical delivery by postal workers. The extension is nonetheless straightforward, even obvious, as there is still a lot that [MAIL] and [EMAIL] have in common: the central role of messages, primarily expressed linguistically; the sequence of writing, sending, receiving, and reading them; their delivery via a fixed distribution network. Thus, by suspending certain specific properties of [MAIL], we obtain a more abstract conception that is fully manifested in [EMAIL]. This abstracted commonality both motivates the extension of *mail* to encompass email and ensures its ready understanding. In fact, one can plausibly argue that it now constitutes a schematic, independently accessible

---

[10] This does not necessarily imply that [ma] is no longer possible. The two pronunciations can coexist indefinitely, perhaps as casual and formal variants.

[11] The relationship between the two senses can be taken as an instance of metaphor, [MAIL] pertaining to the source domain and [EMAIL] to the target domain. The loss of motivation (the "fading" of the metaphor) is a special case of the gradual decrease in analyzability (§3.2.2) that is typical for lexical items.

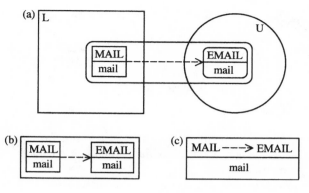

FIGURE 8.4

sense of *mail* subsuming [MAIL] and [EMAIL] as special cases. Note the following exchange:

(1)   **A:** *I got a lot of mail this morning.* **B:** *Email or hard mail?*

As a general matter, extension relies on the implicit apprehension of something common to the source and target. Suppose we think of categorization in terms of the categorizing structure being "recognized" in the target. Its recognition is unproblematic when it is wholly immanent in the target, in which case their relationship is elaborative: ([A] → (B)). When the target conflicts in some respect with the categorizing structure, recognition engenders a certain amount of "strain". It can only come by suspending or at least overriding features of [A], to obtain an abstracted structure, (A′), observable in the target: ((A′) → (B)). As shown in figure 5(a), (A′) is thus an extension from [A] (arising as a stripped-down version of it), as well as being schematic vis-à-vis both [A] and (B). We can therefore posit an intimate relationship between extension and schematization: extension from [A] to (B) facilitates the emergence of a more schematic structure, (A′), with respect to which both [A] and (B) are elaborations. Moreover, the relationships in diagram (a) provide a general model of categorization. Elaboration represents a special case of extension, where [A] is recognizable in (B) without modification. [A] and (A′) then collapse, as seen in diagram (b).

The extent to which (A′) becomes entrenched and emerges as an independently accessible unit no doubt varies. In the case of *mail*, the original, extended, and schematic senses are all well established and capable of being evoked as its meaning, depending on the context. They are thus related as shown in figure 8.5(c), where the heavy-line box indicates that the original meaning [MAIL] (i.e. 'hard mail') is prototypical and most easily elicited. This mini-network is part of a somewhat larger network representing the conventional semantic value of *mail*. In learning to use the word properly, a speaker masters the entire network (not just the schema or the prototype). A lexical item of any frequency tends to be polysemous, having multiple senses linked by relationships of categorization. Its various senses are members of a

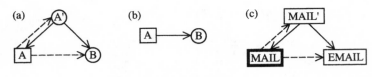

FIGURE 8.5

category that is **structured** by these relationships. It is further said to be a **complex** category because its membership and configuration are not reducible to (or predictable from) any single element.

Complex categories are characteristic of virtually every aspect of linguistic structure: the established senses of a lexical item, the phonetic realizations of a phoneme ("allophones"), the phonological realizations of a morpheme ("allomorphs"), families of grammatical constructions, and so on. They reflect the variation induced by ongoing language change and the constant challenge of adapting existing units to additional contexts and changing circumstances. Starting from a single unit, [A], repeated occurrences of the developments sketched in figures 8.2, 8.3, and 8.5 result in networks of related variants, as suggested in figure 8.6. The individual nodes in such a network can be structures of any kind or degree of complexity (up to and including multilevel constructions). Each categorizing relationship in such a network is itself a conventional linguistic unit, as indicated in figures 8.3 and 8.4. In principle, an important dimension of the network's characterization—merely hinted at by the thickness of boxes—is a measure of each unit's entrenchment and ease of activation. The most entrenched and most readily activated unit will generally be the original structure, [A], which can then be recognized as the category prototype.[12]

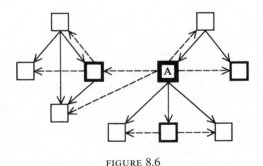

FIGURE 8.6

[12] The structure of a complex category at a given point in time is not necessarily a direct reflection of how it develops, either historically or in language acquisition. In the span of a couple decades, for example, the semantic network of *mail* is being reconfigured, with [MAIL] no longer a clear-cut prototype (hence the term *hard mail* to avoid confusion). We can anticipate [EMAIL] eventually taking over as the prototypical sense, with [MAIL] then being an extension from it. In some circles, this has probably already happened.

Bear in mind that the network model of complex categories is a metaphor. Like any metaphor, it is helpful in certain respects but potentially misleading in others. On the one hand, the network model is useful because it captures some essential properties of complex categories: that there are multiple variants, that these are related in certain ways, and that some are more central (or easily elicited) than others. On the other hand, the model proves misleading if the discreteness it implies is taken too seriously. It suggests that a category has an exact number of clearly distinct members, that it exhibits a unique configuration defined by a specific set of categorizing relationships, and that a target of categorization can always be assigned to a particular category member. Yet these entailments of the metaphor should not be ascribed to the actual phenomenon—if you look for a category in the brain, you will not find boxes linked by arrows. It may well be that the network metaphor has outlived its usefulness. At the very least, it should be counterbalanced with an alternative metaphor that emphasizes continuity rather than discreteness.[13]

Suppose we compare a complex category to a mountain range, with peaks corresponding to category members. Rather than being discrete and sharply distinct, the peaks in a mountain range grade into another, rising from a continuous substrate to their various elevations. The number of peaks cannot be counted with absolute precision—how many there are depends on how high we decide a prominence has to be in order to qualify as such. Moreover, many positions in the range cannot be assigned to any particular peak but are simply part of the substrate from which they all emerge. Despite this basic continuity, it would be quite wrong to insist on the total absence of discreteness. There are indeed peaks in the range, which exhibits a certain configuration (no two ranges are topographically identical). It would be pointless to deny this structure or prohibit the use of discrete terms (count nouns like *peak*, *valley*, *ridge*, etc.) in describing it. Any terms should be used judiciously, of course, and with full awareness of their limitations.

8.2 Assessing Conventionality

Linguists distinguish between expressions that are "grammatical" (or "well-formed") and those that are "ungrammatical" ("ill-formed"). In so doing, they are not **prescribing** how people ought to talk but **describing** the assessments speakers themselves supposedly make. The boundary between well- and ill-formed expressions is fuzzy at best and continually being adjusted as speakers push the limits in normal language use. Still, they can only push the limits if there are limits to push. At a given time, in a given speech community, a large body of conventions are firmly enough established that speakers invoke them as the basis for apprehending expressions. An expression is accepted as conventional to the extent that it conforms to the units invoked for this purpose. It behooves us to understand this process in a fair amount of detail. How are

---

[13] Originally, the network model provided an alternative to the prevalent notion that a single structure was sufficient to define a category. For a general discussion of continuity vs. discreteness, see Langacker 2006.

the units invoked? How do they give rise to judgments of nonconventionality? Can a scheme of this sort impose the proper restrictions (ruling out expressions that are not permitted)?

8.2.1 Interactive Activation

The process of assessing conventionality amounts to categorization. An expression's overall assessment resolves itself into numerous categorizing relationships, each holding between a linguistic unit, [A], and some facet, (B), of a usage event (fig. 8.2). The expression is conventional (well-formed) to the extent that these relationships are elaborative: ([A] → (B)). But now we face a basic problem. How, for a given target (B), is the categorizing unit selected? Out of the countless units comprising the linguistic system, why is unit [A], in particular, invoked to categorize (B)? The choice is critical, for the status of (B) depends on it. Consider the phrase *tall giraffe*. On the one hand, this will be judged conventional if interpreted as manifesting the constructional schema for the modification of nouns by adjectives: ([ADJ N] → (*tall giraffe*)). On the other hand, it is ill-formed if construed as a prepositional phrase, since *tall* is not a preposition and *giraffe* is a simple noun rather than a full nominal: ([P NML] ---> (*tall giraffe*)). You are no doubt objecting that one would never invoke the schema for prepositional phrases to categorize the sequence of an adjective plus noun. While that is true, it begs the question. Why is it, precisely, that [ADJ N] is invoked to categorize *tall giraffe*, and not [P NML]? After all, both schemas are established conventional units.

It would be quite legitimate to argue that linguists should not have to answer this question. Schema selection poses a problem not just with respect to language but for cognition in general. It is thus a matter for psychologists. Whatever general solution they arrive at will presumably prove valid for language as well. We can see the problem's generality by considering its manifestation in a nonlinguistic domain, namely face recognition.

I can distinguish and recognize many individuals from their faces. For each such individual, I have abstracted a schematized image constituting my knowledge of what that person looks like. When I see and recognize someone, I do so by activating the appropriate schema and using it to apprehend the current visual impression. But how do I get it right? Suppose I have just two face schemas, one for Zelda (round face, dark hair, female) and one for Quentin (long face, light hair, male). I know both people well and never fail to recognize them. So when Zelda walks into the room, presenting me with a specific visual impression of her face (Z), I succeed in activating my [ZELDA] schema and using it to effect the proper categorization: ([ZELDA] → (Z)). This is sketched in figure 8.7(a). But what prevents the alternate categorization in diagram (b)? In this case I would activate my [QUENTIN] schema and mistakenly interpret my impression of Zelda as a distorted manifestation of Quentin: ([QUEN-TIN] ---> (Z)). Why, then, do I respond to the sight of Zelda by saying *Hello, Zelda* rather than saying *Gee, Quentin, you sure have changed*?

Although the problem cannot be solved by linguistic methods alone, certain aspects of a general account do seem reasonably apparent. Linguistic units reside in patterns of neural activation. Since the brain is highly interconnected, the occurrence

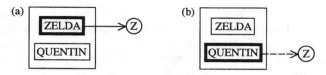

FIGURE 8.7

of a certain pattern either facilitates or inhibits the occurrence of many others. More-over, since neural processing takes place at various levels and unfolds through time, it is constantly influenced by what happens at other levels and earlier stages. The account envisaged is thus dynamic and interactive, with myriad factors helping to elicit the processing activity that constitutes a given mental experience.[14]

For a unit to be invoked as a categorizing structure, one such factor must be preliminary processing of the target itself. When I see a face, for instance, low-level processing of the visual impression might register such coarse-grained features as roundness and surrounding darkness (of the hair), and since these are part of my [ZELDA] schema, they will tend to elicit it. Activation of this unit provides the basis for detailed apprehension of the visual target, in which I recognize Zelda by seeing the face **as hers**. Or suppose the target is *tall giraffe* and that *tall* is recognized at the first stage of processing. Since *tall* is an adjective, and thus embodies the adjec-tive schema, its activation tends to elicit that of the constructional schema [ADJ N]. Invoking this as the categorizing structure facilitates recognition of the following noun (for a noun is thus anticipated) and results in the entire expression being **under-stood as** an instance of the [ADJ N] construction.

In broad outline, then, schema selection can be described as follows. A par-ticular target, T, tends to activate a set of units, each of which has the potential to categorize it. Initially, these units are all activated to some degree. This is sketched in figure 8.8(a), where thickness of lines indicates degree of activation. The potential

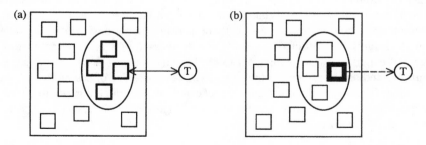

FIGURE 8.8

<hr />

[14] Broadly speaking, these properties are characteristic of a "connectionist" (or "neural network") model of processing based on spreading activation and inhibition (Collins and Loftus 1975; Elman and McClelland 1984; MacWhinney 1987; Regier 1996).

categorizing structures compete for the privilege of serving in this capacity. Most likely they are mutually inhibitory, so as one becomes more highly activated it tends to suppress the others. Eventually (though it is only a matter of milliseconds) one member wins the competition, achieving a high level of activation at the expense of all its rivals. It then serves to categorize T, as shown in diagram (b).

A number of factors encourage a unit's selection as the categorizing structure. The first is degree of entrenchment, translating into inherent ease of activation. In principle (though it is hard to measure in practice), this is one dimension in the characterization of every linguistic unit. A second factor is the influence of context ("contextual priming"). If we have just been discussing Zelda, for example, my schema for her face will be slightly activated and thus more easily elicited than it would normally be. So if a person vaguely resembling Zelda should wander by, I might well mistake her for Zelda until I get a closer look. The third factor is degree of overlap with the target. The more properties a unit shares with the target (as determined by preliminary processing), the more the target tends to activate it. A significant consequence of this last factor is that more specific units have a built-in advantage over more schematic ones in the competition to be selected as categorizing structure. Being characterized in finer-grained detail, a specific unit has more properties that might overlap with the target to boost its level of activation.

There is no requirement that the unit activated to categorize a target be fully compatible with it. In fact, the unit invoked may be less compatible than other candidates, owing its selection to contextual priming or inherent ease of activation. This reflects a fundamental point: namely, that categorization is partially shaped by expectations (proceeding in "top-down" fashion) rather than being solely driven by the nature of the target (in "bottom-up" fashion). Indeed, the target itself is often largely constituted by its categorization. Once invoked by the target based on preliminary processing (which may be rudimentary), the categorizing unit imposes its own content and organization, which can reinforce, supplement, or override those inherent in the target. Supplementation occurs, for instance, when we mentally connect a set of dots to perceive a familiar shape (as in viewing constellations). Overriding the target is a common pitfall in proofreading, where we see a word as it ought to be written, not as it actually is. Whatever the details, a target is never apprehended in a neutral or wholly objective manner; there is always some **basis** for its apprehension. A categorizing unit provides this basis. Its interaction with the target results in a unified experience—not equivalent to either individually—in which the target is **apprehended as** an instance of the category. The experience of seeing Zelda's face **as** her face is not equivalent to seeing her face without recognizing it, nor to invoking the image of her face without actually seeing it. That is, ([ZELDA] → (Z)) is distinct from both (Z) and [ZELDA].

8.2.2 Restrictiveness

An utterance that occurs in a usage event constitutes a linguistic expression by virtue of a substantial number of categorizations (as depicted in fig. 8.2). These categorizations represent the structure ascribed to the expression, i.e. its interpretation with respect to the linguistic system. Of course, a target interpreted as manifesting a particular linguistic unit does not necessarily reflect it without distortion. An expression is nonconventional to the extent that targets deviate from the units invoked to categorize them.

A linguistic system's restrictiveness therefore derives not only from the conventional units it comprises, but also from how they are accessed and applied in usage events. Due to these latter factors, infinitely many expressions are ruled out as ill-formed even though the units themselves are positive in nature, representations of what does occur in the language. Of course, most conceivable expressions are precluded from the outset because they bear no significant resemblance to the language in question. The units of English, for example, provide no basis for even beginning to apprehend expressions in Hopi or Tagalog; these diverge so far from the patterns of English that, except for a few accidental resemblances, they fail to elicit English units as categorizing structures. And since they do not receive a structural interpretation with respect to English, they do not even count as expressions of the language (well-formed or ill-formed). Expressions that do receive a structural interpretation, eliciting units of the language for their categorization, may be judged ill-formed nonetheless when certain categorizations are relationships of extension rather than elaboration.

This model for assessing well-formedness is flexible, dynamic, and interactive. Restrictions on permissible expressions are not stated directly (as explicit prohibitions) but emerge from factors that are matters of degree: entrenchment, extent of overlap, level of activation. A system of this sort is nevertheless able to account for the robust patterns, strict limitations, and clear-cut judgments evident at least in certain aspects of language structure. We can start by observing that, as a special case, such a system allows the emergence of fully general, essentially regular patterns. This occurs when a unit is sufficiently well entrenched and easily elicited, relative to any likely competitors, that it is virtually always invoked as categorizing structure. Internally, moreover, such a unit can be quite specific in regard to the properties a target must have to be fully sanctioned by it.

In an English nominal, for example, a simple adjective directly precedes the noun it modifies: *tall giraffe, elegant dress, sharp knife, serious misgivings*, etc.[15] This regularity is captured by a constructional schema, abbreviated here as [ADJ N], whose semantic pole is as shown in figure 7.5 and whose phonological pole specifies temporal order and adjacency. The pattern is quite general, and judgments are clear-cut: *tall giraffe* is well-formed, **giraffe tall* is not. Though it may seem evident, we need to be explicit about how such judgments are arrived at. Suppose, then, that a target nominal is determined by preliminary processing to include both the adjective *tall* and the noun *giraffe*, the former serving to characterize the latter. Given these

---

[15] This statement pertains to the internal structure of nominals, not to cases where an adjective is external to a nominal it characterizes (e.g. *The giraffe is tall*). What is meant by a "simple" adjective has to be spelled out; included, for instance, are adjectives preceded by certain adverbs (as in **very tall** *giraffe*) but not those followed by a prepositional phrase (****tall beyond belief** *giraffe*). We must also make allowance for multiple adjectives (as in *big, bad wolf*) where only one can precede the noun directly. In principle, such clarifications and qualifications should be offered for almost any example. However, practicality dictates their omission when they do not affect the basic validity of the point at hand.

specifications, how is it ascertained that *tall giraffe* is a proper way of expressing this, while **giraffe tall* is ill-formed?[16]

The constructional schema [ADJ N] provides an accessible option for making these determinations. It is well entrenched and easily elicited. Moreover, it overlaps extensively with the target, since *tall* is a simple adjective, *giraffe* is a noun, and their semantic relationship is just as the schema specifies. If [ADJ N] is indeed activated to categorize the target nominal, only *tall giraffe* will be judged conventional in regard to the placement of noun and adjective: ([ADJ N] → (*tall giraffe*)). The alternative **giraffe tall* violates the word order prescribed by the schema at its phonological pole: ([ADJ N] ---> (*giraffe tall*)). Will these judgments be consistent? That depends on what other units might be available with the potential to be selected as categorizing structure. For simple adjectives there are no serious competitors. In learning English, we are not systematically exposed to expressions like **giraffe tall* and **knife sharp*, so we do not abstract a schema that would sanction them. Should an expression of this sort be produced, it will thus be categorized by [ADJ N] and judged ill-formed.

There is nothing intrinsically wrong with expressions like **giraffe tall*—they simply happen to be nonconventional, given how the language has evolved. It might have turned out otherwise. Imagine a language just like modern English, except that a simple adjective can either precede or follow the noun it modifies: *tall giraffe* and *giraffe tall* are equally acceptable. Exposed to both patterns, learners of this fancied variety of English will abstract both [ADJ N] and [N ADJ] as conventional units. Assuming that both are well entrenched and easily activated, the one that overlaps to a greater extent with a target will win the competition to be selected as the categorizing unit. One respect in which a unit can overlap with a target is word order. On this basis, therefore, a target like *tall giraffe* will elicit the schema [ADJ N] to categorize it (all else being equal), while *giraffe tall* will activate [N ADJ]. Both are judged well-formed: ([ADJ N] → (*tall giraffe*)); ([N ADJ] → (*giraffe tall*)). We see from this example that an expression's conventionality cannot be ascertained by considering just a single unit. The full array of potentially applicable units, and their relative degrees of accessibility, must be taken into account.

When a language has alternate units performing the same basic function, they tend to specialize, so that each is used in a certain range of circumstances (instead of being freely interchangeable). It turns out that English—the real variety—does have a pattern in which an adjective follows the noun it modifies. However, this pattern is limited to adjectives exhibiting certain kinds of complexity, notably by incorporating a prepositional or infinitival phrase: *a giraffe **tall beyond belief***; *students **anxious about their grades***; *anyone **ready to confess***. We must therefore posit two constructional schemas, one in which a simple adjective (ADJ) precedes the noun it modifies,

---

[16] Both interlocutors face this problem, though in slightly different guises. The speaker intends for *tall* to modify *giraffe* and needs to find a conventional means of conveying this. The same structures and categorizations figure in the hearer's understanding of the expression and determine whether it is accepted as normal or perceived as deviant. Also, to some extent each interlocutor assumes the role of the other: the speaker imagines what the hearer faces in trying to understand the expression, and the hearer imagines what the speaker most likely intends in producing it.

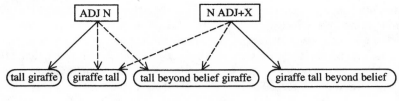

FIGURE 8.9

and one in which a complex adjective (ADJ + X) follows the noun. These alternate units are depicted in figure 8.9, along with four target expressions.

Since both units are accessible, degree of overlap with the target determines the choice of categorizing structure. And since all the targets include a noun and a modifying adjective, the selection hinges on word order and whether the adjective is simple or complex. In the case of *tall giraffe*, these factors conspire to activate [ADJ N] as the categorizing unit; with *giraffe tall beyond belief*, they activate [N ADJ + X]. Hence these two expressions are judged to be well-formed. By contrast, both **giraffe tall* and **tall beyond belief giraffe* overlap with each target in one respect but conflict with it in regard to the other. Thus, while either expression might elicit either unit for its categorization, every combination results in a judgment of nonconventionality. For example, **giraffe tall* can be interpreted either as an instance of [ADJ N] with the wrong word order or as an instance of [N ADJ + X] with the wrong kind of adjective.

For many reasons, judgments are often less crisp and clear-cut. A notorious case is the past tense of "irregular" verbs in English, where speakers are often uncertain about the proper form. I myself am uncertain about the past tense of *dive*: is it *dove* or *dived*? I know that both occur, and while I was taught the former in school, the latter seems more frequent. Although I accept both options, neither feels completely right, and if forced to produce the past-tense form of *dive* I might very well hesitate. The problem arises because there are two potential categorizing units, neither of which is able to fully suppress the other and decisively win the competition to serve in that capacity. One such unit is the constructional schema representing the regular pattern of past-tense formation. Thoroughly entrenched and easily activated, this schema specifies the suffixation of *-d* to mark past tense.[17] The other unit is the symbolic structure *dove* itself, specifically learned by speakers (at least those who use it) as the past-tense form of *dive*. For me, this unit is well enough entrenched that it is activated to some degree even when I hear the form *dived* and recognize it as instantiating the regular pattern. Thus I do not entirely avoid the secondary categorization of *dived* as a distorted manifestation of *dove*. Still, *dove* is not so terribly frequent that its status is wholly secure. It does not spring quite so readily to mind as does the past-tense form of *drive*, nor is its activation strong enough to completely suppress the regular pattern.

---

[17] More precisely, it specifies the suffixation of [d], [t], or [ə̌d] depending on phonological properties of the stem. The schema for the general pattern thus has three well-entrenched subschemas describing the individual variants.

This uncertainty regarding *dived* vs. *dove* comes about because two factors determining the choice of categorizing structure are at odds with one another. The regular pattern has a great advantage in terms of entrenchment and ease of activation. It is used so frequently, and with such a high percentage of English verbs, that it functions as the default, being activated for past-tense verbs unless there is strong motivation to override this choice. The existence of a specific, entrenched alternative—in this case *dove*—provides such motivation. Being an established unit, *dove* itself can be invoked to sanction a past-tense use of *dive*. Compared with the general pattern, it enjoys a major advantage in terms of overlap with the target: if the target is taken as being a past-tense form of *dive*, then it obviously overlaps with *dove* (which is precisely that) in far more respects than with a constructional schema that refers to the verb in only generalized fashion. In my own linguistic system, these two opposing factors are more or less in balance, hence my uncertainty.

The general point is that the factors bearing on the choice of categorizing structure vary from case to case in their relative strength and whether they tend to activate the same or different units for this purpose. The structure selected is not necessarily the most entrenched, the most specific, or the one most compatible with the target. Nor is the outcome necessarily the same from one occasion to the next. It all depends on the specific configuration of the network (for a given speaker, at a given point in time) and how the various elements and factors interact dynamically in the context of a particular usage event.

In taking *dove* as its past-tense form, *dive* follows the same pattern as a number of other monosyllabic verbs: *write/wrote*, *break/broke*, *drive/drove*, *freeze/froze*, *rise/rose*, *strive/strove*. What marks past tense in each case is the substitution $[(\ldots Vy\ldots)_\sigma]$ ---> $[(\ldots ow\ldots)_\sigma]$—that is, occurrence of the vocalic nucleus [ow] in lieu of either [ay], [ey], or [iy], which would otherwise be expected (cf. fig. 6.11(b)). Presumably speakers abstract a constructional schema to capture this limited regularity. If they do, the schema is too weakly established to be invoked for the sanction of novel expressions. When we coin a new verb—for instance *fease* 'make feasible'—the past tense has to be *feased*, not **fose*. The general pattern is so well entrenched that it is accessed by default for virtually all new verbs, eclipsing other alternatives. Unable to compete successfully, schemas representing other patterns are mostly inaccessible for new expressions. These "minor" patterns sustain themselves only because particular instantiations (like *wrote*, *broke*, *drove*, etc.) are specifically learned as conventional units. As such, they are able to compete with the general pattern by virtue of their far greater overlap with the target. In fact, for verbs occurring with any frequency they win the competition quite consistently. Thus we do not apprehend a form like **writed* as a well-formed instance of the regular pattern but as a distorted instance of *wrote*.

This interactive model resolves a number of well-known issues, the first of which is the problem posed by minor patterns like $[(\ldots Vy\ldots)_\sigma]$ ---> $[(\ldots ow\ldots)_\sigma]$. Since a pattern can be discerned, linguists feel obliged to posit a rule describing it. But if such a rule exists, why can it not be applied to other verbs, even novel ones? The model handles this by distinguishing between the mere existence of a schema (a reinforced commonality) and its capacity to win the competition for activation as a categorizing unit. Also accounted for is the clear historical tendency for minor patterns to be most persistent in words with the greatest frequency. The frequent occurrence of specific learned forms like *wrote*, *broke*, and *drove* makes them accessible enough to resist the gradual encroachment of the general pattern. Less frequent forms, like *dove*, *strove*, and the now archaic *hove*, are less readily elicited and therefore tend through time to be supplanted.[18] Finally, the model inherently explains the prevalent phenomenon known as **blocking**, observed in all domains of language structure. The term "blocking" indicates that a general pattern fails to apply in some particular situation because a more specific unit preempts it. Despite their regularity, for example, the past-tense verb **writed* is blocked from occurring by the well-entrenched alternative *wrote*, and the plural noun **mans* by *men*. Likewise, the readily available *thief*, *rapist*, *arsonist*, and *assassin* preempt the occurrence of **stealer*, **raper*, **burner*, and **assassinator* (cf. *killer*, *murderer*, *hijacker*, *embezzler*, *smuggler*, *kidnapper*). Blocking reflects the built-in advantage of more specific units over more schematic ones in competing for activation. A more specific unit is characterized by a larger number of properties, each a potential source of activation through overlap with the target.

A dynamic interactive model can therefore account for the gaps encountered in otherwise regular patterns. Consider one more case, involving a limited set of "postpositions" in Luiseño. As the term suggests, these postpositions are like prepositions, except that they follow the noun expressing their landmark (as suffixes) rather than preceding it (as separate words). The examples in (2) are representative. First, postpositions attach directly to nouns whose referents are inanimate. The constructional schema describing this pattern will be represented by the abbreviatory formula $[N_{inan}$-P$]$. Second, these endings occur on pronouns, whose referents are usually animate. This second pattern is given as $[N_{pron}$-P$]$, since in CG a pronoun is a type of noun (it profiles a thing). However, we see in (2)(c) that postpositions do not attach directly to animate nouns that are "lexical" (i.e. nonpronominal). So instead of a form like **hunwu-yk*, literally 'bear-to', we find the more elaborate expression *hunwut po-yk* 'bear it-to', where the postposition attaches to a coreferring pronoun.[19] Observe that the schema for this pattern, $[N_{an} [N_{pron}$-P$]]$, incorporates the one in (2)(b).

(2)   (a)   *ki-yk* 'to (the) house', *paa-ngay* 'from (the) water', *too-tal* 'with (a) rock' $[N_{inan}$-P$]$

(b)   *po-yk* 'to him', *chaamo-ngay* 'from us', *poomo-to* 'by them' $[N_{pron}$-P$]$

(c)   **hunwu-yk* 'to (the) bear', **nawitma-ngay* 'from (the) girl' $*[N_{an}$-P$]$

(d)   *hunwut po-yk* 'to (the) bear', *nawitmal po-ngay* 'from (the) girl' $[N_{an} [N_{pron}$-P$]]$

Since postpositions occur on both lexical nouns (if they are inanimate) and animate nouns (if they are pronominal), their nonoccurrence with animate lexical nouns is somewhat unexpected. Indeed, the more abstract constructional schema [N-P],

---

[18] For this reason, blatant irregularities—like the various forms of *be* (*am, is, are, was, were*)—survive best in words with the greatest frequency.

[19] The pronoun *po-* is third-person singular, so it translates as either 'him', 'her', or 'it'. The final consonants of *hunwut* and *nawitmal* are noun endings that are omitted with postpositions, in derived forms, and when a noun is possessed.

making no distinction among the types of nouns, might well be expected to emerge as the reinforced commonality of [N_{inan}-P] and [N_{pron}-P]. But if it does, what rules out the expressions in (2)(c), which conform to this higher-level schema? The answer depends on how rules are conceived. A theory embracing constructive rules (§8.1.2) could allow the formation of all expressions conforming to [N-P] at the level of underlying structure. An obligatory rule would then apply to those with an animate lexical noun, inserting a pronoun to bear the postposition: [N_{an}-P] $\Rightarrow$ [N_{an} [N_{pron}-P]]. This transformation would account for both the absence of expressions like (2)(c) and the occurrence of those in (2)(d) to fill the gap. However, it does so at the considerable theoretical cost of permitting derivations from hypothetical underlying structures. By contrast, a theory embracing filters would posit one to screen out the nonoccurring structures: *[N_{an}-P]. The pattern in (2)(d) then has to be dealt with in some other manner.

Neither option is available in CG.[20] Owing to the content requirement, we can only posit schemas that are directly analogous to occurring expressions. Learners of Luiseño will therefore abstract the schemas [N_{inan}-P], [N_{pron}-P], and [N_{an} [N_{pron}-P]], but not [N_{an}-P], since expressions like those in (2)(c) do not occur. Let us further assume, for sake of discussion, that they also abstract the high-level schema [N-P], representing what is common to the first two patterns. We can then account for the data on the presumption that only the lower-level schemas are accessible for the sanction of new expressions. This is quite reasonable since the lower-level patterns are thoroughly entrenched, being experienced on countless occasions, and have the built-in advantage that comes with being more specific than [N-P]. The resulting inaccessibility of the higher-level pattern is indicated in figure 8.10 by enclosing it in a dashed-line box.

The diagram shows how the schemas apply to the different kinds of targets. Based on ease of activation and degree of overlap with the target, the lower-level

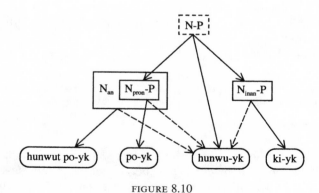

FIGURE 8.10

<hr />

[20] CG's limitation to positive statements (precluding filters) is not a rigid doctrine but a working hypothesis. The framework would not be greatly changed should it be found that speakers sometimes learn specific prohibitions as well. This example shows how filters can be avoided in certain cases that might at first seem to require them.

schemas $[N_{inan}\text{-}P]$, $[N_{pron}\text{-}P]$, and $[N_{an} [N_{pron}\text{-}P]]$ are respectively activated to categorize target expressions like those in (2)(a), (2)(b), and (2)(d). These are judged well-formed. What about (2)(c)? An expression like *hunwu-yk* would indeed be found acceptable were it able to elicit [N-P] for its categorization. The high-level schema is not available, however, being eclipsed by the more specific units. We might speculate that $[N_{an} [N_{pron}\text{-}P]]$ would win the competition, since *hunwut* is fully compatible with N_{an}, but not with N_{inan} or N_{pron}. But since *hunwu-yk* conflicts with each lower-level schema in some respect, it is nonconventional whichever one is chosen.

8.3 Networks of Constructions

A general feature of linguistic organization is the existence of complex categories, in which multiple variants are linked in networks. The individual nodes in such a network can be structures of any size or any kind. As a special case, each node consists of an entire symbolic assembly. The network then defines a category whose members are related constructions. Complex categories of this sort are important in describing both lexicon and grammar, which can be seen as forming a continuum.

8.3.1 From the Grammatical Standpoint

To completely describe the grammar of a language, it is not enough to characterize general patterns. It must also be ensured that the proper elements occur in them. Out of all the elements that might be used in a given pattern, the ones conventionally exploited are often limited to a certain range or even an arbitrary subset. This is the problem of **distribution**.

For many grammatical phenomena, distribution is specified by means of constructional subschemas—structures of intermediate generality—that have to be posited in addition to a higher-level schema describing the general pattern or in lieu of such a schema. We saw this in the case of Luiseño postpositions (fig. 8.10). Even if speakers abstract the general pattern [N-P], they do not exploit all the options it potentially makes available. To specify the actual distribution, we must posit the constructional subschemas $[N_{pron}\text{-}P]$ and $[N_{inan}\text{-}P]$ but not $*[N_{an}\text{-}P]$. We must further posit the more complex schema $[N_{an} [N_{pron}\text{-}P]]$, which fills this gap in the general pattern. It is these lower-level schemas, not [N-P], that actually determine what does and does not occur.

Owing to their built-in competitive advantage, lower-level schemas are frequently invoked and thus essential to language structure. When a high-level pattern is discernible, its actual implementation in conventional usage may still be effected by more specific units. These can be quite specific, to the point of incorporating particular lexical items or grammatical markers. Alongside the schemas mentioned, we can plausibly posit for Luiseño an array of more specific units that incorporate a particular postposition or a particular noun. Here are two such units, along with instantiating expressions:

(3) (a) [N-yk]   *ki-yk* 'to (the) house', *too-yk* 'to (the) rock', *po-yk* 'to him'

(b) [too-P]   *too-yk* 'to (the) rock', *too-ngay* 'from (the) rock', *too-tal* 'with (a) rock'

We must further suppose that numerous specific expressions conforming to these patterns occur sufficiently often to be established as conventional units. Speakers can then invoke them as familiar, prepackaged wholes, rather than having to assemble them from component elements in accordance with constructional schemas. Instantiating expressions like *kiyk* 'to (the) house' and *tootal* 'with (a) rock' might very well be frequent enough to coalesce as units. We can certainly ascribe unit status to most every combination of a postposition and a personal pronoun, like the forms in (2)(b).

In practical terms, we cannot always know whether a particular expression is established as a unit. While this may not be of any great importance (in the grand scheme of things), in principle the degree of entrenchment can be determined empirically. Observed frequency provides one basis for estimating it. Experimentally, one can look for measurable differences in the processing of novel vs. unit expressions (Harris 1998). We have more direct evidence of unit status when an expression consistently displays some idiosyncrasy that does not follow from any regular pattern. Were it not an established unit, for example, there would be no way of knowing that 'to me' is expressed in Luiseño as *neyk*, rather than the expected **noyk* (cf. *noo* 'I'). We must also posit units in the case of a minor pattern when it cannot be predicted which elements participate in it. For instance, the past-tense verbs *wrote*, *broke*, *drove*, *froze*, *rose*, *dove*, and *strove* must all be learned as units. We cannot claim that they are simply constructed when needed by means of the constructional schema describing the pattern $[(\ldots \mathrm{Vy} \ldots)_\sigma] \dashrightarrow [(\ldots \mathrm{ow} \ldots)_\sigma]$. This would imply the schema's accessibility for the sanction of new expressions, but if it were accessible we could not account for its failure to apply with other verbs (e.g. **fose* as the past tense of *fease* or **sote* as the past tense of *sight*).

To indicate that the past tense of *write* is *wrote*, a linguist might flag the stem with a diacritic (or "rule feature") meant to specify that it undergoes a morphological rule ablauting [Vy] to [ow]. Alternatively, one might posit a special subclass of verbs based on this morphological property, listing *write* as one of its members. Yet it seems quite unlikely that anything directly analogous to a diacritic or the symbol for a subclass would be part of the actual mental representation of linguistic structure.[21] In a CG account, the information that *write* takes *wrote* as its past-tense form is provided instead by the specific inclusion of *wrote* among the conventional units of English. The morphological rule is simply a constructional schema—a schematic assembly of symbolic structures—and the instantiating expressions (*wrote*, *broke*, *drove*, etc.) reside in specific assemblies. Thus to describe this subclass of verbs, nothing is posited other than symbolic assemblies linked by categorizing relationships.

An important aspect of the usage-based conception is that large numbers of complex expressions are learned and stored as units, including many that conform to regular patterns (Bybee 2006). The network describing an overall grammatical construction may thus incorporate specific unit expressions instantiating constructional schemas characterized at different levels of abstraction. Usually there is more to the structure of such a network than just elaborative relationships. In addition to these

---

[21] Having no intrinsic semantic or phonological content, such devices are ruled out in CG by the content requirement. Their occasional use for abbreviatory purposes carries no implication that they have any direct analog in cognition.

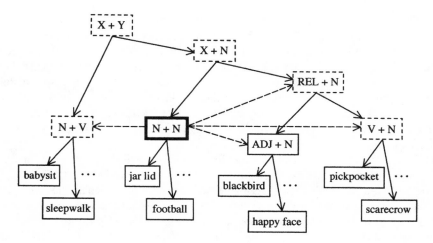

FIGURE 8.11

"vertical" connections, we can also recognize "horizontal" relationships of extension from a category prototype. A particular constructional schema can often be seen as prototypical by virtue of being frequently instantiated and easily invoked for new expressions. It thus defines the category "center", with respect to which other, less commonly exploited constructional variants constitute conventional departures.

Figure 8.11 is a partial sketch of the network for English compounds. The vast majority of examples are compounds of the form [N + N], which can thus be taken as prototypical. Other patterns, including [ADJ + N], [V + N], and [N + V], are shown as extensions vis-à-vis this basic pattern. Also part of the network are various constructional subschemas (not shown), as well as many specific expressions with unit status. Further indicated in the diagram are certain higher-level schemas that might be abstracted as the reinforced commonality of lower-level patterns, such as [REL + N] for compounds where the first element (an adjective or a verb) profiles a relationship. Of the schemas shown, only [N + N] and to a lesser extent [ADJ + N] are commonly exploited in forming new expressions. The others are enclosed in dashed-line boxes to indicate their relative inaccessibility.

Corresponding to a higher-level schema is a wide range of conceivable instantiating expressions. Usually this large space of structural possibilities is only partially, even sparsely, inhabited by expressions (either fixed or novel) that will be accepted as conventional. Moreover, the space is "warped" in the sense that new expressions are more likely to crop up in certain occupied regions than in others. Effecting these limitations are networks of schemas like figure 8.11. To the extent that a high-level schema (e.g. [X + Y]) emerges at all, it is still the overall network that specifies the details of its implementation in actual language use.

8.3.2 From the Lexical Standpoint

At first blush, a lexical item seems simple and straightforward. There is a form (e.g. [cat]), it has a meaning ([CAT]), and the two are paired symbolically:

[[CAT]/[cat]]. But at second blush, when examined more carefully, lexical items prove capable of substantial complexity in a number of dimensions. For now we can ignore the internal complexity of a semantic unit like [CAT], an elaborate conceptual structure recruiting an open-ended set of cognitive domains (§2.2.2). This internal multiplicity (characteristic of any single meaning) has to be distinguished from polysemy, in which a lexical item has not just one meaning but a family of related senses (fig. 2.2).[22] Polysemy in turn is different from symbolic complexity, the extent to which a lexical item is analyzable into smaller symbolic structures (fig. 1.2).

Yet another dimension of complexity pertains to a lexical item's occurrence in larger structural contexts. Typically a lexeme is conventionally established in a variety of contexts, which are describable in either specific or schematic terms. For instance, it is quite standard for *cat* to be directly preceded by a determiner or by an adjective, or to be followed by a complex modifier like a prepositional phrase. As conventional units, we can therefore posit the schematic configurations [DET cat], [ADJ cat], and [cat PP], as well as a considerable number of familiar expressions that instantiate them (e.g. *my cat, the cat, any cat, lazy cat, black cat, cat with kittens, cat on a hot tin roof*). A highly frequent verb, such as *give*, is well entrenched as a component of constructions that specify its various morphological realizations: *gives, gave, given, giving, to give*. Syntactically, it is well established as the lexical head in two kinds of clauses, exemplified in (4). They are distinguished by whether the verb is followed by two nominal complements, as in (a), or by a nominal and a prepositional phrase with *to*. These are commonly referred to as the "ditransitive" and "caused-motion" constructions.[23] The occurrence of *give* in these two patterns is represented by the formulas on the right.

(4) (a) **Ditransitive:** *She gave her boyfriend a new Mercedes.*   [give NML NML]

     (b) **Caused-motion:** *She gave a new Mercedes to her boyfriend.*   [give NML [to NML]]

We can say that lexical items are conventionally used in particular **structural frames** (like [ADJ cat] and [give NML NML]) and that a set of such frames is one aspect of a lexeme's overall description. The lexeme may appear in many frames or just a few. These frames can be of different sizes (so that some incorporate others) and characterized at different levels of specificity (so that some instantiate others). They amount to constructional schemas that contain the lexical item as one component element.[24]

---

[22] A lexical item may also comprise a family of variant forms (FCG1: §10.3.3).

[23] An extensive treatment can be found in Goldberg 1995. A "ditransitive" clause is so called because it is not only transitive but has two object-like complements. The term "caused motion" indicates a relationship to sentences like *He threw the cat over the fence*, where the subject causes the object to move along the path specified by the prepositional phrase.

[24] To the extent that other components are specific rather than schematic, they constitute standard **collocations**. For example, the unit expression *burnt toast* figures in the overall characterization of both *burnt* and *toast*, representing the fact that each commonly occurs (collocates) with the other.

Knowing a large number of lexemes in structural frames is an important aspect of a speaker's mastery of a language. Representing well-rehearsed ways of deploying lexical units, they are in no small measure responsible for the fluency and facility of normal speech. This leads to a subtle but crucial point concerning the relation between a lexeme and its frames. Though standard, it is quite wrong to think of a lexeme as existing independently of its frames. Linguists are guilty of this misconception when they speak of lexical items being "inserted" into syntactic structures. What this overlooks is how lexical items are acquired in the first place: by abstraction from usage events where they occur in particular structural contexts. These contexts provide the initial basis for a lexeme's apprehension, and thus remain—in schematized form—as the learner becomes proficient in using it conventionally. Essential to knowing a lexical item is knowing how it is used. Rather than being obtained **after** a lexeme is acquired, this knowledge is an inherent aspect of its acquisition.[25]

From this usage-based perspective, the issue to be addressed is not how a lexical item comes to be used in certain frames, but to what extent it achieves any independent status vis-à-vis these frames. The abstraction of linguistic units from usage events goes hand in glove with the process of **decontextualization**. A unit is abstracted through the progressive reinforcement of commonalities that recur across a series of events. Excluded from the unit, through lack of reinforcement, are the myriad details that differ from one event to the next. To some extent, therefore, the emergence of a unit results in its detachment from the original supporting contexts. How far this decontextualization is carried depends on how varied the contexts are. Consider the morphological realizations of Luiseño *too* 'rock'. Since the forms in (3)(b) vary only in the choice of postposition, these alone support the emergence of [too-P]. If we add to this the subject form *too-ta*, we have the basis for [too-X], a more schematic frame indicating that *too* occurs with a suffix. But it also occurs with possessor prefixes (e.g. *no-too* 'my rock'), whence the alternate frame [POSSR-too]. Thus it is not the case that *too* consistently appears either with a suffix or with a prefix. Its morphological contexts are varied enough for *too* to be established independently of any particular frame.[26]

To some extent, a lexeme's meaning is shaped by the frames it occurs in. While the effect is often minor—presumably Luiseño *too* means pretty much the same in *too-ta* 'rock', *too-tal* 'with (a) rock', and *no-too* 'my rock'—it is not always quite so negligible. *Send*, for example, has subtly different senses, depending on whether

---

[25] This is especially true for verbs, which are first learned in specific structural contexts and only later generalized (Tomasello 1992, 2003). Of course, it is not denied that some lexemes might be learned in a frame-independent manner (e.g. by looking in a dictionary), or that forms learned in a certain frame can be extended to other contexts characteristic of their grammatical class. The point is simply that the problem of getting lexical items into the proper structural frames is spurious since any strict dichotomy is artificial to begin with.

[26] Still, *too* always occurs as part of a larger word, making it less autonomous morphologically than English *rock*. The suffix *-ta* occurs by default when the noun would otherwise stand alone. Like the endings *-t* of *hunwut* and *-l* of *nawitmal* (see n. 19), *-ta* can be analyzed as being semantically equivalent to the noun schema.

it is used in the ditransitive construction, as a caused-motion verb, or as part of the complex predicate *send for*:

(5) (a) *They sent me another brochure.*   [send$_1$ NML NML]

   (b) *We sent the new letter to all the applicants.*   [send$_2$ NML [to NML]]

   (c) *You can send for more information at any time.*   [[send$_3$ for] NML]

Send has a different kind of landmark in each construction, and since focal prominence is an important aspect of meaning, the semantic values it assumes in these contexts are distinct.

These different senses of *send* are sketched in figure 8.12. The small circles indicate event participants. An ellipse represents a participant's **dominion**, or sphere of control (fig. 3.14). A property shared by all three senses is that the trajector causes (double arrow) another entity to move (single arrow) from its own dominion into that of another participant.[27] The main distinguishing property is the degree of prominence conferred on this other participant, the "recipient", who controls the target dominion. In the case of *send$_1$*, the recipient is focused as landmark, with the consequence that the profiled relationship includes the recipient's subsequent access (dashed arrow) to the mover. By contrast, *send$_2$* confers landmark status on the mover, so that more emphasis falls on the path of motion. Not focused by the verb, the recipient is introduced only indirectly, as the landmark of the *to*-phrase serving to specify this path. With *send$_3$*, the recipient is not even mentioned. The complex verb *send for* deflects attention from what is sent and who receives it, focusing instead on the anticipated result of something moving in the opposite direction, into the trajector's dominion. This second mover functions as the landmark of the complex verb as a whole, not of *send$_3$* individually.[28] Yet some conception of this anticipated motion (dashed arrow)

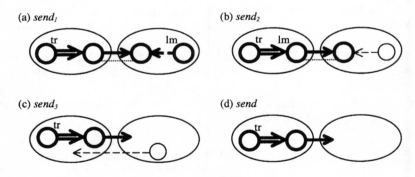

(a) *send$_1$*   (b) *send$_2$*

(c) *send$_3$*   (d) *send*

FIGURE 8.12

---

[27] It is convenient to show the mover in both its initial and final positions. A dotted correspondence line indicates that the entities occupying these two locations are the same.

[28] As evidence for these characterizations, the nominal identified as the verb's landmark (or object) in each case functions as subject of the corresponding passive: *I was sent another brochure*; *The new letter was sent to all the applicants*; *More information can be sent for at any time*.

colors the value of *send₃* itself. Because *send₃* is limited to this larger context, evoking it must to some extent activate the scenario as a whole.

Diagram (d) indicates what is common to *send₁*, *send₂*, and *send₃*. This more schematic sense is thus the meaning *send* has independently of any particular syntactic frame. If it emerges at all, this abstracted meaning is only secondary. From the standpoint of acquisition, it represents a further development in which the decontextualization yielding *send₁*, *send₂*, and *send₃* is carried to the extreme. From the processing standpoint, it is presumably less accessible than the more specific senses. These alternate meanings of *send* can be modeled as a network, shown on the right in figure 8.13. Given with each specific sense is the structural frame that induces it.

Shown on the left in figure 8.13 is a fragment of the network for English ditransitive constructions.[29] Central to this pattern are verbs of transfer, like *give, send, mail,* etc. We can therefore posit the constructional schema [TRANSFER NML NML], as well as subschemas like [give NML NML] and [send₁ NML NML]. An array of more specific structures, such as [give me NML], are also entrenched as units. While the transfer pattern is prototypical, ditransitives are also used in a number of other cases, e.g. with verbs of intended transfer (*promise, owe, grant, bequeath*), verbs of permission and denial (*permit, allow, deny, refuse*), and verbs of creation for someone's benefit (*make, cook, build, bake*). The higher-level schema covering all these possibilities, represented as [V NML NML], is not itself accessible for the sanction of new expressions. The conventional distribution of ditransitives is specified by the entire network, rather than any single node.

Sitting in the middle of figure 8.13, as a node in both networks, is the partially schematic structure [send₁ NML NML]. It belongs to both the lexical network representing the structural frames for *send* (and the meanings they induce) and the

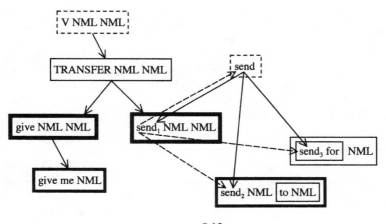

FIGURE 8.13

---

[29] Cf. Goldberg 1995. In examining such diagrams, keep in mind the limitations of the network metaphor (discussed at the end of §8.1.3).

grammatical network for ditransitive constructions. This is in no way problematic but just what we should expect. Lexical items and grammatical constructions are each abstracted from occurring expressions through the reinforcement of recurring commonalities. In either case, the typical result is a network of related variants characterized at different levels of schematicity. How far the process of schematization proceeds, and in what direction, depends on what is shared by the source expressions. From distinct but overlapping sets of expressions, there can thus emerge both constructional schemas (which abstract away from particular lexical items) and lexical variants (first induced by particular structural frames). A structure like [send$_1$ NML NML] represents an initial step with respect to both paths of abstraction. Is it lexical or is it grammatical? The answer can only be "yes", for it is both. This is one of many indications that lexicon and grammar form a gradation (§1.3.2).

8.4 Regularity

It is sometimes maintained that syntax and lexicon are sharply distinct and quite dissimilar in nature. Syntax, on this view, is characterized by regularity and is thus describable by rules, whereas lexicon is the repository of irregularity—a mass of unpredictable idiosyncrasies. CG takes a very different stand on these issues. It offers a unified account of lexicon and grammar (subsuming both syntax and morphology), in which every linguistic unit represents a reinforced pattern and thus embodies a regularity of some kind. To see this more clearly, we need to examine the very notion of regularity and consider some of its less obvious manifestations.

8.4.1 Constructional Meaning and Compositionality

Though linguists seldom bother to explain it, the notion of regularity is anything but self-explanatory. The term subsumes no less than three separate factors: **generality**, **productivity**, and **compositionality**.

1. Generality pertains to the level of schematicity at which a pattern is characterized. For instance, a pattern characterized in terms of a nominal (with no limitation as to kind) has greater generality than one referring to a pronoun in particular. Similarly, the high-level ditransitive schema [V NML NML] is more general than [TRANSFER NML NML] (limited to verbs of transfer), which in turn is more general than [give NML NML] (fig. 8.13). A fully specific fixed expression, such as *Give me that!* or *cat*, represents a pattern with the lowest degree of generality.

2. Productivity pertains to a schema's degree of accessibility for the sanction of new expressions. We have seen that the most general constructional schemas, like [V NML NML] or Luiseño [N-P], are often not available for this purpose. Conversely, a pattern of lesser generality may be fully productive within the scope of the generalization. Luiseño [N$_{inan}$-P], for example, is freely applicable to new combinations of inanimate nouns and postpositions. But a low degree of generality does not ensure productivity. We saw this for the past tense of verbs like *write, break,* and *freeze.* The constructional schema describing the pattern is fairly specific in regard to the verb's phonological pole: $[(\ldots Vy \ldots)_\sigma]$. Yet it cannot be activated to license

new expressions (like *fose* for the nonce-form *fease*). Despite its greater generality, the default pattern (yielding *feased*) is more entrenched and consistently wins the competition for activation. Patterns that correspond to the classic conception of syntax, being both maximally general and fully productive, are actually quite atypical. Likely candidates are schemas describing basic word order, such as [V NML] for a verb and its object.

3. Compositionality is the extent to which a composite structure is predictable from the component structures together with the sanctioning constructional schema. The position taken in CG is that semantics is only partially compositional (§6.2.1). While some expressions (like *jar lid*) approximate full compositionality, others (like *laptop*) diverge quite drastically from what they ought to mean. Some degree of divergence—if only in the guise of greater specificity—is usual for both fixed and novel expressions. So, as with the other two factors, compositionality fails to support the dichotomous vision of a fully regular syntax vs. a wholly irregular lexicon.

Compositionality is only partial because linguistic meanings depend on more than just component structures and constructional schemas. Many additional resources are drawn upon in arriving at composite semantic structures (§2.1.3). An expression's meaning presupposes an elaborate conceptual substrate that supports and shapes it. Furthermore, language users employ a rich array of imaginative and interpretive abilities. Strictly speaking, then, a complex expression's meaning cannot be **computed** from lexical meanings and compositional patterns (the semantic poles of constructional schemas) but is more accurately seen as being **prompted** by them.[30]

Nonetheless, constructional schemas are meaningful and make an essential semantic contribution to complex expressions. If they do not tell the whole story of how composite meanings are arrived at, such schemas at least supply essential information as to how the component conceptions fit together and how their integrated content is construed (e.g. in terms of profiling). They influence the interpretation of component lexical items and may further contribute their own conceptual content. These are all aspects of **constructional meaning**. In these various ways, grammar itself has a substantial and systematic role in determining the meanings of composite expressions.

Only in recent years have linguists come to appreciate the extent to which constructional schemas reinforce, supplement, or even override the conceptual content supplied by component lexical items (Goldberg 1995, 2006). A schema that does not incorporate any specific lexical item may nonetheless be first acquired on the basis of a small number of lexemes that share some essential content, which is therefore retained as the schema emerges (Tomasello 1992; Sethuraman 2002). This aspect of their meaning is then reinforced by the schema when the lexemes are used in the construction it defines. For example, the ditransitive construction is based initially on frequent verbs of transfer, such as *give*, *bring*, *send*, and *tell*. Thus the initial

---

[30] Sweetser 1999 demonstrates that this is so even for seemingly straightforward cases like the combination of an adjective and a noun in the [ADJ N] construction.

constructional schema, [TRANSFER NML NML], retains what is common to these verbs (roughly what is shown in fig. 8.12(a)). Subsequently, both the lexeme and the schema provide this shared content in ditransitive sentences like *She gave him an apple* or *Tell me a story*.

In adult usage, the ditransitive pattern is extended to a variety of situations involving something other than simple transfer. One class of cases are illustrated by the sentences in (6):

(6)   (a) *She made him a kite.   They built us a porch.   I knitted her a sweater.* [creation]

  (b) *He wrote me a check.   She baked them a pie.   Peel me another orange.* [preparation]

  (c) *I bought him a clock.   Find us some old rags.   She got you a fancy car.* [acquisition]

These differ from simple transfer in that the recipient obtains something which is not initially under the subject's control, at least in any usable form. Instead, the subject acts to make it available for the recipient's use by creating, preparing, or acquiring it. Note that all these verbs have other, more basic uses that do not invoke a recipient in any salient manner:

(7)   (a) *She made a kite.*   *They built a porch.*   *I knitted a sweater.*   [creation]

  (b) *He wrote a check.*   *She baked a pie.*   *Peel another orange.*   [preparation]

  (c) *I bought a clock.*   *Find some old rags.*   *She got a fancy car.*   [acquisition]

Thus it is not a matter of these verbs originally having a transfer meaning that enables them to be used in the central ditransitive construction. Instead, they are used in this construction even though they lack this specific content, which the construction itself must therefore supply. The composite meanings in (6) combine the notion of creation, preparation, or acquisition—all of which result in an object's availability for use—with that of transfer to a recipient, contributed by the constructional schema.

This development is sketched in figure 8.14. In the upper box is a partial representation of the constructional schema [TRANSFER NML NML], showing component structures and the correspondences linking them. The box below stands for a verb of creation, preparation, or acquisition, as in (7). The notation is meant to indicate that the trajector does something which causes the landmark to become available in the trajector's dominion. The diagram represents the initial use of such a verb in the basic ditransitive construction, before the pattern in (6) has been established. At this stage, using a verb of creation, preparation, or acquisition to instantiate a schematic verb of transfer constitutes an extension vis-à-vis the sanctioning schema, not merely an elaboration. A dashed arrow is thus employed for this categorizing relationship between the verbs of the constructional schema and the target expression; this is one aspect of the expression's structural interpretation with reference to the schema. Since we are presuming that this usage is previously unfamiliar, the categorization is enclosed in a box with rounded corners.

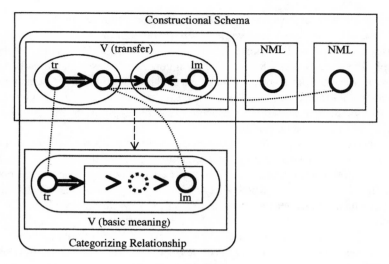

FIGURE 8.14

The result of this categorization is that the verbs in such expressions (e.g. *She made him a kite*) are **apprehended as** verbs of transfer. A categorizing judgment constitutes a unified experience not equivalent to that of apprehending the schema and the target individually (§8.2.1). In the context of this usage, therefore, the verbs in (6) are associated with the unified conception depicted in figure 8.15(a). This blended meaning subsumes the content of both schema and target, and it follows the former in its choice of landmark. When such a verb is first employed in this construction, the blended meaning—like the categorization inducing it—is a novel one. But with repeated use, the entire categorizing judgment is entrenched and established as a unit, including the blended meaning, as shown in diagram (b). At this point, we

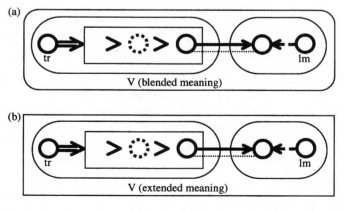

FIGURE 8.15

can reasonably say that the verb has taken on an extended meaning—one that incorporates the notion of transfer, as well as its basic content of creation, preparation, or acquisition. To be sure, it assumes this meaning only in the context of the symbolic assembly sketched in figure 8.14. It is true in general, however, that a verb's meanings are abstracted from its occurrence in particular structural frames, which are part of its characterization (fig. 8.13). To say that a verb "has" a certain meaning is merely to say that its association with this conception, in the appropriate structural context, is established as a conventional unit.

As seen in (6), this type of extension occurs not just with one verb but with many. The repeated use of such expressions leads to the entrenchment, in schematized form, of the entire configuration in figure 8.14. This amounts to a new constructional schema for ditransitives, in which a verb of creation, preparation, or acquisition is employed and apprehended as a verb of transfer. If [TRANSFER NML NML] is prototypical, this new variant is more peripheral to the category, an extension from the prototype. It is conventionally established, however, and accessible for the sanction of new expressions, including those with less frequent verbs not commonly used in this manner. On this basis we can interpret the sentences in (8) and judge them well-formed. Naturally, with repeated use in this construction, these verbs too are capable of acquiring the transfer sense this use induces. It is through such developments that complex categories are gradually built up, starting from their prototypes.[31]

(8)   (a) *She sculpted him an elephant.*   [creation]

       (b) *Skin me another cat.*   [preparation]

       (c) *I stole her a diamond ring.*   [acquisition]

8.4.2 Higher-Order Generalizations

The categorization in figure 8.14 is one aspect of the relationship between an expression and a constructional schema invoked for its structural interpretation. In expressions like (6), a verb such as *make*, *peel*, or *find* instantiates a schematic verb of transfer despite their semantic incompatibility. By virtue of this categorization, such a verb is **apprehended as** a verb of transfer in the context of this construction. The blended meaning that results can be established as a new, extended sense of the verb through repeated occurrence in this frame (fig. 8.15).

Because this happens not just with one verb but with many, the configuration in figure 8.14, including the blended meaning that emerges, is subject to schematization. That is, this context-induced semantic extension constitutes a recurring pattern, which can itself be established as a unit at a level of abstraction determined by the range of verbs giving rise to it. And once established, this unit can itself be invoked to sanction the semantic extension of additional verbs, like those in (8). Our concern in this final section is the nature of such a unit and its place within a linguistic system.

---

[31] I would not claim that the scenario just described necessarily represents the actual course of development for ditransitives. It is only meant to illustrate the kinds of processes that are plausibly invoked for the growth of complex categories and the interaction of lexical and constructional meanings.

It is one representative of an important but little-recognized class of regularities that I refer to as **higher-order generalizations**.

In describing a linguistic system, we are limited by the content requirement (§1.3.4) as to the kinds of units we can posit. The only units permitted are semantic, phonological, and symbolic structures that are (i) parts of occurring expressions, (ii) schematizations of permitted structures, or (iii) categorizing relationships between permitted structures. For example, symbolic structures allowed under (i) are fixed expressions such as *lazy cat*, *clean air*, and *valid argument*, whereas the constructional schema [ADJ N] is permitted under (ii), and the categorization [[ADJ N] → [lazy cat]] under (iii). Thus a schema like [ADJ N], representing part (ii) of the content requirement, emerges as a generalization over instantiating expressions, representing part (i), and their relationship corresponds to part (iii). This is not the only possibility, however. Because categorizing relationships are permitted as units under (iii), and (ii) allows schematizations of permitted structures, schematization can also apply to categorizations.[32] And because it captures what is common to a set of categorizations, the resulting schema constitutes a higher-order generalization.

The structure in figure 8.14 is therefore permitted under the content requirement. We can view it in several different ways, all of which are valid. For one thing, it constitutes an **augmented constructional schema**. It is a constructional schema because it specifies the integration of a verb and its nonsubject complements in sentences like (8), where the verb employed is primarily one of creation, preparation, or acquisition.[33] Moreover, in the scenario outlined above, the structure develops as an augmentation of the central schema for ditransitives based on verbs of transfer. It emerges through application of this central pattern to situations where the profiled action involves transfer only as a secondary consequence. While this usage conflicts with the basic schema, it is well within the usual range of tolerance, and as it recurs, reinforcement of its common features results in entrenchment and schematization of the entire configuration. A new constructional schema thus emerges that is based on and incorporates the original one (which is still independently accessible and prototypical for ditransitives).

This configuration can also be viewed as a partial characterization of the verbs in (6). For each such verb (*make*, *peel*, *find*, etc.), it represents the blended meaning established as one of its senses, as well as the structural frame that induces this extension from its basic semantic value. In schematized form, it represents what is common to such verbs, thus defining a particular subclass of ditransitive predicates.

Finally, the configuration in figure 8.14 can be viewed as a **pattern of semantic extension**. For each individual verb, it represents both the basic meaning (the prototypical semantic value) and the extended meaning induced in this context through its apprehension as a verb of transfer. This aspect of the configuration is separately

---

[32] Furthermore, the relationship between the schematized categorization and any particular categorization is itself a categorizing relationship permitted under (iii).

[33] Bear in mind that fig. 8.14 is simplified in various ways. It does not show constituency, composite structures, or the phonological pole. Nor does it show the blended meaning resulting from the verb's categorization by the schematic verb of transfer (this is given separately in fig. 8.15). And despite the box with rounded corners, we are considering the stage when the entire configuration has the status of a unit.

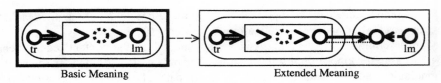

Basic Meaning   Extended Meaning

FIGURE 8.16

shown in figure 8.16. At the schematic level (as part of the augmented constructional schema), it describes an abstracted pattern by which a nontransfer verb develops a transfer sense. We saw in (8) that this pattern is applicable to additional verbs in the same constructional context. As the schematization of a categorization, it constitutes a higher-order generalization.

A generalization of this sort reflects an important aspect of our mental capacity. The abstracted regularity does not pertain to the nature of individual content structures (in this case, meanings) but rather to how such structures are related to one another. This higher-order abstractive capacity has numerous linguistic manifestations. Indeed, since component and composite structures are linked by categorizing relationships, every constructional schema represents the schematization of categorizations. Additional manifestations of this capacity are found in patterns of metonymic and phonological extension.

Although the term is used in various ways, for our purposes metonymy can be characterized as a shift in profile (§3.3.1). An expression that in its basic sense profiles some entity, A, is instead understood as designating another entity, B, which is somehow associated with A and thus mentally accessible through it. This is shown abstractly in figure 8.17.

Here the relevant point is that metonymy often follows conventionally established patterns. To take just one example, the name for a place is commonly extended to designate, instead, a noteworthy (and often tragic) event that occurred there: *Vietnam*, *Chernobyl*, *Oklahoma City*, *Wounded Knee*, *Hiroshima*, *Waterloo*, and so on. A given metonymic usage represents a particular place-to-event extension entrenched as a unit, e.g. [[**VIETNAM**—WAR] ---> [VIETNAM—**WAR**]].[34] Each such unit

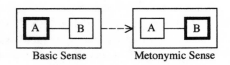

Basic Sense   Metonymic Sense

FIGURE 8.17

[34] The extension occurs at the semantic pole of the place expression. Note that the basic sense is not necessarily the most frequent or cognitively salient. While for most speakers *Chernobyl* evokes the nuclear disaster rather than the place where it occurred, the term is nonetheless still understood as metonymic for the place. Hence the basic sense (as determined by the direction of a metonymic pattern) and the one most easily activated need not be the same. In the case of *Vietnam*, the two senses seem equally well entrenched.

instantiates the schematized extension [[**PLACE**—EVENT] ---> [PLACE—**EVENT**]], which describes the general pattern. Moreover, this schema is commonly invoked for the sanction of new expressions. It was virtually inevitable that in the aftermath of the 2000 presidential election the word *Florida* would come to designate the vote-counting fiasco there (as in *Florida must never happen again*).

Further illustrating the schematization of categorizations is a pattern of phonological extension. Recall the imagined example (§8.1.3) of the vowel [a] being nasalized after [m]. Once established as a regular occurrence, this variant pronunciation is specified by the conventional categorizing unit [[ma] ---> [mã]]. The pattern can be extended to other vowels as well, resulting in units like [[me] ---> [mẽ]], [[mu] ---> [mũ]], etc. As this happens, reinforcement of their common properties produces the schematized extension [[mV] ---> [mṼ]], representing the generalization that any vowel can be nasalized after [m]. Of course, the pattern can also be extended to other nasal consonants, yielding units like [[na] ---> [nã]], [[ŋa] ---> [ŋã]], and the schema [[Na] ---> [Nã]] referring to nasal consonants as a class. As the variant pronunciation generalizes across both vowels and nasal consonants, the schema [[NV] ---> [NṼ]] might eventually emerge as a high-level generalization.[35]

Schematizations of categorizations are noteworthy because the generalizations they embody pertain to the relationship between content structures manifested in different expressions. The generalization expressed by the metonymic pattern [[**PLACE**—EVENT] ---> [PLACE—**EVENT**]], for example, pertains to the semantic value of a place term (like *Vietnam*) in different expressions, as part of different usage events. Likewise, the phonological pattern expressed by [[mV] ---> [mṼ]] pertains to alternate pronunciations of a given syllable on different occasions. We have the capacity, in other words, to generalize over relationships that are not evident in any single expression or usage event, in which case the schematization's scope encompasses multiple expressions. This capacity has another important linguistic manifestation in the emergence of lexical subclasses whose members pattern alike across an array of grammatical constructions. These subclasses constitute higher-order generalizations in the sense that the defining properties are distributed over multiple constructions, in each of which the subclass members behave analogously.

Although this notion has broad applicability, the kind of case I have in mind is a "conjugation class", a set of verbs that follow precisely the same pattern in their inflection for tense, person, number, and so on. It is worth going through an actual example in some detail, as the idiosyncrasies of inflectional paradigms are often considered problematic for semantically based theories of grammar. They are problematic only under the gratuitous and erroneous assumption that such a theory has to predict those idiosyncrasies on the basis of meaning. In CG, however, it is not claimed that they are **predictable**, only that they are **describable** as symbolic assemblies in accordance with the content requirement. While an entire verb paradigm is too extensive to cover here, a small fragment is enough to show the basic approach.

---

[35] Such higher-level schemas capture the sorts of regularities that classic generative phonology handled by means of rules deriving phonetic representations from underlying structures. For a comparison, see FCG1: 443–444 and GC: ch. 4.

	'love'	'sing'	'work'	
1s:PRES	**am**o	**cant**o	**trabaj**o	-o
2s:PRES	**am**as	**cant**as	**trabaj**as	-s
3s:PRES	**am**a	**cant**a	**trabaj**a	Ø
1s:PAST	**am**é	**cant**é	**trabaj**é	-é
2s:PAST	**am**aste	**cant**aste	**trabaj**aste	-ste
3s:PAST	**am**ó	**cant**ó	**trabaj**ó	-ó
	am(a)	**cant**(a)	**trabaj**(a)	

FIGURE 8.18

Chosen for illustration is the most basic conjugation class in Spanish, consisting of "regular" verbs ending in *a*. There are two other major classes, and quite a number of minor ones, but the members of the *a*-class are most numerous. This class functions as a default in that new verbs ending in *a* automatically follow this pattern. Presented with an appropriate verb stem never before encountered, a speaker immediately knows what form it assumes in all the many combinations of person, number, tense, mood, etc. At issue is the question of how this happens. What gives a speaker immediate access to all the inflected forms of any verb in this class?

The data to be considered is presented in figure 8.18. It is a partial set of forms from three common verbs, meaning 'love', 'sing', and 'work'. We will limit our attention to singular forms in the present and past indicative. This amounts to six forms for each verb stem: first-, second-, and third-person singular, in the present and past tense. The stems are given in bold for ease of identification. Observe that the final *a* fails to appear before inflectional endings consisting of a vowel: *-o* '1s:PRES', *-é* '1s:PAST', and *-ó* '3s:PAST'. Note further that the third-person singular present form is zero (Ø), i.e. the stem occurs unmodified. The component elements—stems and endings—are listed in the final row and final column.

Each individual form constitutes a grammatical construction. Two such constructions are sketched in figure 8.19. The stem, either *am* or *ama*, profiles a specific kind of process. The ending, *-o* or *-ste*, evokes a schematic process and relates it to the speech situation in two basic respects: its trajector is identified as either the speaker (1s) or the addressee (2s); and the process itself is either temporally coincident with the speech event or prior to it (cf. fig. 5.10). The two component structures are integrated both semantically and phonologically to produce the composite structure.

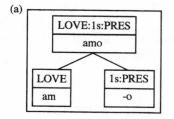
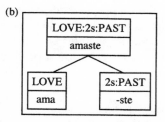

FIGURE 8.19

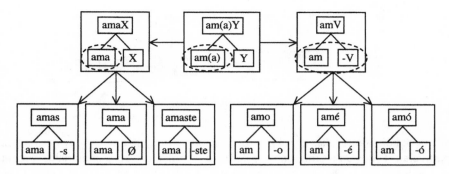

FIGURE 8.20

At the semantic pole, the specific process profiled by the stem is equated with the schematic one evoked by the ending. It is thus the specific process [LOVE] that is related to the speech situation. At the phonological pole, the specific stem *am* or *ama* is identified as the one to which the ending attaches (cf. fig. 6.11).

For a frequent verb like *am(a)*, it is quite possible that all the forms considered achieve the status of units, in which case we can posit the unit constructions in the bottom row of figure 8.20.[36] These are assemblies of symbolic structures, each with a semantic and a phonological pole, but in order to keep the diagrams simple, only the latter is shown. Analogous units can be posited for other common verbs, including *cant(a)* and *trabaj(a)*.

This array of specific assemblies is subject to schematization of different sorts, reflecting the commonalities inherent in different sets of forms. Along one axis it yields the schematic assemblies in the top row of figure 8.20. The schemas on the left and on the right show, respectively, that in certain inflected forms the stem shows up as *ama* and in others as *am*. In the middle is a higher-level schema capturing what is common to those two. The parentheses are meant to indicate that the schematized stem is neutral (unspecified) as to the presence or absence of final *a*. These higher-level schemas provide information often described by linguists in other ways using other theoretical notions. Focusing just on the stem, there is said to be an **alternation** between *ama* and *am*, with *ama* being the basic alternant. It is also said that the "thematic" vowel *a* "drops" before a suffix consisting of a vowel. Generalizing over stems, one might also posit a phonological rule that "deletes" a stem-final vowel before such a suffix. Such statements are not at all invalid from the CG standpoint. They simply correspond to particular facets of networks like figure 8.20.

Let's look at this more closely. From the top row in figure 8.20, the elements enclosed in ellipses are extracted and separately presented in figure 8.21(a). This

---

[36] Ultimately, it makes no difference whether this is actually the case. The schemas defining the conjugation class are capable of emerging regardless of whether the inflected forms of any single verb all have unit status. More generally, the abstraction of a schema requires only the occurrence of sufficiently many varied instantiations to effect the reinforcement of common features. It does not depend on any single instantiation occurring often enough to be entrenched as a unit.

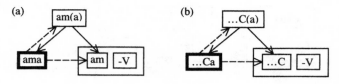

FIGURE 8.21

abstracted diagram makes explicit certain factors left implicit in the previous one; in particular, it shows that the schemas define a complex category comprising variant forms of the stem. The variant *ama* occurs in the widest range of contexts and can be regarded as prototypical. With respect to this prototype, *am* constitutes an extension which only occurs in the context of a vocalic suffix. This is equivalent to stating that *ama* and *am* are alternants, that *ama* is the basic alternant, and that thematic *a* drops before another vowel. Similar complex categories emerge for other stems, such as *cant(a)* and *trabaj(a)*, based on networks analogous to figure 8.20. This array of parallel complex categories is itself subject to schematization, which yields the configuration in figure 8.21(b). This schematic network represents a general pattern of stem alternation. Moreover, the lower two structures—representing the prototype and its context-induced extension—are equivalent to a phonological rule that deletes stem-final *a* before another vowel.

An array of networks like figure 8.20, each representing inflections of a single stem, support the abstraction of other schemas reflecting the commonality of other sets of forms. To take just one example, figure 8.22 depicts a schematization based on the forms in the top row of figure 8.18 (first-person singular, present tense). It should be evident that any patterns discernible within or across inflectional paradigms can likewise be captured by schemas. A speaker's knowledge of such paradigms resides in a vast inventory of specific and schematic assemblies organized in interlocking networks. The specific assemblies represent learned forms, which run the gamut from being completely regular within the system to being wholly idiosyncratic. More schematic assemblies represent the systematicity inherent in the data at any level of abstraction.

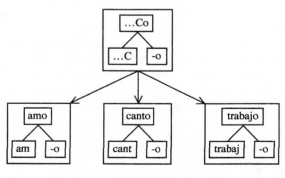

FIGURE 8.22

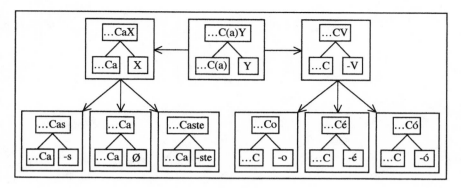

FIGURE 8.23

A schema comparable to that in figure 8.22 is abstracted for each position in a paradigm, e.g. for each row in figure 8.18. These schemas and the higher-level schemas they support constitute the network shown in figure 8.23. Collectively, they provide the characterization of a conjugation class. The entire schematic network (we have of course considered just a fragment) represents a higher-order generalization concerning verb inflection. By invoking it, a speaker presented with a new verb ending in *a* has immediate access to any inflected form and can use it with full confidence that it will be accepted as conventional.

The take-home message is that the central notions of CG are capable of handling an extremely wide range of linguistic phenomena. The few kinds of structures permitted by the content requirement, occurring in various combinations in multiple dimensions and at different levels of organization, straightforwardly accommodate seemingly disparate phenomena that are often treated separately in other frameworks. Moreover, in accordance with basic CG principles, the account they afford is unified, restrictive, and psychologically plausible.

PART III

STRUCTURES

9

Grounding

Consider a skeletal clause consisting of nothing more than the lexical units *girl*, *like*, and *boy*, with *girl* elaborating the trajector of *like*, and *boy* its landmark: *girl like boy*. Though conceptually coherent, this clause is not itself very useful. The profiled relationship is common to innumerable situations that differ not only in detail but also, and more importantly, in how they relate to the speech situation. It figures, for example, in all the following expressions: *the girl likes that boy*; *this girl may like some boy*; *some girl liked this boy*; *each girl likes a boy*; *a girl will like the boy*; *every girl should like some boy*; *no girl liked any boy*; and so on. Despite their shared lexical content, these clauses are semantically quite distinct, saying very different things about the world. The differences pertain to the identification of nominal referents and the status of the profiled process with respect to time and reality. In both cases, this assessment is made relative to the speaker-hearer interaction in the current discourse context.

Bridging the gap between *girl like boy* and the full expressions cited are **grounding** elements. The term **ground** is used in CG to indicate the speech event, its participants (speaker and hearer), their interaction, and the immediate circumstances (notably, the time and place of speaking).[1] A grounding element specifies the status vis-à-vis the ground of the thing profiled by a nominal or the process profiled by a finite clause. Through nominal grounding (e.g. *the*, *this*, *that*, *some*, *a*, *each*, *every*, *no*, *any*), the speaker directs the hearer's attention to the intended discourse referent, which may or may not correspond to an actual individual. Clausal grounding (e.g. *-s*, *-ed*, *may*, *will*, *should*) situates the profiled relationship with respect to the speaker's current conception of reality. In this way grounding establishes a basic connection between the interlocutors and the content evoked by a nominal or a finite clause. If left ungrounded, this content has no discernible position in their mental universe and cannot be brought to bear on their situation. It simply floats unattached as an object of idle contemplation.

---

[1] The same term is more commonly employed in reference to the perceptual opposition known as figure vs. ground. Though not unrelated, the two uses have to be clearly distinguished.

9.1 Subjective and Objective Construal

Although grounding elements serve the specific function of relating a profiled thing or process to the ground, they do not themselves refer to the ground explicitly. As one facet of its meaning, for example, the demonstrative *this* portrays the thing it points to as being "close to" the speaker (not necessarily in a spatial sense). But in contrast to nongrounding expressions like *close to me* or *near me*, which specifically mention the speaker and focus it as landmark, the demonstrative leaves it implicit. Indeed, there is no direct way to mention it overtly—we can say *this person*, but not **this me person* or **the person this me* (cf. *the person near me*). Analogously, the past-tense morpheme *-ed* is roughly comparable to the nongrounding phrase *before now* but does not explicitly mention the time of speaking. One property of the expressions identified as grounding elements is precisely the fact that the ground remains covert. It inheres in the conceptual substrate supporting their meanings without being put onstage as a focused object of conception.

Grounding thereby reflects the asymmetry between the **subject** and **object** of conception: that is, the conceptualizer and what is conceptualized.[2] The subject and object roles are two facets of a conceptualizing relationship, sketched in figure 9.1. The subject (S) engages in conceptualizing activity and is the locus of conceptual experience, but in its role as subject it is not itself conceived. An essential aspect of the subject's activity is the directing of attention. Within the full scope of awareness, S attends to a certain region—metaphorically, the "onstage" region—and further singles out some onstage element as the focus of attention. This, most specifically, is the object of conception (O). To the extent that the situation is polarized, so that S and O are sharply distinct, we can say that S is construed **subjectively**, and O **objectively**. S is construed with maximal subjectivity when it functions exclusively as subject: lacking self-awareness, it is merely an implicit conceptualizing presence totally absorbed in apprehending O. Conversely, O is construed with maximal objectivity when it is

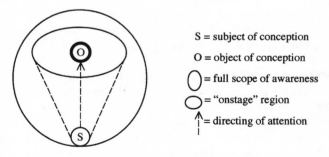

S = subject of conception

O = object of conception

◯ = full scope of awareness

◯ = "onstage" region

↑ = directing of attention

FIGURE 9.1

[2] The subject and object of **conception** must not be confused with subject and object as specifically **grammatical** notions. The speaker and hearer are the principal subjects of conception, even when implicit, whereas grammatical subjects and objects are overt nominal expressions that generally refer to other entities.

clearly observed and well-delimited with respect to both its surroundings and the observer.

These notions are most easily grasped in relation to visual perception. In vision, the perceiving subject is the viewer—in particular the visual apparatus (eyes, etc.), as well as the subjective locus of experience inside the head (the mentally constructed perspective point from which we "look out" at our surroundings). At a given moment, the full scope of awareness consists of everything that falls in the visual field, and the onstage region is the portion presently being attended to. The object of perception, then, is the focus of visual attention—that is, the onstage entity specifically being looked at. The eyes are construed with maximal subjectivity, for they see but cannot themselves be seen. What they see, when examined up close and with full acuity, is construed with maximal objectivity. Construed with a lesser degree of objectivity is everything else currently visible, both onstage and offstage. The scope of awareness even includes parts of the viewer's own body, which is vaguely perceptible at the very margins of the visual field.

Under the inclusive definition adopted in CG, **conception** subsumes **perception** as a special case. Indeed, on the basis of extensive parallels observable between vision and nonvisual conception (Talmy 1996; Langacker 1993, 2001b; GC: ch. 7), terms like **viewing** and **viewer** are used in CG for both. Our interest here lies in conceptions evoked as the meanings of linguistic expressions. For linguistic meanings, the primary conceptualizers are the speaker and the addressee, whose interaction in producing and understanding an expression constitutes the ground. In this guise, both individually and jointly, they function as subjects of conception. An expression's profile, immediate scope, and maximal scope can then be identified, respectively, with the focus of attention, the onstage region, and the full scope of awareness. As the focused object of conception, the profile is construed with the greatest degree of objectivity.

Figure 9.2(a) can thus be offered as a basic scheme for the meanings of expressions. Canonically, the ground (G) consists of the speaker (S), the hearer (H), and their interaction in the context of speech.[3] Since meanings are conceptualizations,

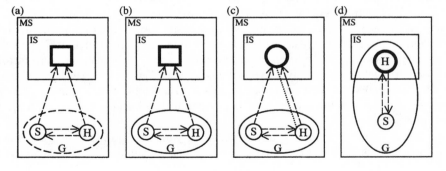

FIGURE 9.2

---

[3] In fig. 9.1, S indicated the subject of conception, but here (as in most diagrams) it represents the speaker. The speaker and hearer both function as subjects in apprehending linguistic meanings.

with S and H as subjects of conception, the ground figures at least minimally in the meaning of every expression. The dashed-line ellipse enclosing G indicates this minimal presence. The dashed arrows represent the directing of attention, which occurs in two different **channels**. First, the interlocutors attend to one another as part of the speech interaction. Second, they direct their attention to the focused entity onstage—the expression's profile—which can be either a thing or a relationship.

Usually the ground's involvement goes beyond this minimal presence. In actual use, almost every expression evokes some facet of the ground in addition to S and H in their role as subjects of conception. Some further connection is thus established between the ground and the onstage situation, as indicated by the solid line in figure 9.2(b). This connection need not be salient and often leaves the ground at the margins of awareness. The word *tomorrow*, for example, evokes the time of speaking as a temporal point of reference but does not refer to it explicitly. Though invoked to identify the profiled entity (the following day), the moment of speech remains offstage and implicit, hence in large measure subjectively construed. A connection with the ground is also inherent in any expression whose import includes the speaker's attitude toward an onstage element (e.g. the pejorative nature of *commie*, compared with *communist*) or its limitation to particular social contexts (e.g. the decreasing formality of *urinate*, *pee*, and *piss*).

As a special case, the connection between the ground and the onstage situation consists in selecting some facet of G as a focus of attention, onstage and objectively construed. The pronoun *you*, for instance, puts the hearer onstage as its profile. In figure 9.2(c) this is shown by means of a correspondence line equating H with the profiled thing. This notation has the advantage of explicitly indicating the hearer's dual role as both subject and object of conception. We obtain the alternate representation in figure 9.2(d) by collapsing the corresponding elements. This notation has the advantage of directly indicating the hearer's onstage role as the nominal referent. Somewhat obscured, however, is the hearer's simultaneous role as subject.

Hence the ground figures in linguistic meanings in myriad ways and with varying degrees of explicit awareness. With the minimal presence shown in figure 9.2(a), it is merely part of the supporting conceptual substrate and is thus construed with maximal subjectivity. At the opposite extreme, exemplified by forms like *I*, *you*, *we*, *here*, and *now*, some facet of the ground is put onstage as the focused object of conception. The profiled entity is then construed with the maximal degree of objectivity possible for such an entity. Its construal can never be fully objective, since one factor that contributes to objectivity is distinctness from the ground. Because of its dual role, a profiled speaker or addressee is construed less objectively than something wholly distinct, and less subjectively than when it functions exclusively as subject of conception.[4]

Under a broad definition, any structure in which the ground has more than just its minimal presence could be said to serve a grounding function. While not

---

[4] Equivalently, we can describe an interlocutor as being construed subjectively in its conceptualizing role and objectively in its role as nominal profile. Its full characterization resides in a blend of these two functions and perspectives.

unreasonable, this would have the consequence that virtually every linguistic unit or expression would qualify as a grounding element (ch. 13). A distinct term would then be needed for certain specific kinds of elements pivotal to the structure of nominals and finite clauses. In CG the term "grounding" is thus reserved for these latter elements and the relations they establish. This should not be taken as suggesting that grounding elements can always be clearly distinguished or that they alone establish connections with the ground.

How, then, are they identified? Several criteria come into play. First, while the ground has more than just a minimal presence, it is offstage and subjectively construed, as in figure 9.2(b). A grounding element profiles neither a facet of the ground nor its connection to the entity being grounded. It is this latter, the thing or process referred to by a nominal or a finite clause, that is put onstage and profiled by the element that grounds it. As a consequence, a full nominal or finite clause has the same referent as its grounding element, which can often be used alone to designate it. While reading, for example, I can refer to the book in my hand as either *this novel* or simply *this*. Excluded from the class of grounding elements (narrowly defined) are expressions that either profile part of the ground (like *I*, *you*, *now*) or invoke it as a focused relational participant (e.g. *before now*, *near me*). These violate the requirement that the ground be subjectively construed.

A second criterion relates to lexical content. The meanings of grounding elements are quite schematic and largely confined to certain basic oppositions of an "epistemic" nature. They offer minimal yet fundamental indications of what the speaker and hearer know regarding the status of events and the identification of event participants. In an English finite clause, the absence vs. the presence of a modal indicates whether the profiled occurrence is accepted by the speaker as being real (e.g. *She is angry*) or merely potential (*She might be angry*). By dividing our mental world into two broad regions, "proximal" vs. "distal", English demonstratives provide a basis deemed sufficient for the hearer to ascertain the intended nominal referent (e.g. *this novel* vs. *that novel*). Compare these with nongrounding expressions such as *tomorrow*, *several miles away*, and *indisputably*. While these too invoke the ground covertly, their conceptual content is considerably richer and less fundamental. They presuppose elaborate cognitive models: that of days occurring in sequence, of a system for measuring distance, or of people disputing a statement's validity. And rather than minimal oppositions, the options they specify are drawn from open-ended sets.[5]

A final criterion concerns the grammatical status of grounding elements. Semantically, they lie toward the grammatical pole of the lexicon/grammar continuum, their schematized meanings residing more in construal than in any specific conceptual content. Usually, moreover, they are well integrated in the grammatical system. They tend to arrange themselves in closed sets of mutually exclusive forms that are partially defined in opposition to one another. For instance, clausal grounding in English consists primarily in the oppositions present ($\emptyset$, *-s*) vs. past (*-ed*) and the

---

[5] Also failing to qualify as grounding elements are expressions that incorporate speaker affect (like *commie*) or a limitation to certain social contexts (e.g. *urinate* vs. *pee* vs. *piss*). While they do invoke the ground, such indications are not epistemic in nature.

absence vs. the presence of a modal (*may*, *can*, *will*, *shall*, *must*). They also tend to be quite limited in how they combine with other elements. Essential to the formation of a nominal or a finite clause, a grounding element is often introduced by a special constructional schema that confines it to a particular structural position.

When grounding is overt and these factors all converge, grounding elements constitute a clearly identified, well-delimited set. This is largely the case in English. The situation is not universal, however, and probably not even typical. While grounding is a universal function, its implementation varies greatly from language to language. Each language has its own inventory of devices subserving this function. They are sometimes covert, or intermediate in their status as grounding elements. But in one way or another, every language provides conventional means for indicating the epistemic standing of a profiled thing or process vis-à-vis the ground.

9.2 Type vs. Instance

Grounding is characteristic of the structures referred to in CG as **nominals** and **finite clauses**. More specifically, a nominal or a finite clause profiles a **grounded instance** of a thing or process **type**. Thus to understand grounding, we must first examine the distinction between a type and an instance of that type.

9.2.1 Nominal and Clausal Organization

The noun and verb categories are universal and fundamental to grammatical structure. Their conceptual characterizations are maximally distinct, in regard to both their prototypes (physical object vs. force-dynamic interaction) and their schemas (thing vs. process). But despite this polar opposition, nouns and verbs are in many respects quite parallel. As discussed in chapter 5, each has two basic subclasses (count vs. mass, perfective vs. imperfective) distinguished in precisely analogous fashion. The noun-verb parallelism further extends to their role in higher-level grammatical constructions. In particular, a noun bears the same relation to a nominal that a verb does to a finite clause.

Nominals and finite clauses resemble nouns and verbs in being universal and grammatically fundamental. Like a noun, a nominal profiles a thing; like a verb, a clause profiles a process. Because they profile things and processes, nominals and finite clauses are themselves nouns and verbs, as broadly defined in CG. They are distinguished from nouns and verbs in the usual, narrow sense—"lexical" nouns and verbs—by further semantic properties pertaining to their cognitive and discourse function. The primary function of lexemes is **classificatory**. As fixed expressions, they provide an established scheme for apprehending the world in terms of culturally sanctioned categories of proven relevance and utility. By contrast, the primary function of a nominal or a finite clause is **referential**. It directs attention to a particular thing or process accorded a certain epistemic status in relation to the ground. Through grounding, its characterization of the profiled entity serves to distinguish it from other members of its category and identify it for immediate discourse purposes.

Lexemes serve their classificatory function by making **type specifications**. A noun designates a type of thing, and a verb a type of process. Through the nouns and verbs of a language, speakers have ready access to immense inventories of thing and process types that are generally recognized and easily expressed. These allow an initial classification of conceived entities for linguistic purposes. The usual starting point for a nominal or clausal expression is thus a lexical noun or verb, which specifies what type of thing or process is being referred to. But for the most part our interest lies with specific individuals rather than general categories—we want to talk about particular people, particular events, and so on. We are able to do this by means of nominals and finite clauses. In addition to a lexical noun or verb, these higher-level structures incorporate elements that take us beyond a type specification to single out an instance of the type. Chief among these are grounding elements, which establish an epistemic relationship between the ground and the profiled thing or process instance.

Let us once more consider the skeletal expression *girl like boy*. What makes it deficient, from the standpoint of English, is the absence of grounding.[6] Because it is merely a lexical noun, *girl* specifies a type of thing—a type with indefinitely many instances—but fails to single out any particular instance as the intended referent. The same of course holds for *boy*. While invoking the type they all instantiate, *boy* does not specifically direct attention to any one of the innumerable boys (real or imagined) that we might have occasion to conceive of and talk about. Analogously, a lexical verb such as *like* does nothing more than specify a process type of which there are many instances. A verb, though, is conceptually dependent: the conception of a process presupposes and incorporates the conception of its participants. A more specific process type is thus defined when its participants are elaborated at higher levels of organization. By itself, *like* makes a highly schematic type specification, there being no description of its trajector and landmark. Their elaboration by *girl* and *boy* yields the composite expression *girl like boy*. This too evokes a process type, obviously more detailed. Yet, since the focal participants are only described as types (not identified as individuals), this process type is still instantiated by countless distinct situations involving different girls and different boys.

In contrast to *girl like boy*, which merely describes a kind of situation, *the girl likes this boy* refers to a specific situation of this sort, involving particular individuals. The difference is due to grounding. By grounding *girl* with the definite article, the speaker directs the hearer's attention to a particular instance of this type, presumed uniquely identifiable by virtue of being the sole instance clearly evident in the current discourse context. The demonstrative *this* likewise singles out a particular instance of *boy*, identifiable on the basis of uniqueness, proximity, or an accompanying pointing gesture. If they occurred independently (i.e. in the absence of clausal grounding), these nominal grounding options would articulate *girl like boy* into *the girl like this boy*.[7] This provides a highly specific type description, one

---

[6] In some languages, expressions directly analogous to *girl like boy* are complete and well-formed. This is due to patterns of covert grounding (more extensive than in English) by means of which a lexical noun or verb is understood in the discourse context as representing a grounded instance of the type it specifies.

[7] Here is one construction where nominal grounding does occur without clausal grounding: *My daughter marry that moron? Impossible!*

limited to relationships between the particular people mentioned. Yet it is still just a type and not an instance. The same girl could like the same boy at various stages of their lives. Such occurrences would constitute different instances of the process type, distinguished by their temporal locations. Through clausal grounding, a particular instance is singled out and accorded a certain epistemic status: *the girl likes this boy*, *the girl liked this boy*, *the girl might like this boy*, etc.

If we define it as subsuming everything we are capable of conceptualizing, our "mental universe" is a very large place. Type descriptions help us deal with this vast expanse by bringing a certain amount of order to it. Each represents a generalization whereby certain conceived entities are judged equivalent in some respect. But the control thus afforded carries with it an inherent limitation: since a given type usually corresponds to an open-ended set of actual or imagined instances, invoking it is not itself sufficient to single out the specific entity we want to talk about. Grounding provides a way of overcoming this limitation. From the array of entities selected by a type specification, it directs attention to the desired instance through an indication of its relation to the ground. The ground functions as a point of reference, allowing mental access to particular individuals.

Yet we do not always avail ourselves of this option. We are often concerned with the general rather than the particular and thus with types rather than instances. Of the various ways to handle this linguistically, the most obvious is simply to leave a noun or verb ungrounded. This is commonly done in English through compounding or morphological derivation. By way of illustration, compare the expressions in (1):

(1)　(a)　*Jennifer loves her cat.*

　　　(b)　*Jennifer is a cat-lover.*

Sentence (1)(a) profiles a specific instance of *love* (grounded by *-s*) involving a specific instance of *cat* (grounded by *her*). Sentence (1)(b) employs the same two lexemes, and thus invokes the same two types, but does not single out any instance. Instead of being grounded, *cat* is incorporated in the compound *cat-lover*, where it merely indicates what type of thing the loving pertains to. In similar fashion, *love* occurs ungrounded as part of *lover*, serving only to specify the type of process in terms of which a type of thing is characterized. The grounded entities are those profiled by the higher-level structures *cat-lover* (a complex noun) and *be a cat-lover* (a complex verb). What the clause thus designates is an instance of the process type *be a cat-lover*, which serves to equate its trajector with an instance of the thing type *cat-lover*. From (1)(b) we might well infer that Jennifer actually does engage in instances of *love* involving instances of *cat*. However, since reference to *love* and *cat* remains at the type level, (1)(b) does not refer to such instances directly.

9.2.2 Instantiation

Hopefully you are now convinced that the type/instance distinction provides a semantic basis for the grammatical distinction between a lexical noun or verb, on the one hand, and a nominal or a finite clause, on the other. But what exactly does this mean?

What is the actual conceptual import of saying, for example, that *cat* merely specifies a type, while *the cat*, *some cat*, or *a cat* designates an instance of that type? Presumably the conception of an instance incorporates that of the type it is based on. At issue, then, is the nature of **instantiation**, the mental operation serving to transform a type conception into an instance conception.

An obvious candidate is profiling. An expression's profile is what it designates, or refers to. Similarly, a nominal is said to single out an instance of the specified type as its referent. One might then propose that instantiation consists of imposing a profile on a type specification, which lacks it. But despite the similarity, a moment's thought reveals that instantiation and profiling have to be distinguished. The reason, very simply, is that profiling is an essential component of type specifications. Recall the example of *hub*, *spoke*, and *rim* (fig. 3.5). Clearly they represent different types of things. Yet as their conceptual base, they all evoke the conception of a wheel—the semantic contrast resides primarily in their choice of profile. Without profiling the three types could not be properly characterized and distinguished.

If not in profiling, perhaps the type/instance distinction lies in specificity. Since a type represents the abstracted commonality of its instances, it must be more schematic than any one of them. Certainly my conception of any particular cat (like Herschel, Racquel, or Metathesis) is more precise and richly detailed than the type conception evoked by *cat* as part of the compound *cat-lover*. There is reason to doubt, however, that instantiation is simply a matter of making a type conception more specific. We often refer linguistically to an instance without having any particular instance in mind or without knowing anything about it. In (2)(a), for example, the nominal *a cat* does not refer to any actual feline but merely one evoked to describe Samantha's wish. This imagined instance need not be characterized in any more detail than the type specification. In (2)(b), the two occurrences of this nominal do refer to actual cats but offer no further description. Despite this lack of specificity, we understand that two different instances are involved.

(2)   (a) *Samantha wishes she had **a cat**.*

    (b) *Since Jennifer had **a cat**, Julie also got **a cat**.*

The greater specificity of an instance vis-à-vis a type may thus be limited to the very fact of its being conceived as an instance. Since it is not reducible to an independent factor (like profiling or elaboration), instantiation must consist in a separate mental operation. A pair of observations suggest its possible nature. The first is simply that the type/instance distinction is nonvacuous only when a type has multiple instances.[8] The second observation concerns the cognitive domains constituting an expression's matrix. In the case of nouns and verbs, one such domain—not accidentally, called the domain of instantiation—has special status. It was mainly described in §5.1.2 as the domain in which the presence or absence of bounding determines categorization as count vs. mass or perfective vs. imperfective. But it was also characterized, more fundamentally, as the domain where instances of a type are primarily thought of as residing and are

---

[8] Proper names represent the degenerate case where a type has just one instance, making the distinction vacuous.

distinguished from one another by their locations. For verbs, this domain is always time. Thus two identical events, involving the same participants in the same places, constitute different instances of the same event type by virtue of occurring at different times. With nouns the domain of instantiation varies, but for physical objects and substances it is usually space. Thus two identical cats constitute different instances of this type by virtue of occupying different spatial locations (at a given moment), whereas a cat viewed at different times can still be recognized as the same instance.

The proposal, then, is that **an instance** (as opposed to a type) **is thought of as having a particular location in the domain of instantiation**, which serves to distinguish it from other instances. Starting from a type conception, instantiation is just a matter of conceiving the profiled entity as occupying such a location. Conversely, starting from instances, a type conception emerges by abstracting away from this notion. Hence the essential difference between a type and an instance conception is that the former suppresses (or at least backgrounds) the thought of the profiled entity occupying a particular, distinguishing location.

An attempt to visualize this contrast is made in figure 9.3. DI indicates the domain of instantiation, the dots represent distinguishing locations, and t abbreviates a type specification. As seen by comparing diagrams (a) and (b), type and instance conceptions have the same essential content. Part of the characterization of *cat*, for example, is the very notion that this type has multiple instances. Likewise, the conception of an instance carries with it the notion that there are other instances of the type it instantiates. Type and instance conceptions differ as to which aspect of this overall configuration they foreground: the abstracted commonality, or the multiplicity with respect to which a single instance is focused as profile. In either case the abstracted commonality is immanent in the conception of any instance, as shown by correspondence lines.

Saying that an instance has a particular location in the domain of instantiation does not imply that the speaker knows the location or even that it could in principle be objectively determined. Instantiation is a mental operation, and for linguistic purposes instances are **conceived** instances, which may or may not represent actual objects or events. Since the cat referred to in (2)(a) is only virtual, it makes no sense to ask just where it is. The cats in (2)(b) are portrayed as actual, real-world creatures, so presumably they have actual, real-world spatial locations. Yet the sentence can be used and understood even if the interlocutors have no idea where the cats are now

(a) Type Conception	(b) Instance Conception
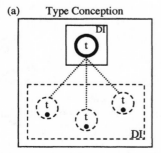	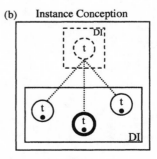

FIGURE 9.3

or where they might ever have been. When it is said that instances have a particular location, this characterization pertains to the very idea of an instance: what it means to be an instance rather than a type. It does not pertain directly to current speaker knowledge of objective reality.

We can talk about anything imaginable. Only a limited portion of our discourse is devoted to actual, real-world situations (despite their privileged status). And when we do talk about actual situations, our descriptions are selective and schematic. Linguistic meanings do not just mirror the situations described, but emerge through an interactive process of construing and portraying them for communicative and expressive purposes. As discourse proceeds, the interlocutors cooperate in building, elaborating, and modifying conceptual structures which, at best, amount to very partial representations of what is being discussed. It is these conceptual representations of situations, not their actual nature, that provide the direct basis for the meanings of expressions. The instances singled out and referred to linguistically are therefore conceived instances of their types, even when they are further identified as specific real-world entities. The locations that distinguish them are thus conceived locations, found within the conceptual representations constructed in discourse. Usually instances are simply assigned to arbitrary locations within these discourse representations.[9] In (2)(b), for example, we envisage separate cats in separate places without any knowledge of what their actual locations might be at any time.

9.2.3 Virtual Referents

Like many linguistic terms, *refer* and its derivatives—*referent, reference, coreference, referential*—are used in a variety of sometimes inconsistent ways.[10] This multiplicity is both a potential and an actual source of confusion, for which CG does not entirely escape responsibility. Recall the apparent inconsistency of saying, on the one hand, that an expression's profile is what it *refers* to and, on the other hand, that a nominal singles out an instance of a type as its *referent*, while at the same time denying (on the third hand?) that instantiation is reducible to profiling. In trying to keep things straight, a key point is that several distinct notions of reference, pertaining to different levels of conceptual organization, are all linguistically relevant. By various linguistic means, we refer to entities at the conceptual level, at the discourse level, and in "the world".

The term "profiling" was specifically adopted for reference at the conceptual level. An expression's profile is its referent **just in the context of its conceptual base**—it is the substructure singled out as focus of attention in contrast to other facets of this same conception. With respect to the concept of a wheel, for example, *hub* refers to the central part only in the sense of directing attention to that part instead of others. Per se, profiling is independent of any particular use in discourse: *hub* profiles

---

[9] This is analogous to the strategy employed for representing discourse referents in American Sign Language: the signer points to an arbitrary location in signing space to establish a referent and subsequently points to the same location as a way of referring back to it. I take this as being a visible manifestation of what we do conceptually in spoken language.

[10] Linguistics comes close to satisfying a definition once proposed for philosophy: the systematic misuse of a technical vocabulary invented for that purpose.

the central part of a wheel even when considered in isolation. Nor does the ground have any role beyond its ubiquitous minimal presence. This measure of discourse independence is what motivates the description of profiling as merely "conceptual" reference (or "reference within a conception").

Of course, the conceptual structures interactively constructed in discourse are also conceptual (just not "merely" so). The statement that a nominal profiles a grounded instance of a type, which it singles out as its referent, pertains to this discourse level. Though it figures in discourse reference, profiling is only one component of this more elaborate notion (others being instantiation and grounding). Both nominals in (3)(a) invoke our knowledge that *hub* designates the central part of a wheel. Nonetheless, since two distinct objects are being talked about, they have different referents in the context of the discourse. The discourse level is also the one alluded to in saying that two nominals are coreferential: that is, they are construed as having the same discourse referent. In (3)(b), for example, the pronoun *it* refers back to the referent of its antecedent, *this hub*.[11]

(3)   (a) ***This wheel's hub*** *is cracked. What about* ***the hub of that other wheel?***

(b) ***This hub*** *is cracked, and I don't think we can fix* ***it***.

In philosophy, and often in linguistics, reference is understood as a relationship between expressions and objects in the world. Many nominals do of course have referents of this sort. The nominals in (3), for example, would normally be taken as referring to actual, real-world hubs. But this classic notion of reference is not appropriate for a general characterization of nominal structure. The referents of many nominals are abstract or problematic in terms of their objective existence (e.g. *the putative irrelevance of moral considerations*). Nor are they limited to real-world entities. We can talk about imaginary worlds as easily (and in the same way) as the one regarded as "real". We use analogous nominal expressions in referring to either girls, boys, cats, and dogs or to unicorns, dragons, hobbits, and jedi.

For the linguistic description of nominals, the main concern is therefore reference at the discourse level. Crucially, discourse referents are not restricted to entities that actually exist in a real, imagined, or possible world. Whatever world we choose to talk about, we commonly refer to entities that are only **virtual** (or fictive) rather than actually existing. Here is just a small sample of nominals with virtual referents:

(4)   (a) *If she had* ***a Porsche*** *she would learn to drive.*

(b) ***A hub*** *is part of* ***a wheel***.

(c) ***Every hobbit*** *owns* ***a unicorn***.

(d) *I don't have* ***any pets***.

---

[11] Usually only nominals are described as having discourse referents, but from the CG standpoint it makes sense to say that finite clauses do as well. Just as *this hub* refers in context to a particular instance of the thing type *hub*, so the clause *this hub is cracked* refers in context to a particular instance of the situation type *this hub be cracked*.

The Porsche referred to in (4)(a) does not exist in reality but only as part of a hypothetical situation presented as being counter to fact. As a generic statement, (4)(b) does not mention any particular hub or any particular wheel. The nominal referents are merely "conjured up" as elements of a virtual situation invoked as a general characterization of such objects. The next sentence likewise makes a general statement about the world it pertains to—it just happens to be an imaginary world inhabited by both hobbits and unicorns. Once again, the nominals do not refer to any specific instances of these types. In response to (4)(c), it makes no sense to ask either (5)(a) or (5)(b). Nor does (4)(d) permit the response in (5)(c). Because it denies their existence, (4)(d) does not mention any actual pets.

(5) (a) *Which hobbit is it who owns a unicorn?*   [in response to (4)(c)]

    (b) *Which unicorn is it that every hobbit owns?*   [in response to (4)(c)]

    (c) *Which pets don't you have?*   [in response to (4)(d)]

Nominals such as these are often described as being "nonreferential". The term is not very satisfactory, however, for while such nominals do lack referents in the world, they nonetheless establish referents at the discourse level. We can see this in (6), where they serve as antecedents for pronouns referring back to them:

(6) (a) *If she had **a Porsche** she would drive **it** to church.*

    (b) ***A hub** lies at the center of the wheel **it** is part of.*

    (c) ***Every hobbit** who owns **a unicorn** believes **he** takes good care of it.*

    (d) *I don't have **any pets**, so I don't have to feed **them**.*

From a linguistic standpoint these nominals are indeed referential, as they single out a grounded instance of a type as their referent. Their special property is that they profile a **virtual** instance rather than an **actual** one.

The pervasiveness and importance of virtuality will gradually become apparent (especially in ch. 14). A general characterization is difficult, if only because the line between what is actual and what is virtual can be drawn in different places. For now the essential point is that instances of a type can either be actual or virtual (whereas types are by nature virtual). The distinction hinges on the **mental space** an instance occupies. Very roughly, we can say that a virtual instance is "conjured up" for a limited special purpose and has no status outside the mental space associated with that purpose. The (a) examples in (4) and (6) invoke a mental space representing how reality would evolve starting from a situation that is both hypothetical and counterfactual. Being confined to this unreal scenario, the Porsche referred to is only virtual. The (b) and (c) examples purport to describe the world's essential nature. They do so by designating virtual situations that constitute the abstracted commonality of actual situations. Being part of these virtual situations, the things referred to (hub, wheel, hobbit, and unicorn) are virtual instances of their types—the abstracted commonality of actual instances. And in the (d) examples, the situation of my having pets is conjured up just in order to exclude it from reality. The virtual pets referred to are only found in the mental space representing this situation.

The same examples show that the actual/virtual distinction can also be made for instances of a process type. Each finite clause in (4) profiles a grounded process instance that is virtual rather than actual. In each case, the profiled occurrence occupies a special mental space evoked for a limited purpose and has no status outside that space. The virtuality is sometimes marked explicitly. In (4)(a), *if* establishes a mental space representing a hypothetical situation.[12] The negation in (4)(d) likewise situates the profiled relationship in a space distinct from actuality. Since *every* and *any* invariably have virtual referents, their use in (c) and (d) implies that the process instance in which their referents participate is also virtual. Still, virtuality is not always marked explicitly (e.g. it is not specifically indicated by anything overtly present in (4)(b)). Moreover, a process instance can be virtual even when its participants are not. In (7), for example, the situation described by *she liked her Porsche* is only virtual even though the nominals refer to actual individuals.

(7)   *If **she** liked **her Porsche** she would drive it to church.*

9.3 Nominal Grounding

It goes without saying (though I will say it anyway) that every language has its own grounding system, which must be described in its own terms. While the English system has no privileged status and is not necessarily even typical, it enjoys the advantage of being accessible and having been studied in depth. By exploring its many subtleties—for nominal grounding in the present section, clausal grounding in the next—we can hope to gain some insights of general validity.

9.3.1 The Grammar of Grounding Elements

Grounding is not a grammatical category (like noun, verb, or preposition). It is rather a **semantic function**, an aspect of conceptual organization by which an expression qualifies as a nominal or a finite clause. In every language, certain overt elements specifically serve this grounding function. But it can also be fulfilled through other means, all exemplified by English nominals. It may be **covert**. In one kind of covert grounding, "zero" (symbolized Ø) stands as one member of a set of oppositions. This is a frequent option with English mass nouns (e.g. *They drank {the / some / Ø} beer*). Grounding can also be **intrinsic**, as with personal pronouns (*we, you, they*, etc.) and proper names (*Abraham Lincoln, California*). Since the very meanings of such expressions imply the identifiability of their referents, they do not require a separate grounding element. A third option is for grounding to be **indirect**, most notably

---

[12] *If* is thus a **space builder** (Fauconnier 1985). Also marking the situation as virtual is the "past-tense" inflection of *had*, which serves more generally to indicate distance from the ground. Since the ground is real and actual (at least by default), a counterfactual situation lies at a certain distance from it epistemically.

with possessives. In *Sheila's camera*, for example, the profiled instance of *camera* is not related to the ground directly, but only indirectly, via the intrinsic grounding of *Sheila*.

Let us focus on overt elements that directly serve a grounding function. For English, we can identify a core system that includes the articles (*the*, *a*), demonstratives (*this*, *that*, *these*, *those*), and certain quantifiers (*all*, *most*, *some*, *no*, *every*, *each*, *any*). These expressions vary considerably in their specific grammatical properties and even in their strategy for singling out a nominal referent. They nevertheless have enough in common to justify their treatment as alternative grounding elements. Among their common features are the semantic properties deemed characteristic of such elements: (i) their role in singling out a nominal referent; (ii) the minimal, epistemic nature of the referent's relationship to the ground; and (iii) the ground itself being subjectively construed. These elements further exhibit a number of grammatical properties which support this semantic characterization.

The first grammatical property is that these elements do not mention the ground explicitly.[13] Even demonstratives, which indicate proximity or distance vis-à-vis the speaker, provide no direct way to mention it overtly: we say *this chair* but not **this me chair* or **this chair me*.[14] The fact that they leave the ground implicit is symptomatic of its being offstage and construed subjectively.

A second property is that most of the nominal grounding elements can stand alone as full nominals.[15] In (8), for example, they function as clausal subjects:

(8)   (a) *{This/That/These/Those} should satisfy the inspectors.*

(b) *{All/Most/Some} were badly damaged.*

(c) ***Each** was more impressive than the previous one.*

(d) ***Any** will be OK.*

This implies that they are themselves schematic nominals, hence that they profile things, even though relationships figure crucially in their meanings. Most obviously, the demonstratives incorporate relationships pertaining to distance and identification. Very roughly, for instance, *this chair* indicates that the chair is near the speaker and uniquely identifiable for both interlocutors. As a paraphrase for *this*, one might therefore suggest the relational expression *near me and identified*

---

[13] More precisely, they do not explicitly mention the speaker, the hearer, or any other facet of the ground. For sake of convenience, I often just refer to the ground (or to G) as an undifferentiated whole, not being specific about which facet is involved. (This practice illustrates whole-for-part metonymy.)

[14] This is not to deny that reference to the speaker can be made periphrastically (e.g. *this chair next to me*, or *this chair which is near me*). Also, some forms of colloquial speech reinforce the demonstratives with the deictic locatives *here* and *there*: *this here chair*, *that there chair*. While these are intrinsically grounded, it is still the case that the speaker—who anchors the distance specification—remains implicit. This kind of reinforcement is one source of new grounding elements.

[15] Why is this not possible for *the*, *a*, *no*, or *every*? Various motivating factors can be cited, such as the availability of well-entrenched alternatives (demonstratives for *the*, *one* for *a*, and *none* for *no*). Still, the distribution is less than fully predictable and has to be learned as a matter of established convention.

to us. Grammatically, however, it patterns as a nominal, as seen in (8)(a). It does not behave analogously to *near me* or *identified to us*, which profile nonprocessual relationships:

(9)   (a)   *The chair was **near me and identified to us***.

    (b)   **The chair was **this***.

    (c)   *An attractive chair, **near me and identified to us**, was next to be auctioned off.*

    (d)   **An attractive chair, **this**, was next to be auctioned off.*

These grammatical properties support the claim that a grounding element profiles the grounded entity, as opposed to either the ground or the grounding relationship. In other words, it exhibits the organization shown abstractly in figure 9.2(b), where the ground is offstage and subjectively construed. As such it cannot be focused as either profile or landmark of a profiled relationship. This leaves only the grounded thing or process—onstage and objectively construed—as the profile of a grounding element.

The examples in (8) indicate that the grounding quantifiers also profile things rather than relationships. Corroborating this point is their behavior in regard to a basic generalization of English grammar. In (10)(a), we observe that *be* combines with a variety of elements to form a complex clausal predicate: adjectives (e.g. *beautiful*), prepositional phrases (*in a pretty vase*), present participles (*drooping*), past participles (*wilted*), and infinitives (*to cheer her up*). What these all share is that they profile nonprocessual relationships (§4.3). We can next observe, in (10)(b), that various quantifiers can also combine with *be* to form a clausal predicate. These too profile nonprocessual relationships, in which the trajector is situated on a scale of quantity. Note, however, that the quantifiers identified as grounding elements do not appear in this construction—the examples in (10)(c) are quite ungrammatical. This is striking evidence that the grounding quantifiers do not profile relationships.

(10)   (a)   *The flowers were {beautiful/in a pretty vase/drooping/wilted/to cheer her up}.*

    (b)   *The problems we face are {three/few/many/several/numerous}.*

    (c)   **The politicians who can be bought are {all/most/some/no/every/each/any}.*

While the facts are complex, there is further grammatical indication that the grounding quantifiers group with articles and demonstratives, both standing in opposition to nongrounding quantifiers like the ones in (10)(b). First, we see in (11)(a) that articles, demonstratives, and the grounding quantifiers are mutually exclusive.[16] This reflects their common grounding function—if one occurs, another is superfluous (and usually semantically incompatible). In contrast, we see in (11)(b) that certain

---

[16] One exception is that *all* can precede a demonstrative or the definite article: *all the(se) oranges*. This construction is best seen as a compact variant of expressions like *all of the(se) oranges*, parallel to *most of these oranges, each of the oranges*, etc. (See CIS: §1.5, GC: ch. 3.)

combinations of grounding elements and nongrounding quantifiers are indeed possible. Their grammatical cooccurrence suggests that the two groups have different semantic functions.

(11)   (a) *_that every_ dog; *_an any_ lawyer; *_those most_ politicians; *_the all_ computers

    (b) **those three** cats; **the many** teachers I have known; **all seven** hummingbirds; **any three** ballerinas

It is not irrelevant that in such combinations the grounding element comes first. As in many languages, a grounding element is generally the "leftmost" component of an English nominal: _the three broken chairs_, but not *_three the broken chairs_ or *_three broken the chairs_. And if we view the lexical noun as the "core" of a complex nominal, a grounding element constitutes its "outermost" structural layer: (_the (three (broken (chairs)))_).[17] There is thus a strong tendency for a grounding element to occupy a peripheral position in the structure of a nominal. This tendency has clear iconic motivation. The external position of a grounding element mirrors its conceptual status as the most extrinsic nominal component. Compared with other components—like a nongrounding quantifier (_three_), an adjective (_broken_), or the lexical noun (_chairs_)—the grounding element provides the least information concerning the nominal referent per se. In _the three broken chairs_, for example, the definite article tells us nothing at all about the chairs themselves. It merely indicates their status as a discourse referent (a matter of how the interlocutors direct their attention to it).

A grounding element can thus be thought of (at least in functional terms) as the final step in putting together a nominal or a finite clause. As the most peripheral component, it specifies an epistemic relationship between the ground and the profiled thing or process, as characterized by the remainder of the nominal or clausal expression. This is shown for nominals in figure 9.4. The grounding element profiles a thing characterized only schematically, but puts it onstage as focus of attention within the immediate scope. The ground is offstage and construed subjectively, so the grounding relationship (represented as a line) remains unprofiled. Whatever its size or internal complexity, the other component structure qualifies as a noun because it profiles a thing (X abbreviates its additional semantic features).[18] A correspondence identifies the schematic and specific things profiled by the two component structures. At the composite structure level, therefore, the grounded entity instantiates the type specified by the noun and incorporates its other semantic properties.

---

[17] With mass nouns (including plurals), zero is one member of the English grounding system. Hence choosing this option has the consequence that some other component appears overtly as the initial component, e.g. ($\emptyset$ (_three_ (_broken_ (_chairs_)))), ($\emptyset$ (_broken_ (_chairs_))), or ($\emptyset$ (_chairs_)).

[18] This component may or may not distinguish between maximal and immediate scope. For sake of simplicity, G is not shown in this component (although it could be in principle) on the presumption that it has nothing beyond its minimal presence. There is no profile determinant because the two profiles correspond (§7.2).

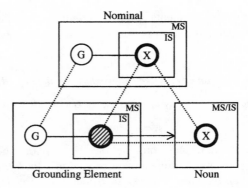

FIGURE 9.4

9.3.2 Basic Grounding Strategies

Our "mental universe" subsumes everything (or every thing) we are capable of conceptualizing. This is clearly a very large set—listing its members is a task best avoided. Yet anything we might conceptualize is also something we might want to talk about, and if we want to talk about it, we need a way of referring to it. Given the size of our mental universe, the problem this poses is far from trivial. A nominal of any sort represents an attempted solution to this problem. A nominal's grounding indicates that reference is achieved, implying (rightly or wrongly) that the interlocutors direct their attention to the same conceived entity.

One can imagine various strategies for achieving nominal reference. An obvious strategy is to have a distinct conventional label (like a proper name) for each and every thing in our mental universe. But this obvious strategy is obviously unworkable. No matter how many labels we learn, there will never be enough for all potential referents.[19] Moreover, most entities we might in principle want to talk about have never even been thought of, so we can hardly have conventional labels for them.

We do of course learn a substantial number of proper names. For the most part, though, we rely on a combination of other strategies. One strategy is the use of descriptions (as opposed to mere labels). I call this the **descriptive strategy**. Through the lexical and grammatical resources of a language, we are able to construct an endless supply of expressions capable of describing any sort of thing imaginable. A simple lexical type specification (e.g. *parrot*) constitutes a minimal description. As need arises, we put together novel descriptions, which can be of any size and can thus characterize their referents at any level of specificity: *parrot > Brazilian parrot > talkative Brazilian parrot > talkative Brazilian parrot with a lisp > talkative Brazilian parrot with a lisp who kept us awake last night > talkative Brazilian parrot with a lisp who kept us awake last night with a constant stream of obscenities*. Whatever its size, a description is usually applicable to an open-ended set of potential referents.

---

[19] What about using numbers, of which there are infinitely many? Unfortunately that is not enough. The numbers too must be named, and if we used all the numbers to name themselves, there would be none left to name anything else.

Even a seemingly unique characterization, like *talkative Brazilian parrot with a lisp who kept us awake last night with a constant stream of obscenities*, could in principle apply to multiple individuals—a whole flock of such creatures might have plagued us.

For this reason, description is normally used in conjunction with another strategy: that of identifying referents not in absolute terms (reference in the world) but in relative terms—that is, reference in the context of a discourse. I call this the **deictic strategy**. The pronouns *I* and *you*, for example, have no constant real-world reference. Depending on who is talking to whom, they refer to different individuals in the context of different usage events. They do, however, have constant reference in relation to the speech situation, referring to the speaker and the addressee, whoever might assume these roles on a given occasion. Similarly, while a demonstrative singles out a particular referent in the context of a discourse, it has no unique referent in the world. Indeed, even its discourse reference can vary from moment to moment. A child let loose in a candy store might very well say *I want this and this and this and this and this*, pointing in turn to five different items. Despite its different reference in the world, *this* has constant reference in the sense that, in each case, it designates the item the child is pointing to at the moment it is uttered.

These two strategies—description and identification relative to the discourse context—work together in nominals with the typical structure sketched in figure 9.4. The noun provides the description. While it minimally consists of a lexical noun that specifies a basic type (like *parrot*), it can if necessary have any desired degree of structural complexity and semantic specificity (e.g. *talkative Brazilian parrot with a lisp who kept us awake last night with a constant stream of obscenities*). Identification relative to the discourse context is effected by the grounding element. We might think of this as a kind of verbal "gesture" through which the speaker directs the hearer's attention to a referent, an abstract analog of the physical pointing that sometimes accompanies demonstratives: *I want this [→]*. But since a description is merely classificatory (not referential), and a verbal gesture hardly points with any precision, individually they are usually insufficient to pick out the proper referent. We overcome this problem by combining the two strategies. The dual strategy is to provide a description, thereby narrowing down the set of possible referents, so that even an imprecise gesture can single out the one intended.

The problem of nominal reference is to direct an interlocutor's attention to one particular thing out of a range of potential **candidates** that is usually open-ended. If not contextually delimited, this candidate set is coextensive with our mental universe, comprising everything we might conceivably wish to talk about (which is every conceivable thing). A large circle represents this maximal pool of candidates in figure 9.5, where diagrams (a) and (b) sketch the deictic and descriptive strategies. Grounding employs the deictic strategy. The effect of grounding, in and of itself, is to focus attention on a candidate identified just in terms of its discourse status, irrespective of whether any type is specified linguistically. I will say that it **singles out** a referent. The effect of description—by either a simple type specification (t) or the more elaborate characterization afforded by a complex expression—is to shrink the pool of candidates to be considered. I will say that a description **selects** a pool of candidates that are **eligible** by virtue of conforming to it. When the two strategies work together, as shown in diagram (c), grounding singles out an eligible candidate as the nominal referent.

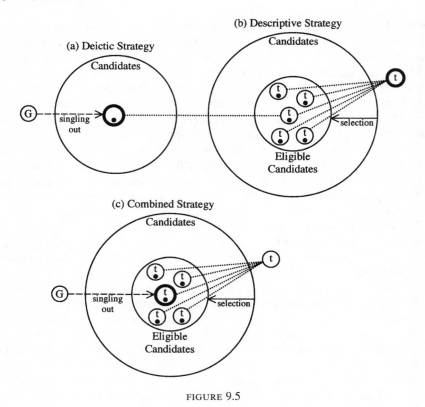

FIGURE 9.5

The three diagrams in figure 9.5 amount to another representation of a grounding construction, more detailed than figure 9.4. Diagrams (a) and (b) represent the two component structures. These are integrated by a correspondence that identifies the thing instance singled out by the grounding element with an instance of the type specified by the noun.[20] The composite structure is represented in diagram (c), which indicates the role of both strategies in determining the nominal referent.

There is one more general strategy to consider. It is most important for the grounding quantifiers: *all, most, some, no, every, each, any*. With these the role of the interlocutors is less apparent than with articles and demonstratives, which specifically invoke them to anchor the grounding relationship. Demonstratives invoke them to specify distance—for example, *this parrot* is identified as the parrot near me (or perhaps near us). The choice of definite vs. indefinite article (e.g. *the parrot* vs. *a parrot*) indicates whether the speaker considers the intended referent to be uniquely apparent to the hearer at the current point in the discourse. But what about the quantifiers? What role do the interlocutors play in the meanings of expressions like *most parrots, no parrot(s)*, and *every parrot*?

[20] It is a moot point whether this noun imposes its profile at the type level (as shown) or at the instance level. Because a type description includes the specification of a profile, and is also immanent in the conception of any instance, the difference is just a matter of whether instantiation remains in the background or is brought to the fore (fig. 9.3). Grounding will bring it to the fore in any case.

Perhaps they have little more than the minimal presence they always have. Even so, these quantifiers still qualify as grounding elements by virtue of their function. They still serve to single out an instance of a type as a discourse referent, momentarily attended to by both speaker and hearer. Moreover, they have basic epistemic import as opposed to specific lexical content, even compared with nongrounding quantifiers. The latter range from being quite specific to rather vague (e.g. *seven* > *several* > *numerous* > *many*), but even the most schematic convey some definite notion of magnitude. This is not really so for the grounding quantifiers (with the natural exception of *no*). What is the actual quantitative import of *most*, *every*, or *any*? They do not imply any specific magnitude or number. Is the set of *all unicorns* larger or smaller than the set of *most angels*? How would you go about counting either one? If *every parrot* seems like a lot of parrots, then why is this nominal singular rather than plural? What about *all months between March and April* vs. *any month between March and April*? Is there any difference at all between them?

The grounding strategy followed by these elements has two key factors: relativity and virtuality. In contrast to the nongrounding quantifiers, which specify magnitude in **absolute** terms (albeit vaguely and flexibly), the grounding quantifiers do so in **relative** terms—that is, in relation to another entity. Moreover, with grounding quantifiers the nominal referent is always virtual. Whereas *seven parrots* or *several angels* may refer to actual individuals, expressions like *every parrot* and *most angels* can only designate virtual entities.

Also virtual is the entity in relation to which their quantity is specified. What is this benchmark entity? It is nothing other than the set of eligible candidates, i.e. everything conforming to the basic or elaborated type description. In the case of *every parrot*, it is the set of all parrots. In the case of *most whiskey*, it is all whiskey. For a given type (t), it will be referred to as the **maximal extension** of that type, abbreviated E_t. This is a virtual entity, a product of conception, not something found in the world.[21] This mental construction reflects a number of conceptual phenomena previously discussed. Through grouping and reification (§4.2.2), conceived instances are "pulled together" and viewed as a unitary entity. The maximal extension further represents a conceptual blend (§2.2.3), combining properties that cannot actually coexist—in particular, those of both count- and mass-noun referents. On the one hand, it is conceptualized as a mass of indefinite extension. We realize that no particular mass of parrots or whiskey can ever be the largest one possible, exhaustive of the type. At the same time, we conceptualize it as a bounded entity, one that is somehow limited in extent. This virtual limit functions as a benchmark, a point of reference for assessing the quantity of a nominal referent.[22]

---

[21] Where would you look to find all parrots or all whiskey? There is no intrinsic limitation to the real world or the present time—parrots or whiskey might be found in any imagined or possible world, at any time in the past or future. (While certain limits may be evident in a particular discourse context, they do not resolve the general problem.)

[22] For this reason, E_t was called the "reference mass" in FCG2. There is no doubt that we are capable of these mental gymnastics. We perform the same conceptual operations, for example, when we talk about the set of even numbers and represent it as $\{2, 4, 6, 8, \ldots\}$. Though noncontiguous in the counting sequence, the even numbers are pulled together and placed in brackets, which function as a virtual boundary even though the set is infinite.

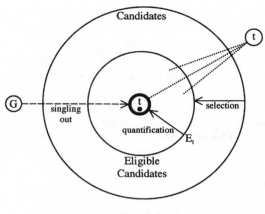

FIGURE 9.6

The basic grounding strategy followed by relative quantifiers is to characterize the nominal referent in relation to the maximal extension. Thus, while the interlocutors do single out the referent in the sense of directing their attention to it, the primary basis for doing so is a relationship that they themselves do not anchor. Instead, as shown in figure 9.6, the profiled instance is related to E_t in terms of quantity. Since it takes the maximal extension as point of reference, this quantity is only relative, its absolute value depending on the size of E_t. In absolute terms, *most days of the year* implies a greater number than *most months of the year*, which in turn is more than *all days of the week* (not to mention *all months between March and April*).

While this **quantificational strategy** has various implementations (§9.3.5), they all entail virtuality: because E_t is a virtual entity, and the profile is identified only in relation to E_t, the profile must also be virtual. Clearly, *every parrot* does not refer to any particular parrot but to a virtual instance conjured up for the sole purpose of making a general statement (one extending to all instances of the category). Likewise, *most parrots* does not single out any specific instance of *parrots* but one identified only as representing a proportion of the maximal extension. The statement *Most parrots are talkative* does not tell us about the volubility of any particular bird. Even in the case of *all parrots*, we are not referring directly to actual instances of *parrot* or an actual instance of *parrots*. Instead, we designate a fictive instance of *parrots* characterized only as being coincident with the maximal extension.

Despite their fictive referents, nominals grounded by relative quantifiers are an important means of thinking and talking about actual situations. By nature they tend to occur in general statements, since their referents map onto any number of actual individuals. They thus provide an essential means of dealing with the world. Certainly a statement like *Polly is loquacious* has the advantage of telling us something definite about a particular situation. On the other hand, while *Most parrots are talkative* is less definitive, it is potentially even more useful, for it bears on an open-ended set of situations.

9.3.3 Demonstratives

Nominals are traditionally described as being either **definite** or **indefinite**. Though elusive, the distinction clearly pertains to the discourse status of nominal referents. We can find its conceptual basis by examining the meanings of nominal grounding elements. These too pertain to discourse, for which the ground is both locus and deictic anchor. How the speaker and hearer interact in singling out discourse referents is the key to their semantic characterization.

In English, the specifically definite grounding elements are the demonstratives (*this, that, these, those*) and the definite article (*the*). The demonstratives in particular bear witness to the dynamic, interactive nature of nominal grounding. Not infrequently, a demonstrative is accompanied by a physical gesture of pointing. Sentence (12), for example, has been uttered on countless occasions (usually to secure what looks like the biggest chunk of birthday cake):

(12)   *I want this [→] piece.*

Through this utterance, the speaker actively directs the listener's attention to a specific referent that is physically present in the discourse context. If successful, this action induces a momentary state of intersubjective awareness, in which the interlocutors share (and know they share) this referential focus. The physical pointing gesture is an overt analog of the mental process referred to here as "singling out", which is characteristic of nominal grounding in general. Demonstratives with pointing embody the "strongest" form of singling out—active, physically manifested, and objectively construed; with other grounding elements it is weakened to varying degrees (cf. Diessel 1999, 2006).

Demonstratives with pointing are thus a natural place to begin the examination of individual grounding elements. How can we describe them explicitly? We must first have a way of representing the ongoing flow of discourse. Useful in this respect is a construct called the **current discourse space** (CDS), defined as everything presumed to be shared by the speaker and hearer as the basis for discourse at a given moment. The CDS is stable in many respects (subsuming an immense body of background knowledge), but as discourse proceeds, it is continually updated as each successive utterance is processed. At any point, the CDS provides the basis for interpreting the next utterance encountered, which modifies both its content and what is focused within it.

Only certain portions of the CDS are specifically invoked and brought to bear on the interpretation of any particular utterance. Those portions—the scope of concern at a given stage of the discourse—constitute a **discourse frame**. As a discourse unfolds, therefore, the interlocutors negotiate a series of discourse frames, each produced by updating the previous one. This is shown abstractly in figure 9.7. The **previous** discourse frame is the one invoked for interpreting the current expression.

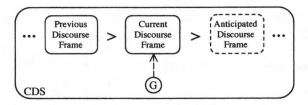

FIGURE 9.7

The **current** discourse frame is the one obtained by updating the previous frame in accordance with the meaning of this expression. Of course, the ground is part of the current discourse space, and so is the ongoing discourse itself, including the sequence of frames and their content.[23]

An important consideration in describing linguistic expressions is how they relate to this general scheme. Viewed from this perspective, an expression's meaning is its contribution to the discourse: both the structure it imposes on the current discourse frame and any expectations it induces concerning other frames. Especially evident is the discourse role of grounding elements. Having little intrinsic content, their meaning resides primarily in the very act of singling out a nominal referent. This is sketched in figure 9.8, which amounts to a schematic characterization of nominal grounding. In all cases the intended result is **coordinated mental reference**, where the speaker and hearer momentarily direct their attention to the same thing instance. Grounding elements differ in their specific means of achieving this, a major factor being the status in the previous frame of the entity singled out in the current frame.

In the case of English demonstratives, additional factors come into play. We make a four-way distinction—among *this*, *that*, *these*, and *those*—on the basis of two binary oppositions. The first pertains to the nature of the nominal referent. Whereas

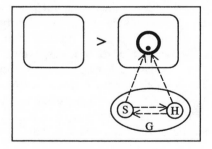

FIGURE 9.8

[23] What counts as a discourse frame is relative to a particular structural phenomenon or level of organization and cannot necessarily be determined with any precision. At each stage the current expression's immediate scope defines its center. Although it is helpful diagrammatically to place G outside the discourse frame, the ground—while offstage—is actually part of it. Placement of G in the diagram can be taken as reflecting the ground's position vis-à-vis the immediate scope.

these and *those* specifically portray it as a plural mass (*these pens, those pencils*), *this* and *that* function as defaults, used with both count nouns (*this pen, that pencil*) and nonplural mass nouns (*this ink, that graphite*). Cross-cutting this opposition is the proximal/distal distinction, where *this* and *these* contrast with *that* and *those* (*{this/ that} pen, {this/that} ink, {these/those} pens*). Importantly, the distance in question need not be spatial. If someone says *I really like this pen*, the proximity coded by *this* might be spatial (the speaker is holding the pen), temporal (the speaker is holding it now), functional (the speaker is using it), attitudinal (the speaker likes it), or any combination of these. The contrast can thus be described more generally as dividing the field of concern into a proximal region (PROX) centered on the speaker and a distal region (DIST) complementary to it, with respect to various dimensions of awareness (cf. Janssen 1995).

All the demonstratives can be used with a pointing gesture: *this [→] pen, that [→] pen, these [→] pens, those [→] pens*. Figure 9.9 shows the pointing use of *this*, where the profile is found in the speaker's proximity. A demonstrative with pointing presupposes a range of possible targets visually accessible from the ground. Four are shown in the diagram. They represent the eligible candidates that fall within the immediate scope of concern.[24] This configuration constitutes the previous discourse frame evoked as "input" by a pointing demonstrative. Based on this input, the demonstrative singles out its referent primarily by means of the physical pointing gesture, represented as a solid arrow. The double arrow indicates that this gesture has directive force: the speaker points with the specific intent of inducing the hearer to focus attention on the entity pointed to. The result, if all goes well, is coordinated mental reference.[25]

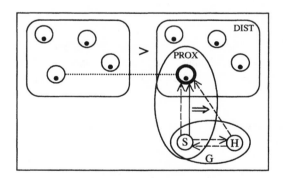

FIGURE 9.9

---

[24] These candidate instances can either be selected by means of an explicit type specification (*I want this [→] piece*), or else the type can be left unspecified (*I want this [→]*). Various factors conspire to determine the immediate scope for purposes of nominal grounding. For demonstratives with pointing, one factor is visual accessibility.

[25] Given the static nature of a printed page, the dynamic nature of demonstratives cannot be fully captured in this two-frame representation. Observe that the arrows indicating both the action (pointing) and its result (coordinated mental reference) are plotted with respect to the current frame. A more adequate (but less practical) representation would directly show the action as inhering in the updating process that produces the result.

In our culture, the canonical pointing gesture—performed with outstretched arm and extended digit—enjoys the status of conceptual archetype. It is often used independently of speech, and provides the model for directional signs and icons (☞). Its incorporation in demonstratives produces grounding elements that are prototypical at least in the sense of representing the "strongest", most salient form of singling out, from which other grounding strategies diverge in various ways and to different degrees. The physical gesture itself is subject to attenuation. Instead of extending the arm, we can simply pivot the wrist so that the finger points in the right direction. A more drastic departure from the archetype is to point with a nod of the head. Perhaps we can even do so with just our gaze.

Of course, the extreme case of attenuation is for there to be no physical gesture at all. If said while dining out, for example, *I really like this restaurant* might well be unaccompanied by pointing. *This* would be diagrammed as in figure 9.9 except for the absence of the solid arrow. In this use the demonstrative still has directive force, constituting an instruction to seek out the intended referent (Kirsner 1993). Especially if the interlocutors have just been discussing various eating places, there is still the presumption that coordinated mental reference has not yet been achieved, so that the restaurant in question needs to be distinguished from other candidates. In the absence of pointing, the burden shifts to the proximal/distal contrast. The choice of *this* vs. *that* can be thought of as a verbal pointing gesture by which the speaker directs the hearer's attention to either the proximal or the distal region. This will often be sufficient to single out the proper referent—provided that this region contains just one eligible candidate. Thus a child confronted with a sliced-up birthday cake is essentially forced to point. By merely saying *I want this piece*, without a gesture, there is no hope of getting the biggest one.

When the pointing is merely verbal, its target need not be physically present. Often it is present only mentally, in the sense of having been evoked in the prior discourse. This gives rise to the "anaphoric" use of demonstratives, so called because—like anaphoric pronouns—they refer back to something previously mentioned. In (13), *this project* refers back to the one just introduced in the previous clause:

(13)   *We've started **a major research project**. The goal of **this project** is to prove the existence of phlogiston.*

An anaphoric demonstrative is sketched in figure 9.10. The directive force is very weak, for instead of having to seek out a new discourse referent, the listener is merely instructed to redirect attention to one already singled out, in a prior episode of nominal grounding. The dashed circles indicate that the presence of other candidates is nonessential.

9.3.4 Articles

Anaphoric demonstratives are often interchangeable with the definite article. If *this* is replaced by *the* in (13), the contrast in meaning is barely discernible. Yet there is a difference. For one thing, *the* neutralizes the proximal/distal distinction (however it might be interpreted). It also represents a more drastic attenuation in

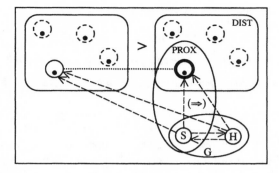

FIGURE 9.10

directive force—essentially its elimination. Very roughly, as shown in figure 9.11, it implies that the relevant scope of consideration contains only one evident instance of the specified type (cf. Hawkins 1978; Epstein 2001; FCG2: §3.1.1). Since there is just one eligible candidate, it is unnecessary to distinguish it from other instances by physical or verbal pointing. Hence *the* represents the degenerate case of mental pointing, where merely indicating the type is sufficient to achieve coordinated mental reference.

In contrast to anaphoric demonstratives (and also pronouns), the definite article does not imply that the referent was singled out or was even particularly salient in the previous frame. As long as it represents the only instance within the relevant scope, it need not have been a previous focus of attention. In (14)(a), for example, the interlocutors were probably unaware of the air conditioner prior to its switching off. Often the referent is not explicitly invoked in the previous frame but can nonetheless be inferred. The first clause in (14)(b) does not specifically invoke a modem, but it does mention a computer, thereby activating our cognitive model of a computer and its parts. This provides the previous frame for purposes of interpreting the second clause, and since the idealized model includes the presence of a single modem, a unique instance of this type is accessible in that context. In this way the modem referred to in the second clause is identified as the one belonging to the computer introduced in the first.

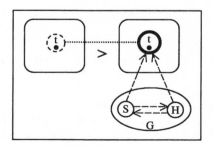

FIGURE 9.11

(14)   (a) *The air conditioner just went off.*

    (b) *She has a computer, but the modem isn't working.*

    (c) *the best way to skin a cat; the only person to have hit a golf ball on the moon*

    (d) *the month between April and June; the nation that shares a border with Canada*

With respect to its status in the previous frame, the unique instance singled out by *the* runs the full gamut—from being salient and explicit, to being latent but directly accessible, to being accessible via inference, to being absent for all intents and purposes. Thus it is often introduced or brought to awareness by the grounded nominal itself. The only requirement is that the type description supplied be sufficient to identify a unique referent in the immediate discourse context. Sometimes the type description ensures uniqueness by its very nature. As observed in (14)(c), it may do so because it incorporates a superlative, like *best*, or a word like *only*, which specifically limits the type to just one instance. Alternatively, it allows us to deduce uniqueness on the basis of other knowledge, as in (14)(d). Often the referent singled out by *the* is unique in a practical sense though not in absolute terms. This happens when a particular instance is so prominent as to be the only one that counts in normal circumstances. That is why we talk about *the moon* despite there being many instances of *moon* in our solar system.

If demonstratives with pointing represent the strongest form of singling out, definite articles represent the weakest form among definite grounding elements. It is quite common for definite articles to descend from demonstratives historically, however. As is typical in the process of **grammaticization** (also called **grammaticalization**), their evolution involves progressive attenuation at both the semantic and the phonological pole (Hopper and Traugott 2003). Phonologically, this has resulted in the definite article being unaccented, having a neutral vowel, and showing a strong tendency to cliticize to the following word (fig. 6.13(b)). Semantically, it has resulted in the absence of directive force: since there is just one instance of the specified type, there is no need to actively seek it out. This is why the English definite article, unlike demonstratives, cannot stand alone as a nominal (*I like {this/*the}*). The article fails to point, either physically or through the proximal/distal distinction. For coordinating mental reference, it relies instead on its referent being the only evident instance of the specified type. Yet its own type specification, being maximally schematic ("thing"), does nothing at all to identify the referent. For its use to be nonvacuous, therefore, *the* requires a more specific type description, which can only be supplied by cooccurring elements.

Many languages lack anything comparable to the English definite article but seem not to suffer from its absence. They partially cover its territory through a wider use of demonstratives. As another means of achieving definite reference, a noun can occur without any overt grounding element. How can a "bare" noun be definite? A language has resources not only for **constructing** expressions but also for **applying** them to the ongoing discourse (ch. 13). Among its conventional units are specific patterns for using and interpreting nominal expressions in particular discourse contexts. We can thus envisage a pattern whereby an ungrounded noun is applied to a discourse frame in which an instance of its type has already been singled out as a discourse referent. If the pattern then identifies that referent with the thing profiled by the noun, it will serve to both instantiate the noun and relate the profiled instance to the ground. It thus amounts to a kind of covert grounding.

With count nouns, the indefinite counterpart of *the* is the article *a(n)*: *an apple*, *a banana*. The prefix *in-* suggests a characterization of the **indefinite** article as being **not definite**. This is in fact a reasonable description. The two articles form an opposing pair such that *a* is used when the conditions for using *the* fail to be satisfied. *The* implies that, in the present discourse context, the type description itself is enough to identify the referent. It may do so because the type description implies the existence of only one instance (i.e. there is only one **eligible candidate**). Alternatively, it can do so because the immediate scope invoked for nominal interpretation contains just a single eligible candidate (i.e. just a single candidate is **available**). Hence the definite article indicates that **just one eligible candidate is available**, and the indefinite article that this is **not** the case.

The indefinite article is thus predicted to be incompatible with a word like *only* or with superlatives, which specify that there is just one eligible candidate. These require the definite article:[26]

(15)   (a) *The United States is {the/*an} only nation that shares a border with Canada.*

     (b) *Your daughter easily solved {the/*a} toughest problem in the chapter.*

Superlatives (marked by *-est*) are usefully contrasted with comparatives (marked by *-er*). If just one problem in a chapter can be the *toughest* one, with respect to a given problem there can be any number of *tougher* ones. Comparatives thus take the indefinite article, as in (16)(a). In (16)(b), however, the comparative takes the definite article—predictably so, for if the context limits consideration to just two candidates, only one can be *tougher*.

(16)   (a) *This is definitely a tougher problem.*

     (b) *Of the two, this is definitely the tougher problem.*

We commonly rely on general knowledge to determine whether just one eligible candidate is available. In (17), for example, our cognitive model of computers and their parts tells us that only one keyboard falls within the relevant scope of consideration (hence *the keyboard*), but many keys (hence *a key*).

(17)   (a) *I can't use my computer—{the/*a} keyboard is malfunctioning.*

     (b) *I can't use my keyboard—{a/*the} key is malfunctioning.*

---

[26] We talk about a person being *an only child*, but there *only child* functions as a complex lexical head. The type it specifies can have any number of instances: *Jill is not the only **only child** in her class—Jack is another **only child**.*

Background knowledge interacts with the meanings of grammatical constructions. By way of illustration, consider nested locatives:

(18) (a) *The body was in the suspect's house, in {a/*the} closet.*

(b) *The body was in the suspect's house, in {the/*a} master bedroom, in {the/?a} closet.*

In this construction, the location specified by one locative constitutes the immediate scope for purposes of interpreting the next (fig. 7.8). Hence the first locative, *in the suspect's house*, establishes the house as the relevant scope of interpretation for what follows. The next locative, **in the closet*, is thus peculiar because, according to our standard cultural model, a house has more than just one closet. On the other hand, *in the master bedroom* reflects the cultural expectation that a house will have only one. Then, in the final locative of (18)(b), the choice of *the* vs. *a* indicates whether the master bedroom has just one closet (the usual case) or whether the suspect is very rich.

The availability of just a single eligible candidate is often purely contingent, depending on either the context of speech or the content of the prior discourse. In (19)(a), the choice of article depends on how many snails are contextually available in the sense of being plainly visible. Choosing *the* implies that only one is visually evident. Choosing *a* implies that the conditions for using *the* fail to be satisfied, which can happen in two distinct ways: either multiple snails are evident or none are.[27] These are, of course, very different circumstances. What they have in common is precisely the fact that they do **not** support the use of *the*.

(19) (a) *Be careful not to step on {the/a} snail.*

(b) *In the room were a puppy and three kittens. She picked up the {puppy/*kitten/*frog}.*

When determined by the prior discourse, the choice of article depends on how many instances of the specified type have been introduced and recently invoked as discourse participants. The first sentence in (19)(b) introduces one instance of *puppy* and three instances of *kitten*. This serves to establish them as discourse referents, in a situation which then functions as the previous frame for interpreting the following sentence. In this context the definite article is felicitously used with *puppy*, as there is just one instance in the frame. But it cannot be used with *frog* (since no eligible candidate is **available**), nor with *kitten* (since there is not **just one**).

With either a definite or an indefinite article, the end result is an established discourse referent that can subsequently be referred to with an anaphoric pronoun:

(20) (a) *In the room were **a puppy** and three kittens. **The puppy** was shaking, so she picked **it** up.*

(b) *In the room were a puppy and three kittens. **A kitten** was shaking, so she picked **it** up.*

---

[27] When no snail is evident, using *the* suggests that a particular snail has special status, making it the only one that counts (e.g. it might be a household pet—cf. *Don't step on the cat*).

Since the pronoun *it* has *the puppy* as its antecedent in (20)(a) and *a kitten* in (20)(b), both nominals succeed in singling out an instance of their type. Yet they differ as to how this coordinated mental reference is achieved. Specifically, they differ as to whether the clause containing the nominal is required for the referent's identification. In (20)(a), we can identify the puppy independently of its shaking, whereas in (20)(b) it is only the shaking that distinguishes the profiled instance of *kitten* from the others in the room. Should someone ask which puppy she picked up, it has two possible means of identification: as either the one that was shaking or the one that was in the room. But if someone should ask which kitten she picked up, it can only be identified as the one that was shaking (since several were in the room).

This difference between definites and indefinites is not limited to nominals grounded by articles. A definite nominal of any sort is presumed capable of identifying its referent independently of the clause containing it. At a given stage of the discourse, therefore, any of the following can single out a particular individual even when not contained in a clause: *the puppy, that kitten, your house, Richard Nixon, the person who sold me this car*. For this reason definites can function as clause-external **topics**:

(21) (a) *{The puppy/That kitten/Your house}, it's shaking.*

    (b) *{Richard Nixon/The person who sold me this car}, he was not to be trusted.*

In each case the first nominal identifies a particular individual, with respect to which the following clause is then interpreted.[28] However, an indefinite standing alone fails to identify any specific individual as its referent: *a kitten, some jello, no house, each president, any salesman*. While they do establish discourse referents, such nominals force us to conjure one up for this purpose—they do not direct attention to any particular instance of the specified type. Hence they cannot function as topic for a clause pertaining to such an instance:[29]

(22) (a) **{A kitten/Some jello/No house}, it's shaking.*

    (b) **{Each president/Any salesman}, he was not to be trusted.*

A referent that has to be "conjured up" is said to be **virtual** (§9.2.3). Could it be that the contrast between definite and indefinite nominals reduces to whether their referents are actual or virtual? It is not quite that simple, since either sort of nominal can have either sort of referent. But the actual/virtual distinction does offer a viable characterization if understood as applying both **locally** and **provisionally**. By "locally", I mean that it applies to the nominal itself, considered independently of the clause containing it, as well as more inclusive structures. By "provisionally", I mean

---

[28] While the topic nominal cooccurs with a clause, the latter does not contain it or contribute to its interpretation. Rather, the topic provides the basis for interpreting the clause.

[29] Indefinites can sometimes function as topics for clauses that do not pertain to particular individuals: *A kitten, I really want one*; *Most houses, they need a lot of work.*

that the referent's status as actual or virtual is subject to being overridden at these higher levels of organization. The suggestion, then, is that definite and indefinite nominals portray their referents as actual and virtual, respectively, when considered locally and on a provisional basis.

For definites, the default case is that their referent is an actual instance of its type, which can thus be identified independently of the clause containing it. Considered individually, for example, *the puppy* induces the default expectation that its referent is an actual creature (not one merely conjured up for a special purpose). This expectation carries over to the clause level in (23)(a), where the puppy is conceived as existing quite independently of its being wanted. The default expectation can, however, be overridden in a larger context, as in (23)(b). There the puppy is virtual, being conjured up as part of a hypothetical situation, and is not conceived as existing in actuality.

(23)   (a) *She wants the puppy.*

       (b) *If a girl sees a puppy and she wants the puppy, she can usually find a way to get it.*

For indefinites, the default expectation is virtuality. Indeed, with the grounding quantifiers the referent is always virtual—expressions like *no house*, *each president*, or *any salesman* cannot designate actual instances of their types. Only with indefinite articles is there even the possibility of actuality. Despite being indefinite, for example, *a puppy* refers to a particular dog in (24)(a). The clause containing this nominal is responsible for its actuality (she could not have actually found a creature that is merely conjured up). Compare this with (24)(b). The verb *want* is compatible with its object being either actual or virtual, and here the default interpretation is virtuality (she just wants a puppy, not any specific one). The larger context can nevertheless impose the opposite interpretation, as it does in (24)(c).

(24)   (a) *She found a puppy.*

       (b) *She wants a puppy.*

       (c) *She wants a puppy. She saw it at the animal shelter.*

Affirming the linguistic importance of virtual entities is the fact that English has considerably more indefinite grounding elements than definite ones. We do with just a single definite article and four demonstratives, but there are several indefinite articles and no fewer than seven grounding quantifiers. The indefinite article *a* is limited to count nouns. For mass nouns (including plurals), we have the option of either Ø (zero) or *sm* (unstressed *some*).[30] In some cases, *sm* and Ø appear to be interchangeable, e.g. in (25). They are however semantically quite distinct.

(25)   *I saw {sm/Ø} {fruit/apples} on the counter.*

---

[30] When fully stressed, *some* functions as a quantifier (e.g. *Sóme unicorns are lazy*). With tertiary stress, it accompanies count nouns and might be analyzed as an article: *Sòme gúy is here to see you. Sòme* contrasts with *a* by emphasizing that the referent is previously unknown.

To appreciate their semantic difference, we need to recall the special properties of mass-noun referents (§5.1.4). A mass exhibits both contractibility and expansibility: any subpart of an instance is itself an instance of the type, as is the union of two instances. In principle, then, any particular mass—such as the water in a swimming pool—is not only an instance of its type but contains within it indefinitely many other instances (arbitrarily delimited "patches" of water or sets of patches). Moreover, the maximal extension of the type (E_t) also qualifies as an instance, by definition the most inclusive one. Thus the **maximal extension** of a type (e.g. all water) is also its **maximal instance**. This is not so in the case of count-noun referents, where instances are usually separate and discrete. Hence they do not routinely contain other instances as subparts, nor does the maximal extension qualify as an instance (the set of all cats is not itself a cat).

The difference between the mass-noun indefinite articles is easily stated: *sm* has individuating force, while *Ø* (iconically) is unrestricted. The instance singled out by *sm* is fairly small and constitutes a single "chunk" or unit with respect to some function. It is natural to say *I see sm water* while looking at a puddle on the floor (a puddle being enough to make it slippery) but hardly while looking at the ocean. This individuating force precludes the use of *sm* with reference to the maximal extension: **The formula for sm water is H_2O*. By contrast, *Ø* imposes no restriction on how large or small an instance can be, so *I see water* is appropriate for either a puddle or the ocean. Due to its unrestricted nature, zero grounding lends itself to making general statements: *The formula for water is H_2O*. Reference to the maximal extension should perhaps be considered the default interpretation, emerging unless the context indicates otherwise. In (25), for example, the profiled instance of *fruit* or *apples* is limited to a quantity that fits on a counter.

Whereas English uses zero grounding for the maximal extension, certain other languages employ the definite article, e.g. French: *Elle aime **le** vin* 'She likes wine'. The proper usage is determined by convention and has to be learned in acquiring either language. Both options are, however, conceptually motivated and consistent with the basic meaning of the grounding element. Since English *Ø* is unrestricted and used with mass-noun instances of any size, use with the maximal instance is an expected limiting case. At the same time, the maximal instance has the uniqueness required by definite articles. If the instance of wine referred to is conceived as being maximal—subsuming all wine—there is no other instance to distinguish it from. To be sure, any subpart of the maximal extension is also an instance of the type. But as we have seen, the uniqueness conveyed by a definite article is often not absolute. We talk about *the moon* because a particular instance of this type is sufficiently prominent (eclipsing all the others, so to speak) that it is normally the only one which counts. In similar fashion, reflecting the general principle that wholes are more salient than their parts, the maximal instance of a type has a special cognitive status that makes it inherently prominent vis-à-vis other instances. When invoked at all, therefore, it tends to be invoked exclusively.[31]

---

[31] Analogous considerations figure in the use of definite articles for masses of limited size. When a mass is singled out, subsequent definite reference picks out the entire mass rather than a subpart. In the following example, *the cats* refers by default to all seventeen, not to any smaller set: *She has seventeen cats and a vicious dog. The cats are very much afraid of the dog.*

9.3.5 Quantifiers

The line between indefinite articles and grounding quantifiers is not a sharp one. I am drawing it on the basis of whether they have the potential to designate actual instances of a type. Because they characterize their referents only in relation to the maximal extension, a virtual entity, the grounding quantifiers always have virtual referents.[32] For the same reason they can also be described as relative quantifiers. They divide into two broad classes: **proportional** quantifiers (*all, most, some, no*) and **representative instance** quantifiers (*every, each, any*). The two classes differ in their basic strategy for singling out the profiled entity in relation to E_t.

The proportional quantifiers are so called because they characterize the profiled entity as some proportion of E_t. Since E_t is a mass, and the profile (P) constitutes some proportion of it, P must be a mass as well. It is thus to be expected that proportional quantifiers occur with mass nouns:

(26)   (a) *{All/Most/Some/No} whiskey is beneficial for your health.*

        (b) *{All/Most/Some/No} alcoholic beverages are beneficial for your health.*

Like E_t, P is a fictive entity created through the mental operations of grouping and reification (where would you actually look to find *most whiskey*?). The conceptual import of these quantifiers derives from the further mental operations of superimposing P on E_t and comparing them in size—matching P against E_t to see how close it comes to covering it. Diagrams are attempted in figure 9.12. In the case of *all*, P succeeds in covering E_t—that is, their boundaries coincide. With *most*, the boundary of P approaches that of E_t but does not quite reach it. *Some* is used for smaller proportions. Naturally, the import of *no* is hard to capture in a diagram. The notation adopted is meant to suggest a mental operation of cancelation: though evoked as a virtual entity, P's existence is effectively canceled out through the specification that the proportion of E_t it represents is zero.[33]

The conceptual operations invoked to describe these quantifiers can be recognized as abstract counterparts of everyday physical actions: grouping a set of objects,

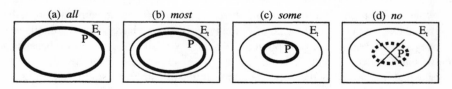

FIGURE 9.12

---

[32] See fig. 9.6. By contrast, nongrounding (or absolute) quantifiers are often used for actual entities (e.g. *I saw {many/numerous/seventeen} cats in the room*).

[33] P thus has a greater degree of virtuality with *no* than with the other proportional quantifiers. However, *no* does evoke a profiled instance of the type and establishes it as a discourse referent: ***No whiskey** tastes as good as **it** looks.*

placing one object on top of another, using one object to measure another, approaching and reaching a boundary, removal or erasure. It can thus be suggested that the quantifiers' meanings reside in **offstage mental simulations** of such actions. As one of its facets, conceptualizing an action involves a mental simulation of it (Barsalou 1999). What this amounts to is the "disengaged" occurrence of the mental operations that occur when we actually perform the action or otherwise experience it (§14.2.1). When disengaged, this processing activity is applicable to abstract or fictive entities, like those evoked by the quantifiers. Of course, when using a proportional quantifier we do not explicitly think about actions like grouping, measuring, or removing, even in the abstract. This is because the simulations constitute the grounding relationship, and a hallmark of grounding relationships is that they are offstage and subjectively construed (fig. 9.4). Hence the simulated actions figure only implicitly in a quantifier's meaning, as a way of mentally accessing the profiled entity onstage.[34]

A striking fact about the representative instance quantifiers is that they occur with singular count nouns, even when used in statements pertaining to all instances of a type:

(27)   *{Every/Each/Any} culture can teach us something of value.*

How can they function as "universal quantifiers" if they only designate a single instance? They can do so because that instance is construed as being **representative**. Anything ascribed to this instance is thus inferred to be valid for all instances.

The profiled representative instance, of course, is not any actual one. It is a virtual instance conjured up to be representative of actual instances. This much—the common denominator of *every*, *each*, and *any*—is shown in figure 9.13(a). As before, a dot indicates a distinguishing location, the very factor that makes an instance an instance. Here, though, an empty dot is used instead of a filled dot in order to make it explicit that the instance is only virtual. Also marking it as virtual is its placement above the ellipse for E_t. This is not to deny that it qualifies as an instance, but rather to show its special status—it is abstracted from other instances precisely to represent their shared property of being instances of the type. As such it corresponds to (and is immanent in) all members of E_t. Likewise, the virtual distinguishing location (empty dot) corresponds to those of actual members but cannot be identified with any particular one.[35]

The profiled instance is thus a mental construction, a conceptual blend that compresses the multiplicity of a type's instances into the discreteness of a single

---

[34] The description of *some* and *no* as proportional in nature is not as obvious as the description for *all* and *most*. An alternative characterization might relate them to the everyday experience of looking inside a container to see whether anything is in it. Since we often find a single object inside, this alternative accounts for *some* and *no* being used with singular count nouns: *There must be some lawyer we can trust; No reputable lawyer would touch this case.*

[35] This virtual location is what differentiates a representative instance from a type conception. The two arise from actual instances through different abstractive processes: the former via neutralization (so that the virtual instance can equally well be identified with any actual one), the latter by abstracting away from the very notion of an instance (fig. 9.3(a)).

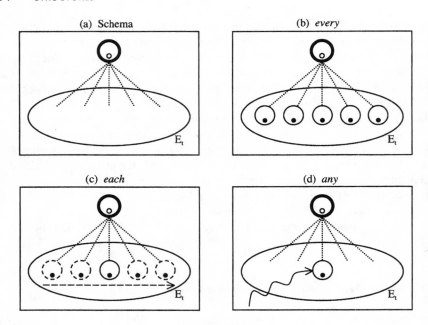

FIGURE 9.13

instance conjured up to represent them all. The structure in figure 9.13(a) amounts to a schema for the meanings of *every*, *each*, and *any*. It is incorporated in the more elaborate mental constructions constituting the distinct meanings of these quantifiers. As with proportional quantifiers, this additional content resides in offstage mental simulations of everyday actions and experiences. Quite naturally (since the profiled instance corresponds to all members of E_t), these involve different ways of accessing the members of a group so as to ensure exhaustive coverage. We have three basic means of doing this: simultaneous viewing, sequential examination, and random selection. *Every* invokes the everyday experience of seeing group members all at once but still perceiving them as individuals—like the members of a choir or the colors in a box of crayons. *Each* reflects the strategy of examining members sequentially, one by one, until they have all been looked at. Represented by a dashed arrow in figure 9.13(c), sequential access has the consequence that just a single instance is being examined at any one moment. Finally, as indicated by the squiggly arrow in figure 9.13(d), *any* is based on random selection. Although random choice results in just a single member being accessed, coverage is exhaustive nonetheless, in the sense that all members have the potential to be selected.

Using *every*, *each*, and *any* does not imply that these everyday activities—simultaneous viewing, sequential examination, and random selection—actually occur in the situation being described.[36] They simply provide an experiential basis

---

[36] Thus (27) does not imply that anybody actually carries out these activities with respect to (all?) cultures.

for conceptualizing the relationship between the virtual profile and the instances it represents. As an aspect of quantifier meaning (part of the mental constructions invoked), they are fictive, abstract, and subjectively construed. These offstage simulations do, however, exert an influence on the choice of quantifier and the meanings of the expressions containing them. It stands to reason that *every*, *each*, and *any* tend to be used for situations that either exhibit the activity they fictively invoke (in which case they reinforce its presence) or could be imagined as exhibiting it (in which case they suggest its presence). The effect is fairly clear in (28): with *every*, we imagine the possibility of seeing all the stars simultaneously; with *each*, we can see them by shifting our gaze from one to the next; and with *any*, we can see whichever one we might happen to choose.

(28)   *Tonight you can see {every/each/any} star in the Milky Way.*

In (29), the use of *each* is most natural given our cognitive model of graduations, where typically the students come up one by one:

(29)   *Each student came up on stage and got her diploma.*

To be sure, *every* is not impossible here, nor does *each* completely rule out the scenario of all the students coming up on stage at once (cf. *Each student threw her cap in the air*).[37]

A glance at figure 9.13 reveals that *any* stands apart from *every* and *each*. Unlike simultaneous or sequential examination, random selection involves accessing just a single instance—the others merely have an equivalent potential of being accessed. This randomness and potentiality confer on *any* an even greater degree of fictivity. Indeed, we find that *any* resists being used in the direct description of actual events:

(30)   (a) *On the show they interviewed {every/each/??any} candidate.*

        (b) *{Every/Each/??Any} contestant is smiling.*

Instead it favors contexts—e.g. interrogative, negative, modal, or conditional—which in one way or another remove the situation from currently established reality:

(31)   (a) *Did you see any movie stars?*

        (b) *I don't see any meat in the freezer.*

        (c) *Any child can assemble this toy.*

        (d) *If you have any questions, don't hesitate to ask.*

---

[37] As in these examples, *each* is normally used only when E_t is contextually delimited (here the relevant students are those in a single class). This may be related to its characterization in terms of sequential examination: it is hard to imagine examining all the members of an open-ended set one by one.

These examples illustrate an additional property distinguishing *any* from *every* and *each*—namely, its occurrence with both plural and nonplural mass nouns. This reflects its characterization in terms of random selection. If I reach into a bag of candy to make a random choice, I can pull out either a single piece or a handful. And if the candy has melted to form a continuous mass of chocolate, I can randomly extract a glob of any size.

9.4 Clausal Grounding

Like a nominal, a finite clause profiles a grounded instance of some type. In both cases the ground and the grounding relationship are subjectively construed; it is only the grounded entity—a thing or a process—that is onstage as the focus of attention (fig. 9.4). This brief exposition of clausal grounding will reveal both similarities to nominal grounding and significant differences.

9.4.1 Clausal Grounding Systems

Among the conceptual archetypes helping to structure our mental universe, few if any are more fundamental than physical objects and events, the respective prototypes for the noun and verb categories. Objects and events pose different epistemic concerns, related to how we typically experience them.

For objects, the basic tendency is to endure. While there are obvious limits and exceptions, our default expectation is that the objects around us will continue to exist indefinitely, unless and until something happens to change this stable situation. We also encounter numerous objects of a given type. An essential feature of our everyday life is the simultaneous existence, in large quantities, of cars, people, buildings, trees, books, spoons, dogs, computers, aspirin tablets, and so on. Thus, in talking about the world, what we generally need to know about an object is not "Does it exist?" but rather "Which one is it?" The primary epistemic concern is not existence but identification. Accordingly, nominal grounding centers on the problem of directing attention to a particular referent from a pool of eligible candidates (E_t).

For events just the opposite is true. By their very nature, events do not endure—rather they occur, and typically their occurrence is quite brief. Nor is it common, for most event types we have occasion to talk about, that there are large numbers of instances that need to be distinguished.[38] When we talk about an event, what we generally need to know is whether it happens, not which one it is; existence, rather than identification, is primarily at issue. As a consequence, clausal grounding is mainly concerned with the status of events with respect to their actual or potential occurrence.

Clausal grounding reflects our lack of omniscience. We do not have a God's-eye view of the world, and with our local perspective we directly experience only a very

---

[38] Since a process is conceptually dependent on its participants, these types include the identification of nominal referents. If our daily life sees many instances of a lexical type like *eat*, there are few if any occurrences of an elaborated type such as *Jeremy's dog eat my porkchop*.

small portion of it.[39] Much of what we know (or think we know) about the world has to be acquired through indirect means: hearsay, records, inference, projection, and the like. Our perspective is also local in a temporal sense. Only the immediate present is directly accessible, and a mere fragment of the past has ever been (as previous present moments). We nevertheless think and talk about the entire sweep of history and the endless reach of the future, knowledge of which ranges from insecure to wholly speculative. This vast discrepancy between what we securely know, on the one hand, and what we contemplate and express linguistically, on the other hand, is the source of clausal grounding. For each situation we describe, there is a need to indicate its epistemic status—where it stands in relation to what we currently know and what we are trying to ascertain.

We are always striving to make sense of our experience and construct a coherent view of the world. This comes with being alive and conscious—we can't help it. As we strive for "epistemic control", each of us develops a conception of **reality**, defined here (for descriptive purposes) as the history of what has occurred up through the present moment. Naturally, each of us has our own take on this history, and none of us knows very much relative to its totality. Thus in discourse the interlocutors advance, negotiate, and adjust their conceptions of reality. Though never identical, usually their reality conceptions have enough in common to allow successful interaction. Their overlap centers on the immediate reality of the ground itself—the here-and-now of the speech situation. The ground and the speaker's conception of reality function as basic points of reference for the epistemic judgments expressed by grounding elements.

What counts as "reality" for this purpose is anything that might be presented as the content of a grounded clause. Reality includes both events and the stable situations that obtain at any period. Besides physical occurrences, it encompasses the social and mental phenomena that constitute so much of the world we experience and talk about. And because it encompasses the mental, reality has many levels and dimensions. One thing we accept as real is the existence of other conceptualizers whose conceptions of reality differ from our own. Moreover, because we conceptualize the content of other conceptualizations, layers of conception—each representing the content of the next—must also be acknowledged as real.[40]

Also existing at the mental level are the imaginary worlds evoked by movies, novels, myths, and the like. Occurrences in these worlds are often portrayed as real (e.g. *Santa Claus has eight reindeer*), just as for the "real world". Nor is reality off-limits to the products of imaginative capacities such as metaphor, blending, and virtuality. What counts as reality for linguistic purposes is what a speaker **conceives** as being real, and in no small measure our conception of occurrences relies on these capacities. An occurrence construed imaginatively can thus be conceived as real by the speaker and presented as real through clausal grounding. For example, a speaker

---

[39] If God speaks a language, Her system of clausal grounding must be very different from ours.

[40] If the event of George telling a lie did not occur, but Martha said that it did, the event of Martha saying this is part of reality. If Louise knows that Martha said this, so is the situation of Louise knowing it. And so on indefinitely. Such layering is one kind of mental space configuration.

can honestly say *The thought just flew right out of my head* (fig. 2.9) to describe what really happened. The reality invoked in a finite clause as the basis for epistemic judgment is therefore not to be identified with either the "real world" or things considered "real" in an ordinary, nonlinguistic sense. It embraces the full range of conceived occurrences to which those judgments pertain, as expressed in finite clauses.

Conceived reality is what a conceptualizer currently accepts as established knowledge. Clausal grounding indicates the status of a profiled occurrence with respect to a reality conception. It may be presented as real, as in *Jill is pregnant*. Or it may have some other status, as in *Jill could be pregnant*, where the pregnancy is only acknowledged as being a possibility. But whose conception of reality is at issue? Whose knowledge is invoked as the basis for the epistemic judgment? As a short answer, we can identify the speaker as the relevant conceptualizer. If I make the statement *Jill is pregnant*, I am indicating that her pregnancy is part of **my** reality conception, not that of the addressee or anybody else. And indeed, I will normally discuss grounding as a matter of speaker assessment. Bear in mind, however, that there is also a long answer, which is far more accurate. A statement (for which the speaker takes responsibility) is not the same as a finite clause—it is, rather, one kind of act for which a finite clause can be employed. It is only in the context of this act that the reality conception invoked by clausal grounding is fully identified with that of the actual speaker. Finite clauses are put to many other uses where this is not the case. Here are just a few:

(32) (a) *According to Jack, Jill is pregnant.*

    (b) *I suspect Jill is pregnant, but we're not sure yet.*

    (c) *It's not the case that Jill is pregnant.*

    (d) *Jill is pregnant—sure, tell me another one.*

Hence the speaker is at best the default conceptualizer for grounding purposes. If we consider a finite clause in isolation, with no larger context to identify it, the conceptualizer invoked for clausal grounding is only virtual.

While every language has clauses describing occurrences and needs some way to indicate their epistemic status, each has its own system of clausal grounding. Naturally, the systems vary in the conceptual models they presuppose, the distinctions made with respect to them, and the extent to which grounding is overt. For overt grounding, languages differ in how it is structurally manifested. It is not necessarily expressed by any single type of element or in any one structural position. In Luiseño, for example, a clause is jointly grounded by means of verb morphology and a clitic following its first word or phrase:

(33) (a) *Waxaam=chamil*   *'owo'a-quṣ.*   'Yesterday we were working.'

       yesterday=2p:PAST   work-PAST:DUR

    (b) *Noo=nupo*   *'exngay*   *'owo'a-an.*   'I will work tomorrow.'

       I=1s:FUT   tomorrow   work-FUT

In these expressions, the first portion of =*chamil* indicates that the clausal trajector is 'we', and the first portion of =*nupo* indicates that it is 'I'. These illustrate a common feature of clausal grounding: namely, schematic reference to the trajector in terms of basic properties—like person and number—which also figure in nominal grounding. This is natural given the conceptual dependence of the grounded process (we cannot conceptualize a process without invoking its participants) and the trajector's prominence within it (primary focal participant). A grounding element of this sort is thus a schematic representation, indicating their epistemic status, of both the profiled process and the participant that anchors its conception.[41]

English clausal grounding does very little by way of specifying the trajector. Except with *be* (*am* vs. *are* vs. *is*; *was* vs. *were*), its only bow in this direction is an ending on present-tense verbs when the trajector is third-person singular: *she knows* vs. *they know*. This can be treated as a special case of present-tense grounding, which is usually coded by zero. Despite some fuzzy edges, the English grounding system has a well-defined core comprising tense and the modals. English has just two basic tenses: "present" and "past". It has five basic modals: *may, can, will, shall, must*. These modals themselves partake of the "tense" opposition, their respective "past-tense" forms being *might, could, would, should,* and *must*.[42] The actual semantic import of notions like "present", "past", and "tense" must be clarified, of course. But let us first clarify the grammatical status of grounding elements.

The modals, along with *have* and *be*, are often described as "auxiliary verbs" (in contrast to the "main" or lexical verb). More broadly, the modals, tense, the perfect (*have* + *-ed*), the progressive (*be* + *-ing*), and the passive (*be* + *-ed*) are taken together as constituting the English auxiliary system (Chomsky 1957). But there is no structural or functional motivation for this grouping (FCG2: §5.1). *Have, be,* and the modals (as well as tense) do share an important semantic property: each profiles a highly schematic process. Hence they are indeed all verbs (due to their profiling), and "auxiliary" verbs in the sense of being nonlexical (owing to their schematicity). Nevertheless, as shown in figure 9.14, the most basic division is not between the "main" verb (V) and the auxiliaries (collectively referred to as "AUX"), but rather between the grounding elements (tense and the modals), on the one hand, and all the remainder, on the other.

This grouping (indicated by double lines) is supported by meaning, semantic function, and grammatical behavior. Semantically, tense and the modals have related epistemic values, specifically invoke the ground, and jointly fulfill the grounding function. By contrast, the ground has no special role (only its minimal presence) in characterizing the perfect, progressive, passive, and lexical verb. Collectively these serve the function of defining the grounded process. Rather than indicating epistemic status, the perfect, progressive, and passive impose particular ways of viewing the process by adjusting the relative prominence of its facets (§4.3.3). Grammatically,

---

[41] Such indications are usually analyzed in terms of "agreement" with the subject. That approach has the fundamental weakness of failing to capture their conceptual basis and epistemic function. (It also runs into descriptive problems, including the absence in (33)(a) of anything for the clitic to agree with.)

[42] *Must* gives no morphological indication of this opposition. There is evidence that this modal simply lacks a nonpresent form (FCG2: 260).

Grounding Elements	Grounded Structure			
Tense Modals	Perfect (*have* + *-ed*)	Progressive (*be* + *-ing*)	Passive (*be* + *-ed*)	Lexical Verb (V)
Auxiliary System ("AUX")				"Main" Verb

FIGURE 9.14

both tense and modality are obligatory in a finite clause,[43] while the perfect, progressive, and passive are optional. Moreover, these latter three appear in nonfinite clauses, both infinitival and participial, from which tense and modals are excluded:

(34) (a) *I would prefer for my proposals to **have** already **been being** discussed for a while.*

    (b) *He resents **having been being** criticized for so long.*

    (c) **I would really like her to {examines/examined/will examine/**might** examine} my proposals.*

    (d) **He really dislikes {criticizesing/criticizing**ed**/**will** criticizing/**might**ing criticize} others.*

The grounded structure consists of the lexical verb augmented, at successively higher levels of organization, by the passive, progressive, and perfect. Each of these latter elements imposes its own processual profile on the structure already assembled (ch. 4, ex. (17)). Since these are optional and occur in any combination, four different verbs have the chance to impose their profile at the highest level: V, passive *be*, progressive *be*, and perfect *have*. The grounded process is the one profiled by the composite structure at the highest level of organization. In the composite expression *have been being criticized*, the grounded verb is therefore *have*, not *criticize*, and in *be criticizing* it is *be*. Only when the options of passive, progressive, and perfect are all declined do the lexical verb and the grounded verb coincide.

9.4.2 Tense

Few linguists would disagree that tense and modality are intimately associated. The source of their association, quite clearly, is that we experience the world sequentially, one moment at a time, so that only the present moment is directly accessible. The past can no longer be experienced directly but only through recall, and the future cannot yet be experienced even indirectly because it has not yet happened—we can only project, speculate, or imagine. In this fundamental way, our degree of

---

[43] This tends to be obscured because each has a zero member: either present tense or the absence of a modal (which carries specific epistemic import).

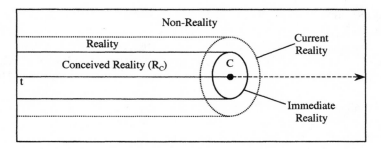

FIGURE 9.15

epistemic certainty about occurrences correlates with their position in time relative to the present.

Depending on how one looks at it, a succession of occurrences either accompanies or constitutes the passage of time. The history of occurrences defines reality, which thus develops or unfolds through time. At a given moment, the portion of reality we call the past has already been defined, the present is still being defined, and the future is yet to be defined. The flow is unidirectional and irreversible—we cannot go back in time, and if something has already occurred, it cannot be made to have not occurred. Metaphorically, we can picture reality as a "growing" cylinder, continually being extended through new occurrences. This is sketched in figure 9.15. The leading face of the cylinder, labeled **current reality**, is the place where growth is occurring. Here matters are still in flux, whereas the past is fixed and the future is free to take whatever form it might.

One thing we know about the world and how it evolves is that we cannot know everything. Thus each of us develops our own **conception** of reality, which we know to be partial, and which we also know—in moments of honesty—is not infallibly accurate. Still, at a given moment there is much we consider to be known (not just suspected or hypothesized). We are not in the process of wrestling with its status but simply embrace it as established knowledge. For a particular conceptualizer, C, this constitutes **conceived reality** (R_C). It is what C accepts as being real. Like reality *tout court*, conceived reality can be pictured as a growing cylinder, continuously augmented through current experience. Its leading face, to be called **immediate reality**, is the portion of current reality accepted by C as real. Immediate reality is basically where we live epistemically, the locus of what we directly experience from moment to moment.

Time and epistemic judgment are thus associated at a very fundamental level. This naturally carries over to their linguistic manifestations, in the form of tense and modality. Tense is normally said to indicate an event's location in time relative to the time of speaking, while modals pertain to its likelihood of occurring. Yet the distinction is anything but sharp, English being a parade example. After all, to indicate future time, English uses the modal *will*. It also uses "tense" for epistemic judgment: the contrast between *it may rain* and *it might rain* does not reflect the time of the event's occurrence but the speaker's assessment of its likelihood. For a wide range of cases, a characterization in terms of time does work quite well for the English "past" and "present" (§5.2.3). In the last analysis, however, these temporal values are best seen as prototypical instantiations of schematic meanings that are epistemic in nature.

At its core, the English grounding system consists of two binary oppositions. Formally, one member of each is zero, and the other is marked overtly. The system is iconic, for in each case the zero member indicates some kind of epistemic immediacy, or closeness to C, whereas the overt marking indicates greater epistemic distance. In the case of tense, the "present" is zero (alternating with third-singular -*s*), and the past is marked overtly. Their semantic contrast, quite analogous to the proximal/distal distinction for demonstratives, is a matter of whether the profiled process is **immediate** or **nonimmediate** to C epistemically. In the case of modals, the zero member is the absence of *may*, *can*, *will*, *shall*, and *must*. The absence of a modal indicates that C accepts the profiled process as being **real**, i.e. as part of R_C. A modal places it outside conceived reality, in a region we can refer to as **irreality** (the complement of R_C). A process grounded by a modal, hence not accepted by C as real, is said to be **unreal**.

When there is no modal, the grounded process belongs to C's conception of reality. "Tense" then specifies where within R_C the profiled occurrence is found. There are just two basic options. With zero (or -*s*), it occupies immediate reality, portrayed in figure 9.15 as the leading face of the growing cylinder. Since this is where the ground is, the designated process is coincident with the time of speaking (e.g. *they like it*). In contrast, -*ed* and its variants place the profiled process in nonimmediate reality—anywhere in R_C except its leading face. Effectively, then, it is prior to the time of speaking (e.g. *they liked it*). When only reality is under consideration, epistemic immediacy and nonimmediacy correlate with present and past locations in time, respectively. In this manner, the temporal specifications "present" vs. "past" arise as prototypical values of these grounding elements. We saw in §5.2.3 how these temporal characterizations account for their pattern of occurrence with perfective and imperfective processes.

It is sometimes claimed that tense in a subordinate clause "agrees" with tense in the main clause. This "sequence of tenses" constraint ensures that when *says* in (35)(a) is changed to *said*, the subordinate verb changes from *is* to *was* in order to agree with it. The examples in (35) clearly demonstrate the untenability of this traditional analysis. There can hardly be agreement between tense in the main and subordinate clauses when all combinations of present and past occur. The sentences are all well-formed, and each has a slightly different meaning. A key point is that the process *be pregnant* is long enough in duration that a previous act of saying and the current speech event can both coincide with portions of it. Also, *say* has an imperfective use in which it describes the stable situation of a person maintaining a position (one sometimes expressed by means of speech). The expressions can thus be glossed as indicated by the bracketed material, where in each case the profiled process is located vis-à-vis the current time of speaking.[44]

---

[44] In (35)(d), Jill presumably said *I am pregnant*, referring to a condition that extends through the present moment, so that the speaker can now say *she is pregnant*. Jill and the current speaker select different temporal portions of the same objective situation to put onstage as the profiled process instance.

(35) (a) *Jill **says** she **is** pregnant.*   [she maintains now that she is pregnant now]

    (b) *Jill **said** she **was** pregnant.*   [she said earlier that she was pregnant then]

    (c) *Jill **says** she **was** pregnant.*   [she maintains now that she was pregnant earlier]

    (d) *Jill **said** she **is** pregnant.*   [she said earlier that she is pregnant now]

The temporal values of these grounding elements are only special cases with respect to their schematic meanings of epistemic immediacy and nonimmediacy. The need for a more abstract characterization is evident from "nonpresent" uses of the "present tense", e.g. for future events and in statements of "timeless" truths:

(36) (a) *They leave next week for Venezuela.*

    (b) *The square of the hypotenuse equals the sum of the squares of the other two sides.*

These nonpresent uses of the present are based on particular mental constructions, which are often tacit but nonetheless crucial to the supporting conceptual substrate. Expressions like (36)(a) evoke an implicit plan or schedule, a kind of mental "document" describing expected future occurrences. Since the schedule is currently in force, a person who knows it has immediate access to the events listed therein. In this way an event has epistemic immediacy for a speaker who consults the schedule and "reads off" an entry. Statements like (36)(b) presuppose another mental construction, a virtual document describing the world's inherent nature—its "essential" structure (as opposed to "accidental" occurrences). Once more, an entry in this document is epistemically immediate for a speaker who consults it. Let me emphasize that, despite their virtuality, the documents invoked in such examples count as aspects of reality in the linguistically relevant sense (§9.4.1). The events described are thus accessible to the speaker as part of immediate reality, even if their actual occurrence does not coincide with the time of speaking.[45]

Further showing the need for a schematic characterization are expressions like (37):

(37) *If I knew what their plans are, I would tell you.*

Despite its past-tense form, the verb *knew* does not refer here to a previous occurrence. The import, rather, is that the hypothetical situation introduced by *if* is counter to fact: the speaker indicates that she does not in fact know what the plans are. Whereas a hypothetical situation might turn out to be actual, the use of *knew* explicitly rules this out by marking its exclusion from immediate reality. The epistemic import of nonimmediacy can thus be manifested even when it does not receive a temporal interpretation. This is also evident from the nonimmediate modals: *might, could, would,* and *should.* The import of *would* in (37) does not pertain to time. Instead it

---

[45] Equivalently, we can say that what counts as the events' occurrence is their apprehension by the speaker in producing the expression; this virtual occurrence does coincide with the time of speaking (Langacker 1999b, 2001a). Nonpresent uses of the present are further considered in §14.2.2.

signals that the speaker is currently unable to make the future projection conveyed by *I will tell you* (in this case, because the condition for that occurrence—knowing what the plans are—is excluded from immediate reality). The temporal values that correlate with immediate vs. nonimmediate reality do not carry over to the modals, which locate the grounded process in irreality.

9.4.3 Modals

The English modals developed historically from lexical verbs with meanings like 'want to V', 'know how to V', and 'have the power to V'. The relationships profiled by such verbs have something in common. Namely, they ascribe to their trajector some kind of propensity, or "potency" which—when unleashed—can lead to its execution of an action (V). While the situations described by these verbs are therefore stable (if I want to do something, I am not now doing it), they do involve some kind of force tending toward V's occurrence. This latent force is represented by the dashed arrow in figure 9.16(a). A correspondence line indicates that the trajector (the locus of the potency) is also the one who carries out the action. While the ground is shown for sake of comparison, it has no special role (merely its ubiquitous minimal presence).

Because they profile force tending toward an action, the source verbs are both **force-dynamic** and **future-oriented**. These ancestral properties are the key to understanding the modern English modals, whose evolution illustrates the diachronic process known as grammaticization. As is usually the case, the resulting grammatical elements are semantically more schematic than their sources. And since the modals are grounding elements, their essential import is offstage and subjectively construed. This import reflects the original notion of potency directed toward an event's occurrence. Being subjectively construed, this potency no longer resides in the clausal trajector (by definition, the onstage focus of attention) but rather in the ground. It constitutes the grounding relationship, as shown in figure 9.16(b). Since grounding elements designate neither the ground nor the grounding relationship, only the grounded process—the target of the force—is left onstage as the profile.

(a)   Lexical Source

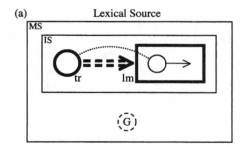

(b)   Grammaticized Modal

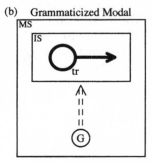

FIGURE 9.16

Precisely how the potency inheres in the ground is the basis for distinguishing two senses of each modal, commonly referred to as a **root** sense and an **epistemic** sense. The root modals pertain to notions like obligation, permission, intention, and ability. For the most part, the modal force is manifested in the realm of social interaction. Obligation, for example, consists of social force directing one to carry out an action, and permission amounts to the removal of social force preventing an action. The modals differ from one another in both the type of force involved and its strength. *Must* conveys a stronger obligation than *should*, and *might* a very weak one (a mere suggestion):

(38) (a) *Rules must always be obeyed.*

(b) *I really should write to my mother.*

(c) *You might help me with the dishes for a change.*

Will expresses intention, and while both *may* and *can* are used for permission, the latter can also indicate ability:

(39) (a) *She absolutely will not sign the waiver.*

(b) *Passengers may not congregate in the aisles or outside the lavatories.*

(c) *The prisoner can leave now—I just received authorization from the warden.*

(d) *OK, so you can leap tall buildings at a single bound. How are you at flipping burgers?*

Saying merely that the root modal force inheres in the ground is rather vague. One would like to be more specific. What is the source of the potency? At whom is the force directed in order to bring about the profiled event? Alas, there is no single answer to these questions. Perhaps the most common pattern is for the speaker to direct the force at the hearer [e.g. (38)(c)]. In this case, the exertion of social force is one aspect of the speaker-hearer interaction. Yet the speaker is not invariably the source of the potency, nor is the hearer always its target. The speaker may simply be conveying an obligation or permission that originates elsewhere [(39)(b)–(c)]. The source is not necessarily a particular individual. It can also be some faceless authority [(39)(b)], or even something diffuse like social expectations [(38)(a)–(b)].[46] The target of force shows comparable variation. Instead of the hearer [(38)(c)], it can be another person [(39)(c)], even the speaker [(38)(b)]. It need not be a specific individual but may also be a general class [(39)(b)] or society as a whole [(38)(a)]. While the target is commonly expressed by the clausal subject [(38)(b)–(c), (39)(b)–(c)], the subject is often not the target [(39)(a)], which is sometimes not expressed at all [(38)(a)].

---

[46] With intention [(39)(a)] and ability [(39)(d)], the source is usually the clausal subject, who carries out the action. These cases most closely resemble the ancestral construction (fig. 9.16(a)). They can nonetheless be analyzed as special cases of the grounding configuration (fig. 9.16(b)): for example, *she can swim* profiles the process *swim*, not the ability to do so.

In general, then, we can only say that a root modal's potency is somehow directed at **effecting** the grounded process. Whether the speaker exerts the force, conveys it, or merely assesses its strength, it bears on the process from the standpoint of bringing it about. By contrast, the epistemic senses of the modals pertain to knowledge. Rather than tending to induce the profiled process, the modal force reflects the speaker's efforts in assessing its likelihood. The potency is directed at incorporating the envisaged process in the speaker's conception of reality (R_C). It represents the speaker's force-dynamic experience in mentally extrapolating the current reality conception—imagining its future evolution—in such a way that R_C comes to include it. Thus it bears on the grounded process not in terms of bringing it about, but rather in terms of **accepting** it as **real**. If root modals are aimed at **effective control** of occurrences, epistemic modals are aimed at **epistemic control**.

Epistemic modals therefore resemble root modals and their lexical sources in being essentially force-dynamic (Talmy 1988a; Sweetser 1990: ch. 3). The notion of force they invoke is more abstract and more subjectively construed, however. If I give permission by saying *You may leave now*, the modal force conveyed has some influence on how things develop out there in the world: you will probably leave. But if I express an epistemic judgment by saying *It may rain this afternoon*, that judgment has no influence on the likelihood of it actually raining. The locus and direct consequences of the potency are internal to the conceptualizer, pertaining to the state of the speaker's knowledge and how it might evolve. The potency inheres in an offstage mental simulation of the speaker's reality conception evolving along a certain path. It resides in the mental effort expended and subjectively experienced in simulating the growth of R_C along a path by which it comes to encompass the grounded process.

Aspects of this mental simulation are sketched in figure 9.17. Metaphorically, we can describe conceived reality as having **evolutionary momentum**, represented by the double dashed arrow. Its evolution up through the current moment imparts a certain impetus, which tends to carry it in certain directions rather than others. The conceptualizer "feels" this momentum in running the mental simulation—that is, in tracking R_C and extrapolating its future course. Some paths are simply precluded: given how things are developing, they cannot be followed in any plausible simulation. Those which are not precluded constitute **potential reality**. Within potential reality, certain paths seem especially likely to be followed: its momentum is such that

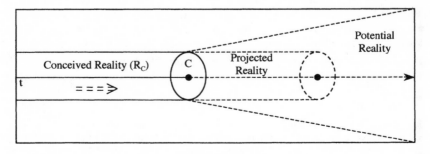

FIGURE 9.17

we can project R_C as evolving along these lines unless something unforeseen should happen to deflect it from this course. These paths constitute **projected reality**.

This scheme provides the basis for describing the epistemic modals. The semantic facts are complex, for each modal form (both immediate and nonimmediate) has developed in its own way and carved out its own special niche. Only a brief overview is possible here, starting with the base forms used in reference to future occurrences.

Of the five base forms (*may, can, will, shall,* and *must*), it turns out that only two are comfortably used in this manner. *Shall* is rarely employed in American English, and then only as a root modal (e.g. *Shall we go?*). *Can* is only marginal as an epistemic. Even with inanimate subjects, as in (40), it tends to be construed as expressing ability (a root modal sense): (40)(a) suggests that the toy is so flimsy that it is able to break, and (40)(b), that the meteorological conditions are still capable of producing rain.

(40) (a) *This toy can certainly break.*

      (b) *It can still rain.*

And while *must* has clear epistemic uses, they do not pertain to future occurrences. If (41) is interpreted epistemically, it pertains to a present situation rather than a future one. If it is interpreted as pertaining to the future, *must* has the root modal sense of imposing an obligation.

(41) *They must be completely satisfied.*

That leaves only *may* and *will*, which are easily described: *may* locates the grounded process in potential reality, and *will* in projected reality. Hence with *may* (42) merely indicates that a close election is possible, but with *will* it amounts to a prediction.

(42) *This election {may/will} be very close.*

We just noted that (41), when interpreted epistemically, pertains to the present rather than the future. How does this square with the notion that the modals are future-oriented? Crucial here is the distinction between the time of occurrences and the time when we know of occurrences. As time passes, we do not just learn of new events encountered along the way—we also learn more about already existing circumstances. At a given moment, therefore, epistemic judgments pertain to either future occurrences or present situations. But in either case a modal indicates that the grounded process is not yet accepted as real. It is future in the sense that its incorporation in the speaker's conception of reality remains to be accomplished. Thus, while modals are typically future-oriented with respect to both the process itself and its incorporation in R_C, they always are in terms of the latter.[47]

---

[47] When modals are used in reference to past occurrences, English resorts to the perfect construction, where the grounded verb is *have: She may have already mailed it.* The modal assessment thus pertains to a present situation—that of a prior event being found in the current sphere of relevance.

For present situations, *may* indicates the potential acceptance of the grounded process in R_C, and either *will* or *must* its projected acceptance:

(43)   *They {may/will/must} be home now—they left three hours ago.*

In American English, *must* is favored over *will* for this purpose. Although both forms project the evolution of R_C to incorporate the profiled process, *must* is stronger because it suggests that evolutionary momentum makes this inevitable.

Let us turn now to the nonimmediate modal forms: *might, could, would,* and *should.* To some extent, each is still analyzable as the combination of the base form (*may, can, will,* and *shall*) with the nonimmediate grounding element ("past tense" in the absence of a modal). But just as their composite forms are only partially compositional (*might* instead of **mayed, could* instead of **canned,* etc.), so are their composite meanings.

In some contexts a nonimmediate form seems to indicate an earlier location in time:

(44)   (a)   *Your sister said that she might drop by this evening.*

(b)   *The painters claimed that they would finish the job next week.*

However, the event located in the past is not the one grounded by the modal (*drop by* or *finish*), but rather the one designated by the main-clause verb (*say* or *claim*). From the adverbs (*this evening* and *next week*), it is clear that the dropping by and the leaving lie in the future. These sentences describe prior speech events in which the previous speaker could have used the immediate form of the modal. The sister probably said "I may drop by this evening", and the painters "We will finish the job next week". What is going on?

The key to these modals is that nonimmediacy is marked on the modal form itself rather than on the grounded verb. Accordingly, it does not serve to locate the grounded process, but to indicate nonimmediacy of the epistemic judgment itself. In using *might* instead of *may,* for example, the speaker implies that the assessment conveyed by *may* is not sanctioned by his own immediate circumstances. One situation involving nonimmediacy of an epistemic judgment arises in reporting the content of a prior speech event where such a judgment occurred. In (44)(a), the use of *may* was appropriate for the sister, reflecting her judgment at the prior time of speaking. By choosing *might* to report her statement, the current speaker indicates the nonimmediacy of these sanctioning circumstances.

The nonimmediate forms are not confined to reported speech. *Might, could,* and *should* can all be used for the speaker's own assessment of either a future occurrence or a present circumstance:

(45)   (a)   *The painters {might/could/should} finish the job next week.*

(b)   *They {might/could/should} be home by now—they left three hours ago.*

Using *might* rather than *may* serves to distance the speaker from the circumstances that justify the latter. Through this specification of nonimmediacy, the assessment of potentiality is rendered more tenuous. Note that *could* and *should* are natural in this context even though neither *can* nor *shall* is unproblematic in epistemic use. *Could* is roughly comparable to *might*. The difference is that *could* offers a positive judgment of (tenuous) potentiality, whereas *might* (like *may*) employs the negative strategy of specifying that the evolution of R_C to encompass the grounded process is not precluded. The import of *should* is just what one would expect for the nonimmediate form of *shall*, if this were used epistemically. *Shall* would place the designated process in projected reality. As its nonimmediate form, *should* indicates that the conditions for this assessment are not currently satisfied. The projection is thus more tenuous: the occurrence is quite likely but cannot be predicted with full confidence.

Finally, *would* is regularly related to *will* in the context of reported speech, as we saw in (44)(b). Outside this context, however, it is more than just an attenuated version of *will* (as *should* is with respect to *shall*). We see this in (46), which does not indicate that the painters are likely to finish the job, but quite the contrary:

(46) *The painters would finish the job next week...*

The sentence feels elliptic—we expect a continuation marking the situation as both hypothetical and counter to fact (e.g. *if you paid them more*). By virtue of being hypothetical and counterfactual, the conditions that would justify using *will* are, of course, nonimmediate.

10

Nominal Structure

The term *noun* is used in CG for any expression that profiles a thing.[1] So defined, it subsumes both lexical nouns and nominal expressions of any size, either fixed or novel. A *full nominal expression* is one that incorporates grounding and thus singles out a discourse referent. More compactly, it is referred to as a *full nominal* or just a *nominal*. In this chapter, I deal with various facets of nominal structure.

10.1 Structure and Function

A nominal corresponds to what linguists often call a "noun phrase" (NP). This term is poorly chosen, since nominals are not always phrases, nor do they always contain a noun (as traditionally understood). An expression does not qualify as a nominal because it exhibits any particular structural configuration. Instead the crucial factors are meaning and function. The schematic characterization of a nominal—that it profiles a grounded instance of a thing type—makes reference to several semantic functions: grounding, instantiation, and type specification. It is due to these semantic properties that a nominal is able to function as it does in larger grammatical structures.

10.1.1 Canonical Structure

There is a natural tendency for the internal structure of nominals to straightforwardly reflect the semantic functions that characterize them. It is normal for the type to be specified by a lexical noun selected from a very large inventory, and for grounding to be indicated by a separate element chosen from a limited set of options. It is not evident that instantiation is ever separately marked, but this too is natural in view of the very slight difference between type and instance conceptions (fig. 9.3). Since they all help specify a single discourse referent, the various components of a

---

[1] This definition avoids arbitrary distinctions and bogus theoretical issues. Since the adjectival form of *noun* is *nominal*, a noun is also described as a *nominal structure* or *nominal expression*.

nominal—grounding element, lexical head, and diverse modifiers—tend to be contiguous and to form a classic constituent (§7.4.1). Moreover, reflecting its status as conceptually the most extrinsic nominal component, grounding is usually the most peripheral component structurally (§9.3.1). It is common, if not typical, for grounding to represent the initial element in terms of linear order and the outermost layer in terms of constituency: (*those* (*two* (*lazy* (*cats*)))).

Important though they are, factors like these have only a general shaping influence. While they motivate overall tendencies, functional considerations provide no basis for predicting the particular details and full diversity of linguistic structure. Each language develops a broad variety of specific nominal structures serving different purposes and responsive to different functional pressures. Although English conforms to the tendencies just noted, it also has nominals without overt grounding (e.g. *nominals without overt grounding*) and some that lack a lexical head (e.g. *some that lack a lexical head*). Other languages differ more fundamentally in their nominal strategies, which, in their own way, are nonetheless quite natural. In some languages, for example, covert grounding is the rule rather than the exception. Not every language requires that a noun and its modifiers all be contiguous. And in languages making systematic use of classifiers (§10.3), a lexical noun is not necessarily the nominal head, being structurally more peripheral (FCG2: §4.3.1).

What to identify as a nominal "head" is a point of some controversy. As is so often the case with theoretical disputes, the issue is terminological rather than empirical. The term "head", of course, is metaphorical. It suggests that whatever is so identified should be the controlling element or one of chief importance.[2] But in a typical nominal, e.g. *those lazy cats*, there are two components with legitimate claim to this status. The first is the grounding element, which is primary in the sense of being the only one a nominal requires (*those* can function alone in this capacity). When it combines directly with a modifier, as in *those with fleas*, the grounding element also exerts control in the sense of imposing its nominal profile on the expression as a whole. The second is the lexical noun (*cats*), which is centrally important by virtue of providing the most extensive semantic content, thereby establishing what type of thing the nominal designates. Thus it is not a matter of which is right but of how we decide to use the term. In CG, the term "head" is used primarily for the profile determinant at any level of organization (not just with respect to nominals). Following this usage, *those* would be the head in *those with fleas*.[3] Yet it is also helpful to follow traditional practice by referring to the central component of a nominal—the one providing its type description—as its **head noun** (or simply its **head**).

Although the head noun is often called a **lexical head**, it is not invariably a lexical item. Besides established lexemes, novel expressions of any size can function in this capacity. We can refer not only to *a cat* or to *a cat-lover* but also—as need arises—to *a cat-lover psychiatric examination*, to *a cat-lover psychiatric examination manual*, to *a cat-lover psychiatric examination manual cover designer*, and so on indefinitely.

---

[2] Pardon the etymological pun. (If you missed it, look up *chief* in the dictionary.)

[3] By analogy, *those* would also be the head in *those lazy cats*. Recall, however, that in canonical expressions the grounding element has the same profile as the grounded noun (fig. 9.4). In such cases neither is considered a profile determinant (in accordance with another terminological decision).

As these examples indicate, head nouns in English are mainly constructed by means of compounding and morphological derivation. Hence the nouns and verbs they incorporate are usually singular and ungrounded.[4] It is only the head noun as a whole that undergoes pluralization: *cat-lovers, cat-lover psychiatric examinations, cat-lover psychiatric examination manuals, cat-lover psychiatric examination manual cover designers*. While the head overall is the pluralized structure, the plural inflection is realized morphologically just on its final word.

Thus for English, at least, nominal heads are defined by several converging properties. Internally, they are formed by compounding and morphological derivation (*cat-lover*), in contrast to the syntactic combination of separate words and phrases observed at higher levels of organization (e.g. *intelligent cat-lover from Vermont*). The head-noun level is also where pluralization occurs to derive a higher-order type (*cat-lover* > *cat-lovers*). Moreover, the type defined at this level is the basic type instantiated by the nominal referent. Whatever type is characterized by the head noun overall, an instance of that type is grounded and profiled by the nominal as a whole. The referent of *an intelligent cat-lover from Vermont* is therefore not a cat but a lover thereof. Likewise, *most intelligent cat-lovers from Vermont* designates a single (fictive) instance of the plural type *cat-lovers*.

The global organization of an English nominal thus tends to be as follows:

(1)   [Grounding [(Modifiers) [Head Noun] (Modifiers)]]

If not a single morpheme, the head noun is built through a combination of compounding and morphological derivation. Pluralization is an option at the highest level, and if chosen, it is realized on the head's final word. Whatever is profiled by the head is profiled by the nominal overall. However, any number of modifiers may combine syntactically with the head and thus refine (or even substantially alter) the basic type it specifies. Finally, since it offers the most extrinsic characterization of the nominal referent, grounding tends to occupy the outermost structural layer.

Canonically, the minimal components of a nominal are a head noun, providing a type description, together with a separate grounding element. Often, however, these two semantic functions are effected by a single form. In some cases there is no need for a detailed type specification. Prime examples of this are pronouns, whose main import resides in grounding. In other cases any need for separate grounding is obviated by the type description. Here the chief examples are proper names.

10.1.2 Pronouns

Pronouns are so called because they stand in for nouns (*pro* = 'for, instead of'). The term is traditionally applied to a substantial variety of forms—properly so, if nouns are broadly defined as in CG. They include both definite and indefinite expressions, as well as those functioning as either full nominals or just head nouns. We might start with a brief look at English *one*, which has a number of uses and related senses.

---

[4] There are some exceptions, such as *arms dealer* and *Clinton hater*.

In expressions like (2)(a), *one* functions as a head noun. Its type description is so schematic—equivalent to the schema for common count nouns—that the nominal it heads needs outside support for meaningful interpretation. It thus requires the availability, in the previous discourse frame (fig. 9.7), of a more specific type specification with which it can be identified. In (2)(a), its type is equated with that of the previous nominal *an expensive car*. This is the import of saying that *one* is a pronoun which "stands for" *car*. In (2)(b), we observe that the plural form *ones* is used analogously (standing for *computers*). Its schematic type description is equivalent to the schema for plural mass nouns. In this construction, *one* and *ones* are simply nouns, not full nominals.[5]

(2)   (a) *My boss has an expensive **car**, but I just have a cheap **one**.*

      (b) *The faculty have fast **computers**, but the students still have slow **ones**.*

One is also simply a noun when it combines directly with a grounding element: *this one, that one, each one, every one, any one*. In a number of cases, the two have coalesced into a single word whose type description is slightly more specific, namely 'person': *someone, everyone, anyone*, and *no one* (also now written *noone*). These composite expressions, which are full nominals, are commonly referred to as indefinite pronouns. Rather than depending on another nominal for a detailed type specification, they are used precisely on occasions when none is necessary: for either an unidentified person, in the case of *someone*, or for general statements where 'person' is itself the type in question. As is true in many languages, indefinite pronouns enter into (partial) paradigms based on schematic nouns for 'person', '(non-human) thing', 'place', 'time', and 'manner': *something, everything, anything, nothing; somewhere, everywhere, anywhere, nowhere; sometime, every time, anytime, *notime; somehow, *everyhow, anyhow, ?nohow*. These offer a flexible means of referring in general terms to most any sort of virtual entity.

One can also stand alone as a full nominal, with two basic variants. The first, exemplified in (3)(a), is used in making statements pertaining to people in general. It thus resembles *someone*, its type specification being 'person', but unlike *someone*, its referent is necessarily virtual. As with *every, each*, and *any*, the fictive individual it designates is taken as being representative, so that anything ascribed to it is valid for all instances. This representativeness obviates the need for separate grounding. Since the virtual instance is abstracted from actual ones, and immanent in their conception, there is no other instance to distinguish it from. Just evoking the profiled instance is sufficient to single it out.

(3)   (a) *One can never be too thin, too rich, or too well-connected.*

      (b) *My friends all have **yachts**. Tom has **several**, Alice has **two**, so I at least want **one**.*

One is also used anaphorically, depending on a previous nominal for its interpretation. An example is (3)(b), where its own schematic type is identified more specifically as

---

[5] For the case of nonplural masses, no single form is fully established in this construction. Sometimes zero suffices: *She bought some wine, and I bought more*. Sometimes *stuff* is pressed into service: *She bought good wine, and I bought cheap stuff*. But there are also cases where neither works: **They don't want just partial freedom, they're holding out for total {stuff/Ø}.*

yacht. In this use, *one* evidently conflates the functions of quantifier and indefinite article. It is a quantifier by virtue of contrasting with other numbers in the counting sequence: *one (yacht)*, *two (yachts)*, *three (yachts)*, etc. At the same time, it is mutually exclusive with the indefinite article *a* (historically derived from *one*), which is otherwise required for singular count nouns: *the yacht*, *a yacht*, *the one yacht*, *a one yacht, *one yacht*. So in this type of use—in a nominal like *one yacht* or as its anaphoric substitute—*one* can be described as an indefinite grounding element with an explicit specification of quantity.

First and foremost, the term "pronoun" calls to mind "personal" pronouns. The label reflects the status of their referents with respect to the speech event participants: the speaker ("first person") and hearer ("second person"), as opposed to others ("third person"). One facet of grounding, that of locating the nominal referent vis-à-vis the ground, is thus intrinsic to personal pronouns. An additional facet, that of singling out the referent, is intrinsic for the first-person and second-person pronouns (*I, we, you*), since these designate either an interlocutor or a group that includes it. With third-person pronouns (*he, she, it, they*), the matter is less straightforward. Their minimal type specifications, like 'animate female' for *she*, select open-ended sets of eligible candidates. Quite a number of candidates are likely to be available in a given discourse context. Nevertheless, the third-person forms are full nominals, presumed capable of singling out the intended referent. How do they accomplish this?

Personal pronouns are closely related to definite articles and also to anaphoric demonstratives. Like a definite article (fig. 9.11), they imply that just a single instance of the specified type is readily accessible in the previous discourse frame. *She* is thus appropriate in (4)(a), where the prior sentence introduces just one eligible candidate, but not in (4)(b), where several are equally available:

(4)   (a)   *I was talking to **an interesting woman**. **She** heads a major corporation.*

      (b)   **I was talking to **several interesting women**. **She** heads a major corporation.*

Unlike articles, pronouns stand alone as nominals and are thus dependent on their own schematic type specification to select the pool of eligible candidates. Also unlike articles, they imply that the referent has already been singled out for joint attention in the previous frame, as shown in figure 10.1. In this respect they resemble anaphoric demonstratives (fig. 9.10). They differ from such demonstratives by lacking directive force, as well as the proximal/distal distinction.

Instead of proximity, a third-person pronoun relies on contextual prominence to identify its referent. It presupposes that a particular instance of its type has not only been singled out in the previous discourse frame, but is salient enough to be the sole instance that counts for anaphoric purposes. In (5)(a), for example, both *the yacht* and *the car* single out referents that satisfy the type specification of *it* ('inanimate thing'). As clausal subject, however, the former has sufficient prominence to eclipse the latter and establish itself as the pronoun's antecedent.[6] *It* thus takes its reference from *the yacht*—they are interpreted as being coreferential.

---

[6] As described in ch. 14, pronominal anaphora is a reference point phenomenon: *the yacht* functions as reference point for interpreting the target pronoun *it* (fig. 3.14). Being determined by a variety of interacting factors (van Hoek 1997), the choice of reference point is sometimes not unique. In the following, for instance, *she* might refer to either Jill or the sister: *When I saw **Jill** talking to **my sister**, **she** was quite agitated.*

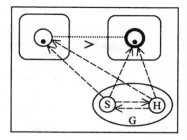

FIGURE 10.1

(5)   (a) ***The yacht*** *is more impressive than **the car**, but I probably can't afford **it**.*

(b) *That **yacht** is certainly impressive, but I can't afford even this cheap **one**.*

By comparison, the anaphoric use of *one* in (5)(b) depends on the antecedent nominal only for its type specification, not its reference: whereas *it* and *the yacht* are construed as designating the same instance of this type, *one* and *the yacht* profile distinct instances. The basis for the contrast is that the anaphoric elements represent different levels of functional organization. *One* in (5)(b) is just a head noun, so only type is relevant for its interpretation. On the other hand, personal pronouns are full nominals, so reference too is at issue.

These two kinds of anaphora are sketched in figure 10.2, where t indicates a specific type and ellipses (...) a more schematic type (cf. fig. 9.3). With a personal pronoun, both the antecedent and the anaphor are full nominals, so each profiles an instance of its type. Effecting their anaphoric relationship is a correspondence serving to identify these profiled instances. The identification of their referents implies that the antecedent's type description is also applicable to the referent of the pronoun. In the other kind of anaphora, the antecedent and the anaphor are simply nouns, the heads within their respective nominals. A correspondence therefore identifies their types but gives no indication concerning the nominal referents. Thus in (5)(b) we know that *this cheap one* is a yacht, albeit not the instance profiled by the subject nominal.

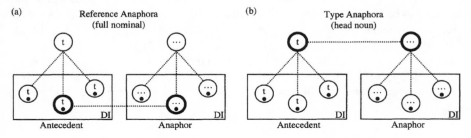

FIGURE 10.2

Recall that a nominal grounding element is itself a schematic nominal, for it profiles a thing and relates it to the ground (fig. 9.4). When it stands alone as a nominal, a grounding element is even more schematic than a pronoun in regard to type. In such cases, the type is often determined anaphorically. Thus we know in (6) that *those* refers to steaks, *most* to students, and *each* to a (fictive) witness:

(6)   (a) *I left **some steaks** out to thaw. You can have **those** for dinner.*

     (b) *We admitted **a thousand new students** last fall. **Most were deficient in reading and math**.*

     (c) ***Numerous witnesses** claimed to have seen the robber's face. **Each** gave a different description, however.*

In effect, these elements are functioning here as pronouns. Note that *those* could be replaced by *them*. And just as in figure 10.2(a), *those* and *some steaks* are related by reference anaphora—they are coreferential. With *most* and *each* the anaphoric relationship is slightly different. Since these quantifiers designate virtual entities, strictly speaking they are not coreferential to the antecedent nominals, *a thousand new students* and *numerous witnesses*, whose referents are interpreted as being actual. Instead these nominals indicate the group with respect to which *most* and *each* specify a quantity. More technically, they identify and contextually delimit the maximal extension (E_t) in terms of which the quantifiers are characterized (figs. 9.12 and 9.13).

10.1.3 Proper Names

Proper names are often claimed to not even have a type description. Indeed, they are often considered meaningless, their sole import residing in their reference to something in the world. This classic view cannot be sustained, however. Many proper names are conventionally employed for particular types of entities (e.g. *Jack* for 'human male', *Jill* for 'human female'). Others evoke substantial bodies of information that is widely shared within a speech community. The name *George Washington* does not just refer to a person, but tends to activate a conventional array of encyclopedic knowledge (army general, first American president, wife named Martha, thought to be honest, and so on). Likewise, *Chicago* does not simply name a city, but evokes an array of widely known properties and associations. To the extent that they are entrenched and conventional, these specifications have to be included in the meanings of such expressions.

The distinguishing feature of proper names is not that they are meaningless, but is rather to be found in the nature of their meanings. As one component of its meaning (one domain in its matrix), a proper name incorporates a cognitive model pertaining to how the form is used in the relevant social group.[7] According to this idealized model, each member of the group has a distinct name, with the consequence that the name itself is sufficient to identify it. The name *Jack*, for example, carries with it the supposition that within the relevant group (e.g. a family) there is just one person

---

[7] This group can be of any size: a family, the students in a class, an occupational group, the members of a culture, and so on. Its specific identification depends on the discourse context.

referred to in this manner. The name can thus be thought of as defining a type—the type 'person named *Jack*'—which (in the context of the group) the model specifies as having just one instance. Since the name itself singles out the only instance, there is no need for separate grounding.

This idealized cognitive model implies that the name itself—that is, the expression's phonological pole—figures in its type description at the semantic pole. Central to the meaning of *Jack* is the specification 'person named *Jack*'. But this property is not limited to proper nouns. Central to the meaning of a common noun, e.g. *yacht*, is the specification that many distinct entities bear this label. One domain in its matrix is the very knowledge that members of the speech community conventionally refer to such entities in this manner. Hence the type description for *yacht* includes the specification 'thing called *yacht*'.[8]

To make these notions explicit, let τ represent a noun's phonological pole, and t its semantic specifications. Its overall type description can thus be given as t/τ: that is, it includes the very fact that things of this sort are symbolized by τ. This is shown in figure 10.3 (a refinement of fig. 9.3). A common noun is one whose type has multiple instances, each of which can also be labeled τ. On the other hand, a proper noun labels just a single entity, so there is no basis for abstracting a separate type. We can either say that the type/instance distinction is neutralized or, equivalently, that the type has just one instance. In the case of proper names, this uniqueness follows from the idealized cognitive model for naming within a social group.[9] And since the name itself is their central defining property, the remaining semantic specifications are often quite schematic (e.g. 'human male' for *Jack*), as shown by using ellipses in lieu of t.

It sometimes happens, though, that the expectations of an idealized cognitive model fail to be satisfied in actual practice. In particular, it is not uncommon for multiple individuals to have the same name within the relevant social group. We thus find expressions like the following:

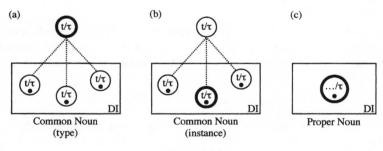

FIGURE 10.3

[8] More generally, an expression's phonological pole is viewed in CG as one aspect of its global meaning (FCG1: §2.2.1). This is by no means problematic, but a key to understanding various phenomena (e.g. onomatopoeia).

[9] This uniqueness can have other sources as well. Within the calendrical cycle, for example, the term for each month (*January*, *February*, . . .) labels just a single entity. Likewise, the terms for basic colors (*yellow*, *red*, *blue*, etc.) designate unique regions in color space (fig. 4.4(a)). While these are not proper names (in a narrow sense), they occur without separate grounding and can thus be considered proper nouns (cf. Coates 2006).

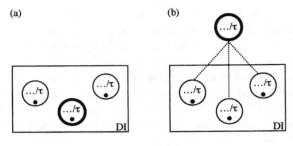

FIGURE 10.4

(7)   (a) *There were four Davids on the soccer team I coached.*

(b) *Are you the **Hank Barnes** who owns the liquor store, or the **one** who ran for mayor?*

In such examples, a proper name functions grammatically as a common noun—it can pluralize, occur with overt grounding, take a restrictive relative clause, participate in type anaphora, and so on. English handles this discrepancy between idealized model and actual situation by suspending the model's requirement that a name be assigned to just one person. A particular name (τ) can thus be used to designate an individual who shares that name with others, as shown in figure 10.4(a). Observe, now, that this situation supports the abstraction of a type, roughly 'person named τ' (.../τ), having each such individual as an instance. The resulting configuration, shown in diagram (b), fully conforms to the characterization of a common count noun (fig. 10.3(a)). The proper names in (7) behave as common nouns because they **are** common nouns.

10.2 Noun Modifiers

Nominals can be of any size and are structurally quite diverse. In large measure this is due to modifiers, which are many and varied and occur in different combinations. Here we can manage just a brief look at noun modifiers and modifying constructions.

10.2.1 Semantic and Formal Variety

Modifiers vary in their size, their grammatical category, and the nature of their semantic contribution. With respect to size, they run the full gamut: from words (*Brazilian parrot*), to phrases (*parrot with a lisp*), to clauses (*parrot who kept us awake last night*). And since phrasal and clausal modifiers can themselves incorporate nominals with modifiers, modifying expressions of any length can be constructed: *that parrot who kept us awake last night > that parrot who kept us awake last night with a constant stream of obscenities > that parrot who kept us awake last night with a constant stream of obscenities that really shocked us > that parrot who kept us awake last night with a constant stream of obscenities that really shocked us by their level of vulgarity...*

Expressions representing a number of different categories can be used to modify nouns: adjectives, prepositional phrases, present participles, past participles (both stative and passive), and infinitives. From the standpoint of CG, these categories all have something in common (§4.3.3). We can make the generalization that noun modifiers profile nonprocessual relationships.[10] The exclusion of verbs, which profile processes, is a natural consequence of modifying relationships being construed holistically. A modifier is only apprehended in relation to the modified noun, which—as the profile determinant—imposes its summary view on the composite expression. Verbs are poor candidates to directly modify nouns because the sequential scanning characteristic of a process cannot be manifested in a summary view. Of course, finite relative clauses do modify nouns, despite their processual profile. Unlike other modifiers, a finite clause is grounded. And since the ground is the vantage point for apprehending the clausal content, the profiled process is to some extent viewed independently (not solely in relation to the head). The separate access afforded by grounding makes possible the sequentiality of a process conception.

In English, whether a modifier precedes or follows the head noun is partly determined by its degree of internal complexity. Adjectives, present participles, and stative past participles often consist of just a single word, in which case they precede the noun they modify: *anxious woman, sleeping child, disfigured statue*. They still precede the noun when they themselves are preceded by a modifying adverb: *very anxious woman, soundly sleeping child, completely disfigured statue*. But when a noun modifier incorporates more elaborate material, which follows it and would therefore separate it from the head noun, the entire complex modifier comes after the noun instead: *woman anxious about her children, child sleeping too soundly to wake up, statue disfigured beyond recognition*. Also following the head are prepositional phrases, passive participial phrases, infinitives, and finite relative clauses. These are always multiword expressions: *house with a view, fire started by vagrants, person to watch out for, lawyer who has never lost a case*.

At least as important as complexity, in determining a modifier's placement, is the kind of semantic contribution it makes. There is a definite tendency in English for a modifier that directly precedes the head to specify an intrinsic or permanent property, whereas post-head modifiers tend to be used for properties of a contingent or temporary character. For example, *an anxious woman* is probably anxious by nature, as a stable personality trait, while *a woman anxious about her children* may simply be waiting for the school bus to arrive. A stative participle describes a property (the "state" resulting from a change) that is likely to endure: *a broken watch, toasted almonds, his sullied reputation*. By contrast, a passive participle profiles an event, often with no persisting result. We can thus refer to *leaves rustled by the wind*, but not to **rustled leaves*; to *an error caught by the proofreader*, but not to **a caught error*; to *that fire started by vagrants*, but not to **that started fire*. More generally, adjectives with the strongest claim to prototypicality are those pertaining to inherent

---

[10] An apparent exception are the initial nouns in expressions like *stone wall, tile floor*, and *paper bag*. Possibly they profile relationships in this construction. Suggesting a relational construal are phrases like *completely tile floor*, where *tile* is modified by an adverb, as well as their use as clausal predicates, e.g. *The floor is tile*.

characteristics of indefinite duration: *big, red, strong, flat, smart*, etc. Post-head modifiers are most typically used for contingent circumstances, such as locations (e.g. *the flowers on her desk*), specific events (*a man I insulted*), and temporary situations (*that spider climbing up your leg*).

Even confining our attention to modifiers traditionally classed as adjectives, we observe considerable semantic diversity and numerous departures from the prototype of describing inherent properties. For example, some adjectives specify position in a sequence or location in time: *my first teacher, our next president, a prior commitment, future events, a former girlfriend*. Others assess the validity of the nominal type specification: *genuine leather, fake Rolex, putative expert, real gold, counterfeit tickets, true patriot*. These shade into adjectives indicating the referent's status with respect to a category: *typical doctor, perfect circle, complete idiot, canonical example, ordinary member, representative instance*. Rather than intrinsic properties, many adjectives describe how a thing is experienced by others: *comfortable chair, scary movie, offensive statement, pleasant evening, welcome break, unsatisfactory answer*. These in turn shade into evaluative assessments whose basis may be entirely subjective: *marvelous report, charming couple, wonderful vacation, darling restaurant, horrible person*. Instead of a property, certain adjectives specify which domain a thing pertains to: *electrical engineer, mental hospital, corporate executive, medical textbook, culinary institute*. Still other adjectives relate to quantity: *abundant resources, rare coins, countless opportunities, infinite patience, meager allowance*. In fact, absolute quantifiers (*many, few, much, little, several, nine*, etc.) qualify as adjectives from both a semantic and a grammatical standpoint.

Permissible combinations of adjectives and their sequencing are a complex matter about which I can offer only some fragmentary observations. There is arguably an overall tendency for proximity to the head to correlate with intrinsicness of the property specified. Quantifiers are always farthest from the head: *nine black cats, *black nine cats, several important visitors, *important several visitors*. Closest to the head are adjectives that directly pertain to type. Domain adjectives have to be adjacent to the head: *excellent culinary institute, *culinary excellent institute, young electrical engineer, *electrical young engineer*. Indeed, since they also resist predicative use (e.g. **The engineer is electrical*), they might best be analyzed as part of the head. Also close to the head are modifiers that assess a type specification's validity: *large fake diamond, *fake large diamond, cheap imitation leather, *imitation cheap leather*. A number of specific patterns are well established. For example, adjectives of nationality follow those assessing validity but precede domain adjectives: *true American patriot, fake Moroccan leather, British mental hospital, German corporate executive, genuine French culinary institute*. Modifiers describing size, color, and material normally occur in that order: *large black woolen coat, small red cardboard box, big blue wooden sign* (but not **blue big wooden sign, *wooden big blue sign*, or **blue wooden big sign*).

The various patterns and tendencies noted are neither exceptionless nor even close to being exhaustive of English nominal structure. But while the facts of noun modification are quite complex, they also show a great deal of systematicity. On the face of it, their description requires a flexible, usage-based model of the sort outlined in chapter 8. A large inventory of constructions and constructional schemas, characterized at appropriate levels of specificity, will serve to capture both local and global generalizations. Moreover, since units vary in degree of entrenchment and ease of activation for the sanction of new expressions, the model accommodates both exceptions and regularities that are less than categorical, representing tendencies of different strengths.

10.2.2 Canonical Constructions

The traditional distinction between complements and modifiers depends on their direction of elaboration vis-à-vis the constructional head (i.e. the profile determinant): a complement **elaborates** a salient substructure of the head, while a modifier contains a salient substructure **elaborated by** the head (fig. 7.14). Given the diversity of modifiers, it is noteworthy that this substructure (the e-site) is almost always the trajector.[11] In *table near the door*, for example, *table* corresponds to *near*'s trajector rather than its landmark. The head also elaborates the trajector of a modifying adjective or participle: *small table*, *table sitting by the door*, *broken table*, *table polished every morning*.[12]

A canonical modifying construction is represented at the left in figure 10.5. The noun profiles a thing and describes its basic type (X). The modifier profiles an atemporal (i.e. nonprocessual) relationship; typically, it ascribes some property (y) to its trajector. Effecting their integration is a correspondence between this schematic trajector and the profile of the noun, which thus elaborates it. The noun is the constructional head, its profile being inherited at the composite-structure level. And since it too profiles a thing, the composite expression is itself a complex noun.

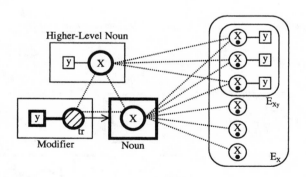

FIGURE 10.5

---

[11] Apart from finite relative clauses (special due to their independent grounding), the one exception in English consists of infinitival modifiers marked by *to*. With these, the head noun corresponds to either the trajector (*the first person to arrive*), the landmark (*a woman to admire*), or even the landmark of a preposition (*something to stir the soup with*).

[12] As evidence for the e-site's trajector status, observe that the same participant is coded by the subject when the modifier functions as a clausal predicate: *The table is {near the door / small / sitting by the door / broken / polished every morning}*.

A modifier allows the profiled entity to be described in greater detail. Starting from the basic type X, modification produces a more elaborate type description consisting of X augmented by property y. Let us call this Xy. Associated with the type at each level is a mental construction referred to here as the maximal extension of that type, i.e. the set of all (contextually relevant) instances. The two maximal extensions, E_x and E_{xy}, are shown in figure 10.5 on the right. Clearly, not every instance of X is also an instance of Xy—being more detailed, Xy selects a smaller pool of eligible candidates. Further modification will shrink the pool still more.

When there is just one modifier, the same noun functions as both constructional head and head noun. *Table* has this dual role in *a table near the door*: it is both the constructional head in its combination with the prepositional phrase and the head noun for the overall nominal. The grounded structure (i.e. all but the indefinite article) is sketched in figure 10.6(a).[13] With respect to the modifying construction, *table* is the head because it imposes its profile at the composite-structure level. With respect to the nominal as a whole, it is the head noun because its profile corresponds to the grounded entity, the composite-structure profile (grounded by *a* at the highest level of organization). These are distinct characterizations, even though they identify the same element as head in certain cases.

The distinction between constructional head and head noun becomes evident in nominals with two levels of modification, e.g. *a small table near the door*. The grounded structure is diagrammed in figure 10.6(b). At the first level of organization, *small* combines with *table* to form *small table*. Since the composite expression profiles the table, the constructional head is *table*. At the second level, *small table* combines with *near the door* to form *small table near the door*. The composite

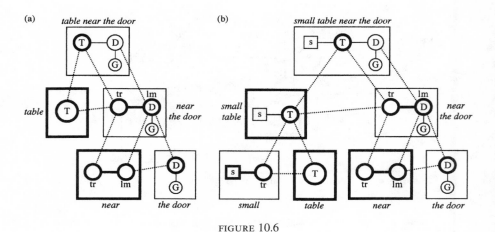

FIGURE 10.6

---

[13] Despite its schematized format—obviously more practical—fig. 10.6(a) is equivalent to the pictorial representation in fig. 7.13. T and D represent the basic types *table* and *door*, while G indicates that *door* is grounded. In diagram (b), s represents the property specified by *small*.

expression once more designates the table (not the locative relationship), so at this level the constructional head is *small table*. The constructional heads are different (*table* vs. *small table*), being locally defined in the context of each construction. By contrast, the head noun is globally defined for the nominal as a whole. The head noun specifies the nominal's basic type, an instance of which is singled out for grounding, and is the lowest-level structure whose profile corresponds to the nominal profile. In *a small table near the door*, the head noun is *table*, an instance of which is grounded by the indefinite article at the highest level of organization.

The nouns at each successive level—*table, small table*, and *small table near the door*—characterize the profiled thing in progressively greater detail. If we say (for sake of uniformity) that each describes a type of thing, the word "type" must be flexibly interpreted. It cannot be limited to the standard, culturally recognized types invoked by lexical nouns, or even to what are called types in ordinary usage: while a *table* is certainly a type of thing, a *small table* would not ordinarily be considered a type of table, and a *small table near the door* would never be. We resort to modifiers precisely because standard, lexically coded types are inadequate for the task at hand, and often the needed description makes reference to nonstandard properties or wholly contingent circumstances.

Furthermore, modifiers contribute semantically in a variety of ways, not merely by adding a property to those defining the basic type (Sweetser 1999). They sometimes have the more drastic effect of suspending aspects of the basic type, commenting on its validity, or indicating a restricted scope of application: *flightless bird, nonalcoholic beer, fake diamond, so-called conservative, imaginary kingdom, hypothetical situation, future president*. In this case the basic type is construed in relation to a broader scenario that permits such assessments. *Fake*, for example, invokes the cognitive model of people creating objects whose appearance is intended to bring about their erroneous categorization as instances of the type in question. But despite such qualifications, the nominal referent is still treated linguistically as an instance of the basic type. Sentences like the following are quite acceptable:

(8)   (a)   *These fake diamonds are the only diamonds I have.*

    (b)   *Nonalcoholic beer is better than no beer at all.*

10.2.3 Nominal Constituents

When there is more than one modifier, the problem of constituency rears its ugly head. How do we know, for example, that *small table near the door* has the constituency shown in figure 10.6(b)? Instead of ((*small table*) (*near the door*)), why not ((*small*) (*table near the door*)), or even ((*small*) (*table*) (*near the door*))? There is no consensus about the internal constituency of nominals, due in part to the matter being quite complex. But let me suggest a more basic reason: that there **is** no definite constituency. As viewed in CG, constituency is neither essential nor fundamental to grammar (§7.4). While certain hierarchical arrangements are fixed and well established, constituency groupings are often flexible and variable, if not just indeterminate. We have no reason to think that the structures constituting a symbolic assembly all have to be arranged in strictly hierarchical fashion, nor does any single hierarchy capture all aspects of grammatical organization.

From the CG standpoint, questions of constituency have to be addressed as part of a broader consideration of symbolic assemblies. A symbolic assembly consists of semantic structures, phonological structures, and symbolic links between the two. Semantic and phonological structures can be of any size. At either pole, complex structures arise through composition, where simpler (component) structures are grouped and integrated to form more elaborate (composite) structures. A symbolic structure consists in the linkage of a semantic structure and a phonological structure (regardless of their size). It cannot be assumed that the groupings at either pole are fully nested (rather than cross-cutting), hence all arranged in a single consistent hierarchy, nor that every grouping participates in a symbolic relationship.[14]

With respect to this general scheme, we can characterize grammatical constituency as a matter of grouping being coordinated at the semantic and phonological poles. Suppose we have three symbolic structures: [[A]/[a]], [[B]/[b]], and [[C]/[c]]. Claiming constituency for [[A]/[a]] and [[B]/[b]] implies both that [A] and [B] are grouped (to the exclusion of [C]) at the semantic pole and also that [a] and [b] are grouped (excluding [c]) at the phonological pole. The respective outcomes of these groupings are the composite conception [AB] and the composite form [ab], whose coordination thus produces the higher-order symbolic structure [[AB]/[ab]]. In assessing the claim of constituency, the critical factor is therefore the status of [AB] and [ab]. We can justify positing these structures by showing that they actually have some linguistic manifestation. If not directly observable, they may be manifested indirectly through the necessity of referring to them for particular descriptive purposes.

Phonological grouping is more accessible to direct observation. To support the constituency shown in figure 10.6(b), we can note the possibility of a slight pause (/) at the putative constituent boundary: *small table / near the door*. At least for this purpose, therefore, *small table* constitutes a phonological grouping. Does it also represent a semantic grouping? Here we can note its role in type anaphora:

(9)   *Do you prefer the **small table** near the door, or the **one** next to the kitchen?*

In (9) we can interpret *one* as referring to either *table* or *small table*. The latter option indicates the conceptual grouping of *small* and *table*, since the type they jointly define is accessible for anaphoric purposes. If *small table* represents both a semantic and a phonological grouping, together these amount to a symbolic grouping, i.e. a grammatical constituent.

Matters are not quite this simple, however. A case can also be made for the "flat" structure ((*small*) (*table*) (*near the door*)), where neither modifier combines exclusively with the head. Phonologically, an absence of intonational grouping is

---

[14] Structures defined in unipolar terms (§6.3) do not per se participate in symbolic relationships. Also, the grouping of structures defined in bipolar terms sometimes yields a higher-order structure that does not itself achieve symbolic linkage. Recall a previous example: *The package arrived that I was expecting* (fig. 7.19(b)). Although *the package* and *that I was expecting* form a natural semantic grouping, the composite conception remains unsymbolized.

characteristic of slow, deliberate pronunciation: *small / table / near the door*. At the semantic pole, *one* refers only to *table* in (10)(a):

(10)   (a) *Do you prefer the small **table** near the door, or the big **one** next to the kitchen?*

      (b) *A SMALL **table near the door** is preferable to a BIG **one**.*

Likewise, the form and meaning of (10)(b) point to the grouping *((small) (table near the door))*. It is possible here to interpret *one* as referring to *table near the door*. And while it is not very natural to effect this grouping by means of a pause (*?small / table near the door*), it is manifested phonologically in another dimension, namely stress. In a discourse context where (10)(b) is appropriate, it is also appropriate for the nominals to be pronounced with reduced stress on all but the adjectives.[15] The grouping of *table* and *near the door* is thus effected on the basis of their diminished accentual prominence.

These conflicting alternatives pose no problem for CG, which eschews the standard assumption of a single, fixed constituency. Rather than being fundamental, constituents emerge within symbolic assemblies as a special case (albeit a typical one) of the configurations their elements can assume. It is only to be expected that the same symbolic components might sometimes be grouped in alternate ways, without significantly affecting the ultimate composite structure. It may also happen that grammatical constituents do not emerge at all. Given three component elements, like *small*, *table*, and *near the door*, nothing prevents them from combining at a single level of organization, with no internal grouping: *((small) (table) (near the door))*. And should grouping occur at one pole, there is no necessity that it be concordant with grouping at the other. In (9), for example, *one* can be interpreted as referring to either *table* or *small table* regardless of whether the intonation is *small / table / near the door* or *small table / near the door*. If *small* and *table* are grouped at only one pole, there is no clear basis for positing a grammatical constituent. Grammar being bipolar in nature, a claim of constituency implies that grouping occurs in parallel at the two poles.

In the absence of clear-cut evidence, the proper analysis may simply be indeterminate—certainly for the analyst, and very possibly even for speakers. Consider the sequence *frisky young horse*. Are there grounds for claiming that *young* and *horse* form a constituent, with *frisky* then combining with *young horse* at a higher level of organization? We have some indication of conceptual grouping in (11), where *young horse* is a possible antecedent of *one*:

(11)   *She wants to ride a frisky **young horse**, not a lazy **one**.*

Moreover, we can perfectly well say that *young* and *horse* are grouped phonologically on the basis of adjacency in the stream of speech. Yet the case is rather tenuous. The evidence for semantic grouping disappears when *one* is interpreted as referring just to *horse*, or in uses where *frisky young horse* has no anaphoric connection. And

---

[15] Small caps indicate their unreduced stress. (Boldface, of course, is not being used for stress but for anaphoric relationships.)

while adjacency is consistent with *young* and *horse* being a constituent, it is also consistent with the tripartite constituency ((*frisky*) (*young*) (*horse*)). Perhaps, then, the proper analysis is not to impose a particular analysis at all.

On the basis of more general considerations, however, I do incline toward treating *young horse* as a constituent in *frisky young horse*. Grouping is such a natural and pervasive phenomenon, and temporal adjacency such a strong grouping factor, that binary structures are often (and not unreasonably) considered the default.[16] Given a modifier sequence, the head and a modifier adjacent to it would thus have a strong tendency to form a constituent, which would then combine—also on the basis of adjacency—with the other modifier. This layering of modifiers is sometimes clearly required on semantic grounds. One example is the contrasting pair *counterfeit American money* vs. *American counterfeit money*. If there were no layering, i.e. if both adjectives modified the head noun directly, we would expect the two expressions to be semantically equivalent. In fact, though, they have different meanings reflecting alternate conceptual groupings. On the one hand, *counterfeit American money* groups *American* and *money*, since *American money* represents an essential conceptual component (the item being imitated). On the other hand, *American counterfeit money* evokes the conceptual grouping *counterfeit money*, describing it as an American product (perhaps an imitation of Japanese currency).

In the case of *frisky young horse*, it makes no evident difference whether *frisky* modifies *horse* directly (implying a tripartite structure) or instead modifies *young horse*. Either compositional path yields the same composite meaning, in which the basic type specification (*horse*) is augmented by two distinct properties (*frisky* and *young*). Here, though, we find possible evidence for constituency by observing a correlation between intonation and word order. *Frisky young horse* would normally be pronounced without any pause, and without one the order of adjectives is fairly rigid—*??young frisky horse* is marginal at best. The reversed order is perfectly natural, however, when pauses are added: *young/frisky/horse*.[17] This intonation suggests a flat structure, with no internal grouping, as shown in figure 10.7.

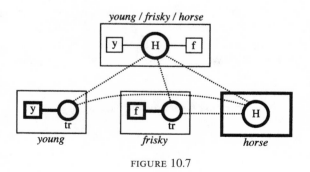

FIGURE 10.7

<hr />

[16] Temporal adjacency is criterial for the "classic" conception of constituency (§7.4). The characterization given above is more inclusive, as it does not specify any particular basis for grouping.

[17] This is written *young, frisky horse*. While the comma represents the first pause, standard orthographic practice neglects the comparable pause between *frisky* and *horse*.

We can therefore posit a distinct modifying construction, where pauses indicate that multiple adjectives directly modify the head at a single level of grammatical organization. If this construction indicates the absence of layering, we can plausibly suppose that the alternative pattern (e.g. *frisky young horse*) results from successive levels of modification.

10.2.4 Noncanonical Constructions

By permitting multiple modifiers at a single level of grammatical organization, the configuration in figure 10.7 is noncanonical for modifying constructions. You can probably guess (given the title of this section) that such constructions can deviate in other ways as well from the typical arrangement (fig. 10.5).

A seemingly drastic departure from the canon are modifying expressions where there is no head noun. Though more limited than in many languages, the phenomenon does occur in English. Apart from certain fixed expressions (e.g. *the poor*), it is largely restricted to complex modifiers occurring with demonstratives (especially *those*) and certain quantifiers: *all who qualified, any with valid complaints, that which he fears the most, those ready to leave, those arriving late, those offended by my remarks.* Our only concern here is with the general nature of such constructions. Why are they possible at all? How can a noun modifier modify a noun that isn't there?

In principle these constructions are unproblematic in CG, since nominals are characterized semantically, not in terms of any particular structural configuration. As long as an expression profiles a grounded instance of a thing type (even a highly schematic type), it counts as a nominal. We have seen that a nominal grounding element is itself a schematic nominal by this definition. And because it profiles a thing, there is no inherent reason why a grounding element cannot itself take a noun modifier. As shown in figure 10.8, we need only specify that the grounded thing instance corresponds to the trajector of the modifier, and that the grounding element functions as profile determinant. In the absence of a lexical head noun, the basic type instantiated by the grounded instance remains schematic. The overall type description is however augmented through the content of the modifier.

Another departure from the canon involves modifiers that play no role in identifying the nominal referent. A well-known case is the contrast between "restrictive" and "nonrestrictive" relative clauses. A restrictive relative clause serves to limit the

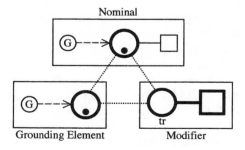

Nominal

Grounding Element   Modifier

FIGURE 10.8

pool of eligible candidates, restricting it to a subset of the basic type's maximal extension. In (12)(a)—where these candidates really are *candidates*—the specified property (really deserving to win) limits the pool to a single candidate, as required by the definite article:

(12)　(a)　*The candidate who really deserves to win ran a positive campaign.*

　　　(b)　*The candidate, who really deserves to win, ran a positive campaign.*

The information supplied by a nonrestrictive clause fails to be exploited in this manner. In (12)(b), the profiled instance of *candidate* is contextually identified independently of deserving to win (rather than on the basis of that property).

To represent the distinction, restrictive relative clauses are usually analyzed as being part of the nominal in question, and nonrestrictive clauses as being external to it. Supporting this analysis are the pauses ("comma intonation") associated with nonrestrictive relatives. In and of itself, however, this structural difference is not sufficient to account for the semantic contrast. This is evident from the fact that the same contrast is observed with modifying adjectives, where there is no difference in constituency. As part of *the tiny mouse*, for example, *tiny* is used restrictively in (13)(a) and nonrestrictively in (13)(b). Only in the former does it help to identify the nominal referent. But in both uses, *tiny* is clearly internal to the nominal.

(13)　(a)　*In the cage she saw a big mouse and a tiny mouse. The tiny mouse was shaking.*

　　　(b)　*In the cage she saw a mouse. The tiny mouse was shaking.*

A general account of the restrictive/nonrestrictive contrast must therefore be independent of the structural difference observed with relative clauses. In the case of adjectives, it turns out that the contrast does not reside in the modifying construction itself, but rather in how the symbolic assembly constituting it is accessed for higher-level purposes. Whether *the tiny mouse* is interpreted restrictively or nonrestrictively in (13), *tiny* itself has the same meaning. The same is true for the composite expression *tiny mouse*. The semantic contrast is, instead, a matter of how this composite expression is integrated with the definite article at a higher level of grammatical organization. The article profiles an instance of some type and indicates its discourse status. The question is, which type? As shown in figure 10.5, two thing types figure in the characterization of a phrase like *tiny mouse*, one specified by the head (*mouse*) and the other by the overall expression (*tiny mouse*). The difference between a restrictive and a nonrestrictive interpretation depends on which of these, in the context of the discourse, is invoked in the higher-level construction.

Let us see in detail how this works. In figure 10.9, diagrams (a) and (b) show how *the* combines with *tiny mouse* in (13)(a) and (13)(b), respectively. The composite structures are omitted because the crucial difference resides in how the component structures are integrated. The internal structure of *tiny mouse*, which by now should be self-explanatory, is the same in both diagrams. Also the same in both is the definite article, which profiles a thing singled out by virtue of being the only instance of its type accessible in the current discourse frame. The type it schematically invokes

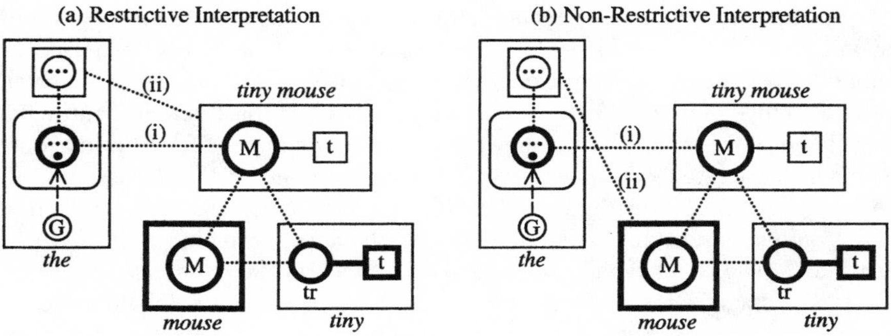

(a) Restrictive Interpretation   (b) Non-Restrictive Interpretation

FIGURE 10.9

is represented at the top. For sake of clarity, separate indications are given of the total type description (rectangle) and the profiled entity (circle).[18]

Under either interpretation, *tiny mouse* is grounded by *the* to form a nominal. As is usual for grounding constructions, their integration involves a correspondence between the profiles of the grounding element and the grounded structure. This basic correspondence—the same in both diagrams—is labeled (i). The difference between a restrictive and a nonrestrictive interpretation stems from an additional correspondence, labeled (ii). This second correspondence identifies the article's schematic type with a more specific type inherent in the grounded structure. In diagram (a), that type is *tiny mouse*. This yields the restrictive interpretation, since the adjectival property figures in the referent's identification. Alternatively, in diagram (b), the type is simply *mouse*. This yields the nonrestrictive interpretation, since the adjectival property does not figure in the grounding.[19]

Though both are often possible, a restrictive interpretation is certainly more usual than a nonrestrictive one. The reason is apparent from the diagrams. In diagram (a), correspondence (ii) holds between elements of the two component structures that directly combine: *the* and *tiny mouse*. In contrast, diagram (b) has the noncanonical feature that one corresponding element is found at a lower level of constituency. That is, *the* combines with *tiny mouse* partly on the basis of a correspondence that connects it, not with *tiny mouse* as a composite whole, but rather with one of its own component structures (*mouse*). While atypical, this is not unique or in any way problematic in CG—it is just one configuration that symbolic assemblies can assume.[20]

[18] In previous diagrams, these have been conflated. This representation of *the* is intended as being equivalent to the one in fig. 9.11 but differs in its details because other factors are now more relevant. In addition to showing the type explicitly, the present diagrams more simply depict the ground and omit the previous discourse frame.

[19] Should correspondence (i) likewise equate *the*'s profile with that of *mouse*? It really makes no difference, since the profiles of *mouse* and *tiny mouse* correspond in any case. The correspondence shown is the one expected on the basis of the general constructional schema for nominal grounding.

[20] Its degree of departure from the canon should not be exaggerated. Since *mouse* is schematic with respect to *tiny mouse*—hence immanent in its conception—we could also say that *the*'s schematic type corresponds to this immanent substructure. The two characterizations are fully equivalent.

We observe a comparable configuration in a modifying construction that is non-canonical in another way as well—namely, a relative clause that is nonadjacent to the modified noun. A previous example, *the package arrived that I was expecting*, was diagrammed in figure 7.19(b). The essentials of this construction (omitting the overall composite structure) are shown once more in figure 10.10. At issue is how the main clause (*the package arrived*) and the relative clause (*that I was expecting*) are integrated. Semantically, the relative clause modifies *package*, whose profile corresponds to its landmark. Grammatically, though, it combines with the main clause as a whole, for which *the package* functions as one component structure. The earlier diagram represented their integration by means of correspondence (i), which identifies the schematic landmark with the main clause trajector. This is non-canonical because the element elaborated usually corresponds to the elaborating structure's entire profile (not just a subpart). An elaborating structure canonical in this respect is, however, available at a lower level of organization—namely, *the package* (or even just *package*, at a still lower level). We can thus posit correspondence (ii) as the basis for integrating the main and subordinate clauses. This is noncanonical because the elaborating structure is a lower-level component. The two analyses are consistent and effectively equivalent, so there is no point in trying to choose between them.

With either correspondence, the construction is noncanonical in several further respects: because the modifier is external to the nominal, because the two are nonadjacent, and because the pivotal correspondence involves the modifier's landmark (instead of its trajector). Can we still legitimately describe this as a modifying construction? Perhaps not under a narrow definition (fig. 7.14(b) and fig. 10.5), but certainly in a looser sense emphasizing semantic relationships. Despite their nonadjacency, it seems quite evident that *the package* and *that I was expecting* constitute a conceptual grouping. As one aspect of the expression's overall meaning, these two elements are specifically construed in relation to one another in order to identify the nominal referent. But since this conceptual grouping fails to be symbolized by any phonological grouping, the nominal and the relative clause are not a grammatical constituent.

It is worth reiterating that the structures in a symbolic assembly are only partially organized into hierarchies based on coordinated grouping at the semantic and phonological poles. No single constituency hierarchy exhausts the structure of complex

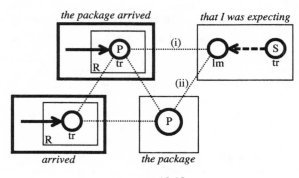

FIGURE 10.10

expressions, nor is every important conceptual grouping directly and individually symbolized by a phonological grouping (let alone one based on linear adjacency). An assembly may thus incorporate an unsymbolized conceptual constituent, with its own internal configuration, irrespective of how its individually symbolized conceptual components are arranged hierarchically in grammatical constituents of the classic sort. Though it is not explicitly shown, the assembly in figure 10.10 incorporates a conceptual constituent established by correspondence (ii), comprising the phonologically discontinuous elements *the package* and *that I was expecting*.[21] It is due to the internal configuration of this unsymbolized constituent (analogous to fig. 10.9(a)) that the relative clause is interpreted restrictively.

10.2.5 Active Zones

We have seen that noun modification involves considerably more than meets the eye or ear. Even seemingly straightforward cases, like the direct, restrictive modification of a noun by an adjective, prove subtle and varied when examined in detail. A lot of this hidden complexity pertains to conceptual integration. We can profit by looking more closely at the basic generalization that the noun's profile corresponds to the adjective's trajector. While this is perfectly valid as a coarse-grained description, there is much to learn from the fine-grained details of particular examples.

Consider first the conceptual integration in phrases like *reluctant agreement*, *informed consent*, and *conscious awareness*. Since the adjective describes an attitude or mental state, one would expect its trajector to be a person (or at least a sentient creature). But in these expressions the modified noun profiles instead an abstract entity that is not itself capable of mental experience. The semantic characterizations of the adjectival trajector and the nominal profile are therefore incompatible.[22] Yet we do not perceive these expressions as being semantically anomalous—their meanings are perfectly coherent. How do they escape anomaly? The answer lies in the specific details of the component meanings and their conceptual integration.

As shown on the right in figure 10.11(a), the modified nouns are nominalizations. They are based on verbal and adjectival stems (*agree*, *consent*, and *aware*) describing

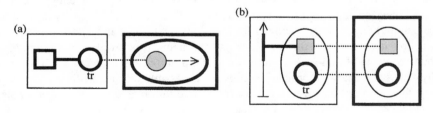

FIGURE 10.11

---

[21] Presumably, the conceptual constituent's internal structure conforms to the semantic pole of constructional schemas describing well-behaved (i.e. continuous) nominals like *the package that I was expecting*.

[22] It is odd at best to say *??The agreement was reluctant*, *?*The consent was informed*, or **The awareness is conscious*.

occurrences that are largely mental in nature. Their trajector is thus a sentient individual engaged in mental activity (represented by a dashed arrow). Semantically, the nominalization consists in the conceptual reification of this activity, producing an abstract thing (bold ellipse) which is profiled by the noun. In this semantic characterization we find a coherent basis for the noun's integration with the adjective. As the diagram indicates, the adjective's trajector is not identified with the reified activity as an undifferentiated whole, but specifically with the sentient individual engaged in it. We interpret *reluctant agreement* as ascribing reluctance to the person who agrees, not to *agreement* per se. Likewise, *informed consent* is consent on the part of an informed individual, and *conscious awareness* is the awareness of a conscious individual. Marked by shading, the individual in question is the noun's **active zone** with respect to its integration with the adjective. The active zone is the entity that anchors the correspondence with the adjective's trajector and directly manifests the property it specifies.

We thus observe a **discrepancy** between the noun's profile and its active zone for combining with the adjective. It is not evident when the construction is viewed at low resolution, where only focused elements (like profile and trajector) rise to the level of awareness. So in a coarse-grained description, it is quite correct to posit a correspondence between the adjectival trajector and the nominal profile. The discrepancy reveals itself when we look at the fine-grained details. At a higher resolution, we find that the correspondence is anchored by a particular conceptual element, the noun's active zone, which is important to its characterization without however being its referent. The active zone therefore **mediates** the profiled entity's participation in the adjectival relationship. For example, it is only in relation to the person who agrees that an *agreement* is said to be *reluctant*.

Further illustrating profile/active-zone discrepancy are combinations like *fast car*, *loud parrot*, and *unhealthy diet*. In these examples we do conceptualize the noun's referent as exhibiting the adjectival property.[23] So even in a fine-grained view, it is not inaccurate to describe the adjectival trajector as corresponding to the nominal profile. Nevertheless, their conceptual integration depends on other elements that are left unexpressed. The adjectives are "scalar". Respectively, *fast*, *loud*, and *unhealthy* locate their trajector—and hence the nominal profile—on scales of rate, amplitude, and health. But in each case, as shown in figure 10.11(b), its placement on the scale is mediated by another entity (represented by a shaded box). This entity is what the scale directly measures: an activity for *fast*, a noise for *loud*, and a person's physical state for *unhealthy*. Yet these entities are not themselves profiled by the modified noun. A *car* is not an activity, a *parrot* is not a noise, and a *diet* is not a person's physical state. These unprofiled entities are accessible as part of the noun's encyclopedic meaning, however: a car moves at a certain rate, a parrot makes a noise, and diet determines a person's physical state. These tacit entities are thus invoked as active zones for the noun's participation in the adjectival relationship.

Profile/active-zone discrepancy is neither unusual nor in any way problematic. It is, in fact, the usual case: an efficient way of accommodating both the multifaceted

---

[23] The following are thus quite natural: *That car is fast*; *The parrot is very loud*; *His diet is unhealthy*.

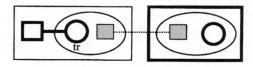

FIGURE 10.12

complexity of linguistic meanings and the special cognitive salience of particular elements. While focused elements (like profile and trajector) are the ones we primarily want to talk about, they are conceived and characterized in relation to any number of associated entities, each providing a potential basis for integration. Figure 10.12 can thus be offered as a general description of adjectival modification. In a coarse-grained view, where only focused elements are clearly evident, the adjective and noun are seen as being integrated by a correspondence between the former's trajector and the latter's profile. But at a higher resolution, where details start to emerge, we find that the focused elements merely deliver us to the relevant conceptual neighborhood, not a specific address. That is, the trajector and profile evoke arrays of associated entities—shown as ellipses—any one of which can be invoked as the specific point of connection. Only as a special case do these points of connection (the active zones) precisely coincide with the focused elements through which they are accessed.

This kind of discrepancy is not a peculiarity of adjectives or noun modifiers, but is typical of grammatical constructions in general. When two salient entities correspond, each provides mental access to an array of associated elements, any one of which can function as its active zone for this purpose. We see this in figure 10.13, where dashed arrows represent a conceptualizer's path of mental access. This sequenced mental access can be recognized as a special case of reference-point organization (fig. 3.14): by directing attention to a salient reference point (R), the conceptualizer can readily access anything in the reference point's dominion (D), one such element being the target (T). This natural and efficient strategy is a basic feature of cognitive processing, evident in numerous aspects of linguistic structure (ch. 14).

A particular sort of profile/active-zone discrepancy occurs in the modification of plural nouns. By their very nature, certain adjectives occur primarily with plurals: *equal portions, parallel lines, identical descriptions, adjacent lots, various possibilities, similar faces, numerous commentators*. Since they specify properties requiring multiple entities for their manifestation, these adjectives have a multiplex trajector comprising a set of constitutive elements. Their integration with a plural noun is thus straightforward. It is represented in figure 10.14(a).

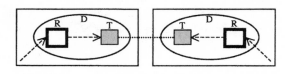

FIGURE 10.13

(a)   (b)

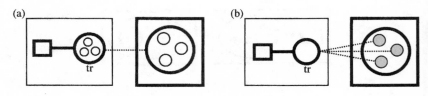

FIGURE 10.14

But plural nouns are also modified by adjectives that specify properties mani-fested individually: *sharp knives, even numbers, intelligent women, long novels, ripe bananas, single mothers, abstract concepts, frisky horses, white kittens, flimsy houses*. How is this possible? If the adjective's trajector is uniplex, and the noun's profile is multiplex, why does their correspondence not result in semantic inconsistency? The answer, it should be clear, is that a global correspondence between focused elements leaves open the specific means of their conceptual integration. Rather than corre-sponding directly to the adjectival trajector, the noun's profile may simply provide mental access to what does—its active zone with respect to their integration. In the case at hand, the point of connection resides in the individual elements that constitute the plural mass.[24] As shown in figure 10.14(b), each constitutive element is an active zone identified with the adjective's trajector. In the composite conception, the adjec-tival property is thus ascribed to each of these elements individually, not the nominal referent as a whole.

10.3 Classification and Quantification

Two aspects of nominal organization that deserve a closer look are noun classes and quantifier constructions. Their intimate relationship is evident in noun classifiers, a major phenomenon in many languages.

10.3.1 Noun Classes

Grammatical classes have varying degrees of semantic motivation. At one extreme lie fundamental and universal categories, notably noun and verb, which are claimed to have a fully consistent (albeit schematic) conceptual basis. At the opposite extreme are classes defined solely by occurrence in a particular grammatical construction with no possibility of semantic characterization. Prime examples here are elements that exhibit some morphological peculiarity, such as nouns where final *f* changes to *v* in the plural: *wife/wives, leaf/leaves*, etc. Most classes lie somewhere in between.

The extreme cases reflect different rationales for classification. Classes like noun and verb are based on fundamental cognitive abilities (like grouping and sequential scanning) inherent in the conception of experientially grounded archetypes (objects

---

[24] Alternatively, we could take the active zone to be the type that these elements all instantiate. Since a type is immanent in the conception of its instances, the two alternatives are equivalent.

and events). While these categories are available for grammatical exploitation, they are not defined in terms of any particular grammatical behavior, and there need not be any single construction in which all members of a class participate. We cannot, for example, define a noun as an element that occurs with articles, since many nouns do not (e.g. proper names and pronouns). Nevertheless, reference to a noun is part of the characterization of innumerable grammatical patterns, even if that alone is insufficient to delimit the set of participating elements. It is clear, moreover, that much of linguistic structure subserves the need for expressions that profile things, ranging from lexical nouns to full nominals (also classed as nouns in CG).

At the other extreme, classes with arbitrary membership arise through accidents of history and the vicissitudes of usage. They reflect the brute-force fact that particular ways of talking have been conventionally established and have to be learned in the acquisition process. For contemporary speakers, the reason *wife* has *wives* as its plural rather than **wifes* is simply that people talk that way. They similarly have to learn—essentially by rote—that a handful of other nouns pattern like *wife* (including *leaf, knife, thief, calf, life, loaf,* and *half*) but that many others do not (e.g. *fife, puff, reef, safe, belief, whiff, cuff, cliff, staff, waif, chief, plaintiff*). This minor variant of the plural construction, where *f* alternates with *v*, implicitly defines a class consisting of those nouns which participate in it. The members of this class cannot be predicted on the basis of their meaning. They have no uniform semantic characterization distinguishing them from other nouns ending in *f*.

Every construction defines a class consisting of the elements that appear in it. Since they pertain to the problem of distribution—that of specifying which elements occur in which patterns—the classes defined in this manner are called **distributional classes**. Knowledge of these classes is clearly vital to speaking a language properly. How, then, is this knowledge represented? In gaining control of this aspect of linguistic convention, what does a speaker specifically have to learn? For the two extremes, simple answers can be imagined. It may well be, however, that neither extreme situation is ever realized in unadulterated form.

Suppose, first, that a distributional class coincides exactly with a semantically defined category (like noun, inanimate noun, or perfective verb). The elements that occur in the construction can then be specified just by invoking this category. What this amounts to, in CG terms, is that the schema for the construction incorporates the schema defining the category as one of its component structures. In this way, the constructional schema correctly describes the distributional facts and captures the appropriate generalization. Even so, it is probably not exhaustive of a speaker's distributional knowledge. We saw in chapter 8 that constructional schemas describing general patterns coexist with more specific structures reflecting their conventional implementation. It is often these lower-level constructional schemas, even those incorporating particular lexical items, that are most important in determining conventional usage.

Suppose, on the other hand, that a distributional class is completely random: there is no semantic (or other) basis for even partially predicting its membership. In this case its members simply have to be learned individually, as an arbitrary list. What this amounts to, in CG terms, is that each element's occurrence in the pattern is specifically learned as a distinct conventional unit. For example, expressions like *wives, leaves, knives,* and so on have to be learned as such, in addition to the constructional subschema representing their abstracted commonality. But seldom, if ever, is a class completely random. Although the list of members may be arbitrary, so that each has to be specifically learned as such, they still tend to cluster in certain regions of semantic and phonological space. Certain members may be similar enough, semantically or phonologically, that their inclusion in the pattern is mutually reinforcing. Schemas can then emerge to capture these local regularities (schematization being merely the reinforcement of recurring commonalities). If so, there is more to a class than just a list of members. A class exhibits some measure of coherence and organization.

Even the class of *f/v* nouns amounts to more than just an unstructured list. While it is hard to make a case for any semantic grouping, in phonological space its members are far from being randomly distributed. First, they are all monosyllabic. Beyond this, most are subsumed by a number of intersecting clusters: (i) *wife, life, knife*; (ii) *leaf, thief, sheaf*; (iii) *life, leaf, loaf*; (iv) *calf, half*. Clusters (i) and (ii) are based on the vocalic nucleus. A member of each is also part of cluster (iii), based on the initial consonant. As for cluster (iv), *calf* and *half* share not only their vowel but also the orthographic peculiarity of silent *l*. In no way do these local regularities obviate the need to specifically learn each plural form. Such regularities do, however, facilitate the acquisition process, giving rise to low-level schemas that help maintain a class and sometimes even attract new members into it.

Distributional classes are quite varied as to the nature and extent of regularities in their membership. These can be based on either semantic or phonological properties, or a combination of the two. A single generalization can be extracted, or any number of local ones. Generalizations differ in their level of specificity, the proportion of the total membership they subsume, and their accessibility for the sanction of new expressions. Despite their variety, CG accommodates distributional classes straightforwardly and in a unified manner—by positing appropriately configured networks of constructional schemas (§8.3). The schemas comprising a network are characterized at various levels of abstraction and further differ in degree of entrenchment and ease of activation. Each captures a local or global generalization concerning the elements permitted in the construction. Whether a given generalization extends to new cases depends on whether the schema that embodies it is able to win the competition for selection as categorizing structure (§8.2.1).

In this usage-based approach, membership in a distributional class does not require separate listing. Rather, it is inherent in a full description of the construction in terms of which the class is defined. Grammatical patterns are not learned in isolation, but are abstracted from expressions consisting of specific elements in every position. In the network describing a pattern, each constructional schema makes some specification concerning participating elements. The lowest-level schemas incorporate particular lexical items that have been conventionally established in the pattern. It is through this combination of regularity and idiosyncrasy (in any proportion) that the proper elements are specified as occurring in it.

Conversely, lexical items are learned in the context of larger expressions containing them. Part of a lexeme's characterization is thus a set of structural frames representing the constructions it occurs in. These frames are nothing other than the lowest-level constructional schemas for the patterns in question (fig. 8.13). In a usage-based perspective, therefore, a lexeme's membership in distributional classes does not require separate specification but is inherent in its full description. For instance, the constructional subschema [send NML NML] provides the information that *send* occurs in the ditransitive construction (§8.3.2)—no special marking is required. Likewise, the very existence of the conventional unit *wives* indicates the participation of *wife* in the pattern of *f/v* alternation.[25]

Important though they are, distributional classes do not exist in their own right as explicit objects of awareness or even as distinct linguistic entities. In a CG account, they are seen instead as being intrinsic to the full, proper characterization of constructions and lexical items. Much the same is true for classes defined semantically. What makes something a noun, for example, is not that it bears any special label, or is found on a list of category members that have to be learned as such. What makes it a noun is rather an intrinsic aspect of its meaning: the fact that it profiles a thing. In similar fashion, the count/mass distinction depends on whether this thing is construed as being bounded, and the common/proper distinction depends on whether the specified type is conceived as having multiple instances (fig. 10.3). When we talk about the schema for such a class, or categorizing relationships between the schema and its members, it is not implied that these are separate and distinct. On the contrary, schemas are immanent in their instantiations and thus inherent in their conception.

We have been considering two basic kinds of classes: distributional classes, and those defined in terms of meaning. A distributional class comprises the elements that occur in a particular pattern or construction. Its members are determined by this single property, irrespective of any semantic regularities they might exhibit. On the other hand, fundamental categories like noun and verb are claimed in CG to have a semantic definition. Although they are central to grammatical organization, and their members participate in many constructions, no particular construction is invoked for their characterization. These two basic sorts of classes are not the only possibilities. Languages also present us with intermediate cases, classes that are partially but not exclusively semantic, and are recognized through occurrence not just in one but in a number of constructions.

I have in mind "gender" classes, so called because the prime examples are noun classes bearing traditional labels like "masculine", "feminine", and "neuter". Linguists are fond of pointing out the inadequacy, if not the downright folly, of such labels. On what rational basis can one say, for instance, that German *Löffel* 'spoon' is masculine, *Gabel* 'fork' is feminine, and *Messer* 'knife' is neuter? These classes are posited not because their members exhibit any consistent meaning, but rather because they pattern alike grammatically, in terms of their inflectional endings and the forms of cooccurring elements (like articles, demonstratives, and adjectives). Still, the traditional labels were not chosen arbitrarily. They are indeed semantically appropriate for a substantial range of vocabulary, where they do reflect biological gender. For instance, *Mann* 'man' functions grammatically as a masculine noun, *Frau* 'woman' is feminine, and *Kind* 'child' is neuter (since a child can be either male or female).[26]

---

[25] Note that *wives* represents an entire symbolic assembly. The component structures are *wife* and a special variant of the plural morpheme: [[...f] ---> [...vz]] (cf. fig. 6.11).

[26] The correlation with biological gender is not exceptionless. Nor is the assignment of gender in other cases wholly arbitrary—indeed, it exhibits a great deal of systematicity (Zubin and Köpcke 1986).

It is quite common for the nouns of a language to be divided into categories of this general sort. Languages vary in the number of classes they exhibit, their degree of semantic coherence, and the semantic properties they are partially based on. In addition to gender, classes can be anchored by a wide range of culturally salient notions: 'person', 'animal', 'deity', 'artifact', 'instrument', 'tree', 'plant', 'fruit', 'collection', 'liquid', 'food', and so on. Languages also differ in the array of grammatical constructions on the basis of which the classes are posited. While descriptively quite complex (from the standpoint of membership, grammatical ramifications, and historical development), these classes can be seen as a natural outcome of general processes. First, they reflect the emergence of complex categories (describable as networks) by extension from a prototype. Second, lexical items are learned from their occurrence in particular structural frames, which are thus retained as an aspect of their characterization.

For convenient illustration, we can take a quick look at Spanish nouns, which clearly divide into two broad categories. The semantic distinction which anchors them is gender: nouns like *hombre* 'man', *hijo* 'son', and *tío* 'uncle' are masculine, whereas *mujer* 'woman', *hija* 'daughter', and *tía* 'aunt' are feminine.[27] However, this category distinction extends to all nouns in the lexicon, for most of which the notions 'male' and 'female' are irrelevant. For instance, *tenedor* 'fork', *mes* 'month', and *techo* 'roof' are masculine, whereas *cuchara* 'spoon', *semana* 'week', and *casa* 'house' are feminine. In general, therefore, the basis for categorization is grammatical rather than semantic. Masculine and feminine nouns are distinguished by a whole series of grammatical properties, of which just three will be mentioned: they differ in the form of the definite article (*el hombre* 'the man' vs. *la mujer* 'the woman'), the indefinite article (*un hombre* 'a man' vs. *una mujer* 'a woman'), and certain modifying adjectives (*hombre simpático* 'nice man' vs. *mujer simpática* 'nice woman').

Given this array of data, what sorts of linguistic units can we posit, in accordance with the content requirement? First, particular expressions can coalesce as units if they occur with any frequency. This is especially likely in the case of articles, so we can reasonably posit a large number of conventional units such as the following: [un hombre], [la mujer], [un tenedor], [el techo], [una semana], etc. Also permitted by the content requirement are schematizations of occurring expressions. On the basis of expressions like *el hombre*, *el hijo*, and *el tío*, we can therefore posit the constructional schema [el N_m], where N_m indicates a noun referring to a male. This schema represents an important generalization concerning the use of *el*. But it does not tell the whole story. Since *el* is further used with nouns like *tenedor*, *mes*, *techo*, and countless others, the highest-level schema simply specifies its occurrence with a noun: [el N]. Analogously, expressions like *la mujer*, *la hija*, and *la tía* give rise to the constructional schema [la N_f] (where N_f is a noun referring to a female), while the further use of *la* with *cuchara*, *semana*, *casa*, etc. supports the higher-level schema [la N].

Likewise, schemas emerge at different levels of abstraction from expressions involving the indefinite article or a modifying adjective. Schemas incorporating the

---

[27] The masculine and feminine categories are strongly associated with the endings *-o* and *-a* (FCG2: §4.4), but to keep things simple we will basically ignore these for now (see §10.4). The points at issue can be made regardless of whether there is any such marking.

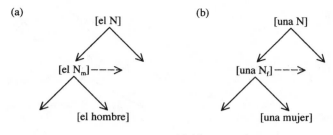

FIGURE 10.15

indefinite article include [un N$_m$], [un N], [una N$_f$], and [una N]. For adjectives we can posit [N$_m$ ... o], [N ... o], [N$_f$ ... a], and [N ... a] (where ... o and ... a represent adjectives ending in o and a). Of course, these various schemas do not exist in isolation from one another. Connecting them are categorizing relationships (also permitted by the content requirement), such as [[el N] → [el N$_m$]], [[el N$_m$] → [el hombre]], and [[una N$_f$] → [una mujer]]. In this way, constructional schemas and instantiating expressions are organized into networks representing both general grammatical patterns and their specific implementation in conventional usage. Fragments of two such networks are shown in figure 10.15.

The networks for constructions are themselves connected in various ways. In particular, a lexical item appearing in multiple constructions provides a point of overlap among them. A frequent noun like *hombre*, for example, is no doubt well established in a number of structural frames: [el hombre], [un hombre], [hombre ... o], etc. Each of these complex units is part of the network describing a general pattern. The frames are not disjoint, for they share the component *hombre*. And since the frames intersect in this manner, so do the networks they represent. In fact, each lexical item that appears in all three patterns is a point of intersection for them.

That *hombre* appears separately in each formula is solely due to the limitations of this notational format. This should not obscure its essential identity in the three frames, or the fact that it ties them together to form a complex symbolic assembly in the paradigmatic plane. To show its identity more directly, we might adopt an alternate notation: [hombre {[el X], [un X], [X ... o]}]. This is meant to indicate that *hombre* functions in the X slot of all three frames. The outer brackets represent the overall paradigmatic assembly they constitute. They can also be taken as indicating the full characterization of *hombre*—not just its basic form and meaning but also the structural frames in which it figures.

(14)   [[el hombre] [un hombre] [hombre ... o]] = [hombre {[el X], [un X], [X ... o]}]

Of course, other lexical items give rise to similar paradigmatic assemblies: [hijo {[el X], [un X], [X ... o]}], [techo {[el X], [un X], [X ... o]}], etc. And to the extent that these assemblies are analogous, they are themselves susceptible to schematization. From animate nouns we thus obtain the schematic assembly [N$_m$ {[el X], [un X], [X ... o]}]. From the full array of nouns that pattern in this manner, we obtain

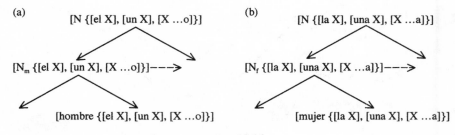

FIGURE 10.16

the still more schematic assembly [N {[el X], [un X], [X ... o]}]. Naturally, the same developments occur with feminine nouns, resulting in the schematic assemblies [N$_f$ {[la X], [una X], [X ... a]}] and [N {[la X], [una X], [X ... a]}]. This is sketched in figure 10.16.

The networks comprising these schemas and their instantiations constitute a description of masculine and feminine nouns in Spanish.[28] The highest-level schemas, [N {[el X], [un X], [X ... o]}] and [N {[la X], [una X], [X ... a]}], describe the categories just in terms of their grammatical behavior. The lower-level schemas [N$_m$ {[el X], [un X], [X ... o]}] and [N$_f$ {[la X], [una X], [X ... a]}], referring specifically to the semantic properties 'male' and 'female', represent the category prototypes. In this way we succeed in capturing the semantic anchoring of the categories, as well as their basically grammatical nature. As outlined in chapter 8, these networks constrain the conventional behavior of familiar nouns and are readily invoked as models for new ones. And although the classification of many nouns is purely arbitrary (a matter of historical accident), a proper description of the categories requires nothing more than assemblies of symbolic structures.

10.3.2 Quantifier Constructions

When the nouns of a language divide into semantically anchored classes, these are often manifested grammatically in the form of **classifiers**. Noun classifiers, which range in number from a handful to several score, are themselves schematic nouns. Their meanings are schematic with respect to the nouns they classify, or at least those representing the category prototype.[29]

Grammatically, noun classifiers are closely tied to quantification, grounding, and anaphoric reference. They typically combine directly with a quantifier, demonstrative, or possessive to form a schematic nominal. This nominal then combines with a lexical noun, deriving a higher-level nominal more specific in type. Here are some examples from Thai:

[28] The descriptions are comparable to that of a verb conjugation class (§8.4.2).

[29] Classifiers are often polysemous, reflecting the diversity of their associated categories. For example, the Thai classifier *tua*, roughly glossed as 'body', is used for animals, furniture, and clothing. (For a useful overview of classifiers, see Allan 1977.)

(15) (a) *khruu   lâaj   khon*   (b) *măa   tua   nán*   (c) *sôm   hâa   lûuk*

         teacher   three   person   dog   body   that   orange five fruit

         'three teachers'   'that dog'   'five oranges'

In (15)(b), for example, the classifier *tua* combines with the demonstrative *nán* to form the schematic nominal *tua nán* 'that body'. The schematic type 'body' can then be elaborated by a noun like *măa* 'dog' at a higher level of structure. Alternatively, the schematic nominal can stand alone and be used anaphorically. In this case *tua nán* is comparable to *that one*, except that *tua* indicates the referent's general category.

Compared with the canonical structure described in §10.1.1, nominals based on classifiers have a fundamentally different organization. In a language like English, it is typically a lexical noun that lies at the core of a nominal, with quantification and grounding representing the outermost structural layers: (*those* (*five* (*rotten* (*oranges*)))). By contrast, in expressions like (15) the lexical noun is peripheral and even optional. The structural core consists of a grounded or quantified classifier, such as *tua nán*, to which a lexical noun may then be added: (*măa* (*tua nán*)). This organization is shown in figure 10.17, where b is the schematic type (glossed here as 'body') specified by the classifier, and D the specific type 'dog'. Observe that the classifier is actually the grounded noun. It is thus an instance of *tua* 'body' that the demonstrative singles out as nominal referent. The lexical noun *măa* 'dog' is not directly grounded but simply elaborates the grounded entity's type. Indirectly, of course, an instance of the lexically specified type is singled out and grounded by the nominal overall.

The same lexical noun is often able to occur with alternate classifiers, each of which imposes a different construal on its content. In Mandarin, for example, the noun *shéngzi* 'rope' occurs with either *tiáo* 'long, thin object', *juăn* 'roll', or *duàn* 'segment', thereby portraying the referent just as a rope, as a coil of rope, or as a piece of rope: *yī-tiáo shéngzi* 'one rope', *liăng-juăn shéngzi* 'two coils of rope', *zhè-duàn*

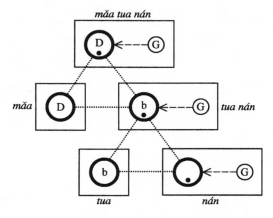

FIGURE 10.17

shéngzi 'this piece of rope'. With the second two examples, we begin to see a transition between simple classification and a related phenomenon that is commonly associated with the same grammatical form. It makes perfect sense to say that a rope belongs to the class of long, thing objects. But can we say that a coiled rope belongs to the class of rolls? Or a short one to the class of segments? It is instructive here to compare the Mandarin expressions with their English equivalents. We use *coil* and *piece* to translate *juǎn* and *duàn*, but nothing to translate *tiáo*: *a coil of rope*, *a piece of rope*, *a rope*.

This other phenomenon, closely associated with classifiers cross-linguistically, is the **unitization** of a mass.[30] Semantically, it consists in some portion of a mass being conceived as a discrete, bounded unit. Though composed of the "substance" constituting the mass, this unit exists in its own right as a distinct and separate entity. A *coil*, for example, is not just rope or wire, but something we can recognize by its shape irrespective of its substance. Similarly, a *stack of plates* is not just plates—it is also a stack, a higher-order entity with its own form and function. Grammatically, unitization is effected by count nouns that profile collections, configurations, constitutive elements, or containers: *flock, pack, cluster, pile, grain, speck, drop, slice, chunk, cup, bottle, bag*, etc. Unitization reflects our propensity to conceptualize the world in terms of discrete objects that we can apprehend as wholes and deal with individually. It allows the application to masses of the semantic and grammatical apparatus based on count nouns.

A unit and the portion of the overall mass it delimits are essentially coextensive. In terms of their real-world reference, a *drop of water* is the same as the water constituting it, and a *flock of geese* consists of nothing more than geese. A container is more distinct from its contents—if I remove the wine from a *bottle of wine*, the bottle still exists. Still, the volume a container encloses is spatially coextensive with a mass that fills it. Due to their coincidence, it may be indeterminate whether the composite expression refers to the unit or just to the mass it delimits. The point is often moot: if I see a flock of geese, I see both the flock (which consists of geese) and the geese (which constitute the flock). Yet the distinction is sometimes indicated linguistically. In (16)(a), the relative salience of unit and delimited mass is reflected in the choice of anaphoric pronoun (*it* vs. *they*), as well as number marking on the verb (*was* vs. *were*). With container nouns, the composite expression refers either to the combination of container and content, as in (b), or else to just the content, as in (c). What is not permitted is for the expression to refer exclusively to the container, as in (d).

(16) (a) *I saw a flock of geese. {It was/They were} clearly visible against the blue sky.*

   (b) *She stacked three bags of mulch in the wheelbarrow.*

   (c) *She spread three bags of mulch around the roses.*

   (d) **The bags of mulch were plastic.*

---

[30] The mass can be continuous, particulate, or replicate (i.e., plural). Unitization is basically the inverse of pluralization: instead of replicating a discrete entity to create a mass, it creates a discrete entity by bounding a mass.

The structure of these expressions, exemplified by *flock of geese*, is sketched in figure 10.18. A key factor is the meaning of the preposition *of*.[31] Described schematically, *of* profiles an **intrinsic relationship** between two things. Prototypically, for example, its trajector is an intrinsic subpart of its landmark (e.g. *the tip of my finger*).[32] The phrase *of geese* thus designates an intrinsic relationship (represented by a double line) that its trajector bears to a mass identified as geese. In accordance with the general pattern for noun modification, its trajector corresponds to the thing profiled by *flock*. A unit noun like *flock* also invokes an intrinsic relationship: one of coextension between the profiled unit (outer circle) and a replicate mass (inner circle). Further integration of the two component structures is thus effected through identification of the intrinsic relationships each is based on. This is reflected diagrammatically in a second correspondence line, connecting the prepositional landmark with the mass unitized by *flock*.

The basic schema for noun modification identifies the modified noun as constructional head (profile determinant). Accordingly, the composite expression *flock of geese* is expected to profile the bounded unit *flock* rather than the mass of geese it delimits. We have seen, however, that either construal is possible. The two interpretations are related metonymically, a matter of alternate profiles on the same conceptual base. The possibility of profiling either the unit or the coextensive mass instantiates a general metonymic pattern of English.

This unitizing construction is the source of more grammaticized expressions which are becoming central to the English quantifier system. In particular, *a lot of* and *a bunch of* are well-entrenched alternatives to the absolute quantifiers *many* and *much*:

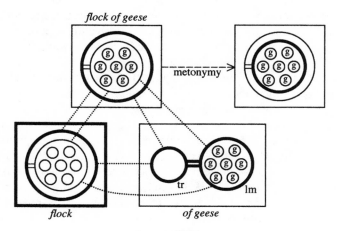

FIGURE 10.18

---

[31] Naturally, CG rejects the prevalent view that *of* is meaningless (a purely "grammatical" element). Its meaning is simply abstract (GC: ch. 3).

[32] Compare this with *the splinter in my finger* (not **the splinter of my finger*). Unlike its tip, a splinter is quite extrinsic to a finger. *Of* is also used to indicate substance (*a ring of fire*), instantiation (*the month of August*), and the relationship inherent in the meaning of certain nouns, such as kin terms (*a descendant of Abraham Lincoln*).

(17)   (a) *We invited {many/a lot of/a bunch of} people to the party.*

    (b) *They drank {??much/a lot of} beer.*

Pivotal to their grammaticization is the fading from awareness of the original concrete sense of *lot* and *bunch*, where *lot* designates a collection of objects (especially for auction) and *bunch* a cluster of objects bound together (e.g. *bunch of grapes*). This loss of content has nearly reached the point where *lot* and *bunch* are pure indications of quantity, denoting a certain extension along a quantity scale. All that remains of their unit sense is the function of delimiting a mass in quantitative terms. And since there is no longer any concrete unit to refer to, the metonymic shift in figure 10.18 becomes obligatory. As an inherent aspect of their characterization, composite expressions of the form *a {lot/bunch} of* N can only profile the quantified mass (N), not the quantifying unit (*lot* or *bunch*). This is evident from both anaphoric reference and number marking on the verb, as seen by comparing (18) with (16)(a):

(18)   *I saw a {lot/bunch} of geese. {*It was/They were} clearly visible against the blue sky.*

Also occurring in an *of*-construction are the quantifiers discussed in chapter 9: *all of those geese, some of the geese, many of these geese, three of his geese*, etc. One difference from expressions with unit nouns is that the prepositional object is overtly grounded and definite. The landmark is thus a contextually delimited mass established independently of the quantification. Another difference is that the noun modified by the *of*-phrase is fully grammaticized as a quantifier,[33] with no vestige of a unit sense analogous to *flock, drop*, or *bunch*. Consequently, reference to the quantified mass does not result from metonymic shift but directly reflects the quantifier's meaning. The overall expression therefore designates a quantified portion of the mass singled out by the prepositional object. The relation this subpart bears to the whole is identified as the intrinsic relationship profiled by *of*.

The case of *some* is diagrammed in figure 10.19. As a grounding quantifier, *some* singles out a profiled thing instance via the quantificational strategy (fig. 9.6). Specifically, its profile represents a non-empty proportion of the maximal extension of a type, E_t (fig. 9.12(c)). In *some of the geese*, what counts as the maximal extension of *geese* (E_g) is the contextually delimited mass singled out by *the*. The portion profiled by *some* corresponds to *of*'s trajector, and E_g to its landmark. The composite expression therefore designates a non-empty proportion of the mass identified in the discourse as *the geese*.

The solid arrow in figure 10.19 indicates that the profiled mass represents a limited portion of the maximal extension. In this construction, the relation the profile bears to E_t is identified with the intrinsic relationship evoked more schematically by *of*. Among the grammaticized quantifiers, *all* stands out as having the special property that the profiled mass and the maximal extension are identical. If we think of a quantifier as singling out the profile by restricting the maximal extension, the restriction imposed by *all* is zero. *All* is therefore vacuous with respect to a prototypical *of*

---

[33] These quantifiers can function as nominals independently of this construction: *{All/Some/Many/Three} are obviously overfed.*

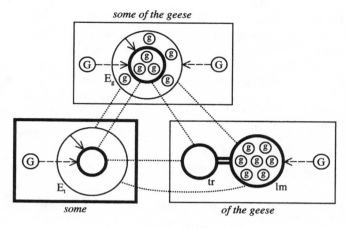

some of the geese

some   *of the geese*

FIGURE 10.19

relationship, where the trajector is an intrinsic **subpart** of the landmark. This special semantic property is reflected in a special grammatical behavior. Alone among
the quantifiers, *all* occurs in an alternate construction lacking the preposition whose
meaning it subverts: we can say either *all of the geese* or just *all the geese* (but not
*{most/some/any/each/many/three} the geese).[34] This construction is diagrammed
in figure 10.20(a). It is simply a matter of *all* combining directly with *the geese*
based on the same correspondence as the one connecting E_t with the prepositional
landmark in figure 10.19.

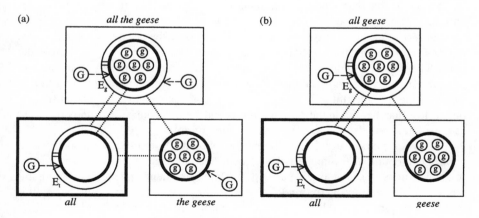

(a)   *all the geese*   (b)   *all geese*

all   *the geese*   *all*   *geese*

FIGURE 10.20

[34] Predictably, *all* shares this behavior with *both*: *both of the geese*; *both the geese*. Like *all*, *both* has the
semantic property that the mass it profiles coincides with the contextually relevant maximal extension,
which is further specified as consisting of just two elements.

In *all the geese*, the grounding quantifier combines with a component structure which is itself a grounded nominal. The composite expression is thus a higher-order nominal that profiles a mass coextensive with one independently singled out as a discourse referent. In this respect *all the geese* contrasts with the simple grounding expression *all geese*, shown in figure 10.20(b). The only difference in constructions (a) and (b) is that *geese* is ungrounded in the latter. Consequently, the default interpretation of *all geese* is that the mass it designates is coextensive with geese in general, rather than any particular subset.

10.4 Inflection and Agreement

A final dimension of nominal structure, quite extensive in many languages, is the marking of nouns to indicate their category, semantic properties, or relationship to other elements. These markings vary as to how internal or intrinsic they are to a noun, with respect to both their semantic import and their formal manifestation.

10.4.1 What's in a Noun?

The most internal markings are those deriving nouns from other categories, exemplified by endings like *-ness*, *-er*, *-ion*, and *-ity*: *sadness, firmness, emptiness*; *driver, boiler, teacher*; *demonstration, persuasion, digression*; *laxity, diversity, stativity*. These are internal to a noun in the strong sense that it is only through their effect that a noun exists at all. Semantically, they create a noun by shifting the profile to a thing associated with the relationship designated by the verb or adjective they attach to. They are thus internal to a noun morphologically because only the composite expression they derive is so categorized: $[[sad]_{ADJ} -ness]_N$.

Markings that derive nouns from other categories are traditionally labeled **derivational**. Of more immediate concern are nonderivational markings, usually referred to as **inflectional**. Not a little ink has been spilled over the issue of how and where to draw the line, but from a CG perspective such discussion is largely beside the point. The very notion that there is a specific line of demarcation rests on theoretical assumptions (e.g. a categorical distinction between lexicon and grammar) viewed in CG as being both gratuitous and empirically problematic. Imposing a strict dichotomy is less than helpful in the case of number and gender, which are usually regarded as inflectional but also function in the derivation of nouns.

Consider pluralization. It is generally thought of as inflectional because it applies to a noun rather than deriving it, tends to be marked by stem-external means (e.g. the suffix *-s*), and often participates in "agreement" phenomena (a plural noun requiring a plural verb or adjective). Yet these points are anything but definitive. While pluralization does apply to a noun, it also derives one—a higher-order noun that specifies a distinct type representing a different category (mass instead of count). Morphologically, its position vis-à-vis the stem is not exclusively either internal or external, for it is often marked by ablaut (e.g. *man* vs. *men*), reduplication (Hopi *saaqa* 'ladder' vs. *saasaqa* 'ladders'), or even full stem suppletion (Hopi *wuùti* 'woman' vs. *momoyam* 'women'). Nor, in CG, is agreement viewed as the "copying" of inflectional features or as having any particular diagnostic value. It is simply a matter of the same information being symbolized in multiple places. As such, it is just a special case of conceptual overlap, which is characteristic of all grammatical constructions.

Also considered inflectional, primarily because they participate in agreement phenomena, are markings for gender and similar categories. With respect to a noun, however, these are often internal and derivational even in the strong sense of being responsible for its categorization as such. Let us return for a moment to Spanish gender (§10.3.1), this time focusing on the endings -o and -a, the general markings for "masculine" and "feminine". For animate nouns, those labels are semantically appropriate: *hijo* 'son' vs. *hija* 'daughter'; *amigo* 'male friend' vs. *amiga* 'female friend'; *gato* 'male cat' vs. *gata* 'female cat'; etc. Through standard morphological analysis, these can be divided into a noun stem that specifies a basic type (*hij-* 'child'; *amig-* 'friend'; *gat-* 'cat') and a gender-marking suffix. Yet this is not viable for the large numbers of inanimate nouns where gender is likewise marked by -o and -a. For instance, *techo* 'roof', *vaso* 'glass', and *año* 'year' function grammatically as masculine nouns, and *casa* 'house', *mesa* 'table', and *semana* 'week' as feminine nouns. But with these there is no separate stem to which the ending attaches. Only as whole does *techo* mean 'roof', *casa* 'house', and so on. In such cases, we have to say that the gender marking is part of the noun itself.

How might these endings be analyzed? They are problematic in classic morphological analysis, where morphemes are construed metaphorically as building blocks. One entailment of this metaphor is that a word should be exhaustively divisible into discrete component morphemes. Consequently, the endings -o and -a in nouns like *techo* and *casa* cannot be recognized as morphemes, for this would leave a nonmorphemic residue (*tech, cas*). In CG, however, morphological description eschews the building-block metaphor. It is based instead on symbolic assemblies, in which composite structures are entities in their own right, motivated by component structures without being literally constructed out of them. It is therefore unproblematic for a composite expression to incorporate material not inherited from any component, and even for a construction to be **defective** in the sense of having only one component, corresponding to just a portion of the composite structure. Nouns like *techo* and *casa* can thus be described as shown in figure 10.21. In contrast to animate nouns like *gato/gata*, they comprise an assembly with a composite structure and only one symbolic component. Though noncanonical, this is one configuration that symbolic assemblies can assume.

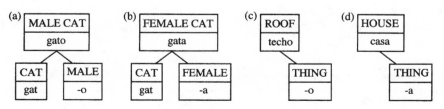

FIGURE 10.21

What about the meanings of *-o* and *-a*? With animate nouns they contribute the meanings 'male' and 'female', which anchor the gender categories. Whether they can be ascribed a specific meaning in cases like *techo* and *casa* is a matter for careful investigation, but let us assume they cannot. In this event *-o* and *-a* are still considered meaningful in a CG perspective. Their meanings are simply quite schematic, probably to be identified with that of nouns as a class (i.e. they profile things). If so, they represent a linguistic phenomenon attested in numerous languages: the existence of morphological elements serving to mark nouns as such without having any additional content or function.[35] Of course, their status as purely grammatical markers is wholly consistent in CG with their treatment as meaningful symbolic elements.

In terms of being internal or external to a noun, number and gender can thus be seen as intermediate. More clearly external are markings whose semantic and grammatical import specifically pertains to relationships with other elements in a larger configuration. With respect to a lexical head, grounding has this character: semantically, it specifies how the nominal referent relates to the ground; grammatically, it is both external to the head noun and tends to be manifested at the outermost layer of nominal organization.[36] More external still are markings that indicate a nominal's syntactic role. The main examples are possessive markers, case inflections, and adpositions. These pertain to an entire grounded nominal (not just a head noun) and specify how it is connected with other elements in larger symbolic assemblies.

A possessive nominal functions as a grounding element with respect to a higher-order nominal (ch. 14). For example, *the man's* serves to ground the head noun *dog* in forming the higher-order nominal *the man's dog*. While internal to the latter, the possessive marker *'s* is clearly external to the lower-level nominal, *the man*. Whereas the plural of *man* is marked internally by ablaut (*men*), the possessive is formed by attaching *'s* to the nominal as a whole.[37] Indeed, it is not even a suffix, in the narrowest sense, but a clitic that attaches to the nominal's final word. We observe the contrast with a complex expression like *the king of Denmark*: plural *the kings of Denmark* vs. possessive *the king of Denmark's* (fig. 6.13(a)). Semantically as well, possession involves the entire nominal, not just the head noun. To serve its grounding function, the possessor itself has to be singled out as a grounded instance of its type.

Just as possessive marking indicates a nominal's role in a higher-order nominal, other markers specify a nominal's role in a clause. They can mark its grammatical status as clausal subject or object. In CG, of course, these are meaningful notions, a matter of primary vs. secondary focal prominence (trajector vs. landmark). Other roles have more tangible conceptual import. It might be specified, for example, that a nominal referent functions as an agent, instrument, patient, recipient, beneficiary, or location with respect to the clausal process. Formally, these roles can marked by inflection, affixation, or a separate word or particle. In unipolar terms their placement

---

[35] Luiseño has a series of noun-marking endings of this sort (ch. 8: nn. 19 and 26).

[36] Grounding is obviously not external with respect to inherently grounded nouns (like pronouns and proper names). And for other nouns, manifestation in the outermost structural layer is typical but not invariant. Grounding is more internal, for example, in a classifier construction (fig. 10.17).

[37] Possessor pronouns (*my*, *her*, etc.) are of course different in this respect.

varies. A preposition, for instance, would normally precede the entire nominal, whereas case inflection appears inside it, on the head noun or on multiple nominal components. Still, in terms of bipolar composition (§6.3) these elements combine with the nominal as a whole.

Semantically, these markers differ in the extent to which they invoke a relationship distinguishable from the profiled clausal process. Toward one extreme lie the prepositions in (19), which mark the knife as an instrument in the process of cutting, Sarah as the agent, and her brother as the beneficiary. As in other uses, these prepositions profile relationships and thus have their own trajector/landmark organization. They serve to specify the clausal role of the participant introduced as their landmark (the prepositional object). In this grammatical use, the relationships they designate are precisely those which hold between a clausal process (their trajector) and a participant in it. These markers tend to be used for participants whose involvement is more peripheral, and are said to introduce them "periphrastically".

(19)   *The meat was cut **with** a knife **by** Sarah **for** her little brother.*

At the other extreme are markers that do not invoke any relationship other than the process itself, but simply register the status of a focal participant as such. A simple example is the object-marking suffix *-i* of Luiseño, as in (20). It does not profile a relationship, have its own trajector/landmark organization, or introduce a participant beyond those invoked by the verb—it merely identifies *'awaal* 'dog' as the clausal landmark. *'awaal* is said to be a "direct" participant of *'ari* 'kick' because it is not introduced periphrastically, by means of a separately coded relationship.[38]

(20)   *Nawitmal=upil*   *'awaal-i*   *'ar-ax.*   'The girl kicked the dog.'

      girl=3s:PAST   dog-OBJ   kick-PAST

If it does not profile a relationship, what does a marker like *-i* designate? Since it does not alter the nominal character of the element it attaches to, it may itself profile a thing. This thing is specified only as being the landmark of some process, as shown in figure 10.22 (where a schematic process is represented by an arrow with ellipses). A correspondence equates the profiles of the noun and the suffix, so the composite expression *'awaali* designates a dog with the role of processual landmark. At a higher level of organization, the schematic process evoked by *-i* is identified with the specific process profiled by the verb, in this case *'ari* 'kick'.[39] In this way the noun is explicitly marked as object of the verb and the clause it heads.

---

[38] There are intermediate cases, and whether a role marker profiles a relationship is sometimes hard to determine. The general correlation of periphrasis with separate words, and affixation or inflection with direct participants, is far from exceptionless.

[39] Recall the notational practice of indicating the identity of two relationships by showing their participants as corresponding.

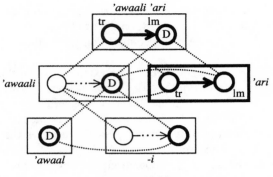

FIGURE 10.22

10.4.2 Morphological Realization

Luiseño *-i* exemplifies what is traditionally referred to as a **case** marker: one that profiles a thing, combines with a nominal as a whole, and specifies its syntactic role in larger structures. Of course, this is not a standard definition, since case is usually considered meaningless (purely grammatical in nature). More pertinent here, though, is the question of whether it really combines with a nominal as a whole. From the standpoint of form, the matter is not all that obvious. Often case is marked on the head, which may be internal to the nominal, or on multiple components, including modifiers and especially a grounding element. For Luiseño, which allows covert grounding, *'awaali* is indeed a full nominal in (20). But a modifying adjective is also marked for object case—for example, *yot-i 'awaal-i* 'big dog OBJ'—and so is a demonstrative: *wunaal-i yot-i 'awaal-i* 'that big dog OBJ'. Yet we do not want to claim, semantically or grammatically, that these elements function individually as objects. Here traditional accounts would seem to be on the right track in saying that case is marked redundantly. This "agreement" in case helps identify the marked elements as all belonging to the same nominal constituent.

Let us see how this works for *yoti 'awaali* 'big dog OBJ'. Figure 10.23 shows *yot* 'big' as first combining with *'awaal* 'dog' in the normal construction for adjectival modification.[40] With respect to bipolar composition, it is the composite expression *yot 'awaal* that is marked for object case. Semantically this is quite straightforward: the thing profiled by *yot 'awaal* is identified by correspondence (i) with the one specified by the object marker as being a processual landmark. What makes the construction noncanonical is the nature of their phonological integration. For one thing, it is atypical because, in unipolar terms, the suffix is doubly manifested, appearing on each nominal component rather than in just one place. It is further atypical because the structures it combines with morphologically are found at a lower level of

---

[40] There is some possibility that an element like *yot* should actually be analyzed as a noun rather than an adjective in Luiseño (so that *yot* would mean something like 'big one' rather than just 'big'). If so, this is just a matter of it profiling the thing instead of the defining relationship, which does not affect the basic analysis.

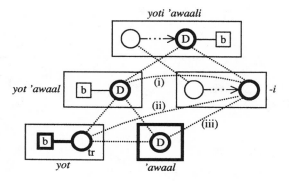

FIGURE 10.23

organization (cf. fig. 10.10). The thing which *-i* marks as landmark figures semantically not just as the profile of *yot 'awaal* but also as the trajector of *yot* and the profile of *'awaal*. These lower-level component structures, identified by correspondences (ii) and (iii), are the ones to which *-i* attaches phonologically. Its parallel phonological integration with each of two components jointly and redundantly symbolizes its semantic integration with the higher-level structure *yot 'awaal*.

If the same semantic element sometimes has multiple phonological manifestations, the converse also happens: multiple semantic notions may have a single phonological realization. Rather than being marked by clearly distinct affixes, two or more categories (e.g. gender, number, case) might be realized together through a single, unanalyzable inflection. A simple example is the marking of gender and number in Italian, as compared with Spanish. The core system in Spanish is transparent: gender is marked by adding *-o* and *-a* to the noun stem, and plural by suffixing *-s* to the result. For Italian, on the other hand, there are four distinct endings, each marking a particular combination of gender and number: *-o* 'masculine singular', *-a* 'feminine singular', *-i* 'masculine plural', *-e* 'feminine plural'. There is no evident way to decompose these into a part indicating gender and another indicating number.

(21) (a) **Spanish:** *tío* 'uncle', *tía* 'aunt', *tíos* 'uncles', *tías* 'aunts'

(b) **Italian:** *zio* 'uncle', *zia* 'aunt', *zii* 'uncles', *zie* 'aunts'

From a symbolic perspective, there is no inherent reason why a single marker should not make multiple semantic specifications. This is different only in degree from a lexical item invoking multiple cognitive domains as the basis for its meaning. To be sure, specifications like gender and number have systematic grammatical relevance (notably in "agreement" phenomena). They do not, however, have to be symbolized individually to be available for grammatical purposes.[41] Ultimately, a

---

[41] For example, since number is inherent in each of the Italian forms, they can be assessed for conformity to a constructional schema requiring that a subject and verb "agree" in number.

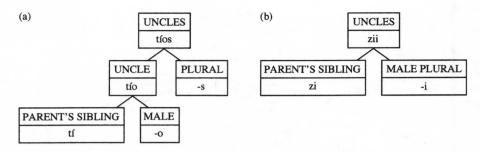

FIGURE 10.24

composite expression provides the same information whether the specifications are made individually at successive levels of composition or simultaneously at a single level. This is shown for Spanish *tíos* and Italian *zii* in figure 10.24.

Decomposability into distinct, individually recognized morphemes is of course a matter of degree. Its graded nature is problematic for the building-block metaphor but easily handled with symbolic assemblies. Two features of such assemblies make its treatment quite straightforward. First, composite structures are entities in their own right, neither limited to what the component structures contribute nor constrained to mirror them faithfully. Second, composite expressions vary in their analyzability (§3.2.2)—that is, the likelihood or extent of components being activated by way of apprehending the composite whole.

Three degrees of decomposability and analyzability (which tend to correlate) are exemplified in figure 10.25. Presuming it to be novel, the possessive nominal *Beverly's* is fully analyzable into the component morphemes *Beverly* and *'s*, each of which is reflected without distortion in the composite expression. Each component structure categorizes the corresponding portion of the composite whole, and in this case both categorizations result in full recognition (solid arrows). By contrast, the possessor pronouns *his* and *my* are well-entrenched units, learned and used as wholes. Decomposability into recognizable morphological components is not required for this purpose, and to the extent that it occurs at all, the expressions are only partly analyzable. In the case of *his*, the components would be *he* and *'s*, the latter being mirrored faithfully, the former only with distortion (dashed arrow) in the quality of the vowel. Finally, although *my* invites categorization by *me*, only the

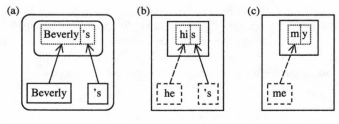

FIGURE 10.25

consonants match. The construction is also defective, in that nothing at the phonological pole individually symbolizes the notion of possession.

In their specific detail, noun inflection and agreement are sometimes quite complex. That complexity arises, however, from the proliferation and interaction of factors that individually are fairly natural and easy to grasp. We have seen how a variety of basic phenomena can be dealt with in CG. There seems little doubt that actual inflectional systems are in principle fully describable by means of symbolic assemblies.

11

Clause Structure

In the broadest sense, the term *verb* is used in CG for any expression that profiles a process. It thus subsumes both lexical verbs and complex verbal expressions, be they fixed or novel. Just as a noun heads a nominal, a verb heads a *clause*, which typically incorporates nominals representing participants in the profiled relationship. Like a full nominal, a *full clause* is one that is grounded: it singles out an instance of the process type and specifies its status vis-à-vis the speech event and the interlocutors. Traditionally, a full clause is said to be *finite* ("finished"). Finite clauses differ in this respect from infinitival and participial expressions, which may otherwise be structurally analogous. By construing a process holistically, infinitives and participles are nonprocessual and thus ungrounded. The grounding of finite clauses is discussed in section 9.4. Here we examine other aspects of clausal organization.

11.1 Global Organization

The things that populate our mental world do not themselves constitute it. What makes it a world—not just an inventory of entities conceived in isolation from one another—are the relationships they enter into. It is a structured world because many relationships persist through time, providing a stable basis for apprehending those defined in terms of change. Whether it persists or changes, a relationship tracked through time is termed a "process". A verb specifies a type of process, and a finite clause designates a grounded instance of a process type. Clauses are thus our basic vehicle for talking about the world and relating occurrences to our own circumstances. Usually a discourse consists primarily of a series of clauses; only rarely does it comprise a series of nominals.[1] The main reason for evoking nominal referents is to describe their participation in relationships.

---

[1] An example of the latter is the list of names read off during a graduation ceremony.

Relationships are conceptually dependent, their own conception presupposing that of their participants. For this reason, nominals are systematically included in clauses (but not conversely). An important dimension of clausal organization is thus the **role** of nominal referents with respect to the profiled process. At issue are both semantic roles (like agent, patient, instrument, etc.) and how these map onto grammatical roles (notably subject and object). A second dimension of organization is the existence of **basic clause types**. Structurally, the types are distinguished by factors like the perfective/imperfective contrast and the number of focused participants. Conceptually, they can be related to salient aspects of human experience (e.g. action, motion, perception, location). A third dimension is how clauses function in **discourse**. Among its manifestations are grounding, devices for introducing new discourse referents, and constructions providing options in choosing and focusing participants (e.g. active vs. passive).

11.1.1 Conceptual Archetypes

Despite its diversity and complexity, clause structure is readily seen as being grounded in basic human experience. It is best described and understood with reference to certain archetypal conceptions representing fundamental aspects of such experience. Conceptual archetypes function as the prototypes for clausal elements and are a major factor in determining their structural arrangement.

One archetype is the organization of a scene into a global **setting** and any number of smaller, more mobile **participants**. At this moment, for example, I find myself in a room containing many other objects: chairs, tables, computer, printer, books, pens, lamp, pictures, and so on. Participants—the most typical being people and discrete physical objects—are so called because they participate in actions and interactions. For instance, I act when I move about the room and interact with the objects there when I use them, touch them, or even look at them. Typical settings are things like rooms, buildings, and geographical regions, which are usually conceived as hosting events rather than participating in them.[2] At a given instant, each participant is found at some **location**. A location is part of the setting (any point or area within it). Accordingly, we think of locations as hosting participants rather than interacting with them—simply being in a place does not, in and of itself, amount to an interaction with it. In short, participants **interact** with one another but merely **occupy** locations.

The notion of interaction inheres in another essential archetype—namely, the **billiard-ball model** (§4.2.1). This is our conception of objects moving through space and impacting one another through forceful physical contact. Some objects supply the requisite energy through their own internal resources; others merely transmit or absorb it. Based on this cognitive model is an additional archetypal conception, that of an **action chain**, sketched in figure 11.1. An action chain is a series of forceful interactions, each involving the transmission of energy (double arrow) from

---

[2] When I move around a room interacting with the objects there, the room is merely hosting these occurrences. I interact with the room (which is then a participant) when I measure it, explore it, or paint it.

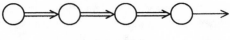

FIGURE 11.1

one participant to the next. In principle, an action chain can be of any length. Quite important linguistically, however, is a minimal action chain consisting of just one link: a single, two-participant interaction. Also important is a degenerate action chain in which the same participant is both the source of energy and the locus of its manifestation: a one-participant action.

Associated with actions and events are various kinds of **archetypal roles**. At one level, the notions setting, location, and participant have this status. At another level, we can distinguish a number of more specific roles for event participants.[3] An **agent** is an individual who willfully initiates and carries out an action, typically a physical action affecting other entities. It is thus an "energy source" and the initial participant in an action chain. Diametrically opposed to an agent is a **patient**, narrowly defined as something that undergoes an internal change of state (e.g. it breaks, melts, or dies). Typically inanimate and nonvolitional, a patient usually changes as the result of being affected by outside forces. It is then an "energy sink" and the final participant in an action chain. An **instrument** is something used by an agent to affect another entity. The typical instrument is an inanimate object physically manipulated by the agent. Thus it is not an independent source of energy but an intermediary in the transfer of force from agent to patient. The term **experiencer** alludes to mental experience, whatever its nature: intellectual, perceptual, or emotive. An experiencer is therefore sentient and normally human. In contrast, a **mover** can equally well be inanimate. It is defined straightforwardly as anything that moves (i.e. changes position in relation to its external surroundings). Finally, the term **zero** is adopted for participants whose role is conceptually minimal and nondistinctive. This is the neutral or baseline role of participants that merely exist, occupy some location, or exhibit a static property.

A different sort of archetype, the **stage model**, pertains to how we apprehend the outside world. The term is meant to suggest that the general process is analogous to the special case of watching a play. We cannot see everything at once, so viewing the world requires the directing and focusing of attention. From the maximal field of view, we select a limited area as the general locus of attention (the analog of looking at the stage). Within this region, we focus our attention specifically on certain elements (analogous to actors and props). Of course, we are less concerned with vision as such than with the parallels it exhibits with conception overall (viewing in the broad sense). The stage model does seem broadly applicable. In particular, the maximal field of view, the onstage region, and the focus of attention correspond respectively to an expression's maximal scope, immediate scope, and profile.

---

[3] Although the importance of participant roles is generally acknowledged, there is little agreement (surprise!) as to their inventory, the terms employed, or even their basic nature (conceptual or specifically linguistic). The roles cited represent salient conceptual archetypes that are commonly exploited linguistically, but the list is not exhaustive, nor are the labels entirely standard.

(a)   Canonical Event Model 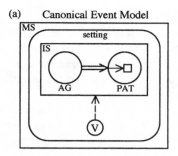   (b)   Default Coding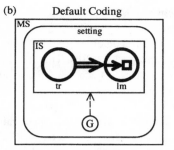

FIGURE 11.2

A final group of archetypes relate to the speech event itself. These include such fundamental notions as speaking, listening, and engaging in a social interaction. Also with archetypal status are the conceptions of basic speech acts (like stating, ordering, asking, and promising). An important and more inclusive archetype is the **default viewing arrangement** discussed in §3.4.1. The default arrangement is that of two interlocutors being together in a fixed location, using a shared language to describe occurrences in the world around them.

These various archetypes are interconnected and capable of being combined. One particular combination offers a convenient point of departure for discussing clause structure. Let us call it the **canonical event model**, for it represents the canonical way of apprehending what is arguably the most typical kind of occurrence. As shown in figure 11.2(a), this occurrence is identified as a bounded, forceful event in which an agent (AG) acts on a patient (PAT) to induce a change of state. This event is the focus of attention within the immediate scope (the onstage region), being apprehended from offstage by a viewer (V) not otherwise involved in it. All of this unfolds within some global setting.[4]

11.1.2 Coding

The term **coding** refers to how conceptual structures relate to the linguistic structures invoked to express them. For example, a conceived event or situation is coded by a finite clause describing it. Certain types of clauses are specially suited for coding particular kinds of occurrences. When related in this fashion, a clause type represents the default means of coding the corresponding occurrences, which are prototypical for it.

Illustrating one such relationship are classic example sentences used by linguistic theorists in different eras: *The farmer killed the duckling*; *Floyd broke the glass*; *John hit Mary*.[5] These instantiate a very basic type of clause: a transitive clause with

---

[4] Fig. 11.2 represents only one possible position of the setting with respect to the maximal scope, immediate scope, and viewer. Its placement depends on vantage point and other factors.

[5] In recent years, *John hit Mary* has been replaced by the politically more correct but less archetypal *John kissed Mary*. While Mary is only partially a patient in the former (since the absorption of energy does not necessarily lead to a change of state), in the latter she is solely an experiencer.

two focused participants. Likewise, the occurrences they describe instantiate a basic conceptual archetype, the canonical event model. Transitive clauses are the normal means of coding such events, which serve as their prototype. This default coding is sketched in figure 11.2(b). The agent-patient interaction is put onstage and profiled, with the agent as trajector and the patient as landmark. The ground is identified with the offstage viewer.

In the default coding of a canonical event, clausal elements assume what is generally taken to be their prototypical values. A prototypical verb is one that profiles an agent-patient interaction. Accordingly, the prototype for clausal subjects is an agent, and for objects it is a patient. Also typical (or at least very common) are a number of other correlations between conceptual archetypes and aspects of clausal organization. A setting is commonly expressed by means of a clause-external adverbial (e.g. *Outside, the crowd was getting restless*). Prepositional phrases are the usual way of coding both locations (*She put it on the shelf*) and nonfocused participants, such as instruments (*He was stirring the soup with a flyswatter*). The offstage position of the viewer correlates with the "unmarked" nature of third-person participants; that is, they represent the general case, first-person and second-person reference being the "marked" or special case.[6] Moreover, a clause is typically positive (as opposed to negative) and declarative in form (rather than interrogative or imperative). These properties reflect the default viewing arrangement, in which the interlocutors observe and describe what happens in the world around them.

These correlations manifest the grounding of clause structure in basic human experience. If every clause conformed to them, no one would question the semantic basis of grammatical notions like subject, object, and verb (e.g. the meaning of "subject" would simply be 'agent'). But matters are obviously much more complicated, for several reasons. First, the coding in figure 11.2 is not the only default relationship. An agent-patient interaction is just one archetypal occurrence, and a two-participant transitive clause is just one basic type. In other pairings, grammatical notions have different semantic import. Second, each clause type is extended to occurrences that deviate from the corresponding archetype. Alongside *Floyd broke the glass*, for instance, we have transitive clauses like *Floyd noticed the glass*, where, instead of agent and patient, the participant roles are experiencer and zero. A third complicating factor is the existence of special constructions allowing even archetypal occurrences to be coded in alternate ways for discourse purposes. Providing alternatives to *Floyd broke the glass* are the passive, "middle", and existential constructions: *The glass was broken (by Floyd)*; *The glass broke easily*; *There was a glass broken*. When the full array of options are considered, it is clear that any general characterization of clausal elements has to be quite schematic.

There is no definitive list of either basic clause types or archetypes with the potential to be invoked as their prototypes.[7] Besides an agent-patient interaction,

---

[6] This is not to deny the frequency of first- and second-person reference—people do like to talk about themselves and each other.

[7] Each can be classified and counted according to variable criteria. The cases cited are chosen just for illustrative purposes.

some archetypes with this potential are the conception of an entity moving through space, having a mental experience, occupying a location, or exhibiting a property. Languages differ in how many clause types they deploy and the range of archetypes each is used for. Like most languages, English expresses movement by means of an intransitive motion verb together with a locative that specifies the path or goal: *They walked {along the river/to the station}*. But English does not have a distinct clause type for mental experience. When that experience involves the apprehension of another entity, we code it with a regular transitive clause: *I {noticed/remembered/liked} the painting*. When it does not, it is commonly expressed with *be* followed by an adjective, the same construction used for properties: *I was {sad/dizzy/nervous}*; cf. *It was {round/heavy/expensive}*. This latter construction represents a special case of a basic clause type employed for static situations. Depending on whether *be* is followed by an adjective, a locative, or a nominal, it specifies a property, a location, or referential identity: *She is {tall/in the garage/my aunt}*.

While English is not unusual in these respects, each language has its own coding strategies. Some, having few if any adjectives (Dixon 1977), instead use intransitive verbs to specify properties. Many languages contrast with English by having a special clause type for mental experience (Klaiman 1981; Bhaskararao and Subbarao 2004). Most commonly, the experiencer is coded by a clause-initial nominal with the same marking as an indirect object, as in German *Mir ist kalt* 'I am cold' (literally: to me is cold). Languages differ as to whether this nominal functions grammatically as clausal subject. English and Samoan display an interesting difference in how they express the mental apprehension of other entities. For this purpose, each language employs a clause type that is primarily associated with another archetype. English has opted for a transitive clause based on an agent-patient interaction: *The boy saw the ship* is structurally parallel to *The pirates destroyed the ship*. In contrast, Samoan prefers the type of intransitive clause used for motion toward a goal (Cook 1993a). The sentences in (1) are thus analogous:

(1) (a) *E   alu   le   tama   'i   le   fale'oloa.*   'The boy is going to the store.'
          IMPRF   go   the   boy   to   the   store

     (b) *Na   va'ai   le   tama   'i   le   va'a.*   'The boy saw the ship.'
         PAST   see   the   boy   to   the   ship

Though different, each strategy represents a natural semantic extension motivated by an abstract similarity. Spatial movement toward a goal, the transmission of force from agent to patient, and the viewing of other entities all manifest the source-path-goal image schema (fig. 2.1).[8] Based on this abstract commonality, each language employs a clause type grounded in physical occurrences for the coding of experiential relationships.

---

[8] Spatial motion provides a metaphorical basis for understanding the other two. We can speak of a *perceptual path* or the *flow of energy* along an action chain, and find it natural to represent all three notions by means of arrows.

While English and Samoan follow different coding strategies, each makes sense in its own terms, exploiting basic cognitive phenomena in accordance with broader patterns in the language. This illustrates an important general point: that clause structure is for the most part natural and well motivated. We can attribute its complexity and diversity to the fact that clauses are used for such a vast array of descriptive and communicative purposes, each potentially achievable in different ways. To accommodate these varied needs, clause types and clausal elements are extended beyond their most typical range of uses. They thus acquire networks of related meanings centered on the conceptual archetypes functioning as their prototypes. It is nonetheless maintained in CG that certain basic notions have schematic meanings valid for all instances, and that certain aspects of clausal organization are either universal or widely shared.

11.1.3 Levels of Clausal Structure

A full, finite clause profiles a grounded instance of a process type. In the simplest case, this type is directly specified by a lexical verb, such as *break* in *Floyd broke the glass*. It is thus a clausal head—analogous to the head noun of a nominal—in the sense that the process it designates is profiled by the clause as a whole. Like a head noun, the verb functioning as clausal head is sometimes novel and often internally complex. An example of one both novel and complex would be the derived form *defunctionalize*. While this alternative to *break* does not (yet) have lexical status, it might well occur in officialese: *Floyd defunctionalized the glass*.

The grounded structure consists of more than just the verb. Minimally, it further includes the verb's "arguments": the nominals that specify its profiled participants. In *Floyd broke the glass*, the past-tense inflection is realized on *break* but grounds the entire structure *Floyd break the glass*. The grounded process is thus an instance not just of *break* but also the more detailed type characterized by that structure. Since a process is conceptually dependent on its participants, a verb evokes them schematically as an inherent aspect of its meaning. The basic type it specifies is thus elaborated by the nominals which identify these participants. The verb being the head, these nominals are complements (§7.3.3) because they elaborate salient substructures of it.

A verb's complements are not limited to the subject and object nominals that specify its focal participants. Often its meaning incorporates additional schematic entities that are sufficiently salient to function as elaboration sites. Among these are participants which happen not to be focused as trajector or landmark. One such participant is the mover in ditransitive expressions, e.g. *She sent him flowers*. Here focal prominence is conferred on the agent and the recipient, making *she* the subject and *him* the object. But what about *flowers*? While the mover in this construction is not a **focal** participant, it is clearly a **central** participant, essential to the meaning of *send* (fig. 8.12(a)). An elaborating nominal—in this case *flowers*—is thus a complement. A verb's semantic structure can also incorporate a schematic **relationship** that functions as an e-site. The verb *put*, for example, makes salient the notion that the profiled action—that of the trajector moving the landmark—results in the latter occupying a new location. Besides a subject and an object, it therefore takes as complement a locative expression that specifies where the object winds up: *He put them in a vase*.

So in the simplest case the verb and its complements constitute the grounded structure. Together they specify a detailed process type (e.g. *Floyd break the glass*), an instance of which is singled out for grounding.[9] But things are not always this straightforward. In particular, there is often a disparity between the grounded process and the process specified by the lexical verb (or a nonlexical analog, like *defunctionalize*). The verb then fails to qualify as the clausal head, even though it supplies the essential content and specifies the basic process type. It is not the head because the clause as a whole profiles an instance of a different process type—a higher-order type derived in some fashion from the basic one.

A major source of such disparities are constructions involving voice and aspect. Consider once more the English passive, progressive, and perfect (discussed in §4.3.3 and §9.4.1). Each combines with a verb to derive a higher-level verb representing a different process type. The passive does this by adjusting the focal prominence of processual participants, conferring trajector status on what would otherwise be the landmark: *criticize* > *be criticized*. The progressive derives a new, imperfective process type by restricting the profiled relationship to some internal portion of the original, perfective process: *criticize* > *be criticizing*. And instead of the verbal process itself, the perfect designates the stable relationship of that process being prior, but still of relevance, with respect to a temporal vantage point: *criticize* > *have criticized*. In each construction, the composite expression designates a process that is based on, but nonetheless distinct from, the one profiled by the lexical verb. Since only this derived process is eligible for grounding,[10] the lexical verb is not the clausal head.

The formation of complex verbal expressions is not the only source of disparity between the process specified lexically and the one that is grounded. It can also happen that a distinct process emerges at the composite-structure level even without morphological derivation or the addition of a higher-level verb (like *be* or *have*). Consider the following construction:

(2)　(a)　*The garden swarmed with bees.*

　　　(b)　*The streets rang with church bells.*

　　　(c)　*In a moment the whole sky will explode with fireworks.*

It is the bees that *swarm*, the bells that *ring*, and the fireworks that *explode*. Counter to the usual pattern, the lexical verb's trajector is not expressed by the subject, but is introduced periphrastically as the object of *with*. The clausal subject serves instead to designate a location suffused with the verbal activity. Though noncanonical, a construction of this sort is unproblematic in CG. It is not required in symbolic

---

[9] This is a functional characterization, not a claim about grammatical constituency. It is neither implied nor precluded that the grounded structure emerges as a classic constituent which combines as a whole with the grounding element.

[10] Instead of being grounded, it may undergo further derivation (e.g. *be criticizing* > *have been criticizing*). The clausal head can be identified as either the entire complex verb derived in this manner, or as the verb *have* or *be* introduced at its highest level. It is on this schematic verb that grounding is realized morphologically (**was** *criticized,* **is** *being criticized,* **has** *been criticizing*).

assemblies that a composite structure precisely match any component structure in its profile or trajector/landmark alignment.[11] What we have in (2) is simply a case where the processes profiled by the lexical verb and at the composite-structure level are non-congruent in these respects. Whereas the lexical verb designates a kind of activity, the composite structure profiles the relationship of a location hosting this activity.

Since a process can emerge at the composite-structure level, without being inherited from any component, there can even be clauses which have no separate verb. A common sort of example are **equative** expressions, like the Luiseño sentence in (3). The structure grounded by the clitic *=up* consists overtly of just two nominals, *Xwaan* and *po-na'*. The equative construction simply juxtaposes these to form a composite expression that profiles their relationship of referential identity. Though not coded by a separate morphological element, this emergent relationship functions as the clausal process, with *Xwaan* as its trajector and *po-na'* as landmark.

(3)   *Xwaan=up*   *po-na'*.   'Juan is his father.'

     Juan=3s:PRES   his-father

Also lacking a separate verb are schematic English clauses consisting of only a subject and a modal: *She may*; *I will*; *Everyone should*. Since a grounding element profiles the grounded process (rather than the grounding relationship), these expressions qualify as finite clauses—the modal profiles a grounded process instance, whose trajector is elaborated by the subject nominal. Of course, the process type is maximally schematic if there is no lexical verb to specify it. Hence these clauses are only useful in a discourse context where the type has previously been specified, e.g. in answer to a question: *Will Betty get the job? She may*.

However the process type is specified, it can be modified by adverbial expressions. Adverbs are quite diverse in terms of their form, the properties they indicate, and the level of conceptual organization they pertain to. Formally, they can be of any size: words (e.g. *then*), phrases (*in July*), or clauses (*while he was being investigated*). They qualify occurrences with respect to such varied properties as time, place, manner, degree, rate, means, reason, purpose, attitude, epistemic judgment, and so on. The examples in (4) illustrate how these properties relate to particular levels of conceptual organization. In (4)(a), *very unsteadily* indicates the manner of walking. It thus pertains to the physical action as such. In sentence (b), *reluctantly* does not so much specify the manner of agreeing as the subject's attitude in doing so. And in (c), the adverb *undoubtedly* describes something inherent in neither the event itself nor its participants. Rather it expresses the speaker's epistemic judgment in regard to the clausal proposition.

(4)   (a)   *She was walking very unsteadily.*

    (b)   *He reluctantly agreed to settle out of court.*

    (c)   *Undoubtedly they made the wrong decision.*

---

[11] That is, some constructions are exocentric (§7.2). This location-subject construction is examined in §11.3.2.

Further dimensions of structure pertain to how clauses function at the discourse level. The previous discourse context determines whether we can use a schematic clause like *She may* in lieu of one that is fully specified (e.g. *Betty may get the job*). More generally, the various discourse notions constituting information structure—notions like topic, focus, given, and new—have a strong shaping influence on clauses, especially with respect to word order. For example, the initial position of the prepositional object in (5)(a) marks it as a clause-level topic. In (5)(b), the inverted positions of the locative and the subject signal their status as given and new, respectively. In accordance with the nonstandard word order, the construction introduces a new participant in the discourse by placing it in a location already invoked. The special construction in (c) marks the element following *it's* as focus. *Zebras* is thus identified as the new and informative part of the sentence (that she's afraid of something is presupposed).

(5) (a) *Political advertising I can do without.*

   (b) *In the box was a kitten.*

   (c) *It's zebras that she's afraid of.*

Also shaping clause structure are the viewing arrangement and the nature of the speaker-hearer interaction. Most obviously, the form of a clause can signal whether it is offered as a statement (*You will solve this problem*), a question (*Will you solve this problem?*), or an order (*Solve this problem!*).

11.2 Subject and Object

Although clauses profile relationships, key problems in their analysis revolve around their nominal components. Pivotal issues are the nature and status of the traditional notions subject and object. Few topics have been subject to more theoretical disagreement, or been the object of more discussion, than these "grammatical relations".

11.2.1 Basic Issues

In *Floyd broke the glass*, the nominals *Floyd* and *the glass* function respectively as subject and object. That much is fairly uncontroversial. Disagreement sets in, however, as soon as we ask what a subject or an object is. There are two basic issues. First, how can these notions be characterized? Second, are they universal? The questions are clearly related: whether subjects and objects can be recognized in every language depends on their characterization.

Factors usually considered as the basis for characterization are meaning, discourse status, and grammatical behavior. In the orthodox view, the first two factors can be quickly dismissed. The relevant aspect of meaning is presumed to be a semantic role. Is there, then, some role that subjects consistently manifest?[12] Evidently not.

---

[12] To keep things simple, I focus primarily on subjects. The lessons learned can then be applied to objects.

Despite a tendency for subjects to be agents, many are clearly nonagentive. Indeed, a subject is not necessarily even the most active participant (e.g. *The glass was broken by Floyd*). An attempt to define subject in terms of discourse status fares no better. Here it is noted that a subject tends to be given (as opposed to new) and also a discourse topic. But once again these are only tendencies, not consistent properties. Recall, for instance, that expressions like (5)(b) serve precisely to introduce the subject referent as a new participant in the discourse.

If the notion subject cannot be characterized in terms of either meaning or discourse status, we are left with grammatical behavior. The standard view is that a certain list of grammatical properties provides a basis for identifying subjects in a given language. Among the subject properties of English (to choose a language at random) are the following:

1. Certain pronouns have special subject forms (*I, he, she, we, they*).
2. A verb agrees with its subject (*Floyd was breaking the glasses* vs. *The glasses were being broken*).
3. The subject inverts with an auxiliary verb in forming questions (e.g. *Was Floyd breaking the glasses?*).
4. A reflexive pronoun cannot be a subject, but usually has a subject for its antecedent (*Floyd admires himself*, but not **Himself admires Floyd*).
5. The subject of an adverbial clause can often be left implicit (e.g. *By breaking glasses, Floyd upsets me*), in which case it is usually interpreted as being coreferential to the main clause subject rather than its object (Floyd does the breaking).

There is thus a broad consensus that subject and object can only be defined grammatically through a list of characteristic behaviors. This has some serious drawbacks, however. For one thing, the defining behaviors turn out to be different from one language to the next. Since the characterizations are therefore specific to individual languages, they fail to capture an aspect of linguistic organization that is widespread if not universal. A more fundamental problem is that a list of grammatical behaviors is merely that: a list of grammatical behaviors. In and of itself, it offers no unifying principle or even any rationale for there being such a list. If the notions "subject" and "object" have any cross-linguistic utility—and I think they do—we still lack a revelatory characterization.

CG offers a fresh perspective on these issues. Being anything but orthodox, it avoids the problems that arise in the orthodox view. Its distinctive approach to linguistic meaning makes feasible the semantic characterization of grammatical constructs, which leads to a different assessment of their universality. Though certainly controversial, the CG definitions of subject and object are not only natural but well motivated, given basic notions of cognitive semantics established on independent grounds. From this perspective, the grammatical behavior used to identify subject and object do not serve to **characterize** these notions but are merely **symptomatic** of their conceptual import.

We will not find conceptual characterizations by looking just at semantic roles like agent and patient; though suitable as prototypes, these archetypes are too specific to cover all instances. For schematic definitions, we must look instead to basic cognitive abilities—in this case, the focusing of attention. Specifically, it is claimed that the subject and object relations are grammatical manifestations of trajector/landmark alignment: a subject is a nominal that codes the trajector of a profiled relationship; an object is one that codes the landmark. Trajector/landmark alignment was established independently as an aspect of linguistic meaning (§3.3.2). It is a matter of focal prominence: trajector and landmark are the primary and secondary focal participants in a profiled relationship. It stands to reason that this conceptual prominence would translate into grammatical "accessibility". The special grammatical behaviors of subject and object can thus be seen as symptoms of their referents being focused relational participants.

This conceptual characterization is not even contemplated in orthodox approaches because traditional semantics does not acknowledge the critical role of prominence and construal. Different views of meaning lead to different views of grammar and thus to different assessments of universality. Among linguists concerned with typological issues, it is widely accepted that many languages lack grammatical subjects. It is simply presupposed that subjects are identified by the sorts of grammatical behavior typical of subjects in familiar European languages, in which case the conclusion is certainly valid. But what if the notion is defined more abstractly? The CG definition of subject as primary focal participant is claimed to be appropriate even for English and other European languages. Although the associated grammatical behaviors vary greatly, this schematic characterization in terms of focal prominence has the potential to be universally applicable.

At issue is the interplay between two basic aspects of conceptual organization: semantic role (pertaining to conceptual content) and focal prominence (a matter of construal). Semantic roles are inherent in the very structure of the conceived occurrence, where each nominal referent participates in a certain manner. Focal prominence is more extrinsic. It resides in the directing of attention, made necessary by the difficulty of viewing a complex occurrence in a global and wholly neutral fashion—we cannot attend to everything equally and simultaneously. As a limited resource, attention has to be allocated, and for a given structure different allocations are possible. Trajector/landmark alignment is simply a linguistic manifestation of this fundamental aspect of cognition. Trajector and landmark can be thought of metaphorically as the onstage elements illuminated by "spotlights" of focal prominence. As a working hypothesis, CG maintains that every language makes some use of a primary spotlight at the clausal level, and that many make use of a secondary spotlight. The grammatical behaviors associated with these focused elements arise by way of either signaling or exploiting their special salience.[13]

At which clausal participants will the spotlights be directed? In this respect languages have different strategies, preferences, and conventions. There are two significant dimensions of typological variation. Along one axis, languages differ in their canonical choice of trajector, selected by default unless there is reason to

---

[13] The characterization of subject as primary focus of attention is supported by experimental evidence (Tomlin 1995, 1997; Forrest 1996).

do otherwise. The two main options are agent and patient. The other dimension of variation is how consistently focal prominence correlates with particular semantic roles. A high level of consistency tends to obscure the role of prominence. If all subjects were agents, for example, the associated grammatical behaviors might simply be analyzed as indications of agentivity. It is only the association of focal prominence with a variety of semantic roles that alerts the analyst to its status as an independent factor.

11.2.2 Agent Orientation

Among the relationships coded linguistically, few are wholly symmetrical. Usually their participants have distinct roles in the profiled occurrence, so that reversing them yields a different conception—a man biting a dog is not the same event as a dog biting a man. Being inherent in conceived events, **role asymmetries** belong to the level of conceptual content. They have to be distinguished from the **prominence asymmetries** imposed on events by linguistic coding. These are matters of construal. The factors that mainly concern us, profiling and trajector/landmark organization, consist in the allocation and focusing of attention for purposes of linguistic presentation. At this level, reversing things does not change the event itself but results in a different way of portraying it. *The man bit the dog* and *The dog was bitten by the man* represent alternate construals of the same conceived occurrence.

A major determinant of clause structure is how the elements at these two levels align with one another. Here we observe a natural tendency for attention to be directed at participants with the greatest cognitive salience. In particular, focal prominence tends to align with semantic roles that (for reasons to be discussed) are plausibly considered intrinsically salient: notably, agent and patient. Perhaps the most typical case is the alignment presented in figure 11.2 as the default coding of a canonical event, where the agent is focused as trajector and the patient as landmark. Certainly this represents a very basic coding strategy. But it is not the only way to make focal prominence line up with salient participant roles. Languages differ in the alignment they adopt as their default coding strategy. And besides this **canonical alignment**, each language provides a range of alternatives to accommodate varied circumstances.

A pivotal factor in canonical alignment is the choice of trajector. The two major strategies align the trajector with either the agent or the theme. These strategies are referred to as **agent orientation** and **theme orientation**. As used in CG, the term **theme** subsumes a number of "passive" semantic roles considered in the following section: patient, mover, experiencer, and zero.[14] Agent and theme orientation are natural strategies because each stems from a fundamental aspect of human experience. Agent orientation reflects our role as sentient, willful creatures forcefully acting on the world, expending energy to achieve and maintain control of our surroundings. Theme orientation reflects the fact that we operate in a world laid out in a certain way, where entities exhibit different properties and occupy distinct locations, so that

---

[14] Terms of course vary. *Theme* is often used for a mover, and *patient* for what is here called a theme. (Recall that *patient* is narrowly defined in CG as a participant that undergoes an internal change of state.) Agent and theme resemble the "macro-roles" labeled *actor* and *undergoer* in Role and Reference Grammar (Foley and Van Valin 1984).

they vary in degree of accessibility and susceptibility to our influence. Both strategies are manifested in every language. What differs is precisely how they are manifested and for what proportion of phenomena.

When nothing much is going on, an event attracts our attention, especially a forceful action effecting a change. The actor tends strongly to be the focus of attention, by virtue of being the most active participant as well as the source of energy. Agent orientation conforms to this tendency by putting the actor in focus at the level of linguistic expression. In the default coding of canonical events, primary focal prominence is conferred on the **head** of an action chain, the agent who initiates the chain of interactions constituting the profiled occurrence. The alignment of clausal trajector with agent is canonical in many languages (if not most), English being a prime example. In a language of this sort, agent is the prototype for subjects, with other subject roles permitted by extension. The wider the range of permitted extensions, the more abstract a schematic characterization of subject has to be. Examining the full range of options makes it evident that focal prominence is the only viable candidate.

Even parade examples like *Floyd broke the glass* are variable in the extent to which the subject is agentive. Instead of acting willfully, Floyd may have broken the glass accidentally. And instead of breaking it actively, through the transmission of force, he may have done so passively by letting it drop or by failing to realize that it shouldn't go in the dishwasher. In cases where it does exert force on the glass, the subject is not necessarily either sentient or the original source of energy. The subjects in (6) are all nonsentient. And while sleepwalkers, dishwashers, and hailstorms function as energy sources, a baseball can only impart the force it acquires by being hit or thrown. From countless expressions like these, we conclude that the agent archetype is merely prototypical for English subjects, which often manifest it only partially, even for physical force-dynamic events. A schematic characterization, fully manifested in all instances, will have to be more abstract. One might then propose that a subject be defined as the **head of a profiled action chain**, i.e. the initial participant in that portion of a chain selected for explicit, focused presentation.[15]

(6)　*The {sleepwalker/dishwasher/hailstorm/baseball} broke the glass.*

Being limited to forceful physical events, this more abstract characterization is still too specific for any representative array of data. For one thing, we have to accommodate events that are force-dynamic, and their subjects agentive, only metaphorically:

(7)　(a)　*The bribery investigation compelled the mayor to resign.*

　　(b)　*His obvious lies damaged the credibility of their star witness.*

---

[15] In (6), the person who hits or throws the baseball heads an action chain leading to the breaking of the glass, but only the baseball-glass interaction is put onstage and profiled. And while Floyd may have put the glass in the dishwasher, thereby initiating the chain of interactions resulting in its defunctionalization, his role in this tragic occurrence is conveniently left implicit.

A large proportion of what we talk about obtains in the mental or social realm, where the force at issue is nonphysical. The subjects in (8) are nonetheless agent-like by virtue of instigating a change that affects another entity:

(8) (a) *We changed the requirements again.*

(b) *The president misled us with his lies.*

(c) *Sheila persuaded my mother to give up smoking.*

(d) *I closed my bank account.*

In other cases, it is dubious that force is involved at all, even metaphorically. The verbs in (9) do not portray the subject as causing a change or exerting influence that in any way impinges on the object. The subject merely apprehends the object, establishing some kind of "mental contact" with it.

(9) *I {saw/liked/remembered/imagined} the painting.*

To handle this wide spectrum of cases, we might generalize the definition of subject by accepting as an "action chain" anything with certain configurational properties, regardless of whether it is physically implemented. This abstracted notion of an action chain comprises a source-path-goal configuration in which the source and goal are both participants. It thus subsumes as special cases the physical or metaphorical transmission of force, the exertion of influence in the mental and social realms, as well as a mental or perceptual path that "reaches" another entity. A subject can then be characterized as the participant that somehow initiates an asymmetrical interaction conceptualized as involving a path from subject to object, or simply as the more active participant in such an interaction.

Despite its generality, this definition still fails to cover all the bases. It says nothing, for instance, about the subjects in (10), where the profiled relationship is symmetrical and neither participant is active in any way. In such cases, the choice of subject is arbitrary from the standpoint of the situation described. We simply impose trajector status on whichever participant seems appropriate in the discourse context.

(10) (a) *Line A intersects line B.*   (a′) *Line B intersects line A.*

(b) *Australia resembles South Africa.*   (b′) *South Africa resembles Australia.*

Truth be known, however, trajector status is always imposed: a matter of construal, it is never inherent in the situation described. Even with canonical events we have an option—for instance, we can use a passive to focus the patient rather than the agent (*The glass was broken by Floyd*). What varies is the extent to which the situation provides **motivation** for a particular choice of subject. With a clear-cut asymmetry, so that one participant is highly active and the other not at all, our attention is naturally drawn to the former. When there is less activity, two participants may compete for attention on a roughly equal basis. The subjects in (11), for example, are both good candidates for primary focal prominence: *she* by virtue of being the locus of mental activity, engaged in apprehending the object; and *his rude behavior* by virtue of inducing her mental experience.

(11)   (a) *She resented his rude behavior.*

    (b) *His rude behavior offended her.*

Symmetrical relationships, as in (10), represent the extreme case where the conceived situation offers no motivation at all for any particular choice of subject—the speaker just has to select one.[16] But in the last analysis, the speaker always has to choose.

It is evident, therefore, that any content-based definition of subjects is doomed to failure. As a characterization that covers all instances, focal prominence stands alone as being both workable and cognitively plausible. And because it is not tied to any specific semantic role or conceptual content, it applies unproblematically even to clauses exhibiting noncanonical alignment (such as passives). It is also applicable whether a language employs the basic strategy of agent orientation, theme orientation, or a combination.

With agent orientation, trajector status is conferred by default on either the agent or the most agent-like of the profiled participants. Consider the sentences in (12), all invoking an action chain in which an agent uses an instrument to effect a patient's change of state. Each sentence profiles a different portion of this overall action chain. What should be noticed is that, in each case, the subject (S) is the head with respect to the profiled portion. When the agent is included in the profile, it is chosen as subject by default. When the profile is limited to the instrument-patient interaction, the instrument is chosen: it is agent-like because it affects the patient and in local terms is the energy source. But if only the patient's change of state is made explicit as the processual profile, the patient functions as clausal subject.[17] It is the most agent-like of the profiled participants by dint of being the only such participant.

(12)   (a) *Floyd broke the glass with a hammer.* $\mathbf{AG_S} \Rightarrow \mathbf{INSTR} \Rightarrow \mathbf{PAT_O} \rightarrow$

    (b) *A hammer broke the glass.* $\mathbf{AG} \Rightarrow \mathbf{INSTR_S} \Rightarrow \mathbf{PAT_O} \rightarrow$

    (c) *The glass broke.* $\mathbf{AG} \Rightarrow \mathbf{INSTR} \Rightarrow \mathbf{PAT_S} \rightarrow$

In languages with a strong agent orientation, the cognitive salience of themes is also made manifest in a variety of ways. A one-participant clause can have a nonagentive theme as its subject, e.g. (12)(c). Available as well are constructions to accommodate situations where, for one reason or another, the theme rather than the agent needs to be focused as trajector (§11.3). For clauses that do select the more agentive participant as primary focal participant, a theme can still be featured as landmark, i.e. as object. The patient has this status in (12)(a)–(b).

---

[16] Of course, the speaker also has the option of choosing them both: *Lines A and B intersect*; *Australia and South Africa resemble one another.*

[17] This hierarchical scheme was first noted by Fillmore (1968), who did not however observe that the hierarchy reflects the transmission of energy along an action chain.

Like subjects, objects have both a prototype and a schematic characterization. If the prototypical object is a patient, it can also be a mover (*I threw it*), an experiencer (*I offended her*), or an unaffected participant with the semantic role of zero (*I remember him*). The profiled relationship need not involve an action chain or anything analogous to one (*She resembles her mother*). A clausal object does not even have to be a participant. It may also be a path (*We hiked a new trail*) or location (*The train reached Chicago*). Depending on how far we stretch the term, an object can even represent some value on a scale of measurement (*It weighs seven pounds*). A schematic definition, one valid for all instances, must therefore be independent of semantic role and any specific conceptual content. If subjects are properly characterized in terms of primary focal prominence, for objects the evident basis is secondary focal prominence.

11.2.3 Theme Orientation

Agent and theme attract focal prominence because each has a kind of cognitive salience that sets it apart from other semantic roles in its experiential realm. Agents belong to the "active" realm—that of action, change, and force, of mobile creatures acting on the world. Here a willful human actor stands out as a paragon with respect to other active roles (like instrument, experiencer, or natural force). On the other hand, themes belong to the "passive" realm of settings, locations, and stable situations, where objects with particular properties are arranged in certain ways. The world thus constituted defines our circumstances, presents both problems and opportunities, and serves as the platform for human activity.

What should we recognize as the paragon with respect to the passive realm? From one perspective, it can be identified with the global setting (or the world as a whole). This is the polar opposite of a point-like mobile actor, and the most representative of what the realm is all about. More relevant, however, is the perspective of the actors themselves. Due to its all-encompassing nature, the setting as a whole tends not to be cognitively salient for viewers within it, hence not a good candidate for focal prominence. We usually take the setting for granted, being more aware of the situation obtaining in a certain limited area. This is the onstage region, the general locus of viewing attention. It is then an onstage participant that is most likely to be a focus of attention and thus attract focal prominence in linguistic coding. The various participant roles in this realm are the ones subsumed under the general rubric **theme**.

The basic thematic roles are zero, mover, patient, and experiencer. The zero role is minimal: it is that of a participant which exhibits a property, occupies a location, or is simply there. It is the most basic thematic role in the sense that these static situations best exemplify the passive realm of settings and stable arrangements. Zero is also the most basic in the sense that the other roles presuppose and incorporate it. A mover, which undergoes a change of location, thus occupies a series of locations through time. Likewise, a patient undergoes a change in a property it exhibits, and an experiencer, to function as such, first has to be there.

Each of these can be the sole participant in a **thematic process**: a minimal, single-participant process in which the theme's role is passive (i.e. it is not construed as a source of energy). Despite its minimality, each clause in (13) is a self-contained whole, conceptually coherent in and of itself. In particular, the profiled occurrence can be apprehended without explicitly invoking an agent or an energy source. When conceived autonomously in this fashion, its construal is said to be **absolute**. This is not to say that notions of energy, force, and causation are totally absent—we know, for instance, that a boat sinks due to gravity, and ice melts due to heat. Yet these are merely background forces, ever-present aspects of our basic circumstances. It is usually only departures from this baseline that count linguistically as external causation or agency.

(13) (a) ZERO: *The pole is long.   She is over there.*

    (b) MVR: *The boat sank.   The door opened.*

    (c) PAT: *The ice melted.   The glass broke.*

    (d) EXPER: *I itch all over.   He was sad.*

Absolute construal is a matter of viewing a thematic process solely in relation to the passive realm. From this perspective, the most typical thematic role is zero, and the most typical thematic process is one with a zero participant. These motivate the basic clause type in (13)(a), where *be* extends through time a stable situation in which the trajector has the property or the location specified by its complement. However, a thematic process can also be viewed in relation to the active realm, where it is seen as the consequence of a force-dynamic interaction. From this perspective the most typical thematic roles are patient and mover (e.g. *Floyd broke the glass*; *I opened the door*). In particular, a patient stands out as being the polar opposite of an agent, their interaction providing the context in which the agent role archetype is most fully manifested. The last thematic role, experiencer, does not belong exclusively to either realm. The kinds of experience described in (13)(d), being passive and involving just a single participant, constitute thematic processes. But an experiencer can also play the active role in a two-participant interaction (e.g. *I see it*).

The two main attractors of focal prominence, agent and theme, display a fundamental asymmetry in regard to their associated processual archetypes. As seen in (13), a thematic process can be conceptualized autonomously, without reference to an agent or agentive causation. The absolute construal of such a process, represented in figure 11.3(a), is conceptually coherent. But the converse does not hold: by its very nature, an agentive process incorporates a thematic process, without which it is conceptually incoherent. As shown in diagram (b), an agentive act consists in bringing about a thematic process and is therefore conceptually dependent with respect to it. There is no counterpart to the absolute construal of a thematic process. Its counterpart would be the configuration in diagram (c), where the agent simply causes or induces, with no conception of the process induced. This is not internally consistent, however—we can hardly conceptualize an agent inducing an occurrence without invoking that occurrence, at least schematically. Thus we do not say things like **He caused*, **He induced*, or **He brought about*, which would be the agentive analogs of the absolute expressions in (13).[18]

---

[18] Fig. 11.3(b) does not imply that an agentive process always has two distinct participants. As a special case, the same participant can function as both agent and theme (e.g. *She jumped*). Nor is every

(a) Thematic Process   (b) Agentive Process   (c) [anomalous]

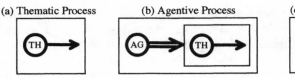

FIGURE 11.3

A typical agentive process thus has the conceptual layering shown in diagram (b). At its core is a conceptually autonomous thematic process, which can often be expressed independently (e.g. *It broke*). This core supports the notion of agentivity, which—being conceptually dependent—is usually not expressed in isolation (**He caused*). Together they constitute a higher-level event conception that is itself autonomous (*He broke it*). Consistent with its foundational role, the thematic process embodies the lion's share of the verb's conceptual content. The verb *shatter*, for example, tells us a great deal about the theme and the process it undergoes, but very little about the agent or its actions (Keenan 1984). We know that the patient is inanimate, glass-like, and brittle and that, through the application of force, it disintegrates instantaneously into many small pieces. The trajector could be a person, a falling rock, an earthquake, a collision, etc. If a person (no doubt Floyd), he could have acted in countless ways: by dropping the object, swinging a hammer at it, throwing a baseball, pushing a button to start the dishwasher, and so on. All we know for sure is that the trajector is somehow responsible for supplying the requisite force.

From the processing standpoint, there are two evident paths for mentally accessing the layered configuration in diagram (b), each natural in its own way. One natural sequence is to follow the transmission of force along the action chain, from agent to theme. The other, based on conceptual autonomy, runs in the opposite direction. The thematic process has a kind of priority because in two respects it anchors the overall conception: as the center of gravity with respect to conceptual content, and by virtue of being presupposed by the notion of agency (required for its full conceptual manifestation). In proceeding along this second path, we start with the conceptually autonomous core, augment it with the notion of agency (which requires its support), and thus arrive at the full conception of an agentive process (also autonomous). At each stage, the structure evoked is self-contained and coherent in and of itself.

If it has clear cognitive motivation, a particular way of ordering or accessing the elements of a complex structure can be called a **natural path**. The first element on a path is its **starting point**. For clauses, we can posit a number of natural paths, each pertaining to a distinct level or dimension of organization. One such path is

---

two-participant process based on a clearly discernible thematic process (*see*, for instance, is not). In many languages, special grammatical properties distinguish a type of clause called "unaccusative", which is generally analyzed as having an underlying object but no underlying subject (Perlmutter 1978). Unaccusatives would instead be analyzed in CG (which does not posit underlying structures) as designating a thematic process construed in absolute fashion.

word order, for which the starting point is the first word encountered in the temporal sequence. A second is the flow of energy along an action chain, which starts with the agent; a third, based on conceptual autonomy, starts with a thematic process. Yet another path is the sequence of access determined by focal prominence: trajector > landmark > other. As a matter of processing efficiency, natural paths tend to coalign (insofar as possible) and their participants to coincide. In *Floyd broke the glass*, for example, *Floyd* is the starting point with respect to the coaligned paths of word order, energy flow, and focal prominence (being the first word, the agent, and the trajector). Herein lies the basis for agent and theme orientation. They represent alternate ways of bringing the path of focal prominence into alignment with one pertaining to conceptual content: its starting point, the trajector, coincides with either agent or theme, the first participant encountered along the path based on either energy flow or conceptual autonomy.

11.2.4 Competing Strategies

Agent and theme orientation are alternate coding strategies. Each is a basic way of bringing linguistically conferred prominence into line with the inherent cognitive salience of an archetypal participant role. Either alignment is capable of being established as the default orientation in a language. To some extent, however, every language makes at least some use of both alignments.

Agent orientation is the coding strategy of selecting an agent as trajector. When this represents the default alignment, the most typical kind of clause is one that profiles a canonical agent-theme interaction, with agent as trajector and theme as landmark (fig. 11.2(b)). This basic clause type is extended semantically to other sorts of occurrences and provides a structural model in terms of which other clause types are partially characterized. We can see this clearly in English, which is strongly agent oriented. We noted in (1), for instance, that English—in contrast to Samoan—uses structurally parallel clauses for an agent-patient interaction (*Floyd broke the glass*) and a perceptual relationship (*The boy saw the ship*). More generally, it employs this type of clause for the mental apprehension of other entities (*I imagined the painting*) and even for symmetrical relationships between two zero participants (*Australia resembles South Africa*).

In terms of their grammatical behavior, the subjects in these semantically varied clauses are essentially all alike. Whether the trajector is an agent, merely agent-like (e.g. an instrument), an experiencer, or even zero, the nominal expressing it acts in all the ways taken as being diagnostic for English subjects: basic word order (SVO), verb agreement, inversion with an auxiliary in questions (*Does he resemble her?*), the formation of question "tags" (*He resembles her, doesn't he?*), and so on. Perhaps more strikingly, the same behaviors are observed in clauses with just a single participant. There may be just one because the same participant functions as both agent and theme, e.g. with a motion verb like *walk* (*He walked*; *Did he walk?*; *He walked, didn't he?*). Agentivity is not required, however. Grammatically, a subject is no less a subject even when its role is purely thematic (*It sank*; *Did it sink?*; *It sank, didn't it?*). Except for the absence of an object, therefore, these intransitive clauses are structurally parallel to canonical transitives.

The strong agent orientation of a language like English is shown in figure 11.4(a), where a dashed-line box encloses elements that function alike grammatically. Three kinds of clause are represented: transitive, where agent and theme are distinct (e.g. *He broke it*); agentive intransitive, where the same participant fills both roles (*He walked*); and nonagentive intransitive, where the participant is only a theme (*It broke*). What the diagram indicates is that the same grammatical properties that distinguish the agent from the theme in a transitive clause are also characteristic of the single participant of an intransitive, even when this itself is a theme. In CG, this cluster of properties is taken as being symptomatic of trajector status—that is, primary focal prominence. This prominence reveals itself as a separate factor precisely because it fails to coincide with any coherently definable semantic role: it can fall on either agent or theme (which are basically opposites) and not on all themes. But in each case it falls on the most agent-like participant.

Shifting now to the alternate coding strategy, the analog of strong agent orientation is strong theme orientation, shown in figure 11.4(c). In languages where theme orientation is the default alignment, the most typical kind of clause profiles a one-participant thematic process. The trajector is then a theme. If theme orientation predominates, the most theme-like participant should be chosen as trajector in other types of clauses. Focal prominence is thus conferred on the theme of a transitive clause, as well as the single participant of an agentive intransitive (which combines the roles of theme and agent). Since all these participants are themes, focal prominence is less obviously independent from semantic role than it is with agent orientation. Examining a wider range of clause types will, however, show their distinctness.[19] Grammatically, trajector status should be evident from an array of behaviors shared by the single participant of an intransitive clause and the theme of a transitive clause.

There are such languages, the most commonly cited example being the Australian language Dyirbal (Dixon 1972). How many there are depends on descriptive and theoretical issues we cannot address here. It hinges on the question of which grammatical properties are best considered diagnostic of subject status—or in CG

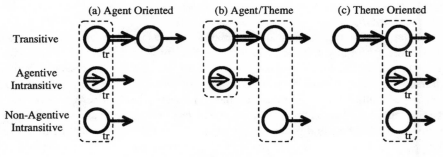

FIGURE 11.4

[19] For example, the trajector can be a setting or location rather than a participant. In the type of construction known as an "antipassive" (which defocuses a theme in the same way that a passive defocuses an agent), it can even be agentive.

terms, symptomatic of primary focal prominence. In theme-oriented languages, where prominence and semantic role are less clearly distinguished to begin with, grammatical behaviors tend to be less consistently attributable to a single factor. For our purposes, the most important thing is to realize that languages employ different strategies—and different mixtures of strategies—in regard to this basic aspect of clausal organization. Yet they all have a common conceptual basis, emerging from the interplay of focal prominence, the inherent cognitive salience of agent and theme, as well as some combination of agent and theme orientation.

These two competing strategies have the consequences shown in figure 11.4(a) and (c). Insofar as agent orientation extends its influence from transitive clauses to intransitives, agents and intransitive themes behave alike grammatically. It is thus a transitive theme, secondary in the sense of not representing the default choice of trajector, which stands out as being different. Conversely, with theme orientation it is a transitive agent that is secondary in this respect and thus stands out as being different. Insofar as this orientation extends its influence, transitive themes behave the same grammatically as intransitive themes. Additionally, there are languages that follow a third basic strategy, shown in figure 11.4(b), where agent and theme orientation are more in balance (Mithun 1991; Velázquez-Castillo 2002). In this type of system, an agent-like participant has the same grammatical behavior in both one-participant and two-participant clauses. A nonagentive theme also behaves alike in both. This consistent correlation between grammatical properties and semantic role calls into question the independent status of focal prominence. Indeed, such languages are often regarded as subjectless (a matter we will return to).

It should not be thought that every language fits neatly into one of three clear-cut types. At best, the idealized schemes in figure 11.4 represent default coding strategies, capturing neither the details of their implementation in a given language nor the full complexity of its clausal structures. Since the strategies are all quite natural, every language probably makes at least some use of each, even if one predominates. In describing a language, they must therefore be considered with respect to individual grammatical phenomena. The natural groupings shown in the diagrams are manifested in various ways: in case marking, the form of pronouns, agreement, verb morphology, and so on. It is common for the grouping evident in one phenomenon to diverge from that observed in others. For example, despite its strong agent orientation, English makes use of the other two schemes in constructions serving to specify the participants of a nominalized verb. A prepositional phrase with *of* specifies either the trajector of a nominalized intransitive verb (e.g. *the sinking of the ship*) or the object of a transitive one (*the sinking of the ship by the pirates*). This is the grouping characteristic of theme orientation. With the preposition *by*, on the other hand, the participant introduced must to some extent be agent-like. In accordance with the agent/theme pattern, this includes both transitive agents and the trajector of agentive intransitives (e.g. *yelling by pirates*) while excluding the thematic trajector of nonagentive intransitives (**sinking by the ship*).

The three basic strategies are most directly evident in case marking. Illustrating the agent-oriented pattern are the Luiseño sentences in (14). The hallmark of this pattern is that transitive and intransitive subjects are marked alike, and a transitive object differently. Here the two subjects, *nawitmal* 'girl' and *'awaal* 'dog', are marked by zero, and the object by the suffix *-i*: *'awaal-i*. The two basic cases in an agent-oriented system are traditionally referred to as **nominative** (NOM) and **accusative** (ACC). As seen in Luiseño, with nominative/accusative case it is typical for nominative to be zero, with only accusative marked explicitly. This marking is iconic since zero indicates a starting point: the origin of the natural path based on energy flow. Only an additional focused participant, encountered farther along this path, is overtly flagged as such.

(14)   (a) *Nawitmal   'awaal-i   'ar-ax.*   'The girl kicked the dog.'

         girl(NOM)   dog-ACC   kick-PAST

     (b) *'awaal   xaar-ax.*   'The dog growled.'

         dog(NOM)   growl-PAST

The Samoan sentences in (15) illustrate a theme-oriented case-marking system. In this type of pattern a transitive agent is specially marked, here by the particle *e* in *e le teine*. The theme has the same marking, namely zero, whether the clause is transitive or intransitive. The two basic cases in such a system are traditionally called **ergative** (ERG) and **absolutive** (ABS). While ergative case is marked overtly, the absolutive is virtually always zero. This marking too is iconic, since zero indicates a starting point: the origin of the natural path based on conceptual autonomy. Only another focused participant, encountered farther along this path, is explicitly marked as such.

(15)   (a) *'ua   tipi e   le   teine le   ufi.*   'The girl cut the yam.'
         PERF   cut ERG   the   girl   the   yam(ABS)

     (b) *'ua   oti   le   teine.*   'The girl died.'
         PERF   die   the   girl(ABS)

The contrast between nominative/accusative and ergative/absolutive case marking comes down to whether the single focal participant of an intransitive clause is marked like the agent of a transitive clause or like the theme. In the third type of system, it is not consistently marked in either fashion. Instead, as shown in figure 11.4(b), an agentive participant patterns like a transitive agent, a nonagentive one like a transitive theme. Illustration is provided by Eastern Pomo, a language of northern California (McClendon 1978). Here case is realized morphologically either with a suffix or by the form of a pronoun. In (16)–(17), we observe that the agentive form of 'I' is *háa* and the thematic form is *wí*, whether the clause is transitive or intransitive. Thus *háa* in (16)(b) indicates that the speaker has the same semantic role as subject of 'go' that it does in (16)(a), as subject of 'kill'. Likewise, *wí* in (17)(b) indicates that the speaker has the same semantic role as subject of 'sneeze' that it does in (17)(a), as object of 'bite'.

(16)   (a) *Háa   míip-al   šaak'a.*   (b) *Háa   wáduukìya.*
         I:AG   he-TH   kill   I:AG   go
         'I killed him.'   'I'm going.'

(17) (a) *Xáas-uulàa*   *wí*   *kookʰóya.*   (b) *Wí*   *'éčkiya.*

rattlesnake-AG   I:TH   bite   I:TH   sneeze

'Rattlesnake bit me.'   'I sneezed.'

While nominative, accusative, ergative, and absolutive are basically names for cases, as just defined, the terms are often extended to other grammatical phenomena. Linguists thus speak of nominative/accusative organization (or just "accusativity") for any phenomenon in which transitive and intransitive subjects behave alike, in contrast to a transitive object. They likewise speak of ergative/absolutive organization (or "ergativity") whenever transitive and intransitive themes behave alike, in contrast to a transitive agent. The terms are even extended to languages: English is thus an accusative language, and Dyirbal an ergative one. This latter extension is problematic, however, since a language as a whole does not exhibit either nominative/accusative or ergative/absolutive organization. There is at best a predominance of one or the other pattern.

Often these patterns are manifested not through nominal case but in the form of the verb. For instance, Classical Nahuatl (the language of the Aztecs) shows nominative/accusative organization in the verb prefixes specifying the person and number of clausal subject and object. We see this in (18), where *ni-* indicates a first-person singular subject, regardless of transitivity (the object form is *neeč-* 'me').

(18) (a) *Ni-k-neki.*   'I want it.'   (b) *Ni-miki-s.*   'I will die.'

1s-3s-want   1s-die-FUT

By contrast, verb prefixation in Lakhota (a Siouan language) follows an agent/theme pattern (Dahlstrom 1983). Thus the agentive form of 'I' is *wa*, and the thematic form is *ma*, whether the verb is transitive or intransitive:[20]

(19) (a) *Wičha-wa-gnayã.*   (b) *Wa-lowã.*

3p:TH-1s:AG-trick   1s:AG-sing

'I tricked them.'   'I sing.'

(20) (a) *Ma-ya-gnayã-pi.*   (b) *Ma-hãska.*

1s:TH-2:AG-trick-PL   1s:TH-tall

'You PL tricked me.'   'I'm tall.'

Luiseño nicely illustrates a mixture of clausal strategies. As seen in (21), it exhibits nominative/accusative organization with respect to three basic phenomena. The first is case, as noted previously. While objects take the suffix *-i*, subjects are

---

[20] Actually, the agent/theme pattern holds only for second person and first-person singular. Even for a single grammatical phenomenon, like case or verb prefixation, it is common for behavior to be "split" between different patterns (FCG2: §9.2.4).

unmarked for case irrespective of transitivity.[21] Next, the grounding clitic that follows the initial word "agrees" with a subject but never an object. Thus the first singular =*n* agrees with *noo* 'I' in (a)–(b), while the third singular =*up* agrees with *hunwut* 'bear' in (c), and the third plural =*pum* with *hunwutum* 'bears' in (d). Finally, the tense-marking suffix on the verb also matches the subject in number, not the object. Hence the singular ending -*q* occurs in (a)–(c), and the plural ending -*an* in (d), for only in (d) is the subject plural.

(21) (a) *Noo=n   hunwut-i   moqna-q.*   'I kill the bear.'
          I=1s:PRES   bear-ACC   kill:SG-PRES:SG

      (b) *Noo=n   hunwut-um-i   qe'ee-q.*   'I kill the bears.'
          I=1s:PRES   bear-PL-ACC   kill:PL-PRES:SG

      (c) *Hunwut=up   pokwa-q*   'The bear runs.'
          bear=3s:PRES   run:SG-PRES:SG

      (d) *Hunwut-um=pum   ngoora-an.*   'The bears run.'
          bear-PL=3p:PRES   run:PL-PRES:PL

Nevertheless, in one basic respect Luiseño clauses follow an ergative/absolutive pattern. A number of common verbs are suppletive, having different stems for singular and plural. We note in (21) that for 'kill' the singular *moqna* alternates with the plural *qe'ee*, while for 'run' the respective stems are *pokwa* and *ngoora*. Whether a verb is singular or plural depends on whether a participant is. But which participant? With intransitives, there is only one focused participant, so the verb agrees with it. The key, then, is whether a transitive verb reflects the number of its subject or its object. It turns out to be the object, as shown in (21)(b). Despite its strong agent orientation, therefore, in verb suppletion Luiseño exhibits the pattern characteristic of theme orientation: the number of the verb is determined by the theme (intransitive subject or transitive object).

11.2.5 Universality

An important factor in the meaning of relational expressions is the degree of prominence conferred on their participants. At a given level of organization, the trajector and landmark of a profiled relationship are the participants accorded primary and secondary focal prominence. These two degrees of focal prominence are offered in CG as schematic characterizations of subject and object. A subject is a nominal expression that specifies the trajector of a profiled relationship. An object (when there is one) specifies the landmark.

How universal are these notions? Does every language have clause-level subjects and objects? These issues are fraught with controversy. The universality of subjects

---

[21] Strictly speaking, case is registered on pronouns by their form, e.g. *noo* 'I' vs. *ney* 'me'. However, this too follows a nominative/accusative pattern (*noo* being used for both transitive and intransitive subjects).

is often questioned—and rightly so, if by "subject" one means an English-type subject, defined in terms of agent orientation and a consistent correlation with numerous grammatical behaviors. However, the conceptual definition proposed in CG casts the issue in a different light. It is not impossible, and arguably not unlikely, that every language makes at least some use of primary focal prominence (trajector status) at the clause level. If so, English-type subjects represent just one way in which it can be manifested. Let us briefly look at some other possibilities.

The grammatical import of focal prominence is most apparent when numerous properties are consistently associated with a clausal element that does not instantiate any single semantic role. While these properties are prototypically linked to an agent (in a language like English) or a theme (in a language like Dyirbal), their extension to other roles indicates the need for a separate descriptive construct. The status of such a construct is often questioned for theme-oriented languages, where grammatical behaviors tend not to be controlled by any one factor, and especially for agent/theme languages, where the controlling factor is evidently semantic role itself.

Samoan exemplifies a theme-oriented language where the need for a separate construct is not clear-cut. Its strong theme orientation is apparent in a number of ways. For one thing, case marking follows the ergative/absolutive pattern:

(22) *Na   opo   e   le   tama   le   teine.*   'The boy hugged the girl.'
     PAST   hug   ERG   the   boy   the   girl(ABS)

Moreover, a two-participant verb like *opo* 'hug' allows the omission of an agent but requires the specification of a theme. One can therefore say *Na opo le teine* 'The girl (got) hugged' but not **Na opo e le tama* 'The boy hugged'. We further noted, in (1), that an intransitive clause describing motion toward a goal provides the structural model for clauses coding perception and other mental contact.

This structural prominence of themes can be taken as symptomatic of their conceptual prominence. But if the distinguished element is always a theme, we have no basis for invoking the notion trajector as an independent construct—the phenomena can be described just by referring to semantic role. We might still interpret the theme's special status as being indicative of primary focal prominence. I would argue, in fact, that this yields the most coherent overall view of clausal structure. But we obviously need more tangible evidence for positing focal prominence as a separate factor. The question, then, is whether Samoan has any relevant phenomena that are not controlled by themes per se. Are there grammatical behaviors—among those commonly associated with subjects—that are better described in terms of a notion like trajector?

A likely candidate is "verb agreement", exemplified in (23)–(24).[22] In the four sentences cited, *ali'i* 'chief' is consistently the agent (hence marked for ergative case), and *'avefe'au* 'messenger' is the theme (with the zero marking of absolutive case).

---

[22] A phenomenon known as "quantifier float" behaves analogously. It is so called because a quantifier "floats" away from the noun it quantifies and appears adjacent to the verb. An example from English occurs in the following sentence: **The Samoan data** is **all** from Cook (1988, 1993a, 1993b, 1999), who has investigated many aspects of Samoan clause structure from a CG standpoint.

(23) (a) *Na   tu-tuli   e   le   ali'i 'avefe'au.* (b) *Na   tu-tuli   'avefe'au   e   le   ali'i.*
         PAST PL-send ERG the chief messenger   PAST PL-send messenger ERG the chief
         'The chief sent the messengers.'   'The messengers were sent by the chief.'

(24) (a) *Na   tu-tuli   e   ali'i le 'avefe'au.* (b) *Na   tuli le 'avefe'au   e   ali'i.*
         PAST PL-send ERG chief the messenger   PAST send the messenger ERG chief
         'The chiefs sent the messenger.'   'The messenger was sent by the chiefs.'

What varies is whether these nominals are singular or plural, as well as their relative order. Number is effectively signaled by the presence or absence of *le*, which indicates the higher degree of definiteness characteristic of a singular referent. Thus in (23) the agent is construed as singular (*le ali'i* 'chief') and the mover as plural (*'avefe'au* 'messengers'), while in (24) we have the reverse (*ali'i* 'chiefs'; *le 'avefe'au* 'messenger'). With respect to word order, agent precedes theme in the (a) examples and follows it in the (b) examples. The key point is that the plurality of a theme (*'avefe'au* 'messengers') is reflected by a plural verb regardless of word order, so both verbs in (23) are plural. By contrast, the plurality of an agent (*ali'i* 'chiefs') is marked on the verb only when the agent nominal directly follows it; the verb is thus plural in (24)(a) but singular in (24)(b). How can this difference be accounted for?

The analysis I suggest recognizes a disparity between the processes profiled by the lexical verb and by the clause as a whole (§11.1.3). The verb itself conforms to Samoan's general theme orientation by choosing the theme as trajector. We can also posit a basic grammatical construction in which (i) a verb combines with a nominal, (ii) the two are integrated phonologically by placing the nominal directly after the verb, and (iii) the nominal referent is focused as trajector at the composite-structure level. This construction has two main variants, differing in regard to which of the verb's participants serves as elaboration site for its combination with the nominal. It is typically the theme that functions as e-site. In this case, the theme is trajector at both the verb level (lexically determined) and the clause level (grammatically determined). This results in the (b) examples. However, there is also a secondary pattern in which the nominal elaborates the verb's schematic agent. This produces the (a) examples, where the verb-level and clause-level trajectors are different: theme and agent, respectively. We can then make the generalization that a plural verb indicates the plurality of the processual trajector, irrespective of level. Only in (24)(b) is the plural participant neither a verb-level nor a clause-level trajector, and only in this sentence is the verb not marked for plurality.

A more straightforward manifestation of focal prominence is found in a well-known feature of Tagalog.[23] Though basically theme oriented, Tagalog has an overtly marked way of calling attention to a clausal participant representing a particular semantic role. The examples in (25) respectively highlight four such roles: agent,

---

[23] The classic description is due to Schachter (1976, 1977). Ironically, Schachter was arguing that Tagalog does not have subjects. He was of course thinking in terms of English-type subjects (not the schematic CG characterization).

theme, location (LOC), and beneficiary (BEN). The choice is doubly marked. For one thing, the focused element is preceded by the particle *ang*, which occurs in lieu of either an article (*ng*) or a preposition (*sa* or *para sa*). In addition, the verb assumes distinct forms to indicate agent focus (AF), theme focus (TF), location focus (LF), beneficiary focus (BF), and so on. Theorists have not known what to make of this phenomenon, since the focused participant is neither a subject (in the classic sense) nor a discourse-level topic. For me it is simply the trajector (TR), hence a subject as defined schematically in CG. What we observe in (25) is the spotlight of focal prominence being directed, in turn, at different onstage elements.[24]

(25) (a) **Mag**-*salis*   **ang** **babae** *ng*   *bigas* *sa*   *sako* *para sa* *bata.*

       AF-will:take:out TR   woman ART rice   LOC   sack   BEN   child

       'The woman will take some rice out of {a/the} sack for {a/the} child.'

    (b) *Aalis*-**in**   *ng*   *babae* **ang** **bigas** *sa*   *sako* *para sa* *bata.*

       will:take:out-TF ART woman TR   rice   LOC   sack   BEN   child

       '{A/The} woman will take the rice out of {a/the} sack for {a/the} child.'

    (c) *Aalis*-**an**   *ng*   *babae* *ng*   *bigas* **ang** **sako** *para sa* *bata.*

       will:take:out-LF ART woman ART rice   TR   sack   BEN   child

       '{A/The} woman will take some rice out of the sack for {a/the} child.'

    (d) **Ipag**-*salis*   *ng*   *babae* *ng*   *bigas* *sa*   *sako* **ang** **bata.**

       BF-will:take:out ART woman ART rice   LOC   sack   TR   child

       '{A/The} woman will take some rice out of {a/the} sack for the child.'

The nonuniversality of subjects has been argued most strongly on the basis of agent/theme languages.[25] Such an argument is made by Chafe (1994: 150) in regard to Seneca (an Iroquoian language). Seneca verbs have two sets of person-marking prefixes. These are not like the subject-marking and object-marking affixes found in many languages (e.g. Classical Nahuatl, in (18)), since only one prefix occurs even when the verb has two participants, and since the prefix chosen can be from either set whether the verb is transitive or intransitive. Hence the marking does not follow the nominative/accusative pattern of figure 11.4(a), but rather the agent/theme pattern of figure 11.4(b). For example, the prefix *(y)e-* specifies third-person female for an agent-like participant in both the transitive *ye-nóǫhgwa'* 'she loves it' and the intransitive *wa'-é-khǫǫni'* 'she cooked'. Similarly, the prefix *(a)go-* indicates a third-person female theme in both the transitive *go-nóǫhgwa'* 'it loves her' and the intransitive *wa'-ágo-hda't* 'she got full'. With a transitive, whether the agent or theme is made explicit depends on which participant the speaker is currently talking

---

[24] Note as well that the focused element is definite (as subjects tend to be), whereas the others may be interpreted as indefinite.

[25] These are usually called "agent/patient" languages, the term "patient" being equivalent to what is here called "theme".

about. Hence both *ye-nǫ́ǫhgwa'* 'she loves (it)' and *go-nǫ́ǫhgwa'* '(it) loves her' indicate that a female is under discussion.

It is clear, then, that the distinction marked by the choice of prefix is agent/theme as opposed to subject/object. It is equally clear that Seneca does not have English-type subjects. It might be argued, however, that a Seneca clause does have a subject, characterized abstractly as primary focal participant. In a given clause, one participant is indeed made salient in a way that subjects commonly are: by being referenced on the verb. I thus suggest that this participant be identified as clausal trajector. On this account, both *(y)e-* and *(a)go-* indicate a third-person female trajector, and further specify it as being agentive or thematic. It would seem to follow that a two-participant verb makes no intrinsic specification for trajector. It is only the prefix that indicates which participant—as determined by discourse salience—has focal prominence at the clausal level.[26]

Whether every language has subjects (in the abstract sense) remains an open question. From the CG standpoint, it makes no essential difference whether the systematic use of primary focal prominence represents an absolute universal or merely a strong universal tendency. In either case, the extent and details of its structural manifestation vary greatly. I suspect that it does have some role in every language, but that is only a suspicion. The universality of objects is even less apparent. At least in agent-oriented languages, there is usually good evidence for positing two focused participants. But if the grammatical role of trajectors is sometimes quite limited (as in Samoan), that of landmarks is even more so. It is not inconceivable that primary focal prominence is systematically exploited in all languages but secondary focal prominence only in some.

11.3 Clause Types

Clauses can be sorted into types with respect to various dimensions of linguistic structure. The clause types known as declarative, interrogative, and imperative are grounded in particular speech acts (stating, questioning, and ordering). Special clause types are also devoted to information structure, notably as ways of indicating topic or focus.[27] But at present our interest lies with distinctions based on the choice of subject and object. Beyond the clauses deemed canonical, a language provides a substantial array of constructions to accommodate discourse needs and varied circumstances.

11.3.1 Voice

If either agent or theme orientation predominates in a language, there has to be some provision for those occasions when the speaker wishes not to focus the participant

---

[26] Tagalog might be comparable, except that there are more options (as seen in (25)) and the trajector need not be the discourse topic.

[27] For example, the special word order of *Squid she won't eat* establishes *squid* as a local topic. In the "pseudo-cleft" construction, the element following *be* is the focus: *What she won't eat is squid.*

in question. The options made available are traditionally referred to as **voice**. In an agent-oriented system, the default alignment is called **active voice**; the alternative (with focused theme) is called **passive voice**. In a theme-oriented system, an **antipassive** construction provides an alternative to the default alignment (which has no standard term).

There are different kinds of passive constructions. Commonly, and perhaps most straightforwardly, passives are formed through verbal derivation. In Hopi, for example, the suffix *-iwa* derives a passive verb from an active one: *ngu'a* 'catch' vs. *ngu'-iwa* 'be caught'. Whereas the active stem confers trajector and landmark status on the agent and theme, respectively, the passive verb selects the theme as its only focused participant. Thus a clause headed by an active verb has both subject and object nominals, as in (26)(a), while a passive clause like (26)(b) has only a subject.

(26) (a) *Pam   tsiro-t   ngu'a.*   (b) *Tsiro   ngu'-iwa.*

       he   bird-ACC   catch   bird   catch-PASS

       'He caught the bird.'   'The bird was caught.'

Figure 11.5(a) describes the formation of a passive verb. The arrow represents a transitive, two-participant interaction, and ellipses (...) indicate schematicity. The verb stem (V) profiles a specific interaction, with the more agentive participant focused as trajector and the more thematic one as landmark. The passive morpheme (PASS) is itself a verb, for it too profiles an interactive process. By itself, however, PASS evokes this process only schematically, selecting the theme as its only (hence its primary) focal participant. The specific and schematic processes are identified by means of the correspondences shown. As is usual for a derivational element, PASS is the profile determinant and imposes its construal on the composite expression. The derived verb is thus a blend combining the specific content of V with the trajector choice imposed by PASS.

The examples in (27), from Greenlandic Eskimo (Woodbury 1977), illustrate an antipassive construction.[28] In sentence (a), representing the default alignment for

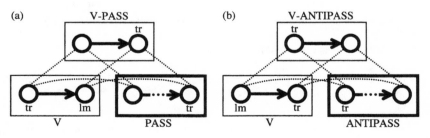

FIGURE 11.5

<hr />

[28] For sake of discussion, the absolutive nominal is presumed to be the trajector (Manning 1996). The final suffix on the verb marks indicative mood.

a theme-oriented language, the trajector is the absolutive *niqi* 'meat'; despite the English translation, the ergative *arna-p* 'woman' has the secondary status of landmark. Imposing the alternative alignment is the antipassive suffix *-nnig*. As shown in figure 11.5(b), its effect on the verb stem it combines with is to shift trajector status from the theme to the agent. Since the theme is left unfocused, the agentive trajector takes absolutive case (zero) by virtue of being the only (hence the most theme-like) focused participant. If necessary, the theme can still be expressed periphrastically, as the object of the instrumental *-mik* 'with'. This is analogous to the periphrastic specification of a passive agent (e.g. *The glass was broken by Floyd*).

(27)   (a) *Arna-p*   *niqi*   *niri-vaa.*   'The woman ate the meat.'

         woman-ERG   meat(ABS)   eat-INDIC

       (b) *Arnaq*   *niqi-mik*   *niri-nnig-puq.*   'The woman ate (some of) the meat.'

         woman(ABS)   meat-INSTR   eat-ANTIPASS-INDIC

That they are specified only periphrastically (if at all) indicates that passive agents and antipassive themes lack focal prominence. This makes perfect sense if (anti)passive constructions are viewed as a means to deny them the focal prominence they would otherwise have. The function served by a passive—that of **defocusing** an agent (Shibatani 1985)—is useful in a variety of circumstances. The agent's identity may be unknown, irrelevant, or best concealed (as when Floyd merely says *The glass was broken*). Often the agent is generalized or undifferentiated (e.g. *The environment is being seriously degraded*). Whatever the reason, defocusing the agent leaves the theme as the only, and thus the primary, focal participant.

Subtly different from passives are **impersonal** constructions. Like a passive, e.g.(26)(b), an impersonal leaves the agentive participant unspecified. This itself amounts to a kind of defocusing: being implicit and unidentified, the agent has no real cognitive salience. But unlike a passive, an impersonal makes no adjustment in trajector/landmark alignment. The primary spotlight of focal prominence is still directed at the agent, albeit vacuously, for there is nothing specific to illuminate. The practical effect is that the theme remains a landmark, illuminated with just the secondary spotlight, despite being the only overtly specified participant. Thus in (28), from Hopi, the patient *taaqa* 'man' takes the object-marking suffix *-t*. The agentive trajector is not specifically identified, although the verbal suffix *-ya* (used with plural subjects) suggests it is not a single individual.

(28)   *Taaqa-t*   *niina-ya.*   '[They] killed the man.'

       man-ACC   kill-PL:SUBJ

When one participant is left unspecified, the other becomes more salient just through the absence of competition. On the other hand, augmenting the salience of one participant diminishes that of others (in relative terms), even when they are fully specified. We have already seen examples of voice distinctions based on this strategy, e.g. the Samoan alternation in (23)–(24). The agent and theme are both fully specified, and have the same form, whichever functions as clausal subject. More striking are the multiple voice options in Tagalog, exemplified in (25). Regardless of which clausal element is put in focus—agent, theme, location, or beneficiary—the others can all still be specified overtly in the usual manner.

In addition to active and passive, many languages have constructions tradition-ally referred to as **middle voice**.[29] Since the term applies to diverse constructions, and in some cases to elaborate families of constructions, any single characteriza-tion is bound to be oversimplified. Still, these varied phenomena do have a center of gravity for which the term "middle" seems appropriate. The configuration most typical for a middle construction is sketched in figure 11.6(b). It is readily seen as being intermediate between a canonical transitive clause in the active voice, shown in diagram (a), and an absolute intransitive, shown in (c). An active transitive clause, such as *I opened the door*, evokes and profiles both an agent's exertion of force and the thematic process it brings about. At the opposite extreme, an intransitive like *The door opened* construes a thematic process in absolute fashion, without refer-ence to the force or agent that induces it. A typical middle is intermediate because it does invoke causation but leaves it unprofiled. In *The door opened easily*, the adverb *easily* implies the willful effort of an agent. Nevertheless, only the theme is made explicit and only the thematic process is profiled.

Although middles resemble passives to some extent, the two constitute distinct alternatives to active transitives. The similarity, seen by comparing diagrams (b) and (d), is that each invokes an agentive process but selects the theme as trajector. The difference is that an English passive designates the entire agent-theme interaction, whereas the middle profiles only what happens to the theme. There is also a func-tional contrast. The primary function of a passive is to provide an alternative to the default agent orientation of canonical transitives. By contrast, middles function as alternatives to both active transitives and absolute intransitives: *The door opened eas-ily* can be viewed equally well as reduced in agentivity vis-à-vis *I opened the door* or as heightened in agentivity vis-à-vis *The door opened*.

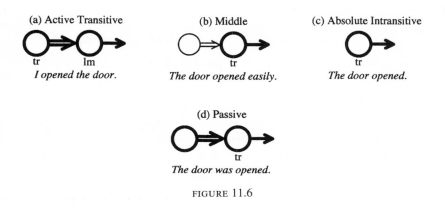

(a) Active Transitive

tr   lm
I opened the door.

(b) Middle

tr
The door opened easily.

(c) Absolute Intransitive

tr
The door opened.

(d) Passive

tr
The door was opened.

FIGURE 11.6

---

[29] For extensive treatments from a cognitive linguistic perspective, see Kemmer 1993, Maldonado 1999, and Manney 2000.

This ambivalence has nicely been shown for Spanish by Maldonado (1988). On the one hand, the Spanish middle—marked by *se*—provides an agentless alternative for an otherwise transitive verb:[30]

(29) (a) *José rompió el vaso.*   'José broke the glass.'

   (b) *El vaso se rompió.*   'The glass broke.'

(30) (a) *El ratero ahogó al anciano.*   'The thief drowned the old man.'

   (b) *El anciano se ahogó.*   'The old man drowned.'

On the other hand, the middle construction adds a force-dynamic component to a thematic process whose construal would otherwise be absolute. For instance, (31)(a) is an absolute intransitive, since the only force involved—the ever-present pull of gravity—is taken for granted. The middle in (31)(b) is nonagentive but nonetheless force-dynamic, at least by comparison. It reflects the normal expectation that a person will exercise the control required to maintain an upright posture. The middle verb *caerse* 'fall down' portrays the event as resulting from a disruption of the balance of forces that maintain it, allowing gravity to prevail.

(31) (a) *La lluvia está cayendo.*   'The rain is falling.'

   (b) *Ricardo se cayó.*   'Ricardo fell down.'

The force implied by a middle need not be physical or even objectively construed. It may just be the subjectively experienced force involved in apprehending an event that runs counter to desire or usual expectations. Thus (32)(a) describes a normal occurrence in a basketball game: after a made basket, the ball is expected to descend (the net is open at the bottom for a reason). But if a ball is placed on a table, it is probably expected to remain there. So in (32)(b) *se* registers the disruption of a stable situation expected to persist.

(32) (a) *La pelota cayó de la canasta.*   'The ball fell down from the basket.'

   (b) *La pelota se cayó de la mesa.*   'The ball fell off the table.'

11.3.2 Nonparticipant Subjects

An archetypal conception with extensive manifestations in clause structure is the organization of a scene in terms of setting, locations, and participants. These notions figure in the canonical event model, as well as the default coding patterns based on

---

[30] The form varies to indicate the person and number of the clausal trajector (*se* is the third-person form). As is common for middles, the marking is the same as in reflexives, where a single participant plays the role of both trajector and landmark. (Thus (30)(b) can also be interpreted as a reflexive meaning 'The old man drowned himself'.) What reflexives and middles have in common is the failure of agentive and thematic roles to be explicitly manifested by distinct participants (Kemmer 1993).

it (fig. 11.2). Perhaps most typical is the pattern exemplified in (33). Trajector and landmark status are usually conferred on participants, coded by nominals (in this case, *Floyd* and *glasses*). By contrast, settings and locations are most commonly introduced by means of relational expressions. Here the global setting is specified by a prepositional phrase external to the clause (as indicated by "comma intonation"), and a location is specified by one internal to the clause. As setting, the kitchen hosts the entire clausal event (that of Floyd stacking glasses on the counter), whereas the counter is merely the location of the glasses.[31]

(33)   *In the kitchen, Floyd was stacking glasses on the counter.*

      SETTING   PARTIC   PARTIC LOCATION

The grammatical structure defining a particular type of clause embodies a particular way of viewing situations. Collectively, factors such as maximal scope, immediate scope, profile, trajector, and landmark constitute a kind of "framework" for apprehending conceptual content and thereby shaping it into linguistic meanings. For a given array of content, different meanings result depending on how this viewing framework is aligned with it. The usual arrangement is for trajector and landmark to align with participants, as in (33). This is just one option, however. Not at all uncommon are alternative alignments in which focal prominence falls on a setting or location. The difference may not at first be apparent, as the distinction between participants and settings/locations is often covert; nonetheless, it has grammatical consequences that allow its detection.

In terms of their form, for example, (34)(a)–(c) appear to be transitive clauses. Each contains two nominals, which appear in the regular subject and object positions (cf. *Floyd broke the glass*). They do not behave like transitives in all respects, however. In (34)(a′)–(c′), we observe that they resist passivization. Since the ability to passivize correlates with transitivity (at least in English), their failure to do so suggests that they actually lack this property.

(34)   (a) *The envelope contained his will.*   (a′) **His will was contained by the envelope.*

      (b) *The lecturer finally reached the end.* (b′) **The end was finally reached by the lecturer.*

      (c) *The train is approaching Chicago.*   (c′) **Chicago is being approached by the train.*

The form of a clause is not itself enough to make it transitive. The key factor in transitivity is conceptual in nature—roughly, the degree of approximation to a canonical agent-patient interaction (Hopper and Thompson 1980; Rice 1987a, 1987b). It is therefore quite relevant that, in the archetypal conception, participants **interact** with

---

[31] This is the default interpretation based on general knowledge, but it is not the only one possible. For instance, Floyd might have been standing on the counter in order to stack the glasses in a cabinet above.

(a) Transitive   (b) Non-Transitive   (c) Non-Transitive

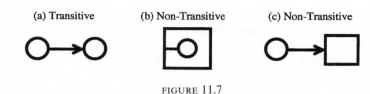

FIGURE 11.7

one another but merely **occupy** locations and settings. A clause can thus be transitive only if its trajector and landmark are both participants. But this is not the case in (34). In each clause, one of the two focal elements is construed as a location: the trajector of *contain* represents the location of its landmark; conversely, with *reach* and *approach* the landmark is the final or projected location of the trajector. Being nontransitive, these clauses lack passive alternants.[32]

In figure 11.7, circles represent participants and boxes stand for settings or locations. Diagram (a) is an abstract depiction of a transitive configuration, where two participants interact (usually asymmetrically). Configurations (b) and (c) are nontransitive because one focal element (either trajector or landmark) is a nonparticipant.[33] This is so whether the participant simply occupies the location, as in diagram (b), or moves with respect to it, as in (c). Despite their grammatical significance, these conceptual contrasts do not entail different syntactic forms. They can all be realized by a clause consisting of subject, verb, and object, in that order.

Numerous grammatical constructions align the clausal viewing framework in such a way that a setting or location is focused as trajector. An example is the construction in (35), which portrays a location as being suffused with activity, making it the locus of an auditory or visual sensation (Dowty 2000). These expressions illustrate a disparity between verb-level and clause-level trajector, for it is actually the insects that *buzz*, the fireworks that *explode*, the shoppers that *bustle* (whatever that is), and the fleas that *crawl*. There being no derivational element, the construction itself shifts primary focal prominence to the encompassing location. It thus portrays the location as hosting the activity, as well as exhibiting the associated perceptual property.

(35)   (a) *The garden is buzzing with insects.*

       (b) *The whole sky exploded with fireworks.*

       (c) *The streets were bustling with shoppers.*

       (d) *My cat is crawling with fleas.*

---

[32] Transitivity depends on how a situation is construed. Under a force-dynamic construal, *contain* is transitive: *The crowd was contained by the security guards.* Similarly, *approach* is transitive when construed in relation to a social interaction: *She was approached by a stranger.*

[33] If I sometimes refer to trajector and landmark as primary and secondary focal **participants**, I am speaking loosely (the distinction between participants and settings/locations not being relevant to the point at hand). Strictly speaking, trajector and landmark should be described as primary and secondary focal **elements**.

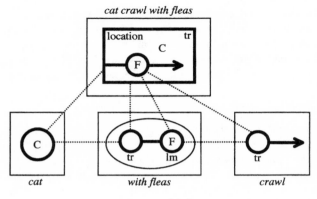

FIGURE 11. 8

Figure 11.8 depicts the relevant aspects of (35)(d). While cats are normally participants, here my cat is merely construed as hosting the fleas' activity. They are connected via the preposition *with*, which profiles a relationship of accompaniment.[34] Correspondences identify its trajector with *cat* and its landmark (*fleas*) with the trajector of *crawl*. The process profiled at the composite-structure level represents a blend of the verbal and prepositional relationships: it inherits its processual nature from *crawl* and its choice of trajector from the *with*-phrase. The profiled process thus centers on the role of this trajector as a location for the fleas and their crawling.

A similar disparity between verb-level and clause-level trajector is observed in (36), where the subject is a spatial or temporal setting:

(36)   (a) *This stadium has seen some thrilling contests.*

       (b) *The last few years have witnessed some major changes.*

A verb like *see* or *witness* has the basic organization sketched in figure 11.9(a): it profiles a perceptual interaction, with the viewer focused as trajector. In contrast, the construction in (36) abstracts away from any particular viewer by way of shifting trajector status to the global setting. It thus portrays the setting as hosting the occur-

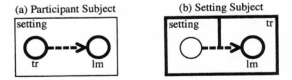

FIGURE 11.9

[34] More precisely, *with* profiles a reference-point relationship (fig. 3.14) such that the landmark is found in the trajector's dominion (shown as an ellipse).

rences specified by the object nominal, while indicating secondarily that anyone in the setting could have viewed them. Since a viewer is invoked in only generalized fashion, it remains implicit and is quite nonsalient.

This setting-subject construction is an instance of the configuration in figure 11.7(b). The sentences in (36) are thus nontransitive, hence they do not readily passivize:

(37)   (a) *Some thrilling contests have been seen by this stadium.

    (b) *Some major changes have been witnessed by the last few years.

From a functional perspective, passive and setting-subject constructions are mutually exclusive because each represents a distinct alternative to the canonical alignment—different ways of reorienting the clausal viewing framework so that primary focal prominence falls on something other than an agent. Both alternatives are natural. The motivation for theme orientation, characteristic of passives, has already been discussed (§11.2.3). And while a setting tends to be nonsalient owing to its all-encompassing nature, this very property provides a rationale for choosing it as subject. A trajector is the starting point with respect to the natural path of focal prominence. As such, a clausal trajector is the initial point of access for purposes of building up to a full conception of the profiled process. An obvious strategy for doing so is to start with the global setting and then "zoom in" to what occurs there.

Closely akin to setting subjects is the *it* that appears in expressions like (38) (a)–(b). Their relationship is suggested by the fact that *it*-clauses do not passivize, even when they are transitive in form (with a nominal in object position, directly after the verb):

(38)   (a) *It's raining big drops.*   (a′) *Big drops are being rained (by it).

    (b) *It seems that he lied to us.*   (b′) *That he lied to us is seemed (by it).

Though usually considered meaningless (a syntactic "dummy"), this *it* is better regarded as being maximally nonspecific in its reference (Bolinger 1977: ch. 4). We might describe it (admittedly impressionistically) as designating the "scope of awareness" invoked as the basis for what follows. In undifferentiated fashion, *it* refers to the full range of circumstances supporting this assessment. Hence *it*-clauses mirror the zooming-in strategy of setting-subject constructions. They are more abstract, however, for instead of being a well-delimited spatial or temporal region, the starting point encompasses any aspect of the conceptualizer's global awareness that might be deemed relevant. With a verb like *rain*, there is of course the potential to interpret *it* as referring to the surrounding atmospheric environment. Still, this is only a special case and is probably too narrow even for such examples.

11.3.3 Objects

In an agent-oriented language, an object is typically a theme. If patients are prototypical (e.g. *Floyd broke the glass*), the other thematic roles are also quite central: mover (*She threw it*), experiencer (*He tickled her*), and zero (*I admired it*). But these are not the only semantic roles of nominals that appear to be objects in terms of their form and (to some extent) their grammatical behavior. In *The train approached the station*, for example, the nominal following the verb is a location rather than a participant. Also nonthematic and noninteractive are the postverbal nominals in expressions like *They stayed the night*, *It cost a fortune*, and *It weighs three pounds*. While these are not traditionally considered objects, they might well be subsumed under a schematic characterization based on secondary focal prominence. This would also cover the ergative agent in two-participant clauses where the absolutive theme is analyzed as subject (as in (27)(a)).

The term **object** is used here very generally, for any nominal landmark (just as **subject** is used for a nominal trajector). Cases that approximate the prototype can then be distinguished by the traditional label **direct object**. The referent of a direct object nominal is thus the final participant on a profiled action chain—either a physical action chain or an interaction construed as being abstractly analogous to one (§11.2.2). If a subject is typically the **head** of such a chain, an object is typically the **tail**.

As in the case of subjects, the choice of object is often flexible. For example, with the same physical action I can either *tie **my shoe***, *tie **my shoelace***, or *tie **a bow** in my shoelace*. And as with primary focal prominence, shining the secondary spotlight on a given element tends to illuminate as well those facets of the overall relationship that it anchors. I *tie my shoe* in order to secure the shoe on my foot, but I *tie my shoelace* to keep the lace from dragging. Naturally, *tie a bow in my shoelace* highlights the bow's creation and thus diverts attention from the shoe. It does not imply that the shoe is on my foot or even that the lace is in the shoe.

There is also flexibility in how something coded as object is construed. For instance, the start of a marathon might equally well be described by either (39)(a) or (39)(b). But while the object nominals refer to the same five-mile path, these sentences construe it rather differently. In (39)(a), *five miles* serves mainly to specify a distance. Its referent is viewed primarily as a point on a scale of measurement, which can be thought of as an abstract location. Since the object is a nonparticipant, the sentence is nontransitive, so its passive counterpart, (39)(c), is infelicitous. By contrast, *the first five miles* is portrayed in (39)(b) as a spatial path to be traversed—a kind of adversary that has to be conquered.[35] Construed as a participant that the runners interact with, *the first five miles* is not just an object but a direct object, so to some extent (39)(b) is transitive. Its passive counterpart, (39)(d), is thus acceptable.

(39)   (a) *All the racers ran five miles.*

    (b) *All the racers ran the first five miles quite easily.*

    (c) **Five miles were run by all the racers.*

    (d) *The first five miles were run quite easily by all the racers.*

---

[35] These contrasting interpretations exemplify a kind of meaning difference discussed in §2.2.2: one based on the ranking of cognitive domains with respect to degree of activation.

Prototypically, a direct object nominal designates a participant viewed as the tail of a profiled action chain. Objects (i.e. nominals with landmark status) approximate this prototype to varying degrees. How the grammatical behavior characteristic of direct objects extends to less typical cases is determined by the conventions of a given language. Many languages make a structurally significant distinction between **direct** and **indirect** objects. In French, for example, indirect objects are marked by the preposition *à* (as opposed to zero), and in the third person they have different pronominal forms:

(40) (a) *Il voit sa mère.* 'He sees his mother.' (a') *Il la voit.* 'He sees her.'

(b) *Il obéit à sa mère.* 'He obeys his mother.' (b') *Il lui obéit.* 'He obeys her.'

Like French *à*, prepositions marking indirect objects usually mean 'to' or 'at'. In languages with case inflections, the case used for indirect objects is traditionally labeled **dative**.

Semantically, an indirect object is usually an experiencer. This role archetype is the prototype for both indirect objects and dative case. A key to their analysis is thus the ambivalence of experiencers with respect to the agent/theme opposition. On the one hand, experiencer (along with patient, mover, and zero) is a basic thematic role: *She was happy; He fainted; I ache all over.* But as the locus of mental activity, an experiencer is also conceived as the source of a mental path establishing mental contact with another entity: *I'm watching you; He imagined it; She remembers me.* In this latter guise it is readily construed as being agent-like, in the sense of being active, volitional, or responsible for initiating an interaction. We can thus distinguish between a **passive** (or **thematic**) experiencer and one that is **active** (or **initiative**). Their distribution tends to follow an ergative/absolutive pattern. That is, passive experiencers are normally coded by intransitive subjects and transitive objects (*I'm happy; That pleases me*), and active experiencers are coded by transitive subjects (*I like that*).

These are only tendencies, however. *Meditate* is intransitive, but its subject is an active experiencer. And in a two-participant clause, a passive experiencer is not invariably a transitive object. An example is (40)(b), where the object is indirect rather than direct. *Obéir* 'obey' is just one French verb considered intransitive for this reason, some others being *plaire* 'please', *convenir* 'suit', *aider* 'help', *parler* 'speak', and *répondre* 'answer'. The direct-object and indirect-object constructions differ in whether the landmark is construed primarily as a passive or as an active participant. With respect to the profiled interaction, both constructions view it as secondary vis-à-vis the trajector (i.e. "downstream" in the flow of influence). What distinguishes them is that the indirect-object construction accords greater prominence to the landmark's further role as active experiencer (Smith 1993). With the verbs that take indirect objects, the landmark's active role is usually quite apparent. A verb meaning 'obey' evokes a previous (unprofiled) event in which the landmark gives an order. The interaction profiled by 'please' depends as much on the landmark's apprehension of the trajector as on the latter's role as stimulus. Especially common in this construction are verbs of communication, where the landmark not only comprehends the message but alternates with the trajector in the roles of speaker and hearer.[36]

Most commonly, indirect objects cooccur with direct objects as complements of three-participant verbs. The prototype is a verb of transfer, notably one meaning 'give' (cf. Newman 1996). Such a verb has three profiled participants—agent, mover, and recipient—with the agent focused as trajector. What, then, should be chosen as landmark? Both the mover and the recipient are central participants with legitimate claims to focal prominence. It is unsurprising, therefore, that languages have different coding strategies. Perhaps the most typical pattern, exemplified in French, is for the mover and the recipient to be coded as direct and indirect objects, respectively. In (41)(a), the position of *ces livres* 'these books' immediately after the verb, as well as its unmarked form, indicate its status as direct object and clausal landmark. The indirect object *mon frère* 'my brother' is marked by the preposition *à*. Both are complements of the verb by virtue of specifying profiled participants, and both sorts of objects are expressed by preverbal pronouns, as seen in (41)(b). Perhaps the indirect object should be considered a secondary landmark. If not, it is at least quite salient as a profiled participant.

(41) (a) *Je donnerai ces livres à mon frère.*   'I will give these books to my brother.'

    (b) *Je les lui donnerai.*   'I will give them to him.'

There are also languages that follow the opposite strategy, such as Khasi, a Mon-Khmer language of India (Dryer 1986). In (42), we note that the recipient, rather than the mover, behaves analogously to the landmark of a simple transitive clause in taking the object marker *ya*:

(42) (a) *Ka   la   yo"ii   ya   'uu   khlaa.*   'She saw the tiger.'
        she   PAST   see   OBJ   the   tiger

    (b) *'uu   hiikay   ya   nga   ka   ktien   phareng.*   'He teaches me English.'
        he   teach   OBJ   me   the   language   English

English tries to have it both ways.[37] With verbs of transfer, we have the option of either the caused-motion construction, where the mover is focused as landmark, or the ditransitive construction, where the recipient is focused instead:

(43) (a) **Caused-motion:** *She sent some monkeys to the zoo.*

    (b) **Ditransitive:** *She sent the zoo some monkeys.*

---

[36] The precise distribution is conventionally determined: which verbs take indirect objects is something speakers have to learn. Still, they do not just memorize an arbitrary list. The verbs most likely to appear in this construction describe occurrences readily construed as conforming to its meaning. This illustrates the linguistic importance of **motivation**, as opposed to strict **predictability** (§1.2).

[37] Recall §8.3.2, especially the first two diagrams of fig. 8.12.

As evidence for the direct-object status of these nominals, observe that they occur as subjects of the corresponding passives:

(44) (a) *Some monkeys were sent to the zoo.*   (a') **The zoo was sent some monkeys to.*

    (b) *The zoo was sent some monkeys.*   (b') **Some monkeys were sent the zoo.*

These alternate choices of landmark manifest different ways of construing an act of transfer. Focusing the mover highlights the similarity to simple transitive clauses that profile the causation of motion (e.g. *He threw it*). In a sentence like (43)(a), the profiled action chain is that of the subject causing the object to move along a path described by the *to*-phrase. Of course, the movement and the path are not exclusively spatial. Further included is the more abstract conception—metaphorically based on spatial motion—of the landmark leaving the agent's sphere of control (its dominion) and entering the recipient's. Indeed, this abstract movement may be primary and even the only one involved (e.g. *He deeded the ranch to his daughter*). But an act of transfer is a social interaction as well. While the caused-motion construction leaves it in the background, the social aspect comes to the fore in ditransitives. By focusing the recipient, the ditransitive construction highlights not only its role in acquiring and controlling the mover, but also its role in apprehending the transfer and interacting with the agent. The profiled action chain may then consist primarily of the agent engaging the recipient and affecting it via the exchange. Owing to this social component, ditransitives typically require a sentient recipient. *The zoo* can thus refer to either a place or an institution in (43)(a), but only the latter in (43)(b). Unlike a place, an institution is construed metaphorically as a person, hence capable of sentience, ownership, and social engagement.[38]

Some languages have even more variety in the choice of object. Through special verb forms, called **applicatives**, landmark status may be conferred on such nonthematic elements as a location, a beneficiary, or an instrument. All of these are options in the Bantu language Kinyarwanda (Kimenyi 1980). The examples in (45) illustrate the instrumental applicative. In sentence (a), the direct object is *íbárúwa* 'letter', with the instrument *íkárámu* 'pen' introduced periphrastically as the landmark of *n'*- 'with'. Sentence (b) has the same translation, but grammatically it is rather different, since the verbal suffix *-iish* shifts secondary focal prominence to the instrument. *Íkárámu* 'pen' is thus the clausal object (specified nonperiphrastically), leaving *íbárúwa* 'letter' as a profiled but nonfocal participant. The object status of *íkárámu* 'pen' is confirmed by the corresponding passive, sentence (c), where it functions as the subject. It is then the agent that has to be specified periphrastically.

(45) (a) *Úmwáalímu*   *a-ra-andik-a*   *íbárúwa*   *n'-ííkárámu.*

       teacher   he-PRES-write-IMPRF   letter   with-pen

      'The teacher is writing a letter with the pen.'

---

[38] Ditransitives comprise an entire family of related constructions, some of which do allow a nonsentient landmark, e.g. *I gave the fence a new coat of paint*. Observe that the caused-motion counterpart is awkward at best: *??I gave a new coat of paint to the fence*. It portrays the event, incongruously, as one in which a coat of paint follows a spatial path.

(b) *Úmwáalímu*   *a-ra-andik-iish-a*   *íbárúwa*   *íkárámu.*

teacher   he-PRES-write-INSTR-IMPRF   letter   pen

'The teacher is writing a letter with the pen.'

(c) *Íkárámu*   *i-ra-andik-iish-w-a*   *íbárúwa*   *n'-úúmwáalímu.*

pen   it-PRES-write-INSTR-PASS-IMPRF   letter   with-teacher

'The pen is being used to write a letter by the teacher.'

In addition to being directed at different elements, the secondary spotlight can sometimes be extinguished. One device for effecting this, known as **object incorporation**, is exemplified in (46), from Classical Nahuatl. Sentence (a) is a simple transitive clause with a specified object, *in nakatl* 'the meat'. Hence the verb *kʷaa* 'eat' has both the prefix *ni-*, for first-person singular subject, and also *k-*, for third-person singular object. In (b), on the other hand, the noun *naka* 'meat' combines directly with *kʷaa* to form the complex verb stem *naka-kʷaa* 'eat meat'. This derived stem is intransitive, so it lacks the object prefix *k-* and does not permit an overt object nominal. While incorporating *naka* indicates that the eating pertains to meat, and to that extent specifies the verbal landmark, it also indicates that the patient is not a focal participant and will not be further identified. Expressed by an ungrounded noun, its characterization remains at the type level.

(46)   (a) *Ni-k-kʷaa-s*   *in*   *naka-tl.*   'I will eat the meat.'

1s-3s-eat-FUT   ART   meat-ABS

(b) *Ni-naka-kʷaa-s.*   'I will eat meat.'

1s-meat-eat-FUT

(c) *Ni-tla-kʷaa-s.*   'I will eat.'

1s-thing-eat-FUT

This defocusing of the landmark is carried one step further in (46)(c), where the type is highly schematic. Since *tla-* specifies only that the patient is nonhuman, it mostly just serves the grammatical function of allowing a transitive verb to occur with only one specified participant. In this respect it resembles impersonals, where the trajector is left unspecified, as well as passives and middles, where conferring trajector status on the theme leaves the agent unfocused (§11.3.1). A transitive verb also has just one participant when marked as **reflexive**. A reflexive construction is one in which a single participant fills the semantic roles of both the trajector and the landmark. Recall the Spanish examples in (30): *El ratero ahogó al anciano* 'The thief drowned the old man' (transitive) vs. *El anciano se ahogó* 'The old man drowned himself' (reflexive). Recall as well that the latter expression can also be a middle: *El anciano se ahogó* 'The old man drowned'. Across languages, it is quite common for these various kinds of constructions—unspecified landmark, unspecified trajector (= impersonal), passive, middle, reflexive—to be formally identical. They can nonetheless be distinguished, as summarized in figure 11.10 (where Δ indicates that a participant is left unspecified).

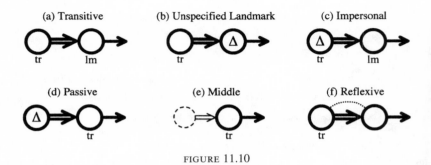

(a) Transitive   (b) Unspecified Landmark   (c) Impersonal

(d) Passive   (e) Middle   (f) Reflexive

FIGURE 11.10

11.3.4 Thematic Processes

A thematic process is a minimal one whose single participant is a passive theme. Such a process can either be incorporated as the conceptually autonomous core of an agentive interaction (e.g. *He broke it*) or can stand alone as the clausal profile (*It broke*). Just as an agentive interaction is the prototype for transitive clauses, a thematic process is prototypical for intransitives. Among the latter, the most representative of the passive realm are imperfective clauses where the subject's semantic role is zero. These designate stable situations in which the trajector exhibits a property, occupies a location, or is simply there.

A thematic process of this sort constitutes the prototype for a basic clause type of English. These clauses lack a lexical verb. Instead, the process they designate is provided by the schematic verb *be* together with its complement. Though typically an adjective or a prepositional phrase, the complement can represent any category that profiles a nonprocessual relationship (§4.3.3). By lending its processual character to this relationship, *be* derives the profiled clausal process.

Figure 11.11(a) shows how this works for a simple adjective. In most uses, *be* profiles a schematic imperfective process. It therefore designates a simplex relationship (inner box) conceived as extending through time without intrinsic bounding. A bar along the time arrow represents the sequential scanning characteristic of a process. Internally to *be*, the relationship followed through time is maximally schematic. It is rendered specific by the complement—in this case, *sad*—which ascribes an emotional state (labeled s) to its trajector. *Sad* is a complement because it elaborates the schematic relation evoked by *be*, which functions as profile determinant. The latter thus imposes its processual profile on the specific content supplied by the adjective. The composite expression *be sad* is a complex imperfective verb which can serve as a clausal head.

The adjective appearing in this construction can also be a stative past participle, e.g. *broken*. Stative participles differ from underived adjectives only by portraying the profiled relationship as the outcome of a change-of-state process (fig. 4.15). With a locative complement, such as *in the garage*, the construction is precisely analogous, for a locative also designates a simplex relationship. The constructions integrating *be* with other sorts of complements represent extensions from this basic pattern. One extension occurs with adjectives like *noisy, careful, naughty, obnoxious*, etc., where

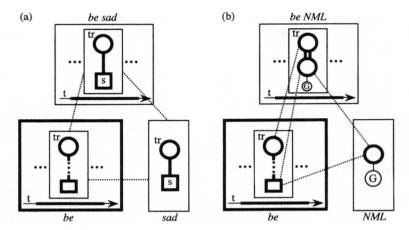

FIGURE 11.11

the property in question is conceived as being subject to willful control. The composite expression, e.g. *be noisy*, is construed as designating an episode of behaving in a way that manifests it. Since the profiled occurrence is bounded, the expression is perfective, hence it takes the progressive: *They were being noisy.* The same extension applies to what are traditionally known as **predicate nominatives**, where the complement of *be* is a nominal: *He is being a jerk*; *Don't be a wimp.* A prior matter, though, is how predicate nominatives arise in the first place. A nominal profiles a thing. How, then, can it elaborate the schematic relationship extended through time by *be*?

Two different kinds of predicate nominatives are usually recognized and considered quite distinct. One kind indicates the referential identity of the subject and predicate nominals: *Joyce is my cousin.* The other kind specifies membership in a category: *Joyce is an actress.* In the CG account, the two variants receive a unified treatment. Both are equative—that is, they predicate referential identity. The difference resides in the status of the second nominal's referent: whether it designates an actual individual or a virtual instance of the specified type. To identify the subject with a virtual instance of a type—an instance conjured up just in order to characterize it—is one way to indicate its category membership. As indefinites always do (§9.3.4), the second nominal invokes its referent as a virtual entity, which may or may not be rendered actual at a higher level of organization. The predicate nominative construction makes it actual by equating it with the referent of the subject.

How, precisely, does it do this? Assuming that *be* has the same schematic meaning as in other uses, the construction is as shown in figure 11.11(b). *Be* indicates only that its trajector bears a relationship to some entity, leaving unspecified both the nature of that entity and how they might be related. The predicate nominative construction specifies both as aspects of constructional meaning. The related entity is equated with the profile of the nominal complement. The relation it bears to the trajector is that of referential identity (rendered diagrammatically by the double line connecting them). Conceptually, this relationship is minimal, essentially just invoking the nominal referents themselves; with no additional content to imply their distinctness, in the composite conception they simply merge. It is thus iconic that identity emerges as an aspect of constructional meaning rather than being independently symbolized.[39]

A distinction is commonly made between *be* as a "copula" (connecting element) and as an auxiliary verb. Copular *be* subsumes the cases already discussed, where the complement is an adjective, locative, or predicate nominative. Auxiliary *be* occurs in passives and progressives. The putative basis for distinguishing them is that copular *be* is the only verb in its clause, hence the true clausal head, whereas auxiliary *be* is subsidiary to a lexical verb which serves in that capacity. However, this rationale confuses two different notions of clausal head: lexical verb and grounded verb. In all cases, *be* can function as the grounded verb, giving temporal extension to a nonprocessual complement: *She is {sad/in the garage/an actress/liked by everybody/ working hard}*. It is true that passive and progressive participles are based on lexical verbs. But at a higher level of organization, where *be* combines with its complement, the constructions are all quite similar and susceptible to a unified account.

A passive participle derives from a transitive verb. Semantically, the participle differs from the verb in two respects: by viewing the profiled interaction holistically instead of sequentially, and by conferring trajector status on the "downstream" participant (the verb's landmark). As in most variants of the *be* construction, the trajector is thus a theme. But since the source is a transitive verb, the trajector can manifest any thematic role—not just zero. A more substantial departure from the prototype, apparent in figure 11.12, is that a passive participle profiles a complex (as opposed to a simplex) relationship, comprising all the component states of the verbal processs.[40] Accordingly, a passive has the potential of being either imperfective or perfective (e.g. *He was liked by his dog* vs. *He was licked by his dog*). The participle inherits its aspect from the verb, and the construction as a whole inherits it from the participle. The passive *be* is therefore neutral in regard to perfectivity, rather than specifically imperfective. This has consequences for how *be* and the participle are integrated. Since the component states may be different, we cannot just say (as in fig. 11.11(a)) that all the states of *be* map onto the same (simplex) relationship profiled by its complement. Instead, the entire complex relationship profiled by *be* corresponds (state by state) to the one profiled by the participle. These merge to form a higher-order process in which the participial relationship is scanned sequentially.

The *be*...*-ing* progressive constitutes another departure from the prototype. From a perfective verb, *-ing* derives a nonprocessual relationship representing some internal portion of the original bounded process (e.g. *work > working*). It further construes this relationship as mass-like, its component states being effectively identical. The progressive *be* is therefore imperfective, but since the complement relationship comprises a series of component states (albeit identical ones), its integration with *be* is analogous to that in the passive. The construction is also nonprototypical because

---

[39] Whether the notion of identity is attributed to the construction or to a specialized sense of *be* itself is moot; *be* assumes this more specific value only in the context of the construction. Conversely, the full characterization of *be* includes the constructional schema as a structural frame (§8.3.2).

[40] By contrast, a stative-adjectival participle profiles just its final state (fig. 4.15). *The glass was broken* is thus ambiguous, describing either a stable situation or a change which results in that situation.

be + Passive Participle

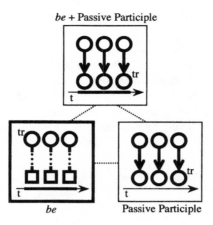

FIGURE 11.12

there is no requirement that the trajector be thematic. A progressive subject instantiates the same semantic role as the verb's trajector, whatever that might be (e.g. an agent in the case of *be working*).

Not every finite clause has an explicit verbal element that renders it processual. Either the profiled relationship itself or its temporal extension can emerge instead as an aspect of constructional meaning. In predicate nominatives, for instance, the profiled relation of referential identity is not specifically inherited from either component structure (fig. 11.11(b)). To illustrate the emergence of temporal extension, let us turn to adjectival clauses in Luiseño. To describe a present situation, it is sufficient to use a noun plus an adjective, with no verb: *'awaal 'oyokval* 'The dog is quiet'. On the other hand, for nonpresent situations the clause contains the verb *miyx* 'be' together with the appropriate tense inflection: *'awaal 'oyokval miy-quṣ;* 'The dog was quiet'; *'awaal 'oyokval miyx-maan* 'The dog will be quiet'. We can reasonably assume that *miyx* extends the adjectival relationship through time, as required for a clausal head. What, then, is the source of this temporality in the present, where *miyx* is lacking?

The question is comparable to that of how a simple noun, like *'awaal* 'dog', can function as a full, grounded nominal (§9.3.4). The answer, once again, is that the conventional units of a language include not only ways of **constructing** expressions but also ways of **applying** them to the ongoing discourse. The speaker-hearer interaction and their apprehension of the onstage situation are part of the meaning of every expression (fig. 9.2). At any moment in the flow of discourse, the interlocutors direct their attention to a particular onstage element—the focus in the current discourse frame (fig. 9.7). For a finite clause, the focused element is the profiled clausal process. The production of the clause delimits the discourse frame's duration, which for a clause is the time span during which the profiled process is apprehended and scanned sequentially.

These notions figure in conventional units specifying how expressions are applied to the ongoing discourse. One such unit allows a structure like *'awaal 'oyokval* to be apprehended as a clause and used to describe a stable situation that continues through the time of speaking. Accordingly, the time span under consideration (the expression's immediate temporal scope) is identified with the duration of the current discourse frame. Likewise, the adjectival relationship is identified with the element focused during this time span. Though not intrinsically processual, the profiled relationship is thereby given temporal extension by the speech event itself, just as it is by *miyx* for nonpresent situations. A process thus emerges in the composite conception obtained by anchoring the overtly symbolized relationship to the speaker-hearer interaction. And because this interaction constitutes the ground, the process is grounded and the clause is finite.

11.4   Complex Verbs

A verb is defined in CG as an expression that profiles a process. Under this broad definition—broad enough to subsume even finite clauses—most verbs are symbolically complex. But even those elements traditionally recognized as verbs are typically complex. If the monomorphemic *break* is a verb, so is the polymorphemic *defunctionalize*, not to mention the phrasal verb *break up* as well as inflected forms such as *broke*, *broke up*, and *defunctionalizes*. Given that those are classed as verbs, it seems arbitrary to leave out more elaborate processual structures like *is breaking*, *broke it up*, and *may have been defunctionalized*. Why, then, should *Floyd broke the glass* be excluded?

Processual structures at any level of organization—ranging from lexical verbs to full, finite clauses—subserve the common function of letting us talk about events and situations. Even if we try to distinguish them, verb structure and clause structure are inextricably bound up with one another. Suppose we define "the verb" of a clause (just for sake of discussion) as a single-word expression that specifies and profiles the grounded process; in *Floyd broke the glass*, the verb is therefore *broke*. So identified, verbs differ enormously in their complexity, as well as in the kinds of elements they incorporate.[41] The verb's internal structure is largely responsible for the grammatical organization of the clause as a whole. It determines not only how the situation is construed but also what remains to be expressed by other means.

How much does the verb contribute to a clause? Minimally, it specifies a basic process type and imposes a particular trajector/landmark alignment. It then consists of just an uninflected stem (like *break* or *defunctionalize*), everything else being conveyed by nonverbal elements that combine with the verb syntactically. But as more is accomplished by the verb itself, through morphological means, there is less that has to be done at higher levels of grammatical organization. For example, if the verb itself incorporates a noun to specify its landmark, there is no need for a separate object nominal. We saw this in (46): whereas Nahuatl *kʷaa* 'eat' takes an object, *naka-kʷaa* 'eat meat' is grammatically intransitive.

A wide and varied array of notions are capable of being coded in the verb. Chief among these are the closely associated notions of tense, modality, and aspect, only

---

[41] Not every clause has such a verb. For instance, there is no such element in Luiseño sentences of the type *'awaal 'oyokval* 'The dog is quiet'. A phrasal verb like *break up* (e.g. *They should break up the demonstration*) is not a single word.

the first of which is marked on the verb in English.[42] Also very common are morphological indications of trajector/landmark alignment (§11.3): passive, antipassive, impersonal, middle, reflexive, applicative, etc. While these pertain to the choice of focal participants, other markings help to identify them, most typically through specifications of person and number. These specifications have varying degrees of morphological independence, ranging from none at all (e.g. *am* vs. *are* vs. *is*) to cases like Nahuatl *ni-k-neki* (I-it-want), where they are clearly segmentable and could even be analyzed as personal pronouns. Additionally, it is not unusual for verbs to incorporate elements that might be considered adverbial. To take just one example, verbs in Cora (a Uto-Aztecan language of Mexico) have prefixes that specify the path, location, or "shape" of the verbal process (CIS: ch. 2). With reference to a candle, for instance, *u-ká-taa-sin* (inside-down-burn-DURATIVE) indicates that the process of burning proceeds in a downward direction at an inside location. The verb is also a frequent host for markings pertaining to higher-level grammatical relationships. A verbal affix can mark a clause as subordinate, for example, or indicate whether two clauses have the same or different trajectors.

In some languages, therefore, it is possible for a clause of some complexity to consist of just a single word. In many more languages, a single verb codes what English expresses periphrastically with both a "main" verb (V) and one or more "auxiliaries": *may V, has Ved, is Ving, will be Ved, had been Ving*, etc. Despite their complexity, these expressions belong to a single finite clause, where V specifies a basic process and the other elements either ground it or impose a particular perspective on it. It is also very common, however, for a verb to incorporate multiple processual notions that in English would have to be expressed with a sentence comprising multiple clauses, each with its own lexical head.

As an example, let us compare the Luiseño sentence in (47)(a) with its English translation. In addition to the modal *will*, the English sentence has three lexical verbs—*make, want*, and *leave*—each a separate word. The grounded verb is *make*. It has three complements: the subject *I*, the object *him*, and the relational complement *want to leave*. This in turn consists of a verb, *want*, with its own relational complement, *to leave*. The two relational complements are traditionally described as subordinate clauses. They are not full or finite clauses, however, because they lack independent grounding as well as an overt subject nominal. Though comparable in some respects, the Luiseño sentence clearly consists of just one clause. The key difference is that the processual notions 'leave', 'want', and 'make' are all coded in a single verb stem, *ngeevichuni* 'make want to leave'. Syntactically, (47)(a) is precisely analogous to (47)(b), with the simple verb stem *'ari* 'kick'. The simple and complex stems are grounded in parallel fashion by the future suffix *-n*. In each case, moreover, the pronouns *noo* 'I' and *poy* 'him' elaborate the stem's trajector and landmark, producing a clause that is further grounded by the clitic *=nupo*. Compared with English, therefore, the Luiseño expression achieves more by morphological means and does less syntactically. By packaging more in the verb, it is simpler in terms of clausal organization.

---

[42] Modals are separate words (*may, will, should*, etc.), and aspect is expressed periphrastically in the perfect and progressive constructions (*have Ved* and *be Ving*). Passive voice is also periphrastic (*be Ved*).

(47) (a) *Noo=nupo   poy   ngee-vichu-ni-n.*   'I will make him want to leave.'

I=1s:FUT   him   leave-want-make-FUT

(b) *Noo=nupo   poy   'ari-n.*   'I will kick him.'

I=1s:FUT   him   kick-FUT

Figure 11.13 shows the internal structure of this complex verb. The lexical root is *ngee* 'leave', which profiles the trajector's movement from a reference location (R). The suffix *-vichu* 'want' designates an experiential relationship (dashed arrow) which the trajector bears to an event that functions as its landmark; an inherent aspect of its meaning, indicated by a correspondence line, is that the desired event is one the trajector itself carries out. This schematic event is specified by *ngee* at the first level of grammatical organization, and since *-vichu* is the profile determinant, *ngeevichu* 'want to leave' designates the process of wanting. At the next level of organization, *ngeevichu* combines with *-ni* 'make', representing a common type of element known as a **causative**. The relationship it profiles consists of the trajector exerting force on the landmark in order to induce a process it performs. Here that process is specified as wanting to leave. Because the head at this level is *-ni*, the composite expression *ngeevichuni* 'make want to leave' profiles an act of inducing this desire. Finally, this causative relationship is grounded by the future suffix *-n* at the highest level of organization. As a grounding element, *-n* profiles the schematic

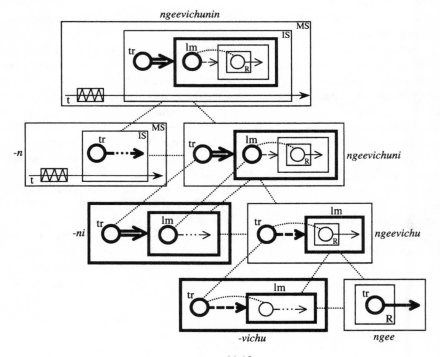

FIGURE 11.13

grounded process, which it specifies as being subsequent to the time of speaking (squiggly-lined box).

Following common practice, we have been referring informally to "the verb" of a clause as a word that specifies and profiles the grounded process. Often, though, this task is performed collectively by elements that do not constitute a single word. Prevalent in many languages are **serial verb** constructions, where multiple words, each processual, are strung together to describe the process profiled by a clause. Typically the component processes are construed as phases of a single event representing a familiar scenario. In English, serial verbs are mostly limited to two-word sequences based on *go* and *come*, such as *Let's go eat* and *Come see this*. In other languages the sequences can be longer and are much more varied. Here is an example from Thai (cited in Takahashi 2000):

(48) *Tua*   *tìk*   *hăn* *nâa* *khâw* *hăa*   *thalee.*   'The building faces toward the sea.'

    body building turn face enter seek sea

Serial verb constructions are sometimes hard to distinguish from phrasal verb constructions, the difference being that in the latter only one component element is processual. English is noteworthy for its prolific use of phrasal verbs, which come in many varieties. We will limit our attention to just a couple basic patterns where the clause is transitive and the profiled process is specified by the combination of a verb and a preposition.[43] The composite V + P expression is thus a complex verb whose landmark is the clausal object.

The sequence V + P + NML can represent several different constructions, each with its own semantic organization and grammatical behavior. Consider the contrasts in (49). In sentence (a), the sequence consists of an intransitive verb followed by a prepositional phrase: [V [P NML]$_{PP}$]. On the other hand, sentence (a′) consists of a complex transitive verb followed by its object: [[V P]$_V$ NML]. Examples (b) and (b′) provide some evidence for the constituency of *through the mall* and the nonconstituency of *through the call*, since only the former preposes as a unit. Likewise, the passives in (c) and (c′) give evidence for the verbal status of *put through*, as opposed to *run through*. Only when V and P form a complex verb is the following nominal a transitive object, as required for passivization. A further difference is seen in (d) and (d′): in a prepositional phrase, the preposition has to precede its object, but with a complex verb, P can either precede the object nominal or follow it.[44]

---

[43] In related patterns, the nonprocessual element can be an adverb (*She pushed it away*), an adjective of result or circumstance (*He wiped it clean*; *I ate it raw*), a nominal (*They elected her president*), or a past or present participle (*She got him fired*; *It sent her sprawling*).

[44] In the latter case, V and P form a conceptual grouping that happens not to be symbolized by a phonological grouping (since the nominal intervenes). This illustrates the general point that a single constituency hierarchy fails to capture all the structures and relationships that need to be posited (§7.4.2). P is often referred to as a "particle", as some participating elements (e.g. *away*) are not prepositions: *throw away the letter* vs. *throw the letter away*. A classic CG account of Verb + Particle combinations is Lindner 1982.

(49) (a) *He ran through the mall.*   (a′) *He put through the call.*

     (b) *Through the mall he ran.*   (b′) **Through the call he put.*

     (c) **The mall was run through.*   (c′) *The call was put through.*

     (d) **He ran the mall through.*   (d′) *He put the call through.*

The trajector/landmark organization of the complex verb has to be distinguished from that of V or P individually. While the complex verb's trajector is consistently the same as V's, its landmark shows more variation. In the case of *put through*, it corresponds to V's landmark (the call is what he "puts") and to P's trajector (the call goes through). We find other combinations in phrases like *wipe your shoes off* and *wipe the mud off*. Only in the former does the phrasal verb's landmark correspond to that of V (we thus say *Wipe your shoes!*, not **Wipe the mud!*). And as for P, the phrasal verb's landmark corresponds to either its trajector or its landmark (the mud goes off the shoes). Despite such differences, these complex verbs are alike in terms of their higher-level grammatical relationships. It is the complex verb as a whole that determines the clausal profile, as well as the trajector and landmark specified by the subject and object nominals.

The construction just described is rather different from another that can also be characterized abstractly as [[V P]$_V$ NML]. Appearing in this latter construction are a large number of familiar collocations: *look at, stare at, talk to, quarrel with, search for, talk about, shoot at, deal with, look for, yell at, grapple with, motion to, ask for, argue about, mess with, wave at, fight over*, and so on. That these are transitive verbs is shown by their ability to passivize: *That will be looked at*; *I was being stared at*; *She should be talked to*. The most obvious difference from the previous construction is that P cannot follow the object nominal. Whereas *put through the call* alternates with *put the call through*, we can only say *look at the wall*, not **look the wall at*. A subtler difference is that this latter construction is consistent in regard to trajector/landmark alignment. As before, the complex verb's trajector is always the same as V's. But in this case the landmark of the complex verb uniformly corresponds to the landmark of P.

Whether the sequence V + P + NML is to be analyzed as [[V P]$_V$ NML] or simply as [V [P NML]$_{PP}$] is not always a clear-cut matter. Indeed, some sequences appear to be ambivalent, each analysis being manifested in certain structural contexts. While all the expressions just cited occur in passives, implying a complex verb, to varying degrees they can still occur in constructions involving a prepositional phrase: *the wall at which he was staring*; *To whom were you talking?*; *With his wife he never quarrels*. But these latter uses seem awkward and are probably vestigial. In casual speech we tend to use alternatives susceptible to a complex verb analysis: *the wall he was staring at*; *Who were you talking to?*; *His wife he never quarrels with*. These familiar V + P collocations are well on their way toward being analyzed exclusively as complex verbs, with P losing its ability to function grammatically like an independent preposition.

What about their semantic development? As one might expect, the grammatical evolution of V + P collocations into complex verbs goes along with the emergence of verb-like meanings. The events they describe lend themselves to construal as two-participant interactions similar to those which transitive verbs commonly express.[45] For instance, to *stare at* someone is not just to fix one's attention on that person—it may very well constitute a social interaction (cf. *ogle*). On the other hand, staring at a wall is less interactive, in the sense that the wall is unlikely to be affected. A passive, which forces a complex-verb interpretation, is thus a bit more natural with a human target: *I was being stared at* vs. *??The wall was being stared at*. Predictably, a phrasal verb emerges only when the following nominal designates a participant, as opposed to a setting or location. For this reason *She was walking in the woods* cannot be passivized: **The woods were being walked in*.

Still, the factors involved are matters of degree and subject to construal. In the proper circumstances, even a canonical location can be viewed as participating in an interaction, resulting in a complex transitive verb (Rice 1987a, 1987b). For example, *play in the sandbox* would normally have the structure [V [P NML]$_{PP}$], as in (50)(a); the sandbox is simply where the children play. Hence the passive in sentence (b) is rather odd. However, the passive in (c) is quite acceptable, evoking a context where the condition of the sandbox is at issue. It is taken as meaning that playing in the sandbox has affected it (e.g. by messing up the smoothly raked sand). With the sandbox construed as a participant, *play in* is analyzed as a transitive verb, which can thus occur in the passive.

(50) (a) *The children are playing in the sandbox.*

(b) *??The sandbox is being played in.*

(c) *The sandbox has definitely been played in.*

This illustrates once more a basic notion of CG: namely, that grammatical structure can only be understood in relation to the conceptual organization it embodies and expresses. One would not think of writing a dictionary that merely listed the lexical forms, with no indication of their meanings. To investigate grammar independently of meaning is equally pointless and misguided.

---

[45] Many V + P collocations can be roughly paraphrased by simple verbs: *look at = examine, search for = seek, talk about = discuss, ask for = request, motion to = signal, wave at = greet*, etc.

12

Complex Sentences

A sentence consisting of more than one clause is said to be **complex**. How, then, are the component clauses related to one another? Traditionally, a distinction is drawn between relationships of **coordination** and **subordination**. In the latter case, a distinction is made between the **main clause** and various kinds of **subordinate clauses**. These differences are not clear-cut, however, nor are the notions themselves very clear. Our first order of business is thus to explore their conceptual and grammatical basis.

12.1 Ordination: Co- and Sub-

Unlike people, not all clauses are created equal. When clauses combine to form a complex sentence, they normally differ in status—one is reasonably described as being subordinated to another. But what exactly does this mean? In fact, there are a number of ways in which clauses differ in status. These various dimensions of subordination are partially independent and have to be carefully distinguished. We speak of coordination in cases where clauses approximate coequal status in regard to all these factors. Yet there is always some asymmetry. Clauses never achieve full equality with respect to every dimension.

12.1.1 Conjoining

In cases of coordination, the clauses are said to be **conjoined**, each is called a **conjunct**, and an element connecting them (such as *and*) is a **conjunction**. To be sure, conjoining is not specifically a clause-level phenomenon. In principle, conjuncts can be of any size, and they can represent any grammatical category. Examples are given in (1), with conjuncts enclosed in brackets. Note that even conjunctions can be conjoined.

(1)   (a) *Conjuncts can [be of any size] and [represent any category].*   [grounded process]

(b) *Conjuncts can be [of any size] or [of any category].*   [prepositional phrase]

(c) *Conjuncts can be of [any size] or [any category].*   [nominal]

(d) *Conjuncts can be of any [size] or [category].*   [noun]

(e) *Conjuncts can be of any size [and] / [or] category.*   [conjunction]

What does it mean to say that conjuncts are coequal in status? Most basically, it means that they participate independently and to the same extent in the same set of grammatical relationships. For example, each conjunct in (2)(a) specifies the landmark of *admire* and is thus its object if considered individually. Their parallel grammatical behavior implies that the conjuncts are also semantically parallel. As full nominals, each of which profiles a grounded thing instance, *the desk* and *my study* are abstractly similar with respect to their content. They are further comparable in their prominence within the clause containing them: the things they profile each have the status of clausal landmark. By contrast, *the desk* and *my study* are not coequal in (2)(b); only the desk enjoys clause-level focal prominence. The nominal *my study* is not itself an object of the verb but of *in*, as part of a prepositional phrase internal to the direct-object nominal. Its referent does not participate in the profiled clausal process but is merely invoked in order to identify the desk in question.

(2)   (a) *She admired [the **desk**] and [my **study**].*

(b) *She admired [the **desk** in my study].*

From the grammatical standpoint, coordination consists of some position in a structural pattern being multiply instantiated. Given the pattern [X Y Z], specified by constructional schemas, a conjoined structure has the form [X [Y$_1$]-[Y$_2$] Z], where [X Y$_1$ Z] and [X Y$_2$ Z] themselves conform to the pattern. Hence this structure represents the conflation of multiple instantiating expressions. From the conceptual standpoint, both Y$_1$ and Y$_2$ profile entities of the requisite sort. The coordinate expression [Y$_1$]-[Y$_2$] thus has two coexisting profiles, each of which participates in the relationships characteristic of the pattern. In (2)(a), both the desk and the study stand in profile, and each corresponds to the landmark of the verb. In (2)(b), by contrast, only

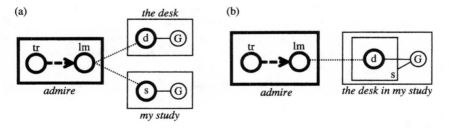

FIGURE 12.1

the desk is profiled and identified with the landmark. The role of clausal object is instantiated only once, by the object nominal as a whole. This contrast is sketched in figure 12.1.

The general requirement that coordinate structures be semantically and grammatically parallel gives rise to many questions concerning its specific implementation. For instance, if conjuncts are grammatically parallel, they ought to represent the same grammatical category. But often they do not, at least on standard accounts. The conjuncts in (3) are traditionally assigned to different categories: in sentence (a), adjective vs. active participial phrase; in (b), adverb vs. prepositional phrase.

(3)   (a)   *He was [sad] and [feeling sorry for himself]*.

     (b)   *She signed the papers [reluctantly] and [with much hesitation]*.

While such cases are problematic in terms of the traditional parts of speech, they are less so with the conceptual characterizations proposed in CG. At an abstract level, *sad* and *feeling sorry for himself* are alike in that each profiles a nonprocessual relationship with a thing as trajector; they are further parallel in that each ascribes a mental state to its trajector, identified as *he* in the context of this construction. Likewise, *reluctantly* and *with much hesitation* are alike in that each profiles a nonprocessual relationship whose trajector is identified with the clausal process of signing the papers; they both fulfill their adverbial function by specifying the subject's attitude in performing this action. Such analogies at the level of conceptual content seem more important than specific grammatical form. In terms of form alone, (4)(a) ought to be worse than either (4)(b), where both conjuncts are prepositional phrases, or (4)(c), where both are nominals. But if anything the reverse is true. All of them commit the semantic faux pas of implying parallelism in the semantic roles of a mental attitude and a physical instrument.[1]

(4)   (a)   *?She signed the papers [reluctantly] and [with a ballpoint pen]*.

     (b)   *??She signed the papers [with reluctance] and [with a ballpoint pen]*.

     (c)   **She signed the papers with [reluctance] and [a ballpoint pen]*.

In addition to matters of parallelism is the question of whether conjuncts participate independently in their relationships with other elements. The same question arose previously in regard to adjectives modifying plural nouns, e.g. *long novels* vs. *similar novels*: whereas each novel is long individually, only collectively are they similar (fig. 10.14). Analogously for *Jack and Jill are tall* vs. *Jack and Jill are compatible*: Jack and Jill are tall individually but compatible only as a pair. A collective interpretation implies the conceptual emergence of a higher-order entity comprising the elements profiled by the conjuncts. By its very nature, coordination encourages this development. The mere fact of successively mentioning the

---

[1] A mistake of this sort is traditionally known as **zeugma**. The examples get worse from (a) to (c) because the clash is made more salient by explicit grammatical parallelism and immediate adjacency.

(a)   (b)

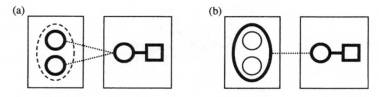

FIGURE 12.2

component elements serves to mentally juxtapose them, so that the higher-order entity exists at least implicitly, as seen in figure 12.2(a). The potential is thus created for a collective construal in which the profile is shifted to this entity, as shown in figure 12.2(b).

The extent to which a higher-order entity emerges and participates as such in correspondences is doubtless a matter of degree. At one end of the scale are numerous fixed expressions, consisting of conjoined nouns, where the composite whole is clearly recognized as an entity in its own right, with its own properties or function: *gin and tonic*; *peanut butter and jelly*; *cup and saucer*; *pencil and paper*; *block and tackle*; *stars and stripes*; *knife, fork, and spoon*; and so on. Drinking a gin and tonic, for example, is not at all equivalent to drinking gin and drinking tonic. The conjuncts in (3)(a) represent an intermediate case. The emotions expressed by *sad* and *feeling sorry for himself* can equally well be construed as distinct, coexisting mental states or as two facets of a single negative outlook. Conjoined clauses would seem to have the best chance of retaining their status as separate, parallel conceptions. Yet even here the issue is not entirely black and white. Clausal coordination is truly felicitous only when the clauses have something to do with one another. In (5)(a), for instance, both clauses can be interpreted as reasons why the speaker is so tired in the evening. On the other hand, (5)(b) seems incoherent because the ideas expressed are totally unrelated.[2] Perhaps the requisite coherence is a matter of the clauses representing facets of a single, multifaceted proposition.

(5)   (a) *[I had three classes today] and [the faculty meeting was acrimonious]*.

(b) *??[The moon orbits the earth] and [the faculty meeting was acrimonious]*.

A further dimension of coordination is how the conjuncts relate to one another, as expressed by conjunctions like *and*, *or*, and *but*. Most typical is *and*-type conjoining, which is minimal and fundamental. Its essential import—inherent in the very notion of coordination—consists in the **mental juxtaposition** of coequal elements. This is simply a matter of elements being conceived together, in a single attentional frame. In and of itself, juxtaposition is a symmetrical relationship. If nothing imposes an asymmetry, the coconceived elements are thus equivalent in status, as well as in their role in higher-level structures. Other coordinate relations are conceptually more

---

[2] More precisely, coherence is harder to achieve because it is harder to imagine a connection. One possibility is that both clauses describe something you can always count on.

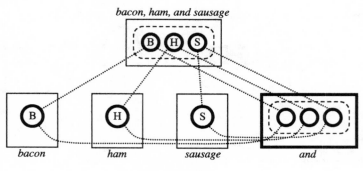

FIGURE 12.3

elaborate. Often their additional content introduces some asymmetry between the juxtaposed elements or affects their role at higher levels of organization.

The essential import of *and* thus consists in mentally juxtaposing coequal elements (rather than in any specific content). As shown in figure 12.3, *and* can be characterized as having multiple, coexisting profiles, all instantiating the same general type.[3] Each profiled entity corresponds to the profile of a conjunct, which serves to elaborate it. In this particular coordinate construction, the conjuncts combine with *and* in parallel, at a single level of organization, even though the conjunction attaches phonologically only to the final one. As just noted, the composite conception is ambivalent as to whether it profiles the conjoined elements individually (the option depicted) or the higher-order entity that emerges from their coconception. It is a matter of whether (or to what extent) the bacon, ham, and sausage are conceptualized as distinct substances or as jointly fulfilling some function (e.g. the toppings on a nonvegetarian pizza).

In other coordinate relations, mental juxtaposition is embedded in a more elaborate conception. The hardest to characterize is *or*-type conjoining. Indeed, with *or* one has to question whether mental juxtaposition is even operative. When we conceptualize a *sausage and pepperoni pizza*, the toppings occur together in a single image: we envisage bits of sausage being interspersed with bits of pepperoni on the pizza's surface. This is not so when we talk about a *sausage or pepperoni pizza*. Here a single coherent image fails to emerge at all. Evoked instead are two alternate pizza images, in each of which one topping occurs to the exclusion of the other. But if they are mutually exclusive, how can we maintain that they are mentally juxtaposed?

In recognition of this difference, *or*-type coordination is commonly described as **disjunction** rather than **conjunction**. Adopting a different label is not the same as offering a conceptual characterization, however. It also obscures the fact that conjoining with *or* really does qualify as conjoining. Despite the contrast noted,

[3] Fig. 12.3 represents the special case of three profiled things. A more schematic characterization would be neutral as to the number of profiled entities (as long as there are more than one) and would allow other types (e.g. process or nonprocessual relationship).

the conjuncts are equivalent in status and grammatically parallel, just as they are with *and*. In a phrase like *sausage or pepperoni pizza*, the referents of *sausage* and *pepperoni* are equally prominent and participate in exactly the same grammatical relationship with *pizza*. These are precisely the factors that motivate the characterization of coordination in terms of coequal structures with coexisting profiles. But is this coexistence not equivalent to mental juxtaposition? I believe it is, so we face an apparent contradiction.

The key is to recognize different levels of conception. *Or* is used in cases of options or uncertainty, when there are multiple candidates to fill a semantic role. Its meaning thus resides in the relationship between two mental spaces: the envisaged situation, where a particular candidate fills the role; and the conceptually more immediate situation, where alternate candidates each have the potential to fill it. In this more accessible situation, the alternatives are simultaneously considered as such on an equal basis, hence mentally juxtaposed in the manner characteristic of coordination. Their exclusiveness pertains to the envisaged situation of the role being filled by just one of them.[4] By placing them in separate mental spaces, *or* divorces the mental juxtaposition of conjoined elements from the envisaged situation of the role being filled. In this way *or* is conceptually more elaborate than *and*, which does not invoke separate spaces. The mental juxtaposition effected by *and* applies directly to the situation described.

Despite its greater semantic complexity, conjoining with *or* is still symmetrical: *X or Y* is equivalent to *Y or X*. This is not so in the case of *but*, whose additional content introduces an asymmetry. *But* is comparable to *and* in the sense that both conjuncts apply directly to the situation described. If a pistol is *small but lethal*, the properties *small* and *lethal* both apply to it. *But*, however, has the additional implication that the second conjunct runs counter to expectations engendered by the first. Thus *small but lethal* presupposes that something small is expected to be ineffective (whereas *small and lethal* is neutral in this respect). By contrast, *lethal but small* carries the supposition that something lethal is expected to be large. Owing to these different suppositions, the two expressions are semantically distinct.

Full equivalence and symmetry may never be achieved in practice. Even in the case of *and*, coordinate structures tend to be interpreted asymmetrically. When the conjuncts describe events, they tend to be understood as occurring in the order expressed. Thus (6)(a) would normally be taken as indicating that she first quit her job and then got married (not simply that both occurred). Juxtaposing events also invites the inference that the first is somehow responsible for the second. From (6)(a), we are likely to infer that quitting her job cleared the way for getting married; from (6)(b), that opening the window caused the alarm to go off.

(6)   (a) *She quit her job and got married.*

   (b) *I opened the window and set off the alarm.*

---

[4] *Or* is sometimes interpreted inclusively, allowing the possibility that both candidates fill the role (e.g. *If there's rain or fog, we'll cancel the party*). The difference between "inclusive" and "exclusive" *or* comes down to whether the conception of a single candidate in the role is taken as a **minimal** or a **maximal** characterization of the envisaged situation.

Other asymmetries pertain to status. In one common pattern of English, the first of two conjoined events is construed as merely preparatory or concomitant with respect to the second, which is the only one of real importance. Both expressions in (6) lend themselves to this construal. More obvious are cases involving motion or posture, such as *go and complain*, where complaining is clearly the main event, or *sit and talk*, where the sitting is subsidiary. Minimally, the very fact that conjuncts are presented in a particular temporal sequence introduces a touch of asymmetry, however inconsequential. As one dimension of construal, sequence of mental access is never completely neutral semantically, irrespective of whether alternate word orders correspond to any difference in the situation described.

Even when conventionally established, such asymmetries may simply embellish the basic conceptual import of coordination (the mental juxtaposition of coequal structures). But if carried far enough, they can effectively override this import, resulting in nonparallel grammatical behavior. One well-known example concerns the usual requirement that a preposed question word has to play an analogous role in all the conjuncts of a coordinate structure.[5] Sentence (7)(a) is thus well-formed, since *what* is the object of both *complain about* and *buy*, while (7)(b) is not, since there it is only the object of *buy*.

(7)   (a) **What** *did he* **complain about** *but still* **buy**?

       (b) ***What** *did he complain to the manager but still* **buy**?

       (c) **What** *did he go to the store and* **buy**?

Why, then, is (7)(c) is acceptable? It seems quite analogous to (7)(b), in that *what* corresponds just to the landmark of *buy*. The apparent reason is that the going is merely subsidiary to the buying. They are not construed as separate and coequal, but as phases of a single occurrence representing a familiar cultural scenario. *What* is therefore the landmark with respect to the emergent conception of the single, complex event *go to the store and buy*. This example nicely shows that grammar is not just a matter of form. Far from being autonomous, it cannot be revealingly described without examining the conceptual structures it embodies and interacts with.

12.1.2 Dimensions of Subordination

There are many ways of combining clauses to form a complex sentence. Coordinate constructions represent the special case of symmetry, parallelism, and coequality among the component clauses. More typically, these properties are lacking by virtue of one clause being subordinated to another. While subordination is therefore quite important, this traditional notion is anything but self-explanatory. It has a number of dimensions that to some extent vary independently.

The first dimension is itself multifaceted. It pertains to the form of a clause: whether it could in principle stand alone as an independent sentence. By this criterion

---

[5] This constraint was first noted by Ross (1986), and cases like (7)(c) are discussed in Lakoff 1986. The complexities of coordination are further explored in Hudson 1988 and 1989, as well as FCG2: §11.2.

alone, the bracketed clause in (8)(a) is nonsubordinate, and the one in (8)(b) is subordinate. While the latter might constitute a full utterance (e.g. in response to the question *What is the worst thing imaginable?*), it is felt to be elliptic. It is not well-formed when interpreted as a complete and independent statement.

(8)   (a) *She claims [she has swallowed a spider].*   (a′) *She has swallowed a spider.*

    (b) *She claims [to have swallowed a spider].*   (b′) **To have swallowed a spider.*

A clause's form can brand it as subordinate due to either what is present or what is absent. For instance, the subordinate clause in (8)(b) is marked as such by both the presence of infinitival *to* and the absence of a subject. Among the varied elements that explicitly mark subordination—remarkably enough, these are called **subordinators**—are those exemplified in (9). A basic theoretical issue is whether subordinators are always meaningful. While some clearly are (e.g. *whether, if, since*), forms like *that*, *-ing*, and *(for)... to* are commonly regarded as purely syntactic. Of course, this is not an issue in CG, where instead the problem is to say just what their meanings are (see §12.3.1).

(9)   (a) *She claims [**that** she swallowed a spider].*

    (b) *She enjoyed [swallow**ing** that spider].*

    (c) *I wonder [**whether** she really swallowed one].*

    (d) *The best spider [**for** you **to** swallow] would be a brown recluse.*

    (e) *[**If** you swallow a spider] you should wash it down with beer.*

    (f) *[**Since** she swallowed a spider] she might as well have a beer.*

Many subordinate clauses are formally distinct because a participant, usually the subject, fails to be overtly manifested. They may then depend on the main clause for its identification. This is how we know that in (9)(b) the subject of *swallow* is *she*, while in (9)(d) its object is *spider*. Equally common is the absence of grounding, as with *to* and *-ing*. Indeed, *to* and *-ing* occur in lieu of grounding precisely because they serve to atemporalize the subordinate process. An ungrounded clause is inherently subordinate in the sense of depending on the main clause to specify the status of the process it is based on. In (9)(b), for instance, only its relation to the grounded clause *she enjoyed* tells us that the swallowing actually occurred (cf. *She might enjoy [swallowing that spider]*).

Atemporalization of the clausal process—viewing it holistically rather than sequentially—is one step in the direction of its nominalization. Many subordinate clauses take the further step of construing the profiled relationship as an abstract thing, making it nominal rather than clausal at higher levels of grammatical organization. The extent to which they are nominal in form depends on whether the structure that undergoes the nominalization—given below in bold—is a full clause, a partial clause, or just a verb. In (10)(a), nominalization applies to the full, finite clause *she would quickly swallow a spider*, so internally the resulting nominal is clausal in form.

In (10)(b), it applies to just the partial clause *quickly swallow that spider*, so only that portion is clause-like in structure, with an adverbial modifier as well as a nominal in the usual direct-object position. The fact that the subject takes the form of a possessive (*her*) argues that the remainder (*quickly swallowing that spider*) is indeed construed as an abstract thing. Comparing this now to (10)(c), we observe that in the latter the subordinate "clause" is completely nominal in form: *her quick swallowing of that spider* is directly analogous to *her beautiful picture of that spider*. Here it is only the verb that is nominalized, so only the resulting noun is available for higher-level combinatory purposes. Apart from being derived from a verb, *swallowing* functions grammatically like any other noun. In (10)(d), for example, it enters into a noun-noun compound parallel to *table tennis*.

(10) (a) *[That **she would quickly swallow a spider**] was unexpected.*

(b) *[Her **quickly swallowing that spider**] astonished everybody.*

(c) *[Her quick **swallow**ing of that spider] was impressive.*

(d) *She is good at both table tennis and spider **swallow**ing.*

Subordinate clauses are thus quite varied in form, running the gamut from being indistinguishable from independent clauses to not really being clauses at all. This dimension of subordination might best be thought of as symptomatic of subordinate status rather than a characterization of it. A second dimension relates to profiling: whether a clause's profile prevails or is overridden at higher levels of organization. Arguably this affords a workable general characterization. That depends, however, on how certain issues are resolved.

An expression's profile is what it designates (or refers to). When component structures combine to form a composite expression, it is usual for the latter to inherit its profile from just one component (§7.2). As a composite whole, for instance, *tasty spider* designates the spider (not the gustatory property), so *spider* is the constructional head, or profile determinant; the adjective's profile is overridden at the composite-structure level. The component clauses of a complex sentence exhibit a comparable asymmetry. Taken as a whole, (11)(a) designates an act of persuading rather than one of resigning. Likewise, the event profiled in sentence (b) is the cutting, not the shaving. In each case the main-clause profile prevails at the composite-structure level, overriding that of the subordinate clause. With a relative clause, as in (c), the profile is overridden even at the nominal level: *this money we stole* profiles the money, not the stealing. The nominal profile is in turn overridden in the main-clause subject construction, where the processual component *is counterfeit* functions as profile determinant.

(11) (a) *They persuaded the CEO [to resign].*

(b) *He cut himself [while shaving].*

(c) *This money [we stole] is counterfeit!*

The subordinate clauses in (11) represent the three basic types traditionally recognized: a complement clause, an adverbial clause, and a relative clause. As a general description, it can therefore be proposed that a subordinate clause is one whose profile is overridden at a higher level of grammatical organization.[6] If we seek a single, simple characterization for all clauses that are traditionally regarded as subordinate, this is in fact the only plausible candidate. But it is not self-evident that we can actually find such a characterization—or even expect to. Indeed, there is no traditional consensus as to precisely which clauses count as subordinate. There is also uncertainty as to how (or even whether) to apply the notion of profiling at higher levels of grammatical structure.

One tip-off that the line between coordination and subordination is not always sharp is the traditional term **subordinating conjunction**. It is used for a variable set of elements, like those in (12), introducing finite clauses whose function (broadly speaking) is adverbial. The ambivalence reflected in the term is not unjustified. On the one hand, the clauses introduced by these elements are to some degree subordinate— formally, because they are specially marked; semantically, because they modify the other clause (e.g. through a specification of time, reason, or circumstance). On the other hand, the asymmetry in status is less apparent than in many complex sentences. Both clauses are finite and fully specified. It would seem, moreover, that their content is equally important and focused to the same extent. In these respects, their relationship resembles coordination.

(12)   (a) *I said it **because** I meant it.*

(b) ***Although** the family was poor, they were always well dressed.*

(c) *They began arguing **before** they even sat down.*

(d) ***While** the term is commonly used, it is never clearly defined.*

One way to resolve the issue would be to argue that *because, although,* and the like do in fact introduce a subordinate clause whose profile is overridden. This is not inconsistent with the clause being comparable in salience and importance to the other. Profiling is a matter of reference, not importance, and while it is a kind of prominence, it is not the only kind. Also, in contrast to the spirit of coordination, the relation between the clauses is inherently asymmetrical: *I said it because I meant it* is quite different from *I meant it because I said it.* Underscoring their asymmetry is the possibility of replacing the clause in question with a nonclausal structure. In (13) this structure is just a modifier, its nonprocessual profile overridden by the processual profile of the clause it modifies.

(13)   (a) *I said it **because of** her comment.*

(b) ***Though** poor, the family was always well dressed.*

---

[6] It would be inaccurate to say that a main-clause profile is not overridden. While valid in local terms, this characterization fails to hold in complex expressions where a main clause is itself subordinated at a higher level. An example is *the spider [she tried [to swallow]]*, where *she tried* functions as a main clause only in relation to the complement clause *to swallow*. In the higher-level relative clause construction, its profile is overridden by *spider*.

(c) *They began arguing **before** dinner.*

(d) ***While** common, the term is never clearly defined.*

With this approach, we are able to maintain a clear and precisely defined distinction between coordination and subordination. But is the distinction really sharp? We have already seen that coordinate structures exhibit various kinds and degrees of asymmetry. Should we not also expect the converse, that certain subordinate structures might tend toward symmetry? Instead of a strict dichotomy, we might well anticipate a fuzzy boundary with transitional cases. A related issue concerns the scope of profile determinance: that is, the maximal size of the structure within which a single profile predominates. It is evident that a single profile prevails in a nominal or a finite clause—*a tasty spider* profiles just the spider, and *she quickly swallowed a spider* profiles just the process of swallowing. It is not so obvious, however, that a complex sentence containing multiple finite clauses should always be analyzed as having only one overall referent. The more complex the sentence (and there is no intrinsic upper limit), the more implausible this seems.

While this issue is unresolved, a reasonable suggestion might run as follows. A crucial factor is grounding. Almost in a literal sense, the ground is the vantage point from which the grounded structure is apprehended. It thus seems natural to propose that grounding might delimit the scope of profile determinance. Each instance of grounding represents a separate act of apprehension, so it makes sense that the material specifically apprehended via that act would have a single overall profile. This would not preclude one grounded structure overriding the profile of another if the latter is central to its characterization. In (11)(c), for example, *this money* overrides the processual profile of the relative clause *we stole*, and *is counterfeit* overrides the nominal profile of *this money we stole*—each grounded structure invokes the previous one and views it from another perspective at a higher level of organization. But in cases like (12), where the two finite clauses are only loosely connected, it is not unlikely that each is apprehended autonomously and related to the other only secondarily.

How clauses are connected is an important topic I will turn to shortly. One particular kind of connection is itself a dimension of subordination. This is the case where one clause elaborates a salient e-site within the other, especially one focused as trajector or landmark. To the extent that it is nominalized, the elaborating clause then constitutes the subject or object of the other. The nominalized clause *my winning the Nobel Prize* is thus the subject of *astonish* in (14)(a) and the object of *resent* in (14)(b). It is subordinate to the main clause in the sense of being a participant in the process profiled by that clause.

(14)   (a) *[[My winning the Nobel Prize] astonished them.]*

(b) *[They resented [my winning the Nobel Prize].]*

Subordinate clauses are often described as being "embedded" in a main (or "matrix") clause. The term implies that the main clause contains the subordinate clause as an internal constituent. This whole-part relationship, indicated by the brackets in (14), would seem self-evident when the subordinate clause functions as the main-clause landmark or trajector. Of course, the subordinate clause may itself have a clausal landmark or trajector, and so on indefinitely. The evident result is the sort of nesting shown in (15)(a), with no intrinsic limit on the number of levels.

(15)   (a) *[Alice said [that Bill believes [that Cindy claims [that Doris swallowed a spider]]].]*

         (b) *[Alice said] [that Bill believes] [that Cindy claims] [that Doris swallowed a spider].*

The constituency in (15)(a) is seldom seriously questioned. But perhaps it ought to be. One factor long recognized as problematic is that the nesting ascribed to such expressions is at odds with their phonological realization. Intonation suggests the nonnested structure in (15)(b): each clause is a separate intonational unit bounded by a slight pause from the one that follows. Furthermore, a primary reason for adopting a layered structure is the tacit assumption that basic grammatical relationships have to be reflected in constituency. In CG this assumption is seen as being gratuitous (§7.4.3). Grammatical relationships have a conceptual basis and can be captured by correspondences irrespective of the order of grammatical combination. A viable description is therefore possible adopting an unlayered structure along the lines of (15)(b).

The structure is sketched in figure 12.4 (showing only essential details). Each clause designates a two-participant relationship. In each but the last, the profiled process consists in the trajector adopting some stance in regard to a proposition, represented as a box; this schematic proposition is its landmark. The component clauses are integrated by correspondences that identify the landmark of one clause with the specific relationship profiled by the next. As a consequence, the composite structure reveals a layered organization such that each clausal relationship incorporates the next one as a participant. This is the nesting depicted in (15)(a). Crucially, though, it is a feature of the expression's conceptual structure, not a matter of grammatical constituency. Instead of holding externally, among the elements of a symbolic

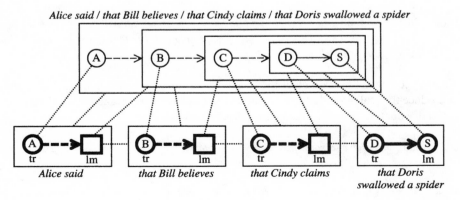

Alice said / that Bill believes / that Cindy claims / that Doris swallowed a spider

FIGURE 12.4

assembly, the layering is internal to the composite structure's semantic pole (hence unipolar rather than bipolar). It constitutes a mental space configuration: the process of Doris swallowing a spider occupies the mental space representing Cindy's claim, which in turn is in the space representing Bill's belief, and so on.

Even if there is no syntactic embedding, each clause is still subordinate to the preceding one conceptually in the sense of functioning as its landmark. What about profiling? Observe that no composite-structure profile is indicated in the diagram. This accords with the previous notion that grounding delimits the scope of profile determinance. Since all the clauses in (15) are independently grounded, each has the potential to constitute an autonomous act of apprehension, with a single overall profile for the content it subsumes. Perhaps they realize this potential despite the conceptual embedding, being apprehended separately and connected only secondarily. As the diagram suggests, the result is then a nonhierarchical, chain-like grammatical structure, where each clause is linked to the next by a correspondence. Semantically, this link consists in the expectation that the schematic landmark will be further specified. At the phonological pole, it is signaled iconically by suspended intonation (hinting that more will follow), in contrast to the falling intonation of the final clause. This linear grammatical organization is not at all inconsistent with a nested mental space configuration—grammar is not to be identified with conceptual structure, but is rather a means of prompting its construction. While a chain-like syntactic structure invokes the mental spaces sequentially, they can nonetheless be summed and integrated to yield the nested conception.

Under what circumstances one finite clause incorporates another—imposing its own profile as part of a single act of apprehension embracing them both—remains an open question. Its answer awaits a coherent overall account of grammar, online processing, and the directing of attention at multiple levels of organization. In the meantime, we should bear in mind that profiling is only one of numerous kinds of prominence that need to be distinguished (even if, in the last analysis, they should all be related). Among these, constituting a final dimension of subordination, are various sorts of discourse prominence. Let us briefly examine just one.

From a discourse perspective, the content presented in subordinate clauses is often the most important. Consider the following discourse fragment:

(16)   *There's something [you simply have to know]. It seems [that Gerald's trophy wife is really a transsexual]. I suppose [they'll get a divorce]. I'm telling you because [he'll need a good lawyer].*

In each sentence the main clause is largely incidental, serving mainly to frame and introduce the real news. In fact, we obtain a perfectly coherent (and basically equivalent) discourse by omitting the main clauses altogether:[7]

(17)   *You simply have to know this. Gerald's trophy wife is really a transsexual. They'll get a divorce. He'll need a good lawyer.*

---

[7] This is decidedly not the case if we omit the subordinate clauses instead: *There's something. It seems. I suppose. I'm telling you because of something.*

It has therefore been questioned whether the clauses traditionally labeled "subordinate" actually deserve that label (Thompson 2002; Diessel and Tomasello 2001; Verhagen 2005). In the sense of conveying essential content, it is often the so-called subordinate clause that plays the leading role. Conversely, it is common for a "main" clause to have a secondary function, such as indicating the status of that content (e.g. *it seems*; *I suppose*) or managing the discourse interaction (*I'm telling you because...*). To the extent that this is so, the complement clause should perhaps be analyzed as imposing its profile on the composite expression, thereby reversing the traditional identification of clauses as "main" vs. "subordinate". Certainly the complement's profile prevails in (18), where the other clause is merely appended as an afterthought. Even so, the complement is subordinate in the specific sense of spelling out the latter's landmark.

(18) (a) *Gerald's trophy wife is really a transsexual, [it seems].*

     (b) *They'll get a divorce, [I suppose].*

     (c) *He'll need a good lawyer, [I'm telling you].*

These observations underscore the need to distinguish various kinds of prominence and dimensions of subordination. Despite the unitary label, subordination is a complicated matter not reducible to any single factor. There is no point imposing a strict dichotomy based on any single criterion—that would be arbitrary as well as misleading. It is only by discerning and investigating the factors involved that we can figure out how complex sentences really work. The following sections explore certain aspects of this problem.

12.2 Clausal Connections

The clauses traditionally regarded as subordinate are roughly divisible into three broad groups: adverbial, relative, and complement clauses. We have seen that these are not invariably subordinate in the sense that their profile is overridden by that of the "main" (or "matrix") clause. Other defining properties—including the presence of a subordinating element and the absence of elements required in a full, independent sentence—are likewise not wholly consistent. There is one more basic factor to consider: that of how clauses are connected to each other. It is primarily on this basis that the three kinds of subordinate clauses are distinguished from the main clause and from one another.

12.2.1 Adverbial Clauses

Adverbial clauses are those whose function vis-à-vis the main clause is roughly analogous to that of nonclausal adverbs. They qualify the main-clause process with respect to such factors as time, means, cause, and purpose, in some cases being introduced by the same elements used in other adverbials:

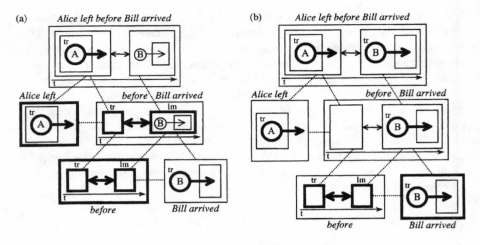

(a) *Alice left before Bill arrived*

(b) *Alice left before Bill arrived*

FIGURE 12.5

(19) (a) *Alice left {before midnight/before Bill arrived}.*

   (b) *They got the contract {through bribery/by bribing the key administrators}.*

   (c) *Progress was slow {because of the rain/because it was raining so hard}.*

   (d) *He'll do anything {for attention/(in order) to attract attention}.*

   Because an adverbial clause can qualify a main clause in many different ways, there is usually some element that specifies the nature of their relationship. Among these **connectors** in English are *before, after, when, while, until, if, by, because, since, despite, unless, although,* and *in order to.*[8] Some of these connectors (*before, after, until, by, since, despite*) also function as prepositions, taking nominal objects. They are all similar to prepositions by virtue of profiling nonprocessual relationships with both a trajector and a landmark.[9] It is through this relationship that the connection between the two clauses is established. The adverbial clause invariably specifies the connector's landmark, and the matrix clause its trajector. In (19)(a), for example, the landmark of *before* is specified by the finite clause *Bill arrived,* and its trajector by *Alice left.* The event of Bill arriving is thus invoked to indicate the temporal location of Alice leaving. The global organization of this sentence is therefore as shown in figure 12.5.

---

[8] By using the neutral term **connector** (in lieu of **subordinator** or **subordinating conjunction**), we avoid the implication that an adverbial clause is necessarily subordinate. In a similar vein, the terms "main clause" and "matrix clause" should not be understood as implying that the clause in question is always more important than the adverbial clause or incorporates it as a constituent. The terminology is far from optimal owing to the complexity and variability of the phenomena.

[9] Whether they actually qualify as prepositions, as narrowly characterized in fig. 4.11(c), depends on whether the adverbial clause is nominalized by conceptual reification (so that the landmark is construed as a thing).

Two alternatives are presented, differing only in what is profiled at the composite-structure level. Figure 12.5(a) presumes that the two expressions in (19)(a) are precisely analogous: they profile only the event of Alice leaving, whether the temporal landmark is a thing (*midnight*) or another event (*Bill arrived*). On this account *before Bill arrived* is merely an adverbial modifier, and *Bill arrived* is subordinate in the sense that its profile is superseded at higher levels. By contrast, figure 12.5(b)—reflecting the ambivalence of the term "subordinating conjunction"—presumes that both finite clauses retain their profile in the overall expression. On this account the sentence is essentially a coordinate structure, with two coexisting profiles. It does not, however, represent a pure case of coordination, where the conjuncts are coequal elements in a symmetrical relationship. They are nonparallel because the connector *before* relates them asymmetrically in terms of trajector/landmark alignment. Even though both events are profiled, *Alice left* is temporally located with respect to *Bill arrived*, rather than conversely.

Which analysis is right? Probably they both are. Because it incorporates grounding, thus relating the profiled occurrence to the interlocutors and the speech event, a finite clause has the potential to be apprehended independently as a complete sentence. Being self-contained in this manner lends it a certain resistance to being subordinated to another clause in the sense of its profile being overridden. It may well be the case that speakers have the option of retaining its profile depending on the heft and importance of its semantic content, as well as its status in the discourse. In examples like (20), where it introduces most of the essential content, there seems little doubt that the *before*-clause is viewed directly in its own terms, not just in relation to *Alice left*.

(20)   *Alice left just before a sprinkler malfunction soaked all the guests.*

Under either analysis in figure 12.5, connectors associate the matrix and adverbial clauses by specifying the nature of their relationship: temporal (e.g. *before*, *after*, *until*), causal (*because*, *since*), concessive (*although*, *despite*), conditional (*if*, *provided that*), and so on. Often there are further connections between them. These are typically anaphoric, like the relationship between a pronoun and its antecedent. Thus in (21)(a), the pronoun *she* refers back to *Alice*. We observe another kind of anaphoric linkage in (21)(b). The verb *do* is maximally schematic in regard to type (equivalent to the verb class schema). It is only through its anaphoric relationship to *leave*, in the matrix clause, that we learn what action Bill engaged in.

(21)   (a) **Alice** *left before* **she** *could thank the hostess.*

(b) *Alice* **left** *before Bill* **did**.

(c) *Alice left before thanking the hostess.*

When it is nonfinite, an adverbial clause commonly lacks an overt subject. An example is (21)(c), where the atemporalizing suffix *-ing* occurs on the verb in lieu of grounding. In such cases the clausal trajector is simply not elaborated by a nominal component. But it may be identified—in (21)(c) it is Alice who thanks the hostess.

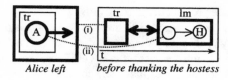

FIGURE 12.6

Its identification is effected through a correspondence with a main clause participant, usually its trajector.[10] The integration of *Alice left* and *before thanking the hostess* is therefore as shown in figure 12.6. Correspondence (i) equates the former with the overall trajector of the latter, just as in figure 12.5(a). This establishes the primary connection between the matrix and adverbial clauses. Additionally, correspondence (ii) identifies the main clause trajector with the schematic trajector of the atemporalized process functioning as the adverbial expression's overall landmark. At the composite-structure level (not shown), Alice is thus identified as both the one who leaves and the one who thanks the hostess.

Of course, we understand (21)(c) as indicating that Alice, despite her role as the one thanking the hostess, did not in fact actually do so. This is a matter of inference, based on the standard party scenario. It presumes that the hostess is in the house where the party is held (not outside on the street) and that thanking the hostess is done immediately and in person (not later, by telephone). Granted these default assumptions, leaving before the thanking prevents the latter from occurring. Observe that changing *before* to *after* reverses the inference: *Alice left after thanking the hostess* implies that she did indeed thank her. Whether the event occurred has to be determined via inference because the clause describing it is nonfinite; without grounding, there is no direct indication of its epistemic status. In contrast, the grounded matrix clause (*Alice left*) explicitly portrays the profiled event as being real (through the absence of a modal) and prior to the time of speaking (through the past-tense inflection). These specifications are then invoked as a partial basis—along with the other factors noted—for inferring the status of the thanking.

The presence vs. the absence of grounding is one asymmetry that motivates the labels "main" vs. "subordinate" clause. In two-clause expressions, the main clause is usually finite, whereas the subordinate clause is very often nonfinite.[11] The latter may then be dependent on the former for various specifications needed for a full proposition. In (21)(c), *Alice left* designates a specific occurrence—a particular instance of leaving on the part of a particular individual—situated with respect to the speech event and the speaker's conception of reality. By contrast, *thanking the hostess* is not itself sufficient to single out a particular instance of thanking or indicate

[10] Here is one example where the correspondent is not the trajector: *It occurred to me just before leaving the party that I should thank the hostess.*

[11] Naturally, a main clause can itself be subordinated as part of a more complex expression. In *Bill persuaded Alice to leave before thanking the hostess*, for example, *to leave* functions as the main clause with respect to *before thanking the hostess*, but as a subordinate clause with respect to *Bill persuaded Alice*.

its epistemic status. If we try to interpret it independently, the designated action is conceived abstractly, as a general characterization applicable to an open-ended set of instances. It is only its connections with the main clause that single out a specific occurrence whose position vis-à-vis conceived reality can be assessed.

A key factor in clausal connections is whether the focal participants of the two clauses—especially their trajectors—are the same or different. In (21)(c), Alice functions as trajector in both the matrix and adverbial clauses, as indicated by correspondence (ii) in figure 12.6. The identity or distinctness of clausal trajectors is important enough that some languages mark it explicitly. In Hopi, for example, connecting elements such as *-t* 'after', *-kyang* 'while', and *-e'* 'if' specifically mark the clausal subjects as being the same (SS). These are all replaced by *-q* when the subjects are different (DS):

(22) (a) *Nu'   paki-t   pu'   qatuvtu.*   'After entering, I sat down.'
          I   enter-after:ss then sit:down

      (b) *Nu'   paki-q   pu'   pam   qatuvtu.*   'After I entered, he sat down.'
          I   enter-DS then he   sit:down

This Hopi construction further illustrates how tenuous the distinction is between main and subordinate clauses, and thus between co- and sub-ordination. While the first clause has adverbial function, the construction would seem to be coordinate in the sense that both events are profiled, in the manner of figure 12.5(b). The adverbial clause is subordinated in the sense of being specially marked by the connecting suffix, which (like English *to* and *-ing*) occurs in lieu of grounding. At the same time, in examples like (22)(a) the adverbial clause is the one with an overt subject and in this respect provides the basis for interpreting the matrix clause. This blurring of traditional distinctions is unproblematic in CG, which invokes them only to the extent that they are useful. Mixed cases are readily described by varying the specific details of symbolic assemblies.[12] What is essential is that every language and every construction be characterized in its own terms.

12.2.2 Relative Clauses

Whereas an adverbial clause modifies another clause, a relative clause modifies a nominal expression. The primary connection is thus a correspondence between the nominal referent and some participant in the process designated by the relative. That participant, sometimes called the **pivot**, has a semantic role in both the relative clause and the matrix clause containing the modified nominal. In (23), for example, the relative clause *I was reading* modifies *book*. The book referred to is the pivot. It is understood as both trajector of the matrix clause, where it functions overtly as the subject, and as landmark of the relative.

---

[12] Sketching the assembly for (22)(a) might prove a useful exercise. You can reasonably assume that the profiling is analogous to fig. 12.5(b), and that the connector *-t* incorporates, as an inherent aspect of its meaning, a correspondence analogous to (ii) in fig. 12.6.

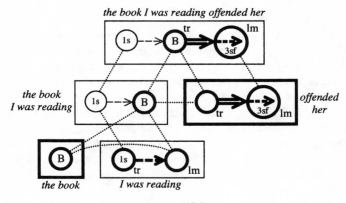

FIGURE 12.7

(23)   *The book I was reading offended her.*

The important details of (23) are presented in figure 12.7.[13] The essential correspondence equates the profile of *the book* with the schematic landmark of *I was reading*. The former being the profile determinant (constructional head), the composite expression designates the book rather than the process of reading it. The result is a complex nominal, *the book I was reading*, which specifies the trajector of *offended her* at a higher level of organization. Hence the topmost structure, representing the composite meaning for the sentence as a whole, shows the book as having two roles: it participates in both the offending (profiled at that level) and the reading.

Languages and constructions vary in regard to the pivot's role within the relative clause. In some languages, only the trajector can function as pivot. Nonfinite relatives in English, e.g. those marked with (nonprogressive) *-ing*, share this limitation.[14] We can thus say *the monkey climbing that tree* but not **the tree that monkey climbing*. In most languages, the pivot can also be the clausal landmark, and often there are further options. English is especially flexible. In finite relatives, the pivot may also be a possessor (*the girl whose cat you stole*), the object of a preposition (*the magazine I got the information from*), or even—when the relative is itself complex—a participant in a complement clause within it (*the dress she persuaded her daughter to buy*).

In all these cases, the pivot has a definite grammatical role within the relative clause. It is typically the trajector or the landmark of an explicit relational element, e.g. the landmark of *read* in figure 12.7. But there are also relative constructions where the connection is semantically open-ended and grammatically indeterminate.

---

[13] Grounding is ignored, as is progressive marking in the relative. The pronouns are given as '1s' (first singular) and '3sf' (third-singular feminine). Dashed arrows indicate mental experience: externally directed in the case of *read*, internal in the case of *offend*.

[14] One exception is that relatives marked with infinitival *to* also allow a landmark to function as pivot: *a good person to know*.

In such constructions, the pivot is not necessarily associated with any particular grammatical position or explicitly coded relationship. It need only be contextually inferrable and interpretable as being related, even indirectly, to the overt content. One construction of this sort are relatives marked by *pu* in Modern Greek (Nikiforidou 2005). For instance, in (24) the head noun *ðieta* has no specific grammatical role in the relative, as it does not correspond to a focal participant of 'die'. A connection with dying can, however, be inferred on the basis of general knowledge, allowing a coherent composite conception to emerge.

(24) *Mu   eðose   mja   ðieta   pu   praɣmatika   peθenis.*

      me   he:gave   one   diet   that   really   you:die

      'He gave me a diet that [if you follow it diligently] you [can] really die.'

Relative pivots are manifested in a variety of ways, quite commonly by zero. In (23), the landmark of *read* is simply not expressed in the relative clause itself. Instead, as seen figure 12.7, its landmark is identified through a correspondence to the profile of the nominal functioning as main-clause subject. Effectively, then, *the book* specifies the landmark of *read*, as well as the trajector of *offend*. The pivot can also be spelled out by a pronoun. This may be a regular personal pronoun appearing in its normal clausal position, as in (25)(a), where *they* refers back to *a cheap pair of glasses*. Alternatively, a minority of languages have special **relative pronouns**, like English *who* and *which*, that typically come at the beginning of the clause. Note that *which* is clause-initial in (25)(c), even though it functions as the clausal object (which normally follows the verb).[15]

(25) (a) *He bought **a cheap pair of glasses** that he doesn't care if **they** get broken.*

     (b) *The people **who** bought that house must be very wealthy.*

     (c) *The book **which** I was reading offended her.*

The book which I was reading is roughly sketched in figure 12.8. In contrast to *the book I was reading* (fig. 12.7), the relative clause does have an overt object: *which* serves this function, despite its position at the beginning of the clause (atypical for objects). The notation for the relative pronoun is meant to indicate that it profiles a thing characterized only as being nonhuman (nh) and as having some role in a process. A correspondence identifies this schematic process with the more specific process designated by the remainder of the clause (*I was reading*). A second correspondence equates the thing profiled by *which* with the landmark of that process, making *which* its object. The resulting relative clause, *which I was reading*, is then integrated with *the book* just as in the previous example. Observe that *the book*

---

[15] In English, personal pronouns tend to be used when a relative pronoun would not be permitted (cf. **He bought a cheap pair of glasses **which** he doesn't care if get broken*). The thorny problem of when a relative pronoun is allowed will be left aside, despite being a major preoccupation of linguistic theorists since Ross 1967. The meanings of relative pronouns are discussed more fully in Langacker 2001c.

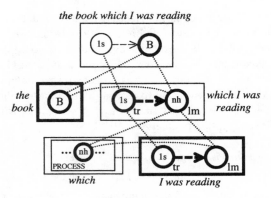

FIGURE 12.8

I was reading and *the book which I was reading* have the same composite semantic structure. Thus *which* does not contribute significantly to the overall expression's conceptual content, but simply makes its structure more explicit.

Canonically, then, a relative construction has two components: a nominal expression that specifies a basic type, and a clause which helps identify a particular instance of that type. They are integrated to form a higher-level nominal through a correspondence between the nominal profile and a schematic clausal participant. The essence of relative clause constructions does not consist, however, in any specific structural configuration. Their essential feature is semantic: a relative clause is one invoked to characterize a nominal referent identified as a participant in the clausal process. While those examined so far may be typical, relative constructions are structurally quite diverse. We have seen, for example, that the nominal and clausal components do not always combine directly to form a grammatical constituent. Figure 10.10 showed the integration of two clauses, *the package arrived* and *that I was expecting*, to derive a complex sentence in which the relative characterizes the subject of the matrix clause even though they are noncontiguous.

More strikingly different (though quite natural in their own way) are relative constructions where the nominal and clausal components are nondistinct. While details vary, a common feature of these constructions is that the lexical head—the noun providing the basic type specification—appears inside the relative clause rather than externally as a separate nominal component. They are thus described as "internally headed" relative clauses (or as "headless", presuming that a head can only be external). Certain relatives in Hopi have this property (Gorbet 1977). In (26), the boy is the one sent home, hence understood as the main-clause object. However, what appears in object position before the verb is the entire clausal structure enclosed in brackets. The nominal containing the lexical head, *mit tiyo'yat* 'that boy ACC', is found within the relative clause, where it is also the object (the boy is the one who gets hit). Since the boy participates as landmark with respect to both the hitting and the sending home, it makes no real difference whether it is lexically manifested in the main clause or in the subordinate clause.

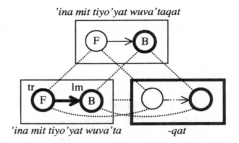

'ina mit tiyo'yat wuva'taqat

'ina mit tiyo'yat wuva'ta   *-qat*

FIGURE 12.9

(26) *Nu'* *['i-na*   *mi-t*   *tiyo'ya-t*   *wuva'ta-qa-t]*   *hoona.*

I   my-father that-ACC   boy-ACC   hit-NR-ACC   send:home

'I sent home the boy that my father hit.'

The bracketed portion of (26) is represented in figure 12.9. It is based on the clausal structure *'ina mit tiyo'yat wuva'ta* 'my father hit that boy', which is in fact a possible sentence. Here, though, it takes the ending *-qat*, whose effect is to impose a nominal construal: the composite expression profiles the boy rather than the process of hitting. This ending decomposes into the nominalizer *-qa* plus the object suffix *-t*. Normally *-qa* is agentive (like English *-er*), but in combination with *-t* it profiles the landmark of the schematic process invoked as its base (rather than its trajector). Hence the composite expression *'ina mit tiyo'yat wuva'taqat* designates a boy characterized as the one the speaker's father hit. It is a full nominal because it profiles a thing identified as a particular instance of its type, and as a nominal it can function as the object of *hoona* 'send home'.[16] It represents a relative clause construction because it invokes a clause to characterize a nominal referent identified as a processual participant.

This way of defining a relative clause does not specifically indicate that its processual profile is overridden. For the expressions diagrammed in figures 12.7 to 12.9, it is reasonably supposed that its profile is indeed superseded at a higher level of organization: in each case, the relative clause is part of a nominal which, taken as a whole, designates a participant in the clausal process rather than that process itself. These are cases where the nominal and clausal components are closely connected and the clause has no other purpose than to identify the nominal referent. Yet there are also many cases where the clause is more loosely connected with the nominal or contributes semantically in other ways. These factors facilitate its being apprehended autonomously and retaining its processual profile.

It is apprehended independently, no doubt, when the nominal and clausal components are discontinuous, as in our previous example: ***The package*** *arrived* ***that***

---

[16] The suffix *-t* is ambivalent as to whether it is part of the relativizing ending *-qat* (as indicated) or simply marks the derived noun as main-clause object. These options are reinforcing rather than contradictory, since the nominal referent functions as landmark in both the main and subordinate clauses.

I was expecting. Since they do not form a grammatical constituent, there is no basis for positing a composite symbolic structure whose semantic pole profiles just the package.[17] The two grammatical components—*the package arrived* and *that I was expecting*—are both finite clauses and profile grounded processes. They are asymmetrically related, in that the former provides the crucial information and the latter is marked by *that*, a general-purpose subordinator. Accordingly, figures 7.19(b) and 10.10 showed the first clause as being the profile determinant, on the assumption that a noncoordinate expression has just one profile overall. While we can reasonably assume this for simpler structures, there appears to be greater flexibility with complex sentences. Profiling involves the focusing of attention, and beyond a certain size, a structure is hard to accommodate in a single "window" of attention with a single overall focus. When loosely connected, there is thus a tendency for finite clauses to realize the potential for a grounded structure to be apprehended independently. Perhaps, then, the sentence is better analyzed as having two processual profiles, accessed in successive windows of attention. In any event, the profile of the relative clause is not overridden by that of the noun it modifies.

Multiple factors interact to determine whether a relative clause retains its profile. One factor is the extent to which it approximates a fully specified clause that could stand alone as a sentence. The relative in (27)(a) is likely to be apprehended independently due to its being grounded and having an overt subject (the relative pronoun *who*). By contrast, the participial relative in (27)(b) is deficient in both respects and thus has a lesser chance of retaining its profile. And in (27)(c), *in this lab* is even less clause-like because it lacks a verb. It is thus considered to be a noun modifier rather than a relative. While there is no clear line of demarcation, simple modifiers have their profile overridden virtually as a matter of definition.

(27) (a) *The effect was discovered by some scientists who were working in this lab.*

      (b) *The effect was discovered by some scientists working in this lab.*

      (c) *The effect was discovered by some scientists in this lab.*

A second factor is the extent to which the content of a relative clause is new or important in the discourse. The relatives in (28) make successively greater semantic contributions encouraging their apprehension in a separate window of attention. In (28)(a), the content supplied by the clause *I read* is neither very informative nor in any way noteworthy. Its semantic unimportance correlates with its phonological "compression": compared with the matrix clause, it tends to be pronounced quite rapidly, with reduced stress, and at a lower pitch. This is not so in the other two sentences, where the content of the relative is more elaborate and less predictable. It is also more essential to the discourse. In (28)(b), the property of making outrageous claims is the key to identifying the particular (fictive) instance of *book* invoked as the basis for making a generalization. In (28)(c), the relative does not so much serve to identify the nominal referent (for which the matrix clause suffices) as to make an

---

[17] Presumably they constitute a conceptual grouping, but it is not symbolized by any phonological grouping to form a composite **symbolic** structure.

additional statement that is actually the major point of the sentence. As we go from (a) to (c), therefore, it seems less and less plausible to claim that the relative clause is subordinate in the sense that its profile is overridden by the head noun *book*.

(28) (a) *There were some outrageous claims in that book I read.*

    (b) *A book which makes outrageous claims is often a best-seller.*

    (c) *I just read a book which makes some outrageous claims.*

Finally, the likelihood of a relative clause retaining its profile is influenced by the closeness of the connection between the nominal and clausal components. With a finite relative, the closest connection is observed in examples like (28)(a): the two components are adjacent, they form a grammatical constituent, they are closely integrated phonologically (the relative being prosodically compressed), the nominal directly specifies the clausal landmark (there being no relative pronoun), and the clause helps identify the nominal referent. Cases where the nominal and clausal components are nonadjacent represent one departure from this configuration. Another kind of departure is a nonrestrictive relative clause:

(29) *I just read a book, which makes some outrageous claims.*

While they are usually contiguous, a nonrestrictive relative is set off from the nominal component by the slight hesitation written as a comma. This prosodic separation is an indication that they occupy separate windows of attention, and are thus in large measure apprehended independently. This is possible because a nonrestrictive relative is not invoked to single out the nominal referent, but to make an additional comment about it. In (29), the relevant type—an instance of which is grounded by the indefinite article—is simply *book*, not *book which makes some outrageous claims* (cf. fig. 10.9). There is no basis for claiming that the relative clause is incorporated into the nominal it modifies, or that its profile is overridden by either that nominal or the clause containing it. Though subordinate in the sense of having a relative pronoun (whose reference depends on the modified nominal), a nonrestrictive relative is coequal with the other clause in terms of profiling. For this reason, expressions like (29) are often likened to coordinate structures.

12.2.3 Complement Clauses

A complement clause is one that specifies a salient participant in the main-clause relationship. In this respect complements are analogous to subject and object nominals, which elaborate the schematic trajector and landmark of a profiled process. Indeed, some complement clauses function grammatically as subject or object of the main-clause predicate. In (30), for example, the bracketed clause occupies the same position as the subject nominal *a loud party*, and like this nominal it follows the first auxiliary verb in a question. Similarly, the complement clause in (31) appears in the same position as the object nominal *a dirty and vicious campaign*, and like this nominal it occurs as subject in the corresponding passive.

(30) (a) *A loud party would bother the neighbors.*

   (b) *[Setting off these fireworks] would bother the neighbors.*

   (c) *Would a loud party bother the neighbors?*

   (d) *Would [setting off these fireworks] bother the neighbors?*

(31) (a) *All the commentators predicted a vicious and dirty campaign.*

   (b) *All the commentators predicted [that he would lose the election].*

   (c) *A dirty and vicious campaign was predicted by all the commentators.*

   (d) *[That he would lose the election] was predicted by all the commentators.*

Can we then say that complement clauses are simply subject or object nominals, obtained by conceptual reification of the complement process? As a general analysis, this fails on multiple counts. First, not every complement clause is parallel to a nonclausal subject or object. For instance, complements directly follow certain adjectives: *I'm {sure/happy/pleased} [he is honest]*. Adjectives do not occur with object nominals, however; we cannot say **I'm {sure/happy/pleased} his honesty*. To express such notions, the adjective is followed by a prepositional phrase: *I'm {sure of/happy about/pleased with} his honesty*. Moreover, a complement that appears to be parallel to a nonclausal subject or object does not always behave like one in all respects. In (32) we observe that a finite complement in subject position is unhappy after an auxiliary verb in a question. Likewise, the examples in (33) show the resistance of infinitival complements to passivization.

(32) (a) *All those lies do not bother the president.*

   (b) *[That he tells so many lies] does not bother the president.*

   (c) *Do all those lies bother the president?*

   (d) **Does [that he tells so many lies] bother the president?*

(33) (a) *The organizers fully expected those problems.*

   (b) *The organizers fully expected [to encounter those problems].*

   (c) *Those problems were fully expected by the organizers.*

   (d) **[To encounter those problems] was fully expected by the organizers.*

Thus complement constructions have to be considered in their own terms. They approximate subject and object constructions in different ways and to different degrees, fully instantiating those constructions only as a special case. By the same token, complement-taking predicates diverge in subtle respects from the meanings they have in noncomplement constructions. The meaning of *sure*, for example, is not precisely the same when followed by a clause or a prepositional phrase. The two senses evoke the same content for their conceptual base. The semantic

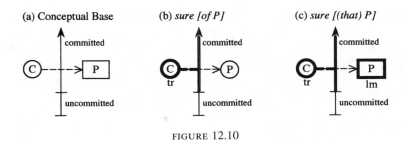

FIGURE 12.10

contrast is a matter of how this content is construed in the context of the larger construction.

The conceptual base is depicted in figure 12.10(a). The dashed arrow represents the stance adopted by a conceptualizer (C) in regard to a proposition (P). Pivotal to *sure* is the extent of C's commitment to accepting the proposition as valid (part of C's conception of reality). A scale measuring degree of commitment is therefore indicated by a solid arrow. While this scale is essentially continuous, a basic distinction is made between C being committed to P (accepting it as real) and being uncommitted. The import of *sure* is that C's stance in regard to P falls well within the region of commitment.

This much is shared by both senses of *sure*. They further share an emphasis on a particular aspect of the conceptualizer's mental attitude—namely, **strength** of commitment to P. In contrast to a verb like *know* or *believe*, where the **fact** of commitment is at issue, the primary thrust of *sure* is that C's stance in regard to P is firm and unlikely to waver.[18] What *sure* profiles, therefore, is not the relationship between C and P (as in the case of *know* and *believe*), but rather where C's attitude falls on the scale of commitment. This is not to deny that C's relationship to P is crucial: it is on that basis that strength of commitment is assessed. The central focus is nonetheless on C's position along the scale, as shown in figure 12.10(b) and (c).

As a consequence, P is not necessarily a focal participant in the profiled relationship. Evidently it is not focal in expressions like *I'm sure of his honesty*, where it combines with *sure* only indirectly, as the object of a prepositional phrase. In the context of this periphrastic construction, P is conceptually reified and construed as an abstract thing, so it is coded by a nominal (*his honesty*) rather than a clause.[19] By contrast, P is expressed nonperiphrastically in sentences like *I'm sure (that) he is honest*. Being directly introduced suggests that P is more salient in the meaning of *sure*, and its clausal form suggests its apprehension as a process rather than a thing.

---

[18] It is not irrelevant that *sure* is etymologically related to *secure*.

[19] It is a moot point whether P's reification is ascribable to the adjective itself or to its being expressed as a prepositional object. The preposition *of* profiles a relationship characterized schematically as holding **intrinsically** between its trajector and landmark (GC: ch. 3). In this periphrastic construction, *of*'s trajector is the entire *sure* relationship, and its landmark—an intrinsic part of the relation—is the reified proposition. This is comparable to *of*'s use to specify the participants of nominalized verbs (e.g. *the dissection of squirrels*).

Accordingly, in figure 12.10(c) P is labeled as a landmark to indicate its prominence, and is also enclosed in a box (instead of a circle) to indicate the absence of reification. A finite clause elaborating P is therefore object-like by virtue of being the landmark in a profiled relationship. It is not however an object in any usual sense, since the term is only used for nominal expressions. The clause elaborating the landmark is a **relational complement** (rather than a nominal complement), and *sure* is thus considered an adjective rather than a preposition (fig. 4.11).

Another example of semantic variation with complement-taking predicates is the verb *expect*. It has at least four variants associated with different constructions, exemplified in (34). Respectively, they take as their complements a nominal, a finite clause, an infinitival clause, and a nominal plus an infinitival clause. Congruent with their occurrence in these constructions, the variants differ in the nature and identification of their landmarks, as shown in figure 12.11.

(34) (a) *The children expect a present.*

   (b) *Her mother expects [(that) she will graduate in June].*

   (c) *The painters expect [to finish on time].*

   (d) *We expect this movie [to make a lot of money].*

With a nominal complement, *expect* profiles a mental relationship (dashed arrow) wherein the trajector conceives of the landmark and anticipates receiving or encountering it. This sense is represented in figure 12.11(a). Since the process is construed as an interaction between participants, the verb is transitive and the nominal elaborating the landmark is not just an object in the broad sense, but a direct object in particular. And being transitive, the resulting clause is susceptible to passivization, as in (33)(c).

When the complement is a finite clause, as in (34)(b), passivization is generally very awkward, though not precluded altogether:

(35) (a) *?*[That she will graduate in June] is expected by her mother.*

   (b) *?[That they would encounter problems] was expected by everybody.*

This is not just a matter of the process being mental instead of physical—note the felicity of (31)(d). It is rather that *expect* (in contrast to *predict*) construes a propositional landmark as relational rather than nominal. As shown in figure 12.11(b), its landmark is a schematic grounded process, apprehended as such (without reification).

 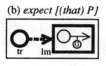 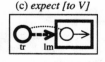 

(a) *expect [NML]*   (b) *expect [(that) P]*   (c) *expect [to V]*   (d) *expect [NML][to V]*

FIGURE 12.11

An elaborating finite clause is thus a relational complement (as opposed to a nominal object), so it is not eligible to be a passive subject. Why, then, are passives sometimes marginally possible, as in (35)(b)? When marked by *that*, finite clauses have the potential for conceptual reification, giving rise to an abstract thing. Propositions are metaphorically conceived as manipulable objects existing independently of any particular conceptualizer. So construed, a finite clause qualifies as a nominal, and as such it combines with the verb's transitive variant.[20]

With variant (c) in figure 12.11, passivization is usually not just marginal but unacceptable, as in (33)(d). Infinitival complements are less susceptible to conceptual reification because they are not sufficiently self-contained to be apprehended independently as usable descriptions of occurrences. The infinitival clause in (34)(c), *to finish on time*, lacks both grounding and an overt subject. In and of itself, therefore, it does not specify any particular event whose reality can be assessed.[21] Integration with the main clause does yield a more specific interpretation, however. The correspondence line in figure 12.11(c) identifies the infinitival trajector with that of *expect*. Thus in (34)(c), where *the painters* and *to finish on time* respectively elaborate the verb's trajector and landmark, we know that the painters are the ones who finish. Moreover, this event's epistemic status is inferrable from the meaning and grounding of the main-clause predicate. The grounding of *expect* situates this attitude in present reality, and its meaning implies that the landmark event is subsequent and less than fully assured. Hence the finishing lies in the future and will not necessarily occur.

Finally, variant (d) in figure 12.11 elevates the infinitival trajector to the status of main-clause landmark. That is, the expectation described in (34)(d) does not address the future in purely general terms, but is specifically an expectation in regard to the nominal object: concerning *this movie*, we expect it *to make a lot of money*. Besides its trajector, this sense of *expect* thus has two salient participants. One is the entity the expectation is directed at; this being focused as landmark, the nominal expressing it is the main-clause object. Also quite salient (a secondary landmark, if you like) is the expectation itself, specified by the infinitival complement. The configuration in figure 12.11(d) makes it automatic that the referent of the object nominal is interpreted as the infinitival trajector.

In sentences like (34)(c), where the matrix subject is equated with the otherwise unspecified trajector of the complement, linguists speak of a **control** relation between them. Although the complement lacks an explicit subject, the control relation identifies its trajector with a main-clause participant, which thus has a dual role in the composite semantic structure: the painters are both the ones who expect and the ones who finish. A controller is established on the basis of the construction and the meaning of the main-clause predicate. That the painters are the ones who finish follows from the meaning of *expect* described in figure 12.11(c), together with the fact that the infinitival complement elaborates its relational landmark.

---

[20] The resulting passives are still marginal for several reasons: (i) they require this extra conceptual operation; (ii) there is competition from the more basic nontransitive construction; and (iii) being quite distant from the transitive prototype, *expect* is not a strong candidate for passivization in the first place.

[21] However, the clause can be reified as another sort of abstract entity—namely, an event type figuring in general statements (e.g. *To finish on time is always desirable*).

English has a large and diverse array of control constructions, even restricting our attention to complement trajectors.[22] We see in (36) that the complement is not always infinitival but can also be marked by -*ing*. Further, the "controller" (given in bold) functions in the main clause as either the subject, the object, or even the object of a preposition. Likewise, the complement clause itself functions in the main clause as either the trajector, the landmark, or a prepositional landmark.

(36)   (a) ***He*** *actually enjoys [being obnoxious].*

    (b) ***He*** *truly excels at [being obnoxious].*

    (c) *[Being obnoxious] never bothers **him**.*

    (d) *[Being obnoxious] is easy for **him**.*

When the main clause has more than one nominal, the issue arises of choosing the controller. Which main-clause participant will serve in this capacity? As is so often the case, this classic syntactic problem proves to be basically semantic. The essential principle is straightforward: the controller is the participant most readily understood as complement trajector when all relevant conceptual factors are taken into account. The most obvious factors are the meaning of the main-clause predicate and the nature of the complement process, but inference and general knowledge are also quite important. Consider (37), where the controllers are different, even though the sentences are grammatically parallel and have the same main-clause predicate. The choice hinges on what we know about the workplace and the respective roles of supervisor and employee. Since an employee's absenteeism comes within the supervisor's purview (but not conversely), we infer that the controller in (37)(a)—the nominal which specifies the complement's trajector—is *me*. And since the supervisor determines an employee's salary (rather than conversely), we infer in (37)(b) that the controller is *my supervisor*.[23]

(37)   (a) *My supervisor talked to **me** about [being absent so often].*

    (b) ***My supervisor*** *talked to me about [approving a raise].*

Many predicates have meanings that strongly favor a particular choice of controller. But even when an alternative is highly entrenched and conventionally well established, there may still be some flexibility. One such case is *ask*. In expressions of the form *X ask Y [to V]*, the controller is almost always Y, as in (38)(a). It stands to reason that a request directed at Y would normally be for something whose

---

[22] We can also speak of control in regard to adverbial and relative clauses: *[When criticized], **he** sulks; **A child** [criticized too often] lacks self-esteem.* Moreover, the "controllee"—the participant whose reference is determined—is not invariably the subordinate-clause trajector. It can also be the clausal landmark or even a prepositional object: ***The book** [I read] was boring; **A noisy office** is hard [to work in].*

[23] These default interpretations can be overridden in special circumstances. Suppose, for instance, that my supervisor likes to confide in me and feels guilty about going to the racetrack every afternoon. In this case (37)(a) would be interpreted with *my supervisor* as controller.

occurrence Y determines. The situation changes, however, with a passive complement based on the verb *allow*, as in (38)(b). Since the trajector of *be allowed to V*
is not responsible for this occurrence, it is most readily identified with the person
making the request instead of the one who grants it. Hence the most natural alignment between the main-clause and complement-clause participants is for X to be
interpreted as the complement's trajector (the one allowed to attend), and Y as the
passive agent (the one who allows it).

(38)   (a) *I asked **her** [to attend the reception].*

    (b) ***I** asked her [to be allowed to attend the reception].*

    (c) ***I** promised her [to attend the reception].*

    (d) *I promised **her** [to be allowed to attend the reception].*

Everything is just the opposite when the verb is *promise*. In expressions of the
form *X promise Y [to V]*, it is Y who makes the request and X who grants it. Accordingly, X is virtually always the controller identified with the complement trajector,
as in (38)(c). Now a promise made in good faith implies the ability to deliver. Thus
if X promises *to V*, the occurrence of V ought to be something that X determines.
With an active verb like *attend*, this is indeed the case: under normal circumstances,
attending is something the trajector willfully does. But once again, the situation
changes when *attend* is replaced by the passive locution *be allowed to attend*, yielding (38)(d). Since the trajector of this process is not responsible for its occurrence,
it is more coherently identified with Y, who makes the request, with X interpreted as
the passive agent.

A distinction is often made between control constructions and "raising" constructions. The difference is covert: in terms of their explicit grammatical form, control
and raising constructions are exactly parallel, for both objects and subjects:

(39)   (a) *She persuaded **him** [to resign].*   [object controller]

    (b) *She expected **him** [to resign].*   [raised object]

    (c) ***He** is happy [to resign].*   [subject controller]

    (d) ***He** is likely [to resign].*   [raised subject]

The putative contrast resides in whether or not the nominal in bold is the real object
or subject of the main-clause predicate. It is in the case of control: there is no question that *him* is the true or "logical" object of *persuade*, and that *he* is the real subject
of *happy*. But is *him* really the object of *expect*? Logically, one can argue, what is
expected is the event—his resigning—rather than the person. By the same token,
the event of his resigning is held to be the true subject of *be likely*, even though *he*
appears overtly in subject position.

A classic analysis handles this apparent discrepancy by positing a "deep" (or
"underlying") level of syntactic structure in addition to its "surface" (or "superfi-
cial") form. At the deep-structure level, *expect* is claimed to have a clausal object

and *be likely* to have a clausal subject: *she expect [he resign]*; *[he resign] be likely.* The surface forms of (b) and (d) are then derived by raising the subordinate subject into the main clause, where it assumes the role of the clause it originates in (which is postposed and marked by *to*). Supporting this analysis is the fact that possible raised nominals are precisely the nominals allowed to occur as subject of the infinitival clause. In (40), for example, the raised noun *tabs* is part of the idiom *keep tabs on*, which occurs in the subordinate clause. Because it is eligible to be the subject of that clause (cf. *Tabs were kept on the protesters*), it is also eligible to be the object of *expect* or the subject of *be likely* in the raising construction. Observe that *tabs* cannot appear in the corresponding position with the nonraising predicates *persuade* and *be happy.*

(40) (a) **She persuaded **tabs** [to be kept on the protesters].*

  (b) *She expected **tabs** [to be kept on the protesters].*

  (c) ****Tabs** are happy [to be kept on the protesters].*

  (d) ***Tabs** are likely [to be kept on the protesters].*

Owing to the content requirement, CG cannot posit derivations from underlying structures. Sentences like (39)(b) and (d) have to be described directly, in their own terms, with *him* as the object of *expect* and *he* the subject of *be likely.* A nonraising analysis can indeed be offered (GC: ch. 11). It straightforwardly accommodates the parallelism with control constructions, as seen in (39), as well as the distributional differences illustrated in (40). The key is to explicitly characterize the meanings of the main-clause predicates.

Persuade and *expect* are compared in diagrams (a) and (b) of figure 12.12, *happy* and *likely* in diagrams (c) and (d). In each case the infinitival complement elaborates the schematic, holistically viewed process represented by the inner box. For each pair of predicates, the essential difference is a matter of whether the trajector of that process has some additional, more substantial role in the process profiled by the predicate. With *persuade* it clearly does: the participant focused as landmark engages the trajector in a communicative interaction (double-headed dashed arrow), is subjected to social force (double arrow), and thereby intends (single dashed arrow) to carry out the infinitival process. Not so with *expect*. Besides its role as infinitival trajector, the landmark of *expect* has no objective involvement. It functions only in a subjective capacity, as the entity to which the trajector's expectation pertains. Anything can function in this capacity, even the idiomatic *tabs* (which roughly means 'contact' or 'surveillance'), so (40)(b) is semantically coherent. But since *tabs* can hardly communicate or intend, (40)(a) is not.

Analogously for *happy* vs. *likely*: only in the former does the infinitival trajector participate directly and substantially in the profiled relationship. *Happy* describes the trajector's emotional state, placing it toward the positive end of the scale. The state is not a general one—someone *happy to resign* can perfectly well be sad overall—but is specifically associated with the trajector's participation in the infinitival process.

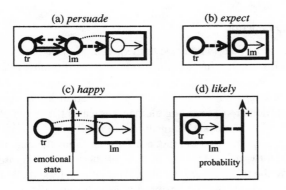

FIGURE 12.12

Still, the trajector must be capable of emotional experience, so its specification by *tabs* in (40)(c) is infelicitous. On the other hand, in (40)(d) *tabs* is unproblematic as the subject of *likely*. The scale invoked by *likely* pertains to the probability of an event's occurrence. That event is specified by the infinitival complement. Its trajector is also focused as the trajector of *likely* and thus corresponds to the main-clause subject. This participant, however, has no objective involvement in the profiled relationship. Besides its role in the complement, it functions only as a point of reference, the entity with respect to which the probability assessment is made. Virtually anything, even the idiomatic *tabs*, can serve in this capacity.

Under this analysis, raising constructions are just a special case of control constructions, where the controller's only substantial role is the one it has in the complement process. But whether or not it figures directly in the profiled relationship, the nominal in question is the "real" subject or object of the matrix predicate. In CG, the schematic characterizations of subject and object make no reference to semantic role but only to focal prominence. Canonically, the spotlights of focal prominence are aimed at entities that participate directly in the profiled relationship. Yet there is no inherent reason why they cannot be aimed at entities participating more indirectly, as proposed for the object of *expect* and the subject of *likely*. This is precisely what the surface facts—the parallels observed in (39)—are trying to tell us. Being based on prominence instead of conceptual content, the CG definitions of subject and object enable us to listen.

12.3 Finite Complements

Though often interchangeable, finite and nonfinite complements are not at all equivalent. They differ not just formally but in their meaning and discourse function. By definition, finite clauses invoke a conceptualizer and indicate its stance vis-à-vis some occurrence. They are thus more closely associated with epistemic judgments and conceptions of reality.

12.3.1 Form and Function

A finite clause is grounded. In addition to the process it designates, which is onstage and objectively construed, it invokes the ground and a grounding relationship, which are offstage and construed subjectively (fig. 9.2(b)). The ground centers on the interlocutors, whose apprehension of the profiled relationship involves an epistemic assessment. In particular, a grounding element indicates the status of the designated process in relation to the speaker's conception of reality.

Because it incorporates grounding, a finite clause has the potential to be apprehended independently as a useful description of the world. Suppose someone says *I kissed a frog*. While this may or may not be true, it is at least the kind of expression whose validity you can assess: it describes a reasonably specific type of event involving a particular individual and portrays an instance of that type as having occurred before the time of speaking. If you accept the statement as valid, it augments your conception of reality (the history of what has occurred up through the present moment). Being independently usable in this manner, a finite clause can often stand alone as a full, nonelliptic sentence. Though common, its use as a complement is secondary.

In contrast, a nonfinite clause cannot itself be assessed for validity or used to augment a reality conception. Take the infinitival expression *to kiss a frog*. Because it lacks both grounding and a specified subject, it describes an event only in generalized fashion, essentially as a type—it fails to single out a particular instance that might be accepted as real. Likewise for a participial expression, e.g. *kissing a frog*. Considered in isolation, such clauses say nothing useful about the world. Thus nonfinite clauses usually cannot stand alone as complete sentences but are more typically used as complements. Through connections with the main clause, they then receive a fuller interpretation and can brought to bear, at least indirectly, on conceptions of reality.

So the form of complements correlates with their typical function. Being fully specified and grounded, finite clauses are geared for independent use. They contain the elements required for this primary function even when pressed into service as complements. By the same token, the form of nonfinite complements correlates with their lack of independence. The formal properties distinguishing them from finite complements all reflect their dependent status. Being subjectless, they depend on the matrix clause for the identification of their trajector. This is accomplished via the control relations discussed in the previous section.[24] In the absence of grounding, the matrix clause also determines their position with respect to time and reality. Determining factors include the meaning of the main-clause predicate and the nature of its grounding. For example, *I want to kiss a frog* implies that the kissing is future and may not ever be realized. We know this because *want* is in the present tense, pertains to subsequent events, and is neutral as to whether they actually occur. By contrast, *I managed to kiss a frog* implies that the speaker did in fact kiss one. *Manage* conveys success in carrying out the action

---

[24] Alternatively, the trajector can be specified periphrastically, as part of the complement itself. The periphrastic element is *for* in the case of infinitival complements: *[For me to kiss a frog] would be out of character*. With participial complements, the subject takes possessive form: *[My kissing a frog] was the highlight of the party*.

expressed in the complement. Hence the profiled instance of *manage* can only be part of past reality by virtue of the action being there as well. With *try* the complement has yet another status. Like *manage*, the verb *try* describes the effort involved in carrying out an action, but unlike *manage*, it does not convey success. With respect to time, *I tried to kiss a frog* is therefore comparable to *I managed to kiss a frog*: since the trying was in the past, the kissing must also have been. But since trying does not ensure success, we cannot infer that it actually occurred.[25]

The status of a nonfinite complement is also affected by the choice of *to* vs. *-ing* as the subordinating element.[26] For instance, with *try to V* the realization of *try* does not entail the realization of V; with *try Ving*, however, it does. The contrast shows up in sequences like the following:

(41)   (a) *I tried to kiss a frog, but I couldn't.*

     (b) *I tried kissing a frog, but it didn't work.*

The meanings and distribution of *to* and *-ing* are complex matters that we can barely touch on here (Wierzbicka 1988: ch. 1; FCG2: §10.2.1). Both are polysemous and hard to disentangle semantically from the varied constructions they appear in. Convention often dictates a particular choice, and when both are possible, the semantic distinction may be subtle at best. For both *to* and *-ing*, a fully general description (valid for all uses) might simply indicate their atemporalization of the complement process (i.e. the suspension of sequential scanning).

Still, the various meanings of *to* and *-ing* center on different prototypes. Most typically, with *to* the complement process is viewed as a whole and is subsequent to the matrix process. *To* manifests this basic sense when used with matrix predicates like *want*, *try*, *persuade*, *expect*, and *likely*, and also in purpose clauses (e.g. *He did it to attract attention*). It is not at all fanciful to see a connection with the preposition *to*, which designates a path-goal configuration (*She walked to the store*). On the other hand, *-ing* most typically takes an internal perspective on the complement process (just as in the progressive) and further indicates that the matrix and complement processes temporally overlap. Among the matrix predicates congruent with this basic sense are *like*, *enjoy*, *see*, *start*, *keep*, and *bother*. With *-ing* there is no clear division between complementation and nominalization. Complements marked by *-ing* show fairly consistent nominal behavior. For example, they follow an auxiliary in questions, as in (30)(d), and function as prepositional objects, as in (37). Also suggesting their nominal character is the use of possessives to specify the trajector: *His being obnoxious never bothers her*. It may be too strong, however, to claim that *-ing* always reifies the complement process.[27]

---

[25] By the process known as **implicature**, the sentence in fact suggests the opposite. If the kissing indeed occurred, the speaker would simply say *I kissed a frog*.

[26] Another option is zero, which occurs with verbs of perception and causation: *I{saw/heard/watched/ let/made/had} them smash her antique vase*. Basically, this option indicates temporal coincidence of the matrix and complement events (GC: 7.5; cf. Kirsner and Thompson 1976). With causation predicates, however, there may be a time lag between them.

[27] For instance, the complement of *keep* gives no indication of being nominal. Observe that the complement of *She enjoyed working* can be replaced by either the question word *what* or the pronoun *it*: *What*

The prototypical values of *to* and *-ing* hint at possible ways of dealing with less typical uses. An initially puzzling case is the use of *-ing* with *anticipate*, as in *I anticipate being nervous*. Because it pertains to the future, it ought to take *to* instead, like its synonym *expect*: *I expect to be nervous*. But synonymy is never exact. One can argue that these verbs reflect two different ways of apprehending a future occurrence. *Expect* incorporates the more straightforward strategy of simply looking into the future from the present vantage point. It governs *to* because, from this perspective, the occurrence lies at the end of a temporal path and can thus be viewed in its entirety. *Anticipate* incorporates the more elaborate strategy of adopting a nonactual vantage point and imagining how things appear from there. It governs *-ing* by virtue of shifting the vantage point to the time of the future occurrence, thus fictively affording an internal perspective on it.[28]

Posing another subtle problem is the distinction between *like to V* and *like Ving*. It is not just a matter of whether the complement process is temporally subsequent to the liking or coincident with it. For one thing, *like to V* differs from *expect to V* in that a subsequent occurrence is not primarily at issue. Rather, as seen in (42)(a), it describes a general positive disposition toward the complement process, presumably based on previous occurrences. And while *like Ving* may be comparable to *enjoy Ving*, where the pleasure accompanies the complement process, it too can describe a general attitude based on previous instances, as in (42)(b).

(42)   (a) *I like to sit in that chair, but I'm not allowed to anymore.*

        (b) *I like sitting in that chair, but I haven't sat there for ages.*

In expressions like these, which abstract away from particular occurrences, temporal relationships figure only indirectly in the *to/-ing* contrast. More directly implicated is another, associated factor: the level at which the positive affect coded by *like* is manifested. With *like Ving*, what is viewed positively is the actual **experience** of *Ving*. By contrast, *like to V* indicates a positive inclination to the **idea** of Ving. It thus introduces specifically mental factors (e.g. judgment, decision, assessment, evaluation) not tied to immediate experience. Because they pertain to different levels, there is no contradiction in saying *I like to run but don't like running*. That is, I like the idea of running (I know it is good for me) but not the experience.

These are only samples of the subtleties and complexities of the *to/-ing* alternation. It may be evident at least that these elements are meaningful and their use semantically motivated, even when a particular choice is conventionally imposed. In the broader picture, their differences are less essential than their shared status as alternatives to clausal grounding. *To* and *-ing* do not serve merely to mark a clause as subordinate but further indicate its relationship to the matrix predicate. Moreover, the

---

did she enjoy?; *She enjoyed it*. With *She kept working*, neither substitution is possible: **What did she keep?*; **She kept it*.

[28] Accordingly, *Don't anticipate my decision!* is an admonition not to act prematurely, as if the decision were already known. Compare this to *Don't expect my decision any time soon!*, where access to the decision lies solely in the future.

clauses they derive are not just formally distinct from finite clauses but semantically very different. The conceptual differences between finite and nonfinite clauses are reflected in how they function in grammar and discourse.

We have noted that finite clauses, by virtue of being grounded and fully specified, have greater suitability for independent use. Only secondarily do they function as complements, in which case they may or may not be explicitly marked as such (e.g. by *that*). When they do function in this capacity, they nevertheless exhibit a fundamental semantic contrast with nonfinite complements, even when the two are seemingly equivalent. Succinctly stated, a finite clause expresses a **proposition**, whereas a nonfinite clause describes an **occurrence**.[29]

An occurrence is something that occurs: an event or a situation. A proposition consists of an occurrence together with an assessment of its epistemic status. It thus invokes a conceptualizer who apprehends the occurrence and makes the assessment. Due to this additional layer, a proposition is more complex and generally more abstract than the occurrence it is based on. Naturally, therefore, complements describing occurrences and propositions are compatible with different ranges of matrix predicates. Some examples are given in (43). Aspectual predicates like *begin*, *keep*, and *finish* focus strongly on occurrences, being solely concerned with their manifestation through time. Since the fact of their occurrence is not at issue, finite complements are precluded. At the other extreme are predicates like *true* and *false*, which require finite complements. They do so because the validity of an epistemic judgment is precisely what is at issue. Only a proposition can be true or false—per se, an event or situation cannot.

(43) (a) *She {began/kept/finished} scraping off the paint.*

(b) **She {began/kept/finished} that she scraped off the paint.*

(c) *That he never takes a bath is {true/false}.*

(d) **His never taking a bath is {true/false}.*

In one way or another, predicates taking finite complements relate to knowledge and conceptions of reality. They pertain, for example, to acquiring knowledge (*learn, suspect, imagine, predict, figure out*), to negotiating it (*persuade, suggest, claim, doubt, agree*), having and maintaining it (*know, believe, sure, certain, convinced*), communicating it (*say, tell, write, inform, announce*), reacting to it (*happy, regret, surprised, astonishing, terrible*), and assessing its validity (*true, undeniable, dubious, seem, probable*). Necessarily, then, such predicates invoke a conceptualizer capable of apprehending the proposition expressed by the complement. The conceptualizer may be explicitly mentioned, in which case it is often a particular individual: *Sam believes that X*; *They persuaded her that X*; *It seems to me that X*. But it can also be left implicit as an unidentified or generalized conceptualizer: *It's*

---

[29] The terms "occurrence" and "proposition" are more or less interchangeable with "process" and "grounded process". The former emphasize the kinds of conception involved, the latter their semitechnical characterization in CG (chs. 4 and 9).

{astonishing/terrible/true/undeniable/probable} that X. Importantly, the conceptualizer associated with such a predicate need not be the one invoked for the grounding of its finite complement. They do sometimes coincide, as in *Sam believes that the
earth is flat*, where Sam adopts the epistemic stance coded in the complement—the
situation of the earth being flat is part of his conception of reality. In principle, however, these conceptualizing roles have to be distinguished. This becomes apparent
with a different matrix verb: *Sam doubts that the earth is flat*. Here the point is
precisely that Sam's view diverges from that expressed in the complement. Sam
entertains the complement proposition, but he cannot be identified with the conceptualizer whose epistemic stance is reflected in its grounding.

Being ungrounded, nonfinite complements do not themselves incorporate such a
stance. The predicates they occur with thus tend to be less concerned with knowledge
than with other ways of engaging the complement process. They pertain, for example, to perceiving the complement occurrence (*see, hear, feel, watch, view*), to causing it (*cause, force, order, make, compel*), or experiencing it (*like, enjoy, easy, fun,
painful*). Also taking nonfinite complements are aspectual predicates (*start, begin,
keep, stop, quit*), as well as those involving desire, intention, and outcome (*want, try,
attempt, aim, intend, persuade, induce, manage, able, fail, wind up*). With all these
predicates, what is directly at issue is occurrence of the complement process rather
than knowledge of its occurrence. Let us say that the relationships they designate
obtain at the **effective** level rather than the **epistemic** level.

Since the boundary between these levels is often fuzzy, it is unsurprising that many
predicates can take either finite or nonfinite complements. The choice sometimes correlates with a palpable difference in the predicate's meaning. In (44)(a), representing
the basic perceptual sense of *see*, both the person and the activity are visually observed.
But in (44)(b) its meaning is more like 'come to know'. I did not necessarily perceive
the activity or even the person; for example, I may merely have seen the instructions and
materials in his room. Nor is it required that vision be involved—I may have deduced
his intentions from various kinds of evidence presented to me verbally.[30]

(44)   (a) *I saw him making a bomb.*

    (b) *I saw that he was making a bomb.*

    (c) *I persuaded him to make a bomb.*

    (d) *I persuaded him that he should make a bomb.*

    (e) *I persuaded him that watermelons are poisonous.*

Likewise, *persuade* has slightly different meanings in (44)(c) and (d). With an infinitival complement, the person persuaded has the intention to carry out the infinitival
process (fig. 12.12(a)). With a finite complement, the person persuaded instead comes
to accept a proposition as valid. Even though (44)(d) suggests that he might intend to

---

[30] Because so much of what we know derives from seeing, semantic extension from vision to
knowledge is very common (Sweetser 1990). It can be "viewed" as either metaphor or metonymy.

make a bomb, this is only an inference prompted by the modal *should*—possibly he agrees that he really ought to make a bomb but has no intention of doing so. And in general, as we observe in (44)(e), the proposition may not even have anything to do with the person who accepts it.

In other cases, a predicate's meaning is basically the same whether it takes a finite or a nonfinite complement. For instance, *happy* describes the same positive feeling in (45)(a) and (b), and *promise* implements the same future commitment in (c) and (d). What differs is whether the predicate relates to the complement process at the effective or the epistemic level. Sentence (a) portrays the positive feeling as stemming directly from the situation of being out of jail, whereas in (b) it stems from knowledge of that situation. But since we can only be happy about a situation we know about, the difference is hardly significant. Similarly, in (c) the speaker commits directly to a future occurrence, and in (d) to the validity of a proposition pertaining to that same occurrence. The expressions are functionally equivalent because the proposition's validity hinges on the occurrence. With either sentence, the speaker's commitment is fulfilled just in case he stays out of trouble. The choice of level is thus a subtle matter of construal, which does not affect the basic content. The resulting semantic distinction has no practical consequences.

(45)　(a)　*I'm happy to be out of jail.*

　　　(b)　*I'm happy that I'm out of jail.*

　　　(c)　*I promise to stay out of trouble.*

　　　(d)　*I promise that I will stay out of trouble.*

A final issue concerning the form of complements is the meaning, function, and distribution of *that*.[31] Though often referred to as a "complementizer", *that* has other subordinating uses, notably in relatives (*the movie that we saw*) and a focus construction known as "clefting" (*It's YOU that I'm angry with*). Moreover, it is limited to finite complements, being mutually exclusive with *to* and *-ing*. Its use with finite complements is generally optional and seemingly of little consequence. If omitted from (45)(b) or (d) it will not be missed. What, then, determines whether it will appear? What does it contribute when it does?

In some cases the use of *that* is obligatory. The best-known circumstance, illustrated in (46)(a)–(b), is its nonomissibility from a complement clause in the grammatical role of main-clause subject. Compare this with the optionality of *that* when the complement appears in nonsubject position, as in (46)(c). A functional explanation can be given in terms of sentence processing. If *that* were omitted from the subject complement, the listener would first interpret *Zelda drinks too much* as an independent expression, and then—upon encountering *is obvious*—would have to

---

[31] I will not consider interrogative complements (marked by *whether* or a basic question word), which can be either finite or infinitival: *I wonder whether she recognized him*; *He asked me where to send it*. Also ignored is the uninflected stem appearing in certain quasi-imperative complements, e.g. *They are demanding that we {be/*are} there on time*. This is reminiscent of what is called the "subjunctive" in other languages.

reanalyze it as being subordinate. By marking the clause as such, the obligatory inclusion of *that* spares the listener this processing inefficiency.

(46)   (a) *[That Zelda drinks too much] is obvious.*

    (b) **[Zelda drinks too much] is obvious.*

    (c) *It's obvious [(that) Zelda drinks too much].*

While the explanation may well be valid, it covers only one small aspect of this element's distribution. To arrive at a coherent overall account, we will have to answer the following basic question: What does *that* mean? Evidently its meaning is abstract and independent of any specific conceptual content. Instead, its import must reside in a particular way of viewing or apprehending the clausal content. My suggestion—admittedly programmatic and impressionistic—is that it explicitly marks the proposition expressed as an **object of conception**—that is, as being construed objectively rather than subjectively (§9.1). Reinforcing its objective construal has the effect of more clearly differentiating the proposition from any conceptualizer who entertains it. This is sometimes described as a "distancing" effect (cf. Borkin 1973).

This abstract characterization helps explain various distributional tendencies. The omission of *that* tends to correlate with a number of factors implying lesser distance between the conceptualizer and the complement proposition: first person, present tense, opinion, simplicity, and informality. These are all exemplified in (47)(a), where using *that* would be quite unnatural. The opposite factors are all exemplified in (47)(d), where *that* is virtually obligatory. In the other two examples, which show a mixture of properties, the likelihood of using *that* varies accordingly.

(47)   (a) *I think he's gay.*

    (b) *She knows (?that) her instructor is gay.*

    (c) *Janice learned (that) her instructor was homosexual.*

    (d) *Janice ascertained that her aerobics instructor was homosexual.*

Furthermore, *that* is obligatory in certain constructions which portray the complement proposition as being established independently of any particular conceptualizer and thus as having a kind of autonomous, objective existence. In one such construction, the complement occurs in apposition to an abstract noun, suggesting its conceptual reification (fig. 7.7): *the {fact/claim/idea/notion/report} that watermelons are poisonous.* Also requiring *that* are certain predicates profiling an emotional reaction to the complement proposition:[32]

(48)   (a) *My parents regret that I never went to college.*

    (b) *She {dislikes/hates/resents/detests} it that only men get promoted.*

    (c) *It {shocked him/bothers me/sucks} that Zelda drinks so much.*

---

[32] The reaction is generally negative, which is quite in line with the distancing function of *that*.

With these "factive" predicates the complement's validity is not at issue, as in (46)–(47), but is simply presupposed.

Why, then, is *that* required with subject complements? The meaning proposed— that it marks the proposition as an object of conception—provides a new way of approaching this stricture. A subject complement specifies the trajector of the process designated by the matrix clause. As matters of definition, the profiled relationship is the onstage focus of attention, and the trajector is its primary focal participant. Within a clause, therefore, the trajector is construed with maximal objectivity—that is, it stands out most distinctly as an object of conception. So it makes sense for *that* to be obligatory in subject complements: it marks them as objects of conception, and among complements they function in this capacity to the greatest degree.

12.3.2 Conceptualizers and Levels of Conception

Our discussion of finite complements has featured a person called the "conceptualizer", affectionately known as "C". It is C who apprehends the complement proposition, construes it with a greater or lesser degree of objectivity, and adjudicates its status with respect to C's conception of reality. Given C's importance, it is reasonable to ask: Who is this person? The question may be simple, but it is not an innocent one and does not have a simple answer. If we round up the usual suspects, the obvious ones to start with are the speaker, the hearer, and the clausal subject. Since there are two clauses, we need to consider both the matrix subject and the complement subject. But we are not limited to subjects—other clausal participants might also have a conceptualizing role. Nor are we limited to conceptualizers that are mentioned explicitly or even specifically identified. Lurking in the shadows are any number of individuals who might be guilty of linguistically relevant conceptualization.

Consider the sentence *Peter told Jane that Henry agreed*. It invokes no fewer than six relevant conceptualizers: Peter, Jane, Henry, the speaker, the hearer, and the person Henry agreed with. While that person may be indentified as Peter, Jane, or one of the interlocutors, it can also be some other individual evident from the discourse context. Each proposition is apprehended by a different array of conceptualizers. All six apprehend the implicit proposition Henry agreed to. Peter, Jane, and the interlocutors function as conceptualizers with respect to the complement proposition (*Henry agreed*). And both interlocutors entertain the matrix proposition (*Peter told Jane*).[33] A full description of the sentence's meaning must therefore indicate, for each conceptualizer (C), which propositions C apprehends and how they relate to C's conception of reality.

In principle, a proposition—the grounded process expressed by a finite clause— can be apprehended by any number of conceptualizers, each with their own vantage point and epistemic stance regarding it. Let us focus on the speaker and the matrix subject, which are generally the most important. The subject's role with respect to a complement clause is roughly analogous to the speaker's role with respect to the

---

[33] Henry was doubtless aware of agreeing but is not specifically portrayed as entertaining a **proposition** to the effect that he did so. Likewise, Peter and Jane were conscious of the telling event but did not necessarily formulate a proposition concerning it.

sentence overall (Achard 1998). In *Jill was sure my cat was hungry*, for example, Jill is the primary conceptualizer for the proposition that my cat was hungry, just as the speaker is the primary conceptualizer for the proposition that Jill was sure of it. The former belonged to Jill's conception of reality, and the latter belongs to the speaker's. One difference, of course, is that Jill and her epistemic stance are onstage and objectively construed, whereas the speaker's involvement is offstage and implicit. Another difference is that the speaker, who formulates the entire sentence, must also apprehend the complement proposition (without necessarily subscribing to it). On the other hand, Jill did not necessarily entertain a proposition concerning the certainty she manifested, nor could she know that the speaker is doing so now.

When multiple conceptualizers entertain the same proposition, the question arises as to whose conception is reflected in a particular phenomenon. In our example, both Jill and the speaker entertain the proposition expressed by the complement clause *my cat was hungry*. Whose conceptualization is the one that matters linguistically? The answer depends on the problem considered. Each conceptualizer is invoked for certain purposes.

The matrix predicate *sure* describes an epistemic assessment of the complement proposition. The assessment is that of its trajector, in this case Jill. The sentence indicates that the proposition was firmly established in Jill's conception of reality. So for that purpose Jill is the relevant conceptualizer, and her reality conception—not the speaker's—is at issue. Indeed, I can truthfully say *Jill was sure my cat was hungry* even if I firmly believe that my cat (who had just engorged three cans of tuna) was actually quite full. But this does not mean that the speaker's conception of reality is totally irrelevant. For one thing, the matrix proposition (that Jill was sure) is accepted by the speaker as real. Moreover, since Jill's certainty pertains specifically to the complement proposition, the latter figures as well in the speaker's reality conception. It serves to characterize what it is that Jill was sure of.

As a crucial aspect of its meaning, the sentence invokes the mental space configuration in figure 12.13(a). P represents the proposition expressed by the finite complement *my cat was hungry*. That proposition was entertained by Jill (J) and was accepted as part of her reality conception (R_J). The proposition concerning Jill and her epistemic stance is apprehended in turn by the speaker (S), who accepts it as real. Thus P also figures—albeit indirectly—in the speaker's conception of reality (R_S). It is not that P itself is taken as being real. Rather, what the speaker accepts as real is that P is accepted by Jill as being real. If we interpret the dashed arrows as representing a path of mental access, we see that S does not access P directly: the only path from S to P runs through Jill and her conception of reality.

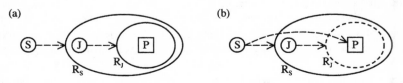

FIGURE 12.13

Sure is usefully contrasted with *realize* in this respect. The sentence *Jill realized my cat was hungry* implies that the speaker also accepts P as real, independently of Jill's epistemic stance.[34] I have shown this in figure 12.13(b) by adding an arrow leading directly from S to P. Also, a dashed-line ellipse is used for Jill's reality conception to indicate that P is included as part of R_S in its own right, not merely as an element of R_J.

The conceptualizers who apprehend a proposition each do so from their own vantage point. In *Jill was sure my cat was hungry*, the complement proposition is apprehended by Jill and by the speaker from different vantage points in time: Jill in the past (hence *was sure* rather than *is sure*), and the speaker right now (at the moment of speaking). Constructions differ as to which vantage point is reflected in the form of the complement clause. The basic pattern in English is for grounding to reflect the speaker's vantage point even when the matrix subject is the primary conceptualizer of the complement proposition. The proposition *my cat was hungry* describes what Jill believed—it was part of her conception of reality (R_J). Nevertheless, the nominal and clausal grounding reflect the speaker's viewpoint instead of Jill's. The cat in question is the speaker's, and the complement describes it as the speaker would: *my cat* (Jill would have referred to it as *your cat*). Likewise, the past-tense form of the complement (*was hungry*) reflects the location of the profiled relationship relative to the time of speaking (Jill would have said *is hungry*). Thus, although the complement proposition is ascribed to Jill, as part of her conception of reality, it is presented linguistically from the speaker's own vantage point. Compare this with another complement construction, the one used for direct quotation. Instead of describing Jill's certainty, the speaker might have chosen to describe what she said, in her own words: *Jill said "Your cat is hungry."* Here the nominal and clausal grounding are based on Jill's apprehension of the complement proposition at the time of her utterance.

We see, then, that the form of a finite complement need not reflect the view of any single conceptualizer.[35] This is so even with respect to clausal grounding. Recall (from §9.4) that English clausal grounding has two basic components. The first is whether the conceptualizer assesses the profiled process as being **real** or **unreal**; this is indicated by the absence vs. the presence of a modal. The second is whether the profiled process is **immediate** or **nonimmediate** to C. In cases of reality, immediacy vs. nonimmediacy amounts to present vs. past in time. But who should we identify as C? It should now be evident that C's identity is variable. It can even differ for the two components of clausal grounding, e.g. for the complement clause in *Jill was sure my cat was hungry*. The clause is grounded by the past-tense inflection (*was*) and the absence of a modal. The profiled process (*be hungry*) is nonimmediate relative to the speaker in the context of the current speech event. It is not however implied that the speaker accepts it as real. The one who accepts it as real is Jill—it is her view

---

[34] For this reason, P's validity for S is unaffected when the main clause is negated: *Jill didn't realize my cat was hungry*. This is one definition of "factive" predicates (Kiparsky and Kiparsky 1970).

[35] What about the "distancing" effected by the subordinating *that* (e.g. in *Jill was sure that my cat was hungry*)? It would seem problematic to identify the relevant conceptualizer exclusively as being either the matrix subject or the speaker.

that the speaker indicates by not putting in a modal. The speaker (who remembers the three cans of tuna) does so despite being certain that her view was false.

The conceptualizer invoked by a grounding element is therefore a virtual entity, in the sense that it cannot in general be identified with any particular individual. By default, C is identified with the actual speaker, but their full identification is often blocked, especially in finite complements. With respect to figure 12.13, the C in question is internal to the box labeled P, which represents the proposition expressed by the complement clause. This proposition consists of the profiled process (e.g. *my cat be hungry*) together with its grounding (its assessment by C as real but nonimmediate). As we have seen, the conceptualizer who makes this epistemic assessment—especially in regard to reality—is largely determined by the meaning of the matrix predicate. The sentences in (49) illustrate the flexibility of C's identification. The absence of a modal consistently indicates that the complement process is accepted as real. The examples differ as to whether this represents the view of the speaker, of Jill, of both, or of neither. In and of itself, the complement does nothing more than present the proposition as something to be considered. Particular conceptualizers may or may not subscribe to the epistemic stance reflected in its grounding.

(49) (a) *Jill was unaware that my cat was hungry.*   [real only for speaker]

  (b) *Jill wrongly believed that my cat was hungry.*   [real only for Jill]

  (c) *Jill was right that my cat was hungry.*   [real for both]

  (d) *Jill gratuitously speculated that my cat was hungry.*   [real for neither]

Despite their default identification, C has to be distinguished from the speaker, and C's conception of reality from the speaker's, even in single-clause expressions. If I say *My cat is hungry*, I would normally be interpreted as indicating that I accept the profiled occurrence (*my cat be hungry*) as part of immediate reality. However, this default is easily overridden:

(50) (a) *Let me guess why you're phoning. My cat is hungry.*

  (b) *My cat is hungry. Sure. Tell me another one.*

  (c) *My cat is hungry. And if you believe that, there's a bridge in Brooklyn I want to sell you.*

Even when it stands alone as a sentence, a finite clause is not always intended as a true statement, nor does its grounding invariably reflect the speaker's epistemic stance. The proposition it expresses might be used for any number of discourse purposes. In general, then, the speaker merely **entertains** the proposition, without necessarily **embracing** it. Only as a special case is C fully identified with the speaker, and C's conception of reality with the speaker's actual one.

Figure 12.14 represents the reality component of grounding for English finite clauses. C is a virtual conceptualizer whose identification depends on clause-external factors. The status of the profiled process is specified by the absence vs. the presence

(a) Absence of Modal   (b) Presence of Modal

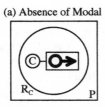
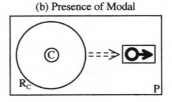

FIGURE 12.14

of a modal: it either is accepted as part of C's conception of reality or remains outside it. In the latter case, the choice of modal (*may*, *should*, *must*, etc.) indicates the strength of C's inclination to accept it as real (§9.4.3). This entire configuration—the profiled occurrence and its epistemic assessment—constitutes a proposition (P).

The proposition expressed by a finite clause is itself a virtual entity if considered independently of its use. Viewed abstractly, for example, the clause *my cat is hungry* makes no specific connection to the world, for it might be uttered at different times, by different speakers, with respect to different cats, and for different discourse purposes. It is only in the context of a particular usage event that specific values are established for these variables, thus converting the proposition into one with actual import. Anchored in this fashion, the clause can either stand alone or be incorporated as part of a complex sentence, notably as a complement.

When the clause stands alone, the default is for the ground invoked by grounding elements to be fully identified with that of the actual speech event. The speaker invoked by grounding is thus the actual speaker, the time invoked is that of the current speech event, and so on. In particular, the speaker assumes the role of C in figure 12.14: the presence or absence of a modal indicates the status of the grounded process with respect to the speaker's own conception of reality. With this interpretation, the clause can be used to make a statement reflecting the speaker's actual assessment. Intended as a statement, for example, *My cat is hungry* indicates that the speaker accepts the cat's current hunger as being real. But full identification with C is only the default. The examples in (50) illustrate various circumstances in which the speaker expresses the proposition but does not embrace it. The extreme case of this is lying, where the speaker purports to embrace a proposition but actually rejects it.[36]

When the clause functions as a complement, the status of the proposition it expresses depends on the larger structure containing it. Its nonindependence has the consequence that full identification of its virtual ground with that of the actual speech event is no longer the default. With respect to immediacy vs. nonimmediacy, the grounding of a complement generally does reflect the vantage point of the actual speaker. Reality, though, is another matter. Usually the matrix predicate indicates

---

[36] More forgivable is to **hedge** its acceptance with a word like *perhaps*. Despite the absence of a modal, *Perhaps my cat is hungry* does not commit the speaker to accepting the hunger as real. *Perhaps* invokes the possibility of a reality conception that includes the profiled occurrence, but it indicates that this is not the speaker's actual conception.

some epistemic stance in regard to the complement proposition. At least implicitly, it thus invokes a conceptualizer responsible for the epistemic judgment. In a complex sentence there may in fact be any number of conceptualizers, including both interlocutors, all of whom apprehend the complement proposition and have some stance in regard to it. The nature of that stance determines whether a given conceptualizer identifies with C and C's conception of reality (Langacker 2004a). In *Jill was sure my cat was hungry*, for example, Jill embraces the complement proposition and accepts C's view of reality as her own (she may well have said *Your cat is hungry*).

Whether this happens is largely dependent on the meaning of the matrix predicate. Such predicates pertain to different phases of the epistemic process. Verbs like *wonder, ask, consider*, and *examine* describe an initial phase of **assessment**, where the trajector considers the complement proposition to determine its possible validity.[37] Other predicates describe an **inclination** to either accept or reject the proposition: *think, believe, suspect, imagine, doubt*. Still others designate the **action** of accepting it as real: *learn, find out, realize, decide, conclude*. And finally, predicates like *know, sure, certain*, and *convinced* indicate the **result** of this action—the stable situation where the proposition has already been incorporated in the reality conception.[38]

Figure 12.15 offers a generalized representation of result and inclination predicates. The conceptualizer is typically (though not invariably) the predicate's trajector. The profiled relationship is that of C accepting P as valid (part of C's conception of reality), or alternatively of C having some degree of inclination to accept it. Observe that these two classes of predicates are analogous to the reality component of clausal grounding (fig. 12.14). Because they specify inclusion in R_C, result predicates are comparable to the absence of a modal. And like epistemic modals, inclination predicates specify the strength of a tendency toward acceptance. There are also differences, of course. For one thing, the predicates profile the epistemic relationship, whereas grounding elements profile the grounded process (the ground and grounding relation being offstage and subjectively construed). For the predicates, moreover, the target of assessment is an entire proposition (P), whereas the target of grounding is simply an occurrence. It is precisely the grounding of a process that **creates** a proposition. Hence the entire configuration in figure 12.14 functions as P in figure 12.15.

The predicates represented in figure 12.15 choose the conceptualizer as their trajector. Though quite natural, this is not the only possible alignment. In addition to being the subject, C can serve grammatically as the object of the verb or a preposition, or it may simply be left implicit:

---

[37] The proposition is marked by *whether*: *She wonders whether he loves her*. However, *whether* can also be used for later phases of the process: *She will soon {find out/know} whether he loves her*. *Whether* differs from *that* by portraying the proposition as one of multiple options (cf. *She wonders whether he loves her or whether he only wants her money*).

[38] Naturally, certain predicates have alternate senses representing different phases. *Believe*, for example, can indicate inclination, action, or result: *She believes he loves her (but she's not sure)*; *He told her he loved her, and she believed it*; *She firmly believes he loves her (nothing will convince her otherwise)*.

(a) Result Predicate   (b) Inclination Predicate

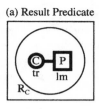   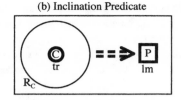

FIGURE 12.15

(51)   *The long series of rigorous experiments {persuaded me/proved to me/demonstrated}*
        that worms are colorblind.

We likewise have various options in choosing the trajector. Rather than C, trajector
status is sometimes conferred on a nonsentient participant, as in (51). As a special
case, exemplified in (52)(a), P itself can function as the matrix subject. Expressions like these are mostly confined to formal writing. In spoken discourse, they
are shunned in favor of the construction in (52)(b), where the pronoun *it* appears in
subject position. This variation reflects the independence of trajector status from any
particular semantic role. The spotlight of primary focal prominence is merely being
directed at different entities within the overall conception.

(52)   (a)   *That worms are colorblind is {possible/likely/doubtful/obvious/true}.*

        (b)   *It's {possible/likely/doubtful/obvious/true} that worms are colorblind.*

What is this spotlight directed at in (52)(b)? What does the pronoun *it* refer to in
such expressions? The standard view is that it refers to nothing at all. *It* is said to be
meaningless in this use, being inserted as a "dummy" subject for purely grammatical
purposes. English finite clauses require an overt subject, so when the complement
"moves" to the end—to avoid the awkwardness of having a full clause in subject
position—the semantically empty *it* takes its place and serves in this capacity. Now
it clearly is the matrix subject in this construction, which does provide a stylisti-
cally preferable alternative to (52)(a). It cannot be meaningless, however. From the
CG perspective, the semantic value of *it* is pivotal to the construction's grammatical
description.

What, then, does it (that is, *it*) mean? I suggested earlier (§11.3.2) that, in this
use, *it* profiles an **abstract setting**. The sentences in (53) illustrate the option of
choosing either a person or a setting as the subject of certain experiential predicates.
In its basic use, *see* profiles the interaction between an experiential subject and the
object of perception (fig. 11.9(a)). By contrast, the setting-subject construction profiles the relationship between a setting and what transpires there (fig. 11.9(b)). It
abstracts away from any particular experiencer, implying that anyone within the setting would see the events in question.

(53)   (a)   *The general saw some catastrophic wars.*

        (b)   *The past century saw some catastrophic wars.*

The contrast in (54) is claimed to be analogous. With a person as subject, *certain* profiles C's epistemic stance toward the complement proposition. The corresponding sentence with *it* abstracts away from any particular conceptualizer. The focus instead is on P's manifestation within the global circumstances. The import is that any conceptualizer, presented with those circumstances, would adopt the stance in question.

(54)   (a) *I am certain that worms are colorblind.*

      (b) *It is certain that worms are colorblind.*

The setting for typical events (like wars) is primarily spatiotemporal. But even when they pertain to such events, propositions are more abstract. They do not consist in the profiled occurrence per se, but rather in its apprehension and epistemic assessment (in the form of grounding). The setting for a proposition must therefore be abstract as well. Though hard to characterize, it can perhaps be described as the **relevant scope of awareness**: everything invoked by C as the basis for apprehending P and making the epistemic judgment expressed by the predicate. In other words, *it* designates the expression's **immediate scope** for this purpose.[39]

Let us summarize by considering the alternate ways of expressing inclination— or in the case of *doubtful* (which occurs in all three patterns), **disinclination**. The first option is for C to be focused as trajector: *I'm doubtful that P.* This was represented in figure 12.15(b). The other patterns share the property of abstracting away from any particular conceptualizer. While an epistemic judgment is still implied, they emphasize other aspects of the overall situation. One option, sketched in figure 12.16(a), is to choose the complement as trajector: *That P is doubtful.* The effect is to highlight P's role as the target of (dis)inclination. The other option, shown in figure 12.16(b), is to confer trajector status on the abstract setting, i.e. the relevant scope of awareness: *It's doubtful that P.* This highlights the role of the global circumstances as the basis for the epistemic judgment.

These latter two constructions allow the speaker to avoid assuming responsibility for the judgment. In saying *I'm doubtful that P*, the speaker directly expresses personal doubt. On the other hand, *That P is doubtful* merely indicates that P merits this

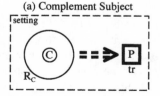 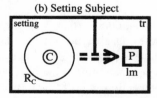

FIGURE 12.16

[39] The meaning imputed to *it* is perfectly consistent with its regular meaning as a referential pronoun, where it commonly refers to abstract and vaguely delimited entities (e.g. **The situation** *is worse than **it** seems*). Using *it* to designate an abstract setting is simply the extreme case of vagueness and nondelimitation (Langacker forthcoming).

negative assessment. Likewise, *It's doubtful that P* merely indicates that the global circumstances warrant this judgment: anyone apprehending these circumstances would come to the same conclusion. To be sure, stating that the attitude is warranted implies that the speaker subscribes to it. It suggests, however, that the speaker—like anyone else—is led to this conclusion simply through awareness of the relevant considerations. If the judgment is wrong, it is not the speaker's fault.

PART IV

FRONTIERS

13

Discourse

Starting from single words, like nouns and verbs, we have worked our way up to successively larger expressions: to multiword constructions, to full nominals and clauses, and finally to complex sentences. The next level is **discourse**, where any number of sentences (or fragments thereof) are connected to form a coherent linguistic production—be it a conversation, a monolog (e.g. a speech), or a written text. Although discourse is often considered a separate topic, requiring different methods and descriptive constructs, the contrast with lower levels is at most a matter of degree. Discourse is in fact the very basis for language structure and is thus essential for understanding grammar.

13.1 The Basis of Language Structure

Discourse is where structure, use, and acquisition come together. Language is learned through its interactive use in social contexts. Its emergence from usage and social interaction is thus a key factor in describing linguistic structure.

13.1.1 Us(ag)e

Discourse is the use of language. Conversely, a language resides in conventional patterns of usage. These patterns, learned from countless instances of use in discourse contexts, are subsequently applied in producing and understanding further discourse. It is the old, familiar story of the chicken and the egg.

A discourse comprises a series of **usage events**: instances of language use in all their complexity and specifity. A usage event has no particular size; depending on our analytical purpose, we can segment a discourse into words, clauses, sentences, intonation groups, conversational turns, and so on. An event is bipolar, consisting in both conceptualization and means of expression. On the expressive side, it includes the full phonetic detail of an utterance, as well as any other kinds of signals, such as gestures and body language (conceivably even pheromones). Conceptually, a usage event includes the expression's full contextual understanding—not only what is said explicitly but also what is inferred, as well as everything evoked as the basis for its apprehension. Thus a usage event, when examined in comprehensive and fine-grained detail, is never precisely identical for the speaker and the addressee. Substantial overlap is usually enough for successful communication, however.

Conventional linguistic units are just one resource exploited in usage events. In speaking and understanding, we draw on our full range of knowledge, mental abilities, and interpersonal skills. Also essential is our apprehension of the context, one facet of which is the ongoing discourse itself. The various factors contributing to usage events should not be thought of as separate and discrete. In particular, the specific contributions of language cannot be segregated or precisely delimited. The linguistic meaning of a word, for example, is not a distinct and self-contained entity, divorced from other knowledge and cognitive abilities—instead it recruits and exploits them. Lexemes offer conventionalized ways of accessing independently established knowledge (encyclopedic semantics). Also, they construe it by means of more general abilities, like the focusing of attention (profiling). "Linguistic" structures are therefore indissociable from other factors involved in language use. They reside in certain aspects of the processing activity that occurs in usage events.

It is through occurrence in usage events that linguistic units arise in the first place. More precisely, they are abstracted from usage events through reinforcement of recurring commonalities. By way of illustration, let (a_1), (a_2), (a_3), etc. stand for roughly similar facets of different usage events. They can be of any kind (expressive, conceptual, or both) and any degree of complexity. For sake of concreteness, suppose they are different renditions of a syllable, as perceived by a language learner. Each rendition is unique in the fine-grained details of its phonetic manifestation. The learner may or may not perceive the differences (represented by the subscripts), but what counts is their coarse-grained similarity (a). Through successive usage events of this sort, (a) recurs and is thereby reinforced, whereas the fine-grained differences are not. The eventual result, given a sufficient number of occurrences, is that (a) is entrenched as a unit: [a]. And since the fine-grained details have been washed out, [a] is schematic relative to each sound experience it is based on.

We can likewise suppose that (A_1), (A_2), (A_3), etc. are roughly similar facets of the conceptual pole in different usage events. By the same process of selective reinforcement, the abstracted unit [A] emerges as a representation of their coarse-grained commonality. It may further happen (concurrently or subsequently) that conceptions of type [A] repeatedly occur in the same events as sound experiences of type [a]: $(\ldots(A_1)\ldots/\ldots(a_1)\ldots)$, $(\ldots(A_2)\ldots/\ldots(a_2)\ldots)$, and so on. Their recurrent pairing could then be entrenched to form the symbolic unit [[A]/[a]], with [A] and [a] as its semantic and phonological poles. While this is surely oversimplified, even for basic lexical items, it at least makes tangible what it means for linguistic units to be abstracted from usage events. In CG, units of any kind or size are seen as emerging in this fashion, even at the discourse level. This is one reason why CG is a **usage-based** approach.[1]

---

[1] Other reasons are (i) the importance ascribed to lower-level schemas, (ii) their coexistence with higher-level schemas they instantiate, and (iii) the role of usage in driving language change.

The units abstracted from usage events are exploited in further events, both in acquisition and throughout our speaking lives. They are immanent in new expressions, representing the contribution of established linguistic precedent. In both speaking and understanding, users activate appropriate units, whose categorization of an expression constitutes its interpretation (or structural description) with respect to the language. As described in chapter 8, their rendition need not be faithful—the targets of categorization are consistently more specific and elaborate than the categorizing structures and very often deviate from their specifications. Language use is always pushing the envelope of established convention. If new renditions or new combinations should happen to recur, they are themselves subject to entrenchment and conventionalization, becoming conventional units available for exploitation. In this way, usage events are both the cradle of language and the crucible of language change.

13.1.2 Interaction

It is generally accepted that the conversational use of language is primary. It is not the most frequent: the award for sheer prevalence goes to the silent verbal thought we engage in at most every moment of our waking lives. Conversation is nonetheless canonical, providing a basic model that other uses of language mimic and adapt as needed. In no small measure, our verbal thought takes the form of imagined dialog, if only with ourselves. A spoken monolog, as in giving a speech or telling a story, can be thought of as the limiting case of dialog, where one interlocutor maintains role of speaker throughout, often with multiple addressees.[2] And when we write, we usually write with a reader in mind, imagining the reader's reaction the way we do a conversational partner's.

A conversation is an inter-action between inter-locutors. It comprises a series of usage events, each of which is an action on the part of each interlocutor. And since expressions are integral facets of usage events, they too are properly viewed as actions. This is so whether we identify expressions as specific occurrences—as when someone says *I love you* on a certain occasion—or as abstract entities independent of any particular occurrence. In the latter case, they constitute potential linguistic actions made possible by the conventional patterns of a language. This potential can be exploited by any speaker at any time. If an expression is used on multiple occasions, as part of different usage events, its realization is never precisely the same (FCG1: §11.2.1).

By definition, conventional linguistic units are abstract entities independent of any particular occurrence. Abstracted from usage events, they are invoked for assembling and assessing subsequent expressions. But they too can be thought of as actions: entrenched patterns of processing activity we can evoke and execute as needed. Learning a language consists in learning to perform these actions properly. Knowing a language is being able to marshal these skills in speaking and understanding. What linguists often refer to as "linguistic knowledge" is more appropriately described as "linguistic ability".

---

[2] A monologic discourse is normally interactive in numerous ways: it is tailored for the listeners, they are often addressed as *you*, their reactions are anticipated, they are sometimes expected to answer or interject, and so forth.

Though mastered by individuals, the skills in question are socioculturally transmitted and interpersonal in nature. The actions they engender are those of the interlocutors in linguistic interactions. From an interactive perspective, linguistic structures are usefully thought of as **instructions** issued by the speaker for the addressee (Harder 1996). We can make this evident by slightly rephrasing the descriptions of various notions.[3] We have described an expression's profile, for example, as the entity it puts onstage as the focus of attention. Alternatively, we might say that it constitutes an instruction to focus attention on that entity. A nominal grounding element, described as singling out a referent from the range of candidate instances, can equally well be characterized as an instruction for the hearer to find the referent. And instead of saying that *believe* invokes a mental space representing the subject's conception of reality, we can describe it as instructing the hearer to invoke it. The directive force of expressions should not be overstated—seldom does it rise to the level of ordering. Usually it is just a matter of eliciting the hearer's cooperation based on default expectations: minimally, that the hearer will attend to what is said and apprehend it in accordance with established convention.

A discourse is thus a series of interactive events, in each of which the speaker exerts some influence on an actual or imagined interlocutor. To qualify as a discourse, the component expressions must be apprehended in relation to one another (not as isolated occurrences). Each pertains in some way to what has gone before—whether by building on it, reacting to it, or just by changing the subject—and sets the stage for what will follow. Hence one aspect of an expression's import, often a crucial one, is how it relates to previous or following expressions. And being abstracted from usage events in discourse, conventional linguistic units also have this property. The discourse connections they specify are inherited by the expressions that incorporate them.

The complete description of units and expressions must therefore indicate the expectations they engender about the prior and later discourse. This is so regardless of their size and level of organization. At a global level, for example, the conventional expression *Once upon a time...* induces the expectation that the following discourse will be a certain type of story. Likewise, *...lived happily ever after* carries with it the supposition of being used to end such a story. We can say that the former is **prospective** and the latter **retrospective**. An essential part of their characterization is thus their position in a story, as shown in figure 13.1. Since these are abstracted linguistic units, the story they invoke is of course schematic rather than specific.

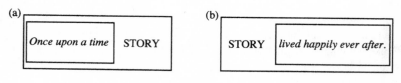

FIGURE 13.1

[3] This rephrasing does not amount to changing them. The alternate phrasings serve merely to highlight the cognitive or the interactive side of the coin.

Prospective and retrospective elements can be found at any level. For instance, expressions like *and so, therefore, nevertheless*, and *at the same time* presage a discourse sequence consisting of at least a clause, but potentially of any length. This makes them prospective. *At the same time*, they are retrospective because they portray this sequence as building on what has just been said (be it as an addition, consequence, qualification, or elaboration). Elements like *if, when, because*, and *although* are prospective by virtue of introducing clauses, and they further induce the expectation that another—the "main" clause—will either precede or follow. At a lower level, *my* is prospective for the nominal it grounds (e.g. *my friend*), whereas *of mine* is retrospective for the nominal containing it (*a friend of mine*). At a lower level still, prefixes and suffixes are *re*-spective-*ly* prospective and retrospective with respect to the stem they attach to. A schematic representation of that stem is thus an inherent part of their characterization. This stem is quite analogous to the story in figure 13.1. As a general matter, prospective and retrospective elements induce the expectation of a structure by invoking it schematically.

From a theoretical standpoint, we can sensibly say that all linguistic elements are both prospective and retrospective. Where they differ is in the specificity of the expectations they engender. At one extreme, these are so general as to be almost vacuous: the mere expectation of the expression being used in discourse. At the other extreme, they are so specific that only one option is allowed (e.g. *fro* occurs only as part of *to and fro*). Most elements are intermediate, being established as part of multiple larger assemblies they have some potential to evoke. In particular, common lexical items are usually established in a number of fixed expressions (consider *red pencil, pencil and paper, pencil lead, pencil in, pencil sharpener, pen and pencil (set), broken pencil*) or schematized structural frames (e.g. the constructional schemas incorporating *send* in fig. 8.13). It is not just specific expressions that carry discourse expectations—schematic structures do as well. If a sentence (like this one) begins with a conditional clause, we expect a consequent clause to follow: *if X, (then) Y*. Nor are expectations limited to the productions of a single speaker. A question carries with it the expectation of an answer. In well-mannered speech, *Thank you* is followed by *You're welcome*. Many interactive patterns of this sort, both specific and schematic, are among the conventional units of a language.

The interactions comprising a discourse unfold in a number of **channels**, both expressive and conceptual. At each pole, we can identify a "core" channel on the basis of its being the most substantive, the most autonomous, and the one speakers are most explicitly aware of. It is no accident that these core channels receive the most attention from linguists and are most consistently reflected in writing. They do not stand alone, however. Though less tangible, the other channels are essential in language and discourse.

On the expressive side, the core channel is what is often referred to as **segmental content**: the series of sounds or phonemes an utterance is composed of.[4] A second channel is prosody, consisting of "suprasegmental" phenomena such as accent, tone,

---

[4] These segments are represented by letters in an alphabetic writing system. While it does reflect an aspect of linguistic organization, this segmentation is neither phonetically realistic nor psychologically primary. Prosody is represented orthographically by devices like punctuation, capitalization, and spacing.

rhythmic grouping, and intonation contours. Obviously the two are intimately related. As suggested by the terms, segmental content is more autonomous and suprasegmentals are more dependent, in the sense that the former "carries" the latter—a vowel, for example, carries primary stress or falling tone, which could not be manifested without it. Less commonly recognized as part of language is the gestural channel, including manual gestures, facial expression, and bodily posture. These are, however, subject to conventionalization and coordination with other linguistic processes. In the case of signed languages, gesture functions as the core expressive channel.

On the conceptual side, we can identify the core channel as the situation being described. Reflecting its role as object of description, we can call this the **objective content**. The objective content itself has central and more peripheral elements, the center being an expression's profile. It further subsumes the expression's immediate scope (the onstage conceptual content), as well as any other content evoked. Another channel consists of the various factors known as information structure (§3.2.1): whether something is given or new, whether it is focused, whether it functions as a discourse topic, and so on. A third channel pertains to the management of discourse. Under this rubric are specifically interactive notions like turn taking, holding the floor, and providing the speaker with feedback or reinforcement.

These expressive and conceptual channels are not necessarily either well delimited or sharply distinct. As integral facets of usage events, they can all figure in linguistic units abstracted from such events. Although each has a measure of autonomy, the various ways of coordinating and connecting them are an important dimension of language structure. We have noted that prosody is "carried" by segmental content, requiring it for its full manifestation. At the conceptual pole, information structure is similarly dependent on the core channel of objective content—without the information there is nothing to structure. There must likewise be speech for speech management.

The dependent channel is often flexible in how it maps onto the carrier. For example, different portions of a sentence can be put in focus because the information they supply is new or otherwise noteworthy. We see this in (1), where *She hates linguistics* shows alternate placements of focus because it responds to different questions. In English, the focused portion retains its full, normal stress (small caps), whereas elements construed as given are phonologically reduced. The same sentence thus has different prosodic manifestations depending on the discourse context.

(1) (a) **A:** *Is there any subject she really despises?*   **B:** *She hates* LINGUISTICS.

     (b) **A:** *How does she feel about linguistics?*   **B:** *She* HATES *linguistics.*

This phenomenon illustrates the symbolization of information structure by prosodic devices. It shows that symbolic relationships do not just link segmental content with objective content—in principle, they can hold between any combination of expressive and conceptual channels. For instance, the segmental "filler" written as *uh* symbolizes the speaker's desire to hold the floor while pausing for reflection: *I think...uh...he's rather...uh...competitive.* Prosody is also used for discourse management. One such case is the contrast between suspended and falling intonation at the end of an utterance, indicating whether or not the speaker intends to continue. Even in spoken language, gesture has a substantial role in symbolizing objective content. The gestures we make while speaking are coordinated with speech and convey information not otherwise provided (McNeill 1992). By holding our hands wide apart, for example, we can signal that something we mention is large. Gesture is sometimes used alone for description, one notorious case being movement of the hands to show a voluptuous woman's shape. It also subserves speech management; for example, a teacher can call on a student with nothing more than a gaze and a nod.

Of course, the teacher might say the student's name as well. In that case, the action of granting the floor is expressed simultaneously by gesture and segmental content. It can also happen that an element simultaneously occupies multiple channels. Consider the physical pointing gesture that accompanies demonstratives in expressions like *I want this [→] one*. In addition to its signaling role, this gesture is part of the situation being described. The sentence describes a relationship in which the speaker goes onstage as a focused participant. Part of this onstage situation is the very fact that the speaker is pointing at something, and the object is specifically identified as what the speaker is pointing at. The gesture, therefore, is both expressive and a facet of what is expressed. In effect, the gesture symbolizes itself.

13.2 Conceptual Substrate

An expression's **maximal scope** has been defined as the full extent of the content evoked as the basis for its meaning (§3.2.3). Invariably, this includes much more than the content overtly expressed. How far it reaches may be indeterminate, and nothing is gained by imposing arbitrary boundaries. The essential thing is to realize that an expression's meaning rests on an extensive and multifaceted **conceptual substrate** which largely remains implicit. Among its facets are the many domains of knowledge invoked, mental constructions (e.g. metaphors), the linguistic interaction itself, and apprehension of the context in all its dimensions.

13.2.1 Context

If someone says *The cat is on the mat*, you are likely to envisage a typical domestic feline reclining on a flat piece of woven material spread out on the floor. This is what we take as being the expression's meaning. But does the sentence really mean this? It would, after all, be quite appropriate for describing other situations. Perhaps, for example, the mat is rolled up in a cylindrical bundle standing on end, with the cat perched unsteadily on top of it. Or perhaps a decorative mat is framed and mounted on a wall, and the cat is clinging to it with its claws. Or a large, voracious cat, having already devoured the curtains, is now eating the mat. Maybe the cat is a tiger in a cartoon, who has just lost a boxing match and is lying unconscious on the canvas. Or suppose we are using a light-colored mat as a makeshift screen for a slide show. To find where to place the projector and how to aim it, you put in a slide with the image of a cat. When the projector is finally positioned properly, I can let you know by saying *OK, the cat is on the mat*.

Since the sentence applies to such diverse situations, what can we identify as its meaning? One option is to distinguish between its specifically linguistic meaning (a matter of semantics) and the fuller meaning it assumes based on extralinguistic resources (a matter of pragmatic interpretation). There is, however, no strict dichotomy between linguistic and extralinguistic knowledge (§2.1.3). And if we try to factor them out, identifying as "linguistic" just those specifications shared by all an expression's varied interpretations, what qualifies will likely be too impoverished to be apprehended independently or recognized as a meaning. To avoid these problems, I have offered a vague, informal definition of linguistic meaning that may prove useful and arguably captures a valid intuition. Besides specifications that are indisputably semantic, an expression's meaning includes any additional structure needed to make the conception coherent and reflect what speakers naively regard as being meant and said, while excluding elements that are indisputably pragmatic and unnecessary for making sense of what is linguistically encoded.

So defined, linguistic meaning subsumes considerably more than what is overtly expressed. The additional aspects of meaning are largely supplied by context. If you have just seen a cartoon tiger get knocked unconscious in a boxing match, you will readily interpret *The cat is on the mat* as describing the prostrate feline on the canvas. But you would not arrive at this meaning in any other context. Most basic features of the scene evoked—notably, that the cat is a cartoon tiger, and the mat the surface of a boxing ring—stem from the context rather than being specifically expressed linguistically. To be sure, one interpetation of comparable specificity arises with no supporting context (e.g. as an isolated example in a linguistics textbook). At the beginning of this section, you probably did understand *The cat is on the mat* as referring to a typical domestic feline reclining on a flat piece of woven material spread out on the floor. This interpretation is not really acontextual, however. It is better described as invoking an imagined context based on default-case knowledge. The default for cats is a domestic feline, the default for cat behavior is sleeping, and the default for mats is that they are spread out on the floor. In accordance with these defaults, the expression evokes a familiar scenario as the basis for its interpretation.

The linguistically relevant context has several overlapping dimensions: physical, cultural, social, and linguistic. It can also be understood in either a narrow or a broader sense. In the narrow sense, it comprises just the immediate, transient circumstances in which a usage event occurs. Understood in a broader sense, it further includes more stable arrangements and shared knowledge in terms of which we apprehend the immediate circumstances. Suppose you yell *The cat is on the mat!* in order to warn me that my beloved Siamese is climbing the valuable decorative mat mounted on my study wall. At your vantage point in the study, the physical context includes the actual scene described, where the cat is clinging to the mat with its claws. For me, in another part of the house, this scene is not part of the context; nevertheless, I will interpret the sentence the way you intend it on the basis of other contextual factors. I know, for example, that there is just one mat in the house, that there is just one cat, that the mat is mounted on a wall, and that cats like to climb. Less obviously (but no less crucially), both of us rely on basic knowledge of possible occurrences given the world's physical nature. The relationship profiled by *on*, for instance, includes the notion of support, thereby invoking gravity and the natural tendency for objects to fall. When you see the cat in contact with the vertically mounted mat, you describe their relationship with *on* because you know the Siamese is not simply floating there unsupported.

The other dimensions of context also figure in this example. Let's start with culture. The way you phrase your warning, and the very fact that you feel obliged to issue one, reflect your interpretation of the scene in terms of standard cultural practices. Why do you say *the cat*—implying unique identifiability—even if you have never before been in my house and have no knowledge of my overall pet inventory? In so doing, you are invoking the cultural model that people keep pets in their home, that cats are one standard pet, and that the default is just one cat per household. If the default were twelve instead of one, you would probably say *a cat* or *one of your cats*. If, instead, the culture proscribed keeping animals as pets, so that the cat must simply have wandered in, you would probably use *some* to label it as a stranger (*Some cat is climbing on your mat!*) or use *there* to announce its presence (*There's a cat on the mat!*). It is due to other cultural knowledge that you feel obliged to yell out a warning in the first place. You know that only things considered valuable are framed and mounted on a wall.[5] You further know that things of value are not routinely sacrificed for the climbing pleasure of cats, and that guests should be mindful of their hosts and their property.

Here, of course, cultural knowledge shades into social knowledge. Guest and host are social roles, and associated with such roles are models of acceptable social behavior. It is normally rude for a guest to shout to a host in another part of the house, but emergencies elicit other expectations (you are not considered rude for yelling *Fire!* when the house is burning). Obviously, social circumstances are reflected in the form of expressions—you hear more and better swear words in the locker room than in church. And a central facet of the social situation is the relationship between the interlocutors, including their degree of intimacy or their relative social status. In most cases, *The cat is on the mat!* is quite acceptable from this standpoint. Suppose, however, that I am a general, and you—a mere private—are working in my house. Despite the emergency, you would probably feel obliged to yell: *Sir! The cat is on the mat!*

The linguistic context likewise has both stable and transient aspects. Chief among the former is knowledge of the language being used, as well as its sociocultural status. Providing a transient linguistic context is the discourse in which an expression occurs. There is no particular limit as to how far back in a discourse the currently relevant context extends; a possible basis for using the definite article with *cat* is that we were discussing this destructive pet several hours ago. Nor is the context limited to prior discourse. When you clue me in by yelling *The cat is on the mat!*, you probably expect an answer (e.g. *Thanks!* or *Not again!*).

A usage event was defined as embracing an expression's full contextual understanding, a portion of which can be identified as its linguistic meaning. A key factor in its meaning is the interaction of the speaker and hearer, each engaged in assessing what the other knows, intends, and is currently attending to. The intended result,

---

[5] Since mats are typically not in this category, you surmise that the one you see is the only one of any consequence in the house. *Mat* thus takes the definite article.

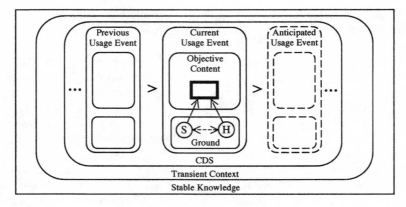

FIGURE 13.2

sketched in figure 13.2, is that the interlocutors arrive at roughly similar conceptions of the objective content and direct their attention to the same element within it (the expression's profile). Crucial in this respect is the common ground provided by the overall context. This common basis for interpretation is called the **current discourse space** (CDS).[6] It comprises everything presumed to be shared by the speaker and hearer as the basis for communication at a given moment. Part of the CDS, of course, is the current discourse itself, including both previous usage events and any that might be anticipated. Also part of the CDS are other mutually evident aspects of the transient context, as well as any stable knowledge required for their apprehension or otherwise invoked. All of these may figure in an expression's full contextual understanding and in those portions that constitute its linguistic meaning.

Linguistic units are abstracted from usage events by the reinforcement of recurring commonalities. Should it recur, any aspect of such events can be incorporated in a unit. The specifications of conventional units are therefore not limited to the core channels of segmental and objective content; in the previous section, we noted the use of prosody for information structure and discourse management, as well as the gestural component of demonstratives. Also, prospective and retrospective elements incorporate specifications about the prior or subsequent discourse (e.g. *You're welcome* directly follows an act of thanking). A personal pronoun, like *she*, carries with it the expectation that its referent will be evident to the hearer by virtue of being salient in the transient context. Usually it is mentioned explicitly: *I asked my lawyer, but she said the case was hopeless*. But it can also be evident on nonlinguistic grounds. If we are both listening attentively to a lecture, for example, I can simply say *She's made some good points*, knowing that you will know who *she* is.

Above and beyond their basic value, units incorporate specifications reflecting sociocultural aspects of the usage events that spawn them. These pertain (inter alia)

---

[6] This notion was introduced in §9.3.3. The objective content in the successive usage events corresponds to the "discourse frames" in fig. 9.7. Be aware that the factors involved are too complex to be represented with full consistency in a single two-dimensional diagram (e.g. fig. 13.2 does not indicate that apprehension of other events in the sequence is part of the contextual understanding comprising any single usage event).

to the interlocutors, conditions for an expression's appropriate use, and even its status in the language. In Spanish, for instance, the pronoun *tu* does more than merely designate the hearer. As an additional aspect of its value (distinguishing it from *usted*), it ascribes to the interlocutors a relationship of familiarity or solidarity. It is quite common, in fact, for units to be appropriate only in limited circumstances, based on register, cultural setting, or the social roles and status of the interlocutors.[7] As part of their conventional import, such units incorporate nondefault specifications concerning the ground or other facets of the transient context. Units can also be recognized as being frequent or uncommon, as belonging to a certain dialect, or as having been borrowed from another language. Though commonly used in English, for example, *enchilada* is recognized as having come from Spanish and *crème brûlée* from French. With respect to properties like these, even the absence of any special value amounts to a kind of value—namely, default-case status. A minimal specification, implicit in every linguistic unit, is the very fact of its being conventionally used and recognized as part of the language by members of the relevant speech community.

13.2.2 The Effect of Viewing Arrangement

Part of an expression's conceptual substrate is the **viewing arrangement**: the relationship between the conceptualizers and the object of conception. An arrangement reasonably taken as canonical finds two interlocutors together in a fixed location, from which they observe and report on actual occurrences. However, there are many and frequent departures from this default: cases where the interlocutors are moving, where they are spatially or temporally separated, where the situation described is nonactual, where the expression is other than a statement, and so forth. The viewing arrangement not only figures in the meanings of expressions but also affects their form (§3.4.1). Semantically, for instance, *I'm not here right now* seems contradictory in face-to-face conversation but quite coherent as the message on an answering machine. With respect to form, *right now* and the present-tense inflection of the verb allude to the time—future from the standpoint of the speaker—when a caller hears the message. In the default viewing arrangement, the speaker would have to describe things differently, e.g. *I won't be here then*.

Even in face-to-face conversation, the viewing arrangement is important and highly variable. Consider an expression's objective content, roughly characterized as the situation being described. Metaphorically, we can think of the speaker and hearer as looking at a monitor displaying this situation. Only so much appears on the screen at any one moment: the expression's immediate scope (the general locus of viewing attention), its profile (the specific focus of attention), and whatever else can fit.[8] As compensation for this limited coverage, the display changes from one usage event to the next as the camera pans, zooms, or saccades. Importantly, the

---

[7] For example, *prostitute*, *hooker*, and *whore* belong to successively lower registers (levels of formality), and *Your Honor* is only used for addressing the judge in a courtroom. Hence the following judgments: *I object to calling this witness, Your Honor, because she's known to be a {prostitute/??hooker/*whore}.*

[8] The objective content is more inclusive than the immediate scope whenever there is reason to distinguish onstage and offstage content within the situation described, e.g. in progressives (fig. 5.9).

camera can be directed at anything at all. We can think and talk about any time or place. The situations described can be observed, recalled, or imagined. They can be physical, mental, or social in nature. Much of what we talk about could not actually exist, being constructed by mental processes like metaphor and blending (§2.2.3). And rather than directing the camera outward, we can aim it at the ground or at ourselves. If we choose to talk about it, even our innermost experience can appear on the monitor.

When the ground figures in the situation being talked about, there is some flexibility in how it is viewed. In particular, an interlocutor participating in a profiled relationship has a dual role as both subject and object of conception. Either role may then be chosen as the basis for linguistic expression. If someone asks me what I think about the president, I can give the same basic response in two different ways: I would probably say *I don't trust him*, but I can also be more casual and omit the first-person pronoun, saying simply *Don't trust him*. With the former, I put myself onstage as an object of conception, explicitly mentioned and focused as clausal subject. Effectively, I portray the situation as being external to the ground, as if it involved another person. Despite their referential identity, indicated by the correspondence line in figure 13.3(a), to some extent I mentally split myself into two individuals, the conceptualizer and an object of conception.[9]

The alternative expression, *Don't trust him*, is not just a matter of my being too lazy to use a subject pronoun. Instead, as shown in figure 13.3(b), it presents the situation as I actually experience it. I am really a single individual, functioning as subject of conception for both the attitude and the sentence describing it. The sentence directly reflects this by treating me solely as an offstage conceptualizer. This dual-capacity role is coded linguistically in the usual way—namely, by being left implicit—hence the lack of an overt grammatical subject. There is thus a discrepancy between the objective content (OC) and the expression's immediate scope (IS). The former, representing the situation described, includes me in my guise as trajector of the process profiled by the verb. Linguistically, however, I present myself merely as

(a) *I don't trust him.*   (b) *Don't trust him.*

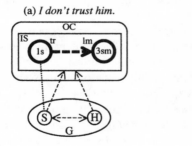 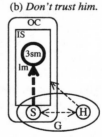

FIGURE 13.3

[9] The "split self" phenomenon, which has many linguistic manifestations (Talmy 1988a; Lakoff 1996), is based in part on the apprehension of other minds and the nature of their experience. Notably, the speaker simulates the hearer's view of the scene, and from H's standpoint S is indeed a distinct individual (Langacker 2007).

the subject of conception—or rather I do not present myself at all, preferring not to venture onstage within the scope of viewing attention.[10] Expressions like these correlate with lesser formality, as they invite the hearer to construe the situation from the speaker's own vantage point.

In commands, we observe a similar alternation with respect to the hearer, who likewise has a dual role as both interlocutor and participant in the profiled event. The subject pronoun *you* is said to be optional in imperatives: we can either say *You leave!* or simply *Leave!* These are not exactly equivalent, however, the former being stronger or more formal. Once again, the difference comes down to whether the hearer's role as participant or as interlocutor is coded linguistically. Viewing the hearer as an onstage participant has a distancing effect that naturally correlates with greater formality. And since it reflects the speaker's more objective construal of the hearer (rather than the hearer's subjective construal of self), it correlates with the speaker being firmly in control.[11]

Imperatives are a striking example of how the viewing arrangement affects an expression's form. Let us first consider the nonimperative *She ordered him to leave*. As a declarative, it merely **describes** an act of ordering instead of **constituting** one. In figure 13.4(a), this action is shown as a double arrow to indicate its force-dynamic nature: through verbal means, the trajector exerts social and psychological force on the landmark with the intent of causing the latter to do something. The expression profiles their interaction, which is thus the focus of attention within the immediate scope. There being no overlap with the ground, the event and its participants are objectively construed. Sentence (b), *I order you to leave!*, represents the opposite extreme, where the profiled event and the speech event do not just overlap but are fully coincident. A sentence like this is called a **performative**, since its utterance (under appropriate conditions) constitutes a performance of the act described (Austin 1962). As shown in figure 13.4(b), the speaker-hearer interaction in the ground is itself an instance of ordering (not the default of simply stating). The speech event is thus identified with the profiled event onstage,[12] and the interlocutors with its participants. Their identification produces a special viewing arrangement in which the objective content subsumes the entire ground. We can show this directly by superimposing corresponding elements, thereby obtaining figure 13.4(c). The diagrams in 13.4(b) and (c) are equivalent (notational variants).

While performatives are more explicit, simple imperatives have the advantage of being more succinct. We do not need a verb like *order* to issue a command: saying

---

[10] This subjective self-construal, imposed at the level of the overall construction, overrides the focal prominence of the verb's trajector. Japanese has a similar construction which takes this one step further by reinterpreting the verbal landmark as clause-level trajector: *Sake-ga hosii* (sake-NOM want) 'I want sake'. Once the verb's trajector is pulled offstage and subjectively construed, the landmark (in this case *sake*) is the only remaining focal participant, hence the trajector at the higher level of organization. The difference between English and Japanese is a matter of whether constructions depending on subject or object status make reference to the lower level of organization or the higher one.

[11] The inclusion of *you* is therefore inconsistent with *please* or with a sympathetic appeal to the hearer's self-interest: *Please, (*you) leave!*; *For your own sake, (*you) leave!*

[12] Their identity—hence their temporal coincidence—is responsible for performative verbs appearing in the simple present tense, which is normally problematic for perfectives (§5.2.3).

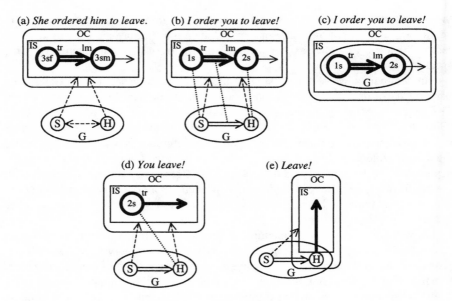

FIGURE 13.4

Leave! or *You leave!* is usually quite sufficient. As a salient feature of the conceptual substrate, the speaker-hearer interaction is part of an expression's meaning, whether or not it is put onstage and profiled. Leaving it implicit does, however, greatly affect an expression's form. Shown in figure 13.4(d) and (e), the simple imperatives consist of just a single clause, with or without an overt subject. Since the ordering is offstage and subjectively construed, the leaving stands alone as the object of description. The presence or absence of *you* depends on whether the hearer is coded as a participant or as an interlocutor.

13.2.3 Speech Acts

The kinds of actions described by performatives—actions like stating, ordering, asking, requesting, promising, vowing, proclaiming, and christening—are known as **speech acts** (Austin 1962; Searle 1969). While most full sentences, in actual use, are understood as representing some kind of speech act, true performatives are rather infrequent. Questioning is very common, but instead of saying *I ask you whether she is home yet*, we would normally just ask *Is she home yet?* Even the traditional *I now pronounce you man and wife* is being replaced by the more informal *You are now husband and wife*. Under the proper circumstances, the couple is married either way. The speech-act force is no less real or valid when it is left implicit as part of the conceptual substrate.

 Speech acts are based on standard cultural models. As recognized ways of interacting in the society, these models are invoked as cognitive domains for various linguistic purposes. They function as the meanings of speech-act verbs: *ask, order, promise, proclaim, sentence*, and the like. Such verbs can either be used performatively (*I hereby sentence you to life in prison*) or descriptively (*The judge sentenced him to life in prison*). The most basic speech acts (stating, ordering, and asking) function as the prototypical values of basic sentence types (declarative, imperative, and interrogative). An expression can also evoke a speech act as part of its meaning even when it is not explicitly indicated. Although the word is not used, the solemn statement *I will never again smoke marijuana* may well be interpreted as a promise.

The cultural models invoked by speech acts are familiar scenarios of social and linguistic interaction. Schematically, they represent any preconditions required for a valid performance of the act;[13] the various participants and their roles; the action itself; the intended outcome; and expectations about the sequence, form, and content of the expressions employed. The interactive event constituting a speech act is characterized by its place in such a scenario. As part of an abstracted cognitive model, the speech act and its participants are of course only virtual entities—like the referents of *I* and *you* or the conceptualizer in a grounding element (§12.3.2). In a particular instance of language use, they are identified with an actual interaction on the part of the current interlocutors.

An expression's overt content may therefore represent just one of several levels of organization that figure in its full conceptual import. Suppose someone says *I'll be there* and understands this as being a genuine promise. There is more to this sentence than just the finite clause *I'll be there*. In and of itself, a finite clause does not constitute a promise or any other speech act; it merely expresses a proposition with no intrinsic epistemic status. It may, for example, be part of a larger sentence that specifically denies its validity: *It's not the case that I'll be there*. If accepted as valid, *I'll be there* might simply be a statement about the future, with no intent of promising. When the clause is in fact understood as a promise, it is by virtue of being embedded in the promising scenario, in which the speaker makes a commitment to bring about the profiled occurrence: [Promise Scenario [*I'll be there*]]. Of course, this promise could be made by any speaker at any time. The expression receives a specific interpretation—a particular speaker committing to a particular occurrence—only in the context of an actual usage event: [Usage Event [Promise Scenario [*I'll be there*]]].

This dimension of an expression's meaning is often more elaborate, incorporating multiple scenarios configured in a certain way. Sentence (2)(a) exemplifies one well-known pattern, where a question about the ability to do something actually constitutes a request to do it. At one level it is in fact a question, as indicated by its form, as well as the possibility of answering *Yes*. But (2)(a) is not just a question, as indicated by the possible inclusion of *please* and by the inappropriateness of answering *Yes, I could* and then doing nothing. It instantiates a complex interactive schema in which the question scenario is embedded in the request scenario: [Request Scenario [Question Scenario [Clause]]]. The question is not a genuine one, for it is only posed by way of making the request.

(2) (a) *Could you (please) pass the salt?*

(b) *Go ahead, leave! See if I care!*

---

[13] These are often called "felicity conditions". If I should say to you *I hereby sentence you to life in prison*, you will not have to worry, since I do not have the authority to perform this act.

Similarly, *leave!* is not a genuine order in the context of (2)(b). The speaker merely pretends to give an order as a way of presenting the consequences of the imagined action. The order scenario is therefore incorporated into a more elaborate mental construction that overrides its force. Despite their covert nature, complex scenarios of this sort have the status of conventional linguistic units.

Three very basic speech act scenarios are those of stating, ordering, and questioning. Conventional units of English specify their default-case pairings with three basic clause types: [Statement Scenario [Declarative Clause]], [Order Scenario [Imperative Clause]], [Question Scenario [Interrogative Clause]]. To be sure, each clause type can also be used in other ways.[14] Conversely, speech acts have different manifestations. The examples in (3) illustrate some alternate pairings of clause types and scenarios. We see in (a) that a clause with the special word order of an interrogative can also be used as an exclamation. Despite its imperative form, the first clause in (b) is not an order to flirt with the speaker's wife. And in (c), we note that intonation allows a declarative clause to function as a question or an order.

(3) (a) *Isn't she cute!* [cf. *Isn't she ready?*]

(b) *Flirt with my wife and I'll break your arm.*

(c) **A:** *You'll leave.* **B:** *I'll leave?* **A:** *Yes, you'll leave!*

English declaratives are structurally basic in the sense that the other clause types are readily described in reference to them. Imperative clauses lack two basic features of declaratives: grounding (by tense and modals) and an overt subject. And in contrast to declaratives, where auxiliary verbs all follow the subject, in an interrogative clause the first auxiliary precedes it. As one might expect, the most basic clause type is typically paired with the most basic speech-act scenario. Statement has the same relation to other speech acts that vanilla has to other flavors. While this speech act is often called "assertion", that term is overly pretentious. It evokes an argumentative situation where the speaker has to assert the validity of a proposition, by force of evidence, to an interlocutor who does not previously subscribe to it. But this is not how people ordinarily talk. Though a statement is often informative, it is seldom advanced with confirming evidence to overcome an interlocutor's resistance. Indeed, it is often not even informative. Much of our everyday talk consists in stating what is already plainly evident to the listener. Witness the following statements, given in bold:

(4) (a) *Take it easy. Remember,* **you have a heart condition**.

(b) *Omigod!* **Someone's knocking on the door**. *Get some clothes on!*

(c) **You're late. You should have called to let me know.**

(d) **It's already dark. The days are getting shorter.**

---

[14] Declarative, imperative, and interrogative clauses are defined in terms of their structure. Despite the standard labels, they acquire interactive force only in combination with speech-act scenarios.

How, then, do we characterize a statement? In normal interactive use, every expression is intended to have some effect or elicit some response. Intended results are inherent in speech-act scenarios: a promise commits the speaker to a course of action, a question obliges the addressee to answer, and so on. Among the different-flavored speech acts, stating is special just by being so bland. It represents the most neutral flavor, minimal in terms of intended effect and hearer response. In and of itself, a statement carries with it nothing more than the baseline expectation—characteristic of all expressions—of being heard and understood. This is not to deny, of course, that speakers intend and achieve much more by making statements. It is just that such effects are above and beyond the basic statement scenario.

Another feature of the statement scenario is that the speaker subscribes to what is said. This does not prevent people from lying—it is, rather, what makes it possible to lie. It is only because a statement purports to represent the speaker's view that it can actually be used to misrepresent it. There are, to be sure, many cases (short of lying) where a speaker says something without subscribing to it. These result from embedding the statement scenario in more elaborate mental constructions that override it. In one complex scenario, the speaker merely echoes what has just been said:

(5)   *I've just been nominated for the Nobel Prize. Sure. Tell me another one.*

Here the speaker suspends his own reality conception and provisionally identifies with the (purported) view of the previous speaker. Reiterating the proposition keeps it alive for further consideration, often leading to its rejection. Another case is irony, where the speaker says something that is clearly false and intended to be recognized as such. To take just one example, *That was a brilliant move* is nearly always said in response to doing something stupid. The speaker goes through the motions of stating the brilliance of the move, with the clear understanding that it is not a genuine statement. The presumption that the speaker subscribes to what is said is overridden when the statement scenario is incorporated into the more complex scenario of stating with ironic intent.

In its basic variant, diagrammed in figure 13.5(a), the statement scenario evokes a usage event in which the speaker produces a finite clause. Shown at the top is the proposition expressed by the clause, consisting of a grounded process. The relevant aspect of its grounding is that the conceptualizer (C) adopts an epistemic stance (e) toward the profiled occurrence (primarily by the presence or absence of a modal). A correspondence line indicates that the speaker assumes the role of C in this regard; that is, the speaker subscribes to the proposition. Dashed arrows represent the intended outcome: the baseline expectation that the hearer will momentarily join the speaker in attending to the proposition. Though statements are sometimes forcefully made, this is not intrinsic to the scenario. It specifies only the minimal speaker-hearer interaction (double-headed arrow), where the interlocutors apprehend one another and attend to what is said. A potential result of the usage event is that the hearer also identifies with C and subscribes to the proposition. The diagram shows the arguably typical case where the statement is informative, so that the hearer did not subscribe to it previously.

The order scenario is rather different. As seen in figure 13.5(b), the content expressed (e.g. *Leave!*) is not a proposition but simply a process. Whereas statements pertain to the **epistemic** level, thus invoking a conceptualizer and an epistemic stance, orders pertain to actions per se, at the **effective** level (§12.3.1). For this reason, an imperative clause does not contain a separate grounding element: its verb cannot be inflected for tense (**Left!*) or take a modal (**Will leave!*).[15] So instead of the speaker being identified with C, the hearer is identified with the trajector of the profiled process. The speaker does have a stance in regard to this process, however: the **effective** stance—indicated by a dashed double arrow—of intending to bring about its occurrence. To realize this intent, the speaker subjects the hearer to social and psychological force, represented by the solid double arrow. The projected outcome is that the hearer will share this intent and act accordingly.[16]

The question scenario is more complex, for it shares certain features of statements and orders. As with statements, the clause expresses a proposition. As with

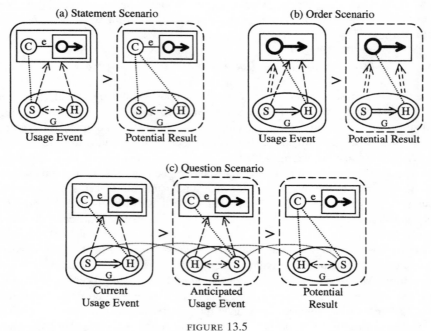

FIGURE 13.5

[15] An order like *You will leave!* represents a blend, where imperative force is superimposed on what would otherwise be a statement. The futurity and modal force conveyed by *will* are identified with those inherent in the order scenario.

[16] Though not internally grounded, an imperative clause is grounded by the speech act itself. As with root modals (e.g. *You should leave*), grounding occurs at the effective rather than the epistemic level (§9.4.3). Ordering counts as grounding because it relates the profiled process to the interlocutors, specifying their effective stance in regard to it. It also has epistemic import, since something not yet effected is not yet real.

orders, the speaker obliges the hearer to act, specifically by answering the question. The usage event is thus prospective in the sense of presaging a subsequent usage event. Correspondence lines indicate that the speaker in the first event functions as hearer in the next, and conversely. Because a question requests information rather than offering it, the initial hearer is the one who is first identified with C, being presumed to have an epistemic stance in regard to the profiled occurrence. It is anticipated that the hearer will then, in the guise of speaker, provide an informative statement which makes this stance explicit.[17] A potential result of the second event is that the questioner will also identify with C. If the question is *Will it rain?*, the answer *Yes, it will* indicates that the responder assumes the role of C with respect to the proposition *It will rain*. Accepting the response as valid implies that the questioner also assumes that role, so that *It will rain* expresses what is subsequently the questioner's own epistemic assessment.

13.2.4 Expressives

A word should also be said about expressions like *Hi*, *Thanks*, *Yes*, and *Damn!*, as well as **vocatives**, where a person is addressed by name. Because their essential import resides in facets of the speaker-hearer interaction, these might well be regarded as special kinds of speech acts. What makes them special is their relationship to the situation described—or rather their nondistinctness from that situation. They deviate from the canonical arrangement with stating, questioning, promising, and so on, where the interaction constituting the speech act is separate from the expression's objective content. Instead, their "content" is a facet of the interaction itself. In this respect they resemble performatives, where the profiled event and the speech event are the same (fig. 13.4(c)). Unlike performatives, however, they focus on only one aspect of the interaction, whose status as the linguistically coded occurrence is necessary rather than incidental. They are thus nonclausal and cannot serve as descriptions of external occurrences.

For want of a better term, I call such elements **expressives**. Their function is not to describe (implying an external situation) but is better characterized as expressive, emotive, or interactive. The differences should not be exaggerated. Many other expressions have expressive or emotive import (e.g. *gay* vs. *queer*, *good* vs. *absolutely marvelous*, or *fail to save* vs. *kill* vs. *butcher* [with reference to a surgeon]). And every expression is to some extent interactive, a tacit instruction to evoke an array of content and construe it in a certain fashion. For their part, expressives are not altogether lacking in descriptive content. They too invoke cognitive domains and impose a particular construal. Rather than being sharply distinct, expressives form a continuum with more descriptive expressions.

For one thing, certain expressives are to some extent still recognizable as elliptic versions of descriptive statements. *Awesome!* evokes the fuller *That's awesome!* (whereas *Wow!* does not suggest **That's wow!*). We can still interpret *Congratulations* as abbreviating *Let me offer my congratulations*, and while it is only vestigial, an

---

[17] This rudimentary description pertains specifically to "yes/no" questions. A generalized version is needed for "content" questions with *who*, *what*, *where*, *when*, etc.

analogous understanding of *Greetings* or *Thanks* is not impossible. Expressives not interpreted as elliptic may be recognized as special uses of elements also employed descriptively. *Damn!*, for instance, retains its association with the corresponding verb, and *Hell!* with the corresponding noun. A name is clearly recognized as such, whether the person named is being addressed (e.g. *I see, Joe*) or merely referred to (*I see Joe*).

Like expressions used descriptively, expressives evoke conceptual content and direct attention within it. Among the cognitive domains invoked are interactive scenarios: those of people meeting and exchanging greetings (for *Hi, Hello, Greetings*), of asking and answering a question (*Yes, No*), of helping one another and being polite (*Please, Thanks, You're welcome*), and so on. Some domains pertain to sensation and emotional reaction (*Ouch!, Yuck!, Damn!*, and other four-letter words). Expressives emphasize particular facets of their domains. For example, *Yes* is what one says in responding positively to a question. It therefore calls attention to the response phase of the question scenario, conveying that the responder subscribes to the proposition at issue. *Please* is what one says in making a polite request. As such, it highlights the speaker's deferent attitude (suggesting that the hearer need only respond if it **pleases** her). *Ouch!* gives vent to a mild, brief episode of pain. It thereby directs attention to this bodily experience, as opposed to its cause, its locus, or the possibility of injury. A crucial feature of expressives is that central participants in the scenarios are specifically identified as interlocutors in the speech event. *Please* is what the speaker says to the addressee in making a request, and *Ouch!* expresses the speaker's pain, not that of anybody else.[18] However, the interlocutors are usually left implicit, especially the speaker (*Damn you!* occurs, but not **I ouch!*). This indicates that expressives invoke the interlocutors in their offstage role as subjects of conception.

What do expressives profile? Perhaps nothing, at least in a narrow sense of the term. An expression's profile is the onstage focus of attention, objectively construed by definition. But at least from the standpoint of the speaker, expressives are not about viewing and describing onstage content. In using one, the speaker is either performing a social action or vocally manifesting an experience—rather than **describing** a scenario, he **enacts a role** in it.[19] For the speaker, then, the action or experience is subjectively construed. While an expressive evokes and calls attention to it, the prominence it thus receives is not that of a focused object of description. If we stick to the narrow definition, therefore, expressives are principled exceptions to the generalization that every expression has a profile.

Vocatives are slightly different. When I address someone by name, the name certainly does profile that individual. The reason for the difference is that names are not intrinsically expressive. Often, if not typically, they are used descriptively: *I saw Joe yesterday*. Vocatives are not a separate type of expression, but rather

---

[18] This does not prevent me from saying *Ouch!* by way of empathy if I see someone else bump his head. I then identify with the experiencer and emulate his likely reaction based on a mental simulation of the experience.

[19] By contrast, a performative describes (and thus profiles) a speech act in addition to enacting it (fig. 13.4).

a matter of names being recruited for interactive use. By addressing Joe as *Joe* (instead of *you*), I indicate that his status as interlocutor is not secure. There are two basic patterns. If we are already engaged in conversation, mentioning his name serves only to reaffirm his status as addressee: *It seems to me, Joe, that you really should get married.* Alternatively, I can call his name to attract his attention and thereby establish him as the addressee: *Joe! I can use your help over here.* In either case, Joe is an onstage participant in an otherwise tacit scenario—the visible tip of an interactive iceberg.

Vocatives resemble expressions like *Fire!* and *Water!*, which likewise evoke scenarios by explicitly mentioning just one, crucial element. Although these are nouns, they are understood as calls to action, the specific action depending on general and contextual knowledge. Fire being a dangerous thing, yelling *Fire!* is usually a warning to avoid it, while *Water!* is normally taken as requesting this substance. Context, of course, may reverse these default interpretations (imagine a bursting dam or the prospect of eating raw meat). *Help!* can be understood as either a noun or a verb. As a verb, it is essentially an imperative, though weaker in force than an order; it is rather a plea, directed at anyone able to respond. Canonical imperatives (e.g., *Leave!*) might be analyzed as a special case of these minimally explicit calls for action. They all share the property of relying on the conceptual substrate to indicate the desired course of action with respect to the overtly mentioned element.

13.3 Discourse Genres

As a long-term goal, CG envisages an integrated account of linguistic structure in all its varied manifestations. One aspect of this challenge is to accommodate, in seamless fashion, both individual expressions and connected discourse. Also contributing to the challenge are the myriad ways of using language. These give rise to numerous kinds or **genres** of discourse, both spoken and written.

13.3.1 Uses of Language

Although speech is primary, writing is so ubiquitous in modern societies that a comprehensive account of language cannot ignore it. Indeed, some people (myself included) routinely have more encounters with the written word than with the spoken. Writing is not just a semisuccessful attempt to represent speech. It has a life of its own, with its own conventions and special uses. It also has an impact on the spoken language. An obvious case is the prevalent use of acronyms, a major source of nouns in modern English.[20] Or note the common practice of reproducing quote marks in speech and gesture: *He's rather quote/unquote* [gesture made by crooking two fingers on each hand] *high-spirited.*

---

[20] The individual letters can be pronounced either individually (*USA, CIA, VIP, IBM, UFO, DNA, PVC, NFL*) or as if they spelled a word (*NATO, FEMA, NOW, PETA, BART, NIMBY, WYSIWYG*). The possibility of the latter has become a major consideration in choosing new names. The National Organization for the Reform of Marijuana Laws (NORML) was not so named by accident.

Both speech and writing occur in various genres. The term is used in literature for general types of works such as novels, short stories, and epic poems. By extension, we can usefully apply it to any recognizable type of linguistic production. Ordinary conversation is thus a spoken-language genre, as are lectures, sermons, job interviews, play-by-play accounts of sporting events, menus for automated phone responses, and instructions shouted out by drill sergeants. And quite apart from literature, written-language genres are numerous and highly varied: personal letters, business letters, email, signs, labels, recipes, menus, class schedules, course descriptions, newspaper headlines, computer manuals, assembly instructions, linguistics articles, various kinds of legal documents, and many more. It should be obvious that alternate classificatory schemes can be proposed, and that many linguistic productions do not fit neatly in any single category. Still, the genres mentioned are probably all familiar to you, and in each case you have at least a rough idea of their typical properties.

To the extent that they are standard in a speech community, discourse genres are characterized by conventional linguistic units. In principle, their CG description is comparable to that of other aspects of language structure. Our knowledge of a given genre consists in a set of schemas abstracted from encountered instances. Each schema represents a recurring commonality in regard to some facet of their structure: their global organization, more local structural properties, typical content, specific expressions employed, matters of style and register, etc. Individually and collectively, the schemas embody our expectations about the genre and serve as templates in producing and apprehending new instances. They are not necessarily very different from templates created for practical purposes, such as the template for a business letter in your word-processing program, or the schematic will in a package of do-it-yourself legal software. This is not to say, of course, that every genre is so straightforwardly described.

Genres are based on cultural scenarios representing familiar kinds of linguistic interaction. Most imply a viewing arrangement that is quite different from the canonical one involving two interlocutors engaged in face-to-face conversation. With sermons, there is one speaker and many listeners. In the case of answering machine messages, there are many potential addressees, and the partners in any actual exchange are not together in either time or space. For writing, of course, separation in time and space is the usual situation. The objective in most written genres is to produce a text to be read as appropriate at some future time. The intended reader may be a specific group or individual, even oneself (as with sticky notes and diaries). But typically the text is meant to be accessible for anyone who might encounter it at any time. In the broadest sense, this still involves a linguistic interaction: via the text produced, the writer expects to have some effect on any potential reader.

The scenario for a discourse genre is part of the conceptual substrate for linguistic productions that manifest it. The scenario includes a purpose and a viewing arrangement. In different ways and to varying degrees, these factors determine the form of productions based on it. For example, a drill sergeant need only produce a series of terms for the actions to be executed. The drill scenario ensures that these will be interpreted as commands and rules out any other content.[21] The template for

---

[21] Hence the following is not a well-formed instance of the genre: *Shoulder arms! Right Face! I prefer Mozart over Beethoven. Forward harch!*

a legal document may be almost as rigid, but in view of its purpose the form and content are very different. Instead of short commands, it consists of full sentences, often quite elaborate, which attempt to spell out in full, explicit detail all the relevant background, obligations, contingencies, parties to the action, and so on. The words *I* and *you* are very frequent in conversation and personal letters, but they hardly occur at all in newspaper headlines. A poetic genre might well impose restrictions concerning rhyme, meter, and number of lines per stanza, yet be totally free in regard to content. By contrast, a restaurant menu is very limited in subject matter but is not expected to rhyme.

While every discourse scenario has roles analogous to those of the speaker and hearer in ordinary conversation, the details vary greatly. The writer of a diary is also the sole intended reader. In the case of a menu, these roles correspond respectively to the faceless restaurant management and the faceless mass of potential customers. On a given occasion, the menu effects a linguistically mediated interaction whereby a particular customer learns what the management's representatives have to offer and is able to respond accordingly. Some genres have multiple speaker-type and hearer-type roles. A typical sportscast has two announcers, one who does the play-by-play, the other an ex-jock doing "color". Interspersed with the play-by-play, they take turns addressing one another, but at the same time both of them are speaking to and for the audience.

Of course, multiple speaker and hearer roles are characteristic of the most basic discourse genre: ordinary conversation. Here the default scenario specifies just two interlocutors, who alternate in the two capacities. If there are more than two, the norm is for one to be speaking and the others listening at any given time. A "turn" is the stretch of discourse during which a single speaker "holds the floor". Among the conventional units of a language are various ways of negotiating turns (an aspect of speech management). For instance, by using suspended (level) intonation at the end of an utterance, a speaker signals the intention to continue, whereas falling intonation gives the listener a chance to intervene. Conventional units are not limited to single turns but can also make specifications concerning turn sequences. One such case is the question-answer scenario, sketched in figure 13.5(c). Naturally, the ideal of alternating turns, with just one person talking at a time, is often honored in the breach. The rough and tumble of actual conversation is marked by overlap, interruption, two people talking simultaneously, and so on. But this too is subject to conventionalization and is often cooperative rather than competitive. Commonly, for example, one person finishes an utterance by supplying a word or phrase the other is searching for. The full utterance is then the product of "co-construction" by the interlocutors.

At least in conversation, the production of a discourse is clearly social, negotiable, and effected through multiparty interactions. Can it be dealt with, then, in "cognitive linguistics" and "Cognitive Grammar"? It does of course require special methods for collecting and analyzing data, as well as special descriptive notions, such as "turn" (Sacks, Schegloff, and Jefferson 1974). Cognitive and social phenomena are not mutually exclusive, however. Conversation is constructed by sentient creatures who apprehend the expressions produced and are constantly engaged in assessing the knowledge and conscious state of their interlocutors. Though flexibly employed (like any others), the conventional units invoked are learned by individuals as entrenched patterns of neural and neurally directed activity. It is true that language is grounded in social interaction. But it is equally true that social interaction is grounded in cognition.

13.3.2 Levels of Organization

Linguistic productions can be of any size. For all but the smallest, their composition proceeds through levels of organization, such that the "output" from one level of composition functions in turn as "input" for the next. We have dealt extensively with grammatical constituency, where at each level component structures are integrated to form a composite structure, successively producing phrases, clauses, and complex sentences. The sentence is not, however, the highest level of discourse organization. In this book, for example, sentences are grouped into paragraphs, paragraphs into subsections, subsections into sections, sections into chapters, and chapters into parts. These constitute the body of the text, which combines with supplementary materials (preface, index, etc.) to form the whole.

Structures at a given level have to be characterized in relation to constitutive elements of the proper sort. There is no point describing a chapter directly in terms of phrases, or a complex sentence in terms of words. It is not just that skipping levels yields an incomplete description—it actually makes the descriptive task far more difficult. A complex sentence is not just a string of words. Its words are organized into clauses, whose formation follows certain patterns. With clauses established as structural elements, characterized independently, we can proceed to examine patterns for combining them. But if no reference is made to clauses, it is hard to see how the description of complex sentences could ever get off the ground. It is not really feasible to describe them exclusively in terms of lower-level elements such as articles, adjectives, nouns, and verbs (or intermediate structures like nominals and prepositional phrases). A string of words is a well-formed complex sentence only when certain substrings happen to constitute clauses.

The higher the level of organization, the more likely it is for conventional units to be schematic. If we consider specific expressions learned as units (i.e. lexical items as defined in CG), we find that their number correlates inversely with their size: we learn thousands of words and phrases, many fewer clauses, still fewer complex sentences, hardly any lengthy passages, and probably not a single novel. The larger the expression, the less chance it has of being repeatedly useful and thus frequent enough to be entrenched and conventionalized. Also, schematic characterizations are more abstract at higher levels. Among the schemas describing nominals are templates for particular structural sequences involving specific categories (e.g. noun, demonstrative, adjective) and even specific forms. For the most part, schemas at higher syntactic levels abstract away from such details and simply refer to nominals as such. Generally, for instance, the internal composition of nominals is of little consequence in describing the formation of complex sentences. And in schemas characterizing higher-level discourse structures, there need be no specifications at all about grammatical form. Beyond the fact that it consists of a series of sentences, what can one say in general about the syntactic form of a paragraph?

Though beyond the scope of syntax (as usually conceived), higher-level structures like paragraphs, sections, and chapters are subject to description. They can even be considered symbolic, since their characterization involves both formal and semantic properties. In standard prose, for example, a paragraph prototypically has a certain approximate length. Semantically, it is expected to address a single point concerning a particular topic, being more or less complete and self-contained in this respect. It should, moreover, be coherent and well organized, by properly introducing the point addressed, developing it systematically, and finishing with a summary or conclusion. This is, to be sure, both vague and tenuous. It is not entirely vacuous, however, and conscientious writers invoke it as a guide.

Similar descriptions can be offered for more inclusive structures like sections and chapters. A section is a series of paragraphs addressing multiple aspects of a common topic. A chapter comprises a number of sections all pertaining to a more general topic. These are clearly matters of degree and interpretation. There is no essential difference between a section and a chapter—a section in a longer work might well be a chapter in a shorter one.[22] And naturally, the number and kinds of levels posited depend on the discourse genre. The relevant point is simply that high-level structures like these have the potential to emerge as conventional units with discernible properties, however tenuous or schematic they might be. Their schematicity is to be expected given their level of organization.

In view of memory limitations, higher-level structures like paragraphs and sections are more characteristic of writing than of spoken discourse. This is not to say that they are absent in speech. Close analogs are found in intermediate genres, such as orally delivered lectures written or planned beforehand. Even in casual conversation we have a certain capacity for planning and high-level organization. But spontaneous conversation does carry with it the pressure of constructing expressions on the spot for immediate communicative purposes. The demands of conversation are seen as being responsible for various aspects of language structure, including some peculiar to this basic genre. The recording and analysis of conversation give a rather different picture than descriptions based on artificially constructed examples or on writing. If anything, the structural features characteristic of conversation are more fundamental than those of other genres.[23]

To take just one example, conversation exhibits a dimension of organization that I refer to here as **attentional frames**.[24] These are short stretches of discourse initially identified phonologically, but which also have conceptual import. Phonologically, the frames are cohesive intonation groups set off from one another by various prosodic features, represented here by double slashes:

---

[22] This is one respect in which language exhibits a "fractal" organization, where the same structural feature repeats itself at successively higher levels. More on this below.

[23] Along with other theories, CG has been criticized for not being based on conversational data. Certainly the special features of this genre have tended to be neglected. However, CG is not inherently tied to any discourse genre. It applies perfectly well to conversation without essential modification.

[24] The notion is due to Chafe (1994: ch. 5), who calls them "intonation units". Chafe cites the examples in (6) and discusses the intonational properties on the basis of which such units are delimited. Langacker 2001d provides further detail about their treatment in CG.

(6) (a) *Have the animals // ever attacked anyone in a car?*

(b) *Cause I had a thick patch of barley there // about the size of the kitchen and living room // and I went over it // and then // when I got done // I had a little bit left // so I turned around // and I went and sprayed it twice // and it's just as yellow as can be.*

Semantically, these frames are plausibly characterized as successive windows of attention, each subsuming a manageable amount of conceptual content—the amount readily invoked at a given moment in the planning and production of the discourse. Attentional frames tend to coincide with clauses; witness the last five frames in (6)(b). But some are nonclausal (e.g. *and then* in (6)(b)), and a single clause is often split into multiple frames (e.g. (6)(a)). The converse is also possible. If the phrasing in (7)(a) is normal for conditionals, we can nonetheless squeeze both clauses into a single frame, in the manner of (7)(b).

(7) (a) *If she said it // then it's true.*

(b) *If she said it then it's true.*

Though commas often correspond to their boundaries, attentional frames are not systematically represented in writing. They are mostly a feature of spoken language, reflecting the processing constraints of real-time speech production. Thus attentional frames do not fit neatly in the traditional scheme—primarily based on writing—whereby words are combined into phrases, phrases into clauses, clauses into sentences, and sentences into longer texts. With respect to this scheme they constitute a distinct and often cross-cutting dimension of organization. Why, then, do the frames tend to correlate with clauses? Probably because a clause represents another, more codified response to the same processing constraints. The essential elements of a clause are a single event and its central participants, often expressed anaphorically. Typically, then, the content of a clause fits naturally in a single window of attention. We can take this as functional motivation for the universality of clauses as basic elements of grammatical structure. Of course, not every clause is typical, so their correlation with attentional frames is only partial. The latter, being more flexible in regard to content, are more consistently able to accommodate online processing needs.[25]

Clauses are basic structural elements for spoken language even if they do not always coincide with attentional frames. The same cannot be said for sentences. If a full clause is described schematically as an expression that profiles a grounded process, an analogous conceptual characterization of sentences does not seem possible. A well-known traditional definition—that a sentence expresses a "complete thought"—is vague and clearly insufficient.[26] There is some truth to the view that segmentation into sentences is merely a convention of writing; a sentence is then

---

[25] Whereas a clause resides primarily in objective and segmental content, an attentional frame is defined in terms of non-core channels: attention (an aspect of information structure) and intonation. There are no inherent restrictions on the core-channel content it subsumes.

[26] For example, this definition does not discriminate sentences from larger productions. And since a sentence can be of any length, it can express any number of complete thoughts.

definable (roughly) as a sequence bounded by spaces that begins with a capital letter and ends with a period. But segmentation is often arbitrary,[27] and many sequences written in this fashion are not traditionally considered sentences. Like this one, for example. Because the sentence level (however defined) has no privileged status in CG, we will not pursue this matter any further. The important thing is that symbolic assemblies allow the description of expressions, and the patterns they instantiate, irrespective of size and level of organization.

A significant aspect of language structure, not yet sufficiently explored, is a kind of "fractal" organization, whereby some feature recurs at successively higher levels. An obvious case is profiling. In a constituency hierarchy, the composite structure produced at each successive level has its own profile (which may or may not be inherited from a component structure). Similarly for focal prominence: when relationships are profiled at successive levels, each exhibits its own trajector/landmark alignment. These features recur up through the level of a nominal or a finite clause and extend to certain complex sentences (§12.1.2). Whether they have analogs at higher levels of discourse organization is less straightforward. It does not seem fanciful to view the overall topic of a paragraph (in the present case, fractal organization) as being analogous to a clausal trajector. As for profiling, a possible analog is the essential content of a passage[28] or the main story line of a text. Whether these are in fact manifestations of the same, more general, phenomena will have to be determined by broader considerations.

The size of expressions is not the only dimension in which levels of organization can be discerned. More abstractly, we have to posit a number of levels pertaining to semantic and discourse function. Suppose a speaker says *I like it*, intending this as a true statement describing her attitude. Analytically, we have to recognize no less than four functional levels: [Usage Event [Statement Scenario [Grounding [Objective Content]]]]. Each involves a conceptualizer with a distinct role in regard to the expression's overall import. The objective content, the level overtly expressed, comprises the profiled process and its participants. In the case at hand, *like* designates a mental relationship in which an experiencer (*I*) has a positive attitude toward a stimulus (*it*). The objective content is grounded to form a finite clause. In this case, zero grounding indicates that the profiled relationship is immediate to the ground and accepted by C as real. Recall that C, intrinsically, is only a virtual conceptualizer and is not invariably identified with the actual speaker (§12.3.2). Nor does the grounded process represent any particular speech act; intrinsically, it is merely a proposition, with the potential to be used in different ways. When used for a speech act, a proposition is embedded in the appropriate scenario (here the statement scenario), which— as an abstracted linguistic unit—invokes the interlocutors in generalized fashion. It is only in the context of an actual usage event that the virtual speaker and hearer are identified with specific individuals.

The default is for the conceptualizers at different levels to be identified. When *I like it* is uttered as a true statement, the actual speaker assumes the role of speaker

---

[27] Should the content of n. 26 be written as one sentence or as two?

[28] For illustration, see examples (16) and (17) in ch. 12.

in the statement scenario, the role of C in the grounding element, and the role of experiencer in the profiled relationship. The roles are nonetheless distinct, each corresponding to a different function, and they are often filled by different conceptualizers. If we change *I like it* to *He likes it*, the onstage experiencer is no longer identified with the speaker. In *Perhaps he likes it*, the adverb insulates the speaker from the role of C in the clausal grounding: unlike C, the speaker does not necessarily accept the profiled process as being real. C can likewise be distinct from the speaker in a speech-act scenario, as in questions (*Does he like it?*), or when an apparent statement is overridden as part of a complex scenario:

(8)   (a) *He likes it. Sure. Tell me another one.*

   (b) *He likes it. And a fish likes hooks.*

It is further possible for the actual speaker to remain distinct from the one invoked by the speech-act scenario. In (9), the speaker merely reports a statement made by another individual. The speaker herself need not subscribe to its content.

(9)   *He likes it, his mother says—but I really don't think so.*

Since these levels are all characteristic of a single-clause expression, they are not a matter of size. Nevertheless, they exhibit a fractal organization, where the conceptualizer at one level figures in the conception entertained at the next higher level. In *He likes it*, the onstage experiential relationship is apprehended by the C of the grounding element. The grounded process constitutes the proposition apprehended by the speaker in the statement scenario, which in turn is apprehended by the actual speaker in a usage event. These levels define an axis extending from the entities construed most objectively (the profiled process and its trajector) to the ultimate subject of conception.[29]

Along another axis, which tends to correlate with subjectivity, there is evidence for positing three levels of organization: the **effective** level, pertaining to occurrences; the **epistemic** level, pertaining to knowledge of occurrences; and an intersubjective **discursive** level, where the relevant occurrences are those of the discourse itself. These can be illustrated by different uses of *because* (Sweetser 1990: ch. 4):

(10)   (a) *The candle went out because the oxygen was exhausted.*   [Effective]

   (b) *He was mad at me because I flirted with his wife.*   [Effective]

   (c) *She must be home, because her lights are on.*   [Epistemic]

   (d) *Are you busy tonight, because I've got tickets to the game?*   [Discursive]

Each sentence has the form *Y because X*, and in each case X is the cause or reason for Y. They differ, however, in regard to which aspect of Y participates in the

---

[29] A comparable fractal organization, involving nested conceptualizations at successively higher levels, is possible in an expression's objective content: *Sharon claims that his mother believes that he likes it.*

causal relationship. In (10)(a)–(b), Y is engaged at the effective level, pertaining to the profiled occurrence itself (the candle going out, his being mad at me). The causal interaction is physical in (a), social and emotive in (b), but in both cases, what is caused is the onstage occurrence per se. By contrast, (10)(c) does not indicate that her lights being on causes her being home (if anything, the opposite is true). What it means, instead, is that the situation is the basis for the epistemic judgment expressed by the modal: because her lights are on, it *must* be the case that she is home. Y is thus engaged at the epistemic level. What X induces is not the objective occurrence described in Y, but rather an epistemic assessment of that occurrence. Finally, the causal relation in (10)(d) obtains at the discourse level: having tickets for the game is the reason for asking the question. What X induces is not the occurrence of being busy, or knowledge of that occurrence, but the speaker's decision to perform an act of questioning.

These levels show up in other linguistic phenomena. For instance, root and epistemic modals (§9.4.3) are distinguished by whether the modal force pertains to occurrences or knowledge of occurrences:

(11) (a) *You **must** be there—it's essential.*   [Effective]

  (b) *You **must** be very tired, having walked so far.* [Epistemic]

We have also observed (§12.3.1) that predicates taking finite clauses as complements (*suspect*, *know*, *regret*, *true*, *astonishing*, etc.) profile relationships at the epistemic level, while those taking nonfinite complements (*see*, *force*, *enjoy*, *start*, *try*, etc.) pertain to the effective level. Numerous adverbs are conventionally used at different levels. In (12)(a), *again* specifies repetition of the event described. On the other hand, the event repeated in (12)(b) is not the necessity of being careful, but rather the discourse event of the speaker saying that this is so.

(12) (a) *I've lost my keys **again**.*   [Effective]

  (b) ***Again**, you have to be more careful.* [Discursive]

Then is used at all three levels. In each case, it evokes a series of events and points to some location within it. The location in question is characterized as following an event already indicated and as hosting an event to be specified subsequently. At the effective level, these events are the ones explicitly described. In (13)(a), *then* directs attention to a time after his finishing the beer and indicates that the event of his ordering scotch can be found at this temporal location. By contrast, the relevant events in (13)(b) are not the profiled occurrences but stages in the process of reasoning: should it be established that his alibi is valid, we can *then* conclude that he is innocent. Analogously, the relevant events in (13)(c) are stages in the discourse.

(13) (a) *He finished his beer, **then** he asked for scotch.*   [Effective]

  (b) *If his alibi stands up, **then** he's clearly innocent.* [Epistemic]

  (c) *As I was saying, **then**, you need to get more rest.* [Discursive]

13.4 Structure Building

Discourse is not just a sequence of words, clauses, or sentences. It is also—and more essentially—a series of conceptions associated with these forms. Nor is it the case that these conceptions are separate and discrete. On the contrary, each develops from and builds on the previous one, so as discourse proceeds an integrated conceptual structure of progressively greater complexity is being constructed. The structure already assembled is part of the conceptual substrate for each successive expression. It is a major component of the current discourse space serving as context at each stage for the current usage event (fig. 13.2).

13.4.1 Basic(s and) Principles

As a discourse unfolds, at each stage we have some memory of what has gone before. Briefly, at least, we are able to recall the specific form of expressions and hence the construal they impose on the content evoked. For a longer period, sometimes extending through a considerable stretch of discourse, we remember the content expressed, i.e. the conceptual structure that has been progressively built up. Over a longer term, even when memory of a discourse has long been forgotten, some of that content may be retained in the guise of expanded knowledge, altered beliefs, and the like.[30]

Structure building no doubt proceeds simultaneously at multiple levels of organization involving different time scales. It ranges from conceptual integration at the lowest levels of grammatical composition to apprehension of the global import of entire texts. There is reason to think, however, that clauses (especially finite clauses) are basic discourse units, and that the conceptual structure progressively assembled in discourse tends to be updated on a clause-by-clause basis. More generally, attentional frames—which typically coincide with clauses—suggest themselves as primary units of discourse processing. Clauses and frames will thus be our main concern.

Canonically, then, a discourse is a series of clause-sized expressions, each constituting an attentional frame. As a minimal representation, each clause is thus as shown in figure 13.6(a): the process it profiles is the focus of attention within its objective content, which occupies the window of attention imposed by the frame. But in one way or another, most clauses carry expectations about the preceding or the following discourse, if not both. They then require a more complex representation,

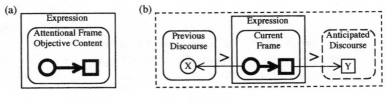

FIGURE 13.6

---

[30] At least roughly, these types of retention correspond to the psychological notions of short-term, working, and long-term memory (Barsalou 1992).

including a previous and/or an anticipated frame, as shown in figure 13.6(b). One basic kind of expectation is that a schematic element evoked in the current frame will be specified in finer detail either earlier or later in the discourse. In effect, then, this element functions as a discourse-level elaboration site. Conventionalized expectations of this sort are part of an expression's overall characterization (indicated by the dashed-line box).

The discourse in (14), which is made up but perhaps not too implausible, will serve as a concrete illustration of structure building:

(14)   *I just ran into Jill. // She's upset. // She really thinks // her daughter might move, // so she won't see her any more.*

Each expression in the sequence invokes the structure already assembled as the basis for its interpretation. The incorporation of its content produces an updated structure invoked by the next expression. The following diagrams (obviously simplified) show the connections thus established. Represented in the top row are the current frames of the successive expressions, and in the bottom row, the structures produced at each stage.

We start with the box at the lower left in figure 13.7. The box is empty on the assumption that there is no prior discourse, so nothing has yet been built.[31] The correspondence line connecting it to the first expression, *I just ran into Jill*, indicates that the latter initiates a discourse through which a structure will be built. The first structure produced is equivalent to this expression in terms of both content and construal: its content involves a recent event in which the speaker (S) encounters Jill (J), and it profiles that occurrence. Since nothing indicates otherwise, the event is situated in reality—the default mental space for a discourse.

The next expression, *she's upset*, is retrospective. In particular, the subject pronoun *she* carries the expectation that its referent is uniquely identifiable in the current discourse space, having already been singled out as a focus of attention (fig. 10.1). The structure in place does in fact include just one salient individual—Jill—who meets the pronoun's schematic specifications as being third-person, singular, and

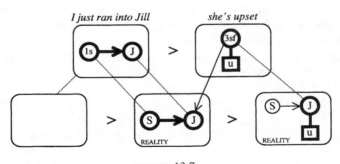

FIGURE 13.7

---

[31] This is not to say that structure building starts from nothing; on the contrary, it presupposes a vast conceptual substrate (§13.2). It is just that nothing has yet been introduced by the discourse itself.

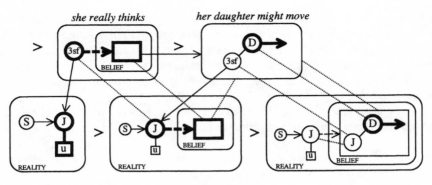

FIGURE 13.8

feminine (3sf). Jill is thus identified as the pronoun's referent. A solid arrow indicates this elaborative relationship, which provides the conceptual overlap allowing the expression's content to be incorporated into the structure being built. In the updated structure, Jill both participates in the encounter and exhibits the property of being upset (u). The latter is more prominent at this stage by virtue of having just been mentioned. As each successive expression imposes its own profile on the structure being assembled, previously focused elements gradually fade from awareness.

The continuation of this discourse is shown in figure 13.8. The next expression, *she really thinks*, is both retrospective and prospective. It is retrospective due to the pronoun *she*, which once again refers to Jill. It is prospective due to the verb. *Think* profiles a relationship in which the trajector inclines to accept a proposition as valid. It thus evokes a mental space (labeled BELIEF) representing the conceptions the trajector provisionally accepts, one of which is the proposition in question (the verb's landmark). Moreover, it induces the expectation that this schematic proposition will be specified in the following discourse. The next expression, *her daughter might move*, is then interpreted as fulfilling this expectation. In the structure updated by this clause, the profiled event—that of the daughter moving—is therefore incorporated in Jill's belief space. And since there is no other candidate in the previous discourse, the possessor invoked by *her* is also identified as Jill. Observe that Jill is represented twice, once in each mental space, as she has a role in both.

Introducing mental spaces, establishing their content, and determining their configuration are essential aspects of structure building (Fauconnier 1985; Fauconnier and Sweetser 1996). In the current discourse, for example, it is crucial to realize that the speaker, in producing the clause *her daughter might move*, is neither subscribing to that proposition nor inclining to its validity. It is not presented as being real for the speaker but merely as something Jill thinks, in the space representing her tentative beliefs. Only indirectly does it figure in the speaker's conception of reality: it is part of this conception that Jill inclines to certain propositions, one of them being that her daughter could be moving.

The importance of mental space configurations is further evident from the final expression, *so she won't see her any more. So* is retrospective, indicating that the proposition it introduces follows (⊃) from something already expressed. In the present discourse, this is identified with the event of the daughter moving and not, say, with Jill's thinking this might happen. The profiled relationship (*she won't see her any more*) is thus incorporated in Jill's belief space, as a consequence of the anticipated move. It is not introduced as something the speaker subscribes to.[32] The expression is also retrospective due to the subject and object pronouns. Figure 13.9 shows the most likely interpretation, in which the former refers to Jill and the latter to the daughter. The opposite alignment is not absolutely precluded, however.

Clearly, the structures produced in discourse are quite diverse and extremely complex. There are, however, certain conventional patterns of discourse construction, as well as some basic principles. Though little explored, the patterns would seem to form a continuum with the constructional schemas employed in grammatical composition. In figure 13.8, for instance, the clause *her daughter might move* elaborates the schematic proposition invoked by *think*. The updating effected by this expression is thus an instantiation of the constructional schema for combining a matrix clause with its complement. The structure building in figure 13.7 instantiates a familiar way of starting a discourse. The pattern is flexible in regard to grammatical form, pertaining more to the channel of information structure. It specifies that the first clause (*I just ran into Jill*) is of no real significance—it is simply a vehicle for introducing an important discourse participant (Jill).[33] This participant is then the topic for a stretch of discourse that immediately follows (*She's upset. She really thinks...*).

Effective discourse tends to follow some basic principles. The first is to build on what has already been established (Gernsbacher and Hargreaves 1992). This was amply illustrated in figures 13.7 to 13.9, where points of attachment were readily found for the retrospective elements in each successive expression. A second principle, especially important in conversation, is to present new material at a manageable

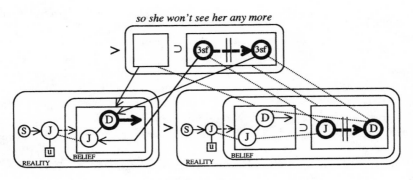

FIGURE 13.9

<hr />

[32] Indeed, the speaker may know that the daughter is not in fact moving and will continue seeing her mother.

[33] Here are some other options: *I saw Jill last night*; *Jill stopped by*; *Remember Jill?*

rate. Here we find the motivation for dividing a discourse into a series of attentional frames, as well as the tendency for a single clause or frame to introduce just one new participant or significant new idea. This too is evident in (14). For instance, the two new participants (Jill and the daughter) are introduced in separate attentional frames, and the longest expression (*so she won't see her any more*) conveys just one new substantive idea.

Other principles pertain to the sequence of presentation. For one thing, a discourse flows more smoothly when the structure produced at each stage is self-contained, not requiring later expressions for a coherent interpretation to emerge. It is for this reason that pronouns normally follow the antecedent nominals introducing their referents.[34] The following is thus less natural than (14) as a way to start a discourse:

(15)   *??I just ran into her. // She's upset. // Jill really thinks…*

If nothing indicates who the pronominal referent is, the listener has to build a structure that represents her with a mental question mark attached. A pronoun implies that its referent is immediately identifiable, but it is not until the third expression that this expectation is fulfilled. Another ordering principle is to avoid the need for **backtracking**—either undoing or redoing what has already been accomplished. With respect to (14), structure building might have to be undone if the speaker intended the last expression to mean not that Jill would no longer see the daughter but rather the opposite. A **repair** is then in order:

(16)   *…so she won't see her any more. // What I mean is, // the daughter won't see Jill any more.*

An additional sequencing principle is that the order of presentation should conform to a **natural path** of mental access, i.e. a conceptual ordering established on nonlinguistic grounds. An obvious case is temporal sequencing: processing is easier if events are recounted in the order of their occurrence. This usually correlates with another conceptual ordering, where one event causes or somehow leads to another. In (14), the last two expressions conform to both these natural paths—the daughter's moving precedes Jill's not seeing her as well as being responsible for it. The first two expressions also conform to both paths, in the sense that the speaker's encountering Jill both precedes and makes possible the observation of her mental state. Here, though, one of the sequenced events remains covert. The second expression (*She's upset*) simply describes Jill's state, without explicitly mentioning the speaker's observation of it. We nevertheless infer this event, based on the standard scenario of meeting someone and finding out how they are doing. Despite its inferential basis, the event sequence is salient enough to determine the order of presentation. With the opposite order, the discourse flows less smoothly. The beginning in (17) is awkward, even though Jill was presumably upset prior to the encounter.

---

[34] There are exceptions, of course, as we are dealing here with tendencies rather than ironclad rules. The kinds of optimality embodied by the various principles are not always consistent with one another and are often overridden by other factors.

(17)   *??Jill's upset. // I just ran into her. // She really thinks // her daughter might move...*

Two further principles are that a discourse should be **coherent** and **cohesive**. Coherence is basically a matter of everything hanging together and making sense. There may be specific indications of how things fit together, e.g. *so* in (14), which tells us that the occurrence it introduces (*she won't see her any more*) follows from what has just been said (*her daughter might move*). Often, though, coherence depends on factors that are left implicit. There is no explicit indication in (14) that Jill's being upset is due to the fear that her daughter might move. We nonetheless infer this connection—otherwise, juxtaposing *She's upset* and *She really thinks her daughter might move* would be pointless. One reason for the awkwardness of (17) is precisely the fact that an intervening clause (*I just ran into her*) makes it harder to establish this relation between Jill's mental state and its cause. The order of the first two clauses is a source of incoherence in other ways as well. Starting with *Jill's upset* suggests that her mental state is responsible for the occurrence mentioned subsequently, which turns out to be *I just ran into her*, but this makes little sense. Also, the clausal sequence obscures the actual connection between the two occurrences: namely, that encountering Jill made it possible for the speaker to discern her mental state. Thus (17) is notably less coherent than (14).

Cohesiveness is a matter of tying things together, typically through overlapping form or content. An example of cohesiveness in the present text is the parallelism between the second sentence of the preceding paragraph (*Coherence is basically a matter of everything hanging together...*) and the first sentence in this one (*Cohesiveness is a matter of tying things together...*). One factor in the cohesiveness of (14) is that every clause makes some reference to Jill. More abstractly, the discourse is cohesive in that Jill is consistently mentioned first and her daughter subsequently. Thus *Jill* occurs in the first expression, *her daughter* only in the fourth. Within the latter nominal, *her* precedes *daughter*. And in the final expression (*so she won't see her any more*), the preferred interpretation is for *she* to be identified as Jill, and *her* as the daughter. A certain amount of cohesiveness greatly facilitates processing. But there are of course limits. The discourse in (18) has more cohesion than is needed or easily tolerated.

(18)   **I just ran into Jill. // Jill's upset. // Jill really thinks // Jill's daughter might move, // so Jill won't see Jill's daughter any more.*

13.4.2 Grammar and Discourse Function

Grammatical peculiarities can often be plausibly explained in terms of discourse. Observe, for instance, that clauses introduced by *because* and *since* have the option of preceding the clause they combine with, while clauses headed by *so, thus, therefore*, and *hence* can only follow:

(19)   (a) *He refused the bribe, {because/since} he was honest.*

       (b) *{Because/Since} he was honest, he refused the bribe.*

(c) *He was honest, {so/thus/therefore/hence} he refused the bribe.*

(d) **{So/Thus/Therefore/Hence} he refused the bribe, he was honest.*

Why should this be so? We find a basis for the contrast in the discourse principle that the order of presentation should conform to a natural path of mental access. The relevant natural path is that of one occurrence causing or somehow leading to another: $X \supset Y$. In the case of *because* and *since*, the basic order in (19)(a) runs counter to this natural path, as the caused event is specified first (*Y, because X*). The alternate order in (19)(b) allows the order of presentation to reflect the causal sequence (*because X, Y*). On the other hand, with *so*, *thus*, *therefore*, and *hence* the order in (19)(c) already conforms to path of causation (*X, so Y*). The alternate order would therefore serve no purpose.

But it is not just grammatical idiosyncrasies that have discourse motivation. There is no exaggeration in saying that all of grammar is shaped by discourse and only exists to make it possible. It is atypical for the structures examined in grammar—such as phrases, clauses, and even sentences—to be used in isolation. Normally they occur as integral parts of longer discourse sequences that provide the reason for their being assembled and assuming the form they do. Fundamental grammatical notions can be characterized in terms of their discourse function. For example, the function of a full, grounded nominal is to single out a discourse referent (§9.3). Clauses serve the function of saying something useful about the referents thus established. So usually a discourse consists primarily in a series of clauses, seldom in a series of nominals. Clauses are basic units of structure building, especially when they coincide with attentional frames.

Clausal subjects have an important discourse role. A subject has aptly been described as a **starting point**, an accessible point of departure from which a clause moves on to make its own new contribution (Chafe 1994: ch. 7).[35] As such, its referent tends to be given—that is, already available in the current discourse space (CDS). In this way a clause conforms to the basic discourse principle of building on what has previously been established. Recall the beginning of (14). In the first clause (*I just ran into Jill*), the subject refers to the speaker, who is always part of the CDS (figure 13.2). From this starting point, the clause proceeds to introduce a new participant, Jill, who is then part of the CDS for subsequent expressions. The next two clauses (*She's upset* and *She really thinks...*) build on this foundation by taking Jill (the referent of the subject pronoun *she*) as their point of departure. Subjects also interact with the discourse principle that the order of presentation should conform to a natural path of mental access. As the starting point for structure building, subjects should tend to occur toward the beginning of a clause rather than at the end. This turns out to be a complex matter, with many factors at work. Still, in most languages the subject of a clause precedes an object in the most basic (or semantically neutral) word order.

The discourse function they serve is central to the characterization of many grammatical constructions. Some constructions have the function of allowing structure

---

[35] We will see in ch. 14 that this functional description of subject is quite consistent with its conceptual characterization in CG as primary focal participant (trajector).

building to follow the natural progression from given to new. This is one motivation for using a passive.[36] In (20), for example, the discourse flows more smoothly when the second clause is passivized. The active in (20)(a) is awkward because its subject (*a rattlesnake*) is new to the discourse. With the passive in (20)(b), the referent of the clausal subject (*he*) is already established in the CDS.

(20)   (a) *We got some bad news about Clarence. ?A rattlesnake bit him.*

     (b) *We got some bad news about Clarence. He was bitten by a rattlesnake.*

Another construction subserving this function is the preposing of a locative, as in (21):

(21)   (a) *I looked in the kitchen. ?Several dead rats were on the counter.*

     (b) *I looked in the kitchen. On the counter were several dead rats.*

Once again, version (a) is awkward because the subject of the second clause (*several dead rats*) is new to the discourse (and presumably unanticipated). Here, though, the situation cannot be remedied with a passive, for the clause is intransitive. It is mitigated in version (b), however, by the alternate order of presentation. While *several dead rats* is still the grammatical subject, its role as starting point is overridden by the locative preposing construction, which superimposes on the clause a path of mental access that starts with the specified location. In the discourse context, the counter is already accessible in the CDS—it has not been explicitly mentioned, but the kitchen has been, and in a kitchen one expects to find a counter. Thus, in accordance with the special word order, structure building follows the natural progression from given to new. With attention focused on the kitchen, the counter becomes an accessible location. Invoking this location induces the expectation that something new will be introduced there. The mental progression from kitchen to counter to rats represents the conflation of three natural paths: the order of presentation, the path from given to new, and a natural path of search (from setting to location to target).

Of course, discourse does not always flow this smoothly. Discourse is not—indeed, it cannot be—just a matter of following natural paths in efficiently building a single, consistent conceptual structure. This is due in part to the processing demands of real-time speech production. But it also reflects the inherent complexity of discourse and the myriad, often conflicting considerations that come into play. Even in a well-planned discourse, structure building does not consist exclusively in adding to what is already in place; besides addition, we engage in repetition, cancellation, qualification, even contradiction. For instance, we have many ways of indicating that what follows runs counter to an expectation just created: *but, however, even so,*

---

[36] There are others, notably the possibility of omitting any reference to an agent. This is useful when the agent is unknown (*Several paintings were stolen*), hard to specify (*Thirty billion burgers are consumed in this country every year*), or painful to reveal (*I'm afraid your favorite cup was dropped and got broken*).

yet, still, on the contrary, nevertheless, by contrast, on the other hand, etc. Instead of being orderly, disposing of one topic before moving on to the next, we commonly talk about several things at once, intermingling expressions that contribute to the building of different structures. At the extreme, expressions are sometimes interrupted by wholly extraneous material:

(22)   *Then she told me that I would have to use—Are you warm enough? If you're not, I can turn up the heat—that I would have to use another credit card.*

Even when we are being orderly, there is discontinuity in the flow of discourse whenever we close off one topic and begin another. We then start building a new conceptual structure, or at least a new branch of the old one. The transition in (23) illustrates a familiar pattern for explicitly changing topics. It informs the listener that the structure centered on Jill is now complete, and that a new one anchored by Jack is being initiated.

(23)   *...But she could never satisfy her mother. Well, so much for Jill. Now what about Jack? The last time I saw him...*

An important factor in smoothly flowing discourse is the introduction and "tracking" of participants. When a discourse referent is first introduced, it has to be specified by a nominal with sufficient descriptive content to single it out. A definite nominal can serve this function provided that its meaning implies that there is only one relevant candidate. A variety of definites have this property, including proper names (e.g. *Jack* in (23)), possessed nouns (*Jack's house*), superlatives (*the tallest building in Asia*), and nominals with uniquely identifying modifiers (*those dead rats on the kitchen counter*). Canonically, however, nominals introducing new participants are indefinite. Once a referent is established in the CDS, nominals referring to it are usually definite and less descriptive, as identification has already been achieved. The least descriptive, being highly schematic in regard to type, are personal pronouns. The progression in (24) is thus a natural way of introducing rats in the discourse and repeatedly referring back to them. Note that the last expression (*Without tails?*) succeeds in evoking the rats without explicitly mentioning them.

(24)   *There were **several dead rats** on the counter. For some reason **those rats** really bothered me. I couldn't stop looking at **them**. What were **they** doing there? Without tails?*

Certain syntactic positions are better suited than others for introducing new discourse participants (Du Bois 1987; cf. Herring 1989). In view of the natural flow from given to new, they are commonly introduced as objects, only awkwardly as subjects:

(25)   (a) *We saw **a lion**. It was chasing **a gazelle**.*

      (b) *We saw **a gazelle**. ?**A lion** was chasing it.*

      (c) *We saw **a gazelle**. It was being chased by **a lion**.*

As its starting point, the subject of a clause is more naturally used for a participant already established in the CDS. The passive in (25)(c) conforms to this alignment and allows the new participant to be introduced as the object of a preposition. Another grammatical role not well suited for introducing a participant is that of nominal possessor, the reason being that—like the subject within a clause—a possessor is the starting point within a nominal (ch. 14). Thus (26)(a) is quite infelicitous as a way of establishing the lion as a discourse referent. In (26)(b), the problem is avoided by introducing the lion in the prior clause.

(26) (a) *A *lion's* mane was magnificent. It was resting contentedly in the sun.

  (b) We saw *a lion*. Its mane was magnificent. It was resting contentedly in the sun.

There is no blanket prohibition on introducing a new participant as clausal subject. In fact, it is quite common for intransitive subjects to serve this function—but not just any intransitive subject. This tactic works best with verbs like *appear* and *enter*, whose meaning is precisely that of bringing the trajector into the scene. It also works with an action that calls attention to the subject, like the roaring in (27)(c). Events of this sort are objective counterparts, within the situation described, of what happens subjectively when a new participant enters the interlocutors' scope of awareness. Other intransitive clauses lend themselves less readily to the introduction of discourse referents. The static situation of merely being somewhere, as in (27)(d), is not anything that actively calls attention to the subject, but it does at least create the potential for its being noticed. A stable property like being old is even further removed from any notion of bringing the subject into the scene.[37]

(27) (a) Suddenly *a lion* appeared.

  (b) *A lion* entered the clearing.

  (c) *A lion* was roaring in the distance.

  (d) ?*A lion* was in the clearing.

  (e) *A *lion* was old.

Introducing new participants is a basic function of certain constructions. One of these is locative preposing, exemplified in (21)(b) and (28)(a). The latter, while it has the same elements as (27)(d), flows more smoothly because the preposed locative provides an alternate starting point already established in the discourse. Initially invoking this location creates the expectation of finding something there.

---

[37] Why, then, is (26)(b) felicitous, even though the second clause (*its mane was magnificent*) introduces a new participant (the mane) as an adjectival subject? Primarily because the mane is not entirely new to the discourse. Mentioning a lion suggests the existence of a mane (just as mentioning a kitchen suggests the existence of a counter). Thus the mane is easily accessed, especially with the link provided by the possessor pronoun *its*.

(28)   (a) *In the clearing was **a lion**.*

       (b) *There was **a lion** in the clearing.*

Also serving this function is the "existential" construction with *there*, as in (28)(b). Grammatically, *there* is the clausal subject.[38] Conceptually, it resembles *it* (§11.3.2) in that it designates an abstract setting. We can roughly describe this setting as a "locus of existence". As such, it is a natural starting point for purposes of mentally accessing a new participant whose existence is thus announced.

13.4.3 Covert Grounding

In English, the status of a discourse referent as given or new is generally indicated by whether the nominal referring to it is definite or indefinite. Some nominals, like proper names and personal pronouns, are inherently definite. In the case of common nouns, definiteness is signaled by grounding, e.g. *the bear* vs. *a bear*. In many languages, however, it is usual for nouns to occur without explicit grounding. One such language is Luiseño. An example is (29), where *hunwut* 'bear' occurs without overt grounding and is interpretable as either definite or indefinite:

(29)   *Hunwut xaari-q.*   '{The/A} bear is growling.'

       bear   growl-TNS

Evidently, languages can manage quite well without consistently marking this distinction.[39] If you think about it, the status of the bear is ambivalent only when (29) is viewed in isolation. In the context of an ongoing discourse, the matter is usually clear: either a bear has already been established as a participant, in which case *hunwut* refers to it, or it has to be introduced. So if anything is problematic, it is the redundancy of an English-type system, where explicit indication has to be given of something apparent on other grounds.

Since definiteness is usually marked by grounding elements, unmarked nouns like *hunwut* in (29) pose the question of whether or not they are grounded. Is *hunwut* a full nominal, which (by definition) profiles a grounded instance of its type? Or is it simply a noun, which specifies a type without singling out an instance? In and of itself, of course, *hunwut* is just a noun. But what about cases where it functions syntactically as a clausal subject or object, roles that are normally reserved for full, grounded nominals? Semantically, it then qualifies as a nominal. A clause like (29) does not invoke 'bear' as just a type: it ascribes the act of growling to a particular instance of that type. If it is grounded, however, the grounding is covert, with no

---

[38] Observe, for instance, that *there* follows the first auxiliary in questions: *Was there a lion in the clearing?* The plural verb in sentences like *There were lions in the clearing* is just one indication that a verb's inflection for person and number is an independent semantic specification, rather than being mechanically induced by "agreement" with the subject (Reid 1991).

[39] When necessary, such languages generally indicate definiteness with a demonstrative and indefiniteness with the numeral 'one'.

direct reflection in grammatical form. This apparent discrepancy results from considering a clause in isolation rather than as an integral part of an ongoing discourse. By removing the artificial boundary between grammar and discourse, we can describe covert grounding straightforwardly.

As a basis for comparison, let us first reconsider the English definite article (§9.3.4), sketched in figure 13.10(a). Like other grounding elements, it profiles a thing construed as an instance of some type (t). The distinctive property of *the* is how the profiled instance relates to the prior discourse frame. Very roughly, it indicates that this instance is already evident in the discourse context and is the only instance of t with this status. When *the* combines with a lexical noun, such as *bear*, the composite expression imposes these requirements on an instance of the type it specifies. The resulting nominal, shown in figure 13.10(b), is therefore retrospective: it carries the expectation of there being just one salient instance of *bear* in the CDS. Figure 13.10(c) represents the application of this nominal to the ongoing discourse.[40] Observe that the prior discourse frame of the nominal corresponds to the conceptual structure previously built, and its current frame corresponds to the updated structure it produces. In a felicitous application, the previous structure does contain just one salient instance of *bear*, which is identified with the instance profiled by the nominal. The effect of applying the nominal is thus to direct attention, within the updated structure, to the instance it profiles.

Let us now return to (29). Although its subject consists of just a noun, it is part of a clause which in turn is part of a discourse. While the noun is not grounded by a separate overt element, the overall assembly fulfills the grounding function. Imagine a discourse context where a sole instance of *hunwut* 'bear' has already been established in the structure being built. The effect of using (29) is then to update this structure by means of a clause that evokes the notion 'bear' as a focused element. Figure 13.11(a) depicts the noun's contribution to this updating. Since the structure contains just one instance of 'bear', the noun is naturally interpreted as referring to it. The noun's type specification is thus instantiated through the very act of applying it to the discourse. Suppose, on the other hand, that there is no salient instance of 'bear' in the CDS. In this case, the noun is naturally interpreted as an instruction

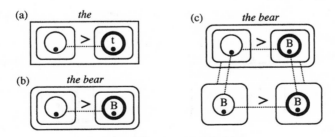

FIGURE 13.10

---

[40] For simplicity, the diagram shows the nominal applying independently. Normally it would do so as part of a clause containing it (e.g. *The bear is growling*).

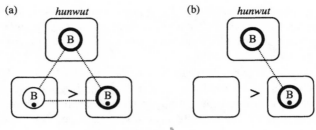

FIGURE 13.11

to introduce one there, as shown in figure 13.11(b). Either way the outcome is the same: the updated structure contains an instance of 'bear', identified as the trajector of *xaari* 'growl'.

Importantly, these interpretations are not just natural but also conventional. They represent established patterns in the language, usable with any common noun—it is only by virtue of these conventional units that speakers produce expressions like (29) in the first place, confident that their interlocutors will accept them and know what to do with them. Shown in figure 13.12, the patterns in question are simply schematized versions of the configurations in figure 13.11. They are not constructional schemas in the narrow sense (i.e. templates for combining smaller expressions into larger ones). Instead, they are standardized ways of applying expressions to the discourse, using them to update the structure being built. They nonetheless resemble constructional schemas in being schematic symbolic assemblies linked by correspondences. They are, if you like, constructions lying at the interface of grammar and discourse, in accordance with the CG view that these form a continuum. The interpretations they sanction are part of an expression's conventionally determined meaning (which always relies on a conceptual substrate that includes the current discourse). In effect, they fulfill the function of nominal grounding despite their covert nature.

Analogous descriptions can be suggested for covert clausal grounding, as well as cases where relational participants identifiable from the discourse context remain implicit. Such phenomena illustrate several basic points. First, languages differ in how they fulfill semantic functions (like grounding). They further differ as to where they draw the line between overt expression and reliance on the conceptual substrate.

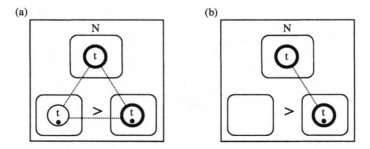

FIGURE 13.12

Second, conventional units relevant to grammar are not limited to those employed in constructing complex expressions. In particular, some consist in conventional patterns for applying expressions to the ongoing discourse, without contributing additional phonological content. Finally, there is no definite boundary between grammar and discourse. This is not to deny that much can be learned by examining them independently. But ultimately, any attempt to maintain a strict separation is both pointless and misguided.

14

Engaging the World

Some have questioned whether a "cognitive" approach to language can accommodate either its social function (as a means of interaction) or its referential function (as a means of describing the world). These concerns are unfounded. They stem from the erroneous idea that what goes on inside the skull is isolated from everything outside it, including other minds. But this is simply not so. In the sense that cognition resides in activity of the brain, it does indeed take place inside the skull. The brain, however, is the nexus of a nervous system that runs all through the body, connecting with the sensory and motor organs through which we perceive and act on the world. Neither is the brain's activity isolated from other minds. An essential aspect of cognition is our awareness of other people and our recognition that they, too, are cognitive agents. We are quite adept at reading their intentions, as well as imagining the nature of their mental experience. Thus cognition, far from being insulated from the world and the other people in it, is our primary means of engaging them.

In this final chapter, I deal with two related properties of cognition, both essential to understanding grammar. The first is temporal sequencing. As neurological activity, cognition necessarily takes place through time. Precisely how it does so—the time course of conception—is often critical. A second key property is that cognition consists of far more than sensory and motor interactions. What happens in the social, cultural, and imaginative spheres is as real and important to us as physical occurrences. Moreover, we are not just concerned with immediate reality. We further engage the world through memory, anticipation, prediction, generalization, and contemplation of alternatives. Involving many kinds and levels of mental construction, these phenomena transcend immediate bodily experience. However, they also prove to be grounded in it.

14.1 Dynamicity

Because it occurs through time, conceptualization—even the activation of established concepts—is inherently dynamic. In cases of any complexity, different facets of the total conception are activated at each successive instant. This may or may not result in their all being active simultaneously, but either way the sequence of activation is part of the overall mental experience. It is consequential even when the time scale is small enough that it stays below the threshold of conscious awareness.[1]

14.1.1 Paths of Mental Access

Some conceptions lead to others. If you think of the letter A, you are likely to think of B. This facilitates the activation of C, which in turn leads to D, and so on. One conception can lead to another due to an established connection between them, as with the alphabet, or just by virtue of creating the conditions for its emergence. For example, imagining a hypothetical circumstance makes it possible to imagine what would happen in it: if you won the lottery, you could quit your job. Connections of this sort tend to be asymmetrical, conception moving more readily in one direction than the other. Learning the alphabet, so that you can quickly run through the progression from A to Z, does not automatically give you the ability to smoothly recite it backward. It does, though, provide the means to figure out the opposite sequence. For example, to determine what "follows" T in the reverse ordering, I can recite a string containing it ($\ldots Q > R > S > T \ldots$) and thereby observe that the adjacent letter is S.

A series of conceptions where each leads readily to the next is called a **natural path**. Quite a number of natural paths have a significant role in language structure. An obvious one is the order of presentation, where words are produced or encountered in a certain sequence. Another is a chain of elaborative relationships—that is, a series of elements, each of which contains a schematic elaboration site specified by the next. One such case is a chain of complement clauses, as in (1), where the clausal landmarks function as e-sites (fig. 12.4).

(1)   *[Alice said] [that Bill believes] [that Cindy claims] [that Doris swallowed a spider].*

The paths just mentioned involve the linguistic expression itself. Others inhere in the conception expressed. At the conceptual level, two very basic natural paths—closely correlated in our experience—are the order of event occurrence (where X precedes Y) and the sequence of causation (where X induces Y). Also very basic are paths consisting in a series of whole-part relations, such as body > arm > hand > finger > knuckle. At each step in such a chain, the conception of the whole provides the context (immediate scope) for conceiving of the part (fig. 3.3). Additionally, any kind of scale (like cost, weight, or temperature) is a natural path defined by its successive values.

The origin of a natural path is a **starting point**. It should not be surprising that the starting point is often either the conceptualizer or something to which C has immediate access. The default conceptualizer (C_0) is the current speaker, who anchors a

---

[1] For various reasons, however, conceptualization is not strictly linear. Processing occurs simultaneously in various dimensions and at multiple levels of organization. There is not invariably any natural sequence of access for the elements of a complex conception, nor is one fully adhered to in actual practice.
And given the pressures of online processing, any actual rendition is likely to be discontinuous and complicated by factors like backtracking and reconceptualization.

number of linguistically relevant paths. One such path is a chain of conceptualizers $(C_0 > C_1 > C_2 > C_3 \ldots)$, each of whom apprehends the next and to some extent simulates their mental experience. We have such a chain in (1): S > Alice > Bill > Cindy > Doris. A path of this sort is also a path of access to successively embedded mental spaces. The starting space is the speaker's conception of reality. Successively embedded within it are the spaces representing the content of Alice's statement, Bill's belief, and Cindy's claim (fig. 12.4). Other paths correspond to "distance" from the speaker in various dimensions: speaker > hearer > other; human > animate > inanimate; concrete > abstract; actual > virtual; given > new. They reflect the speaker's special status as initial conceptualizer and as an actual person always accessible in the discourse.

There is a tendency for starting points to coincide and natural paths to correlate with one another. In (1), at least four natural paths coalign: order of presentation; sequence of elaboration; chain of conceptualizers; and successive embedding of mental spaces. Moreover, all of them start with Alice (metonymically speaking): she is mentioned first, her clause provides the first elaboration site, she is the first onstage conceptualizer, and hers is the first mental space introduced.[2] Being overt and ever-present, word order tends to correlate with numerous paths of mental access. The coalignment of paths facilitates processing. Thus (2)(a), where the order of locatives corresponds to a natural path of search, is easier to process than (2)(b), where the order is random. And in (3) to (5), the (a) examples flow more smoothly than the (b) examples because the order of presentation follows a natural sequence.

(2) (a) *The article is in today's paper, in the sports section, on the last page, near the bottom.*

(b) *??The article is in the sports section, near the bottom, in today's paper, on the last page.*

(3) (a) *The distance from San Diego to Los Angeles is about 120 miles.*

(b) *?The distance to Los Angeles from San Diego is about 120 miles.*

(4) (a) *The rainy season begins in January and ends in March.*

(b) *??The rainy season ends in March and begins in January.*

(5) (a) *In the evening stores are open between 7 and 10.*

(b) *?*In the evening stores are open between 10 and 7.*

We can plausibly assume that any conception of ordering or directionality requires seriality at some level of cognitive processing. Additional processing effort is thus implied when a conception incorporates natural paths requiring that the same elements be accessed in opposite sequences. Consider (3)(b), where *from* and *to* impose a directional construal. We apprehend its directionality by tracing a mental path from San Diego to Los Angeles—at some level of processing, we mentally

---

[2] As default starting points, the speaker and the speaker's conception of reality have an ambivalent status with respect to natural paths. They are indeed starting points, but since defaults are taken for granted, they can be ignored for certain purposes.

access the cities in that order. But the order of presentation leads us to invoke them in the opposite sequence: *to Los Angeles from San Diego*. To grasp the import of this expression, we must therefore reconceptualize the path (§3.4.2), construing it in the manner specified by the prepositions.

The conception of a scale has an inherent directionality, normally depicted by an arrow. A scalar adjective, such as *long, heavy, angry*, or *intelligent*, indicates the extent to which the trajector manifests a defining property. The origin of a scale—its starting point—corresponds to the lack of anything noteworthy: to either a default value or the property's total absence.[3] Successive values on the scale, representing degrees of departure from this baseline, thus constitute a natural path of mental access. Although we have the ability to move along a scale in either direction, there is some inclination for this scanning to observe its inherent directionality. Suppose we want to describe the relative intelligence of two individuals. If they are equal in discourse salience (neither being the current topic), we would tend to say *X is more intelligent than Y*, rather than the logically equivalent *Y is less intelligent than X*. The reason is that *more* induces scanning that conforms to the scale's directionality, while the scanning induced by *less* runs counter to it.

The preference for coalignment emerges quite clearly when comparison is conceived metaphorically in terms of motion. We can say that *X surpasses Y in intelligence*, or *X is beyond Y in intelligence*, where X moves along the scale in a positive direction. But we do not find expressions implying motion in the opposite direction (e.g. **Y subpasses X in intelligence*).[4] There is an alternative where Y is the mover—namely, *Y falls short of X in intelligence*. Here, though, Y moves in the positive direction, being construed metaphorically as a projectile that fails to reach its target. In another alternative, X and Y are both conceived as moving, so either can function as subject: *X is ahead of Y in intelligence*; *Y is behind X in intelligence*. In this case, the motion of both X and Y conforms to the scale's inherent directionality.

The processing efficiency achieved by coaligning natural paths is reflected linguistically in different ways. A minimal result is for one expression to be slightly favored over another (e.g. *X is more intelligent than Y > Y is less intelligent than X*). In more egregious cases, nonalignment results in diminished acceptability, exemplified by the (b) examples in (3) to (5). Processing efficiency also tends to correlate with coding efficiency: that is, simpler forms. It is no accident, for example, that *more* alternates with the suffix *-er* (*longer, brighter, easier*, etc.), while *less* has no reduced alternative. Likewise, an active (*X broke Y*) is formally simpler than a passive (*Y was broken by X*), where the order of presentation (Y > X) runs counter to the action chain (X $\Rightarrow$ Y). With the coalignment of natural paths, coding efficiency can also be achieved through greater reliance on iconicity. For instance, (6)(a) strongly

---

[3] In expressions like *This cord is only a foot long*, the starting point for assessing length is zero. By contrast, *This cord is long* bases the assessment on the usual length of cords. For properties based on a norm, there is often a complementary property representing departure from it in the opposite direction—for example, *This cord is short* (meaning that its length is less than the norm, not that it is less than zero). See also Croft and Cruse 2004: ch. 7.

[4] Of course, we can achieve the same effect by using the complementary scale, with the opposite inherent directionality: *Y surpasses X in {stupidity/lack of intelligence}*.

encourages the inference that events occurred in the order stated. If the opposite order is intended, it has to be made explicit, so (6)(b) is more complex.

(6)   (a) *She criticized him. He went to his room and kicked his dog.*

      (b) *She criticized him. He had gone to his room after kicking his dog.*

Paths of mental access are many, varied, and linguistically important. When the elements of a path are discrete and have a certain amount of salience, it can be described as a chain of **reference point relationships**. Depicted in figure 14.1(a), a reference point relation consists in the mental progression from a **reference point** (R) to a **target** (T) accessed through it. The set of entities accessible via R (each a potential target) constitute its **dominion** (D). Figure 14.1(b) shows a chain of such relations, where each successive target (T_i) functions in turn as the next reference point (R_{i+1}).

Being a matter of sequential mental access, reference point relationships are intrinsically dynamic but have no intrinsic content. They represent a general aspect of conceptual organization that proves essential to the semantic characterization of some basic linguistic phenomena. One of these is metonymy, in which an expression's usual referent provides mental access to the entity it is actually construed as designating. In (7), for example, *Vietnam* does not refer to the country per se, but rather to a war that was fought there. Coherence demands that the subject designate an event, and knowledge of recent history leaves little doubt as to which event is intended. Owing to their strong association, naming the country readily calls the war to mind.[5]

(7)   *Vietnam marked a turning point in American history.*

Reference point relationships also figure in nominal compounds, where two nouns combine to form a composite expression that is also a noun: *jar lid, basketball net, sheep dog, baseball glove, bicycle seat, axe handle, window shade, fishing pole, book*

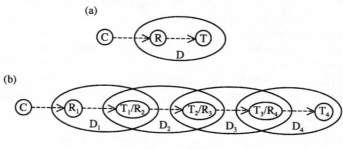

(a)

(b)

FIGURE 14.1

---

[5] This metonymic interpretation is a well-established sense of *Vietnam*. It instantiates a general pattern productively applied to new occurrences. If everything goes wrong on your vacation in Rhode Island, you can subsequently describe the experience by saying *Rhode Island was a disaster*.

cover, fingernail, trout stream, pencil sharpener, tomato worm, tree root, wine bottle, etc. The basic pattern is for the first noun to evoke a range of knowledge with respect to which the second is interpreted. There are many kinds of nets, for example, but only one accessible via basketball. By virtue of this association, *basketball net* is understood as referring to a net of this type (as opposed to a fishing net, butterfly net, mosquito net, or hair net). The interpretation is usually based on familiar scenarios. *Sheep dog* means what it does due to the cultural model of dogs herding sheep—it would mean something different if the standard model involved dogs being docile like sheep or eating them. Naturally, a compound can also derive its meaning from the context or any situation we might imagine, no matter how outlandish. A given compound can therefore be interpreted in different ways. While an *airplane diaper* would probably be understood as a diaper carried on an airplane for infant emergencies, it would also be appropriate for a massive piece of cloth wrapped around a plane to soak up leaking fuel.

14.1.2 Possession

Reference point relations are the key to understanding the linguistic phenomenon known as **possession**. What (you might ask) is the meaning of a possessive marker like English *'s*, or the import of a possessive construction like *Zelda's quilt*? The term notwithstanding, possession encompasses far more than relationships of owning or possessing. These are at best prototypical, along with kinship and whole-part relations (*my sister, the rat's tail*). Indeed, possessive expressions are used for an extremely diverse array of relationships: *Zelda's drink, the kitten's fleas, our bus, her trial, the store's location, my headache, Sean's attitude, their average intelligence, the diamond's value, his predicament, the year's top story, the photo's glossy finish, our existence, the bullet's trajectory, Lincoln's assassination,* and so on. Thus a general characterization can hardly be based on specific conceptual content. What, then, do possessives all have in common? Various considerations point to a reference point relationship being the shared feature (Langacker 1995; Taylor 1996; GC: ch. 6). A schematic description, valid for all instances, is simply that the possessor functions as a reference point providing mental access to the entity possessed, its target.

As noted previously (§3.4.2), a reference point characterization is sufficiently abstract to accommodate the full range of possessive expressions. Since it does not specify any particular content, it is compatible with any kind of conceived relation between possessor and possessed. But there are also limitations, and these too are accommodated. For the most part, possessive relationships are irreversible; we would not, for example, say **the quilt's Zelda, *the tail's rat, *the value's diamond,* or **the trajectory's bullet*. This irreversibility reflects the inherent asymmetry of reference point relationships—the path of mental access leads from R to T rather than in the opposite direction. The direction of access correlates with certain natural paths, including whole > part, concrete > abstract, and human > animate > inanimate. If two entities are equivalent in this respect, it may be possible for either to function as possessor, as in *the doctor's lawyer* and *the lawyer's doctor.*[6]

---

[6] Additional factors bear on the choice of possessor. One is information structure: *the doctor's lawyer* takes the doctor as given and introduces the lawyer as a discourse referent. Another is contextual

In a usage-based approach, the schematic description of possessives does not stand alone. The schema coexists with any number of conventional instantiations characterized at different levels of specificity (including many expressions with unit status). Within this array of established uses, some have good claim to being prototypical, among them ownership, kinship, and whole-part relations.[7] These are all clear examples of reference point organization. By their very nature, kin terms invoke a reference individual (fig. 3.6)—one is not a sister, a grandson, or an aunt in any absolute sense but only in relation to a certain person. Likewise, a part is only apprehended as such in relation to a larger whole (fig. 3.2). Though we might well recognize a tail in isolation, we can only identify it **as** a tail by invoking its position within the overall configuration of a body. In the case of ownership, reference point organization reflects the cognitive salience of people vis-à-vis nonhuman entities, as well as the cultural model whereby every person owns, controls, or has privileged access to a certain set of entities (which we call "possessions"). There are many fewer people than possessions, and we are much more likely to know them as individuals. To identify possessions with reference to their owners (*Zelda's quilt*) is thus a more efficient strategy than the opposite.

Possessives illustrate a general proposal of CG (§2.1.2): namely, that fundamental and universal grammatical notions have semantic characterizations at both the prototype and schema levels. Functioning as their prototypical values are conceptual archetypes that reflect basic aspects of everyday experience (e.g. physical object, in the case of nouns). The schematic meanings—valid for all instances—consist in basic cognitive abilities not tied to any specific conceptual content (e.g. grouping and reification). The abilities are initially manifested in the corresponding archetypes, providing the basis for their apprehension, and are later extended to other, less central cases.

In possession, the archetypes of ownership, kinship, and whole-part relations function as prototypical values. The reference point ability provides the schematic meaning. It is due to this ability that we are able to conceptualize ownership, kinship, and whole-part relations in the first place—that is, a reference point relationship is inherent in their conception. These archetypes have a basic directionality, involving a mental progression from R to T. We apprehend a kinship relation, such as *cousin*, by tracing a mental path from reference individual, through linking relatives, to profiled target: R ---> parent ---> sibling ---> child (T). Likewise, the conception of a part implies sequential access to the levels of a whole-part hierarchy, as body (R) ---> arm ---> hand ---> finger ---> knuckle (T). With ownership, a key notion is that of the possessor controlling the possessed: R $\Rightarrow$ T. The asymmetry of this relationship, the directionality in the flow of influence, is apprehended through seriality in the evocation of participants, whereby we first conceptualize R and then T. Their content being

---

accessibility. If you find a disembodied tail on the kitchen counter, you might wonder where *the tail's rat* has gone. Expressions like *the car's owner*, *the hotel's occupants*, and *the country's ruler* reverse the usual alignment (human > nonhuman) because the possessed noun derives from a verb (*own*, *occupy*, *rule*) and profiles its trajector. The identification of its landmark is thus a natural basis for singling out an instance of the type it specifies.

[7] These uses are frequent and readily come to mind as examples of possessive expressions. In some languages, the relevant nouns have to be possessed.

very different, what the possessive archetypes all share is precisely the invocation of R to mentally access T. Less typical uses of possessives result from applying this same ability to other kinds of circumstances.

Reference point relationships are a special case of sequential mental access, where R and T are discrete and salient enough to be individually recognized. As an aspect of conceptual organization, they are independent of any specific linguistic phenomena. They can thus be exploited linguistically in different ways, each of which imposes its own construal on the content so organized. The intrinsic salience of R and T is therefore not to be identified with the kinds of prominence imposed by grammatical constructions. The same reference point relationship can be reflected in multiple expressions involving alternate choices of profiling and trajector/landmark alignment.

There are, for example, both nominal and clausal possessive constructions, which differ in these respects. We have thus far focused on nominal possessives, such as *Zelda's quilt*. The same relationship can often be expressed in clausal form: *Zelda has a quilt.*[8] The basic difference between them is that the former profiles the entity possessed, whereas the latter designates the possessive relation itself. The verb *have* is highly polysemous and appears in a wide array of constructions (Brugman 1988). In simple clauses like *Zelda has a quilt*, it profiles an imperfective process with two focal participants. The range of senses it exhibits in this construction includes the possessive archetypes, established extensions from the prototype, and schemas at different levels of abstraction. Its most schematic value, devoid of any specific conceptual content, is simply that of a reference point relationship, with R focused as trajector and T as landmark. In forming a clause, these are specified by full nominals in accordance with the general subject and object constructions.

Nominal and clausal possession have different functions. *Zelda has a quilt* profiles a possessive relationship, which it introduces in the discourse. By contrast, *Zelda's quilt* presupposes this relationship and invokes it to identify a nominal referent. This identifying function qualifies *Zelda's* as a nominal grounding element. The noun *quilt* specifies a thing type of which there are many instances. The possessive marker *'s* evokes a reference point relationship and, more generally, the notion of there being many possible reference points, each with its own dominion. This provides the basis for distinguishing instances of a type from one another: one way to single out a quilt, distinguishing it from all other things of this sort, is to identify it as the instance occurring in the dominion of a particular individual. Of course, that individual must itself be identified. This is the function of the possessor nominal, in this case *Zelda*, which bears the possessive marking. *Zelda's quilt* is thus identified, for discourse purposes, as the one accessible via Zelda (whether through ownership or some other relation evident in the context).

This construction is sketched in figure 14.2. The conceptual base for *'s* is a reference point relationship. As a schematized grounding element, *'s* profiles the grounded entity, namely T, rather than the grounding relationship (§9.3.1). The schematic reference point functions as an e-site at the first level of composition. Its elaboration by *Zelda* produces the specific grounding element *Zelda's*, in which the

---

[8] While these are not atypical, there are numerous other kinds of nominal and clausal possessive constructions, in English and other languages (Langacker 2004b).

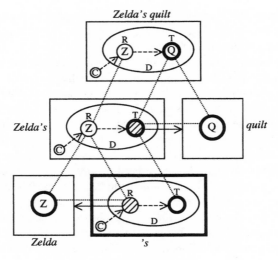

FIGURE 14.2

profiled target remains schematic.[9] At the higher level of organization, *quilt* elaborates T to specify the type of the grounded instance. The integration of *Zelda's* and *quilt* exhibits a characteristic property of grounding constructions (fig. 9.4): since their profiles correspond, neither stands out as profile determinant.

14.1.3 Pronominal Anaphora

Possession is one example of reference point relationships playing a role in the identification of nominal referents. They also help determine use of the definite article, which implies that only one instance of the specified type is accessible in the current discourse space. They do so by providing a scope of interpretation where a profiled instance has the requisite contextual uniqueness. In (8), the first sentence introduces a quilt into the discourse and establishes it as a topic. The following sentence is thus interpreted with respect to it. In particular, the quilt serves as reference point for interpreting *the pattern* and *the colors*, its dominion constituting the immediate scope for this purpose. And since a typical quilt has just one pattern and one set of colors, within this scope the nominal referents are the only instances of their types.

(8)   *I really like **Zelda's quilt**. **The pattern** is neat and **the colors** are striking.*

Pronominal anaphora is another reference point phenomenon, with R being the antecedent nominal and T the pronoun. T is mentally accessed via R in the sense that the antecedent determines the pronoun's reference. In (9), for example, *it* is interpreted via *Zelda's quilt*. Like *the pattern* and *the colors* in (8), *it* is taken as referring

[9] Evidence for this profiling is the fact that *Zelda's* can stand alone as a nominal used anaphorically: *This quilt is nicer than Zelda's.*

to an element of the quilt's dominion: as something associated with the quilt (hence mentally accessible through it). The special property of a pronoun is that this element is identified as the reference point itself—of all the elements in its dominion, R itself is the easiest to access. So with *Zelda's quilt* as the antecedent nominal, *it* is taken as referring to the quilt. The two are said to be **coreferential**.

(9) ***Zelda's quilt*** *is beautiful. Everyone likes **it**.*

A reference point tends to function as such in multiple respects, pertaining to different aspects of linguistic organization. In (8) and (9), R gives access to T in terms of both content and expression. With respect to content, R's dominion comprises the entities mentally associated with R through either established knowledge or a conceived situation in which they figure. Our standard knowledge of quilts is such that *Zelda's quilt* primes us to think about its pattern and its colors, not to mention the quilt itself. At the level of expression, R's dominion consists of that portion of the ongoing discourse within which R is sufficiently prominent to impose itself as the basis for interpretation. We see in (8) and (9) that a nominal in one sentence is able to exert its influence at least through the following sentence.

In regard to pronominal anaphora, the extent of a reference point's dominion is a classic problem of great complexity (Langacker 1969; Reinhart 1983). Its solution in CG (van Hoek 1995, 1997) can be sketched here only in the briefest terms. Stated most generally, the likelihood of a nominal being invoked as reference point depends on its prominence, and the likelihood of an element being included in its dominion depends on the closeness of their conceptual connection. Among the factors contributing to a nominal's prominence are profiling, trajector status, discourse salience, and role as conceptualizer. In (9), *Zelda's quilt* is highly prominent due to being trajector of the process profiled by the sentence containing it, which further establishes it as a discourse topic. Thus it is readily invoked as antecedent for a pronoun in the sentence that directly follows. The topic relationship is one conceptual connection between *Zelda's quilt* and the elements of the latter sentence. They are further connected through emergence of a coherent overall conception, in which the beauty of the quilt is taken as being responsible for everyone liking it. Hence the pronoun *it* falls within the dominion of *Zelda's quilt* and will almost certainly be interpreted as coreferential with it.

The closest conceptual connections hold among the elements of a single sentence, as reflected in its grammatical organization. Perhaps the strongest is the connection between the trajector and the landmark of a profiled relationship. This is the prototypical configuration for using a reflexive pronoun, as in (10), where coreference of *the president* and *himself* is the only option. But since every grammatical link represents a conceptual connection, coreference is generally possible even between elements whose grammatical association is only indirect. Thus in (10) the possessor pronoun *his* can also be taken as referring to the president.[10] Their connection is effected through a chain of grammatical relations: *private office* specifies the target of *his*; *his private*

---

[10] Stated more precisely, *his* refers to the entity possessed (the private office), with the president identified as reference point. Although *his* is only partially analyzable morphologically, at the semantic pole it still incorporates a pronominal element that participates in anaphoric relationships.

office is the landmark of *in*; *in his private office* modifies the clausal process; and *the president* elaborates the trajector of that process. Despite this indirectness, the connection is clear, and due to its prominence the subject functions as antecedent. Here, though, it is not the only option—in the proper discourse context, *his* could be taken as referring to another individual previously established as the topic of discussion.[11]

(10)   *In **his** private office **the president** was admiring **himself**.*

Usually the positions of a pronoun and its antecedent cannot be happily reversed. With coreference intended, for example, (11)(a) is at best rather awkward (we tend to interpret *he* as referring to someone other than the president) and (11)(b) is completely unacceptable:

(11)   (a)   *??In **the president**'s private office **he** was admiring himself.*

    (b)   **In his private office **himself** was admiring **the president**.*

These asymmetries reflect the inherent directionality of anaphoric relationships. Because it provides the basis for interpreting the pronoun, the antecedent nominal has conceptual priority with respect to it. Consequently, the felicity of anaphoric relationships depends on the antecedent preceding the pronoun along natural paths of mental access. The most obvious path is order of presentation—normally the antecedent precedes the pronoun in the flow of speech. The opposite order is often problematic. In contrast to (9), the following is very marginal (assuming that the quilt has not yet been established in the CDS):

(12)   *??**It**'s beautiful. Everyone likes **Zelda's quilt**.*

But order of presentation is not the only relevant path, or even the most important. Thus a pronoun sometimes does precede its antecedent, as in (10), where *his* precedes *the president*. In such cases, the antecedent has conceptual priority with respect to other natural paths.

One relevant path is a chain of elaborative relationships, notably with complement clauses (as in (1)). Another is the natural path of access from a conceptualizer to the conception entertained. In (13)(a), the antecedent precedes the pronoun with respect to both these paths, as well as order of presentation: *the president* is in the matrix clause, *he* in the complement; *the president* functions as conceptualizer in regard to the complement; and *the president* comes before *he* in the temporal sequence. This represents the optimal configuration for an anaphoric relationship, since all three paths coalign with its inherent directionality. Conversely, in (13)(b) we observe the worst configuration: the pronoun precedes its supposed **antecedent** along all three natural paths.[12]

---

[11] For example, (10) might appear in a story about the director of the CIA, with prior indication that the president has come to CIA headquarters.

[12] The sentence is perfectly grammatical if *him* and *the president* are taken as referring to different people, but only judgments based on coreference are relevant here. Well-formedness is always assessed relative to specific interpretations.

(13)   (a) *It never bothers **the president** [that **he** lies].*

    (b) **It never bothers **him** [that **the president** lies].*

Other examples show that all three paths are relevant for anaphora. Note first that (14)(a) is fully acceptable even though the pronoun precedes the antecedent in the temporal sequence, while (14)(b) is marginal (assuming coreference) even though the pronoun follows. Evidently this factor is outweighed by the other two: despite the effect of word order, the more acceptable sentence is the one in which the antecedent is in the matrix clause and functions as conceptualizer with respect to the complement.

(14)   (a) *The fact [that **he** lies] never bothers **the president**.*

    (b) *??The fact [that **the president** lies] never bothers **him**.*

While these latter factors often work together, each makes its own contribution to sanctioning anaphoric relationships. How might one demonstrate that path of conceptualization has an effect? We can see this by comparing the sentences in (14) to those in (15), which are parallel except that the antecedent (*the book*) is not a conceptualizer. In this case the sentences are equally acceptable. The relative infelicity of (14)(b) must therefore be ascribed to the pronoun's role as conceptualizer for the clause containing its antecedent.

(15)   (a) *The fact [that **it**'s full of lies] doesn't diminish **the book**.*

    (b) *The fact [that **the book** is full of lies] doesn't diminish **it**.*

Likewise, we can assess the role of a complement chain by comparing sentences with complements to analogous sentences with modifiers. In (16)(a)–(b) the clause introduced by *that* is a preposed object complement (the landmark of *realize*), while in (16)(c)–(d) the *when*-clause is adverbial. The crucial examples are (b) and (d). In the former, *the president* resists interpretation as the antecedent of *he* even though it precedes it in the linear sequence. This is due in part to *he* being a conceptualizer with respect to the complement. But only in part, as shown by comparison with (d). Here too *he* functions as conceptualizer in regard to the preposed clause, yet coreference is unproblematic. The difference is that the complement clause in (b) bears an elaborative relationship to the matrix predicate, whereas the adverbial clause in (d) does not. It is only in the former that *realize* provides an elaborative path connecting the subject pronoun to the clause containing its antecedent.

(16)   (a) *[That **he** is a liar] **the president** certainly realizes.*

    (b) *??[That **the president** is a liar] **he** certainly realizes.*

    (c) *[When **he** is lying] **the president** realizes it.*

    (d) *[When **the president** is lying] **he** realizes it.*

Pronominal anaphora has often been approached from a purely syntactic standpoint. Attempts to describe the position of a pronoun vis-à-vis its antecedent have tended to focus on formal properties, especially linear order and grammatical constituency. But while these are not irrelevant, a comprehensive description has to be based on dynamic conceptualization. In anaphoric relationships, the antecedent nominal provides mental access to the pronoun in the sense of determining its reference. Whether it can do so—whether the pronoun falls in its dominion—depends on its prominence and the closeness of their conceptual connection. These in turn reflect the complex interaction of numerous factors, each involving precedence along a natural path. Two such factors deserve to be looked at in greater depth: the status of a nominal as a topic or as a subject.

14.1.4 Topic vs. Subject

Topic and subject have an important role in pronominal anaphora. A nominal is readily invoked as antecedent for a pronoun in the stretch of discourse over which it has topic status. For example, *this computer* antecedes *it* in (17)(a), an explicit topic construction. An explicit topic has a strong tendency to be invoked as reference point. We observe in sentence (b) that the positions of the pronoun and antecedent cannot be reversed: the topic nominal can only function as R, not as T, in the anaphoric relationship. Indeed, we note in (c) that a nominal in the pronoun's position cannot escape the topic's influence. If coreferential with the topic, it has to be expressed as a pronoun—repeating the full nominal (*this computer*) wrongly implies that its referent would not otherwise be apparent.

(17) (a) ***This computer***, *I just can't get **it** to work.*

  (b) ****It**, I just can't get **this computer** to work.*

  (c) ****This computer**, I just can't get **this computer** to work.*

In similar fashion, a subject tends strongly to be invoked as reference point with respect to all other clausal elements.[13] The effect of subject status is shown by the data in (18). In sentence (a) the anaphoric relationship is optimal because the antecedent *Harvey* not only precedes the pronoun but is also the clausal subject. Conversely, sentence (b)—where a subject pronoun precedes its antecedent—is flatly ungrammatical. The difference is not solely due to linear order, which proves to be a secondary factor. We observe this in (c) and (d), where the initial element in the anaphoric relationship is not the clausal subject but rather its possessor. In this case both sentences are acceptable, though (d) is somewhat marginal because the pronoun comes first. Still, its relative acceptability indicates that the pronoun's status as subject is primarily responsible for the ungrammaticality of (b).

---

[13] We saw this previously in the contrast between (10), *In **his** private office **the president** was admiring himself*, and (11)(a) *??In **the president**'s private office **he** was admiring himself.* The former is more acceptable despite the order of presentation.

(18) (a) ***Harvey*** *resembles* ***his*** *dog.*

   (b) ******He*** *resembles* ***Harvey****'s dog.*

   (c) ***Harvey****'s dog resembles* ***him****.*

   (d) *?****His*** *dog resembles* ***Harvey****.*

Their role in pronominal anaphora suggests that topic and subject are themselves reference point phenomena. As a reference point, a topic or a subject provides
mental access to the elements of its dominion. Should one of these elements be a
pronoun, the topic or subject will tend to be invoked as the basis for its interpretation.
This reflects the inclination—a matter of cognitive efficiency—for natural paths to
coalign and for reference points to serve as such in multiple respects. If a nominal
and a pronoun function as R and T in regard to a topic or subject relation, they will
also tend to do so for anaphoric purposes, with the same alignment.

How, then, can a topic or a subject be characterized? The two notions are closely
associated grammatically and sometimes hard to distinguish. It happens, moreover,
that topic constructions develop historically into subject constructions.[14] Given their
evident affinity, and their common description as reference point phenomena, what
precisely is the difference?

Let us start with topics. As with many fundamental notions, it is hard to find a
verbal definition that does not seem hopelessly vague. Almost invariably, linguists
merely say that the topic of a sentence is "what the sentence is about". This is quite
compatible with its CG characterization, which does, however, have the advantage of
relating this notion of "aboutness" to a general and basic feature of conceptual structure. Topics represent a particular kind of reference point organization, distinguished
from others by the nature of the target.[15] In contrast to possessives and pronominal
anaphora, where the target is a thing, for topics the target is a proposition (P), i.e. a
grounded process. The basic configuration is thus as shown in figure 14.3.

A topic's dominion is the range of associated knowledge—a set of propositions
in which it has some role and which can thus be accessed through it. The import of

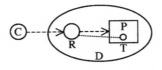

FIGURE 14.3

---

[14] This process is happening in French, being most apparent in questions. It comes about when a sentence like *Sophie, est-elle heureuse?* 'Sophie, is she happy?' (where *Sophie* is a clause-external topic)
is reanalyzed as *Sophie est-elle heureuse?* 'Is Sophie happy?' (where it functions as a clause-internal
subject). For a general discussion of topic vs. subject, see Li and Thompson 1976.

[15] In the cases to be considered, the reference point is always a thing. A question worth pursuing is
whether preposed adverbials (like the one in the previous sentence) should be analyzed as topic expressions that profile relationships.

a topic relationship is that the target proposition belongs to this body of knowledge. P is an integral part of D, whether it is already established there or has to be introduced. For both the speaker and the hearer, D provides the context for apprehending P and interpreting it. A proposition can only be interpreted in R's dominion if R somehow figures in its content. The small circle in figure 14.3 represents R's manifestation in P: that is, the element of P it corresponds to. This is called the **pivot**.[16] While the pivot may have any role in P, it tends to be a focal participant, as in (19)(a)–(b). And while it is often expressed overtly by a pronoun, it may also remain implicit. The pivots in (19)(c)–(d) are quite peripheral (at least in terms of grammar), and in (d) the pivot is left unexpressed.

(19)   (a) *That mural, it's really starting to depress me.*

        (b) *That mural, I like it less and less every day.*

        (c) *That mural, we would be better off if someone sprayed graffiti all over it.*

        (d) *That mural, we never should have given permission.*

As in the case of anaphora, a topic has a dominion in regard to both content and expression. At the level of expression, R's dominion is the stretch of discourse during which it enjoys topic status. Minimally this is just a clause, but it can also be a complex sentence or a discourse of any length. In (20), for example, the first sentence introduces the topic of writing a dissertation, and the succeeding sentences are all interpreted with respect to it. There is clearly the potential for the disquisition to continue indefinitely, until someone "changes the topic".

(20)   *It's really hard to write **a dissertation**. You have to find a subject. Then you have to come up with some ideas and do lots of preliminary analyses. When you do the background reading, you find that most of those ideas have already been proposed and rejected. So you have to work for a number of years before anything viable starts to take shape. You have to worry about continued financial support. Then you have to satisfy five committee members with mutually incompatible notions about what you should be doing. You have to go through about seven drafts. Then . . .*

The topic in (20) bears no special marking but is simply a verbal object introduced via the regular object construction. Nor does anything explicitly indicate that the following clauses are interpreted with respect to it; in fact, they fail to even mention it. Topic relationships are first and foremost a discourse phenomenon. As a discourse unfolds, the organization they impose is inherent in the conceptual structure being built, even when they have no distinct grammatical realization. There are, however, topic markers and explicit topic constructions. The sentences in (19) represent a basic topic construction in which the initial nominal is established as a topic at least

---

[16] The term is also used with relative clauses (§12.2.2). The difference between topic and relative clause constructions is that a relative clause is part of the nominal expressing R and helps identify its referent, whereas a topic is a separate nominal whose reference is established independently.

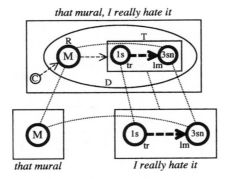

that mural, I really hate it

that mural   *I really hate it*

FIGURE 14.4

for the proposition that follows. In unhurried speech, the nominal and target clause are separated by the slight pause written as a comma, suggesting that each occupies its own attentional frame.

An instance of this construction is sketched in figure 14.4. The two component structures are a nominal, *that mural,* and a finite clause, *I really hate it.* Semantically, their integration hinges on a correspondence between the nominal profile and the clausal element functioning as pivot—in this case, the referent of the object pronoun. Phonologically, their integration consists in temporal adjacency and the suspended intonation between them. There being no topic marker, the topic relationship emerges only at the composite-structure level; it is not a property of either component structure, considered individually, but rather of the construction as a whole.[17] The composite structure is shown as having two distinct profiles: the reference point and the target process. This is because the expression comprises two attentional frames, each a window of attention with its own attentional focus. An analysis positing a succession of profiles (instead of a single overall profile) captures the evident dynamicity of this construction.

In this construction, the topic nominal is clearly external to the target clause, as shown by intonation as well as by the fact that the clause is structurally complete. The same considerations lead to the opposite conclusion in sentences like the following: *That mural I really hate.* In this expression, there is no intonational disjuncture between the topic and the remainder, nor is the latter a complete clause in and of itself. Here the topic nominal is an integral part of the target clause, functioning not only as topic but also as clausal landmark. It is thus internal to the clause, both semantically and syntactically.

Shown in figure 14.5, this construction amounts to a blend of the topic and object constructions. It represents a variant of the object construction because *that mural* elaborates the schematic landmark of *I really hate.* It resembles the topic construction

---

[17] In some languages, the topic nominal does take an overt marker, Japanese *wa* being a well-known example. English *as for* is roughly comparable: *As for that mural, I really hate it.* The topic construction is then analogous to the one shown for possessive *'s* in figure 14.2 (apart from profiling and the nature of the target).

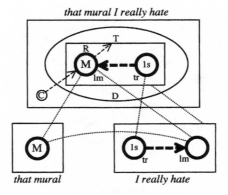

that mural I really hate

that mural   *I really hate*

FIGURE 14.5

in that the topic comes first, but it differs by virtue of there being just a single attentional frame with a single overall profile. Thus the mural's invocation as reference
point is simultaneous with its invocation as clausal landmark. Another way to put it is
that there is no distinction between topic and pivot, the topic nominal being internal
to the clause expressing the target proposition.

Topics thus occur at different levels of organization, holding sway over dominions of different sizes.[18] The dominion can be a passage of any length, a complex sentence, or a single clause. The smaller the dominion, the closer the connection tends to
be between the reference point and the target proposition. Structurally, the topic can
be in a separate sentence, in the same sentence but external to the target clause, or an
integral part of that clause. But even in the latter case, a topic functions as reference
point for discourse reasons, not by way of coding the clausal proposition. Being a
matter of information structure, a nominal's role as topic is superimposed on its role
as clausal participant. Conceptually, its status as topic is extrinsic to the proposition,
determined by discourse factors rather than by objective content. Hence the same
proposition can usually be expressed with alternate topics (*That mural, I really hate
it* vs. *As for me, I really hate that mural*) or none at all (*I really hate that mural*).

Like a topic, a subject functions as reference point for a target proposition. This
is the basis for their similarity. The difference is that a subject is both **structurally
internal** to a clause and **conceptually intrinsic**. A topic is a reference point in discourse, directing the hearer to the proper realm of knowledge for interpreting the
target proposition. Its role as reference point is thus extrinsic to the clause's objective
content. By contrast, the subject's role as reference point is inherent in the apprehension of the clausal content. A subject specifies the trajector of a profiled process, and
the trajector—it will be argued—functions as reference point for the very purpose of
conceptualizing that process.

An entity invoked as reference point for one purpose is likely to serve in that
capacity for other purposes as well. So it stands to reason that a subject, being a

---

[18] This illustrates the fractal organization of language structure (§13.3.2).

clause-internal reference point, would also tend to be a discourse topic. Still, their coincidence is only a tendency. Topic and subject are distinct notions, pertaining to different channels. When the same nominal serves in both capacities, it is a reference point with respect to both information structure and objective content.[19]

14.1.5 Subject and Object

The subject of a clause is a nominal that elaborates the trajector of the process it designates. I am now suggesting that the trajector of a profiled relationship, previously described as its primary focal participant, can also—and more fundamentally—be characterized as a reference point with respect to it. Similarly, an object elaborates the landmark of a profiled relationship, previously described as its secondary focal participant. By analogy, then, a relation's landmark can be characterized as a secondary reference point with respect to it. These notions are hardly self-explanatory, but when properly understood they prove both psychologically plausible and linguistically revealing.

Let us start with the idea that the focal participants of a profiled relationship are **intrinsic** reference points with respect to it. In contrast to a topic, which locates a proposition in a larger conceptual context, the trajector and landmark of a process are inherent in its conceptualization—they function as reference points for the very purpose of building up to its full conception. This follows from the earlier observation (§4.2.1) that relations are **conceptually dependent** on their participants: we cannot apprehend a relationship without invoking the participants that support its manifestation. Because they make its conception possible, participants are reasonably described as providing mental access to a relation. This, of course, is tantamount to saying that they function as reference points in regard to it.

Figure 14.6 represents the contrast between extrinsic and intrinsic reference point relationships with a profiled process as target. Diagram (a) corresponds to a clause-external topic construction, like the one in figure 14.4. The reference point relation is above and beyond the target's characterization and is thus extrinsic to it, even though R somehow figures (as pivot) in the overall content of this proposition. R's dominion is the range of associated knowledge, within which T is interpreted. Diagram (b) depicts the intrinsic reference point relation involving a process and its

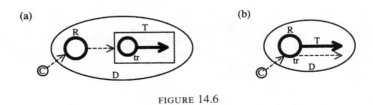

FIGURE 14.6

<hr>

[19] This is not inconsistent with the common observation that certain constructions, like the passive, allow a discourse topic to be expressed as clausal subject. The nature of a subject should not be confused with the factors that influence its choice.

trajector. In this case R and T are not distinct. "Reaching" the target is simply a matter of conceptualizing it, so the dashed arrow representing the path of mental access is coextensive with the solid arrow repesenting the temporal unfolding of the profiled relationship. And since T is conceptually dependent, the path of mental access runs through R. Here R's dominion (the set of potential targets) consists of all those processes it might anchor in this fashion.

Granted that trajector and landmark are intrinsic to the conception of a profiled process, how does their reference point characterization relate to their description in terms of primary and secondary focal prominence? Describing them as **focal** participants is equivalent to describing them as reference points. Focal participants are commonly referred to by linguists as **central** (or **core**) participants. This notion of centrality cannot, of course, be understood in a literal, spatial sense. Rather, it is invoked metaphorically to indicate that the participants in question are essential to the relationship: without them, it would either be incoherent or constitute a different relationship. This amounts to saying that a relation's central participants provide mental access to it. And since a profiled relationship is by definition a **focus** of attention, its essential participants are **focal** participants.

To the notion of centrality (obligatory access) the reference point characterization adds the notion of dynamicity (sequential access). Here we find the basis for distinguishing trajector and landmark: they are **primary** and **secondary** focal participants by virtue of being the **first** and **second** reference points evoked in building up to the full conception of a profiled relationship. According to this analysis, trajector/landmark alignment consists in a natural path of mental access, with the trajector as its starting point: trajector > landmark > relationship. It is thus suggested that the two degrees of focal prominence are at least partially attributable to sequentiality.

A relationship with both a trajector and a landmark is sketched in figure 14.7. The labels R_1 and R_2 indicate their status as first and second reference points. The overall target process, T, has been factored into two subprocesses, T_1 and T_2, representing those facets of T that directly involve R_1 and R_2. With a verb like *smash*, for instance, T_1 consists in the trajector's exertion of force, and T_2 consists in the landmark's resultant change of state.[20] The proposal, then, is that the conception of a two-participant relation involves a mental progression from R_1 to R_2, and thus from

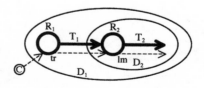

FIGURE 14.7

---

[20] This is not to say that T_1 and T_2 are always nonoverlapping or clearly distinguishable. In the case of *smash*, the notion of causation (T_1) is conceptually dependent on the change induced (T_2) and thus invokes it schematically. Likewise, the change of state is hard to conceptualize independently of the force inducing it.

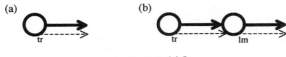

FIGURE 14.8

T_1 to T_2, the subrelations they respectively anchor. In view of this progression, it is also apparent that R_1 heads a path of access subsuming both T_1 and T_2. Figure 14.7 can thus be seen as a special case of figure 14.6(b), where $R = R_1$ and $T = T_1 + T_2$.

For ease of representation, I will adopt the simplified diagrams of figure 14.8. The labels R, T, D, and C are suppressed, and neither the conceptualizer nor the dominions are shown explicitly. It suffices to indicate the path of mental access.

Importantly, a path of mental access is usually not exclusive. With a situation of any complexity, there are alternate ways to access constitutive elements in building up to a full conception of it. Comprising one range of alternatives are different options in regard to profiling—which facets of the overall situation will be singled out as the focused relationship. Depending on the choice of profile, different participants are central enough to its conception (if not indispensable) to be considered reference points with respect to it.[21] A relationship can also be accessed by evoking the same participants in alternate sequences. These differences are matters of construal and are possible even if the total conceptual content should be identical. Since meaning includes both content and construal, expressions that contrast in these ways are semantically nonequivalent.

As brief illustration, consider the three-way contrast among expressions of the form *X give Y Z*, *X give Z to Y*, and *Y receive Z*. Applied to a simple act of physical transfer, they share the conceptual content sketched in figure 14.9(a). The effect of the transfer is that Z moves from X's dominion (sphere of control) into Y's. The dominions are shown as ellipses, and Z's movement as a single arrow. The double-shafted arrow indicates that X initiates this movement. The double-headed arrow represents the event's interactive nature: X intends for Y to have Z, Y is cognizant of this intent, the exchange has social import, and so on. Finally, multiple arrows stand for Y's role in assuming possession of Z: observing its approach, physically accepting it, and then controlling it.

Shown in figure 14.9(b)–(d) are the alternate construals the expressions impose on this content.[22] The verbs are distinguished in terms of profiling. Whereas *give* designates the overall event, comprising all the relationships indicated, *receive*'s profile is limited to Y's interaction with Z. This difference correlates with the choice of trajector, the starting point for mentally accessing the profiled process. With the agent X as starting point, the profile extends to all the occurrences X initiates: Z moving, Y interacting with Z as a consequence, and Y being affected at the mental and social levels (e.g. in apprehending the change and being recognized as the new controller).

---

[21] Does the profiled relationship determine the focal participants, or conversely? Let me simply say that these factors are interdependent. It may well be a chicken-and-egg situation.

[22] For sake of clarity, the dominions are not represented.

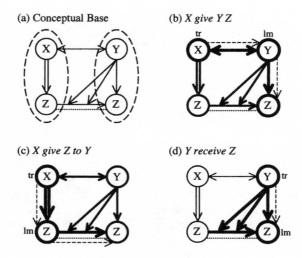

(a) Conceptual Base   (b) *X give Y Z*

(c) *X give Z to Y*   (d) *Y receive Z*

FIGURE 14.9

On the other hand, with the recipient Y as starting point, the profile is confined to the occurrences Y initiates: the physical and experiential aspects of accepting and controlling Z.

In the case of *give*, a further difference stems from the choice of landmark, the second reference point evoked in mentally accessing the profiled process. The landmark can be either the recipient, in what is known as the ditransitive construction, or the mover, as an instance of the caused-motion construction (§11.3.3). With either option, the profile encompasses all the relationships shown. The reference points do, however, represent alternate ways of building up to the full conception. Naturally, choosing one or the other serves to highlight those facets of the overall relationship it figures in most directly. This is shown by the heavier lines in figures 14-9(b) and (c). When the access from X proceeds via Y (note the dashed arrows), there is greater emphasis on the action affecting Y, mainly by effecting its status as controller. By contrast, access via Z serves to highlight the causation of Z's movement.[23]

In addition to there being alternate paths of access, processing occurs at multiple levels of organization. This is exemplified by the relation between a transitive verb, such as *throw*, and its corresponding passive, *be thrown*. At the lower level of organization, the verb *throw* profiles the causation of motion, with the agent as trajector and the mover as landmark. Shown at the left in figure 14.10, this represents an optimal alignment, in that the path of mental access follows the natural paths of causation and temporal sequencing. The passive provides an alternative for cases where, for discourse purposes, the same content is more conveniently accessed with the mover as starting point. The effect of the passive construction (and more specifically, the past

[23] This contrast results in different patterns of usage. For instance, the caused-motion construction allows omission of the recipient, which is not on the main path of access: *She could only give $5*. In cases where there is no actual movement on the part of Z, the only option may be to use the ditransitive, which highlights the end result: *The noise gave him a headache*; **The noise gave a headache to him*.

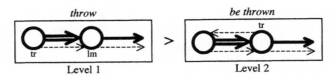

FIGURE 14.10

participial inflection) is to superimpose on the basic conception a higher-level construal in which the mover functions as trajector. In the derived expression *be thrown*, the same content is accessed through (hence viewed in relation to) the mover. It is not that the basic alignment disappears—it is simply overshadowed at the composite-structure level. To some extent we have to backtrack, and follow the natural path anchored by the agent, in order to apprehend what happens to the mover.[24]

The proposal that trajector/landmark alignment is based on sequence of mental access, and is thus essentially temporal in nature, may not be intuitively obvious. This is only to be expected in view of the small time scale involved. At the most basic level, the sequentiality is intrinsic to the meaning of a single lexeme (e.g. *throw*), whose conception is measured in milliseconds. It is only at higher levels of organization, where the time scale is larger and elements are separately expressed, that we can reasonably anticipate their sequential access being subject to introspection. The proposal is a special case of the broader notion (§14.1.1) that conceptions of ordering and directionality reside in serial processing, which is a basic aspect of conceptual experience even when it remains below the threshold of conscious awareness. In this respect trajector/landmark alignment is seen as comparable to the intrinsic directionality of a scale.

Though not self-evident, neither is the proposal merely speculative. There is quite a bit of evidence that trajector and landmark are properly characterized as sequentially accessed reference points. Some evidence is only circumstantial, like the well-known fact that in most languages a subject precedes an object in the basic (most neutral) word order. This is only circumstantial because the subject and object nominals, while they express the trajector and landmark, cannot (strictly speaking) be identified with them. Trajector and landmark are conceptual entities, inherent in the meaning of a verb or a larger predicate. Their sequential access is thus internal to the predicate, a matter of apprehending the profiled relationship, so per se it has nothing to do with the order of presentation. On the other hand, subject and object nominals are symbolic structures. As such, they have phonological expression and occur in a certain order. Their status as subject and object does not depend on word order, however, but on correspondences between their profiles and the clausal trajector and landmark. Even when used to identify subject and object, clause-level

---

[24] A similar kind of backtracking occurs with clause-internal topics, as in *That mural I really hate* (fig. 14.5). Here, though, it is not a matter of deriving a higher-level predicate with alternate trajector/landmark alignment. Instead, backtracking occurs with a finite clause containing subject and object nominals, as a function of the special word order. The reference point relation it introduces is extrinsic to the conception of the profiled clausal process (fig. 14.6).

word order is influenced by information structure and other considerations. There is, nonetheless, a definite tendency for a subject to precede an object in the absence of overriding factors, which is only to be expected if trajector/landmark alignment also has a temporal basis. The default ordering reflects the processing efficiency achieved through the coalignment of natural paths.

Also suggesting the sequentiality of trajector/landmark alignment is the well-known **grammatical accessibility** of the subject and object roles. Compared with other clausal elements, the two are highly active grammatically: they are most likely to trigger verb agreement, to function as pivot in relative clauses, and so on. In autonomous theories of syntax, grammatical relations are often ranked for "syntactic prominence", with subject and object the first two items on the list. In such approaches, however, terms like "prominence" and "accessibility" have no independent content—they simply label the fact that some grammatical roles figure in more phenomena than do others. By contrast, the CG account derives the ranking from something more fundamental. The syntactic prominence of subject and object reflects the conceptual prominence of trajector and landmark, established independently as essential constructs for semantic description (§3.5). We have now taken the further step of explicating trajector/landmark alignment in terms of sequence of mental access, providing a direct basis for their grammatical accessibility.

One manifestation of their accessibility is the key role of subject and object in pronominal anaphora. Though many factors are involved, one can make the basic generalization that a subject can serve as antecedent for any other clausal element, and an object for any element except the subject (van Hoek 1995, 1997). We see in (21)(a) and (b), for instance, that a subject can serve as antecedent for the possessor of an object, but not conversely. Likewise, (21)(c) and (d) show the unidirectionality of an anaphoric relationship between a clausal object and an element of a prepositional phrase.

(21)　(a) *The kitten* was chasing *its* tail.

　　　(b) **It* was chasing *the kitten*'s tail.

　　　(c) We observed *the baboons* in *their* native habitat.

　　　(d) **We observed *them* in *the baboons*' native habitat.

Accepting that anaphora is itself a reference point phenomenon, the generalization dovetails with the characterization of trajector and landmark as first and second reference points for apprehending the clausal process. Reference points invoked for one purpose tend to be used as such for other purposes as well.

Supporting the analysis even more directly is the use of possessives to specify the participants of a nominalized verb, as in *Booth's assassination [of Lincoln]* and *Lincoln's assassination [by Booth]*. When a verb is nominalized, the process it designates is construed as an abstract thing; the noun *assassination* profiles a thing comprising one instance of the process *assassinate*. The event's construal as a thing is represented by the heavy-line ellipse in figure 14.11. If the trajector and landmark of a process are reference points with respect to it, and the process is construed as

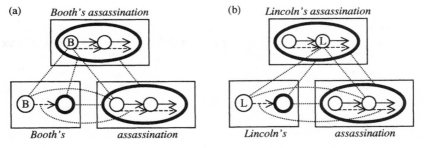

(a) *Booth's assassination*   (b) *Lincoln's assassination*

Booth's   *assassination*   *Lincoln's*   *assassination*

FIGURE 14.11

a thing, then each participant's relation to it constitutes a possessive relationship (defined schematically as a reference point relation between two things). Hence the analysis correctly predicts that possessives should commonly be used to specify the participants of a reified process.

The expressions are quite analogous to basic possessives like *Zelda's quilt* (fig. 14.2), the only difference being that the target is a reified process. So in both expressions *assassination* elaborates the schematic target of the possessor phrase (*Booth's* or *Lincoln's*). The special feature of this periphrastic construction is that the target noun itself incorporates reference point relations—those inherent in the verb's trajector/landmark alignment—one of which is identified with the possessive relation. The possessor thus corresponds to either the trajector or the landmark of the reified process, and its reference point relation to the target is the same one it has intrinsically as part of the verbal meaning. In this way, the possessive construction serves to specify a processual participant.

A final piece of evidence comes from **equative** expressions, as in (22). These are of two basic sorts. In (22)(a)–(b), the subject and predicate nominals refer to specific, actual individuals. What these sentences profile is the relationship of referential identity: that is, the nominals refer to the **same** individual.[25] In such examples the nominals are often reversible, identity being a symmetrical relation. But in other examples, like (22)(c)–(d), the nominals do not refer to specific individuals. And in this case they are typically not reversible, as witnessed by the infelicity of (22)(d). How can we describe such expressions? And why are they irreversible?

(22) (a) *My cousin Harvey is the guy who got drunk at our wedding.*

   (b) *The guy who got drunk at our wedding is my cousin Harvey.*

   (c) *A tiger is a feline.*

   (d) **A feline is a tiger.*

---

[25] I noted previously that identity is the limiting case of a reference point relation, where the path from R to T has a length of zero. Since it has so little content, identity is commonly expressed simply by juxtaposing two nominals, emerging as an aspect of constructional meaning (fig. 11.11). As in other uses, *be* gives temporal extension to this relationship (in case you were wondering what the meaning of *is* is).

Expressions of this latter sort also profile a relation of referential identity. The basic difference is that the nominal referents are virtual rather than actual: they are fictive instances of their types, conjured up in order to make a general statement. The key factor is a kind of directionality that tends to be obscured with actual referents but emerges more clearly with fictive referents evoked as representatives of their types. The import of (22)(c), very roughly, is as follows: if you start with an instance of *tiger*, you will always find that it coincides with an instance of *feline*. This accords with our standard taxonomic model, in which tigers are a subclass in the class of felines. But (22)(d) runs afoul of this taxonomy: if you start with an instance of *feline*, it is not always true that it coincides with an instance of *tiger* (e.g. it might be a leopard).

So even though it predicates identity, the equative construction implies a direction of assessment, invoking the first nominal's referent as a starting point—the one whose identification is at issue. Where does this directionality come from? The only evident source is trajector/landmark alignment. As clausal subject, the first nominal specifies the trajector of the profiled identity relationship. The trajector is the starting point by virtue of being the first reference point evoked in conceptualizing this relation.

14.2 Fictivity

The tiger and the feline referred to in (22)(c) are fictive (or virtual) instances of their types, as opposed to actual individuals. They join the growing menagerie of fictive entities that we have seen to be linguistically significant. Among these (to mention just a few) are the products of metaphor and blending (§2.2.3), an imagined vantage point (§3.4.1), virtual bounding (fig. 5.4), the conceptualizer (C) invoked by a grounding element (§12.3.2), and the fictive invocation of a speech-act scenario (§13.2.3). Its prevalence is such that fictivity has to be recognized as a basic feature of cognition with a fundamental role in language structure.

14.2.1 Disengaged Cognition

We live in a real world.[26] Since our view of this world is mentally constructed on the basis of experience, each of us apprehends it somewhat differently, and quite differently from creatures with other mental capacities. Despite this variability, the constructive process is shaped and constrained by the world's actual nature—otherwise, there would be little chance of survival. The process is further constrained by our position in the world. We always apprehend it at the present moment, from our current location, through our own senses, and with our own mental faculties. Omniscience is not an available option.

Ultimately, the world we construct is grounded in our experience as creatures with bodies who interact with their surroundings through physical processes involving sensory and motor activity. This is known in cognitive linguistics as **embodiment**.

---

[26] Or at least we think we do. If not, the illusion is quite compelling.

But obviously, our mental life transcends the limits of immediate bodily experience. Various cognitive processes give rise to mental structures, at successive levels of organization, whose connection with such experience is progressively more remote. Not only do these structures allow us to cope with the real world more efficiently, but also they define—and vastly expand—what constitutes it. From our standpoint, the world we inhabit and engage has not just physical but also social, cultural, and intellectual dimensions. Once they are cognitively established, we can operate in these realms in largely autonomous fashion. Discussions of investment strategies, or ruminations concerning linguistic theory, are basically independent of immediate physical reality; nonetheless, they are means of engaging certain aspects of our mentally and socially constructed world.

Thus a great deal of our cognitive activity is disengaged (to varying degrees) from immediate bodily experience. How do we manage to transcend it? One way is through memory, consisting in the partial revival of a previous experience. Another is anticipation, where the observation of a present situation affords a basis for projecting its future development. This can be as elemental as the default expectation that a physical object will continue to exist from moment to moment. But it can also be based on patterns that are learned through previous occurrences. Patterns are learned by **abstraction**, a fundamental means of transcending immediate experience.

Abstraction comes about through the reinforcement of what is common to multiple experiences. Since features that fail to recur are not reinforced, an abstracted structure is always impoverished relative to the experiences it derives from. And since commonalities are often apparent only in a coarse-grained view, involving lesser precision, abstracted structures are usually schematic relative to these experiences. Though immanent in all of them, an abstracted structure is independent of any particular instantiation. It represents a generalization with the potential to be invoked in subsequent processing. Without the capacity for abstraction, every experience would be unique and unrelated to every other. A structured view of the world could not emerge.

The conventional units of a language are abstracted from usage events. Once learned, a unit transcends the events giving rise to it, with the potential to be employed in further events involving new expressions (ch. 8). It is disengaged from immediate experience in the sense that it is part of a speaker's linguistic repertoire, available for implementation, even when not currently being used. As a consequence of this disengagement, an entity crucial to a unit's meaning may be virtual in nature when the unit is considered independently of its use. Obvious cases are the pronouns *I* and *you*, which—viewed as conventional units—refer to the speaker and hearer in abstracted, generalized fashion. It is only in the context of a particular usage event that they refer to specific, actual individuals. The same holds for a speech-act scenario, as well as for the conceptualizer invoked by grounding elements and predicates of propositional attitude (§12.3.2). More generally, the entity profiled by a lexical noun or verb is merely a type of thing or process, and a type per se is always virtual. It is only when grounded to form a nominal or a finite clause that the profiled entity is conceived as an instance of its type. And it is only in the context of a particular usage event that this instance can be identified as an actual individual in the world.

It is not the case, however, that abstracted entities are always identified with actual ones in the context of usage events. In some linguistic structures, their abstracted nature is precisely the reason for invoking them. This is so when, instead of being grounded, a noun or verb is used as the first element of a compound or as the base for morphological derivation. A *mosquito net* is intended to offer protection from mosquitoes in general, rather than any one in particular. Similarly, describing someone as a *complainer* would normally be taken as indicating a general propensity to complain, not a specific instance. But while the absence of grounding results in virtuality, its presence does not itself ensure actuality. For example, *A tiger is a feline* is a full, finite clause containing two grounded nominals. Yet all the referents are virtual: the tiger, the feline, and thus the profiled identity relation. Instead of being actual, an instance of a type may simply be conjured up for a special purpose, one of them being to make a general statement.[27] In this case, the instance referred to is construed as being **representative** of its type (§9.3.5), hence an abstraction vis-à-vis particular instances.

Types and representative instances arise from actual entities through different kinds of abstraction, indicated in figure 14.12. Recall that an instance is thought of as having a particular, distinguishing location in the domain of instantiation (DI). We obtain a type conception by abstracting away from this property. While the overall description of a type includes its connection with instances (this is, after all, what it means to be a type), instances and their locations remain in the background (fig. 9.3). In the conception of a representative instance, on the other hand, the notion of instances and distinguishing locations is itself an aspect of the abstracted commonality. The virtual instance is abstracted from actual ones precisely to represent their shared property of being instantiations of the type (fig. 9.13).

Representative instances of a type figure in numerous linguistic phenomena. They are pivotal to the meaning of the grounding quantifiers *every*, *each*, and *any* (§9.3.5). They are further used for making both local and global generalizations. For example, the following sentence describes what is common to three distinct events involving different customers and different snakes:

(23)   *Three times this morning a customer bought a python.*

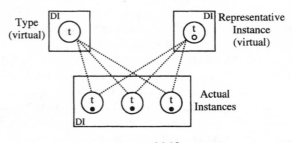

FIGURE 14.12

---

[27] Examples of other reasons for invoking a virtual instance are negation (*I don't have a dog*) and the description of desires (*I would like to have a dog*).

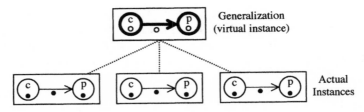

FIGURE 14.13

Despite this multiplicity, the subject and object nominals occur in the singular. The profiled customer and python are not any actual instances, but virtual instances of their types, construed as being representative of the actual ones. They participate in an instance of buying that is also virtual, being representative of three actual instances. As shown in figure 14.13, this fictive occurrence is the one the sentence puts onstage as the profiled process. It is abstracted as a generalization over three actual occurrences, the connection between them being specified by the adverbial expression *three times this morning*. The sentence's meaning includes this entire configuration—both levels and the nature of their relationship.[28]

Analyzed in similar fashion are **generic** statements employing indefinite nominals, e.g. *A tiger has stripes*. With generics, the generalization is global rather than local: instead of applying to a limited number of occurrences that happen to be analogous, it is offered as a characterization of the world's essential nature (Goldsmith and Woisetschlaeger 1982; Langacker 1997). It thus applies to an open-ended set of occurrences, and is expected to be valid for every instance of the qualified type (in this case, *tiger*). Generics make no explicit reference to the notion of the world having an essential structure, or to the type's maximal extension (E_t). These mental constructions are part of the supporting conceptual substrate.

Virtual instances also play a role in **quantifier scope**, where one quantifier figures in the conception to which the other applies. On the relevant interpretation, for example, *Two boys ate seven apples* ascribes the feat of eating seven apples to each of two boys. It is said that *two* has *seven* **in its scope** (or that *two* has **wide scope**, and *seven* **narrow scope**). Interpreted in this manner, the sentence implies that a total of fourteen apples were consumed. Why, then, does it mention only seven? The reason is that the profiled occurrence *eat seven apples* is a fictive event abstracted to represent the commonality of two actual events, one on the part of each boy. The two boys are actual, but the seven apples are virtual.

By nature, an abstraction conforms to the structures it is based on but is less detailed. As a representation of what they share, it is immanent in these structures but not exhaustive of them. Another basic means of transcending direct experience, one that exhibits the opposite properties, is **conceptual integration** (Fauconnier and Turner 2002). Conceptions are integrated through correspondences between their elements. The result is often a new conception substantially different from any previously entertained. An obvious

---

[28] These levels can also be described as mental spaces: "actuality" and a "generalization space". Fictive entities occupy special mental spaces by their very nature.

case is metaphor, in which a source domain is used to apprehend a target domain, resulting in a blended structure (fig. 2.9). Another is semantic composition, where component structures are integrated to form a composite conception. Patterns of composition—the semantic poles of constructional schemas—allow the formation of conceptions that are familiar (e.g. *lazy cat*), novel but possible (*purple bread*), purely imaginary (*invisible elephant*), or even conceptually incoherent (*square circle*).

Conceptual integration lets us deal with the ever-changing circumstances of real life. At the other extreme, it is used in producing works of fiction where the characters, the story, and even the world itself are imaginary. In between is the practice of invoking fictive entities as an indirect means of dealing with actuality. Large-scale examples include mathematics, scientific theories, and systems of philosophy (Lakoff and Núñez 2000; Lakoff and Johnson 1999). On a more modest scale, we find linguistic devices that specifically indicate the nonactual status of occurrences. In (24)(a)–(c), for instance, the fictive nature of the dog speaking French is indicated by negation, the verb *imagine*, and the conditional construction with *if*, respectively. Invoking this situation does however serve a purpose in regard to actuality. Knowing that something is not the case, or will only be the case under certain conditions, may very well have consequences for what we actually do. And if Jane is deluded about her dog speaking French, the fact that she imagines it is nonetheless a real situation we may have to cope with.

(24)   (a) *Jane's dog does not speak French.*

    (b) *Jane merely imagines that her dog speaks French.*

    (c) *If her dog speaks French Jane can make a fortune.*

In a final means of transcending direct experience, mental operations inherent in a certain kind of experience are applied to situations with respect to which their occurrence is extrinsic. This is called **subjectification**, indicating that the operations come to be independent of the objective circumstances where they initially occur and whose apprehension they partially constitute. A previous example is the reference point characterization of possessives (§14.1.2). The mental operation of invoking R to access T (C ---> R ---> T) is immanent in the conception of the possessor controlling the possessed (R $\Rightarrow$ T). In many possessive uses, the objective notion of control is attenuated to the point that sequential mental access is all that remains. Another example is nominalization, e.g. *assassinate > assassination*, whereby an event is conceived as an abstract thing (fig. 14.11). Here the mental operations are grouping and reification (§4.2.2), which apply transparently in collective nouns such as *stack*, *team*, and *archipelago*, and below the level of conscious awareness with prototypical nouns such as *dog*, *rock*, and *pencil*. With a noun like *assassinate*, the entities grouped and reified are the component states of the verbal process (the relationships profiled at each successive instant).

One product of subjectification is the phenomenon known as **fictive motion**.[29] For instance, the expressions in (25)(a)–(b) incorporate elements used primarily for

---

[29] See, for example, CIS: ch. 5; Langacker 2005a; Matsumoto 1996a, 1996b; Talmy 1996. There is experimental evidence that the processing of fictive motion expressions is indeed linked to the conception of actual motion (Matlock 2004; Matlock, Ramscar, and Boroditsky 2004).

spatial movement: the motion verb *run*, as well as the path prepositions *from* and *to*. Moreover, they appear to indicate movement in opposite directions. Yet both describe the same situation, which is static and has no inherent directionality. In such expressions, cognitive operations inherent in the conception of spatial motion are applied to static scenes as a way of mentally accessing them.

(25)   (a) *An ugly scar runs from his elbow to his wrist.*

  (b) *An ugly scar runs from his wrist to his elbow.*

  (c) *The pitcher ran from the bullpen to the mound.*

We conceptualize an actual motion event, such as (25)(c), by tracking the mover's progress along a spatial path. This is shown in figure 14.14(a): through processing time (T), we successively conceptualize the mover as occupying—through conceived time (t)—a series of locations that collectively constitute the path. An inherent aspect of this conception is that the conceptualizer scans mentally along the same path which the mover traverses physically; to properly apprehend this event, C must access the successive locations in the same order that the mover reaches them. The dynamic conception of a path is therefore immanent in the conception of actual motion. In fictive motion expressions, the same mental operations are applied to a static scene, as shown in figure 14.14(b): through processing time, C scans along the path by successively invoking the constitutive locations. Here, though, the analog of the mover is a spatially extended object (like a scar) that occupies all these locations simultaneously. Instead of tracking an object's movement, C scans along the path by way of building up to a full conception of the object's spatial configuration. And at least for this purpose, conceived time has no significant role in the expression's objective content (OC).[30]

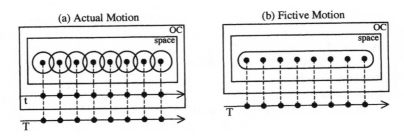

FIGURE 14.14

[30] Expressions like (25)(a)–(b) involve summary scanning along this path (fig. 4.7). At a higher level of conceptual organization, the entire configuration built up in this fashion is portrayed as stable through time, so *run* designates an imperfective process. Fictive motion expressions can also be perfective, e.g. *The trail rose quickly near the summit.* These involve sequential scanning, reflecting the experience of a moving viewer. Though actually different, the successively encountered portions of the object traversed are fictively construed as the same entity, which is thus perceived as changing position through time, just as in fig. 14.14(a).

Through subjectification, the dynamicity inherent in the apprehension of events is transferred to the conception of static scenes. A verb like *run*, which profiles objectively construed motion by its trajector, comes instead to designate a configuration apprehended through subjectively construed motion (i.e. sequential mental access) by the conceptualizer. We observe a similar transfer of dynamicity in cases of **fictive change** (Matsumoto 1996c; Sweetser 1997). Let us briefly examine two basic kinds.

One kind involves past participles used as adjectives, as in *broken vase*, *detached retina*, and *scattered marbles*. Derived from change-of-state verbs, these participles designate the state resulting from the verbal process (fig. 4.15). A vase is described as *broken*, for example, only when it has undergone the process *break*. However, not every use of a stative-adjectival participle implies an actual change. A *broken line* has never undergone the process of breaking. Likewise, a *detached garage* has never been attached, nor have *scattered villages* ever been clustered together. In such uses, the change designated by the verb stem is only virtual, serving to specify how the actual situation deviates from one considered neutral or more typical. A *broken vase* and a *broken line* are comparable in terms of the profiled state—the vase and the line are both in pieces—which in each case differs from the state of being whole. But *broken vase* invokes an actual change through time, a physical progression manifested in the vase itself, hence objectively construed. By contrast, the change invoked by *broken line* is subjectively construed. It does not inhere in the line itself, but rather in the conceptualizer, as a mental progression in which the profiled state is viewed as departing from the canonical one. Being only virtual, the change is not conceived as unfolding through time. The mental progression (residing in sequential access through processing time) is, nonetheless, a vestige of *break*'s dynamicity.

The following sentence exemplifies a second kind of fictive change:

(26)   *Our Christmas tree gets smaller every year.*

This may describe an actual change, of course: we cannot afford a new tree every Christmas, so we use the same one over and over, and each year it loses additional needles and branches. More likely, though, the sentence means that the tree we buy each year is always smaller than the (different) one we bought the previous year. On this interpretation the change is only fictive—no tree actually gets any smaller. Nor does the subject refer to any actual tree. The sentence invokes the abstracted conception of a family celebrating Christmas, a cultural scenario in which a tree has a prominent role. *Our Christmas tree* is a **role description**: the tree it refers to is the virtual one that occurs in this scenario (as it applies to the speaker's family). This role is filled by a series of actual trees, each presumably constant in size. It is through the fictive identification of these instantiations, imagining them to be a single entity, that we obtain the notion of a tree changing size.

Even this small sample should indicate how often we resort to fictive entities and other mental constructions. What explains their prevalence? Why is cognitive activity so often disengaged from immediate experience? For the most part we are not attempting to escape reality by constructing an imaginary world. More typically, it is in fact the real world that concerns us. While it does not refer to them directly, for example, (26) does pertain to actual trees and an aspect of real-world experience. The main purpose of disengaged cognition is not to escape but to cope. The mental capacities we have discussed here are crucial for constructing and negotiating the world we live in. Though disengaged from immediate bodily experience, they allow us to engage the world at other levels.

14.2.2 Covert Scenarios

We understand (26) by invoking the cultural practice of decorating a pine tree during the Christmas season. We have an explicit basis for doing so: the compound *Christmas tree* provides direct access to this familiar scenario. Quite commonly, however, we rely on scenarios that are left implicit or suggested only indirectly.[31] Faced with seeming incoherence, we may simply infer them as a way of making everything make sense. Many invoked scenarios are fictive in nature. Like fictive motion and fictive change, they are often a source of dynamicity in the conception of stable situations.

An example that nicely illustrates these points is the following (cited in Talmy 1988b):

(27) *There's a house every now and then through the valley.*

This sentence comprises an existential expression, *there's a house*, together with two adverbs, *now and then* and *through the valley*. The sentence is natural and readily understood, but when we try to analyze it, questions arise about its semantic and grammatical coherence. The adverb *now and then* specifies that an event occurs intermittently. Usually, however, the existence of a house is a stable situation. And even though *through the valley* describes a path of motion, (27) does not contain a motion verb and does not refer explicitly to anything that moves. What, then, do the adverbs modify?

We make sense of (27) by invoking the scenario of a traveler (I imagine someone riding on a train) who observes the scenery along the way. The adverb *through the valley* describes this imagined path of travel. A traveler has a limited field of view, so as he moves along the path, only a portion of the valley is visible at a given moment. This provides the basis for the adverb *now and then*. It describes the intermittency of a certain kind of viewing event: occasions when, at the moment in question, a house appears in the field of view. It is, of course, a different house on each occasion. In the context of this scenario, *there's a house* construes the house and its existence as virtual entities representing the abstracted commonality of multiple viewing experiences. The travel and the traveler are also fictive. While it is not precluded that the speaker might be recalling the observations made during an actual journey, the sentence itself does not imply this. The import is rather that anyone traveling through the valley would have this experience.

Travel is only one activity allowing the sequential observation of multiple entities. If they can all be observed from one place, like the fielders on a baseball team, we can access them sequentially just by shifting our gaze. If they are moving one by

---

[31] This is usually the case with speech-act scenarios (§13.2.3).

one across our field of view, like the cars of a passing train, we can simply watch them. We also perform various actions to bring them successively into view: turning the pages of a book, removing plates from a stack, pressing a button to scroll through a text, and so forth. From these varied kinds of experience, we abstract a generalized conception of sequential examination. Let us call it the **scanning scenario**.[32] Like the travel scenario in (27), the schematic scanning scenario is tacitly invoked in many sorts of expressions. The scanning is usually fictive—we do not actually conceptualize the entities one by one but merely imagine doing so. This simulated scanning lends dynamicity to the apprehension of static situations. It also provides the connection between a generalization and the range of instances supporting it.

One element invoking the scanning scenario is the quantifier *each* (§9.3.5).[33] It is used quite naturally in expressions describing actual sequential observation, like (28)(a). The scanning, though, is only simulated—understanding this sentence does not require that we actually observe all the graduates one by one. And since the scanning is only simulated, *each* is also used in expressions like (28)(b), where, in actuality, there is no sequential examination. *Each* profiles a virtual instance of a type taken as being representative of a set of actual instances. The notion of serial access provides a link between the representative instance and those it represents: the property ascribed to the former (e.g. having its own recipe for tiramisu) holds for all the instances reached in this manner. If we examined them one by one, checking them for the property, in every case we would find it.

(28)   (a) *As they filed across the stage, she called out the name of each graduate.*

      (b) *Each restaurant has its own recipe for tiramisu.*

Even when in the background of awareness, covert scenarios are not only part of the meanings of expressions but are also reflected in their forms. We see this in (29), where frequency adverbs appear to function as nominal quantifiers. Normally these adverbs specify the frequency of events (e.g. *She {always/usually/often/ seldom/never} pays cash*). Here, though, the more likely interpretation concerns the proportion of instances of a type who exhibit a certain property. On this reading, the sentences in (29) are equivalent, respectively, to those in (30), with the quantifiers *all, most, many, few,* and no. How can this be? How can adverbs quantify nouns?

(29)   (a) *Linguistic theorists are **always** arrogant.*

      (b) *Professional basketball players are **usually** tall.*

      (c) *Moral crusaders are **often** closet perverts.*

---

[32] This is not to be confused with **sequential scanning**, defined quite narrowly as the processing mode characteristic of verbs (§4.2.3): as the profiled relationship is tracked through time, its component states are accessed serially but without summation—that is, only one is focused at each moment of processing time.

[33] *Each* contrasts in this respect with *every* and *any*, which invoke abstracted scenarios that are based, respectively, on simultaneous viewing and random selection (fig. 9.13).

(d) *University professors are **seldom** rich.*

(e) *Movie stars are **never** good role models.*

(30) (a) ***All** linguistic theorists are arrogant.*

    (b) ***Most** professional basketball players are tall.*

    (c) ***Many** moral crusaders are closet perverts.*

    (d) ***Few** university professors are rich.*

    (e) ***No** movie stars are good role models.*

This apparent anomaly is due to a covert scenario. The adverbs in (29) do in fact specify the frequency of events, but these cannot be identified with the profiled clausal process. Each sentence ascribes a property (e.g. being arrogant) to its subject (linguistic theorists). We understand the sentences by invoking a version of the scanning scenario: the notion of progressing through life (or moving through the world), in the course of which we encounter enough instances of a given type to constitute a representative sample. What the adverbs describe is the frequency of events in which the instance encountered exhibits the property in question. And since the frequency of events correlates directly with the proportion of instances with the property, the effect is the same as with nominal quantification. The events, of course, are only fictive—(29)(a) does not imply that the speaker has ever been fortunate enough to actually meet a linguistic theorist (let alone all of them). They serve as a means of apprehending the static distribution of properties in terms of the dynamic process of exploration.

Numerous adverbial expressions prompt the simulation of a scanning experience. Compare the uses of *still* in (31). Canonically, as in sentence (a), it indicates that the profiled situation continues longer than expected. In this case, both the situation (being undecided) and its continuation through time are aspects of the expression's objective content—that is, the scene being viewed and described. To a basic apprehension of the scene, *still* adds the instruction to scan along the temporal axis by way of assessing the duration of the profiled relationship, and it specifies that the requisite scanning goes beyond an expected cut-off point. While this scanning per se is a mental operation, hence subjectively construed, it does have an onstage counterpart: the progression through time of the profiled situation.

(31) (a) *She is still undecided about buying a new car.*

    (b) *She can't stand sports like football or hockey, and golf is still too violent for her.*

By contrast, the scanning prompted by *still* in (31)(b) lacks a counterpart within the objective scene. It proceeds along a scale comprising a series of sports ranked in decreasing order of violence: football > hockey > soccer >...> volleyball > tennis > golf.[34] Here, also, *still* indicates that the profiled situation (a sport being too

---

[34] Once more, the scanning is only fictive: we do not actually have to run through every sport in sequence in order to understand the sentence. It is enough to imagine doing so by means of a small-scale simulation of that experience.

violent for her) continues longer than expected. But how do we interpret "longer than expected"? It does not pertain to the duration of the situation (presumably this is permanent). Rather, it reflects the process of scanning along the scale by way of assessing the situation's extension on it, i.e. the set of values for which it exhibits the property. Hence the import of *still* in sentence (b) is not that the **situation** continues longer than expected through **conceived** time but rather that the **scanning** continues longer than expected through **processing** time.

The preposed adverbials in (32) illustrate various ways of inducing fictive scanning. In sentence (a), we understand *through the ages* by simulating the experience of tracing a mental path through the time span of human history. In (b), *from the brightest to the dumbest* invokes the scenario of examining all the students one by one in the order of their intelligence. Sentence (c) recalls the experience of reading a graph, its two axes representing body size and gestation period. *As body size increases* is a case of fictive change, obtained by viewing the sizes of different species as if they were a single entity. The matrix clause is likewise a case of fictive change, obtained by identifying different gestation periods. We further conceptualize these changes in terms of movement along the respective axes. Finally, we understand the changes as affecting the same virtual creature, representing the different species. Based on this mental construction, the sentence tells us that the changes occur in tandem: as the virtual creature's body extends along the scale of size, at the same time its gestation period stretches out along the scale of length.

(32) (a) *Through the ages, some great intellects have changed our view of the world.*

     (b) *From the brightest to the dumbest, the students all work very hard.*

     (c) *As body size increases, the average gestation period gets longer.*

Covert mental constructions are also the basis for nonpresent uses of the English present tense. Three such uses are exemplified in (33): the "scheduled future", the "historical present", and generics (sometimes described as "timeless"). Prototypically, the English present specifies that the grounded process coincides with the time of speaking (§5.2.3). Schematically, it indicates that this process is **immediate** to the conceptualizer (C) invoked by clausal grounding (§9.4.2). Nonpresent occurrences seem problematic with respect to either characterization. Future, past, and timeless events can hardly coincide with the time of speaking. And what does it mean to describe them as immediate to C?

(33) (a) *The party starts at midnight.*   [scheduled future]

     (b) *I get home last night and see a note on my door.*   [historical present]

     (c) *A kitten chases a piece of string.*   [generic]

The key is to recognize that the profiled occurrences are only virtual. They figure in tacit mental constructions, and while they correspond to actual occurrences, they cannot be identified with them. Sentences like (33)(a) invoke the scenario of consulting a plan or schedule (hence the term "scheduled future"). A schedule comprises representations of events, together with their anticipated times, and once in place it is always available for consultation. In this sense a schedule and its entries are directly accessible—hence immediate—to anyone who knows it. Using (33)(a) amounts to consulting a mental schedule and "reading off" an entry. Apprehending the event consists in activating its representation—that is, simulating its occurrence at the specified time. Although it pertains to the future, this simulation coincides with the time of speaking.

Other uses of the present are comparable, apart from being based on different mental constructions. The historical present reflects our capacity for reliving past events by replaying them in our minds. We do not confuse this mental replay with the original events themselves—we know full well that they are simulations or re-creations of those events, available through memory for "viewing" at the present moment. Producing a sentence like (33)(b) is not too dissimilar from watching a videotape and describing each event as we see it. Generics are quite distinct. They arise through generalization instead of memory, and rather than particular events they represent the abstracted commonality of many occurrences. Generics invoke a cultural model that views the world as having an essential structure we can discover and describe. Producing a statement like (33)(c) amounts to "reading off" an item in such a description. Because they inhabit a representation of the world, not the world per se, the event and its participants are only virtual (representative instances of their types).

14.3 Simulation and Subjectification

Cognition is **embodied**. It resides in processing activity of the brain, which is part of the body, which is part of the world. At the most basic level, we interact with the world through our senses and physical actions. There are other levels, of course: much of the world we live in is mentally and socially constructed. But either directly or indirectly, the world we construct and apprehend is grounded in sensory and motor experience.

In the last section we explored various ways of disengaging cognition from immediate physical experience. They all share the property shown abstractly in figure 14.15. Diagram (a) represents an act of engaged cognition, where a person

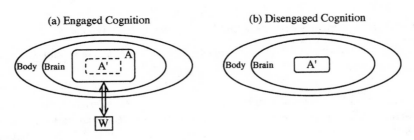

FIGURE 14.15

interacts directly, at the physical level, with something in the world (W). This inter-action (double arrow) is effected through the body, primarily via sensory and motor organs. The box labeled A indicates the role of the brain in this engagement: A is the processing activity, minimally including sensory input and motor commands, that constitutes the interactive experience. Diagram (b) shows comparable processing taking place without engagement. Certain facets of A—labeled A'—come to occur autonomously, in the absence of any current interaction with W. Though not neces-sarily either well delimited or easily segregated, A' is immanent in A, so it occurs whenever A does. Thus its independent occurrence amounts to a shadow version of the experience constituted by A.

A' is said to be a **simulation** of A. In various guises and under different labels, simulation is widely recognized as having a fundamental role in conceptualization and cognitive semantics (e.g. Johnson 1987; Barsalou 1999; Matlock 2004; Hampe 2005; Bergen 2005). One of its guises is sensory and motor **imagery**, well estab-lished as a psychological phenomenon (Shepard 1978; Kosslyn 1980). Without the usual perceptual stimulation, we can conjure up the visual image of a cat, the audi-tory image of a baby crying, or the tactile image of sandpaper. Without actually mov-ing, we can imagine what it feels like to walk, swim, or throw a rock. These kinds of images have a significant role in lexical semantics. Included in the meaning of *apricot*, for example, are images of what one looks like and how it tastes. Included in the meaning of *throw* are visual and motor images of throwing. Activating appro-priate images—simulating the experiences they represent—is a nontrivial aspect of apprehending such expressions.

Simulation is not confined to lexical semantics. As a general feature of cogni-tion, it has many linguistic manifestations. It is a significant factor, for example, in expressions that invoke a fictive vantage point or viewing circumstances. In grasping the import of (34)(a), one thing we do is simulate the experience of seeing Catalina under the conditions indicated. Simulation is also essential for recognizing other conceptualizers and the nature of their mental experience. In understanding (34)(b), we have to imagine being in the senator's place in order to figure out where the wife and lover are in relation to him. And to some extent we simulate his mental state by way of apprehending the finite clause. Other obvious cases include the fictive travel invoked in (27) [*There's a house every now and then through the valley*], as well as the mental replay narrated in the historical present, as in (33)(b) [*I get home last night and see a note on my door*]. The basic point, however, is that simulation—in the broad sense of figure 14.15—occurs to some degree in virtually all expressions.

(34)   (a) *If it were clear, we could see Catalina from the top of that mountain.*

(b) *With his wife seated on his left and his lover on his right, the senator was getting nervous.*

Simulation is always **attenuated** relative to engaged experience. Because it is not driven by immediate perceptual input, or harnessed to actual motor activity, it lacks the intensity or "vividness" of such experience. (Given the choice between burning my hand and merely imagining the pain this involves, I would probably choose the latter.) Simulations are also less elaborate, A' being just a portion of A. The visual image of a cat is bound to omit certain features that are evident when actually seeing it. The image is more schematic, lacking fine-grained detail.

Attenuation is a matter of degree. Naturally, lesser intensity and more rarified content translate into diminished awareness of the simulations carried out. Consider some previous examples. We understand (27) by imagining the experience of traveling through the valley. This being a fairly specific notion, we are easily made aware of it. Less so in the case of (29)(b), *Professional basketball players are usually tall.* This too invokes a scenario involving travel and successive encounters. But since no specific path is indicated, the travel conception is rather nebulous—the generalized notion of moving through the world in the course of life. Indeed, its spatial component is tenuous enough that it might fade away altogether. If so, we are left with something approximating the scanning scenario: the abstract conception of sequential examination. The scanning scenario is central to the meaning of *each* (distinguishing it from *every* and *any*). But owing to its rarified content, speakers are not explicitly aware of it.[35]

One dimension of attenuation is the extent to which elements are **objectively** or **subjectively construed** (§9.1). Elaborate conceptual content lends itself to being construed objectively. Thus (27) may well engender explicit awareness of a person traveling through the valley and watching the scenery. But we can also construe this content more subjectively by imagining how things look through the eyes of the traveler. In this case we have lesser awareness of the mover, as well as the circumstance of traveling and observing: instead of being onstage as objects of conception, they remain implicit as features of the (imagined) viewing situation. With more rarified content there is less to construe objectively. In this respect, the travel scenario of (27) and the scanning scenario invoked by *each* lie toward opposite ends of the spectrum. On the one hand, travel makes possible the sequential observation of scenes along an extended spatial path. On the other hand, the sequentiality of *each* is fully generalized: it is not limited to travel, to spatial extension, to visual observation, or even to the physical realm. This abstracted notion has little by way of tangible content. Instead of presenting a situation to be viewed, it is better described as a manner of viewing, potentially applicable to any sort of content. It is then subjectively construed, inhering in the subject rather than the object of conception.

Sequential examination functions as an object of conception when we conceive of someone engaging in it (e.g. in watching a general inspect a line of troops). In relation to this onstage role, its status in *each* exemplifies **subjectification** (§14.2.1): mental operations inherent in experiences of a certain kind are used in abstraction from their content and applied to other circumstances. The individuation effected by *each*, reflecting the discreteness of examining objects one by one, can thus be imposed on any sort of conception. Through subjectification, many abstract meanings can be related to everyday experiences. Among the other grounding quantifiers, *every* and *any* are based respectively on simultaneous viewing and random selection. The proportional quantifiers *all*, *most*, and *some* reflect the basic experience of

---

[35] They do find the characterization reasonable when it is presented to them, however.

superimposing two objects and assessing their relative sizes. The scanning involved in fictive motion (*A scar runs from his wrist to his elbow*) mirrors the continuous observation of movement along a spatial path.

Subjectification is often manifested diachronically. The use of verbs like *run* for fictive motion develops historically from their original import of describing actual movement, objectively construed. Possessive verbs like *have* derive historically from verbs of physical control, with meanings like 'seize', 'catch', 'hold', 'carry', 'get', and so on (Heine 1997). Immanent in the conception of R controlling T is a reference point relation, where R is invoked as a basis for apprehending T. This mental progression from R to T is all that remains when a verb is extended to general possessive use, becoming independent of any specific conceptual content. Owing to its highly schematic nature, a verb of this sort is usually regarded as "grammatical" rather than "lexical". Subjectification is thus a factor in the diachronic process of **grammaticization**: the evolution of grammatical elements from lexical sources.[36]

Recall, for example, that the English modals (*may, will, must*, etc.) derive historically from verbs with meanings like 'want to', 'know how to', and 'have the power to': they describe a potential force or potency tending toward the execution of an action (§9.4.3). Even in their epistemic uses, the grammaticized modals retain a vestige of their force-dynamic origin. For instance, *must* indicates compulsion (a force that cannot be resisted), and *may* the absence of a barrier (Sweetser 1982; Talmy 1988a). This force is subjectively construed, experienced as part of a mental simulation. It is the force we experience in extrapolating our current conception of reality so that it "reaches" the grounded process.

To take just one more example, it is common for a verb meaning 'go' to grammaticize into a marker of future time. English *be going to* is well along this evolutionary path. *Tom is going to mail a letter* can still describe Tom's spatial motion toward a goal with the intent of mailing a letter upon reaching it. More likely, though, it simply means that Tom will mail a letter (perhaps just by clicking a mouse). In the former case, the conceptualizer scans through time by way of tracking the subject's movement through space. On the future interpretation, this subjective temporal scanning occurs independently of any conception of spatial motion. It is merely a way of mentally accessing an event's location in time.

I do not claim that all grammatical markers arise in this manner. But it is striking how many grammatical notions are plausibly described as subjective counterparts of basic aspects of everyday experience, i.e. conceptual archetypes. This brings us back to a general CG proposal (§2.1.2) that has framed a sizeable portion of our discussion. It is suggested that certain fundamental and universal grammatical notions can be characterized semantically in terms of both a prototype and a schema. Providing the prototypical meaning is an objectively construed conceptual archetype.

---

[36] See Heine, Claudi, and Hünnemeyer 1991; Hopper and Traugott 2003; CIS: ch. 12; GC: ch. 10. The term "subjectification" is commonly used in a related but slightly different sense. As defined by Traugott (1982, 1989), subjectification indicates a shift in meaning from something objectively discernible to something in the mental and textual realms—for example, the semantic extension of *while* from temporal to "concessive" import ('at the same time as' > 'although'). For different perspectives on subjectification, see Athanasiadou, Canakis, and Cornillie 2006.

The schematic meaning resides in a domain-independent cognitive ability, initially manifested in the archetype and later extended to other domains of experience. Clearly, this relation between the prototype and the schema is nothing other than subjectification: mental operations immanent in the archetypal conception come to be used in abstraction from its content and applied to other circumstances.

At a minimum, the proposal was made for the notions noun, verb, subject, object, and possessive. Let us briefly review how it applies to them.

1. The schematic basis for possessives is the conceptual operation of invoking a reference point to mentally access a target. This mental progression is immanent in the conception of ownership, kinship, and whole-part relations, the possessive archetypes.

2. Subject and object are also defined schematically in terms of reference points. They correspond to the trajector and landmark of a profiled relationship, i.e. its primary and secondary focal participants. Their focal prominence consists in the trajector and landmark being the first and second reference points accessed by way of building up to a full conception of the profiled relation. This mental progression from trajector to landmark is immanent in the conception of an agent acting on a patient. It is in clauses describing such interactions that subject and object assume their prototypical values.

3. Agent-patient interactions are prototypical for verbs as well. In actually observing such events, we scan them sequentially: at a given point in time, we can only observe the situation manifest at that instant. The schematic characterization reflects this aspect of the archetypal experience while abstracting away from all specific content. A verb profiles a process, a relationship scanned sequentially in its evolution through time.

4. Finally, a noun profiles a thing, defined abstractly as the product of grouping and reification. These mental operations are immanent in the conception of physical objects, the prototype for nouns.

14.4 Mind, Meaning, and Grammar

As their names suggest, cognitive linguistics and Cognitive Grammar view language as an integral part of cognition. Conceptualization is seen (without inconsistency) as being both physically grounded and pervasively imaginative, both individual and fundamentally social. Being conceptual in nature, linguistic meaning shares these properties. And being symbolic in nature—hence intrinsically meaningful—grammar does as well.

Grammatical meanings are schematic. At the extreme, they are nothing more than cognitive abilities applicable to any content. The more schematic these meanings are, the harder it is to study them, but also the more rewarding. Grammatical analysis proves, in fact, to be an essential tool for conceptual analysis. In grammar, which abstracts away from the details of particular expressions, we see more clearly the mental operations immanent in their conceptual content. These often amount to simulations of basic aspects of everyday experience: processing activity inherent in conceptual archetypes is disengaged from them and extended to a broad range of other circumstances. In this respect, grammar reflects an essential feature of human cognition.

What sets us apart from other creatures is the extent to which conceptualization transcends immediate experience. Though grounded in such experience, the world we live in and talk about is mentally constructed through processes involving abstraction, conceptual integration, and subjectification. These means of disengagement are clearly reflected in grammar. At the semantic pole, grammar consists in abstracted patterns of conceptual integration. Grammatical meanings are schematic and often represent the subjectification of basic experience, consisting in the autonomous occurrence of mental operations inherent in such experience. In this way, grammar itself is a means of transcendence. Through the conceptions it allows us to construct and symbolize, we can engage the world in all its richness and complexity.

REFERENCES

Achard, Michel. 1998. *Representation of Cognitive Structures: Syntax and Semantics of French Sentential Complements.* Cognitive Linguistics Research 11. Berlin: Mouton de Gruyter.

Allan, Keith. 1977. Classifiers. *Language* 53:285–311.

Athanasiadou, Angeliki, Costas Canakis, and Bert Cornillie (eds.) 2006. *Subjectification: Various Paths to Subjectivity.* Cognitive Linguistics Research 31. Berlin: Mouton de Gruyter.

Austin, J. L. 1962. *How to Do Things with Words.* Cambridge: Harvard University Press.

Barlow, Michael. 1992. *A Situated Theory of Agreement.* New York: Garland.

Barlow, Michael, and Suzanne Kemmer (eds.) 2000. *Usage-Based Models of Language.* Stanford: CSLI Publications.

Barsalou, Lawrence W. 1992. *Cognitive Psychology: An Overview for Cognitive Scientists.* Tutorial Essays in Cognitive Science. Hillsdale, N.J.: Erlbaum.

———. 1999. Perceptual Symbol Systems. *Behavioral and Brain Sciences* 22:577–660.

Bergen, Benjamin. 2005. Mental Simulation in Literal and Figurative Language Understanding. In Seana Coulson and Barbara Lewandowska-Tomaszczyk (eds.), *The Literal and Nonliteral in Language and Thought,* 255–278. Łódź Studies in Language 11. Frankfurt am Main: Peter Lang.

Bhaskararao, Peri, and Karumuri Venkata Subbarao (eds.) 2004. *Non-Nominative Subjects.* Typological Studies in Language 60–61. Amsterdam: John Benjamins.

Birner, Betty J. 1994. Information Status and Word Order: An Analysis of English Inversion. *Language* 70:233–259.

Bolinger, Dwight. 1965. The Atomization of Meaning. *Language* 41:555–573.

———. 1977. *Meaning and Form.* London: Longman.

Borkin, Ann. 1973. *To Be* and Not *To Be. Papers from the Regional Meeting of the Chicago Linguistic Society* 9:44–56.

Brugman, Claudia. 1988. The Syntax and Semantics of HAVE and Its Complements. Ph.D. dissertation, University of California, Berkeley.

Bybee, Joan. 1985. *Morphology: A Study of the Relation between Meaning and Form.* Typological Studies in Language 9. Amsterdam: John Benjamins.

———. 2006. From Usage to Grammar: The Mind's Response to Repetition. *Language* 82: 711–733.

Bybee, Joan, and Paul Hopper (eds.) 2001. *Frequency and the Emergence of Linguistic Structure*. Typological Studies in Language 45. Amsterdam: John Benjamins.

Chafe, Wallace. 1994. *Discourse, Consciousness, and Time: The Flow and Displacement of Conscious Experience in Speaking and Writing*. Chicago: University of Chicago Press.

Chomsky, Noam. 1957. *Syntactic Structures*. Janua Linguarum 4. The Hague: Mouton.

————. 1965. *Aspects of the Theory of Syntax*. Cambridge, Mass.: MIT Press.

Coates, Richard. 2006. Properhood. *Language* 82:356–382.

Collins, Allan M., and Elizabeth F. Loftus. 1975. A Spreading-Activation Theory of Semantic Processing. *Psychological Review* 82:407–428.

Cook, Kenneth W. 1988. A Cognitive Analysis of Grammatical Relations, Case, and Transitivity in Samoan. Ph.D. dissertation, University of California, San Diego.

————. 1993a. A Cognitive Account of Samoan Case Marking and Cliticization. *Studi Italiani di Linguistica Teorica e Applicata* 22:509–530.

————. 1993b. A Cognitive Account of Samoan *lavea* and *galo* Verbs. In Richard A. Geiger and Brygida Rudzka-Ostyn (eds.), *Conceptualizations and Mental Processing in Language*, 567–592. Cognitive Linguistics Research 3. Berlin: Mouton de Gruyter.

————. 1999. Samoan as an Active Zone Language. In Leon de Stadler and Christoph Eyrich (eds.), *Issues in Cognitive Linguistics*, 391–405. Cognitive Linguistics Research 12. Berlin: Mouton de Gruyter.

Croft, William. 1990. *Typology and Universals*. Cambridge: Cambridge University Press.

————. 2001. *Radical Construction Grammar: Syntactic Theory in Typological Perspective*. Oxford: Oxford University Press.

Croft, William, and D. Alan Cruse. 2004. *Cognitive Linguistics*. Cambridge Textbooks in Linguistics. Cambridge: Cambridge University Press.

Dahlstrom, Amy. 1983. Agent-Patient Languages and Split Case Marking Systems. *Proceedings of the Annual Meeting of the Berkeley Linguistics Society* 9:37–46.

Deane, Paul. 1992. *Grammar in Mind and Brain: Explorations in Cognitive Syntax*. Cognitive Linguistics Research 2. Berlin: Mouton de Gruyter.

Diessel, Holger. 1999. *Demonstratives: Form, Function, and Grammaticalization*. Typological Studies in Language 42. Amsterdam: John Benjamins.

————. 2006. Demonstratives, Joint Attention, and the Emergence of Grammar. *Cognitive Linguistics* 17:463–489.

Diessel, Holger, and Michael Tomasello. 2001. The Acquisition of Finite Complement Clauses in English: A Corpus-Based Analysis. *Cognitive Linguistics* 12:97–141.

Dixon, R. M. W. 1972. *The Dyirbal Language of North Queensland*. Cambridge Studies in Linguistics 9. Cambridge: Cambridge University Press.

————. 1977. Where Have All the Adjectives Gone? *Studies in Language* 1:19–80.

Dowty, David. 2000. "The garden swarms with bees" and the Fallacy of "Argument Alternation". In Yael Ravin and Claudia Leacock (eds.), *Polysemy: Theoretical and Computational Approaches*, 111–128. Oxford: Oxford University Press.

Dryer, Matthew S. 1986. Primary Objects, Secondary Objects, and Antidative. *Language* 62:808–845.

Du Bois, John W. 1987. The Discourse Basis of Ergativity. *Language* 63:805–855.

Elman, Jeffrey L., and James L. McClelland. 1984. Speech Perception as a Cognitive Process: The Interactive Activation Model. In Norman Lass (ed.), *Speech and Language*, vol. 10, 337–374. New York: Academic Press.

Epstein, Richard. 2001. The Definite Article, Accessibility, and the Construction of Discourse Referents. *Cognitive Linguistics* 12:333–378.

Evans, Vyvyan. 2007. *A Glossary of Cognitive Linguistics*. Edinburgh: Edinburgh University Press, and Salt Lake City: University of Utah Press.

Evans, Vyvyan, and Melanie Green. 2006. *Cognitive Linguistics: An Introduction*. Mawhaw, N.J.: Erlbaum.

Evans, Vyvyan, Benjamin K. Bergen, and Jörg Zinken (eds.) 2006. *The Cognitive Linguistics Reader*. London: Equinox.

Fauconnier, Gilles. 1985. *Mental Spaces: Aspects of Meaning Construction in Natural Language*. Cambridge, Mass.: MIT Press, and London: Bradford.

————. 1997. *Mappings in Thought and Language*. Cambridge: Cambridge University Press.

Fauconnier, Gilles, and Eve Sweetser (eds.) 1996. *Spaces, Worlds, and Grammar*. Chicago: University of Chicago Press.

Fauconnier, Gilles, and Mark Turner. 1998. Conceptual Integration Networks. *Cognitive Science* 22:133–187.

————. 2002. *The Way We Think: Conceptual Blending and the Mind's Hidden Complexities*. New York: Basic Books.

Fillmore, Charles J. 1968. The Case for Case. In Emmon Bach and Robert T. Harms (eds.), *Universals in Linguistic Theory*, 1–88. New York: Holt.

————. 1982. Frame Semantics. In Linguistic Society of Korea (ed.), *Linguistics in the Morning Calm*, 111–137. Seoul: Hanshin.

————. 1988. The Mechanisms of "Construction Grammar". *Proceedings of the Annual Meeting of the Berkeley Linguistics Society* 14:35–55.

Fodor, Jerry A. 1979. *The Language of Thought*. Cambridge: Harvard University Press.

————. 1983. *The Modularity of Mind*. Cambridge, Mass.: MIT Press, and London: Bradford.

Foley, W. A., and R. D. Van Valin Jr. 1984. *Functional Syntax and Universal Grammar*. Cambridge: Cambridge University Press.

Forrest, Linda B. 1996. Discourse Goals and Attentional Processes in Sentence Production: The Dynamic Construal of Events. In Adele E. Goldberg (ed.), *Conceptual Structure, Discourse and Language*, 149–161. Stanford: CSLI Publications.

Geeraerts, Dirk. 1993. Vagueness's Puzzles, Polysemy's Vagaries. *Cognitive Linguistics* 4:223–272.

————. (ed.) 2006. *Cognitive Linguistics: Basic Readings*. Cognitive Linguistics Research 34. Berlin: Mouton de Gruyter.

Gentner, Dedre. 1981. Some Interesting Differences between Verbs and Nouns. *Cognition and Brain Theory* 4:161–178.

————. 1982. Why Nouns Are Learned before Verbs: Linguistic Relativity versus Natural Patterning. In Stan Kuczaj (ed.), *Language Development I: Syntax and Semantics*, 301–334. Hillsdale, N.J.: Erlbaum.

Gernsbacher, Morton Ann, and David Hargreaves. 1992. The Privilege of Primacy: Experimental Data and Cognitive Explanations. In Doris L. Payne (ed.), *Pragmatics of Word Order Flexibility*, 83–116. Typological Studies in Language 22. Amsterdam: John Benjamins.

Givón, Talmy. 1984. *Syntax: A Functional-Typological Introduction* (2 volumes). Amsterdam: John Benjamins.

————. (ed.) 1983. *Topic Continuity in Discourse: A Quantitative Cross-Language Study*. Typological Studies in Language 3. Amsterdam: John Benjamins.

Goldberg, Adele E. 1995. *Constructions: A Construction Grammar Approach to Argument Structure*. Chicago: University of Chicago Press.

————. 2006. *Constructions at Work: The Nature of Generalizations in Language*. Oxford: Oxford University Press.

Goldsmith, John, and Erich Woisetschlaeger. 1982. The Logic of the English Progressive. *Linguistic Inquiry* 13:79–89.

Gorbet, Larry. 1977. Headless Relatives in the Southwest: Are They Related? *Proceedings of the Annual Meeting of the Berkeley Linguistics Society* 3:270–278.

Grady, Joe, Sarah Taub, and Pamela Morgan. 1996. Primitive and Compound Metaphors. In Adele E. Goldberg (ed.), *Conceptual Structure, Discourse and Language*, 177–187. Stanford: CSLI Publications.

Haiman, John. 1978. Conditionals Are Topics. *Language* 54:564–589.

———. 1980. Dictionaries and Encyclopedias. *Lingua* 50:329–357.

———. 1985. *Natural Syntax: Iconicity and Erosion*. Cambridge Studies in Linguistics 44. Cambridge: Cambridge University Press.

Hampe, Beate (ed.) 2005. *From Perception to Meaning: Image Schemas in Cognitive Linguistics*. Cognitive Linguistics Research 29. Berlin: Mouton de Gruyter.

Harder, Peter. 1996. *Functional Semantics: A Theory of Meaning, Structure and Tense in English*. Trends in Linguistics Studies and Monographs 87. Berlin: Mouton de Gruyter.

Harris, Catherine L. 1998. Psycholinguistic Studies of Entrenchment. In Jean-Pierre Koenig (ed.), *Discourse and Cognition: Bridging the Gap*, 55–70. Stanford: CSLI Publications.

Haspelmath, Martin. 1997. *Indefinite Pronouns*. Oxford Studies in Typology and Linguistic Theory. Oxford: Oxford University Press.

Hawkins, John. 1978. *Definiteness and Indefiniteness: A Study in Reference and Grammaticality Prediction*. London: Croom Helm.

Heine, Bernd. 1997. *Cognitive Foundations of Grammar*. New York: Oxford University Press.

Heine, Bernd, Ulrike Claudi, and Friederike Hünnemeyer. 1991. *Grammaticalization: A Conceptual Framework*. Chicago: University of Chicago Press.

Herring, Susan C. 1989. Verbless Presentation and the Discourse Basis of Ergativity. In Bradley Music, Randolph Graczyk, and Caroline Wiltshire (eds.), *Parasession on Language in Context*, 123–137. Chicago: Chicago Linguistic Society.

Holmqvist, Kenneth. 1993. *Implementing Cognitive Semantics*. Lund: Department of Cognitive Science, Lund University.

Hopper, Paul J., and Sandra A. Thompson. 1980. Transitivity in Grammar and Discourse. *Language* 56:251–299.

Hopper, Paul J., and Elizabeth Traugott. 2003. *Grammaticalization*. 2nd ed. Cambridge Textbooks in Linguistics. Cambridge: Cambridge University Press.

Hudson, Richard A. 1988. Coordination and Grammatical Relations. *Journal of Linguistics* 24:303–342.

———. 1989. Gapping and Grammatical Relations. *Journal of Linguistics* 25:57–94.

———. 1992. Review of Ronald W. Langacker, *Concept, Image, and Symbol: The Cognitive Basis of Grammar. Journal of Linguistics* 28:506–509.

Huffman, Alan. 1997. *The Categories of Grammar: French* lui *and* le. Studies in Language Companion Series 30. Amsterdam: John Benjamins.

Jackendoff, Ray. 1983. *Semantics and Cognition*. Current Studies in Linguistics 8. Cambridge, Mass.: MIT Press.

———. 1994. *Patterns in the Mind: Language and Human Nature*. New York: Basic Books.

Janssen, Theo. 1995. Deixis from a Cognitive Point of View. In Ellen Contini-Morava and Barbara Sussman Goldberg (eds.), *Meaning as Explanation: Advances in Linguistic Sign Theory*, 245–270. Berlin: Mouton de Gruyter.

Johnson, Mark. 1987. *The Body in the Mind: The Bodily Basis of Meaning, Imagination, and Reason*. Chicago: University of Chicago Press.

Keenan, Edward L. 1984. Semantic Correlates of the Ergative/Absolutive Distinction. *Linguistics* 22:197–223.

Kellogg, Margaret Kimberly. 1994. Conceptual Mechanisms Underlying Noun and Verb Categorization: Evidence from Paraphasia. *Proceedings of the Annual Meeting of the Berkeley Linguistics Society* 20:300–309.

————. 1996. Neurolinguistic Evidence of Some Conceptual Properties of Nouns and Verbs. Ph.D. dissertation, University of California, San Diego.

Kemmer, Suzanne. 1993. *The Middle Voice.* Typological Studies in Language 23. Amsterdam: John Benjamins.

Kimenyi, Alexandre. 1980. *A Relational Grammar of Kinyarwanda.* University of California Publications in Linguistics 91. Berkeley: University of California Press.

Kiparsky, Paul, and Carol Kiparsky. 1970. Fact. In Manfred Bierwisch and Karl Erich Heidolph (eds.), *Progress in Linguistics,* 143–173. The Hague: Mouton.

Kirsner, Robert S. 1993. From Meaning to Message in Two Theories: Cognitive and Saussurean Views of the Modern Dutch Demonstratives. In Richard A. Geiger and Brygida Rudzka-Ostyn (eds.), *Conceptualizations and Mental Processing in Language,* 81–114. Cognitive Linguistics Research 3. Berlin: Mouton de Gruyter.

Kirsner, Robert S., and Sandra A. Thompson. 1976. The Role of Pragmatic Inference in Semantics: A Study of Sensory Verb Complements in English. *Glossa* 10:200–240.

Klaiman, M. H. 1981. Toward a Universal Semantics of Indirect Subject Constructions. *Proceedings of the Annual Meeting of the Berkeley Linguistics Society* 7:123–135.

Kosslyn, Stephen Michael. 1980. *Image and Mind.* Cambridge: Harvard University Press.

Kövecses, Zoltán. 2000. *Metaphor and Emotion: Language, Culture, and Body in Human Feeling.* Cambridge: Cambridge University Press.

————. 2005. *Metaphor in Culture: Universality and Variation.* Cambridge: Cambridge University Press.

Lakoff, George. 1986. Frame Semantic Control of the Coordinate Structure Constraint. In Anne M. Farley, Peter T. Farley, and Karl-Erik McCullough (eds.), *Papers from the Parasession on Pragmatics and Grammatical Theory,* 152–167. Chicago: Chicago Linguistic Society.

————. 1987. *Women, Fire, and Dangerous Things: What Categories Reveal about the Mind.* Chicago: University of Chicago Press.

————. 1990. The Invariance Hypothesis: Is Abstract Reason Based on Image-Schemas? *Cognitive Linguistics* 1:39–74.

————. 1996. Sorry, I'm Not Myself Today: The Metaphor System for Conceptualizing the Self. In Gilles Fauconnier and Eve Sweetser (eds.), *Spaces, Worlds, and Grammar,* 91–123. Chicago: University of Chicago Press.

Lakoff, George, and Mark Johnson. 1980. *Metaphors We Live By.* Chicago: University of Chicago Press.

————. 1999. *Philosophy in the Flesh: The Embodied Mind and Its Challenge to Western Thought.* New York: Basic Books.

Lakoff, George, and Rafael E. Núñez. 2000. *Where Mathematics Comes From: How the Embodied Mind Brings Mathematics into Being.* New York: Basic Books.

Lakoff, George, and Mark Turner. 1989. *More Than Cool Reason: A Field Guide to Poetic Metaphor.* Chicago: University of Chicago Press.

Lambrecht, Knud. 1994. *Information Structure and Sentence Form: Topic, Focus, and the Mental Representations of Discourse Referents.* Cambridge Studies in Linguistics 71. Cambridge: Cambridge University Press.

Langacker, Ronald W. 1968. *Language and Its Structure: Some Fundamental Linguistic Concepts.* New York: Harcourt, Brace and World.

————. 1969. On Pronominalization and the Chain of Command. In David A. Reibel and Sanford A. Schane (eds.), *Modern Studies in English*, 160–186. Englewood Cliffs, N.J.: Prentice Hall.

————. 1982. Space Grammar, Analysability, and the English Passive. *Language* 58:22–80.

————. 1987. *Foundations of Cognitive Grammar*, vol. 1: *Theoretical Prerequisites*. Stanford: Stanford University Press. [cited as FCG1]

————. 1990. *Concept, Image, and Symbol: The Cognitive Basis of Grammar*. Cognitive Linguistics Research 1. Berlin: Mouton de Gruyter. [cited as CIS]

————. 1991. *Foundations of Cognitive Grammar*, vol. 2: *Descriptive Application*. Stanford: Stanford University Press. [cited as FCG2]

————. 1993. Universals of Construal. *Proceedings of the Annual Meeting of the Berkeley Linguistics Society* 19:447–463.

————. 1995. Possession and Possessive Constructions. In John R. Taylor and Robert E. MacLaury (eds.), *Language and the Cognitive Construal of the World*, 51–79. Trends in Linguistics Studies and Monographs 82. Berlin: Mouton de Gruyter.

————. 1997. Generics and Habituals. In Angeliki Athanasiadou and René Dirven (eds.), *On Conditionals Again*, 191–222. Current Issues in Linguistic Theory 143. Amsterdam: John Benjamins.

————. 1999a. *Grammar and Conceptualization*. Cognitive Linguistics Research 14. Berlin: Mouton de Gruyter. [cited as GC]

————. 1999b. Virtual Reality. *Studies in the Linguistic Sciences* 29(2):77–103.

————. 1999c. Assessing the Cognitive Linguistic Enterprise. In Theo Janssen and Gisela Redeker (eds.), *Cognitive Linguistics: Foundations, Scope, and Methodology*, 13–59. Cognitive Linguistics Research 15. Berlin: Mouton de Gruyter.

————. 2001a. The English Present Tense. *English Language and Linguistics* 5:251–271.

————. 2001b. Viewing and Experiential Reporting in Cognitive Grammar. In Augusto Soares da Silva (ed.), *Linguagem e cognição: A perspectiva da linguística cognitiva*, 19–49. Braga: Associação Portuguesa de Linguística and Universidade Católica Portuguesa, Faculdade de Filosofia de Braga.

————. 2001c. What WH Means. In Alan Cienki, Barbara J. Luka, and Michael B. Smith (eds.), *Conceptual and Discourse Factors in Linguistic Structure*, 137–152. Stanford: CSLI Publications.

————. 2001d. Discourse in Cognitive Grammar. *Cognitive Linguistics* 12:143–188.

————. 2004a. Aspects of the Grammar of Finite Clauses. In Michel Achard and Suzanne Kemmer (eds.), *Language, Culture and Mind*, 535–577. Stanford: CSLI Publications.

————. 2004b. Possession, Location, and Existence. In Augusto Soares da Silva, Amadeu Torres, and Miguel Gonçalves (eds.), *Linguagem, cultura e cognição: Estudios de linguística cognitiva* (2 volumes), vol. 1, 85–120. Coimbra: Almedina.

————. 2005a. Dynamicity, Fictivity, and Scanning: The Imaginative Basis of Logic and Linguistic Meaning. In Diane Pecher and Rolf A. Zwaan (eds.), *Grounding Cognition: The Role of Perception and Action in Memory, Language and Thinking*, 164–197. Cambridge: Cambridge University Press.

————. 2005b. Construction Grammars: Cognitive, Radical, and Less So. In Francisco J. Ruiz de Mendoza Ibáñez and M. Sandra Peña Cervel (eds.), *Cognitive Linguistics: Internal Dynamics and Interdisciplinary Interaction*, 101–159. Cognitive Linguistics Research 32. Berlin: Mouton de Gruyter.

————. 2006. On the Continuous Debate about Discreteness. *Cognitive Linguistics* 17:107–151.

————. 2007. Constructing the Meanings of Personal Pronouns. In Günter Radden, Klaus-Michael Köpcke, Thomas Berg, and Peter Siemund (eds.), *Aspects of Meaning Construction*, 171–187. Amsterdam: John Benjamins.

————. Forthcoming. On the Subject of Impersonals.

Lee, David. 2001. *Cognitive Linguistics: An Introduction*. Melbourne: Oxford University Press.

Levinson, Stephen C. 1997. From Outer to Inner Space: Linguistic Categories and Non-Linguistic Thinking. In Jan Nuyts and Eric Pederson (eds.), *Language and Conceptualization*, 13–45. Language, Culture and Cognition 1. Cambridge: Cambridge University Press.

Li, Charles N., and Sandra A. Thompson. 1976. Subject and Topic: A New Typology of Language. In Charles N. Li (ed.), *Subject and Topic*, 457–489. New York: Academic Press.

Lindner, Susan. 1982. What Goes Up Doesn't Necessarily Come Down: The Ins and Outs of Opposites. *Papers from the Regional Meeting of the Chicago Linguistic Society* 18: 305–323.

MacWhinney, Brian. 1987. The Competition Model. In Brian MacWhinney (ed.), *Mechanisms of Language Acquisition*, 249–308. Hillsdale, N.J.: Erlbaum.

Maldonado, Ricardo. 1988. Energetic Reflexives in Spanish. *Proceedings of the Annual Meeting of the Berkeley Linguistics Society* 14:153–165.

————. 1999. *A media voz: Problemas conceptuales del clítico* se. Publicaciones del Centro de Lingüística Hispánica 46. Mexico City: Universidad Nacional Autónoma de México, Instituto de Investigaciones Filológicas.

Manney, Linda Joyce. 2000. *Middle Voice in Modern Greek: Meaning and Function of an Inflectional Category*. Studies in Language Companion Series 48. Amsterdam: John Benjamins.

Manning, Christopher D. 1996. *Ergativity: Argument Structure and Grammatical Relations*. Dissertations in Linguistics. Stanford: CSLI Publications.

Matlock, Teenie. 2004. The Conceptual Motivation of Fictive Motion. In Günter Radden and Klaus-Uwe Panther (eds.), *Studies in Linguistic Motivation*, 221–248. Cognitive Linguistics Research 28. Berlin: Mouton de Gruyter.

Matlock, Teenie, Michael Ramscar, and Lera Boroditsky. 2004. The Experiential Basis of Motion Language. In Augusto Soares da Silva, Amadeu Torres, and Miguel Gonçalves (eds.), *Linguagem, cultura e cognição: Estudios de linguística cognitiva* (2 volumes), vol. 2, 43–57. Coimbra: Almedina.

Matsumoto, Yo. 1996a. Subjective Motion and English and Japanese Verbs. *Cognitive Linguistics* 7:183–226.

————. 1996b. How Abstract Is Subjective Motion? A Comparison of Coverage Path Expressions and Access Path Expressions. In Adele E. Goldberg (ed.), *Conceptual Structure, Discourse and Language*, 359–373. Stanford: CSLI Publications.

————. 1996c. Subjective-Change Expressions in Japanese and Their Cognitive and Linguistic Bases. In Gilles Fauconnier and Eve Sweetser (eds.), *Spaces, Worlds, and Grammar*, 124–156. Chicago: University of Chicago Press.

McLendon, Sally. 1978. Ergativity, Case, and Transitivity in Eastern Pomo. *International Journal of American Linguistics* 44:1–9.

McNeill, David. 1992. *Hand and Mind: What Gestures Reveal about Thought*. Chicago: University of Chicago Press.

Mithun, Marianne. 1991. Active/Agentive Case Marking and Its Motivation. *Language* 67:510–546.

Newman, John. 1996. *Give: A Cognitive Linguistic Study*. Cognitive Linguistics Research 7. Berlin: Mouton de Gruyter.

Newmeyer, Frederick J. 1983. *Grammatical Theory: Its Limits and Its Possibilities*. Chicago: University of Chicago Press.

Nikiforidou, Kiki. 2005. Conceptual Blending and the Interpretation of Relatives: A Case Study from Greek. *Cognitive Linguistics* 16:169–206.

Palmer, F. R. 1981. *Semantics*. 2nd ed. Cambridge: Cambridge University Press.

Perlmutter, David M. 1978. Impersonal Passives and the Unaccusative Hypothesis. *Proceedings of the Annual Meeting of the Berkeley Linguistics Society* 4:157–189.

Reddy, Michael J. 1979. The Conduit Metaphor: A Case of Frame Conflict in Our Language about Language. In Andrew Ortony (ed.), *Metaphor and Thought*, 284–324. Cambridge: Cambridge University Press.

Regier, Terry. 1996. *The Human Semantic Potential: Spatial Language and Constrained Connectionism*. Cambridge, Mass.: MIT Press, and London: Bradford.

Reid, Wallis. 1991. *Verb and Noun Number in English: A Functional Explanation*. London: Longman.

Reinhart, Tanya. 1983. *Anaphora and Semantic Interpretation*. Chicago: University of Chicago Press.

Rice, Sally. 1987a. Towards a Cognitive Model of Transitivity. Ph.D. dissertation, University of California, San Diego.

———. 1987b. Towards a Transitive Prototype: Evidence from Some Atypical English Passives. *Proceedings of the Annual Meeting of the Berkeley Linguistics Society* 13:422–434.

Riemer, Nick. 2005. *The Semantics of Polysemy: Reading Meaning in English and Warlpiri*. Cognitive Linguistics Research 30. Berlin: Mouton de Gruyter.

Rosch, Eleanor. 1978. Principles of Categorization. In Eleanor Rosch and Barbara B. Lloyd (eds.), *Cognition and Categorization*, 27–47. Hillsdale, N.J.: Erlbaum.

Ross, John R. 1967. Constraints on Variables in Syntax. Ph.D. dissertation, MIT, Cambridge, Mass. [Published as Ross 1986.]

———. 1986. *Infinite Syntax!* Norwood, N.J.: Ablex.

Ruhl, Charles. 1989. *On Monosemy: A Study in Linguistic Semantics*. Albany: State University of New York Press.

Sacks, Harvey, Emanuel A. Schegloff, and Gail Jefferson. 1974. A Simplest Systematics for the Organization of Turn-Taking for Conversation. *Language* 50:696–735.

Sadock, Jerrold M. 1974. Read at Your Own Risk: Syntactic and Semantic Horrors You Can Find in Your Medicine Chest. *Papers from the Regional Meeting of the Chicago Linguistic Society* 10:599–607.

Schachter, Paul. 1976. The Subject in Philippine Languages: Topic, Actor, Actor-Topic, or None of the Above? In Charles N. Li (ed.), *Subject and Topic*, 491–518. New York: Academic Press.

———. 1977. Reference-Related and Role-Related Properties of Subjects. In Peter Cole and Jerry M. Sadock (eds.), *Syntax and Semantics*, vol. 8: *Grammatical Relations*, 279–306. New York: Academic Press.

Searle, John R. 1969. *Speech Acts: An Essay in the Philosophy of Language*. London: Cambridge University Press.

Sethuraman, Nitya. 2002. The Acquisition of Verbs and Argument Structure Constructions. Ph.D. dissertation, University of California, San Diego.

Shepard, Roger N. 1978. The Mental Image. *American Psychologist* 33:125–137.

Shibatani, Masayoshi. 1985. Passives and Related Constructions: A Prototype Analysis. *Language* 61:821–848.

Smith, Michael B. 1993. Aspects of German Clause Structure from a Cognitive Grammar Perspective. *Studi Italiani di Linguistica Teorica e Applicata* 22:601–638.

Sweetser, Eve. 1982. Root and Epistemic Modals: Causality in Two Worlds. *Proceedings of the Annual Meeting of the Berkeley Linguistics Society* 8:484–507.

———. 1990. *From Etymology to Pragmatics: Metaphorical and Cultural Aspects of Semantic Structure*. Cambridge Studies in Linguistics 54. Cambridge: Cambridge University Press.

————. 1997. Role and Individual Interpretations of Change Predicates. In Jan Nuyts and Eric Pederson (eds.), *Language and Conceptualization*, 116–136. Language, Culture and Cognition 1. Cambridge: Cambridge University Press.

————. 1999. Compositionality and Blending: Semantic Composition in a Cognitively Realistic Framework. In Theo Janssen and Gisela Redeker (eds.), *Cognitive Linguistics: Foundations, Scope, and Methodology*, 129–162. Cognitive Linguistics Research 15. Berlin: Mouton de Gruyter.

Takahashi, Kiyoko. 2000. Expressions of Emanation Fictive Motion Events in Thai. Ph.D. dissertation, Chulalongkorn University, Bangkok.

Talmy, Leonard. 1988a. Force Dynamics in Language and Cognition. *Cognitive Science* 12:49–100.

————. 1988b. The Relation of Grammar to Cognition. In Brygida Rudzka-Ostyn (ed.), *Topics in Cognitive Linguistics*, 165–205. Amsterdam: John Benjamins.

————. 1991. Path to Realization: A Typology of Event Conflation. *Proceedings of the Annual Meeting of the Berkeley Linguistics Society* 17:480–519.

————. 1996. Fictive Motion in Language and "Ception". In Paul Bloom, Mary A. Peterson, Lynn Nadel, and Merrill F. Garrett (eds.), *Language and Space*, 211–276. Cambridge, Mass.: MIT Press, and London: Bradford.

————. 2000a. *Toward a Cognitive Semantics*, vol. 1: *Concept Structuring Systems*. Cambridge, Mass.: MIT Press, and London: Bradford.

————. 2000b. *Toward a Cognitive Semantics*, vol. 2: *Typology and Process in Concept Structuring*. Cambridge, Mass.: MIT Press.

Taylor, John R. 1996. *Possessives in English: An Exploration in Cognitive Grammar*. Oxford: Oxford University Press/Clarendon.

————. 2002. *Cognitive Grammar*. Oxford Textbooks in Linguistics. Oxford: Oxford University Press.

————. 2004. *Linguistic Categorization: Prototypes in Linguistic Theory*. 3rd ed. Oxford: Oxford University Press/Clarendon.

Thompson, Sandra A. 2002. "Object Complements" and Conversation: Towards a Realistic Account. *Studies in Language* 26:125–164.

Tomasello, Michael. 1992. *First Verbs: A Case Study of Early Grammatical Development*. Cambridge: Cambridge University Press.

————. 2003. *Constructing a Language: A Usage-Based Theory of Language Acquisition*. Cambridge: Harvard University Press.

Tomlin, Russell S. 1995. Focal Attention, Voice, and Word Order. In Pamela Downing and Michael Noonan (eds.), *Word Order in Discourse*, 517–554. Typological Studies in Language 30. Amsterdam: John Benjamins.

————. 1997. Mapping Conceptual Representations into Linguistic Representations: The Role of Attention in Grammar. In Jan Nuyts and Eric Pederson (eds.), *Language and Conceptualization*, 162–189. Language, Culture and Cognition 1. Cambridge: Cambridge University Press.

Traugott, Elizabeth. 1982. From Propositional to Textual and Expressive Meanings: Some Semantic-Pragmatic Aspects of Grammaticalization. In Winfred P. Lehmann and Yakov Malkiel (eds.), *Perspectives on Historical Linguistics*, 245–271. Amsterdam: John Benjamins.

————. 1988. Pragmatic Strengthening and Grammaticalization. *Proceedings of the Annual Meeting of the Berkeley Linguistics Society* 14:406–416.

————. 1989. On the Rise of Epistemic Meanings in English: An Example of Subjectification in Semantic Change. *Language* 65:31–55.

Tuggy, David. 1993. Ambiguity, Polysemy, and Vagueness. *Cognitive Linguistics* 4:273–290.

————— 2003a. The Nawatl Verb *kīsa*: A Case Study in Polysemy. In Hubert Cuyckens, René Dirven, and John R. Taylor (eds.), *Cognitive Approaches to Lexical Semantics*, 323–362. Cognitive Linguistics Research 23. Berlin: Mouton de Gruyter.

—————. 2003b. *Abrelatas* and *Scarecrow* Nouns: Exocentric Verb-Noun Compounds as Illustrations of Basic Principles of Cognitive Grammar. *International Journal of English Studies* 3(2):25–61.

Turner, Mark. 1987. *Death Is the Mother of Beauty: Mind, Metaphor, Criticism*. Chicago: University of Chicago Press.

Tyler, Andrea, and Vyvyan Evans. 2003. *The Semantics of English Prepositions: Spatial Scenes, Embodied Meaning and Cognition*. Cambridge: Cambridge University Press.

Ungerer, Friedrich, and Hans-Jörg Schmid. 2007. *An Introduction to Cognitive Linguistics*. 2nd ed. London: Pearson Longman.

Vandeloise, Claude. 1991. *Spatial Prepositions: A Case Study from French*. Chicago: University of Chicago Press.

van Hoek, Karen. 1995. Conceptual Reference Points: A Cognitive Grammar Account of Pronominal Anaphora Constraints. *Language* 71:310–340.

—————. 1997. *Anaphora and Conceptual Structure*. Chicago: University of Chicago Press.

Velázquez-Castillo, Maura. 2002. Grammatical Relations in Active Systems: The Case of Guaraní. *Functions of Language* 9:133–167.

Vendler, Zeno. 1967. *Linguistics in Philosophy*. Ithaca, N.Y.: Cornell University Press.

Verhagen, Arie. 2005. *Constructions of Intersubjectivity: Discourse, Syntax, and Cognition*. Oxford: Oxford University Press.

Wierzbicka, Anna. 1985. Oats and Wheat: The Fallacy of Arbitrariness. In John Haiman (ed.), *Iconicity in Syntax*, 311–342. Amsterdam: John Benjamins.

—————. 1988. *The Semantics of Grammar*. Studies in Language Companion Series 18. Amsterdam: John Benjamins.

—————. 1995. Dictionaries vs. Encyclopaedias: How to Draw the Line. In Philip W. Davis (ed.), *Alternative Linguistics: Descriptive and Theoretical Modes*, 289–315. Current Issues in Linguistic Theory 102. Amsterdam: John Benjamins.

—————. 1996. *Semantics: Primes and Universals*. Oxford: Oxford University Press.

Woodbury, Anthony C. 1977. Greenlandic Eskimo, Ergativity, and Relational Grammar. In Peter Cole and Jerry M. Sadock (eds.), *Syntax and Semantics*, vol. 8: *Grammatical Relations*, 307–336. New York: Academic Press.

Zubin, David A., and Klaus-Michael Köpcke. 1986. Gender and Folk Taxonomy: The Indexical Relation between Grammatical and Lexical Categorization. In Colette Craig (ed.), *Noun Classes and Categorization*, 139–180. Amsterdam: John Benjamins.

INDEX